Cheetahs of the Serengeti Plains

Cheetahs of the

T. M. CARO

WILDLIFE BEHAVIOR AND ECOLOGY
George B. Schaller, editor

Serengeti Plains

GROUP LIVING IN AN ASOCIAL SPECIES

THE UNIVERSITY OF CHICAGO PRESS • CHICAGO AND LONDON

Tim Caro is associate professor in the Center for Population Biology and the Department of Wildlife and Fisheries Biology at the University of California, Davis.

The University of Chicago Press, Chicago 60637
The University of Chicago Press, Ltd., London
© 1994 by The University of Chicago
All rights reserved. Published 1994
Printed in the United States of America
03 02 01 00 99 98 97 96 95 94   5 4 3 2 1

ISBN (cloth): 0-226-09433-2
ISBN (paper): 0-226-09434-0

Library of Congress Cataloging-in-Publication Data

Caro, T. M. (Timothy M.)
    Cheetahs of the Serengeti Plains : group living in an asocial
species / by T.M. Caro.
        p.   cm. — (Wildlife behavior and ecology)
    Includes bibliographical references and index.
        ISBN 0-226-09433-2 (cloth). — ISBN 0-226-09434-0 (pbk.)
        1. Cheetah—Behavior—Tanzania—Serengeti Plain.   2. Social
behavior in animals.   3. Cheetah—Tanzania—Serengeti Plain.
I. Title.   II. Series.
QL737.C23C35   1994
599.74′428—dc20   93-35466
                                                            CIP

In memory of Roger Stater and his wicked sense of humor.

Contents

An adolescent male cheetah looks inquisitively at the observer. Its head still has the fluffy appearance typical of cubs. (Drawing by Dafila Scott.)

Preface

The central aim of this book is to explore the evolutionary causes of social behavior. The cheetah is particularly interesting in this regard because it exhibits great variation in social organization, enabling hypotheses about group living to be tested without the confounding effects of phylogeny. Some segments of cheetah society live in small groups, some permanent, some less so, and appear to be teetering on the edge of sociality. They therefore present several independent tests of why individuals embark on the evolutionary route to sociality.

In addition, the causes of group living in carnivores are themselves currently under close scrutiny. Until recently, it had been tacitly assumed that large carnivores live in groups because they enjoy greater hunting success, and by implication, foraging advantages. Preliminary data and theory suggest that direct reproductive benefits are more likely to drive sociality in these species, but too few studies are currently available to support the generality of this conclusion.

In this book, I use cheetahs to explore the costs and benefits of group living in carnivores in three ways: by examining why cheetah cubs stay with their mothers for a full year after weaning; by exploring the reasons that adolescent littermates remain together as temporary units; and by looking at the causes and consequences of living in permanent associations for male cheetahs. The different answers to these three questions each bear on the evolution of social behavior in mammals.

The second and corollary aim of the book is to examine the behavior

of cheetahs from a functional perspective. The social organization of cheetahs is exceptional in that it lies somewhere between lions, which live in
groups, and other, solitary members of the cat family in which adults associate only at mating. Male cheetahs often live in small groups or coalitions, as do male lions, while female cheetahs live alone or with dependent
cubs, as do tigers or ocelots. As animals' social organization depends so
much on female distributions (Trivers 1972; Bradbury and Vehrencamp
1977; Wrangham 1979), it is reasonable to categorize cheetahs as being
asocial. Since male lions are known to form groups in order to defend a
pride of several females, explanations for group living in male cheetahs
must be sought elsewhere, and offer a chance to explore the ecological
causes of differences in breeding systems.

Cheetahs are also distinct from other cats in a morphological sense,
showing a variety of canid-like traits and employing an extremely fast
chase to capture prey. Hitherto it has been assumed that these hunting
skills require a protracted period of parental care over which to develop.
The species therefore offers an opportunity to investigate developmental
mechanisms that might hasten the acquisition of hunting techniques:
these include rudimentary hunting attempts in cubs and maternal encouragement of cubs' predatory skills. It also allows the benefits of parental care for offspring, and its costs for parents, to be explored; research on
these issues is currently hamstrung by a dearth of specific predictions and
by difficulties in measurement (Clutton-Brock 1991).

My third and interrelated aim is to provide a synthetic account of the
biology of cheetahs in the wild. Studies that use a species or ecological
system to tackle a theoretical issue are crucial to advancing understanding
of evolutionary processes, but do not always stand the test of time. Theo-
ries move forward, and data collected for a specific purpose are often
unsuitable for testing the next generation of ideas. There is great value
therefore in presenting baseline information that can be used by others
interested in basic and applied science in ways that are not always apparent to the author. I have endeavored to provide such quantitative data on
most aspects of the cheetah's ecology and behavior in Serengeti. Some of
this may prove useful for captive breeding programs and future reintroductions. Last, I have not been shy of supplying descriptive material and
anecdotes to fill out the dry numbers and statistics. These give important
ecological background for understanding the cheetah's lifestyle and convey, I hope, a flavor of the problems cheetahs have to surmount in a
savannah environment.

The organization of the book follows the basic grouping patterns of
different age-sex classes of cheetah society, starting with females and
moving on to mothers, cubs, independent offspring, and finally, males.
Comparative discussions and statistical tests are located at the end of each

chapter. The book ends with an examination of the evolution, ecology, and conservation needs of the species. Chapter 1 briefly reviews the principal hypotheses on the evolution of grouping in animals, focusing particularly on carnivores. Chapter 2 describes the Serengeti study site and provides an up-to-date and thorough review of our current knowledge of cheetahs, their morphology, taxonomy, reproduction, feeding, and social structure, thereby clearing the way for examining their social behavior in depth. Chapter 3 describes methods of data collection during 5,000 hours of observation.

In chapter 4 I give a background to reproduction in females, including seasonality of estrus and births, and describe causes of cub mortality, which is exceptionally high in cheetahs. Periods of dependence on the mother and cub adoptions are also discussed. Chapter 5 outlines the changes in females' hunting and foraging success and vigilance that occur when they have cubs. I then examine the short-term costs that adult females incur by living with a group of cubs. Comparisons between mothers and solitary females demonstrate that while mothers endure reduced food intake, those with large cubs can benefit from the antipredator advantages of group living, which brings into question the usual assumptions about costs of parental care.

Chapter 6 investigates the advantages that cubs gain from staying with their mother so long after weaning. Contrary to common belief, quantitative analyses of the development of hunting skills show that there is little improvement during this period, despite maternal encouragement of cub hunting behavior. Benefits of offspring dependence change as cubs grow older: cubs first derive enormous benefits from their mother's antipredator behavior and vigilance; later, the most important benefit is her provisioning.

Chapter 7 focuses on adolescents. Changes in hunting skills from the attempts of newly independent adolescents to the proficiency of adults are reported. Then the importance of remaining with siblings is investigated. Analyses show that group members do not benefit from enhanced foraging success, as is generally believed for dispersing juvenile carnivores. Rather, group membership allows individuals to lower personal vigilance and suffer reduced harassment from dangerous predators. Female philopatry and male dispersal are also covered.

Female cheetahs occupy huge home ranges; and while some males defend small territories within areas of female overlap, others wander the Park as nomads. Chapter 8 examines the phenotypic differences between the two types of males, presents new data on patterns of serial territory ownership that have just emerged from this long-term study, and most important, relates female cheetah concentrations on the plains to the location and stability of territories.

Chapters 9, 10, and 11 are concerned with permanent associations of males. Chapter 9 reviews the relationship between coalition size and territoriality, examines the changing advantages of group size for males over the course of the study, and calculates lifetime reproductive payoffs for males living in different-sized coalitions. Chapter 10 addresses the issue of cooperative hunting. It shows that individual foraging success increases with group size because of changes in prey preferences but not because of collaboration during hunts. As coalition formation is rare among male mammals, chapter 11 examines the social behavior that ties male cheetahs to one another, and investigates the short-term benefits and costs of living in a coalition. Unlike those of many primates, coalitions of cheetahs appear egalitarian.

Chapter 12 highlights some of the key evolutionary and ecological themes to emerge from the book: life history traits of cheetahs are compared with those of other felids, and the ecological factors favoring the cheetah's unique breeding system are examined. Returning to the main theme of the book, it draws attention to the different reasons that cheetahs live in different sorts of groups, none of which are related to cooperative hunting in this species. These findings are compared with data from other carnivores for which cooperative hunting is frequently assumed but has rarely been shown to occur.

The last chapter addresses the wider issue of how cheetahs can be conserved. Habitat destruction is the principal threat to their survival in the wild, while high predator densities may limit population growth in protected areas. The cheetah shows extreme lack of genetic variability; after discussing the possible causes of this problem, its consequences for both juvenile mortality and disease resistance are discussed, since these factors have potential import for conservation programs. I conclude by suggesting that the cheetah's poor breeding performance in captivity may hinge on behavioral rather than genetic or physiological problems.

Acknowledgments

I first became intrigued by cheetahs while writing up my Ph.D. thesis on domestic cat behavior in Cambridge. In 1978 my interest in behavioral ecology was growing rapidly from my interactions with members of the Kings' College Sociobiology Group and out of frustration in being unable to interpret the functions of different aspects of behavioral development in the laboratory. When Brian Bertram suggested that I follow up the work that he had begun on cheetahs in Serengeti, it seemed an ideal opportunity to extend my research on cats into a natural setting, and having been a field assistant there in 1970, I knew the area already. After Brian had left Serengeti, George and Lory Frame had carried work on cheetahs much further, and, now back from the field, they were gracious in allowing someone to take over the study and actively encouraged me to do so. During that time in Cambridge I received intellectual and moral support in writing grant applications from Pat Bateson and Richard Wrangham.

When funds and permissions had been obtained, I purchased an ex-Army Land Rover, with the expert help of Martin Sharman, from a fleet of 150 that had just returned from Germany. Instead of shipping the vehicle and flying out to Tanzania, I convinced my girlfriend, and now wife, Monique Borgerhoff Mulder, to drop her job and drive out overland with me. She bore the brunt of obtaining visas to cross the continent while I prepared and stocked the vehicle for the journey. We left London in November 1979 and arrived in Serengeti on 1 March 1980. Driving overland to East Africa is a wonderful way of appreciating the changing biogeography and cultural diversity of the African continent, and I recommend it to any biologist or anthropologist planning to work there. In southern Sudan I saw a cheetah cross the road in front of us, and a few minutes later a Murle warrior appeared, tracking it.

It is a great privilege for anyone to live in Serengeti National Park, and I will always be thankful to the Tanzanian National Scientific Research Council, UTAFITI (now COSTECH); Tanzania National Parks (TANAPA); and the Serengeti Wildlife Research Institute (SWRI) for granting me permission to work there for over ten years. In particular I would like to thank Professor Karim Hirji, former coordinator of research at SWRI, for his enthusiasm for research, great knowledge of Tanzanian bureaucracy, and unstinting help in getting permits in Dar es Salaam and Arusha. David Babu, the Chief Park Warden of Serengeti National Park when I arrived and later Director of Tanzania National Parks, took a keen interest in what I was doing and generously allowed me to radio-collar cheetahs despite its controversial aspects.

In Seronera, L. M. Ole Moirana and Bernhard Maregesi, subsequent Chief Park Wardens, continued to grant me the hospitality of their park and also their garage workshop. At the Serengeti Wildlife Research Centre (SWRC), Acting Directors Frank Silkiluwasha, Mvula Bruno, and Hassan Nkya offered me their facilities, including a series of houses, and provided moral support when times were difficult. With a study area of over 2,000 km², my series IIA Land Rover began to suffer and needed regular repair in both the SWRC and Seronera garages. In the former I would like to thank Awadhi Musa and the late Barnabas Sumley, and in the latter Abisolem Mbise (Matanya) and Daniel Kibwe, for their help in repairing my vehicle and in teaching me sufficient mechanical skills to deal with problems that might arise at long distances from home.

In the early years my friends and neighbors at the Centre were Msuya Alawi, Gaspar Amworo, Rob Blumenschine, Dick and Runi Estes, Kisiri Konyokonyo, Craig Packer and Anne Pusey, Jon and Hazel Rood, Alan and Joan Root, Roger Ruess, and Makonge Rugatiri. Occasionally they provided me with useful cheetah sightings, as did Monique Borgerhoff Mulder, Sara Cairns, Mitsuaki Iwago, Leo Kunkel, Lois Piercy, Jon and Sue Pollock, Rick Thompson, and Hugo van Lawick. Alan and Joan Root were particularly helpful in flying down from Nairobi with vegetables and mail in the early days. Simone and Joe Cheffings moved important papers out of their small safe in Nairobi and let me pack copies of my data into it as insurance against accident. In fact this proved absolutely critical to completing the study after I lost all the originals in a house fire in November 1981. Barbie Allen kindly allowed me to use her mailing address and store data with her in the second half of the study.

Outside Serengeti, in Nairobi and Arusha, a group of close friends provided enormous and unfailing hospitality when I turned up on their door-steps. Andrew Hill introduced me to the best restaurants. Peter Hetz hosted me in royal fashion by providing whiskey, a group of lively friends, and access to the best rock and roll tape collection south of the equator. He had a talent for recommending obscure garages and spare parts stores for my ailing vehicle and could tell me where to purchase anything from cheap mattresses to pin-striped jackets. Along with Peter, Sue Praill and Marianne Kuitert provided a continuous set of bases in Nairobi, and talked me out of my bush mentality over long and delicious breakfasts. Debbie Snelson played the essential role of bringing me up to date on Nairobi gossip and conservation realities. In Arusha, Peter Swan and Bee McGrath let me stay with them under crowded circumstances and helped me drop my gearbox (twice); they also started the myth that I could live solely on boiled potatoes for weeks on end. Last, through greeting, visit-ing, and drinking tea with ten householders a day in rural southwestern Kenya, Monique showed me that anthropological fieldwork could be just as difficult as any faced by biologists. All these friends made periods away from work highly enjoyable and let me recharge my batteries.

A series of colleagues on the cheetah project kept up the long-term demographic records after 1983. Tony Collins, and my students Clare FitzGibbon and Karen Laurenson, worked incredibly hard at collecting demographic data while running their own studies at the same time. Tony, in particular, managed to keep the project alive when fuel was in short supply. All have been extremely generous in sharing demographic, behav-ioral, and census data that are so critical to studying long-lived organisms. Mary Holt provided much-needed veterinary help for a field season, and Donna Jefferson helped with estimates of interobserver reliability. Fi-nally Markus Borner, Serengeti's troubleshooter, helped me locate radio-collared cheetahs during hours of unnerving flying. Through his own example, and through a haze of cigars and sundowners, he convinced me that people can have an impact on preventing the natural world from dis-appearing and that every person's effort counts. I was lucky to be able to work with such a group of friendly and diligent people.

Analysis of field data began when I was based at the University of Cam-bridge, and I am grateful to Pat Bateson for putting up with me there. He provided persistent encouragement throughout the study, visited me in Serengeti, and took on the onerous task of carrying back an upduplicated microfiche of 15 months' data in his top pocket without mishap. At Cam-bridge, I benefited from Steve Albon's statistical and computational skills, though he would not like to be associated with all of the results, I suspect. Wrangling with Tim Clutton-Brock over Large Animal Research Group lunches kept me on the straight and narrow. After moving to the Univer-sity of Michigan, I had discussions with Warren Holmes and Richard

Wrangham that were both enjoyable and profitable, although I wished Warren could have chosen some other Japanese restaurant for our venue. John Pepper helped with analyses of ecological data. I finished the book at the University of California, Davis. There, Marcella Kelly carried out painstaking work on many aspects of the book, but especially on the comparative analyses, and it would have taken much longer to complete without her impressive organizational skills. I am also grateful to Brenda Gunn and Neil Pelkey for help in analyzing the female distributions. Barbara Wittman graciously allowed me to include her comprehensive cheetah bibliography, Dafila Scott kindly drew the plates at the front of each chapter, Lynn Matteson rephotographed the figures, Norma Roche copyedited the manuscript, and Susan Abrams encouraged me over the hurdles of publishing. Blackwell Scientific Publications kindly granted permission to use figures 2.12, 2.13, and 8.6; the American Association for the Advancement of Science to use figure 2.15; the National Geographic Society to use figure 4.1 and tables 4.1, 4.6, and 4.8; Academic Press to use table 8.1 and figure 8.3; and John Wiley and Sons to use tables 11.7 and 11.9.

Many colleagues found time to criticize earlier drafts of chapters. Marc Bekoff, Monique Borgerhoff Mulder, David Burney, Tim Clutton-Brock, Sarah Durant, Clare FitzGibbon, Paule Gros, Mart Gross, Sandy Harcourt, Marc Hauser, Kim Hill, Warren Holmes, Karen Laurenson, Walter Koenig, Don Lindburg, Steve O'Brien, Craig Packer, George Schaller, Dave Scheel, John Silk, Barb Smuts, Judy Stamps, Nadja Wielebnowski, David Wildt, and Truman Young all provided helpful comments.

The project was supported primarily by three grants from the Royal Society of Britain and by three from the National Geographic Society. Their policies of continuing to finance research in far-off regions of the world deserve great credit. The Frankfurt Zoological Society kindly let us locate cheetahs from the air at no cost. Funding was also provided by the Nuffield Foundation, the Scientific and Engineering Research Council of the United Kingdom (to FitzGibbon), the Leverhulme Trust and Messerli Foundation (to Laurenson), the University of California, the Max-Planck-Institut für Verhaltensphysiologie, and the Department of Zoology and Sub-Department of Animal Behaviour at Cambridge.

Throughout all stages of the study, driving out, data collection, analysis, and writing up, Monique Borgerhoff Mulder provided a host of stimulating ideas and comments, and tolerated the long hours I spent working when we could have been up to no good.

Finally, a word about Serengeti itself. This vast expanse of plains, circumscribed by a plateau to the west, the Crater highlands and Gol Mountains to the south and east, and the wide belt of woodlands to the north, is extraordinarily beautiful. Being alone, out on the plains, 50 km from the nearest person, watching the sun go down over Oldonya Rongai is something I will always cherish. But it is the sights and sounds of the animals that make the deepest impression. Going to sleep in the back of the vehicle surrounded by thousands of wildebeests stretching as far as the eye can see, hearing them gallop off en masse in the night as the whoops of spotted hyenas get louder, or waking up to the vibrations of a cheetah cub chewing on my tire meant that I gained a close appreciation of the lives of some of these species, perhaps all the more so because I was on my own with them. Serengeti is therefore a very special place for me, as it is for many people, and together with the Tanzanians to whom it belongs, we must work vigorously to preserve its integrity against exploitation from both outside and inside its borders. We have a duty to do this for future generations. As for the cheetahs themselves, I can only apologize for my intrusion into their lives. Perhaps the knowledge in this book will contribute toward our efforts to prevent the species' disappearance, for it is only we who can block their path to extinction.

Cheetahs of the Serengeti Plains

An adult female slowly raises herself from a crouching to a sitting position as she approaches a herd of Thomson's gazelles unseen. (Drawing by Dafila Scott.)

1
GROUPING AND COOPERATIVE HUNTING

Benefits of Grouping

Natural selection favors individuals that leave the most surviving offspring (Trivers 1985), and it is generally believed that selection at the group or species level is unimportant compared with that operating at the level of the individual or gene (Maynard Smith 1964; Williams 1966; Wilson 1975; Dawkins 1982). Groups composed of individuals that compromised their own reproductive interests for the benefit of the group would soon be invaded by individuals that were selfish, unless selfish groups quickly became extinct or dispersal rates between groups were extremely low (Maynard Smith 1976). Such conditions are very uncommon in most organisms and especially in vertebrates. It is therefore necessary to invoke individual advantages to explain why animals form groups and endure the substantial costs of group membership, such as having to share food and mates. Broadly, such advantages are thought to result from an enhanced ability to escape predation, from an increased food intake, or from environmental or social constraints forcing individuals to aggregate (Alexander 1974).

Group membership can reduce an individual's risk of predation in a number of ways (Bertram 1978a; Pulliam, Pyke, and Caraco 1982). First, the ability to detect approaching predators may be enhanced because more individuals are present to monitor the environment (Powell 1974; Lazarus 1979). For example, larger groups of gazelles detect cheetahs at greater distances than smaller groups (FitzGibbon 1990b). In addition, groups may enable individuals to be less vigilant, allowing them more time

3

for other important activities (Caraco 1979). Second, an individual can reduce the probability that it will be selected in an attack by associating with conspecifics (Hamilton 1971), or can benefit from hiding behind conspecifics (Hamilton 1971; Triesman 1975a,b). Grouping may also confuse a predator during flight (Neill and Cullen 1974) or even deter its attack, as illustrated by muskoxen forming a defensive circle against wolves (Mech 1970).

Grouping can enhance an individual's food intake in several ways as well. Larger groups may displace smaller groups from a territory containing many resources (e.g., wedge-capped capuchin monkeys: Robinson 1988) or successfully defend localized food sources (e.g., chimpanzees: Wrangham 1980), or occupy high-quality areas (e.g., vervet monkeys: Cheney and Seyfarth 1987). Grouping may also increase individual access to food if it leads to more efficient prey capture, as, for instance, when jacks pursue anchovies (Major 1978) or killer whales hunt porpoises (Martinez and Klinghammer 1970). Individuals may also be able to follow other more knowledgeable animals in the group to a food source (Ward and Zahavi 1973; Wilkinson 1992).

In many species, however, individuals that live in groups are forced together because of environmental constraints, as when seabirds nest in huge colonies on remote islands or seals pup on isolated beaches (Riedman 1990), or because of social constraints that prevent dispersal to neighboring territories (see Brown 1987; Stacey and Koenig 1990). Other benefits unrelated to predator avoidance or feeding include huddling together to survive cold temperatures (Arnold 1990).

Although members of social species could theoretically benefit from grouping in several of the ways outlined above, research on small diurnal species, such as ground squirrels and house sparrows, has concentrated on the antipredator advantages of grouping (Sherman 1977; Elgar and Catterall 1981). Conversely, studies of large animals, such as primates, have interpreted grouping patterns as strategies for increasing access to food (Janson 1992). Only recently has the importance of predation pressure been seriously considered in efforts to understand patterns of grouping between (van Schaik, Warsano, and Sutrino 1983) and within (van Schaik and van Noordwijk 1985) primate species (see Cheney and Wrangham 1987).

GROUPING IN CARNIVORES

The same bias is evident in studies that attempt to understand the reasons that large carnivores live in groups, even though most members of this order, 85–90% of species, do not aggregate outside of the breeding season (Bekoff, Daniels, and Gittleman 1984; Gittleman 1986). With these animals, perhaps, the tendency to relate grouping to food acquisition is more excusable, since their spectacular and alarming mode of catching prey has so colored the way we view them that much of their behavior has been interpreted as related to hunting. Researchers have suggested several benefits that might be gained by carnivores living in groups. By forming groups, carnivores might better be able to lower the risks of prey capture while hunting (Gashwiler and Robinette 1957); they might increase the diversity and size of prey that they can capture (Kruuk 1972); or they might improve their hunting success (Kruuk 1975). Group-living carnivores might collectively be able to drive off dangerous predators larger than themselves (Rood 1975), or might keep other scavenging species away from their carcasses more easily (Lamprecht 1978b). In addition, groups might be better at defending cubs against infanticidal males (Packer and Pusey 1983), or defending their carcasses against conspecifics (Packer 1986). I have placed these hypotheses chronologically in order to show that only recently have we got around to the idea that food may not be the principal force responsible for the evolution of sociality in carnivores. Nevertheless, the third reason, improved hunting success as a result of cooperative hunting, is still the most widespread and is certainly the popular view as to the evolutionary cause of sociality in large carnivores (Kleiman and Eisenberg 1973; Fox 1975; Kruuk 1975; Wilson 1975; Zimien 1976; Mills 1978). The idea that carnivores are like other mammals, subject to a host of different selective pressures favoring or disfavoring group living, is still not taken seriously.

Cooperative Hunting in Carnivores

It is very difficult, however, to demonstrate that communal hunting results in improved hunting success, and that this in turn is an evolutionary cause of sociality, for at least four reasons. First, many carnivores live in groups larger than those in which they hunt (lions: Schaller 1972c; Packer 1986; spotted hyenas: Kruuk 1972; Cooper 1990). Second, individuals may choose to hunt large prey to satisfy the demands of the temporary aggregation or permanent group in which they are constrained to live for other reasons, not because large groups are any better able to capture large quarry. Third, large groups may be better at defending carcasses from conspecifics (Packer 1986) or from other predators (Lamprecht 1978b) and hence may make capture of large prey a worthwhile proposition. Fourth, it cannot be assumed that all members of a hunting party are actually involved in hunting the same quarry. Some may be hunting other members of the herd independently, as described for certain wild dog hunts (Kuhme 1965). Alternatively, some members may not be hunting at all but simply tag along in order to be on hand when the kill is made, as described for lionesses hunting warthogs (Scheel and Packer 1991).

Even if group members target the same quarry, it is still necessary to demonstrate that hunting success increases as a result of the actions of members hunting together.

At this juncture, approaches to cooperative hunting fall into three camps. Some argue that hunters must show some form of organization between them so that their activities are coordinated in space or time, without hunting success necessarily increasing over that of a solitary hunter (Boesch and Boesch 1989). Others reason that hunting success on a given prey item must increase beyond that of two individuals hunting separately, without necessarily specifying the means by which this increase occurs (Packer and Ruttan 1988). Yet others point out that cooperative hunting can evolve only when the per capita rate of food intake for hunting group members exceeds that of an individual hunting alone (Pulliam and Caraco 1984; Clark and Mangel 1986).

Each of these approaches has advantages and drawbacks. In the first, demonstrating coordination circumvents the potential problem of new individuals having to learn to cooperate before there is any improvement in hunting or foraging success (Boesch 1990). Nevertheless, this approach leaves open the question of what benefits accrue from such complex behavior. The second approach explores the relationship between group size and hunting success and has proved important in specifying the conditions under which cooperative hunting might be favored. In a series of game-theoretical analyses, Packer and Ruttan (1988) showed that cooperative hunting is unlikely to evolve when individual hunting success is already high, when groups capture only a single prey item per hunt, when large prey items that can be scavenged by noncooperators are pursued, or when a large number of hunting individuals are involved. While these predictions are certain to be influential in future studies of communal hunting, they do not consider the effect that group size may have on prey preferences. Group size–related changes in prey preferences might easily overshadow the influence of group size on food intake through their effect on hunting success. The third approach can incorporate changes in prey preferences and hunting success with group size but leaves open the mechanisms by which individuals achieve enhanced intake while hunting together.

Ideally, a comprehensive study of cooperative hunting needs to adopt all three approaches. Furthermore, to determine whether cooperative hunting is the evolutionary cause of sociality, it is additionally necessary to show that access to food is the most important determinant of per capita reproductive success, with other benefits of group living being of lesser import.

Given these formidable difficulties, it was not surprising that early studies initially favored the idea that optimal predator group size was related to prey size (Caraco and Wolf 1975; Nudds 1978), once factors such as kinship (Rodman 1981) or intruder pressure (Sibly 1983; Pulliam and Caraco 1984) had been taken into account. As more evidence has accumulated, however, and as more species have been studied, there is growing recognition that communal hunting is not necessarily the evolutionary force driving group living in carnivores (MacDonald 1983; Gittleman 1989) although it may be a consequence of residing in a group. New studies increasingly interpret grouping as a response to a wide array of factors, including food availability (e.g., European badgers: Kruuk and MacDonald 1985), predation (dwarf mongooses: Rasa 1986), and competition for mates (male lions: Packer and Pusey 1982), although many of these conclusions are based on studies of other, intuitively significant aspects of grouping rather than on refuting the importance of communal hunting per se.

Advantages of Studying Cheetahs

The principal theoretical aim of this book is to examine the costs and benefits of living in social units in the context of an in-depth study of one species, the cheetah, and thereby to scrutinize the idea that food acquisition is the key force driving social behavior in large carnivores. Cheetahs are well suited to studies of the costs and benefits of group living because they have a very variable social organization. Animals in three separate age-sex classes may live either alone or in groups: females and mothers with cubs, independent adolescents, and males (table 1.1; fig. 1.1). Although links between ecology and patterns of social behavior have been profitably studied using cross-species comparisons (e.g., Crook and Gartlan 1966; Clutton-Brock and Harvey 1977; Terborgh 1983), such

TABLE 1.1 Associations between Cheetahs

Found alone	Found in groups	Duration of grouping
Pregnant females	Mothers with cubs	Months
Lactating females with cubs in lair		
Single adolescents	Adolescent sibgroups	Months
Single males	Groups of males	Years
	Adolescents or lost cubs attached to a family	Months or days
	Males and females in a mating association	Days

Fig. 1.1 Patterns of grouping shown by cheetahs in the wild. (*a*) Mother (center) and two dependent cubs over a year in age about to leave a termite mound where they have been scanning for prey. (*b*) Three independent adolescent littermates walking past a remaining pool of water in mid-dry season; note the thin, gracile appearance of the two in the background. (*c*) Three adult males with full bellies eating a yearling wildebeest kill. The one on the right is checking his surroundings between feeding bouts.

studies are problematic insofar as they do not provide independent points for analysis. This is because species share characteristics through common descent from shared ancestors, especially if they are closely related (Harvey and Pagel 1991). Capitalizing on variation within species is therefore a powerful method of relating grouping patterns to ecological and social parameters (Brown 1964; Lack 1968; Orians 1969b).

Cheetahs also have the advantage of being mainly diurnal, a trait unusual among carnivores and unique among felids (Gittleman 1986a). This enables extensive and detailed behavioral observations to be made. Although radio telemetry and night vision equipment allow nocturnal and crepuscular species to be located and followed in ways that were unimaginable twenty years ago (Amlaner and MacDonald 1980), it is still difficult

b

c

to score subtle details of behavior with accuracy under these conditions. This is especially true of hunting behavior, which has played such a prominent role in hypotheses about grouping in carnivores. Also, observers of hunting behavior must maintain some distance from the predator and prey so as not to influence the outcome of predation attempts. In the cheetah study I was able to obtain data on prey preferences, success of individuals hunting alone and in groups, behavior of individuals during group hunts, changes in food intake with group size, and estimates of the relative importance of food for individual fitness, all of which are necessary to reject or accept the idea that cooperative hunting is responsible for group living.

Disadvantages of Studying Cheetahs

Although research on cheetahs can clearly contribute to the study of behavioral ecology, and of the causes of sociality in particular, there are profound difficulties in working with an elusive predator. Carnivores live at low population densities compared with herbivores, and this problem is exacerbated with large species occupying high trophic levels. Thus sample sizes are inevitably small by the standards of fieldwork conducted on most mammals or birds. With small sample sizes it becomes necessary to combine data across individuals on at least some measures of behavior. This is, in fact, common practice in studies of carnivore prey preferences or hunting success, but it nonetheless introduces potential biases if one individual is, say, particularly selective or poor at hunting; this problem is known as the pooling fallacy (Machlis, Dodd, and Fentress 1985). Whenever possible, I tried to compare individuals, rather than repeated samples from the same and different individuals lumped together, in statistical tests. Where sample sizes were too small to do this, I reported and tested data from pooled samples, but compared individual scores by eye to check whether the findings were in the same direction.

Furthermore, species that hunt by stealth are secretive by nature and difficult to detect in their habitats (fig. 1.2). Because most cheetahs traverse very large areas in search of prey, chances of finding specific individuals are not improved by repeatedly searching a small part of the study area, as can be done for a territorial animal. This meant that the majority of cheetahs were difficult to relocate on a regular basis, even after radio telemetry was used, since it was possible to collar only a small proportion of the population. As a consequence, the demographic records have large gaps in them despite prolonged hours in the field, since subjects could not be found on any sort of regular schedule. The strength of this study therefore lay in its behavioral rather than in its demographic records, and this is reflected in the book.

Fig. 1.2 Cheetahs were often difficult to locate even at close range. One is in the center of the figure looking left.

Finally, in species that feed opportunistically and therefore sporadically, some subjects may be recorded as not hunting or eating over a short observation period, whereas others may be sampled during a period of intensive foraging. While it is possible to minimize these differences by following individuals for long periods (ideally a week in this study), this could not always be achieved since the majority of behavioral observations were made without the aid of radio telemetry. This problem introduced considerable variance into certain data sets, making it difficult to employ parametric tests in analysis; using nonparametric statistics in turn limited opportunities for multivariate statistics.

Previous Studies

Cheetahs had been studied in the wild on several occasions prior to this study. Pienaar (1969) furnished a monumental data set on cheetah-prey relations covering a 24-year period in Kruger National Park, which showed that cheetahs selected mainly impalas in that habitat. McLaughlin

(1970) was the first to study the behavior and ecology of free-living individuals in detail. Based in Nairobi National Park, his study concentrated on cheetahs' hunting techniques and food habits. Combining data collected in the same park with observations made in captivity, Eaton published a series of papers on the cheetah's behavior, culminating in a volume (1974) that covered a variety of topics, including reproduction, development, and conservation. Labuschagne (1979) used spoor to study the movements and activities of cheetahs in the Kalahari Gemsbok National Park; he found that springboks were the main prey chosen there.

In the Serengeti ecosystem, five studies of cheetahs had been conducted, albeit of different scales. Kruuk and Turner (1967) described hunting techniques and prey selection by cheetahs, while Schaller (1972c) and Bertram (1978b) each included a chapter on cheetahs in their books on lions, the former being a particularly carefully researched account of their distribution and numbers, movements, population dynamics, social structure, and ecological effects as predators. In the Masai Mara Game Reserve in Kenya, Burney (1980) studied interactions between cheetahs and both tourists and Masai, directly addressing policy decisions for managing this species in protected areas. In my view, this work has not received the attention it deserves. Finally, Frame and Frame (1981) expanded the study of individual cheetahs initiated by Bertram, and for the first time provided detailed qualitative accounts of certain individuals' behavior and reproductive careers.

With this comprehensive coverage it is reasonable to ask, what else could be accomplished? Most of these studies were carried out either before or during the period when the discipline of behavioral ecology was developing (Wilson 1975; Krebs and Davies 1978; Trivers 1985; Alcock 1989). Consequently the studies centered on careful behavioral descriptions and on the ecological effects that cheetahs had on prey populations, topics that were prevalent at that time. Missing was an account of individual cheetahs' behavioral strategies based on quantitative analyses and interpreted in the light of modern evolutionary theory. This book is an attempt to fill that gap by presenting new data on cheetahs and additionally by reviewing recently published work of colleagues. Though I have published a series of scientific papers and popular articles on cheetahs elsewhere, their topics are not rehashed here; the reader is referred to the original articles referenced in the Bibliography.

Summary

1. The principal reasons that animals form groups are to reduce the individual risk of predation and to gain enhanced per capita access to food. Among carnivores, in particular, food acquisition has been viewed

as the main factor underlying group formation since they are generally believed to hunt cooperatively.

2. Cooperative hunting has several meanings. It can refer to coordinated activity during group hunts, simultaneous hunting by group members that leads to improved hunting success, or simultaneous hunting that results in increased per capita foraging returns. Rigorous proof that cooperative hunting is the evolutionary cause of sociality will have to incorporate all three measures and show that foraging returns are the most important determinant of reproductive success.

3. There are strong motives for studying the causes and consequences of grouping using cheetahs because three segments of cheetah society live both alone and in groups. Cheetahs are also diurnal and can be observed closely.

4. On the other hand, cheetahs live at low densities, are secretive, and feed opportunistically. These problems impose limits on what can be accomplished in terms of demographic records and constrain statistical analyses.

5. Several previous studies of free-living cheetahs examined their feeding ecology, hunting behavior, and management. This study attempts to interpret their behavior in the light of current evolutionary theory.

Two 5-month-old cubs pat each other during a bout of social play. (Drawing by Dafila Scott.)

2

SERENGETI, AND THE TAXONOMY AND NATURAL HISTORY OF CHEETAHS

Serengeti and cheetahs are emotive words that conjure up vivid impressions, hence each merits careful introduction. In this chapter I briefly describe the history, location, landscape, flora, and fauna of the Serengeti ecosystem and my study area within it. Next I discuss the morphology of cheetahs and current understanding of their taxonomic position within the Felidae. Finally, I outline the background natural history of the species to provide a context in which subsequent chapters can be easily placed, and to convey the existing knowledge that was available to me when my study began and hence the way it influenced my research agenda.

The Study Site

BRIEF HISTORY OF SERENGETI

The name Serengeti derives from the Datoga or Masai word *Siringet,* meaning "tending to extend." The Serengeti area has been occupied by hominids for more than 3 million years. Most famous are the wealth of fossil hominids found in Olduvai Gorge in the center of the region (e.g., Leakey 1967; see Blumenschine 1987 and Foley 1987 for discussions of hominid ecology). More recently, archeological evidence shows that humans seasonally occupied the plains 6,000 years ago and had permanent habitations in the woodlands (Bower 1973). Only 200 years ago, Datoga pastoralists grazed their cattle on the plains before being ousted by the Masai (Borgerhoff Mulder, Sieff, and Merus 1989). The first European to see Serengeti was the German explorer Baumann, who entered from Oldeani Mountain at the southwest of the Crater highlands in 1892. Colonial hunters did not penetrate Serengeti to a significant extent until World War I, but, later, during the 1920s and 1930s, they shot enormous numbers of mammals (see Turner 1987).

In response to this pressure, Serengeti was granted the status of a game reserve and hunting was banned there in 1937; however, Masai continued to occupy the area. In 1951, it was designated as the first national park in Tanganyika Territory. In the 1960s, the boundary between the Serengeti National Park and the Ngorongoro Conservation Area was redrawn, and important extensions to the northern corridor (the Lamai wedge) and to the western corridor (the Grumeti extension) were added to the park. Masai, Wasukuma, Waikoma, and Wangirimi peoples were completely evicted from the park only in 1960. In 1957, Bernhard and

Fig. 2.1 My first home base at SWRI between March 1980 and November 1981, together with the Land Rover in which I conducted fieldwork throughout the study.

Michael Grzimek carried out the first systematic animal count in the area and established a research project in the park. This later became the Serengeti Research Institute (later Serengeti Wildlife Research Institute and now Centre), at which I was based (fig. 2.1). During the period of my study, approximately 1,700 people employed by Tanzania National Parks and three tourist lodges lived permanently in the park. Visitor numbers increased rapidly during the second half of the 1980s (fig. 2.2a); without doubt, these visitors constitute the greatest human impact Serengeti has experienced in historical times. Visitors have a consistent but localized presence around Seronera throughout the year, relieved only during the heavy rains in April and May (fig. 2.2b).

LOCATION OF SERENGETI

My entire study was conducted within the confines of the Serengeti ecosystem. This region is usually defined as the area used by migratory wildebeests. It lies about 500 km inland from the Indian Ocean and straddles the Tanzania-Kenya border to the east of Lake Victoria (1° 15' to 3° 30' south, 33° 52' to 35° 42' east) (fig. 2.3). About 25,000 km² in area, it is principally contained within the administrative areas of the Serengeti National Park and Ngorongoro Conservation Area, where I worked, but also includes the Maswa Game Reserve, the Loliondo, Grumeti, and Ikorongo Game Controlled Areas in Tanzania, and in Kenya, the Masai Mara Game Reserve (fig. 2.4).

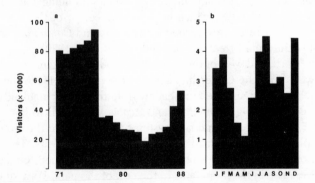

Fig. 2.2 (*a*) Number of visitors entering Serengeti National Park per annum between 1971 and 1988 (Tanzania residents and nonresidents combined). The border with Kenya was closed between 1977 and 1983. (*b*) Average number of visitors entering the park in each month of the year between 1985 and 1988. (Data from Serengeti National Park wardens' reports.)

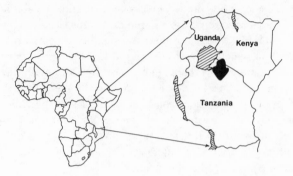

Fig. 2.3 Location of the Serengeti ecosystem in Africa (solid area), defined as the approximate area used by migratory wildebeests. Hatched areas denote lakes.

TOPOGRAPHY

The Serengeti ecosystem is a huge plateau situated at an altitude of 1,200–1,800 m; the Crater highlands, rising to 3,587 m, delineate its eastern and southern boundaries. The southeastern portion of the ecosystem is characterized by vast (5,200 km²), undulating plains punctuated by groups of granite and gneiss outcrops known as kopjes (fig. 2.5). The size and beauty of the plains make you catch your breath. Two topographical features break up the plains (see fig. 2.4). The Gol Mountains, dry quartzite and gneiss hills, run north to south along the eastern side, separating the Salei plains from the main plains to the west. Olduvai Gorge dissects the plains south of these mountains, seasonally draining Lake Lagarja (also called Lake Ndutu), which lies near the center of the main plain. Both of these features are adorned with *Acacia* and *Commifora* trees, in contrast to the almost treeless surroundings (Sinclair 1979).

To the north and west of the plains the woodlands begin. Volcanic ash, blown west from the Crater highlands in the past, has made the soil in these areas coarser, and the rain shadow from the Crater highlands is less pronounced, allowing *Commifora* and *Acacia* woodlands to flourish (de Wit 1977). Three major drainage systems flow west into the woodlands off the plains: the Simuyu, Mbalageti, and Seronera rivers. The largest rivers, however, are in the woodlands. There the Grumeti, Orangi, and Mara rivers rise in the mountains to the east of the park. Wasukuma cultivation delineates the western boundary of the woodlands outside the Maswa Game Reserve, and at the end of the western corridor lies Lake Victoria. The northern corridor of the ecosystem is also bounded by intense cultivation on its western side where the Wanata, Waikoma, Wakuria, and Waikesa live. In the north section of the northern corridor the

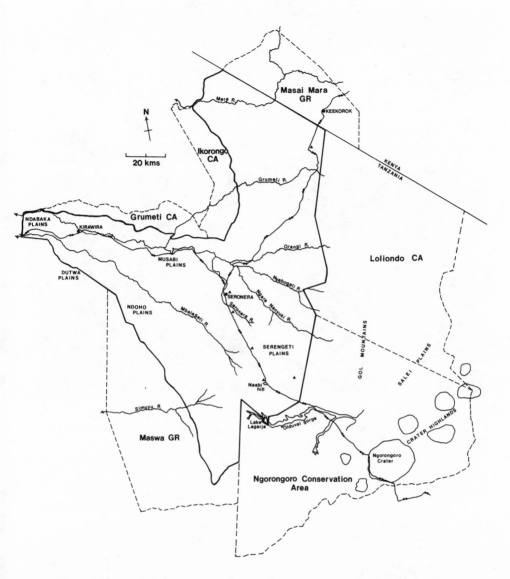

Fig. 2.4 The Serengeti ecosystem, showing the main topographical features, administrative regions, and place names. The Serengeti National Park, shaped like a T lying on its side, is bounded by the thick black line. The western strut of the T is called the western corridor, and the extension to the north, the northern corridor. The Lamai wedge is located between the Mara River and the border with Kenya. Main roads are marked by occasional double filled circles. Dashed lines denote administrative boundaries. Rain gauges (triangles) referred to in the text are, starting at Naabi Hill and moving north along the main road, Naabi North, Simba kopjes, Seronera-south, and Seronera meteorological station. The Southeast kopjes rain gauge is to the east of Naabi Hill, and Bologonja is close to the international boundary. CA = Controlled Area; GR = Game Reserve.

Fig. 2.5 A kopje in the eastern portion of the Gol kopjes complex. A mother and her three cubs walk southeast in search of groups of Thomson's gazelles remaining on the short grass plains in the dry season.

woodlands break up and are replaced by the tall grass plains that characterize the Masai Mara Game Reserve in Kenya. Several large plains are found in the western corridor: the Musabi, Ndoho, Ndabaka, and Dutwa plains.

THE SEASONS

During a typical year, there are two pronounced seasons: a wet season from November to May and a dry season from June to October (fig. 2.6a). In some parts of East Africa, such as Nairobi, rainfall is usually higher in November and December (the short rains) than in January and February (the short dry season) and then becomes very heavy in March, April, and May. In Serengeti, however, the short dry season is less pronounced (see fig. 2.6a; Sinclair 1977). Rain starts in November and continues to fall sporadically until March or April, when it becomes very heavy. Toward the middle to end of May, the afternoon rains stop and a northeasterly wind springs up, signaling the start of the long dry season. Few years are

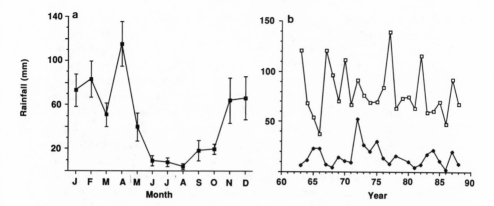

Fig. 2.6 (*a*) Average (and SE) rainfall in each month at Naabi North rain gauge in the center of the Serengeti plains between 1980 and 1988. (*b*) Wet season (November to May, open squares) and dry season (June to October, solid diamonds) monthly average rainfall each year from 1963 to 1988 at Naabi North. (Serengeti Ecological Monitoring Programme, unpublished data.)

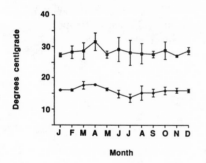

Fig. 2.7 Average (and SD) maximum (upper line) and minimum (lower line) temperatures for each month at the Serengeti Wildlife Research Institute from March 1980 to December 1983; each month's averages are derived from between 2 and 4 years of data. (Serengeti Wildlife Research Institute, unpublished data.)

typical, and the onset and severity of seasons vary widely. For example, during the 1970s, dry seasons were relatively wet (fig. 2.6b). The lack of a pronounced short dry season, and more importantly, the fact that most migratory ungulates remain on the plains from November to May, are the reasons that I refer to only two seasons throughout this book. Temperatures are clement in Serengeti, with a maximum rarely exceeding 30°C, providing a climate conducive to work (fig. 2.7).

THE VEGETATION

The driest part of Serengeti is the eastern plains (fig. 2.8, Southeast kopjes rain gauge). Large parts of this area are covered with grasses less than

10 cm high. These are the short grass plains; the most important flora here are *Microchloa kunthii, Digitaria macroblephara, Harpachne schimperi,* and a sedge, *Kyllinga nervosa.* Proceeding north and west, rainfall increases (fig. 2.8, Simba kopjes rain gauge), with vegetation height rising to about 60 cm in the dry season. These intermediate grass plains consist of the grass species listed above and in addition *Andropogon greenwayi* and *Sporobolus fimbriatus;* herbs such as *Indigofera, Solanum,* and *Heliotropium* are found here too. Farther north and west, long grass plains appear in response to the greater rainfall (fig. 2.8, Seronera-south rain gauge). The dominant species here are *Themeda triandra, Pennisetum mezianum, Digitaria macroblephara,* and *Aristida adoensis,* which grow up to 1 m in height. In most years fires, set by TANAPA authorities in the early dry season but later by poachers and cattle rustlers, burn the long grass plains to varying extents (fig. 2.9).

Seronera marks the northwestern corner of the Serengeti plains, and beyond this to the north and west, the ecosystem is dominated by woodlands. Rainfall is high throughout this area (fig. 2.8, Seronera meteorological station and Bologonja rain gauge). The principal tree species are *Acacia tortalis, Commiphora trothae, Acacia clavigera, Acacia senegal, Acacia hockii,* and the whisting thorn, *Acacia drepanolobium.* Gallery forest is found along the major drainage systems. (Extensive synopses of Serengeti vegetation can be found in McNaughton [1983, 1985].)

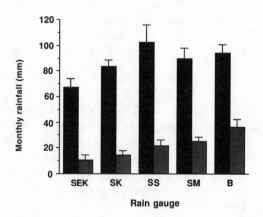

Fig. 2.8 Average (and SE) total wet (solid bars) and total dry (hatched bars) season rainfall from 1980 to 1989. Rain gauges, from south to north and left to right: SEK, Southeast kopjes; SK, Simba kopjes; SS, Seronera-south; SM, Seronera meteorological station; B, Bologonja; see fig. 2.4 for locations.

Fig. 2.9 A fire on the eastern side of Mukoma Hill set by TANAPA personnel in the early dry season of 1989. Trees in the foreground follow drainage lines on the plains, while those in the background represent the beginning of the woodlands.

MIGRATORY HERBIVORES

In terms of its effect on plant biomass, the most important mammalian herbivore is the wildebeest. Probably as a result of the disappearance of the rinderpest virus, its numbers increased from 0.2 million in the late 1950s to a stable 1.3 million during the 1980s (Sinclair, Dublin, and Borner 1985); a further increase was noted in 1989 (Campbell 1989) (table 2.1). From December to May wildebeests are found on the short grass plains (fig. 2.10) (Pennycuick 1975), principally south of Lake Lagarja. The soils of these plains are rich in minerals, particularly magnesium, phosphorus, and calcium, that the females need for lactation, which follows calving in February (McNaughton 1990). Some wildebeests are also found on the Salei plains and in the Loliondo Controlled Area east of the park during the wet season. As the plains dry out in May, wildebeests move north and west off the Serengeti plains into the woodlands, following the Simuyu, Mbalageti, and Seronera rivers, and then on into the northern reaches of the western corridor. From June to August, they move into the Grumeti and Ikorongo Controlled Areas before heading into the western region of the northern corridor, and then on north. Some wildebeests move north and northeast off the plains through the Loliondo Controlled Area and thence north. Between August and November most wildebeests are found in the Masai Mara Game Reserve in Kenya or in the northern part of Serengeti National Park. Depending on the timing of the onset of the rains, they move south through the central woodlands onto the Serengeti plains in November or December, following a forage mineral gradient (McNaughton 1990). Three additional much smaller resident populations of wildebeests remain in Ngorongoro Crater, at Kirawira, and in the Masai Mara year round.

The second most important herbivore is Burchell's zebra. Zebra numbers have remained at approximately 0.2 million animals since counts began in 1966 (Sinclair and Norton-Griffiths 1982). Zebras spend the wet season on the plains and move north into the northern corridor and the Masai Mara during the dry season, returning via the same route.

TABLE 2.1 Numbers of Large and Medium-sized Ungulates in the Serengeti Ecosystem in May 1989

Species	Total	Standard error
Migratory species		
Wildebeest	1,686,079	175,658
Zebra	257,387	20,590
Thomson's gazelle	440,845	42,285
Grant's gazelle	31,276	2,219
Eland	13,813	811
Resident species		
Impala	109,677	13,695
Topi	77,966	8,593
Buffalo	67,339	15,419
Hartebeest	22,771	2,485
Giraffe	12,450	768
Warthog[a]	5,624	524
Waterbuck	1,418	461
Ostrich	6,604	339

Source: Campbell 1989.

Note: Numbers of ostriches counted on the plains are also shown. The survey covered Serengeti National Park (12,467 km²), the Grumeti (589 km²) and Ikorongo (845 km²) Game Controlled Areas, parts of the Ngorongoro Conservation Area (4,445 km²), Loliondo Game Controlled Area (2,648 km²), and areas adjacent to the Serengeti National Park (4,035 km²), 27,451 km² in total, but did not include the Masai Mara Game Reserve.

[a] Warthogs showed a significant decline during the 1980s.

Fig. 2.10 Herds of wildebeests amassed on the short grass plains in the wet season. (Copyright K. Laurenson 1990.)

The last numerous migratory ungulate is the Thomson's gazelle; its numbers stood at 0.44 million at the 1989 count (Campbell 1989). The population may have declined from 0.7 million animals in the early 1970s, but the severity of this decline is controversial due to the use of differing counting techniques and censusing under suboptimal conditions (Borner et al. 1987; Dublin et al. 1990). The current consensus is that numbers have remained relatively stable since surveys began. Thomson's gazelles graze the short grass plains during the wet season and move to the plains-woodland border during the dry season (Durant et al. 1988), traveling farther on into the woodlands as the season progresses. They return to the plains in the opposite direction.

Approximately 30,000 Grant's gazelles are found throughout the ecosystem. Some of those inhabiting the plains remain there throughout the year, whereas an unknown proportion of individuals move to the woodlands when the plains become very dry. Approximately 13,800 elands also migrate on and off the plains annually (Campbell 1989).

RESIDENT HERBIVORES

Most nonmigratory ungulates are found in the woodlands, which contain a much greater density of flora and fauna than the plains, although warthogs, topi, and Coke's hartebeests are also found on the plains during the wet season and, since the mid-1970s, during the dry season as well (Hanby and Bygott 1979). In the woodlands, ungulate distributions are related to local mineral concentrations (McNaughton 1988). Table 2.1 gives estimates of large and medium-sized resident herbivores in May 1989.

THE PREDATORS

The huge ungulate biomass supports large predator populations. Serengeti was regarded as a superb area for shooting lions at the beginning of this century (Turner 1987), and lions are still hunted by foreigners on the park boundaries. Tourists on photographic safaris are particularly attracted to Serengeti because of its large carnivores. Although predators are difficult to census because driving transects underestimates their numbers (Bertram 1976), long-term, labor-intensive studies in Serengeti have provided approximate estimates unavailable in most other ecosystems (app. 2).

STUDY AREA

My study area comprised the central region of the Serengeti plains and plains-woodland border, and was approximately 2,200 km^2 in size (fig. 2.11). The plains were chosen because cheetahs were more easily located in grasslands, where wide areas could be scanned with binoculars, than in the woodlands, where vegetation reduced visibility. Ability to follow individuals easily was also a consideration. In addition, the bulk of the Thomson's gazelle population, reportedly the main food of cheetahs in the Serengeti (Kruuk and Turner 1967; Schaller 1972c), occupied this area for most of the year (Maddock 1979).

Some of the woodlands bordering the plains were also included in the study area, as gazelles collected along the Seronera, Nyamara, and Ngare Nanyuki rivers to the northwest and north of the plains in the dry season. The woodlands along the western border of the plains at the base of Oldonya Olbaye plateau, and west of the Moru kopjes were not searched for cheetahs for reasons of inaccessibility, despite gazelles concentrating there in the dry season (see fig. 2.11). Difficult driving conditions in the wet season sometimes precluded visits to the Moru kopjes themselves and limited my excursions to Hidden Valley, so these were eventually excluded from the study area too.

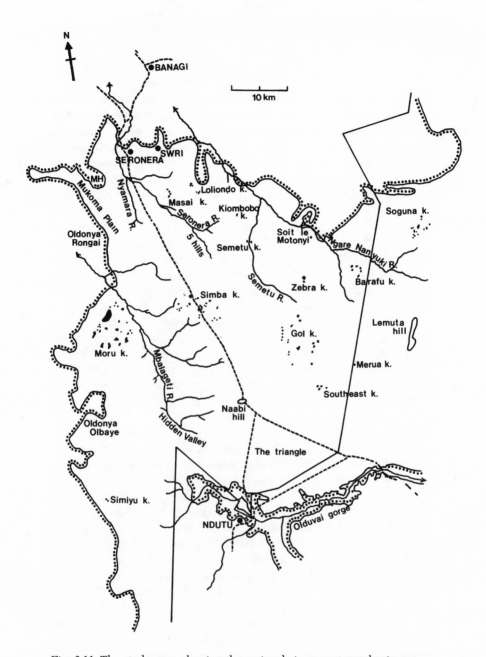

Fig. 2.11 The study area, showing the major drainage systems, kopje systems (marked k.), and principal roads (dashed lines). The continuous solid line denotes the Park boundary. The line bordered by dots denotes the woodland edge, with woodlands on the side of the dots; MH refers to Mukoma Hill. The Serengeti Wildlife Research Institute (SWRI), later renamed Centre, was my base.

DISTRIBUTIONS OF MIGRATORY PREY IN THE STUDY AREA

Schaller (1968) had found that on the plains, approximately 90% of chee-tahs' kills consisted of Thomson's gazelles (app. 3), so gazelle distribution in the study area was assumed to have a strong influence on cheetahs' whereabouts. Figures 2.12 and 2.13 show the distribution of Thomson's gazelles on the Serengeti plains over the course of the year. From January to April Thomson's gazelles were concentrated on the eastern boundary of the Park, although in January many were farther east in the Ngoro-ngoro Conservation Area, not shown in the figure. During May and June gazelles moved northwest so that by July they were concentrated in the vicinity of Seronera but especially to its south. Some gazelles moved into the woodlands after July, but concentrations nevertheless remained high in the Seronera area until October. During that month some gazelles re-turned to the short grass plains, and by November most were found on the plains again, where they moved progressively east until January.

Both wildebeests and Grant's gazelles were also consumed by cheetahs. Figure 2.14 shows that wildebeests were virtually absent from the study area during dry season months and were present for roughly half the wet season months on the short grass plains, more so on the southern plains. In contrast, Grant's gazelles were present almost everywhere throughout the study area during all months of the year.

STUDY PERIODS

I arrived in Serengeti on 1 March 1980 and stayed until 20 December 1983, aside from a 6-week period of absence in December and January 1980–81. Anthony Collins arrived in November 1983 and collected demographic records until October 1984. Clare FitzGibbon and I re-turned in January 1985, and after I left in February, she remained in the field until March 1987 studying the antipredator behavior of Thomson's gazelles in relation to cheetahs and wild dogs. During this time she con-tinued to collect demographic records on cheetahs. I visited Serengeti three times during her stay, in July and August 1985 (with Steve O'Brien, David Wildt, and Mitch Bush), in January and February 1986 (with Mary Holt), and in August and September 1986; each time I collected blood samples, radio-collared cheetahs, and took further demographic records.

In 1987 I was in the field from May until October, when Karen Lau-renson arrived to start a study of female cheetahs' reproductive strategies, which terminated in September 1990. I made two further visits during this period in June and July 1988 and in May 1989. The emphasis placed on overlap between personnel allowed us to take standardized demo-graphic and behavioral information on cheetahs continuously for over 10 years.

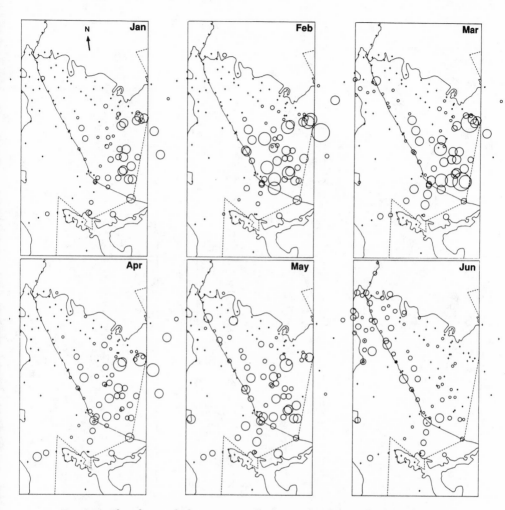

Fig. 2.12 Abundance of Thomson's gazelles at 142 locations, 1 km in radius, on the Serengeti plains each month during the first half of the year, between February 1982 and July 1985. For each month, a median number of gazelles was derived from counts made in different years. The woodland border and Olduvai Gorge are shown, as is the park boundary (dashed line) and main road (solid line). Numbers of gazelles were divided into seven categories: 1–10, 11–50, 51–100, 101–200, 201–500, 501–1,000, and >1,000, and are represented by seven sizes of circles increasing in area in proportion to the median number in these categories. Points at which no gazelles were seen are denoted by +. (From Durant et al. 1988.)

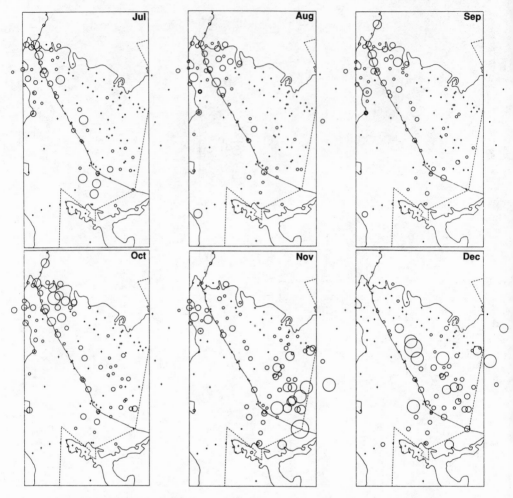

Fig. 2.13 Abundance of Thomson's gazelles at 142 locations, 1 km in radius, on the Serengeti plains each month during the second half of the year, between February 1982 and July 1985, excluding November and December 1984. Symbols are as for fig. 2.12. (From Durant et al. 1988.)

Morphology and Taxonomy of Cheetahs

Cheetah is a word derived from the Hindu *chita,* meaning "spotted one." The species was first described as *Felis jubata* by Schreber in 1776; since then the nomenclature has changed several times. Generic names have included *Cyanilurus, Guepardus,* and *Cynofelis* (reviewed in McLaughlin

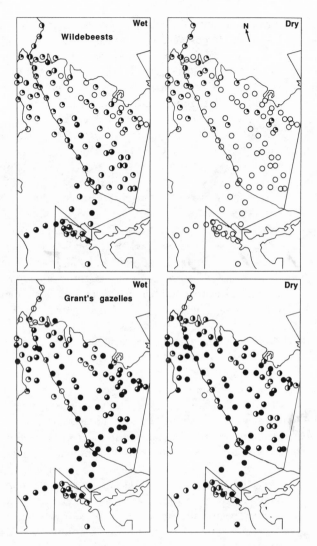

Fig. 2.14 Presence of wildebeests (top) and Grant's gazelles (bottom) at 111 locations on the Serengeti plains during wet season months (left, $N = 8$ or 9 counts
for most locations) and dry season months (right, $N = 9$ counts), between July
1983 and February 1985 (excluding November and December 1984). The woodland border and Olduvai Gorge are shown, as are the park boundary and main
road. Circles denote the percentage of months in which each species was seen at
each location: open circles, never seen; quarter solid circles, seen on 1–25% of
months; half solid, 26–50%; three-quarters solid, 51–75%; full solid, present in
76–100% of months.

1970). It is currently known as *Acinonyx jubatus. Acinonyx* may have been derived from the Greek *akaina,* "a thorn," and *onyx,* "a claw," or alternatively from the Greek prefix *a* and *kineo,* "to move," referring to its nonretractable claws. *Jubatus* (Latin) refers to the crest or mane seen in young individuals and in certain adults. Cheetahs, especially from Asia, were also referred to as "hunting leopards" in older literature.

Cheetahs have several unique morphological features absent in other extant cats. They have a slight build, long, thin legs, a deep, narrow chest, and a small, delicate domed skull (Pocock 1916b; Brown and Yalden 1973). Their small rounded ears, set far apart, are black when viewed from behind. Their light brown pelage is covered with solid round black spots, the smaller of which are interspersed with larger ones. No two cheetahs have the same arrangement of spots on their bodies or faces. A tear streak extends from the medial corner of the eye to the upper lip just behind the canines. Compared with other extant felids, cheetahs are medium-sized cats, similar in size to leopards and cougars. Cheetahs that were weighed in this study were lighter than those in other studies (app. 4) but resembled captive animals in North American zoos, most of which were from southern Africa (captive males, $N = 60$, $\bar{X} = 40.2$, range 27.9–51.0 kg; females, $N = 68$, $\bar{X} = 35.0$, range 25.0–46.4 kg: Wildt et al. 1993). In Serengeti, males were significantly heavier than females [1] and had larger chest girths, an important measure of body size in mammals (Bertram 1975b), and longer tails [2]. Other linear dimensions did not differ significantly between the sexes [2].

The cheetah's peculiar morphology, superficially resembling that of a greyhound, formerly caused it to be placed in a monophyletic group, *Acinonychinae,* separate from the *Pantherinae* and *Felinae* (Pocock 1917). It is usually considered to be one of the earliest divergences in felid evolution (Hemmer 1978; Neff 1983). Nevertheless, cat systematics are in confusion because of the great size variation and convergent morphology within the family (Wozencraft 1989). For example, Herrington (1986) suggested that cheetahs may share a common ancestor with the manul or Pallas's cat, whose own position within the family is unknown! Using albumin immunological distances, Collier and O'Brien (1985) constructed a molecular phylogeny of the Felidae. They found that the family was composed of three lineages. The ocelot lineage (e.g., ocelot, Geoffroy's cat, margay) diverged first from the rest of the felids about 10 million years ago in the Miocene. A second lineage, the small species of *Felis* (e.g., European wildcat, black-footed cat), diverged about 2 million years later. A third pantherine (e.g., lion, lynx, bobcat) lineage broke away from this group about 5 million years ago. Surprisingly, cheetahs sit firmly within this third lineage, being more closely related to lions, tigers, and lynxes than (in decreasing order of resemblance) to servals, clouded leopards,

Asiatic golden cats, or cougars. According to this phylogenetic reconstruction, the cheetah's unique morphological traits may have arisen recently and rapidly, possibly within the last 2 million years.

Paleoecological records show that cheetah-like cats ranged across Asia, Africa, and North America as little as ten thousand years ago (Kurtén 1968). *Acinonyx jubatus* is an Old World species, and there were at least two other species of Old World cheetahs that might have existed at the same time. *Acinonyx pardinensis,* weighing perhaps 95 kg, occurred in Europe during the Villafranchian period, 1.9 to 3.8 million years ago, earlier than suggested by the molecular phylogeny, and a smaller species, *A. intermedius,* found in the mid-Pleistocene, had a range extending from Europe eastward to China.

Many cursorial predators lived in North America in the late Pleistocene. Two large (ca. 95 kg) extinct species of cheetahs have been described from this period, *Miracinonyx studeri* and *Miracinonyx trumani* (van Valkenburgh, Grady, and Kurtén 1990). Each had skull morphology similar to that of *Acinonyx jubatus,* with small upper canines, a short face, a broad, domed forehead, and enlarged internal and external nares, presumably to facilitate oxygen intake during chases (fig. 2.15). Most striking is their lack of a postcanine gap, which, among extant cats, is uniquely absent in cheetahs (Adams 1979). These two New World species have now been placed in a new subgenus or genus *Miracinonyx,* depending on the authority (see Adams 1979; van Valkenburgh, Grady, and Kurtén 1990, respectively) rather than being classified as cheetah-like cats in the genus *Felis* (Martin, Gilbert, and Adams 1977).

Miracinonyx and *Acinonyx* are distinguished from other species by features related either to facial shortening or to nasal expansion, and both groups may have undergone a reduction in head mass and enlargement of respiratory passages to facilitate very fast and prolonged running

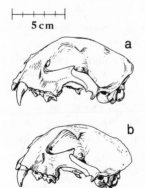

5 cm

a

b

Fig. 2.15 Comparison of the skulls of *Acinonyx jubatus* (top) and the extinct New World species *Felis trumani* (bottom) (from Martin, Gilbert, and Adams 1977). The latter was later reassigned to the genus *Miracinonyx* (van Valkenburgh, Grady, and Kurtén 1990).

(van Valkenburgh, Grady, and Kurtén 1990). *Miracinonyx* is believed to be closely related to *Puma*, which is restricted to the Western Hemisphere. If the similarities between *Miracinonyx* and *Acinonyx* are the result of common descent, this would suggest that cheetahs originated in North America (Adams 1979), not in Eurasia as previously believed. Indeed, contrary to the molecular classification, *Acinonyx* and *Puma* are thought by some to be descended from a common ancestor among the Pseudaelurini (see Adams 1979). Alternatively, the similarities between *Acinonyx* and *Miracinonyx* may simply be a case of parallel evolution. Convergent evolution among carnivores occupying similar niches in the Old and New Worlds has occurred in the case of jackals and coyotes, leopards and jaguars, and wild dogs and wolves (Martin 1989), so there is a strong precedent for this hypothesis. Clearly the cursorial features found in modern-day cheetahs had selective advantages in many different ecosystems in the past.

Until quite recently there was taxonomic controversy over the number of extant cheetah species. Individuals with a blotched coat pattern resembling that of a serval had been collected from eastern Botswana, northern South Africa, and Zimbabwe (Hills and Smithers 1980), and a specimen has now been reported from Burkina Faso (Frame 1992). This morph was originally classified as *Acinonyx rex*, the king cheetah (Pocock 1927a; see Wrogemann [1975] for an excellent history of the controversy), and much has been made of the rarity and uniqueness of these individuals (e.g., Bottriell 1987). Recently, definitive evidence from a successful captive propagation program in South Africa has shown that king cheetahs are simply *A. jubatus* individuals with a single recessive gene trait homologous to *tabby-blocked* in domestic cats (van Aarde and van Dyk 1986). There is growing but controversial interest in breeding these cheetahs in North American zoos.

Seven subspecies of cheetahs are recognized today (app. 5), but *A. j. velox* is normally subsumed under *A. j. raineyii*, while *A. j. raddei* is presumed extinct, reducing the number to five. Subtle morphological differences separate these groups, but only two, *A. j. jubatus* and *raineyii*, have been compared using electrophoretic methods. Surveys of allozymes showed that both subspecies were extremely homozygous compared with other free-living species examined so far (O'Brien et al. 1983, 1987). Southern African individuals were monomorphic at all 47 loci sampled, whereas East African individuals exhibited polymorphisms at only 2 out of 49 loci (O'Brien et al. 1987). The Nei genetic distance using these 49 loci was 0.004 between the two subspecies, whereas that between human races is approximately 0.03. This finding calls into question the subspecific classification (app. 5), at least in reference to *A. j. jubatus* and *raineyii.*

Distribution and Density

At the time of Christ, *Acinonyx jubatus* probably had a wide distribution throughout Africa and southwestern Asia (fig. 2.16). Since then its range has contracted (fig. 2.17). In the early 1970s a survey conducted by Myers (1975) showed that between 7,000 and 23,000 cheetahs survived in twenty-five African countries; only in Botswana, Namibia, and Kenya did numbers reach 2,000 animals. The species' range at the time of writing is almost certainly smaller than in the 1970s, but new data are unavailable.

Compared with those of sympatric carnivores such as lions and spotted hyenas, cheetah densities are low (table 2.2). For example, their numbers range from 0.25/100 km² in the Tarangire area in Tanzania (Lamprey 1964) to 5.0/100 km² in the Timbavati Nature Preserve in South Africa (Myers 1975). Seasonal densities are far higher, however, reaching 40/100 km² on the Serengeti plains at certain times of year (calculated from Schaller 1972c), although overall densities were 0.8–1.0/100 km². Similar local concentrations have been reported in Nairobi National Park (25/100 km²: McLaughlin, reported in Burney 1980) and in the Kalahari (Labuschagne 1974). Historically, cheetah densities may always have been low because the factors that contribute to high adult male mortality (intrasexual combat) and high cub mortality (principally predation) would

Fig. 2.16 Possible former distribution of cheetahs at the time of Christ (from Wrogemann 1975). Star denotes location of confirmed reports of a contemporary remnant Asiatic cheetah population in Iran.

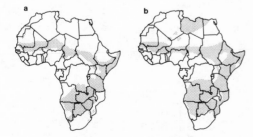

Fig. 2.17 (*a*) Distribution of cheetahs in Africa in 1973 (adapted from Myers 1975). (*b*) Distribution in 1970s (adapted from Smithers 1983).

TABLE 2.2 Estimated Numbers of Large Predators Living in Some Regions of Africa

	Area		
	Nairobi National Park (Foster and Kearney 1967)	Kruger National Park (Pienaar 1969)	Serengeti ecosystem (Borner et al. 1987)
Date	1960s	1964	1980s
Lion	17	1,120	2,135–2,535
Leopard	3	650	800–1,000
Spotted hyena	18?	?	5,161
Wild dog	Rare	335	46
Cheetah	10	263	564

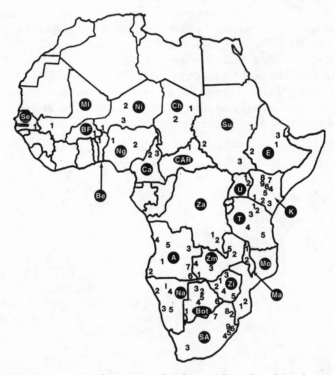

Fig. 2.18 Major protected areas in sub-Saharan Africa thought to be currently used by cheetahs. (Data from MacKinnon and MacKinnon 1986; P. Gros, pers. comm.) NP/PN refers to national park; GR, game reserve; P, parks; NR, nature reserve; CA, conservation area.

Angola (A)
1 Bikuar NP
2 Iona NP
3 Kameia NP

4 Kisama (Quicama) NP
5 Luando NR
6 Luina NR
7 Mavinga NR

Benin (Be)
1 Reserve de Biosphere de la Penjari
(for PN du W see Niger)
Botswana (Bot)
1 Gemsbok NP–Mabuasekube GR
2 Nxai Pan NP
3 Moremi R
4 Central Kalahari GR–Khutse GR
5 Makgadikgadi Pan GR
6 Bamanmashati GR
Burkina Faso (BF)
1 Reserves de l'Arly–Pama–Singou
(for PN du W see Niger)
Cameroon (Ca)
1 PN de Waza
2 PN de Faro
3 PNs de Benoue et de Bouba Ndgida
Central African Republic (CAR)
1 PN de Manovo-Gounda–St. Floris
Chad (Ch)
1 R Fada Archei
2 R de Ouadi Rime–Ouadi Achim
Ethiopia (E)
1 Awash NP
2 Gambella NP
3 Yangudi Rassa NP
Kenya (K)
1 Masai Mara GR
2 Amboseli NP
3 Tsavo NP
4 Meru NP–Kora GR
5 Nairobi NP
6 Buffalo Springs NR–Shaba NR–
Samburu NR
7 Marsabit NR
8 Sibiloi NP
9 Mt. Kukal R
Malawi (Ma)
1 Nyika NR
2 Kasungu NP
Mali (Ml)
1 PN de la Boucle du Baoule
Mozambique (Mo)
1 PN do Banhine
2 PN do Zinave
Namibia (Na)
1 Etosha NP
2 Skeleton Coast P
3 Namib-Naukluft P
4 Waterburg Plateau P
5 Hardnap NR

Niger (Ni)
1 PN du W
2 RN de l'Air et du Tenere
3 R Gababedji
Nigeria (Ng)
1 Kainji Lake NP
2 Yankari GR
Senegal (Se)
1 PN de Niokolo-Koba
South Africa (SA)
1 Kalahari Gemsbok NP
2 Kruger NP–Timbavati GR–Sabie
Sand GR–Groot Letaba GR
3 Rolfontein NR (reintroduced)
4 Umfolozi GR (reintroduced)
5 Hluhluwe GR
6 Mkuzi GR (reintroduced)
7 Pilanesberg NP
8 Hans Merensky NR
9 Itala NR
Sudan (Su)
1 Dinder NP
2 Radom NP
3 Boma NP
Tanzania (T)
1 Serengeti NP
2 Ngorongoro CA
3 Tarangire NP
4 Ruaha NP/Rungwa GR
5 Selous GR
Uganda (U)
1 Kidepo NP
2 Matheniko GR–Pian-Upe GR
Zaire (Za)
1 PN de l'Upemba
2 PN des Kundelunga
Zambia (Zm)
1 Sioma Ngwezi NP
2 South Luangwa NP
3 Blue Lagoon NP
4 Liuwa Plain P
5 Kasanka P
Zimbabwe (Zi)
1 Chizarira NP
2 Wankie (Hwange) NP–Kazuma Pan
NP–Matesi NP
3 Mana Pools NP
4 Rhodes Matapos NP
5 Gonarezhou P

probably have been severe in the past. Cheetah species became extinct before sympatric lion species did in North America and Europe, supporting the view that they were poor competitors. In historical times, the opposite has occurred in Iran, Uzbekistan, and Egypt, however (D. Burney, pers. comm.).

Cheetahs are classified as vulnerable by the IUCN and are listed under Appendix I of CITES, although an annual quota of 150 live animals or hunting trophies from Namibia, 50 from Zimbabwe, and 5 from Botswana per year was passed at the 1992 CITES meeting. Habitat encroachment and reduction in their ungulate prey, principally stemming from cultivation and direct shooting, are primarily responsible for reducing the cheetah's range, although direct persecution occurs in Namibia and Zimbabwe (Morsbach 1987). There seems no reason to suppose that these pressures will become less severe, and in the long term, the cheetah's best hope of survival is through protection in multiple-use areas or national parks (fig. 2.18). A relict Asian population of *A. j. venaticus* still survives in Iran and possibly in northwestern Afghanistan, although their numbers are unknown (Jackson 1990; Karami 1992).

Natural History of Cheetahs

HISTORICAL REFERENCES TO CHEETAHS

Cheetahs can probably run faster than any other land mammal over short distances of 300–400 m (see Gray 1968). Bourlière (1964) claimed that a cheetah can accelerate to 93 kph in 2 seconds from a standing start, and observed a cheetah running at an average speed of 112 kph over 700 m. Hildebrand (1959, 1961) filmed a cheetah reaching this velocity. Schaller (1969) stated that cheetahs can attain 95 kph and can outrun gazelles that reach 70–80 kph, as estimated by driving parallel to them. Regardless of its exact speed, I can attest to the exhilaration of watching a cheetah chase a gazelle.

The hunting behavior of cheetahs has attracted the nobility for centuries. Captive animals were used for coursing in Asia prior to the Assyrian dynasty (Simon 1966) and in Libya during the reign of the pharaohs (Harper 1945). Drawings of a Dionysian procession in Alexandria during the reign of Ptolemy II (309–246 B.C.) show a cheetah on a leash, while a silver ornament found in a Scythian burial site in the Caucasus (700–300 B.C.) depicts a cheetah wearing a collar. In A.D. 439, cheetahs were sent to Anastasius, Emperor of the East in Constantinople, and from there the sport quickly spread to Italy, where it became a badge of extravagance among the wealthy (Harper 1945). There are also records of hunting with cheetahs at Kiev in Russia (Novikov 1956). Between the thirteenth and sixteenth centuries Mongol emperors used cheetahs for sport in India, and Akbar the Great is said to have kept 3,000 trained cheetahs to hunt antelope. Cheetahs were used to hunt blackbuck and chinkara well into the twentieth century.

According to Sterndale (1884), a hunting cheetah was taken to within 300–400 m of a herd, and its hood was removed. If it killed a male antelope it was allowed to feed from the hindquarters and then gently pulled off so that the attendants could disembowel the prey; the viscera were then given to the cheetah in a special bowl. If the cheetah killed a female, it was not allowed to feed as punishment. Within six months the cheetahs learned to select only male prey. Fitzsimons (1919) described the practice differently. He observed that while a cheetah was choking its victim attendants would open the prey's hindleg vein and fill the feeding bowl with blood. The cheetah would release its stranglehold and lap up the blood, allowing attendants to drag the carcass away. Indian male cheetahs were usually used for coursing, but when they became scarce (due in part to collection by sportsmen) East African animals were imported. Only young adult cheetahs were used, as hand-raised cubs could not be trained to chase, capture, and kill prey.

In several regions of Africa and Asia, cheetahs have been treated as vermin, especially by European settlers. In colonial times they were run down by dogs or on horseback and then shot (Roosevelt 1910). Cheetahs are still persecuted in Namibia and Zimbabwe today because they take livestock, while they are shot for recreation in some regions of the Sahel. Nevertheless they are protected in most of the countries where they still occur; fortunately this is the case in Tanzania.

PREY CONSUMED BY CHEETAHS

The majority of studies of free-living cheetahs have centered on their feeding, and in some cases, hunting behavior. Appendix 3 shows the range of prey species eaten by cheetahs across Africa; small prey are underrepresented because the information is partially based on carcass remains. Not surprisingly, food habits differ between study locations, reflecting differences in prey species and their abundance. Whereas Thomson's gazelles, Grant's gazelles, and impalas were equally represented in cheetah kills in Nairobi National Park, Thomson's gazelles were the most important prey item in four studies conducted in Serengeti National Park. Puku were eaten most frequently in Zambia; impalas in South Africa. By far the most impressive data base is that of Pienaar (1969), who found 2,523 cheetah kills over a 24-year period. These included a cheetah, a porcupine, two buffalo calves, and two giraffe calves. By dividing numbers of prey species taken by the numbers available, he found that reedbuck were the most preferred prey item in Kruger National Park. This method shows that Thomson's gazelles were most preferred in Nairobi National Park (McLaughlin 1970).

In all studies, young prey animals are taken in preference to adults, especially when medium-sized ungulates such as wildebeests are considered. For example, FitzGibbon and Fanshawe (1989) found that fawns and half-grown Thomson's gazelles constituted 53.7% of cheetahs' kills but only 5.9% of the gazelle population. FitzGibbon's (1990c) detailed study in the Serengeti revealed that single adult (usually female) cheetahs preferentially selected Thomson's gazelles that were on their own or in small groups, were in high vegetation, were less vigilant, were on the edge of the herd, and were farther from their nearest neighbors. Such individuals were usually males, and although cheetahs were actually more successful in capturing single female than single male Thomson's gazelles, more males were killed because they suffered such a high number of attacks. Circumstantial evidence suggests that cheetahs do not select unhealthy prey (FitzGibbon and Fanshawe 1989), but more work is required to determine this; for example, there are anecdotes of injured individuals being preferentially attacked (FitzGibbon 1990c).

Some attempts have been made to calculate the effects of cheetah depredation on prey populations by estimating the percentage of available prey killed per annum, or by calculating the percentage of yearly recruitment of prey taken by cheetahs. From the frequency with which cheetahs made kills in Nairobi National Park (once every 25–60 hours), McLaughlin (1970) estimated that cheetahs took 39–47% of the impalas, 53–64% of the Grant's gazelles, and a huge 64–92% of the Thomson's gazelles recruited into these populations annually. So despite living at low densities, cheetahs can have a substantial impact on prey populations in some areas.

HUNTING BEHAVIOR

Cheetahs spend most of the day resting. They hunt by sight, mainly during the day, especially between 0700 and 1000 and between 1600 and 1900 (Schaller 1972c). The cheetah has five main hunting methods (see Estes 1991). It may wait crouched or even sitting upon seeing an unsuspecting herd moving toward it. It may slowly walk toward a herd of gazelles in full view of them, and then break into a sprint from 60 or 70 m away if they have not run off. If prey are grazing and oblivious to its presence, it may start its rush from as far as 600 m, particularly if a neonate gazelle stands or nurses. In most attempts on vigilant adult prey, however, it will stalk toward the prey walking semi-crouched, freezing in mid-stride or dropping to the ground in a crouch if the quarry looks up, interspersing these behaviors with trotting or sitting immobile until it is close enough to launch an attack. Cheetahs also flush concealed prey such as hares or neonate gazelles from vegetation and pursue them briefly as soon as they run off (Frame and Frame 1981). On the open Serengeti plains, the last two methods are the predominant modes of prey capture (FitzGibbon 1988). Schaller (1972c) noted that independent cheetahs were successful in 53.5% of 56 runs made at gazelles older than neonates, whereas 100% of 31 runs at small fawns resulted in capture.

Cheetahs kill most prey by strangling, but hares are bitten through the skull. Cheetahs make no attempt to defend their kills against spotted hyenas or lions, and according to Schaller, lose up to 13% of their kills in this way in Serengeti. In contrast, they usually ignore jackals and vultures, although the latter have occasionally driven a cheetah from a kill (G. Schaller and K. Laurenson, pers. comm.).

REPRODUCTIVE ACTIVITY IN FEMALES

Females are polyestrous, cycling approximately every 12 days (range 3 to 27 days) in captivity (Bertschinger et al. 1984; Asa et al. 1992). Based on receptivity to males, the length of estrus varied from 1 to 3 days and was shorter when mating occurred (Bertschinger et al. 1984); however, others have described females as being receptive for 10 to 14 days (Seager and Demorest 1978). An intensive laparoscopic survey of sixty-eight captive females in North American zoos (Wildt et al. 1993) concluded that cheetahs were induced ovulators, based on the absence of luteal scars (see also Wildt et al. 1981). Bertschinger et al. (1984) also demonstrated that baseline plasma progesterone levels failed to rise in the absence of mating, indicating that the luteinizing hormone surges necessary for ovulation took place only following copulation. The survey disclosed luteal scars in four females that had had no opportunity to mate, demonstrating that females can occasionally ovulate spontaneously.

Females are reported to be capable of reproduction at 13 to 16 months of age (Wrogemann 1975). Five of eleven females less than 26 months of age had ovarian follicles in Wildt et al.'s study. Females aged between 16 and 20 months, however, showed a lower percentage of well-rounded ovaries and luteal scars and a higher percentage of small (less than 2 mm) follicles than those over 5 years of age, which might be indicative of poor reproductive performance. An old female of 182 months still showed follicular activity.

REPRODUCTIVE ACTIVITY IN MALES

Captive males have sired offspring in their third year of life, and all males aged between 15 and 26 months in Wildt et al.'s survey produced motile spermatozoa in ejaculates. Nonetheless, mean motile sperm per ejaculate and circulating testosterone levels were lower in this age group than in males aged 5–10 years. If testosterone is responsible for aggressiveness and libido, low titers could explain why young captive cheetahs do not usually breed.

More than 75% of sperm from captive males were pleiomorphic (Wildt et al. 1993), a level similar to that in free-living populations (Wildt, O'Brien, et al. 1987). These pleiomorphisms have been related to the cheetah's lack of heterozygosity, as determined from isozyme analysis of this and other species (Wildt, Bush, et al. 1987; Wildt, O'Brien, et al. 1987). In standardized tests, these abnormalities reduce cheetah sperm's ability to penetrate domestic cat oocytes compared with leopard cat sperm (Wildt et al. 1993), and combined with reduced motility (Donoghue et al. 1992), compromise fertilization. Nevertheless it is not known whether these problems affect natural fertility. Wildt et al. speculate that the proportion of structurally abnormal sperm in cheetahs is just below the threshold of sterility.

ESTRUS AND MATING

Estrous behavior is difficult to detect both in the wild and in captivity, although certain females show elevated rates of rolling, head rubbing, tail twitching, calling, frisky behavior, or even spray marking (see Sarri 1991; S. Wells, unpublished data). The most reliable sign is rolling in the presence of a male (Bertschinger et al. 1984). There is circumstantial evidence that the presence of males and intermale aggression triggers estrus within 24 hours (Herdman 1972a; N. Hulett, pers. comm.). There may also be a seasonal component to estrus, but this remains unresolved. For example, Brand (1980) found that more than three-quarters of matings in the De Wildt Breeding Centre, Pretoria, occurred in December and January. Nevertheless, there is great geographical variation even within southern Africa; for example, July to September is the breeding season in Namibia. In general, any peaks are superimposed on a background of matings throughout the year (Eaton 1974). Moreover, studies identifying estrus peaks are usually based on small sample sizes and, in the wild, are derived from backdating sightings of newly emerged cubs, which are confounded by neonatal mortality.

As much as 2 to 3 weeks prior to mating, males and females stutter-call or stutter-bark and exhibit mild aggression toward each other. Though breeding animals remain in close contact for 2 or 3 days, mating occurs in minutes and can be followed by gaps of 8 hours before the next episode (Tong 1974; Frame and Frame 1981). Mating often occurs at night (Wrogemann 1975) and to my knowledge has been seen only five times in the wild.

BIRTH AND CUB DEVELOPMENT

Gestation is 90 to 95 days in length, and up to eight cubs can be born in a litter, although six is normally the most that emerge from the lair in the wild. Litter sizes are larger than those found in most other felids (app. 6). Cubs remain in a lair, usually in a marsh, tall vegetation, or a rocky outcrop, for approximately 8 weeks (Laurenson 1993). All mothers observed by Laurenson carried cubs to new lairs during this period. Cubs are born weighing 250–300 g but can average 463 g in captivity (Wack et al. 1991). They have a thick covering of long bluish-gray or smoky gray hair that appears on the nape, shoulders, and back soon after birth. Its function is the subject of controversy (Eaton 1976b) but camouflage seems the most likely explanation (see Caro 1987a); it disappears at about 3 months of age, but a short mane is retained into adolescence and for longer in some individuals. Between 3 and 6 weeks a peculiar set of milk teeth erupts (Broom 1949), being replaced by adult teeth at about 8 months of age. Nursing terminates when cubs are approximately 4 months old.

Cubs accompany their mothers on hunts from 8 weeks onward and are introduced to solid food. Cheetah cubs are noted for their playfulness, especially during the first 6 months of life. From 6 months onward they practice rudimentary hunting skills but are still not adept at 13 to 20 months when they leave their mothers (Schaller 1972c). Opinion differs as to whether family fissioning is abrupt (Schaller 1970) or occurs gradually, with mother and cubs rejoining one or more times (Frame and Frame 1981). After separation from their mother, littermates remain together for variable periods of time. Mothers with dependent cubs can mate again successfully, but families separate before the birth of the subsequent litter. Many of the above statements taken from the literature are based on only a handful of observations, and although approximately correct, may obscure important and biologically meaningful variation between individuals.

Litter losses in the lair are high (chap. 4) and are caused by a variety of factors including predation, abandonment by mothers, and the elements. Cub mortality is also high after cubs emerge from the lair and before they reach 3 months of age. Schaller (1972c) observed that a third to a half died during this period. In the Masai Mara Game Reserve, 41% of cubs that emerged died before 3 months of age (Burney 1980). Five were killed by lions, three by spotted hyenas, six in a flood, three by automobiles, and four died as a result of unknown causes. After 3 months of age most cubs survive to independence. Pienaar (1969) reported a 50% mortality rate from emergence to maturity in Kruger National Park, and McLaughlin (1970) noted a 43% figure for Nairobi National Park. Mothers resume estrus quickly if they lose their litters prematurely (Schaller 1972c).

SOCIAL STRUCTURE

Published reports indicate great variability in cheetah group size. A questionnaire survey in East Africa (Graham and Parker 1965; Graham 1966) showed that of adult cheetahs apparently unaccompanied by young, 27% were solitary, 34% were sighted in groups of two, 19% in groups of three, and 20% in groups of four to twelve. The survey also found that although 63% of litters were accompanied by one adult, 21% were accompanied by two, and the rest by three or four adults. Eaton (1970b) apparently witnessed one group of three adult males and two adult females hunting together. In contrast, McLaughlin (1970) and Schaller (1972c), working in two different areas, never saw adult females living together, although they occasionally met inadvertently.

These disparate observations have been more or less resolved by detailed long-term studies of known individuals carried out by Burney (1980) in Masai Mara Game Reserve, and by Frame and Frame (1981) in Serengeti. They concluded that female cheetahs live alone, whereas males may be found alone or in groups of two, three, or even four (as reported by Foster and Kearney [1967] in Nairobi National Park). For instance, Frame and Frame (1976b) found females associating together in only 1 out of 390 female sightings. They also determined that sisters leave their siblings at about the time of first estrus, but brothers remain together throughout life (Frame and Frame 1981). In addition, unrelated males may join up to form permanent coalitions (Caro and Collins 1987b). In sum, adult females are unsociable, but some males live permanently in small all-male groups.

The discrepancy between these in-depth studies and the sightings survey must hinge on misidentification of large cubs, temporary male interest in females, and possibly, parasitic associations by young individuals incompetent at hunting (see table 1.1). Since cubs continue to associate with their mothers until they are almost fully grown, daughters may be as large as their mothers, and sons may be even larger, although they are slimmer and less stocky than adults. If such a family group were seen at a distance, or encountered by an inexperienced observer, they might be taken for a group of adults. When littermates leave their mothers they usually remain together for several months. Such groups may be composed of up to six brothers and sisters, or be single-sex groups. Again, some of these groups might be recorded as a mixed-sex group of adults.

A male or group of males maintains close proximity to either a single female or a mother and cubs when seeking to mate with her. Such an association may last for a few minutes to over 2 days, and participants may even hunt together at this time. Clearly a trio of males associating with a mother and 12-month-old daughter could account for Eaton's observation, for example, and for some of the larger documented group sizes.

Finally, cubs that are not fully grown and that have lost contact with their family through ill fortune will attempt to associate with unrelated cheetah families or even male groups for as long as they can, sharing meat caught by the adult female or by the males (see chap. 4). For incompetent hunters this may be the only means of survival. Single adolescents or sibling groups may also attach themselves to an unrelated family. Despite suffering aggression from the mother, such cheetahs may stay with a family for many months, and would add to further confusion over group size and group composition.

Paradoxically, the large number of reasons that account for observations of groups of cheetahs, and the added burden of relying on experienced and knowledgeable observers, make it difficult to provide convincing evidence that adult females *do* live together in long-term associations (see chap. 12). At present, the weight of evidence points to obligate asociality in adult females and facultative sociality in adult males.

A final controversy concerns whether cheetahs are territorial. In Serengeti, Schaller noted that cheetahs followed the Thomson's gazelle migration and stressed that several families used the same area at the same time but that they avoided meeting through visual and olfactory means. Both Eaton (1974) and McLaughlin (1970), working in Nairobi National Park, also recorded considerable spatial overlap in individuals' ranges and little temporal overlap. In the Kalahari Gemsbok National Park, Labuschagne (1974) recognized that females with cubs were temporarily territorial, and that some individuals were nomads, while a third category was strictly territorial. Individuals in this last class would defend areas against intruders, although few fights between free-living cheetahs have been seen. Frame (1984) resolved some of these reports by finding that females and males showed different movement patterns. In Serengeti, females and their cubs ranged over 800-km² home ranges following migrating gazelles, as subsequently documented by Durant et al. (1988), whereas some groups of males defended much smaller areas of 30 km² against other males, although these were not entirely exclusive since some males passed through them. He was unsure as to why some males set up territories, and when I began my study the causes and consequences of territoriality were poorly understood.

In conclusion, cheetah social organization had been well described by the 1970s, but no study had attempted to investigate the reasons for variation in cheetah grouping patterns. Understanding this variation requires knowledge of why cubs need to stay with their mothers until they are almost fully grown, why littermates remain together as adolescents, and the causes and repercussions of group living for males. These topics are the subject of this book.

Summary

1. Human ancestors lived in Serengeti 3 million years ago, and over the last 6,000 years a number of different peoples have occupied the area sporadically.

2. The Serengeti ecosystem represents the extent of the woodland and plains used by wildebeests during their annual migration. There is a wet season from November to May and a dry season from June to October.

3. During the wet season, the most numerous herbivores, wildebeests, zebras, and Thomson's gazelles, occupy the short grass plains. The central portion of these plains was chosen as the study site for reasons of ease of observation and accessibility.

4. A number of cheetah species lived during the Pleistocene, including two in North America, but only *Acinonyx jubatus* is extant. Despite its slight build, thin legs, and deep chest compared with other felids, recent molecular techniques suggest that the cheetah is closely related to the pantherine lineage and question its inclusion in a monospecific genus *Acinonyx*.

5. The king cheetah, formerly *Acinonyx rex*, is an *A. jubatus* mutant. Seven subspecies of *jubatus* have been recognized in Africa and Asia, although genetic techniques show that subspecific differences are minor.

6. The distribution of cheetahs was reasonably widespread across Africa in the 1970s although densities were low everywhere. Since then further range contraction has almost certainly occurred.

7. Cheetahs have been caught and tamed by humans for millennia, and in Asia were still used as coursers to catch antelopes in the twentieth century.

8. Different prey species assume varying degrees of importance in the diet in different locations; young prey animals are taken in preference to adults everywhere.

9. Cheetahs are induced ovulators and evidence for seasonal breeding is weak. A high proportion of spermatozoa show abnormalities, but it is not known whether this affects natural fertility. In the wild, cheetahs normally produce from one to six cubs that remain dependent on their mother for over a year.

10. All segments of the cheetah population show variation in grouping patterns. Females live alone or with dependent cubs, littermates of both sexes may remain together for a time after gaining independence, and a proportion of males form lifelong associations.

Statistics

1. Weights of Serengeti male cheetahs were greater than those of females: $N = 23$, 19 individuals respectively, Student's t test, $t = 3.291$, $P = .002$ (see app. 4).

2. Linear dimensions of Serengeti male and female cheetahs: Head and body length, $N = 24$, 16 individuals respectively, Student's t test, $t = -0.933$, $P > .3$; tail, $N = 24$, 19, $t = 2.113$, $P = .041$; hindfoot, $N = 24$, 18, $t = 1.454$, $P > .1$; chest girth, $N = 21$, 12, $t = 2.164$, $P = .038$; upper canines, $N = 22$, 7, $t = 0.925$, $P > .3$ (see app. 4).

Members of a trio of adult males, showing the lines of spots on their faces. (Drawing by Dafila Scott.)

3
SAMPLING METHODS AND TECHNIQUES

This chapter describes my methods of data collection, starting with how cheetahs were located in the field, the information collected at sightings, and the way cheetahs were recognized individually. As the main thrust of this book concerns the behavior of cheetahs, rather than their demography, I present my methods of recording behavior in some detail. Decisions had to be made as to which animals to follow and for how long a period, which types of behavior were pertinent to the questions I was asking, and at what time of day it was appropriate to collect different types of information. These issues, together with behavioral definitions, form the core of the chapter. Next, techniques used for immobilization of cheetahs and for counting Thomson's gazelles are presented. Finally, I make some general statements about my use of statistical analyses; specific statistical data are found at the end of each chapter.

Locating Cheetahs

OBSERVING CHEETAHS DIRECTLY

During most days of the study, a predetermined area of the park was searched for cheetahs. Observations were invariably made from a white long-wheelbase Land Rover (see fig. 2.1), which was driven to locations providing a good view of the surroundings, such as rises, watersheds, and hilltops. The area was then scanned slowly, and normally twice, using 10 × 50 Zeiss binoculars, from inside the vehicle, as both habituated and fearful cheetahs sometimes took time to sit up and show themselves. Certain shapes or other cues that might indicate the presence of a cheetah were scrutinized through the glasses. These were, in approximate order of importance, a clear silhouette of a moving cheetah (which might be mistaken for a lion or almost any other mammal if it was more than 2 km away!); a triangular silhouette of a cheetah sitting up, which was more difficult to see, but whose thin shape was less likely to be confused with other predators (except occasionally jackals); a thin, light-colored oblong shape of a recumbent cheetah; and finally, a light spot in a patch of dark vegetation that might indicate the position of a cheetah's head (see fig. 1.2).

BEHAVIOR OF PREY

Ungulates also gave clues for locating subjects. Gazelles, for instance, adopt a characteristic stare posture upon seeing a predator in which they hold the back straight and keep the head erect (Walther 1969); they approach and follow cheetahs on 52% of occasions they encounter them (FitzGibbon in press; fig. 3.1). The direction in which such gazelles were staring was examined carefully through binoculars, although jackals, spotted hyenas, lions, wild dogs, and even smaller carnivores such as caracals and bat-eared foxes could elicit this response in adult gazelles. Similarly, fleeing ungulates, especially Thomson's gazelles, usually signified the presence of a predator, often a cheetah.

CARCASSES

Carcasses could also indicate that a cheetah was in close proximity, although there was no guarantee that it had necessarily made the kill or was still in the vicinity. Vultures descending rapidly to the ground, standing together, or perching provided a marker for locating a carcass. Those taking off or ascending in thermals might have left a dead animal recently, but such carcasses had often been vacated by carnivores some time earlier and were more difficult to find. If spotted hyenas or lions were seen, the search area was widened or abandoned, as cheetahs would normally leave a kill if these predators approached.

APPROACHING CHEETAHS

Cheetahs could be sighted from as far away as 2.5 km and were then approached slowly, but not directly, until the vehicle was about 200 m away. Further approach was made in a zigzag fashion while circling the vehicle away from the subject at each "tack" rather than driving directly toward it. If the cheetah ran away, the vehicle was halted and the engine turned off; only when the animal had stopped moving was it approached again (see Burney 1982). When animals appeared very shy and unlikely to stop

Fig. 3.1 A herd of Thomson's gazelles have approached and now stare at a cheetah walking in the foreground.

running off, attempts were made to get a few pictures by driving parallel to the fleeing cheetah.

Sightings were made during daylight only (0630–1845). If cheetahs had not been found by 1030, searching was usually terminated until 1700 or the next day because the morning heat haze made long-distance scanning impossible. Also, cheetahs usually became less active at this time unless the day was very overcast, in which case searching was extended.

Information Collected at Each Sighting

Sightings were numbered in order, and the date, time of finding the cheetah and leaving it, and its location were recorded. Number and sex of cheetahs was catalogued by noting presence or absence of testes, although this was difficult with small cubs. At first, location was written in longhand and subsequently mapped onto a 500 × 500 m grid square map (by M. Kelly); later the grid square was recorded in the field. Grid squares in which unsuccessful scans were made and those immediately adjacent to them were also noted and were later used to gauge the distribution of cheetahs corrected for search area.

AGING CHEETAHS

Exact birth dates of most individuals were unknown. Ages of cubs accompanying their mothers were based on comparison of cubs' body sizes with those of known-aged animals. An aging chart was kindly provided by G. and L. Frame, which was subsequently amended in the light of Laurenson's (1992) study of female reproduction. Laurenson located females on a monthly basis using aerial radiotelemetry and assessed their reproductive status on the ground after the flight. Well-developed mammary glands and a protruding abdomen indicated advanced pregnancy, whereas brown rings around nipples and full mammae indicated that females were lactating. Date of parturition could be pinpointed to within a few days by noting these changes and the time when pregnant females' movements became restricted to a lair. The lair sites of lactating females were located by radiotracking from the vehicle at daybreak, when mothers were usually nursing their cubs. On days when the mother left the lair to hunt and could no longer see it, Laurenson would search the dense vegetation on foot in order to count and weigh the cubs. Litters were no more likely to be abandoned by their mothers or killed by predators due to Laurenson's observation schedule than to die of causes unrelated to it, such as fire or exposure (Laurenson and Caro, in press). As a result of this research, she found that cubs left the lair at approximately 8 weeks. The aging scale was therefore recalibrated as follows.

Cubs with black manes and less than one-quarter of their mother's height at the shoulder were estimated at 2 months old. Cubs with black manes but less than a third of their mother's height were estimated at 3 months; more than a third of her height and with shoulders still fluffy, 4 months; just under half her height, 5 months; just above half her height, 6 months. After this, sexual dimorphism could be discerned. If sons were two-thirds or daughters five-eighths of their mother's height, they were estimated at 7 months old. If sons were three-quarters or daughters two-thirds of her height, they were scored as 8.5 months old; if sons were seven-eighths or daughters three-quarters, as 10.5 months old. If sons were as large or larger, or daughters were seven-eighths as large or as large as their mothers, they were estimated at 12.5 months or older. Female cubs in this last age category could be distinguished from their mothers by their slighter build, fluffier manes, and round cublike faces. Aging was facilitated if the family contained both sons and daughters, but these criteria were used even when only a single offspring was present. Repeated sightings of the same family at different times confirmed that these estimates of cub age were highly reliable.

Fig. 3.2 An adolescent cheetah, showing the long light hairs on her nape.

Cubs from large litters appeared to have slightly smaller body sizes, and an effort was made to take this into account when aging animals; however, Laurenson (in press-a) could find no effects of litter size on the growth rates of cubs in the lair once individual differences had been taken into account. Aging became more inaccurate as cubs grew older, so the first sighting was used to backdate birth dates. To increase sample sizes, the nine age classes were combined into three larger categories in many of the analyses: 2- to 4-month-old cubs were termed *young;* 5- to 7-month-old cubs, *middle-aged;* and dependent cubs 8.5 months old or older were called *old* cubs. *Youngster* referred to dependent offspring of any age. Ages of dependent cubs reported in my previous publications may be underestimates by as much as 2 weeks.

Independent cheetahs, defined as those without their mothers, were divided into four age classes. *Adolescents* (approximately 14 to 22 months) had a slight, gracile appearance and rounded cublike faces when viewed from the front. They had manes consisting of long light hairs that partially obscured the black spots on the nape (fig. 3.2). Littermates stayed together for several months after they stopped accompanying their mother and before male and female siblings separated from each other. *Young adults* (approximately 23 to 42 months) were full size but had a cleaner appearance than adults, and retained some of their manes; females also had rather circular faces. At this age males were never seen with female siblings, and females were never accompanied by littermates. *Adults* (>3.5 years) usually had no mane, the black and light nape hairs being of about equal length. Often they had callused elbows where the fur had been worn away. The age at which I judged females to enter full adulthood was somewhat variable as it depended for the most part on the length of mane, which showed individual variation (G. Frame, pers. comm.). *Old* individuals had prominent black hairs on the mane, and the tail appeared thin because the light hairs had become shortened in both regions. Males were heavily scarred by this age. These four age classes were derived from those employed by G. and L. Frame and accorded with those individuals for whom birth dates were known with greater certainty. They corresponded to Burney's (1980) subadult, young adult, prime, and old adult categories, respectively. For the purposes of analysis, old individuals were combined with adults.

BELLY SIZE ESTIMATES

At each sighting, an estimate was made of every individual's level of hunger by scoring its belly size on a scale from 1, when the animal was very emaciated, to 14, when it looked as if it had swallowed a basketball and would voluntarily leave a kill that still had meat on it (fig. 3.3). Cheetahs normally started hunting when their bellies had declined to size 4. Belly size estimates have been used reliably by other researchers on both cheetahs (Frame and Frame 1981) and lions (Bertram 1978b; Packer 1986), and experienced observers of cheetahs (C. FitzGibbon, K. Laurenson, and I) almost always scored individuals identically. Moreover, in sixteen trials with a relatively inexperienced observer (D. Jefferson), her belly size scores matched mine in six trials (38%), differed by one point in seven trials (44%), and never differed from mine by more than two points. Belly size scored when the subject was first sighted, usually at the beginning of the day, was used in analysis.

TAMENESS

From 1984, individuals were scored according to their degree of habituation to the vehicle. Animals that allowed an approach to within 15 m without moving off were assigned a tameness score of 0; those that moved off at this distance, a score of 1; those that moved off at 30 m, 2; at approximately 50 m, 3; individuals that crouched down until the vehicle arrived but then ran off, 4. Cheetahs that ran off at 500–1,000 m, as soon as or before the vehicle moved toward them, were given a score of 5. It

Fig. 3.3 An adolescent male with belly size 14 is about to leave an adult female Grant's gazelle kill with flesh still on it; his brother continues to gnaw at a bone.

was difficult to obtain photographs of these last individuals that could be used for identification purposes. Although some subjects became more tame as a result of being observed or encountering tourist vehicles, and others became more shy, presumably as a result of being harassed by tourists, the six categories proved helpful in matching sightings to one another.

STATUS OF MALES

Males that were seen repeatedly in one area and that scent-marked were termed *territorial males*. In order to determine the status of each male, the incidence or absence of scent marking was recorded when males were encountered. Scent marking involved spraying urine on prominent features of the environment such as upright and fallen trees, rocks, or bushes or urinating close to the ground in a semi-squatting position and repeatedly raking the ground with the hindfeet (see also Burney 1980). Territorial males also sought out prominent landmarks on which to defecate. The positions of territories were determined from the location of sightings. Nonterritorial males were those that were sighted at several locations in the park, often many kilometers apart. They urinated infrequently, almost never sprayed rocks or trees, and did not defecate on prominent landmarks (see chap. 8).

Recognition of Individuals

When a cheetah was approached to within 50 m or less, several black-and-white photographs were taken using a 400-mm lens mounted on a Nikkormat camera body. It was known already that each individual had a unique pattern of spots on its body (Bertram 1978b) and bands on its tail (Burney 1980). Attempts were made to obtain clear photographs of each side of the face taken at right angles (preferably while the animal was sitting or lying down with its head raised), as this part of the body had been used to match individuals in the past (by B. Bertram and G. Frame). Sometimes pictures of the front of the chest were also snapped when the subject was sitting on its haunches. Shots taken at right angles when the animal was walking or standing gave additional views of the side of the face, body, tail, and inside of the forelegs. As the study progressed, a special effort was made to photograph both sides of the tail while the animal was standing or walking. All the photographs taken at a given sighting were affixed to cards, accompanied by a sighting number, date, age-sex class of the animal, and other cheetahs present. Some individuals with torn ears or particularly patterned tails could be recognized immediately in the field and did not require photography.

Pictures took up to 4 months to be incorporated into the photographic index because negatives and contact sheets had to be processed in Nairobi before prints could be developed in the SWRC laboratory or elsewhere. As a consequence, it was difficult to match animals in the field to recently photographed cheetahs, the most obvious candidates. Sifting through all the cards while following a cheetah could take me an hour or more, and was often unsuccessful during the first 5 years of the study when the rate of sighting of new animals did not level off (Caro and Collins 1986). With the limited time available for finding cheetahs (about 3.5 hours in the dry season or 4.5 in the wet), these difficulties forced me to take photographs at most sightings instead of attempting to match in the Land Rover. Although these photographs proved useful while initiating the card index, it may, in retrospect, have been better to reduce the number of photographs and carry out more matching on the spot because the process of comparing sightings took years to complete after fieldwork was over.

MATCHING SIGHTINGS

I compared photographs by eye or with a magnifying glass, studying similar parts of the body, most notably sides of the face, chest, and tail. The pattern of banding on tails was subsequently used as a method of determining relatedness (Caro and Durant 1991). A 2 × 2 matrix of sightings was compiled and each cell was filled in as a true negative (if the animals were different); as a probable negative (almost certainly different animals but the photographs were poor or were taken at angles that made comparisons troublesome); or as a definite positive (the sightings were of the same animal). In this third case, all the cells in the matrix belonging to the second sighting were scored out entirely, and the cheetah was assigned a name if it did not have one already; the two cards were then put together.

For females, either sightings from a given year, or individuals on whom I had behavioral data, were compared with one another. For males, all sightings of single males from the first 5 years of the study were compared with one another, then pairs were compared with pairs, and trios with trios, because I already knew that group membership was fairly stable (Frame 1980); eventually males from different group sizes were compared.

Criteria Used to Follow Cheetahs

The primary aim of the first part of the study was to examine parental behavior and to relate ontogenetic changes in offspring behavior to the changing social and ecological circumstances in which they grew up. This required detailed and prolonged observation of cheetah families at nine different ages spaced approximately 1 month apart. Most behavioral observations were conducted without radiotelemetry, however, and it proved impossible to relocate a family at will a month after a period of observation. Instead I watched a minimum of four different families at each age, which enabled me to monitor ontogenetic changes in behavior using a minimum sample size. Only litters of up to four cubs were observed because the behavior of more than five cheetahs could not be recorded accurately, especially at kills. In any case, litter sizes of more than four were very rare in older age categories. At first I followed any family that I could find, but as numbers built up I became increasingly selective. Toward the end of the study, I also focused on single-cub litters. Table 3.1 shows the number of litters eventually observed at different cub ages. I did not attempt to increase the number of large and small litters or the number of litters containing daughters in the sample as these factors were not the focus of attention. As it was, it took 4 years to fill the table.

To determine why female adolescents remained with their littermates, sibling groups containing one or more females and single adolescent females were followed. Young females and adult females without cubs were also observed so that changes in behavior, especially in hunting abilities, could be traced after independence (table 3.2).

Male cheetahs were also watched intensively so that the behavior of males living in different-sized groups could be compared. Individuals and groups of males were followed when none of the right females were avail-

TABLE 3.1 Size and Composition of Litters Observed at Different Ages during the Study

				Age (months)				
2	3	4	5	6	7	8.5	10.5	≥12.5
M 7	F 6	FF 6	MF 6	F 2	F 5	MM 7	MM 6	M 1
F 4	MF 5	MMF 7	FF 4	MF 7	MF 1	MM 6	MF 5	M 3
MF 1	MMF 7	MMF 7	MMF 3	MF 7	MMF 7	MF 7	MF 2	MM 7
MMF 7	MMF 7	MMF 7		MMF 5	FFF 7	MF 1	MF 1	MF 7
MFF 2	MMF 1	FFF 7		MMFF 7	MMFF 7	FF 6	FF 1	MF 6
MMMF 5	MMMF 3	MMFF 7				FFF 4	MMF 5	MF 1
MFFF 3							MMF 2	MF 1
								MMF 5
								MMF 1
MF 4	MMM 1			MF 2		FF 3		
MF 3								

Note: M = male; F = female; number = number of days each family was followed. Not all litters were included in every analysis. A few of these litters suffered a loss of cubs during periods of observation and their new composition is shown below the line; the latter were excluded from analyses.

TABLE 3.2 Independent Females Observed at Different Ages during the Study

	Single Females		
Sibgroups	Adolescents	Young	Adults
MF 7	F 7	F 7	F 7
MF 6	F 7	F 5[a]	F 4
MF 6	F 5	F 4[a]	F 3
MF 2	F 4[a]	F 3[a]	F 2
FF 3	F 2	F 3	F 2
MMF 4	F 1	F 2	F 2
MMF 1	F 1	F 2	F 1
FFF 4	F 1	F 2	F 1
MMMF 2		F 1	F 1
		F 1	F 1
		F 1	F 1
			F 1

Note: M = male; F = female; number = number of days each was followed. Size and composition of sibgroups are also shown: not all were included in every analysis.

[a] Data provided by K. Laurenson.

TABLE 3.3 Adult Male Groups Observed during the Study

	Singletons	Pairs	Trios
Adults	M 8	MM 6	MMM 9
	M 7	MM 6	MMM 7
	M 6	MM 5	MMM 6
	M 5	MM 5	MMM 6
	M 4[a]	MM 4	MMM 1
	M 3	MM 4[a,b]	
	M 2	MM 3	
	M 2	MM 1	
	M 1	MM 1	
	M 1	MM 1	
	M 1		
	M 1[a]		
Adolescents	M 4	MM 2	MMM 4
	M 3	MM 1	
	M 1		

Note: Numbers = number of days each was followed. A few males not shown here were observed for even shorter durations. Not all males were included in every analysis.

[a] Data partially provided by C. FitzGibbon.

[b] Data partially provided by A. Collins.

able for observation; sample sizes were built up slowly over the course of 7 years (table 3.3). Trios were underrepresented because habituated groups were scarce. On a few measures unrelated to hunting, groups of adolescent males were included in male comparisons.

Observation Periods

A family of cheetahs was followed during daylight hours from the time it was located until 1900. Observations were usually made at a distance of 0 to 150 m by eye or with the aid of 8 × 40 binoculars, which I could hold in one hand while writing with the other. Families were usually relocated the next and on six subsequent mornings; thus watches lasted between 1 and 7 days (see table 3.1). The seven-day length was chosen so that a representative sample of successful hunts and meals could be witnessed. In retrospect, this may have been overly long, given that measures unrelated to feeding were subsequently found to change little from day to day. Consecutive days were chosen because it was far easier to find families the next day (they often moved little overnight) than several days later. Furthermore, watching on consecutive days allowed me to calculate the total number of meals eaten per unit time, since occasional overnight meals could be discerned from dusk-to-dawn increases in belly sizes.

To relocate families the next day, the area where they were last seen was searched first, then an area 2 km in radius around this spot. Next, the direction in which the family was last seen heading was scanned carefully; this was followed by a large sweep 5 km in radius during which regular stops and scans were made. Next, an even wider area was covered, especially near concentrations of Thomson's gazelles if the mother had been hungry the night before. If the family had not been located by 1130 after 5 hours of searching, the full procedure was repeated the next day. If the family was found, I continued the watch until 7 days' data had been collected. If I had no luck, the family was abandoned. A small number of families that had been lost were fortuitously found a few days later (<10 days) and were observed again, with both periods being treated as a single watch. In general, mothers with young cubs were easier to relocate because they moved little overnight, while families with old cubs moved long distances, possibly at the instigation of the cubs. Finding families the next day constituted the most worrisome and difficult part of the study.

At first, I attempted to watch adolescents for seven consecutive days, but quickly established a good sample of hunts because so many of their attempts failed. Therefore, I switched to 4-day follows. This was a relief because sibling groups moved long distances overnight, frustrating relocation the next day. Young females and adult females without cubs were sometimes watched for 3 or 4 days, but generally data on these animals were collected as other commitments allowed (see table 3.2).

Males also moved long distances overnight and could rarely be found on consecutive days; even those that were radio-collared later on in the study were difficult to find next day from the ground. Data on males were therefore collected on an ad hoc basis: for example, if I found a male on whom I had some data already, I followed him for the rest of the day.

Behavioral Observations

TIME BUDGETS

Throughout the day, the activities of each cheetah were noted every 15 minutes. Five main categories of behavior were recorded: *resting,* lying with flank and hindquarters touching the ground; *observing,* sitting on backlegs with forelegs vertically supporting the body, or standing; *moving,* walking or running; *hunting;* and *eating.* Hunting started when the subject either crouched at, stalked, trotted toward, rushed at, or chased prey. Just one or up to all five of these behaviors could characterize a hunt. A hunt could start or stop with any of them, although it normally began with one of the first three behaviors. After that, one behavior might be repeated several times in a row, interspersed with bouts of sitting, or the sequence might alternate between any of the activities, except that rushing was followed only by chasing or termination of the hunt, while chasing led to termination of the hunt or occasionally to another chase. Two rarer behavior patterns, walking toward prey with the head held high and ears forward (usually through tall vegetation), and sitting with the head positioned low relative to the scapulae, were not included as part of a hunt because they were difficult to identify. In some analyses moving, observing, and hunting were summed together and called *searching* for prey because cheetahs often moved toward a gazelle group and then sat and watched it before starting to hunt, or walked through stands of vegetation to flush concealed prey.

Eating was defined as chewing meat or bones. Less frequent activities were *grooming*, licking self; *social behavior*, licking another individual; *sniffing*, sniffing an object; *scent marking* (defined above); and *playing*, apparently nonfunctional activity in which movements were exaggerated or repeated (Martin and Caro 1985). The percentage of instantaneous samples (Altmann 1974) in each of the five main categories was calculated each day and an average taken for all the days in each watch.

THE DAYTIME REST PERIOD

During the middle of the day (0930 to 1700 hours), between the main hunting periods, time was allocated to recording cheetahs' vigilance in detail. When an individual or group had obviously settled down, usually in the shade of a bush or tree, a 3-hour observation period was initiated during which the behavior of individuals was recorded every 5 minutes on the minute. *Vigilance* was defined as eyes open and looking around (looking at the ground or at another individual was excluded). When an animal had its eyes open, the 90° quadrat into which it was looking was recorded. Postures scored were *lying flat out*, lying prone with head on the ground (occasional rolling over was included); *lying out*, lying prone with head raised; *lying alert*, lying with flank and hindquarters on the ground but forelegs tucked under the body; and *sitting up*, sitting on backlegs with forelegs vertically supporting the body (fig. 3.4). Each individual's height off the ground was noted every 5 minutes, estimated to the nearest .5 m.

Every 5 minutes any physical contact between individuals was noted, as was the estimated distance between each cub and its mother or the distances between all individuals in the cases of male and sibling groups. Distance estimates were repeatedly checked against a series of jerry cans placed at known distances from the porch of my house.

a

b

c

Fig. 3.4 An adult female cheetah (*a*) lying flat out, (*b*) lying out, (*c*) lying alert; (*d*) a different female sits up. A sitting cheetah enabled me to discern the unique pattern of spots on the chest and inside of the forelegs.

d

If the rest period was interrupted by a hunt, or any individual in the group was recorded as walking for more than two consecutive 5-minute scans, the observation period was terminated and only data from previous whole half-hour blocks were used in analysis. After a hunt had finished or when the cheetahs had settled again, a new observation period was started until 3 undisturbed hours' observation had been made that day. These stringent criteria ensured that cheetahs were sampled only when they were relatively relaxed.

The percentage of 5-minute instantaneous samples in which each individual was vigilant, or was in a particular posture, and so on, was calculated for each day. (If, for example, there were two 1.5-hour observation periods on a given day, a mean of the two was taken to represent that day). An average was then calculated over all the days of the watch. The distance between two individuals was calculated by summing all recorded distances between the two cheetahs and dividing by the number of scans during that observation period.

HUNTING BEHAVIOR

Hunts were observed from distances of 200–500 m from the cheetah to minimize disturbance of predator and prey. Date, time, and belly sizes of cheetahs at the beginning of the hunt were recorded, along with the species of prey and the number, age, and sex of individuals in the group being hunted. I relied on Walther's (1973) age criteria for gazelles and on horn development in assessing other ungulates' ages; most species were sexually dimorphic in horn size and shape. If the quarry could be discerned, either because one animal was chased or because a prey animal was alone, its age and sex were noted specifically. The number of bouts of stalking, crouching, trotting, rushing at, or chasing prey by each cheetah involved in the hunt (i.e., each individual that performed any one of these activities) was recorded. A bout was considered to have ended when one of these behavior patterns was replaced by another or by walking or sitting. These records allowed me to calculate the percentage of hunts in which these behaviors occurred and the rate at which they were performed. If more than one cheetah was present, the identity of the individual that initiated the hunt and, separately, the individual that was at the front of the advancing group were recorded, as these were not necessarily the same. For the sake of consistency, cubs' hunting behavior directed at both *appropriate* and *inappropriate* prey (the latter defined as species or age-sex classes of prey not attempted by adults) was recorded as a hunt, although in many cases it could have been playful.

It was easy to determine when a hunt had ended: cheetahs stopped their advance after prey had seen them, walked away from prey they had been hunting, failed to catch their quarry at the end of the single chase that usually characterizes cheetah hunts, or else captured their quarry. When cheetahs rested or even dozed off in the course of a hunt but had not been detected by prey, and then resumed hunting the same group, I recorded this as a single hunt. (It is worth noting that FitzGibbon, Laurenson, and I found it difficult to reach a consensus on this issue.) The duration of a hunt, its outcome, the estimated distance from the nearest prey group member when it was abandoned, and the reasons for failure were written in longhand. A ratio of successful hunts to all hunts was calculated for each individual or group of cheetahs watched and for different sizes of prey attempted.

BEHAVIOR OF CHEETAHS AT KILLS

Once the prey had been captured and killed, I drove to the carcass, stopping 15 to 20 m away. I never noticed mammalian or avian scavengers being drawn to my vehicle in other circumstances, so I suspect that my presence did not attract competitors. Shy predators, however, would be unlikely to come near to scavenge or drive cheetahs away. A stopwatch was started as soon as the first member of the cheetah group started to feed and was allowed to run until the last member left the carcass. The times when each member started and finally stopped eating could be recorded in this way. Between these events, the number of times and number of seconds for which each cheetah stopped feeding and raised its head to observe the surroundings was also recorded (see fig. 1.1c). Later, these data were expressed as the rate at which each individual looked up from the carcass and the percentage of time it spent not feeding and looking around during this period; for each cheetah, averages were calculated across all kills made during a watch.

These measures enabled me to calculate precisely the amount of time that each cheetah spent eating from each carcass, as well as the proportion of time each individual fed compared with the total amount of time all individuals ate from the carcass. I used this second measure as a means of reckoning the proportion of the meat eaten by each animal. From a parallel study, I had total flesh weights and weights of flesh from different parts of the body of several age-sex classes of bovids eaten by cheetahs (Blumenschine and Caro 1986). By noting the parts of the carcass that remained when cheetahs left a kill voluntarily or were displaced from it, I could subtract unit flesh weights from the total weight of flesh known to be on that age-sex class of prey, which allowed me to estimate the amount of flesh that had been eaten. Then, by multiplying the proportion of time each individual had been eating by the number of kilograms of meat that had been consumed, I could ascertain the weight of flesh each individual had eaten at a kill. Summing these weights across kills and dividing by the total time cheetahs were watched, the number of kilograms of meat eaten per daylight hour could be estimated to the nearest 0.1 kg.

These computations assumed that each cheetah consumed flesh at the same rate while eating. Though some cheetahs would gnaw bones while others were still chewing muscle, rates of aggression were low, and I had no indication that certain individuals were consistently deprived of profitable carcass elements. The pattern of consumption was that all individuals ate muscle and viscera first and subsequently cleaned off the bones and scraps when there was little meat left. Thus each individual probably suffered temporarily lowered rates of flesh consumption to an approximately equal extent. When similar-sized individuals were feeding, I assumed that each ate the same amount of flesh per minute. In families in which cubs were smaller than their mothers and had smaller mouths this assumption was invalid. Here I estimated that young cubs ate a third as much as their mothers; middle-aged cubs, two-thirds as much; and old cubs, the same amount as their mothers per unit time.

Aggression at kills was recorded by summing instances of slapping or biting another cheetah or the carcass; growling was noted but not separated by individual because it was difficult to tell who was vocalizing. Totals of aggression and growling were then divided by the total time any member of the group was feeding and by the number of cheetahs present to obtain average rates per cheetah per hour.

SOCIAL BEHAVIOR

Most social behavior among adult cheetahs consisted of *social grooming,* licking the fur of another animal and capturing and eating hippoboscid flies and ticks. I recorded all bouts of social grooming (which had to be separated by more than 10 seconds) throughout the day, noting the actor, recipient, and whether grooming was reciprocated; that is, whether the recipient started to groom its partner while being groomed. I also registered which individuals *initiated group movements.* This occurred when one individual moved off and, while still walking, was followed by all other group members, each of whom had previously been resting or sitting up.

The vocalizations I recorded were *yipping,* a short, high-pitched bird-like call cheetahs made when looking for a lost companion (Adamson 1969) or when they were fearful, and *growling, hissing,* and *yowling* (a drawn-out moan of variable pitch), all characteristic of low-level aggression. I also scored *churring,* a single soft chirrup or series of chirrups, by which cheetahs invited others to join them. Churring also occurred in the context of male-female liaisons but was much louder and was usually uttered by males. In captivity it is called stuttering or stutter-barking and has been described as a throaty series of short sound bursts of low frequency (600–700 Hz) that last 0.6 seconds each, emitted with an open mouth (Eaton 1974). In captivity, males may stutter almost continuously during periods of excitement (Degenaar 1977). Vocalizations were recorded ad libitum in the field.

When mothers and cubs were subjects of observation, nursing was recorded. The cubs in a litter normally all nursed at the same time. The length of time each cub spent nursing throughout the day was timed to the nearest second. If a cub could not gain hold of a nipple or quickly disengaged and tried the same or another nipple again, I guessed that it was unsuccessful in gaining milk and did not score this as nursing. Though time spent nursing does not necessarily approximate to offspring weight gain (Mendl and Paul 1989), it is a reasonably good measure of weaning (Konig and Markl 1987).

BEHAVIOR BETWEEN MALES AND FEMALES

When independent male and female cheetahs were encountered together, the number of times each male *approached* (also called *investigated*) the female, *sniffed* her, or sniffed where she had been resting (*sniffed object*) were recorded. Instances of *slapping* and *growling* (combined with yowling) by each male directed either at the female or toward other males were noted, as were *self-grooming*, *rolling over*, and *moving off* away from the female. The number of times the female slapped a male, growled, rolled over, groomed herself, and moved off were scored as well. *Yipping*, a short high-pitched vocalization similar to a contact call, was also recorded. In this context, however, it almost certainly represented fear in females, as they often yipped when a male made a sudden movement toward them; males too gave yips in this tense situation. Distances between a male or males and the female were estimated and marked down each time a participant changed his or her position.

ANTIPREDATOR BEHAVIOR

During watches, I noted all the occasions when I saw dangerous predators, such as lions, leopards, and spotted hyenas, from my position near the cheetah group. Also included in this list were striped hyenas, golden jackals, black-backed jackals, side-striped jackals, olive baboons, and male and female cheetahs, all of which could pose a threat to small cubs or steal meat from cheetahs. I noted whether any cheetah in the group saw the predator and, if possible, who noticed it first. Cheetahs might simply *watch* the predator pass by, from a resting, sitting, or standing position. Or they might respond by *leaving*, walking or slinking off while apparently trying to remain hidden, or trotting away; by *crouching*, usually if the predator came to within 40 m; or by *hissing*, standing with an arched back and piloerected hair and hissing at the predator, when it was less than 5 m away. These three behaviors and watching were termed *defensive* actions (differing from Caro 1987a). Cheetahs might also react by *stalking* toward the predator; *chasing*, which included rushing at the predator, as cheetahs would normally veer away from lions, and spotted hyenas often stood their ground; or *contacting* the predator, usually slapping it on the hindquarters. These latter three were termed *offensive* actions. If a mother reacted to a predator in several of the ways above, only the one that brought her into closest proximity to the predator (the most dangerous one) was used in analysis. Other rare behavior patterns, such as mothers apparently drawing predators away from hidden cubs (Ammann and Ammann 1984), were not examined.

Immobilization of Cheetahs

In order to examine the condition and ranging patterns of cheetahs, a small sample of females and males, both territorial and nonterritorial, were immobilized, and some were fitted with radio collars. Only individuals of tameness 0 or 1 were selected, as these could sometimes be approached within 10 m in the Land Rover. A 3-ml mini-ject syringe (3064 Dist-inject) with a 1.5 × 30 mm (K1530V Telinject) sleeved needle and tailpiece (Zoolu Arms of Omaha) containing 1–1.5 ml of tiletamine hydrochloride and zozalepam hydrochloride at a concentration of 200 mg/ml (Zoletil, Virbac) was shot at the animal using a three-stage 183-cm-long hand-held blowpipe (Zoolu Arms of Omaha). Later on in the study a dart rifle (Zoolu Arms of Omaha) was employed, which increased the firing range to almost 20 m. Darts were usually aimed at the hindquarters but sometimes struck the animal's back or shoulder with no ill effects. In Laurenson's subsequent study (1992), syringe darts containing 100 mg of ketamine (Vetalar, Parke Davis and Co., U.K.) and 125 mg of xylazine (Rompum, Bayer, U.K.) were used. The effects of this drug combination could be reversed using RX 821002A (Rickett and Coleman, U.K.), enabling Laurenson to immobilize mothers briefly without their cubs becoming separated from them.

Struck animals often growled or yelped at the dart's impact and characteristically ran 30 to 50 m but then settled down quickly. They showed signs of sedation within 3 to 5 minutes and were recumbent within 10 minutes. To minimize further disturbance and facilitate smooth anesthesia, they were not followed during this period, although their movements were watched very carefully through binoculars to monitor the rate at which the drug took effect and the exact location where they lay down. Darting animals was much easier with two people, one of whom could follow the subject's movements in the long grass before the anesthesia took effect.

When the subject had been down for about 2 minutes, the vehicle approached it. The animal's tail was lifted to determine whether additional anesthetic was required (usually 0.25 ml if at all). A 20- or 30-ml blood sample was then taken from the femoral vein; this was done as quickly as possible to avoid the problem of changes in red blood cell parameters that occur after the onset of anesthesia in this species (Hawkey et al. 1980). Usually 5 ml of blood was mixed with dipotassium salt of ethylene diamine tetracetic acid (2K EDTA), while 20 ml was allowed to clot. All blood samples were placed in a coolbox at approximately 0°C.

Individuals then received a physical examination in which eyes, ears, teeth, tongue, and gums were checked, scars and pelage examined, all lymph nodes palpated, and ticks counted all over the body. In addition, three measures of general condition were scored (reported here in order of best to worst). First, the ease with which the dorsal spinous process vertebrae could be palpated was scored (3, palpable with strong pressure; 2, palpable with moderate pressure; 1, easily palpable). Second, coat quality was recorded as soft or coarse. Third, the degree of mange on each ear was recorded (0, none; 1, tips of ears only; through 5, severe, where the entire pinnae were covered). Lengths of head and body, tail, hindfoot, chest girth immediately distal to the forelegs, testes, and both upper canines were measured. The animal was then weighed in a net attached to a spring balance that was read while lifting it up with two hands. This last task was a difficult procedure and was greatly facilitated by an additional person.

Fig. 3.5 A 545-g radio collar has just been attached to male S_2, still under anesthesia; it appears loose because it is resting on the ground. Note the position of the transmitter below the collar and the aerial protruding above it.

In some cases a radio collar with external antenna was fitted (Advanced Telemetry Systems, Minnesota). The collars weighed between 260 and 545 g; heavier ones were placed on males (fig. 3.5), lighter ones on females. I made sure that I could get just four fingers between the animal's neck and the collar but no more, and I always asked an assistant to check whether the collar was too tight or too loose before affixing it permanently. Excess collar was then cut off, and the two bolts protruding from the collar's exterior were cut and filed smooth after the self-tightening nuts had been fastened. These precautions ensured that there were no sharp edges on which the animal or a companion could cut itself while grooming.

The procedures outlined above took 30 to 45 minutes, during which time the cheetah was always kept in the shade of the vehicle (fig. 3.6). If recovery from anesthesia was imminent, forcing the vehicle to depart, the animal was doused with water which was rubbed into the fur in order to keep it cool. If there was still some time before the animal came round, it

Fig. 3.6 Author checking the radio collar on the neck of a male that is beginning to recover from anesthesia. Note that most of the cheetah is in the shade of the Land Rover.

was carried to the shade of a nearby bush or stand of tall herbs to keep it cool. If no shade was available nearby, it was placed on the mattress in the back of the vehicle and driven to a large tree or bush where it could recover. Whatever the case, I then moved the vehicle 100 to 500 m away and kept watch until the cheetah had recovered sufficiently to avoid dangerous predators such as lions or spotted hyenas.

Blood samples were then taken back to the laboratory, with 24 hours set as the maximum storage time before they reached the refrigerator. At SWRC, total red and white cell numbers were counted by standard techniques using a Neubauer counting chamber (Dacie and Lewis 1984). Packed cell volumes and hemoglobin concentrations were measured using Microcompur centrifuges. Blood smears were made, air-dried, and fixed in methanol. They were returned to the UK under license, where personnel in the Veterinary School, Cambridge, stained them with Giemsa stain and performed differential white cell counts.

RELOCATING COLLARED CHEETAHS

Radio-collared cheetahs were relocated from the air on approximately a monthly basis. Aerials were mounted on each wing strut of a Cessna 182 and connected by coaxial cables to a switch box (kindly loaned by C. Packer) attached to a receiver that could sequentially scan the frequencies of the cheetahs currently collared. The pilot (M. Borner) flew at an altitude of 2,000 feet along a predetermined route until the first signal was detected, sometimes from as far as 40 km but usually 10 km away. He then switched back and forth between antennae so that we could discover from which side of the airplane the signal emanated. By cutting the engine, dropping to tree height, and then making a series of right-angled turns, we could pinpoint the exact location of the signal and mark it on a 500-m grid map. This frequency was then deleted from the receiver, and the plane ascended again and flew on until the next signal was detected and the procedure repeated. After the flight was over (and the passengers had recovered), some individuals were relocated from the ground by driving the vehicle to the appropriate grid square and finding the animal using a hand-held yagi radio antenna. Individuals were also located on a day-to-day basis in this way from the ground.

Estimation of Thomson's Gazelle Birth Peak and Recruitment

From 1985 onward, numbers of Thomson's gazelles in different age-sex classes were counted at the end of each calendar month (principally by C. FitzGibbon and K. Laurenson) in order to determine the birth season and recruitment. Gazelles were counted by driving transects through the main concentrations, stopping at 0.25 km intervals, and recording the age and sex of Thomson's gazelles within 200 m of a 180° arc of the front of the vehicle (see Bradley 1977). Gazelles were categorized as neonates (1 to 2 weeks) and fawns (3 to 8 weeks), but these were not always separated; half-growns (2 to 4.5 months); adolescent females (4.5 to 8.5 months); adolescent males (4.5 to 12.5 months); subadult and adult females (> 8.5 months); and subadult and adult males (> 12.5 months) (see Walther 1973). Recording was terminated when more than 1,000 adult females had been counted each month. (Fawns were combined with neonates, and adolescents with subadults, in analyses of hunting behavior.)

The total numbers of neonates and fawns counted each month were summed and divided by two to give a monthly age-sex class occupance and then divided by 62%, which was the average percentage of time these age classes remained in hiding (FitzGibbon 1988). The resulting figure was then divided by the total number of subadult and adult females to give the percentage of young per reproductive female produced each month. The method of calculating recruitment into the adult population is given in appendix 7.

Comparative Data

To compare life history variables of different felids, M. Kelly reviewed as many literature sources as possible for each species (see app. 6). For studies in which a variable was reported as a range, the midpoint was used. A single figure reported as an average was also used. Figures based on a single individual were omitted, however. Subsequently a mean value was calculated across studies for each species. Life history variables for cheetahs were calculated in the same way, with data from this study included along with data from others. We did not use Gittleman's (1984) important data set on carnivores because we required additional information on smaller cats.

Statistical Analyses of the Data

In general, parametric statistics, particularly analysis of variance, were the preferred method of analyzing behavioral measures (Sokal and Rohlf 1981). First, I examined the data by eye against a normal distribution generated by an SPSSX program while simultaneously checking that the ratio of skewness to its standard error differed little from unity. For data that were not normal, $\log_{10}$ transformations (+1) were applied and the data were reexamined. If transformations failed to normalize the data, which often occurred since I was strict about excluding nonnormal data, then nonparametric statistics were used instead (Siegel 1956). This sometimes resulted in apparently parallel data sets being analyzed using different statistics. For each behavioral measure, watches lasting a single day were compared with longer watches using t tests or Mann-Whitney U tests to determine whether short watches were unrepresentative of cheetahs' behavior. If significant differences were found ($P < 0.1$), single-day watches were dropped from subsequent analyses of that measure.

Families were observed on 54 occasions but some litters were observed at more than one age (27 once, 4 twice, 5 three times, and 1 four times). Also, some mothers were observed more than once, either with different or with the same litters (22 once, 5 twice, 2 three times, and 4 four times). Previous analyses (Caro 1987a, 1990) had examined whether individual differences between mothers were an important source of variation in maternal behavior, but there had been few measures in which significant ($P < 0.1$) effects were found. This held particularly when sample sizes (and hence replicates) were reduced after dropping single-day watches. Furthermore, in the many nonparametric tests it was very difficult to control for any maternal effects when examining how cub age influenced behavior because of the uneven number of replicate litters or mothers. For all three reasons, individual differences between mothers or litters were not investigated in analyses presented here. Similarly, when independent cheetahs living in different-sized groups were compared, the occasional individual that was represented in both samples was treated as being independent (two females only in comparisons between 12 group-living and 8 solitary adolescents; one male only in comparisons of 11 singletons, 10 pairs, and 5 trios of males).

Individual rates of behavior for males and adolescents living in a group were examined to see if they were independent, and if not, a mean for each group was calculated. This reduced sample sizes and, as a consequence, data from pairs and trios subsequently had to be combined in some male analyses. As both territorial and nonterritorial males contributed to the male samples, they were first compared, and if significant differences were found, territoriality was controlled for in subsequent analyses of variance comparing male groups. Rates of behavior of individual cubs in a litter were always averaged to give a litter mean (Abbey and Howard 1973; Martin and Bateson 1986).

The number of hunts and kills made by different-sized groups of males or adolescents and the various size classes of prey that they attempted were often compared. To make maximum use of the data, I wanted to use hunts and kills made by cheetahs followed for short periods as well as those of intensively studied subjects. Cheetahs observed for short periods usually hunted just once or twice, however, and were often unsuccessful. This lowered mean hunting success when calculated across individuals or groups. In common with most other predator studies, I therefore decided to use hunts or kills as units of analysis rather than subject averages in order to include all the data. Although repeated sampling of individuals (pooled data) could have been a source of pseudoreplication, there was no a priori expectation that it would bias outcomes of tests. This did not seem to be an empirical problem either. For example, considering data on prey preferences, only one cheetah seemed to be a (wildebeest) specialist, and inclusion or exclusion of this animal in male group size analyses made little difference to the results. When analyzing foraging success per unit time, however, only intensively studied groups and singletons were used.

Comparisons of hunting and feeding behavior were often made with different sample sizes. Correspondence between the number of successful hunts and the number of times subjects were seen to eat was not exact, because individuals were located on a kill without my having witnessed the hunt, or because kills were stolen by spotted hyenas immediately after a successful hunt, or very occasionally, because I did not watch the carcass being eaten.

Not all sightings made during the 10-year study had been matched at the time of writing. Thus some variables collected at sightings, for example, belly sizes or litter sizes, might have lacked independence if these were repeated sightings of the same individuals. Consequently I tried to verify findings based on these measures by reporting them in conjunction with other independently derived measures. In general, however, the possibility of consistent bias at sightings seemed remote; for example, there was no reason to believe that I was more likely to spot thinner animals in one group size but fatter animals in another.

Interspecific comparisons can be confounded by nonindependence as a result of shared ancestry (Harvey and Pagel 1991). This problem can be overcome by using computer software that takes branch lengths of the phylogenetic tree into account. Unfortunately these programs are inappropriate for taxa such as felids for which generic assignments are in dispute (Wozencraft 1989) because minor adjustments to the tree can greatly affect results. Collapsing the number of species to five genera is controversial for the same reason and reduces predictive power. Therefore I presented $\log_{10}$ data for individual species but did not attempt statistical tests. As a check, the same data were analyzed by genera but in no case did they differ from conclusions based at the species level.

Throughout the book, two-tailed tests are used to provide levels of significance. I took $P < 0.1$ as the level of rejection for the null hypothesis because sample sizes were generally small due to the number of topics covered. However, when $0.05 < P < 0.1$, the results are always qualified and interpreted cautiously, allowing readers to assess the biological significance of the findings for themselves. Data are reported as means and standard errors unless stated otherwise. Statistical data and tests are presented at the end of each chapter, however, means are omitted if they can be found elsewhere in tables. Numbers in brackets within the text refer to these statistical sections.

Summary

1. Cheetahs were located by sighting them directly or by finding them in the vicinity of alert prey or carcass remains.

2. Information collected at each cheetah sighting included location, size of group, age of its members, level of hunger as estimated from belly size, and whether males were territorial or not.

3. Cheetahs were photographed and identified by subsequent matching of photographs to one another. Later on in the study some individuals were identified immediately in the field.

4. Behavioral data were collected on mothers and their cubs, adolescent cheetahs, and males living in different-sized groups during daylight hours and usually on consecutive days.

5. Time budgets were collected throughout the day, while data on vigilance were taken during a 3-hour midday rest period. Information on hunting and feeding was recorded as it occurred. Patterns of social behavior, interactions between the sexes, and antipredator behavior were also scored.

6. Some cheetahs were immobilized, weighed and measured, had blood samples taken, and were then followed with the aid of radiotelemetry.

7. Age-sex classes of Thomson's gazelles were counted every month in order to determine availability of neonates and fawns and annual recruitment.

8. A review of the felid literature allowed comparative analyses to be made at a species level.

9. If behavioral data were normal, they were analyzed using parametric statistical techniques, but in many cases nonparametric statistics had to be employed. Two-tailed tests were used, and the null hypothesis was rejected at $P < 0.1$.

A young adult female surveys her surroundings during the heat of the day. (Drawing by Dafila Scott.)

4
FEMALE REPRODUCTION
AND CUB MORTALITY

Understanding female reproductive patterns, particularly patterns of receptivity, is important for appreciating the extent of male competition over access to females (Emlen and Oring 1977; Clutton-Brock and Parker 1992). For example, in a species in which females enter estrus throughout the year and are widely dispersed, males will have to search over large distances to secure matings (e.g., elephants: Barnes 1982). If, however, females are receptive simultaneously and live in groups or aggregate in small areas during a breeding season, competition over females will be especially intense (e.g., elephant seals: Le Boeuf 1974). The period over which females are receptive and how they are distributed in space therefore affects many aspects of male competition, including body size, weaponry, social relations, and ranging behavior. In addition, seasonality of estrus is an important issue for zoo managers since cheetahs' poor breeding performance in captivity has been attributed to disinterest on the part of females in numerous cases. The first part of this chapter documents the timing of conceptions and births in cheetahs over the course of the year.

In the past, variation in life history traits across taxa has usually been attributed to differences in body weight (Western 1979; Western and Ssemakula 1982), brain weight (Sacher 1959; Sacher and Staffeldt 1974), or metabolic rate (McNab 1986). For example, allometric associations might arise if genes that control the production of growth hormone and hence body size also influence the onset of reproduction. Recent work, however, has shown that once the effects of body size are removed (Read and Harvey 1989; Harvey, Pagel, and Rees 1991) and data are scrutinized using improved statistical techniques (Harvey and Pagel 1991), mortality schedules are far more important predictors of life history traits than are allometric variables (Harvey and Zammuto 1985; Harvey, Promislow, and Read 1989; Read and Harvey 1989). Juvenile mortality, in particular, is associated with a range of variables including gestation length, neonatal weight, and litter size across mammalian families, whereas adult mortality is of lesser import, predicting only age at maturity (Promislow and Harvey 1990). Sources of mortality can be divided into extrinsic sources, which are not sensitive to changes in reproductive decisions, and intrinsic causes, which are (see Stearns 1992), so although high intrinsic mortality is a priori likely to be associated with fast life history schedules, high extrinsic mortality is not. Unfortunately, data on mortality are poorly documented in the literature, and the extent to which its causes are intrinsic or extrinsic is often unknown. In the second part of the chapter, therefore, the extent and causes of juvenile mortality in cheetahs are presented to set the stage for subsequent comparative analyses of felid life histories. Finally, two sections describe associations between family members and their duration; these findings provide important background to subsequent chapters that examine the costs and benefits of living in families and in adolescent sibgroups.

Patterns of Reproduction

Most of the radio-collared female cheetahs reproduced during the study (table 4.1). Of the three that did not, two had reproduced previously, while one young female may have been monitored for an insufficient period, judging from the time it took other young females to give birth. Taking young and adult females together, 95% ($N = 20$ females) had given birth. This figure contrasts markedly with data from captive animals; only 15.7% ($N = 108$ females) listed in the 1986 cheetah studbook had ever reproduced in captivity (Marker 1987).

SEASONALITY OF CONCEPTIONS

Cheetahs on the Serengeti plains were more likely to conceive successfully in wet season months than in the dry season [1] as determined from backdating litters examined in their lairs (fig. 4.1; Laurenson, Caro, and Borner 1992). This resulted principally from females being somewhat more likely to conceive in the wet than in the dry season following the loss of an unweaned litter [2]. The difference could not be attributed to higher litter mortality in the wet season [3]. Rather, females that lost their litters in the dry season took longer to conceive successfully than those that lost theirs in a wet season month [4].

TABLE 4.1 Reproductive Histories of Radio-Collared Females

Female identity	Total number of days female was collared	Number of days from collaring to birth of next litter	Number of litters born to female while collared
Immobilized as adults			
MK	535	0[a]	4
TGG	520	36	3
EMM	476	11	3
KC	330[b]	52	3
SKU	491	87	2
SGY	274[c]	27	2
MSH	249	39	2
MV	197[c]	35	2
MQ	181	0[a]	2
DUT	166	108	1
NDO	161	83	1
SOF	158[b]	103	1
KSA	161	—	0[d]
SRH	280	—	0[e]
Immobilized as young adults			
MTT	592	2	4
BTX	561	262	2
BHT	768	327	2
RGL	173	114	1
AM	356	264	1
MKA	226	—	0

Source: Laurenson, Caro, and Borner 1992.

[a] Collared while lactating.

[b] Decollaring date was taken as the date of mother's death.

[c] Date of collaring was taken as the date the previous grown cubs were estimated to have separated from their mother.

[d] Female had raised two daughters to independence and was collared just after another 5-month-old cub had disappeared; she was subsequently seen with another litter (S. Durant, pers. comm.).

[e] Female had given birth previously but was never seen heavily pregnant or lactating while collared.

Conceptions may have increased in the wet season because availability of neonate and fawn Thomson's gazelles rose sharply at this time (fig. 4.2). Young gazelles were the preferred prey of young and adult female cheetahs (FitzGibbon and Fanshawe 1989; also compare apps. 7 and 8) because they were relatively easy to catch (FitzGibbon 1990a). Thus seasonal increases in these age classes may have been responsible for enhanced food intake by females in the wet season (see chaps. 5 and 7), which may have improved their condition and promoted estrus. The possibility that fawn availability additionally affected successful gestation

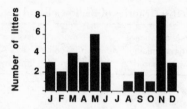

Fig. 4.1 Number of litters conceived in each month between November 1987 and August 1990, derived from repeated checking of 20 radio-collared females' reproductive condition ($N = 36$ litters). The wet season spanned November to May, the dry season June to October. (From Laurenson, Caro, and Borner 1992.)

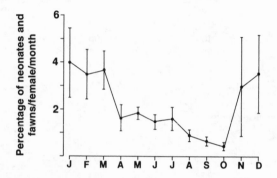

Fig. 4.2 Mean (and SE) percentage of reproductive female Thomson's gazelles that had neonates or fawns during each month of the year. Counts of gazelles were made at the end of every month between February 1985 and August 1990 except for January 1986 and March 1987 and then averaged for the same month each year (see Methods). The wet season spanned November to May, the dry season June to October.

seems more remote because in domestic cats, at least, peak energetic requirements of pregnancy (1.5 to 1.7 above baseline levels: Loveridge 1986) occur in the last trimester when resorption is unlikely.

Although evidence for an association between the timing of conceptions and fawn availability is not strong, other factors can be excluded on logical grounds. Seasonal availability of adult gazelle prey did not change markedly because female cheetahs followed the migration closely from the plains to the woodland border and back again (Durant et al. 1988). Scarcity of male cheetahs was unlikely to be an issue, as females were found on some male territories in dry season months (Caro and Collins 1987a) and nonterritorial males tracked female movements year round (chap. 8). Last, day length, which might have triggered onset of estrus, varies little just south of the equator. If estrus is indeed facilitated by an abundant and readily available supply of food in Serengeti, this suggests that differential timing of breeding in other regions of Africa may be linked to fluctuating availability of target age-sex classes of prey in each region (Wrogemann 1975).

BIRTHS

Females gave birth throughout the year, with no difference in the number of litters born in wet and dry season months in either Laurenson's sample or in a larger sample over the 1980s [5]. Nevertheless, there appeared to be a somewhat greater number of births in February, March, and April and in August in both the early 1970s and late 1980s (fig. 4.3). This bimodal pattern of births might be explained by a combination of an increased rate of conception at the start of the wet season and high neonatal mortality (see below). Females that lost their litters in the wet season would quickly conceive again and give birth 4 to 6 months later (allowing for individual differences in litter age at death and time taken to conceive again).

Cubs were born in lairs situated in marshes ($N = 11$ lairs), in patches of thick vegetation ($N = 13$) (fig. 4.4), along seasonal drainage lines ($N = 4$), and in kopjes ($N = 3$) (Laurenson 1993). A mean of 3.5 cubs were born, with the modal litter size being 3 (fig. 4.5). The mean was probably a slight underestimate since litters were not examined at birth but, on average, 15 days after the estimated date of parturition (range 6 to 35 days) and some cubs may have died before counting. For comparison, 3.7 was the average litter size of cubs born in captivity in North America from 1956 to 1985 (Marker and O'Brien 1989) and 3.9 was the average for litters in South Africa between 1973 and 1977 (Degenaar 1977). Sex ratio

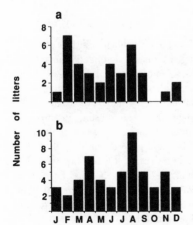

Fig. 4.3 Number of litters born in each month on the Serengeti plains (*a*) from 1969 to 1976 (data from Frame 1975–76), and (*b*) from 1987 to 1990 (data from Laurenson 1992). The wet season spanned November to May, the dry season June to October.

Fig. 4.4 Three 2- to 3-week-old cubs in a lair under thick vegetation. They have their eyes open and are somewhat mobile. (Copyright K. Laurenson 1990.)

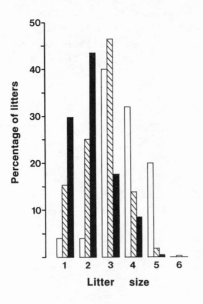

Fig. 4.5 Percentage of litters of differing size on the Serengeti plains. Open bars denote sizes of litters as determined from examining 25 litters in the lair between 1 and 5 weeks after birth (data from Laurenson, in press-b). Hatched bars show sizes of litters in 399 sightings of litters that had emerged from the lair but were less than or equal to 4 months of age. Solid bars show sizes of litters in 849 sightings of dependent litters aged greater than 4 months.

of cubs in the lair did not differ from unity [6]. In captivity, the secondary sex ratio was approximately 1:1 as well (111 males:122 females: Degenaar 1977). Composition of larger litters was not biased toward males (Caro 1990) as in free-living lions (Packer and Pusey 1987).

Cub Mortality

TIMING OF MORTALITY

Mortality among free-living cheetah cubs in the lair was very high. Of 36 litters born, only 27.8% emerged from the lair, or 28.8% of the 125 cubs estimated to have been born (table 4.2). Cub mortality was still very high in the first 2 weeks after cubs emerged from the lair, with only 26 or 27 of the 36 cubs that emerged still alive at the end of the first week (25.0–27.8% mortality since emergence) and only 19 or 20 at the end of the second week (44.4–47.2% mortality since emergence) (Laurenson, in press-b). This rate was similar to the 50% mortality quoted by Schaller (1972c). By 4 months of age only 10 to 12 of the original 125 cubs remained, and by independence, this was reduced even further to only 5 to 7 animals (table 4.2). Indeed, each of the 10 litters emerging suffered some reduction in numbers. Long-term records show that the proportion of small litters increased as cubs grew older while the proportions of litters containing three, four, and five cubs declined (see fig. 4.5).

CAUSES OF MORTALITY IN THE LAIR

Laurenson (in press-b) knew the cause or probable cause of 16 instances of litter reduction in the lair, and stringent checks ruled out the possibility that these were influenced by visits to the lair or intensive observation schedules (Laurenson and Caro, in press). Ten were due to predation, two due to abandonment, one from exposure, one from a grass fire, and two probably a result of poor health (table 4.3). In her study, lions were the

TABLE 4.2 Mortality of Cheetah Litters and Cubs

	Number in lair	Number emerging from lair	Number alive at 4 months	Number alive at 14–18 months
Litters	36	10	5–6	3–4
	(100.0)	(27.8)	(13.9–16.7)	(8.3–11.1)
Cubs	125[a]	36	10–12	5–7
	(100.0)	(28.8)	(8.0–9.6)	(4.0–5.6)

Source: Laurenson, in press-b.

Note: Percentages are shown in parentheses.

[a] Six litters that died before being counted were estimated to consist of the average of 3.5 cubs.

most important predator of very young cubs in the lair, and in the Serengeti ecosystem as a whole, they were responsible for 82.4% ($N = 17$ litters) of fatal attacks on litters, although they rarely ate their victims (table 4.4). Lions sometimes located cheetah lairs by seeing the mother sit up, but may also have stumbled upon them while the mother was absent on a foraging excursion. If the mother was present she defended the cubs by rushing at and threatening the lion (Laurenson, in press-b) but she could not drive it off. During these encounters, very young cubs were hampered by their relative immobility and tried to burrow into the grass (K. Laurenson, pers. comm.). In many cases this was an inadequate antipredator strategy and led to the whole litter being taken (table 4.4). In only 15.4% of all cases of litter loss in the den ($N = 26$ litters) could predation definitely be ruled out as a cause of death.

Mothers abandoned two litters and possibly another three. Prey availability and the difficulty of securing food apparently affected whether cubs were abandoned. The total number of gazelles counted near the lair was much lower for lairs that were abandoned than for those from which cubs emerged (Laurenson, in press-b). One young female, a poor hunter (see chap. 7), had her lair in a marsh approximately 12 km from the main concentrations of gazelles (Laurenson 1991b). She ate a third as much food as 14 mothers of other litters. On one occasion she spent 3 days attempting to catch Thomson's gazelles 9 km from her lair but never re-

TABLE 4.3 Causes and Extent of Cheetah Litter and Cub Mortality

Cause of mortality	Litters[a]	Cubs[b]
Predation	10	35.5
	(62.5)	(73.2)
Abandonment	2	4
	(12.5)	(8.2)
Fire	1	4
	(6.3)	(8.2)
Exposure	1	3
	(6.3)	(6.2)
Inviable cubs	2	2
	(12.5)	(4.1)
Unknown	23	69.5–71.5
Total dead	39	118–120

Source: Adapted from Laurenson, in press-b.

Note: Percentages due to known sources of mortality are shown in parentheses.

[a] The number of litters is inflated by 3 because in one litter a cub was inviable while the remainder were abandoned but then killed by a predator before starvation occurred. In another litter a cub was inviable but the remainder suffered predation.

[b] Litters that were not examined in the lair were assigned an average of 3.5 cubs.

turned. Her cubs, weighing less than 2 kg, were reasonably alert and not severely dehydrated when they were examined on the fourth day after their mother left. Another mother abandoned a single male cub.

Other carnivores desert their dens when prey is scarce. Cub mortality in lions is far higher in the dry than in the wet season on the Serengeti plains (Packer et al. 1988); one lioness abandoned two barely mobile cubs that were starving. Similarly, wild dogs leave their pups to die in the den if prey becomes very scarce before they are mobile (Reich 1981).

Two litters also succumbed to the elements: one was burnt in a grass

TABLE 4.4 Circumstances Surrounding Predation on Cheetah Cubs

Number killed	Predator	Cubs eaten?	Certainty	Cub age	Lair	Source[a]
Before emergence						
2/2	Lion	1 half	Definite	4 wk	Marsh	1
4/4	Lion	No	Definite	5 wk	Marsh	1
3/4	Lion	No	Definite	4 wk	Kopje	1
4/4	Lion	No	Definite	4 wk	Marsh	1
3/3	Lion	No	Definite	4 wk	Marsh	1
All	Lion	No	Definite	?	Marsh	1
All	Lion	?No	Definite	?4 wk	Kopje	1
All	Lion	?No	Definite	?4 wk	Kopje	1
1 alive	Lion	?No	Definite	6 wk	Kopje	1
5/5	Lion	?No	Definite	2 wk	?	2
5/5	Lion	No	Probably	4 wk	?	3
3/3	?Lion	Some	Definite	5 wk	Vegetation	1
All	?Lion	?	Probably	1–2 wk	Marsh	1
2/2	?Lion	?	Possibly	4 wk	?Bush	4
3/3	Spotted hyena	?	Definite	?	?	2
1/4	Secretary bird	?	Definite	?2 wk	Vegetation	1
2/2	?Male cheetah	?	Possibly	1 wk	?	2
After emergence						
1/3	Lion	Yes	Definite	8 wk	—	5
2/4	Lion	Yes	Definite	8 wk	—	5
1/2	Lion	No	Definite	6 mo	—	1
1/4	Spotted hyena	Yes	Definite	8 wk	—	1
4/4	Spotted hyenas	Yes	Definite	9 wk	—	1
2/4	Maasai dogs	?	Possibly	3 mo	—	2
1/4	Leopard, then spotted hyena	No	Probably	9.5 mo	—	2

Source: Adapted from Laurenson, in press-b.

[a] 1, Laurenson, in press-b, or pers. comm. to Laurenson; 2, Burney 1980; 3, Ammann and Ammann 1984; 4, Frame and Frame 1981; 5, Caro, pers. obs.

fire, while three members of the other disappeared one by one during a period of intense rain. One of these three cubs was found sodden, emaciated, and hypothermic; a histological examination revealed a pneumonia infection. There were two additional instances of individual cubs dying in an otherwise healthy litter for unknown reasons.

CAUSES OF MORTALITY AFTER EMERGING FROM THE LAIR

Cheetah cubs that had left the lair were still subject to predation by both lions and spotted hyenas (see table 4.4). Now that they were mobile, cubs scattered and hid when rushed at by a predator and were sometimes able to avoid detection. This may have accounted for the lower proportion of cubs being killed in those litters that were attacked by predators after they had quit the lair [7]. After hiding, cubs later slipped away from the source of danger to rejoin their mother.

By 16 to 18 weeks, cubs were fleet and could normally outrun predators, and there are few records of cubs dying after this period (fig. 4.6). M. Smits van Oyen reported (to K. Laurenson) a 6-month-old cub killed by a lion, and Burney (1980) noted a 9.5-month-old cheetah cub wounded by a leopard and finished off by spotted hyenas. I saw a very weak 8.5-month-old cub die of disease-related causes.

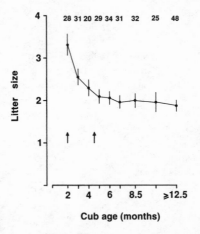

Fig. 4.6 Mean litter size (and SE) plotted against cub age in months; numbers of litters seen over the 10-year study are shown above the graph. Most litters were not seen at every age, and new litters might be first seen at any age, which could result in the average litter size increasing. Left-hand arrow indicates time of emergence from the lair: before this time cubs were susceptible to predation and abandonment. Right-hand arrow shows the approximate age at which cubs could outdistance predators other than cheetahs; before this time they were still susceptible to predation.

In conclusion, an average of only 4.8% of the cubs that were born survived to independence, and predation accounted for 73.2% of mortality from known causes (see table 4.3). In the Serengeti ecosystem lions were the principal predator of cheetah cubs (table 4.5).

High cub mortality has probably affected cheetahs throughout their recent evolution. In the past lions and spotted hyenas must have been abundant in the areas supporting a high ungulate biomass where cheetahs lived. For example, historical accounts indicate that the Serengeti lion population was higher in the early part of this century than it is today. Cheetahs living on seasonally productive grasslands must also have abandoned their litters in the past because such areas attract ungulates for only a few months of the year (Sinclair and Fryxell 1985). Thus cheetahs in the Sahel zone or in areas such as the Athi Plains south of Nairobi, the Simanjiro Plains east of the Tarangire River, or in the Amboseli basin probably would have experienced ephemeral prey concentrations after giving birth and would have been subject to starvation in the lair as they are today.

RESUMPTION OF ESTRUS

On average, adult females mated within 3 weeks of losing their previous litter (table 4.6); for three females, conceptions occurred at first resumption of estrus, between 2 and 8 days later. This was reminiscent of lions, which conceived again an average of 24 days following the loss of unweaned offspring, providing they mated with the same males that fathered their previous litter (Packer and Pusey 1983).

The interval between the death of the previous litter and the next birth was longer for young than for adult females (see table 4.6), although the reasons for this are unknown [8]. As it was males rather than females that principally sought out and investigated the opposite sex, the possibility

TABLE 4.5 Percentage of Cheetah Cubs Killed by Different Predators in the Serengeti Ecosystem

Predator	In lair ($N = 53.5$)[a]	After emergence ($N = 12$)	Total (birth to independence) ($N = 65.5$)
Lion	88.8	33.3	78.6
Spotted hyena	5.6	41.7	12.2
Leopard	—	8.3	1.5
Cheetah	3.7	—	3.1
Masai dog	—	16.7	3.1
Raptor	1.9	—	1.5

Source: Adapted from Laurenson, in press-b.
[a] Litters that were not counted in the lair were estimated to consist of an average of 3.5 cubs.

TABLE 4.6 Number of Days between Reproductive Events

Female identity and litter number		Estimated number of days from death of previous litter to next birth	Estimated number of days from death of previous litter to next successful conception
Adult females			
TGG	1	117	24
	2	131	38
MK	1	108	15
	2	115	22
	3	120	27
EMM	1	98	5
	2	223	130[a]
MV	1	101	8
SKU		140	47
MSH		105	12
KC	1	95	2
	2	110	17
MQ		106	13
SGY		106	13
$\overline{X}$		111.7	18.7
Young females			
MTT	1	157	64
	2	116	23
	3	123	30
BTX		161	68
BHT		245	152
$\overline{X}$		160.4	67.4

Source: Laurenson, Caro, and Borner 1992.

[a] A female with pyometra of the uterus was not included in calculation of the means.

that young females were slower to find mates than were adults was unlikely to account for this result. Though age differences have been found in the shape of ovaries and size of ovarian follicles in captive cheetahs (Wildt et al. 1993), the effect this might have on the probability of conception is unclear.

DOES INFANTICIDE OCCUR IN CHEETAHS?

Rapid resumption of estrus raises the possibility that males might gain reproductive advantages by killing a female's cubs fathered by other males, and then mating with her themselves. Among mammals, infanticide is restricted mainly to primates, rodents, and carnivores (Hausfater and Hrdy 1984). Among carnivores, it has been studied principally in lions, in which males taking over a pride kill cubs fathered by previous residents (Packer and Pusey 1983). Infanticide has also been reported in tigers (Schaller 1967), cougars (Seidensticker et al. 1973), and leopards (Ilany 1990). In these and other felids, a new resident male would have exclusive access to bereaved females at a later date.

There has been no direct observation of infanticide in cheetahs. None-theless, a female was seen fighting with a male near her lair on the day she lost her litter (J. Scott, pers. comm., cited in Burney 1980). The day after the same female gave birth to a subsequent litter, Burney saw her fight with a male who was apparently searching up and down a stream-bed as if looking for cubs. If some females rapidly resume estrus (see table 4.6) despite migrating large distances (as in Serengeti), or if they take some time to start cycling again but remain within the same male's territory (as may have been the case in Burney's nonmigratory population in the Masai Mara Game Reserve), there could be positive selection on infanticide in cheetahs.

Adoption

Estimates of cub mortality were based on changes in the number of cubs seen with particular mothers and to a lesser extent on witnessing cubs' deaths. Absent cubs were presumed to have been killed, fallen terminally ill, or to have lost their families. Without mothers, cubs were bound to starve because their hunting skills were rudimentary until 10.5 months of age and only poor thereafter (chap. 6). Nevertheless, some cubs managed to attach themselves to unrelated adult cheetahs, usually families, and sur-vive by scavenging food; these we assumed were cubs who had lost contact with their mothers or whose mothers had died. Table 4.7 shows that these associations lasted from a few days to periods approaching a year in du-ration (3 months on average) and that adoptees and family members could be the same age or differ by many months. Adoption did not involve non-offspring nursing, since only cubs of 6 months or older or adolescents were seen to join families. Nevertheless this possibility cannot be ruled out, given that younger cubs occasionally got mixed up. For instance, A. Root (pers. comm.) saw two mothers near each other, each with three cubs roughly 2 months old. One of the mothers temporarily left her cubs to hunt, while the other, shyer female ran from his vehicle. When the first mother called to her cubs to follow, all six ran to her. She hissed and slapped the ground when the unrelated cubs were a meter away. It took several hours before the families were reunited, and one cub was still missing when Root left. I saw a similar incident in which cubs were at-tracted to the closest female that was calling them.

The chief benefit that adopted cubs and adolescents gained from these associations was the opportunity to rob the family of food. I witnessed eight kills made in the presence of adoptees, who obtained at least some food in six of them (an estimated average of 61.0%, SE = 13.4% of the meat in these cases). At some kills, adoptees slapped the biological cubs and ran off with the whole carcass. It may have been coincidence, but the one family in which I actually saw a cub die (probably from disease-related causes) was accompanied by a 12.5-month-old male who stole large quantities of food. The sick 8.5-month-old daughter ate a half and a quarter of the amount consumed by her two siblings during the 4 days I saw her alive (an estimated 0.4 kg in total). I had little doubt that, allowed greater access to carcasses, she would have eaten more, which might have improved her condition. It is possible that certain groups of unrelated adult males originated from associations between male adoptees and male cubs (chap. 9), given that adoptees were still with some families at the last sighting (see table 4.7).

Superficially, adoptees appeared to be tolerated by families, but close inspection revealed that mothers' behavior toward them varied from indifference, at best, to overt aggression, slapping and hissing when they

TABLE 4.7 Cases of Involuntary Adoption by Cheetahs

Composition and age of cheetah group when first seen with adoptee	Age and identity of adoptee when first seen with group	Estimated period adoptee was with group (days)		
		Min	Probable	Max
2 adult males	(6)M	29	37	44[a]
Mother + 4(11)MMFF	(6)M	160	216+	271+[b]
Adult female	(7)F	1	20	39
Mother + 2(11)MF	(9.5)?	1	56	111
Mother + 2(10.5)MF	(10.5)F	12	68	124
Mother + 2(6)MM	(10.5)M	287	312+	337+[b,c,d]
Mother + 2(11.5)MF	(11.5)M	36	104+	172+[b]
Mother + 3(4)FFF	(11.5)M	1	2	3[a]
Mother + 3(7)FFF	(12.5)M	7	119+	230+[b,c]
Mother + 2(8)MF	Adol F	21	44	67[e]
Mother + 2(12.5)FF	Adol MF	5	29	53
Mean		50.9	91.5	131.9

Note: Figures in parentheses refer to the age of the cubs in months, M and F to their sex.

[a] Separation from the adopting group was seen (see text).

[b] Adoptee was still with the family at last sighting.

[c] One cub died while adoptee present.

[d] Male adoptee stayed at least until the time the son left his mother and possibly longer.

[e] Family lost a biological cub between previous sighting and when it was first seen with adoptee; the adolescent female was seen alone before and after she joined.

approached too close. Only once did I ever see a mother briefly groom an adopted cub. Cubs were more tolerant, occasionally playing with the visitor. Maternal errors involving mistaken identity were not a factor in this species as they are in some instances of adoption in pinnipeds (Riedman 1990).

Adoptees were wary of the family moving off and leaving them behind. They attempted to maintain closer proximity to the mother than did her biological cubs, and almost always were the first to stand in readiness to leave when the mother did so. On two occasions I saw adopted cubs lose their providers. Once the mother suddenly left to hunt after resting for 20 minutes, and the 11.5-month-old male failed to notice the family's departure for 3 minutes; by this time they were more than 100 m distant. On the other occasion, a 7-month-old male lost the two adult males with whom he had been associating for a month. He shared their kills and was even present when they pinned down females. He lost contact on a day they had located and chased a new female. Walking in a semicircle, he searched for his companions and called for over an hour until dusk, but he had still not found them the next day. A week later he had tacked onto a mother and two fully grown sons that I found 7 km away. Forty-two hours after the cub had lost contact with the male pair, I found the two males together, and one of them yipped 20 times. This is the vocalization used by mothers to attract lost cubs, so he may have been trying to regain contact with the cub, but I could not be sure.

In conclusion, adoption must have enhanced orphans' survival considerably, since single cubs under 10 months of age would die without provisioning. Moreover, some associations carried a cub from this vulnerable period to a stage when it might have a chance of securing food for itself (as in the second case in table 4.7). For a family, the cost of feeding an extra mouth was divided among its members and appeared to be of insufficient magnitude to cause the mother to kill her unwanted guest, a possibility given the size difference in some cases.

Instances of adoption in cheetahs are unusual in that they do not fall into any of the major categories of adoption in mammals as outlined by Riedman (1982). Mothers do not obtain inclusive fitness benefits by adopting cubs, benefit from cub cooperation in, for example, capturing prey, or gain reciprocal benefits by having future litters allomothered at a later time. Nor are they likely to obtain additional parenting experience, since they have a litter already. Exploitation of infants, as reported for some primates (Hrdy 1976), cannot apply here. Finally, it seems highly improbable that mothers are committing a reproductive error, as reported for pinnipeds (Riedman and Le Boeuf 1982), since they discriminate against nonoffspring. In further contrast to most other mammals, adoption in cheetahs does not involve nonoffspring nursing (Pierotti 1991;

Packer, Lewis, and Pusey 1992). Rather, it is reminiscent of cases of adoption in some birds. For example, herring gulls may adopt when a chick moves into their territory because its own family has been driven off by intruders, or because the chick is brought in alive by a cannibal (Graves and Whiten 1980; see also Holley 1981). Though foreign chicks risk attack from the adoptive parents, they spend far more time on the nest than biological chicks and crouch down when attacked, both of which inhibit adults' aggression. Foreign chicks are provided with food and gain weight; of ten chicks that moved to nonbiological parents, six fledged (Graves and Whiten 1980).

Periods of Association between Family Members

Cubs that survived and retained contact with their own families stayed with their mothers for an average of 509.4 days ($N = 17$ litters, SE = 10.5, range 433 to 577 days) or 18.2 months. Although cubs were born throughout the year, they were slightly more likely to become separated from their mothers in the wet than in the dry season [9]. This was unrelated to the timing of births: of eight litters known to have been born in the wet season, six left in the wet, and all of the nine born in the dry season left in wet season months (birth dates were not known with accuracy for four litters). Since newly dependent adolescents were poor hunters (chap. 7), they must have benefited from family dissolution in the wet season when easy-to-catch gazelle neonates and fawns were numerous (see fig. 4.2). Bias toward wet season departure probably accounted for the variation in length of dependence (15.5 to 20.6 months) observed in this and an earlier study (Frame 1984).

TABLE 4.8 Evidence that Females May Conceive before Their Previous Cubs Separate from Them

Female identity (and litter number)	Date previous litter left (± days error in estimation)	Estimated date of conception of next litter	Estimated birth date of next litter	Conceived before previous litter left?
MQ (1)	6 Feb 88 (±58)	2 Jan 88	4 Apr 88	Possibly
MQ (2)	27 Jul 89 (±16)	30 May 89	1 Sep 89	Yes
EMM	16 Mar 88 (±12)	21 Jan 88	23 Apr 88	Yes
NDO	10 Nov 88 (±34)	5 Dec 88	7 Mar 89	Possibly
MV	16 Jan 89 (±30)	19 Nov 88	20 Feb 89	Yes
SKU[a]	28 Feb 89 (±59)	28 Apr 89	24 Jul 89	No
SGY	13 Apr 90 (±29)	6 Feb 90	9 May 90	Yes

Source: Laurenson, Caro, and Borner 1992.

[a] Cub may have died as it was only 12 to 13 months old at separation.

In some instances females next conceived when their previous litter was still accompanying them, while in others this occurred after family dissolution (table 4.8). Adamson (1969) even reported a female giving birth to her second litter while accompanied by the first. Mothers had more to gain from leaving their offspring than vice versa (chap. 5) and these gains could have been intensified in mothers that were already pregnant. Congruence of maternal conceptions and family separations in the wet season is therefore not surprising.

After offspring left their mothers, they remained together as a sibling group for an average of 186.9 days (6.7 months, SE = 74.2 days, $N = 8$ sibgroups). Thus females left their littermates between 647 and 760 days of age (23.1 to 27.1 months old, $N = 8$ sibgroups). Females first conceived at 1,043 days of age on average (SE = 33.6 days, $N = 5$ females), or when they were 37.3 months old, and always in the wet season (Laurenson 1992). Ages at first successful conception approximate those of captive females (2.5 to 3 years), although supplemented free-ranging and captive cheetahs can first conceive at younger ages (Adamson 1969; Marker and O'Brien 1989).

As first conception occurred 158.8 days, or 5.7 months (SE = 91.5 days, $N = 5$ females) after females left their siblings (Laurenson 1992), they may have left before first cycling. Alternatively, they may have departed around the time of first estrus (see Frame and Frame 1981) but have required several cycles to conceive.

It seems unlikely that the proximate cause of females leaving their littermates was to avoid sib matings. First, females did not leave mixed-sex sibgroups earlier than they did all-female sibgroups [10]; second, males may not have been behaviorally capable of mating at 2 years of age even though they were already spermatogenic (Wildt et al. 1993); and third, dates of first conception occurred nearly 6 months after sibgroup dissolution. Nonetheless, better data on timing of first estrus in relation to group fissioning, the probability of conceiving during early estrus periods, and the mating competence of adolescent males are required to determine the role of inbreeding avoidance in the dissolution of sibgroups.

Summary

1. Most adult females in the population gave birth, in contrast to females in captivity.

2. Successful conceptions were more likely to occur in wet season months, possibly as a result of increased food availability in the form of newborn Thomson's gazelles. There was no seasonal birth peak, however.

3. Only 28.8% of cubs born emerged from the lair. Predation by lions

was the principal source of mortality, although some mothers abandoned their litters when herds of Thomson's gazelles were too far from the lair.

4. Cubs continued to suffer high mortality after emerging from the lair, again from predation, with 8.8% of cubs surviving to 4 months of age. Cubs had only a 4.8% chance of reaching independence.

5. Females rapidly conceived again following the loss of an unweaned litter, with adults being quicker to reproduce again than young females.

6. Cubs that had lost their mothers sometimes joined unwilling families and stole food from them. These associations enabled the adopted cubs to survive.

7. Cubs remained with their mothers for an average of 18.2 months. Most litters left their mothers in the wet season, probably to take advantage of gazelle fawns that appeared then. Offspring then remained together as a sibgroup for an average of 6.7 months. Females first gave birth when they were over 3 years old.

Statistics

1. Number of litters conceived in wet and in dry seasons as determined from monitoring radio-collared females, 29 and 7 litters respectively, $\chi^2 = 6.320$, df = 1, $P < .02$.

2. Number of females that next conceived in wet and in dry seasons following the death of their previous litter, 15 and 4 females respectively, $\chi^2 = 3.322$, df = 1, $P < .1$.

3. Sixteen litters died in the wet season while 10 died in the dry season, $\chi^2 = 0.110$, df = 1, $P > .8$.

4. Number of days between the loss of an unweaned litter and the next conception in the dry season ($N = 5$ losses) and in the wet season ($N = 9$ losses), $\bar{X}s = 49.4$, 15.0 days respectively, Mann-Whitney U test, $U = 8$, $P < .1$.

5. Number of litters born in wet and in dry season months in Laurenson's detailed study, 20 and 16 litters respectively, $\chi^2 = 0.114$, df = 1, $P > .8$.

Across 10 years of study, 115 and 87 litters respectively, $\chi^2 = 0.017$, df = 1, $P > .9$.

6. Number of male and female cubs sexed in lairs, 57 males and 41 females, binomial test, $z = -1.520$, $P > .2$.

7. In 14 of those 17 litters that were attacked by predators before cubs emerged and for which data were available, all the cubs were killed, whereas all the cubs were killed in only 1 of the 7 litters that suffered predation after emergence, Fisher exact test, $P = .004$ (see table 4.4).

8. Number of days between death of the previous litter and next birth

was shorter in adult females ($N = 9$) than in young females ($N = 3$) (averages were taken of those females represented more than once), $\bar{X}$s = 17.8, 86.3 respectively, Mann-Whitney U test, $U = 1$, $P = .02$.

9. Number of litters leaving their mothers in wet and in dry seasons, $N = 16, 5$ litters respectively, $\chi^2 = 2.755$, $P < .1$.

10. Estimated age at which siblings separated from one another in groups that contained only females ($N = 4$ groups) and in those that contained cubs of both sexes ($N = 4$ groups), $\bar{X}$s = 713, 694 days respectively, Mann-Whitney U test, $U = 6$, $P > .6$. Scores were derived by taking the midway point between minimum and maximum estimated dates.

A mother and her two 3-month-old cubs rest together; mothers with young cubs quickly dozed off in quiet moments. (Drawing by Dafila Scott.)

5
COSTS OF FAMILY LIFE FOR MOTHERS

Parental investment is defined as "any investment by the parent in an individual offspring that increases the offspring's chance of surviving (and hence reproductive success) at the cost of the parent's ability to invest in other offspring" (Trivers 1972). Since the effects of current reproductive effort on the parent's survival and future reproduction are difficult to measure (Clutton-Brock 1984; Reznick 1985), measurements of the amount of time or energy that parents expend on offspring (parental expenditure) or of behavior that increases offspring's fitness (parental care) are often used instead (Clutton-Brock 1991). Maternal care is predicted to vary with environmental conditions, as well as with the characteristics of the mother and her offspring (see Sargent and Gross 1986; Montgomerie and Weatherhead 1988). For example, in mammals, studies have shown that mothers discriminate against sons when environmental conditions are harsh (wood rats: McClure 1981); that dominant mothers invest more in sons than in daughters in accordance with males having a higher variance in reproductive success than females (red deer: Clutton-Brock, Albon, and Guinness 1986); and that mothers modify their behavior according to the age of their offspring (yellow baboons: Altmann 1980; see Clutton-Brock 1991 for review).

Changes in maternal behavior according to offspring age, the focus of this chapter, are nevertheless hard to predict. One could argue that as offspring grow older and are better able to fend for themselves, their probability of survival increases and they therefore assume greater importance in contributing to parental fitness. Hence, parents might be expected to expend more energy or suffer greater costs in caring for older offspring (Andersson, Wiklund, and Rundgren 1980). Alternatively, it could be argued that parental expenditure will be greatest when offspring are young since its effects on offspring growth and survival are likely to be highest at this time (Clutton-Brock 1991). Certainly in primates and ungulates, in which lactation is the principal form of parental care, time and energy expended on offspring decline as offspring mature and increasingly come to rely on their own foraging to meet energy demands (e.g., rhesus monkeys: Berman 1980; ungulates: Ralls, Lundrigan, and Kranz 1987). In carnivores, however, in which mothers initially provide solid food for offspring after lactation ceases, it is unclear whether parental expenditure will rise or decline as offspring grow larger and their demands for solid food increase.

Most studies of parental care in mammals have been conducted on social species. In species in which adults do not associate outside the breeding season, however, the postweaning period is the only time when adult females experience the advantages and disadvantages of group living. Up to now, the economics of group living have not been considered as a factor affecting parental investment decisions, but they need to be incorporated into calculations about parental expenditure.

In this chapter, the costs of caring for cubs of different ages in terms of lactation, hunting, feeding, and vigilance are examined. (Antipredator behavior of mothers and cubs is treated in chap. 6.) These costs of care are then contrasted with costs experienced by lone adult females. Consideration of both the benefits and costs that mothers may derive from offspring and the costs of independence for cubs leads to a discussion of which party might benefit most from family dissolution. Changes in maternal behavior associated with litter size and sex composition have been discussed elsewhere (Caro 1987a; 1990).

Changes in Maternal Behavior

THE TIME COURSE OF LACTATION

It was impossible to record details of nursing while cubs were in the lair (K. Laurenson, pers. comm.), but cubs regularly nursed in the early morning. On average, mothers left the lair 179 minutes (SE = 15, N = 69 cases) after 0630 (Laurenson 1992), but this was brought forward if they were hungry, and there were considerable differences among individuals (Laurenson 1993). As a consequence, mothers with cubs in the lair killed few prey before 0930 compared with lone females (Laurenson 1992). After cubs had quit the lair, they nursed up until 0800, and I sometimes found it difficult to locate tame mothers with 2-month-old cubs because

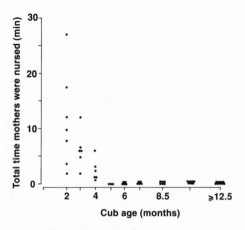

Fig. 5.1 Summed total number of minutes that mothers were nursed by cubs per daylight hour, plotted against cub age in months. Each point represents one litter.

they rarely sat up during the first 2 hours of the day. At this time, mothers allowed cubs to nurse for an average of 18.8% of daylight hours. This proportion declined rapidly as cubs grew older (fig. 5.1) [1].

During the midday rest period, particularly between 1130 and 1300, 2- or 3-month-old cubs might spend up to an hour suckling while their mother lay resting with her ventral surface exposed. When cubs were 4 months old, mothers rolled over, covered their nipples with their hind-legs, or sat up to avoid suckling attempts during this period of the day. Now cubs nursed for an average of only 4% of daylight hours, perhaps as a result of this maternal behavior (see Gomendio 1991). After 4 months, cubs received no milk, judging from their short bouts of contact with their mother's ventral surface, the loud sucking noises that often ended nursing attempts, and their efforts to find another nipple. After 8.5 months, I saw only one litter attach to the teat, although adolescents would occasionally nuzzle the ventral surface of a sibling during intense bouts of grooming. The proportion of the offspring dependency period over which lactation lasted (roughly 20%) appeared typical for felids and canids; in bears, hyenas, and mustelids lactation endures relatively longer (Gittleman 1986b). Larger litters nursed for slightly longer on average than smaller litters, once cub age had been taken into account [1].

CHANGES IN PREY PREFERENCES WITH REPRODUCTIVE STATE AND CUB AGE

Compared with lone females without cubs, lactating females with cubs in the lair and females whose cubs had just quit the lair chose to hunt an increasing proportion of prey larger than hares or neonate fawns (here termed large prey), and hunted large prey more often per hour (Laurenson 1992). They also had somewhat greater hunting success on large prey than did lone females (fig. 5.2), primarily because their chases were more successful. As a consequence, lactating females killed a greater number of large prey items per hour than did lone females (fig. 5.3). In contrast, hunting success on small prey was always high and did not change with females' reproductive status.

Mothers' preference for larger prey, such as adult Thomson's gazelles, remained high until cubs were 8.5 months old but then declined [2]. Attempts on even larger items weighing over 20 kg, such as Grant's gazelles and wildebeests, occurred only rarely [2], perhaps because of low success rates (7.0%, $N = 43$ attempts).

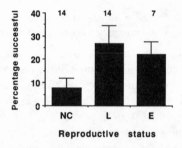

Fig. 5.2 Mean (and SE) percentage of hunts of large prey (i.e., prey other than hares or gazelle neonates and fawns) by young and adult females that were successful, separated according to whether they had no cubs (denoted as NC), had cubs in the lair (L), or had newly emerged cubs (E). Numbers of females are shown above the bars. (From Laurenson 1992.)

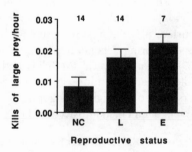

Fig. 5.3 Mean (and SE) number of kills of large prey (i.e., prey other than hares or gazelle neonates and fawns) made per hour by young and adult females, separated according to whether they had no cubs (denoted as NC), had cubs in the laire (L), or had newly emerged cubs (E). Numbers of females are shown above the bars. (From Laurenson 1992.)

CHANGES IN HUNTING BEHAVIOR WITH REPRODUCTIVE STATE AND CUB AGE

Females' hunting behavior changed once their cubs were born. Those with cubs in the lair or with newly emerged cubs spent a greater proportion of the day hunting than did lone females (Laurenson 1992). From then on, however, time spent hunting declined [3]. In contrast, the number of hunts per hour undertaken by females was unaffected by their reproductive state (Laurenson 1992) or by the age of their cubs [4] when all types of prey were considered. Laurenson suggested that time spent hunting initially rose after cubs were born because an increasing proportion of hunts were of large prey and these hunts took longer to complete. In addition, mothers with emerged cubs spent more time specifically in hunts of these large prey than mothers with cubs in the lair.

In general, mothers with young cubs that were still lactating put more effort into hunting than mothers with older cubs. Combining hunts of all types of prey, they spent more time in each hunt [5], put somewhat more time into successful hunts [6], and had marginally greater hunting success [7], at least when cubs had just come out of the lair (fig. 5.4). Nevertheless, some of the extra time spent hunting resulted from mothers of young cubs falling asleep! This was because cubs remained behind or accompanied their mother for just a few meters but then sat and watched her move forward (see chap. 6), advancing only if called. Freed of nursing attempts and being played upon, a mother had a chance to close her eyes for up to 10 minutes between bouts of advancing toward prey. Prey often wandered off as a consequence, and hunts were abandoned at marginally greater distances from prey when cubs were younger than when they were older (fig. 5.5) [8].

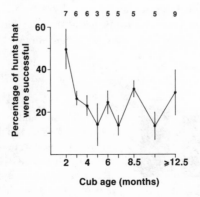

Fig. 5.4 Mean (and SE) percentage of mothers' hunts that were successful, plotted against cub age in months. Numbers of families are shown above the graph.

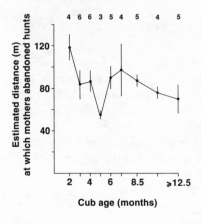

Fig. 5.5 Mean (and SE) estimated distance in meters at which mothers abandoned their hunts (in which prey escaped), plotted against cub age in months. Only those mothers seen to hunt five or more times are included. Numbers of families are shown above the graph.

CHANGES IN FOOD INTAKE WITH REPRODUCTIVE STATE AND CUB AGE

As a result of their preference for large prey, mothers with cubs in the lair, and later with newly emerged cubs, showed a steady increase in the proportion of the day they spent eating and the number of kilograms eaten per hour (fig. 5.6). Intake doubled from 0.12 kg per hour of observation for females with no cubs to 0.23 for females with newly emerged cubs. Subsequently, both of these measures declined as cubs grew older (fig. 5.7) [9], although weight of prey that mothers captured per hour did not change with cub age [10]. Reduced maternal intake resulted from having to share meat with increasingly voracious offspring; mothers fed for an average of only 27.5% of a family's total feeding time on a carcass when their cubs were 8.5 months old or older ($N = 13$ litters, see Caro 1989b for a fuller discussion).

In contrast to these results, maternal belly size scores did not increase across reproductive states (Laurenson 1992) or decline with cub age. Indeed, in dry season months, belly sizes of mothers with young cubs were

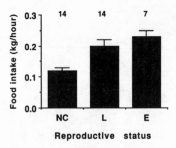

Fig. 5.6 Mean (and SE) kilograms of flesh eaten by young and adult females per hour, separated according to whether they had no cubs (denoted as NC), had cubs in the lair (L), or had newly emerged cubs (E). Numbers of females are shown above the bars. (From Laurenson 1992.)

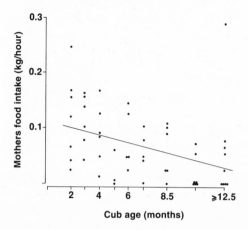

Fig. 5.7 Kilograms of flesh mothers ate per hour, plotted against cub age in months ($y = 0.113 - 0.007x$, $N = 54$, $r = -.382$, $P = 0.004$). Absolute amounts of flesh eaten by mothers with young cubs are lower than those for mothers with newly emerged cubs in fig. 5.6 because the samples are not strictly comparable. Laurenson (1992) assumed that each cub ate 4.5% of what its mother ate at kills and devalued maternal intake accordingly. I calculated maternal intake based on the proportion of time each family member spent feeding but assumed that young cubs ate a third as much as their mother per unit time (see chap. 3). Each point represents a mother from one litter.

significantly smaller than those of mothers with middle-aged or old cubs [11] and were smaller than in the wet season. The lack of correspondence between changes in maternal food intake and maternal belly size with cub age probably reflects more rapid absorption rates in lactating females despite their eating a greater amount per unit time.

Energetic Demands of Lactation

In mammals, lactation is the most energetically costly component of reproduction, with the demands of milk production sometimes exceeding those of the rest of the body (Hanwell and Peaker 1977; Pond 1977; Bauman and Currie 1980; Oftedal 1985). In cheetahs, females lost condition while lactating (Laurenson 1992). On average, lactating females were 0.9 kg lighter than lone females, had thinner skin fat folds, and had lower muscle mass as determined by palpating vertebral processes. Their health seemed unaffected, however. They did not carry higher ectoparasite burdens and were not eosinophilic compared with lone females. Female cheetahs met the energetic demands of lactation primarily by increasing their food intake, as they switched to larger prey and had greater success hunting it (Laurenson 1992). Though this option is open to lone females too, Laurenson suggests that a buildup of body reserves might hamper a lone cheetah's running speed and hunting efficiency with little immediate benefit. Females with cubs in the lair also spent more time drinking (Laurenson 1992).

Other species also increase food intake during lactation. For example, gelada baboons show a steep rise in time spent foraging during lactation (Dunbar and Dunbar 1988), and red deer more than double their food intake (Clutton-Brock, Guinness, and Albon 1982; see also Gittleman and Thompson 1988).

Cheetahs also met the demands of lactation by tapping body stores, judging from their elevated urea and lowered creatinine levels, which are indicative of protein catabolism and reduced muscle mass (Laurenson 1992). Lactating females also had raised cholesterol levels, signifying breakdown of fat stores for use in milk production. Thus females metabolized both fat and muscle tissue during lactation in addition to increasing their food intake.

Mothers with older offspring ate less than lactating mothers with young cubs because the former were apparently unable to adjust their prey preferences, hunting success, or hunting rates further to accommodate the increasing demands of growing progeny. This finding is reminiscent of California gulls, in which food is withheld from offspring as they mature (Pugusek 1990). In the few carnivores that share large packets of food, costs resulting from direct behavioral competition with large offspring could plausibly match the energetic costs of lactation under certain

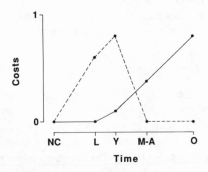

Fig. 5.8 Hypothetical costs of reproduction in female carnivores that must share food items with dependent offspring, plotted against time over the reproductive cycle. NC, no cubs; L, cubs in the lair; Y, young cubs that have emerged; M-A, middle-aged cubs; O, old cubs. Dashed line shows possible energetic costs of lactation; solid line, costs incurred through loss of food to offspring. The scale on the y-axis is arbitrary and the heights of the curves are unknown.

environmental conditions, although the relative magnitude of each is uncertain (fig. 5.8). In such species costs of postweaning care are likely to be greater than in insectivorous species, such as dwarf mongooses, in which dependent offspring forage individual items of insect prey for themselves (Rood 1986). In both groups of species, however, philopatric offspring that remain in their natal range may continue to impose costs on mothers (Clutton-Brock, Albon, and Guinness 1982).

Changes in Mothers' Vigilance

Compared with lone females, mothers with newly emerged cubs spent a greater proportion of the day observing their surroundings and were more vigilant during the midday rest period (Laurenson 1992, in press-b) but these measures declined as cubs grew older [12]. Statistically, these measures of vigilance are associated with hunting behavior (Caro 1987a), although cheetahs may also have scanned their environment for other reasons. Though mothers benefited by locating prey and predators, vigilance also carried costs in terms of lost opportunities for resting. These costs fell primarily on mothers with young cubs.

At kills, mothers with cubs just out of the lair spent a greater percentage of time observing their surroundings than those with cubs in the lair or lone females (Laurenson, in press-b), but this measure also declined as cubs grew older [13]. Vigilance at kills (see figs. 1.1c; 5.9) was statistically associated with antipredator behavior on the part of the mother (Caro 1987a) and seemed to reflect cubs' changing vulnerability to predation. Once cubs left the relative safety of the lair where they were hidden from

Fig. 5.9 A mother maintains vigilance while her two middle-aged cubs eat the abdominal contents of an adult female Thomson's gazelle she has captured.

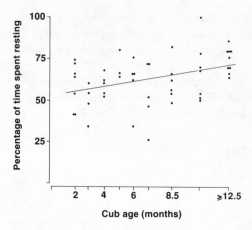

Fig. 5.10 Percentage of 15-minute scans mothers spent resting during the course of the day, plotted against cub age in months ($y = 52.416 + 1.558x$, $N = 51$, $r = .401$, $P = .004$). Each point represents a mother from one litter.

predators, maternal vigilance at kills rose and stayed high until 4 months of age, the period during which cubs were principally affected by predation (Laurenson, in press-b; chap. 4). Similar changes in maternal vigilance have been recorded in vervet monkeys. The proportion of time vervet mothers scanned the environment in response to the playback of an alpha male's leopard alarm call was sensitive to ontogenetic changes in offspring vulnerability (Hauser 1988). As a result of the greater proportion of time they spent observing, hunting, and eating throughout the day, females with cubs spent a lesser proportion of time resting than lone females (Laurenson 1992), or mothers with older cubs (fig. 5.10) [14].

Although mothers became progressively less vigilant as cubs matured [15], this change was not associated with increasing levels of cub vigilance

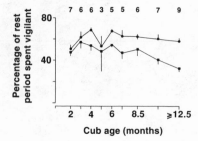

Fig. 5.11 Mean (and SE) percentage of 5-minute scans during the midday rest period in which a mother (solid squares) or at least one family member (solid circles) had its eyes open and was observing its surroundings, plotted against cub age in months. Numbers of families are shown above the graph.

[16]. In fact, the percentages of time mothers and cubs spent observing their surroundings were positively correlated, as a result of all parties sitting up to observe events or passing animals simultaneously. Since young cubs did not always recognize predators or respond to them appropriately, and became fully competent at detecting sources of danger only when they were 10 months old or older (chap. 6), mothers' apparent lack of confidence in their cubs was well founded. That said, at least one member of the family group had its eyes open and was observing the surroundings for approximately 60% of the midday rest period over the period of maternal care (fig. 5.11) [17].

In summary, the energetic costs of maternal care fell principally on those mothers whose cubs had recently emerged from the lair. These individuals were lactating and spent a greater proportion of time hunting and a lesser proportion of time resting than lone females, mothers with cubs in the lair, or mothers with older cubs (table 5.1). Mothers with young cubs countered high energetic requirements by capturing larger prey and having greater hunting success. Vigilance associated with hunting and with scouting for predators was also greatest in mothers with young cubs. According to my estimates, lactating mothers whose cubs had left the lair ate approximately 1.4 kg of meat per day, while using a different formula, Laurenson (1992) put the figure nearer 2.8 kg/day for mothers with newly emerged cubs. I estimated that cheetah mothers with old offspring ate as little as 0.5 kg/day as a result of competition from their

TABLE 5.1 Principal Changes in Females' Behavior with Reproductive State and Cub Age

Females' behavior	Reproductive state[a]	Cub age[b]
Nursing	Increases?	Declines
Hunting		
Preference for large prey	Increases	No effect[c]
Rate of hunting	No effect	No effect
Time spent hunting	Increases	Declines
Hunting success	Increases	Declines
Feeding		
Amount eaten	Increases	Declines
Vigilance		
Vigilance during the day	Increases	Declines
Vigilance at kills	Increases	Declines
Resting	Declines	Increases

[a] Changes in behavior with reproductive state: from pregnant, to lactating with cubs in the lair, to lactating with newly emerged cubs. (Data from Laurenson 1992.)

[b] Changes in behavior with cub age: from 2 to ≥12.5 months. (Data from this study.)

[c] Declines in old cubs.

large cubs. Being freed from lactation, however, their energy demands were low and they appeared to be on an equivalent or higher nutritional plane than lactating females. In this carnivore, therefore, costs of parental care declined with offspring age.

Effects of Litter Size on the Behavior of Mothers

The number of cubs in a litter generally had little effect on maternal behavior when cubs were young, although mothers spent a progressively greater proportion of the day searching for prey as little size increased (Caro 1989b). When cubs were old, litter size assumed greater importance because large cubs each ate a greater percentage of the food available for family consumption. As a result, mothers' belly sizes were smaller if they had three or four cubs in their charge than if they had one or two [18]. To compensate, mothers with three *old* cubs attempted to capture large prey (here adult Grant's and adult and subadult Thomson's gazelles) more often than mothers with one or two cubs [19], but they did not increase their rate of hunting (see above). Despite a maternal focus on larger prey, mothers with large litters of old cubs did not kill a greater proportion of these large prey, presumably because they were more difficult to catch [20].

Effects of litter size on maternal condition and behavior are well documented in mammals, especially during the period of lactation (Mendl 1988). Broadly, maternal energy expenditure increases with litter size because mothers produce more milk (Sadlier 1980), and as a consequence they increase their food intake and spend less time resting. This information is derived mainly from rodents, but domestic cats show the same pattern (Hall and Pierce 1934; Loveridge 1987). In cheetahs too, mothers were nursed for longer periods by larger litters, but following weaning, effects of litter size on maternal care were limited to just a handful of measures (see below and also Caro 1987a, 1990). In some rodents, the next reproduction is delayed following a large litter. In cheetahs, the number of days a litter was alive multiplied by its size, an estimate of cost imposed on the mother, was positively correlated with the length of time from its premature loss to the next conception (Laurenson 1992).

Comparisons between Mothers and Lone Adult Females

MOVING

To understand the reasons that mothers tolerated offspring associating with them for so long, it is useful to compare the short-term behavioral costs of being a mother with the costs suffered by lone adult females. Adult cheetah mothers with young, middle-aged, and old cubs all spent a significantly greater proportion of the day moving than did lone adult females unaccompanied by cubs (table 5.2) [21].

While mothers with young cubs had to travel to find the food necessary to support lactation (Laurenson 1992), mothers with older cubs sometimes had to travel because their cubs initiated so many family movements [22], up to 25% of group sorties (fig. 5.12). The greater the number of old cubs in the party, the more marked the effect [23]; daughters in particular were active in moving off in search of prey (see below).

HUNTING AND FEEDING BEHAVIOR

Overall I found the hunting behavior of mothers to be very similar to that of lone adult females. Whatever the age of their cubs, their prey preferences, success rates, time spent hunting, and hunting rates did not differ significantly from those of lone females [24], despite cub age–related differences between mothers as reported above. Laurenson (1992) found that females with newly emerged cubs (aged 2 months in my sample) chose to hunt a greater percentage of prey larger than neonate gazelles or

TABLE 5.2 Mean Percentage (and SE) of 15-Minute Scans Adult Mothers and Lone Adult Females Spent Moving and Resting

	Mothers with cubs that were			
	Young $N = 16$	Middle-aged $N = 12$	Old $N = 22$	Adult females $N = 13$
Moving				
	14.2	12.8	12.4	5.9
	(1.3)	(3.6)	(1.5)	(1.7)
Resting				
	56.8	62.3	68.7	71.3
	(2.8)	(4.3)	(2.8)	(5.4)

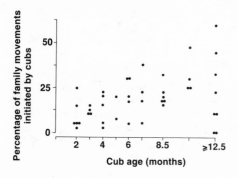

Fig. 5.12 Percentage of family movements that were initiated by cubs, plotted against cub age in months. Each point represents one litter.

hares, and hunted and killed them at higher rates than did females without cubs. It is difficult to reconcile our findings, but her mothers were lactating heavily and were hence under greatest pressure to increase their intake by catching large prey, whereas lactation had dropped off markedly in some of my mothers with young cubs aged 3 or 4 months (see fig. 5.1). Additionally, her lone females were sampled systematically over 5 days, whereas mine were sampled more opportunistically over shorter time periods (table 3.2). This might have inflated my measures of hunting if I had (unwittingly) sampled lone females that were hungry or about to hunt.

Mothers with older cubs spent less time feeding than lone females [25] and ate fewer kilograms of meat per hour [26]. On average, mothers with old cubs consumed less than a third as much food per unit time as females living alone (fig. 5.13). Old cubs had jaws of nearly adult size and could chew meat as fast as their mothers. In the face of this competition mothers attempted to maximize access to food by spending a lower proportion of time off kills than lone adult females [27], although instances of overt aggression between family members were rare. Increased litter size exacerbated competition still further, with mothers of old cubs both spending less time feeding per hour and eating less meat as family members rose in number [28]. Even mothers with middle-aged cubs ate less than half as much as lone females. Belly sizes taken from a wider sample of individuals suggest higher maternal intake rates than those obtained from direct observations, but they confirm that lone adult females were not as hungry as mothers [29].

The reduced intake rates experienced by cheetah mothers that had ceased lactating contrast sharply with data from ungulates and primates, which show that lactating females forage more than nonlactating females (e.g., sheep: Arnold and Dudzinski 1967; olive baboons: Altmann 1980; red deer: Clutton-Brock, Guinness, and Albon 1982; gelada baboons: Dunbar and Dunbar 1988). Again, this suggests that the constraint of having to share individual food packets with offspring can result in additional costs to carnivore mothers as compared with other mammalian taxa.

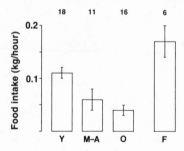

Fig. 5.13 Mean (and SE) number of kilograms of flesh eaten per hour by adult mothers of young (Y), middle-aged (M-A), and old (O) cubs, and by adult females with no cubs (F). Sample sizes are shown above the bars.

What prevented mothers from altering their hunting behavior to ameliorate the effects of competition from growing cubs? Mothers with older cubs differed little from lone females in the proportion of the day they spent resting (see table 5.2) [30], so time was not limiting, yet mothers of old cubs hunted for an average of just 1.2 minutes per hour compared with lone females' 2.6 minutes per hour. At least four explanations for low maternal intake rates are possible. First, mothers with old cubs might have required less food than lone females, many of whom were pregnant (chap. 4). Nevertheless, energetic requirements in the last trimester of pregnancy are only 1.5 times that of nonreproductive needs in domestic cats (Loveridge 1986) and, anyway, some mothers with old cubs may themselves have been pregnant (see table 4.8). Second, to make a full recovery from the energetic demands of lactation, mothers of older cubs might have been prepared to sustain reduced food intake, as low as 0.5 kg per day over week-long stretches, in return for resting for two-thirds of the day. Third, mothers may have been unable to capture prey of any larger size on a regular basis; recall that mothers with large litters attempted larger prey but could not secure it. Fourth, intake during daylight hours may have underestimated true intake, since mothers with old cubs hunted more often at night than mothers with younger cubs. None of these explanations is entirely satisfactory, and the topic warrants further examination.

Short-Term Benefits of Family Life for Mothers

When cubs were young, responsibility for detecting predators and defending the family lay with mothers, but older offspring of 10 months or more showed levels of vigilance that approached those of adults (see chap. 6). This observation suggested the possibility that mothers themselves could obtain group-related benefits from their association with large cubs. Mothers in the company of old cubs were somewhat less vigilant during the midday rest period than lone adult females; there was a suspicion that they spent a greater proportion of time lying flat out (table 5.3) [31]. These differences stemmed from increasing group size, since adult females were less vigilant and somewhat more relaxed with increasing numbers of cubs (fig. 5.14) [32]. These observations are remarkable given that mothers with old cubs were hungry, particularly those with large litters, and might therefore be expected to be on the lookout for prey.

Theory argues that animals obtain benefits from grouping because predators are more likely to be detected early by a group (Pulliam 1973). In addition, an individual in a group can reduce the amount of time it spends being vigilant without reducing the probability of the group detecting a source of danger (Elgar and Catterall 1981). Numerous studies have demonstrated a decline in individual vigilance with increasing group size. Although Elgar (1989) has argued that many of these findings are subject to confounding variables, most of these can be dismissed in the case of cheetahs relaxing during their midday rest period. Time of day, distance from cover, or objects obstructing the view of group members were unlikely to differ among group sizes. Reduced vigilance resulting from a lower proportion of group members being on the edge of large groups has little bearing, since all individuals were on the edge of such a small group anyway. As cheetahs were not feeding when data were collected, increased competition over food in larger groups cannot explain lowered individual

TABLE 5.3 Mean Percentage (and SE) of 5-Minute Scans during the Midday Rest Period that Females Spent Vigilant, Lying Flat Out, and Lying Out

| | Mothers with cubs that were | | | |
	Young $N = 19$	Middle-aged $N = 12$	Old $N = 22$	Adult females $N = 14$
Vigilance	52.8	47.0	39.6	51.7
	(2.8)	(3.5)	(2.5)	(5.7)
Lying flat out	9.2	11.3	16.7	15.6
	(1.4)	(2.1)	(2.7)	(6.8)
Lying out	31.4	41.5	41.1	35.3
	(2.7)	(4.5)	(3.1)	(5.3)

Note: All comparisons between lone adult females and each of the other groups, and between adult females and the other groups combined, were nonsignificant except those between lone females and mothers with old cubs on vigilance and on lying flat out.

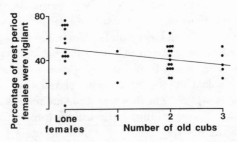

Fig. 5.14 Percentage of 5-minute scans during the midday rest period that adult females and adult mothers had their eyes open and were scanning the surroundings, separated by the number of old cubs they had accompanying them ($y = 50.408 - 4.685x$; $N = 36$, $r = -.317$, $P = .060$. Each point represents one female, or mother from one litter.

vigilance levels either. Admittedly, group members differed in age, since the groups were composed of mothers and cubs, but it was the adult females in the different-sized groups that were being compared. The fact that adults may have been compensating for less vigilant offspring would not affect the overall conclusion that adults showed reduced vigilance as group size increased.

Why did mothers exhibit reduced vigilance in larger groups of old cubs? I have no direct evidence that larger groups detected predators earlier than smaller groups, since I took no records on this, but data in chapter 7 show that associating individuals can reduce personal vigilance without compromising the vigilance of the group. Mothers' reduced vigilance and relaxed demeanor in the company of old cubs indicated that they probably benefited in this way.

In addition, carnivores, particularly jackals and cheetahs (usually females), seemed intimidated by mothers with middle-aged or old cubs, since they were more likely to move away from them than from cheetah families with young cubs [33]. I had insufficient data on interactions between predators and lone adult females to test whether they were harassed more than were families, but, again in chapter 7, I show that single adolescent cheetahs were more likely to be approached by spotted hyenas and male cheetahs than were groups of adolescents. Since predators would find it difficult to distinguish mothers with large cubs from groups of adolescent cheetahs at even moderate distances, the antipredator benefits of grouping should pertain equally well in comparisons between lone adult females and mothers with large cubs. In sum, mothers could treat old cubs as something approaching equals in respect to vigilance and antipredator behavior, and they benefited in terms of reduced personal vigilance as a consequence.

Who Gains Most from Family Dissolution?

Evolutionary considerations predict that a mother will terminate parental care when its cost to her is more than half the benefit to her offspring. An offspring, however, should favor continued parental care until the costs of care to its mother's fitness exceed twice the benefits to itself (Trivers 1974). In a monogamous breeding system parents and offspring are related equally to the parents' future offspring; therefore the costs of an act of parental care will be identical for both parent and current offspring, but its benefits will differ. As current offspring are related to themselves by 100% but to each parent by half this amount, the benefits of parental care will always be greater for offspring than for parents, and conflicts of interest will occur throughout the period of parental care (Lazarus and Inglis 1986). Though parent-offspring conflict has been explored theoretically (e.g., MacNair and Parker 1978; Godfray 1991; see Mock and Forbes 1992), there are few empirical data on the short-term costs and benefits experienced by both parties at the time parental care ceases (but see Davies 1976), especially in mammals (Berger 1979). This is unfortunate, since the short-term cost-benefit ratios of both parties will help to determine the total reproductive costs on the basis of which natural selection should mold decisions about the termination of investment.

In this study it was relatively easy to assess the short-term costs experienced by cheetah offspring after the cessation of parental care because sibgroups showed little change in ranging patterns and remained within the study area (fig. 5.15). On average, as much as 79.5% ($N = 5$ sibgroups, SE = 9.9%) of their home range fell within the natal range. Comparisons between dependent cubs and independent adolescents were separated by sex because females had significantly lower belly sizes than males during these periods [34] and were more active in instigating family movements [35]. Daughters often rose from resting and moved off toward prey, even

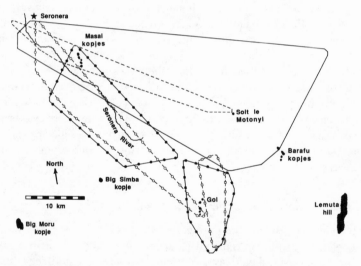

Fig. 5.15 Location of mothers' ranges and their offspring's ranges after they had left their mothers but while littermates remained together; ranges of both generations are underestimates because most of these individuals were not radio-collared and the number of sightings was low (see app. 9). Shown are the ranges of mother 1, collared (solid line), and the range of her three-daughter sibgroup (dashed line) 18 to 73 days after last being seen with their mother; mother 2 (solid line and circles) and the range of her two-daughter sibgroup (dashed line and circles) 44 to 244 days after last being seen with their mother; mother 3 (solid line and squares) and the range of her son-and-daughter sibgroup (dashed line and squares) 21 to 156 days after last being seen with their mother. Topography as in fig. 2.11.

in the middle of the day, with family members following reluctantly be-hind; as adolescents, females would usually start walking toward patches of herbs in order to search for concealed prey before their brothers did. Thus females might be disposed to leave the family first.

For males, there were disadvantages in being separated from their mothers. Males spent a lower proportion of time resting [36] and a greater proportion of time hunting and searching for prey after independence [37]. Male laziness accounted for these differences, since males were re-luctant to hunt in family groups. Sometimes they continued to rest while their mother and sisters stalked prey, or else they just walked on behind, relying on their mother to capture prey for them. I saw dependent male cubs initiate hunts 30 times in total but saw dependent females do so 50 times, even though there was a predominance of males in old litters (see table 3.1). In sibling groups, however, males kept up with littermates since they could play an important role in taking over the chase and knocking prey down if a sibling was reluctant to contact the quarry (chap. 7).

Measures of food intake did not differ between the final stage of de-pendence and independence for either males or females, but both sexes had significantly smaller belly sizes once they became independent [38]. Thus adolescents' belly sizes declined more rapidly despite their eating as much as when they were with their mothers. Being forced to become more involved in attempting to capture prey after independence, adoles-cents may have absorbed food more rapidly and consequently may have been hungrier. Thus offspring, especially sons, were unlikely to have been the first to initiate family dissolution.

Mothers' long-term reproductive considerations were probably the most important factor causing families to split up. A pregnant mother would be unwilling to give birth while still in the company of her previous litter. In contrast, cubs' reproductive considerations were negligible since they were unlikely to conceive at this age (see chap. 4). Nevertheless, the exact timing of family dissolution probably depended on short-term con-siderations, with food intake being the most important proximate factor. Food intake was especially important at this time because offspring were still growing in size, whereas mothers may have needed to put on fat for the next bout of reproduction (Bronson 1989). Differences in the per-centage of time spent eating, amount of food ingested, and belly size be-fore and after family dissolution all indicated that mothers had more to gain from leaving the family than either daughters or sons (table 5.4). Other proximate factors might also influence who left the family first. These include mothers obtaining greater antipredator benefits from re-maining in the family than cubs, since they would be alone after dissolu-tion while littermates would remain together. Also, daughters might be more prone to leave because they were better hunters than their brothers.

TABLE 5.4 Mean (± SE) Values of Feeding Behavior before and after Family Dissolution

	Belly size	Food intake (Kg/hr)[a]	Percentage of time spent eating
Mothers	5.9 ± 0.2 (98)	0.03 ± 0.02 (6)	2.0 ± 1.0 (5)
Lone females	6.5 ± 0.2 (297)	0.17 ± 0.03 (6)	5.4 ± 1.4 (14)
Dependent female cubs	6.1 ± 0.3 (74)	0.07 ± 0.01 (3)	2.6 ± 0.9 (7)
Adolescent females	5.3 ± 0.2 (75)	0.10 ± 0.02 (16)	3.8 ± 0.7 (20)
Dependent male cubs	6.7 ± 0.3 (76)	0.04 ± 0.01 (8)	1.7 ± 0.6 (7)
Adolescent males	6.1 ± 0.3 (62)	0.07 ± 0.02 (16)	2.6 ± 0.5 (16)

Note: Values are for individuals in a family when cubs were aged 12 or more months old and after dissolution of the family. Belly sizes were taken from sightings (number shown in parentheses) and feeding measures from observation periods (numbers of individuals shown in parentheses).

[a] Animals watched for 12 or more hours.

Data presented in chapter 7 show that adolescent cheetahs could expect to suffer low rates of food intake for some years after independence due to their poor hunting skills. The surprising result of the analyses presented here was that cubs' poor feeding regime started before independence (note the intake rates of cubs and lone females in table 5.4). Intuitively, I expected intake rate to start declining at the time the mother disappeared. Also surprising were mothers' depressed feeding rates compared with those of lone females. If a mother's subsequent bout of reproduction was successful, she might achieve a high nutritional plane only between the departure of her litter and her next conception (ca. 1 month) and during pregnancy (3 months). For the remaining 15 to 20 months, she would suffer the costs of lactation and increasingly severe competition from cubs. Put in this light, sequences of litter losses through predation and other causes (chap. 4), though devastating for her reproductive success, would allow a female to maintain a high nutritional plane for extended periods of time. Thus greater reproductive success might have been linked to lower adult survival through the depressed feeding returns associated with cub dependency.

Summary

1. Mothers nursed their cubs until they were 4 months of age, then continued to care for them for approximately a year after weaning.
2. Lactating mothers attempted to capture a greater proportion of

prey larger than hares or neonate gazelles, were more successful at catching them, and killed them at higher rates than females without cubs. Lactating mothers also spent more time hunting than either lone females or mothers with old cubs and apparently put more effort into securing prey.

3. Females therefore met the energetic demands of lactation by almost doubling their food intake, although they apparently used food more rapidly than lone females or mothers with older cubs. In addition, lactating mothers mobilized fat and muscle tissue as determined from blood biochemistry.

4. Mothers did not adjust prey preferences or hunting success further as their cubs grew older, despite having to share food with increasingly demanding cubs. As a result, mothers ate progressively less, but their energy demands were in decline and they were not particularly hungry. For carnivores that catch large prey items that have to be shared with offspring, the costs of postweaning care must be more severe than for insectivores or herbivores that do not divide food items.

5. Mothers were most vigilant after cubs had left the lair and before they were 4 months old. The subsequent decline in maternal vigilance was contingent upon the age of the cubs but was not associated with increasing cub vigilance.

6. When cubs were old and competition over food was marked, larger litter size resulted in mothers being hungrier, and they attempted to catch larger prey.

7. In comparison with lone adult females, mothers traveled more but ate less meat per hour because they had to share it with their offspring. Mothers appeared unable to ameliorate increased feeding competition from growing cubs.

8. Mothers benefited from the company of older cubs in two ways: they could afford to be less vigilant than lone adult females, and predators avoided cheetah families containing older cubs. This finding demonstrates that in polytokous solitary species mothers can gain temporary antipredator benefits from family life.

9. Both sons and daughters suffered as a consequence of separating from their mother. After independence, males spent more time hunting and searching for prey, and both sexes became hungrier because they were forced to capture food for themselves.

10. Regarding short-term energetic demands, mothers had more to gain from leaving their offspring than vice versa, since their food intake increased dramatically when they were freed from their cubs.

Statistics

1. Total time that mothers with young litters ($N = 19$), middle-aged litters ($N = 13$), and old litters ($N = 22$) were suckled by one or more

cubs, $\overline{X}$s = 6.88, 0.05, 0 min/hr respectively, $F_{2,50}$ = 56.478, $P < .0001$, using logged data controlling for litter size.

Total time that mothers with small litters (1 and 2 cubs) (N = 30 litters) and with large litters (3 and 4 cubs) (N = 24 litters) were suckled by one or more cubs, $\overline{X}$s = 0.75, 4.54 min/hr respectively, $F_{1,51}$ = 3.248, P = .077, using logged data controlling for cub age.

2. Number of attempts mothers made on adult male and female Thomson's gazelles when they had young (N = 276 attempts), middle-aged (N = 159 attempts), and old cubs (N = 207 attempts), $\overline{X}$s = 24.6%, 27.0%, 16.4% respectively, G test, G_2 = 7.218, P = .031.

Number of attempts mothers made on prey larger than 20 kg when they had young, middle-aged, and old cubs (Ns as above), $\overline{X}$s = 4.7%, 6.9%, 9.2% respectively, G test, G_2 = 3.787, $P > .1$.

3. Time spent hunting by mothers with young cubs (N = 19 litters), middle-aged cubs (N = 13 litters), and old cubs (N = 22 litters), $\overline{X}$s = 2.5, 1.8, 1.2 min/hr respectively, $F_{2,51}$ = 2.895, P = .064 on logged data.

4. Rate of hunting by mothers with young (N = 17 litters), middle-aged (N = 12 litters), and old cubs (N = 15 litters), $\overline{X}$s = 0.22, 0.23, 0.25 hunts/hr respectively, $F_{2,41}$ = 0.413, $P > .6$.

5. Length of time spent in each hunt by mothers with young (N = 19 litters), middle-aged (N = 13 litters), and old cubs (N = 19 litters), $\overline{X}$s = 10.2, 7.8, 5.7 sec respectively, $F_{2,48}$ = 3.637, P = .034 on logged data.

6. Length of time spent in each successful hunt by mothers with young (N = 19 litters), middle-aged (N = 11 litters), and old cubs (N = 14 litters), $\overline{X}$s = 6.2, 5.4, 3.7 min/hr respectively, $F_{1,26}$ = 3.460, P = .080, on logged data controlling for individual differences between mothers.

7. Percentage of hunts of all prey that were successful for mothers with young (N = 19 litters), middle-aged (N = 13 litters), and old cubs (N = 19 litters), $\overline{X}$s = 33.9%, 18.0%, 25.5% respectively, $F_{2,48}$ = 2.620, P = .083 on logged data.

8. Spearman rank order correlation coefficient between the estimated distance from prey at which mothers (seen to hunt 5 or more times) abandoned failed hunts and cub age, N = 42, r_s = −.257, P = .1.

9. Effects of cub age on the number of minutes mothers of young (N = 17 litters), middle-aged (N = 12 litters), and old cubs (N = 15 litters) spent eating per hour, $\overline{X}$s = 2.6, 1.3, 1.0 min/hr respectively, $F_{1,16}$ = 14.302, P = .002, controlling for individual differences between mothers.

Effects of cub age on the number of kilograms of meat mothers of young (N = 19 litters), middle-aged (N = 13 litters), and old cubs (N = 22 litters) were estimated to eat per hour, $\overline{X}$s = 0.11, 0.06, 0.04 kg/hr respectively, $F_{1,20}$ = 3.189, P = .089, controlling for individual differences between mothers using logged data. Note: Intake rates for mothers with young cubs are lower than those for mothers with emerged cubs shown in fig. 5.6 because (*a*) assumptions about cub intake rates differed between this and Laurenson's study (see legend, fig. 5.7), and (*b*) data are derived from different cub age groups (2 to 4 months here, but only 2 months in fig. 5.6); and, as a consequence, (*c*) sample sizes differ.

10. Effects of cub age on the number of kilograms of edible flesh mothers of young (N = 19 litters), middle-aged (N = 13 litters), and old cubs (N = 22 litters) captured per hour, $\bar{X}$s = 0.54, 0.40, 0.39 kg/hr respectively, $F_{1,20}$ = 0.004, $P > .9$, controlling for individual differences between mothers.

11. Belly sizes taken from sightings of mothers with young (N = 65 sightings), middle-aged (N = 86 sightings), and old cubs (N = 115 sightings) in the dry season, $\bar{X}$s = 4.7, 5.2, 5.3 respectively, Kruskal-Wallis test, H = 5.188, df = 2, $P < .0001$.

Belly sizes taken from sightings of mothers with young (N = 109 sightings), middle-aged (N = 80 sightings), and old cubs (N = 115 sightings) in the wet season, $\bar{X}$s = 5.5, 5.4, 5.6 respectively, Kruskal-Wallis test, H = 0.998, df = 2, $P > .3$.

12. Effects of cub age on the percentage of 15-minute scans mothers of young (N = 14 litters), middle-aged (N = 12 litters), and old cubs (N = 15 litters) spent observing their surroundings, $\bar{X}$s = 18.1%, 17.1%, 16.1% respectively, $F_{1,14}$ = 8.511, P = .011, controlling for individual differences between mothers and excluding single-day watches.

Effects of cub age on the percentage of 5-minute scans mothers of young (N = 19 litters), middle-aged (N = 13 litters), and old cubs (N = 22 litters) were vigilant during the midday rest period, $\bar{X}$s = 52.8%, 48.1%, 39.6% respectively, $F_{1,49}$ = 17.424, $P < .005$, controlling for litter size.

13. Effects of cub age on the percentage of time mothers of young (N = 17 litters), middle-aged (N = 11 litters), and old cubs (N = 10 litters) spent off carcasses they ate from, $\bar{X}$s = 32.6%, 27.0%, 15.7% respectively, $F_{2,35}$ = 8.022, P = .001.

14. Effects of cub age on the percentage of 15-minute scans mothers of young (N = 16 litters), middle-aged (N = 13 litters), and old cubs (N = 22 litters) spent resting throughout the day, $\bar{X}$s = 56.6%, 60.0%, 68.7% respectively, $F_{1,32}$ = 3.392, P = .082, controlling for individual differences between mothers.

15. Pearson correlation coefficient between the percentage of 5-minute scans during the midday rest period mothers were vigilant and cub age, y = 57.570 − 1.743x, N = 54, r = −.477, P = .0003.

Spearman rank order correlation coefficient between the frequency at which mothers looked up from the carcass and cub age, N = 42, r_s = −.258, $P < .05$.

Spearman rank order correlation coefficient between the percentage of time mothers spent off the carcass and cub age, $N = 42$, $r_s = -.530$, $P < .001$.

Pearson correlation coefficient between the percentage of 15-minute scans mothers spent observing their surroundings and cub age, $y = 18.561 - 0.243x$, $N = 41$, $r = -.152$, $P > .3$.

16. Pearson correlation coefficient between the percentage of scans mothers and cubs were vigilant, $y = 47.977 - 0.059x$, $N = 54$, $r = -0.036$, $P > 0.8$ not controlling for other variables.

Spearman rank order correlation coefficient between the frequency at which mothers and cubs looked up from the carcass, $N = 42$, $r_s = -.128$, $P > .2$.

Spearman rank order correlation coefficient between the percentage of time mothers and cubs spent off the carcass, $N = 42$, $r_s = .128$, $P > .2$.

Pearson correlation coefficient between the percentage of scans mothers and cubs spent observing their surroundings, $y = 7.923 + 0.700x$, $N = 41$, $r = .463$, $P = .002$, not controlling for other variables.

17. Effects of cub age on the percentage of 5-minute scans during the midday rest period for which any family member had its eyes open and was observing the surroundings, young ($N = 19$ litters), middle-aged ($N = 13$ litters), and old cubs ($N = 22$ litters), $\bar{X}s = 59.8\%, 62.6\%, 59.8\%$ respectively, $F_{2,50} = 0.884$, $P > .4$, controlling for litter size.

18. Belly sizes, averaged over the days they were watched, for mothers with small litters of 1 and 2 cubs ($N = 30$ litters), and those with large litters of 3 and 4 cubs ($N = 24$ litters), $\bar{X}s = 5.3, 5.2$ respectively, $F_{1,20} = 10.377$, $P = .004$, controlling for individual differences between mothers.

19. Numbers of large prey (adult Grant's and Thomson's gazelles, and subadult Thomson's gazelles) attempted by mothers with cubs of different ages. Mothers of young cubs: small litters of 1 and 2 cubs ($N = 89$ attempts), large litters of 3 and 4 cubs ($N = 189$ attempts), 29.2%, 30.2% respectively, G test, $G_1 = 0.026$, $P > .8$.

Mothers of middle-aged cubs: small litters ($N = 77$ attempts), large litters ($N = 82$ attempts), 33.8%, 35.4% respectively, G test, $G_1 = 0.045$, $P > .8$.

Mothers of old cubs: small litters of 1 and 2 cubs ($N = 154$ attempts), large litters of 3 cubs ($N = 53$ attempts), 18.8%, 34.0% respectively, G test, $G_1 = 4.853$, $P = .023$.

20. Number of large kills (adult Grant's and Thomson's gazelles, subadult Thomson's gazelles) made by mothers with old cubs, small litters of 1 and 2 cubs ($N = 42$ kills), large litters of 3 cubs ($N = 13$ kills), 23.8%, 23.1% respectively, Fisher test, $P > .2$.

21. Percentage of 15-minute scans that adult mothers with young ($N = 16$ litters), middle-aged ($N = 12$ litters), and old cubs ($N = 22$ litters) spent moving compared with adult females ($N = 13$), Mann-Whit-

ney U tests, $U = 32$, $P < .002$; $U = 41$, $P = .05$; $z = 2.584$, $P = .01$ respectively (see table 5.2 for means).

22. Spearman rank order correlation coefficient between the percentage of family movements initiated by cubs and cub age, $N = 44$, $r_s = .417$, $P < .01$.

23. Spearman rank order correlation coefficient between percentage of 15-minute scans adult females or mothers spent moving and group size, lone adult females ($N = 13$), mothers with 1 old cub ($N = 2$ litters), mothers with 2 old cubs ($N = 15$ litters), mothers with 3 old cubs ($N = 5$ litters), $\bar{X}s = 5.9$, 10.4, 12.3, 13.4 respectively, $r_s = .439$, $P = .008$.

24. Number of hunting attempts on large prey (adult Grant's and Thomson's gazelles, subadult Thomson's gazelles) for adult mothers (29.0%, $N = 635$ attempts) and lone adult females (34.0%, $N = 47$ attempts), G test, $G_1 = 0.528$, $P > .4$. In this and the three subsequent tests, there were no significant differences between lone females and mothers in each of the three cub age categories, so only comparisons with all the mothers together are presented.

Percentage of hunts on all prey that were successful for adult mothers ($N = 39$) and lone adult females ($N = 4$) seen to hunt 5 or more times, $\bar{X}s = 25.5\%$, 18.8% respectively, Mann-Whitney U test, $z = 1.172$, $P > .2$.

Time spent hunting per hour by adult mothers ($N = 46$) and lone adult females ($N = 15$), $\bar{X}s = 2.06$, 2.57 min/hr respectively, Mann-Whitney U test, $z = -0.720$, $P > .4$.

Number of hunts made per hour by adult mothers and lone adult females (Ns as above), $\bar{X}s = 0.25$, 0.30 respectively, Mann-Whitney U test, $z = -0.178$, $P > .8$.

25. Number of minutes that adult mothers with young ($N = 18$ litters), middle-aged ($N = 11$ litters), and old cubs ($N = 16$ litters) spent eating compared with lone adult females ($N = 6$) for those individuals watched 12 or more hours, $\bar{X}s = 2.6$, 1.3, 0.9, 3.6 min/hr respectively, Mann-Whitney U tests, $U = 40$, $P > .1$; $U = 10$, $P < .05$; $U = 11$, $P < .02$.

26. Number of kilograms of meat that adult mothers of young ($N = 18$ litters), middle-aged ($N = 11$ litters), and old cubs ($N = 16$ litters) were calculated to eat per hour compared with lone adult females ($N = 6$) for those individuals watched for 12 or more hours, $\bar{X}s = 0.11$, 0.06, 0.04, 0.17 kg/hr respectively, Mann-Whitney U tests, $U = 32.5$, $P > .1$; $U = 7.5$, $P < .02$; $U = 8$, $P = .002$.

27. Percentage of time adult mothers of old cubs ($N = 12$ litters) did not eat from carcasses while they were available compared with lone adult females ($N = 9$), $\bar{X}s = 13.7\%$, 31.6% respectively, Mann-Whitney U test, $U = 23$, $P < .05$.

28. Spearman rank order correlation coefficient between number of

minutes adult females or mothers spent eating per hour and group size for those animals watched for 12 hours or more, lone adult females ($N = 6$), mothers with 1 old cub ($N = 2$ litters), mothers with 2 old cubs ($N = 10$ litters), mothers with 3 old cubs ($N = 4$ litters); $\bar{X}s = 3.6, 0, 1.3, 0.6$ min/hr respectively; $r_s = -.490, P = .021$.

Spearman rank order correlation coefficient between number of kilograms adult females ate per hour and group size for those animals watched for 12 hours or more (Ns as above), $\bar{X}s = 0.17, 0, 0.05, 0.03$ kg/hr respectively, $r_s = -.507, P = .016$.

29. Belly sizes taken from sightings of mothers with young, middle-aged, and old cubs compared with lone adult females. Wet season: $Ns = 109, 80, 115, 153$ sightings, $\bar{X}s = 5.5, 5.4, 5.6, 6.9$ respectively, Mann-Whitney U tests, $z = -4.476, P < .0001; z = -4.381, P < .0001; z = -4.081, P < .0001$.

Dry season comparisons to lone adult females: $Ns = 65, 86, 115, 144$ sightings, $\bar{X}s = 4.7, 5.2, 5.3, 6.1$ respectively, Mann-Whitney U tests, $z = -4.388, P < .0001; z = -2.561, P = .01; z = -2.831, P = .005$.

30. Percentage of 15-minute scans adult mothers with young ($N = 16$ litters), middle-aged ($N = 12$ litters), and old cubs ($N = 22$ litters) spent resting compared with lone adult females ($N = 13$), t tests, $t = -2.24$, $P = .034$ on logged data; $t = -1.28, P > .2; t = -0.47, P > .6$ respectively (see table 5.2 for means).

31. Percentage of 5-minute scans during the midday rest period lone adult females ($N = 14$) and mothers with old cubs ($N = 22$ litters) were vigilant, $\bar{X}s = 51.7\%, 39.6\%$, t test, $t = 1.96$, df $= 18.20, P = .066$.

Percentage of 5-minute scans during the midday rest period lone adult females and mothers with old cubs (Ns as above) lay flat out, $\bar{X}s = 15.6\%, 16.7\%$, Mann-Whitney U test, $z = -1.641, P = .101$.

32. Percentage of 5-minute scans during the midday rest period lone adult females ($N = 14$), mothers with 1 old cub ($N = 2$ litters), mothers with 2 old cubs ($N = 15$ litters), and mothers with 3 old cubs ($N = 5$ litters) were vigilant, $\bar{X}s = 51.7\%, 32.5\%, 41.0\%, 38.2\%$ respectively, $r_s = -.351, P = .036$.

Percentage of 5-minute scans during the midday rest period they were lying flat out (Ns as above), $\bar{X}s = 15.6\%, 15.3\%, 14.8\%, 23.1\%$ respectively, $r_s = .326, P = .052$.

33. Combined responses of carnivores (spotted hyenas, lions, cheetahs of both sexes, and jackals) to cheetah mothers with cubs of different ages. Percentage of instances when predators left (as opposed to approached or stood and watched) the cheetah family when cubs were young ($N = 55$ instances) versus middle-aged and old ($N = 117$ instances), $\bar{X}s = 14.5\%$, 32.5%, G test, $G_1 = 6.619, P = .013$; cases of predators being chased by cheetah families were excluded because these were sometimes playful.

Percentage of instances when jackals left (as opposed to approached or stood and watched) the cheetah family when cubs were young ($N = 12$ instances) versus middle-aged and old ($N = 9$ instances), $\overline{X}$s $= 25.0\%$, 88.9%, Fisher test, $P = .006$.

Percentage of instances when female cheetahs or families of cheetahs left (as opposed to approached or stood and watched) the cheetah family when cubs were young ($N = 18$ instances) versus middle-aged and old ($N = 25$ instances), $\overline{X}$s $= 5.6\%$, 52.0%, Fisher test, $P = .001$.

34. Belly sizes, averaged over the days watched, for male and female dependent cubs over 12 months old and males and females in sibling groups (if there was more than one animal of a given sex, a mean figure was calculated) ($N = 9$ groups). Females $\overline{X} = 6.1$, males 6.6; Sign test, $P = .04$ using groups watched for more than 1 day where at least one member of each sex was present.

35. Number of group movements initiated by male and female dependent cubs over 12 months old and males and females in sibling groups (if there was more than one animal of a given sex, a mean figure was calculated) ($N = 8$ groups). Females $\overline{X} = 17.1$, males 9.2; Sign test, $P = .07$, using groups in which two or more group movements were scored and where at least one member of each sex was present.

36. Percentage of 15-minute scans that male cubs aged 12 or more months in family groups ($N = 7$) and males in independent adolescent groups ($N = 16$) spent resting, $\overline{X}$s $= 71.4\%$, 62.4%, t test, $t = 2.39$, $P = .026$, excluding single-day watches.

37. Percentage of 15-minute scans that male cubs aged 12 or more months in family groups ($N = 7$) and males in independent adolescent groups ($N = 16$) spent hunting, $\overline{X}$s $= 0.9\%$, 3.7%, Mann-Whitney U test, $U = 21.5$, $P < .05$, excluding single-day watches.

Percentage of 15-minute scans that male cubs aged 12 or more months in family groups ($N = 7$) and males in independent adolescent groups ($N = 16$) spent searching (moving, observing, and hunting combined), $\overline{X}$s $= 24.6\%$, 32.8%, t test, $t = -2.41$, $P = .025$, excluding single-day watches.

38. Belly sizes taken from sightings of dependent male cubs aged 12 months or more, and from independent adolescent males (if more than one male was in a group a mean was taken). All year: Ns $= 76$, 62 sightings, $\overline{X}$s $= 6.7$, 6.1 respectively; Mann-Whitney U test, $z = 1.489$, $P > .1$. Wet season: Ns $= 34$, 27 sightings, $\overline{X}$s $= 7.1$, 5.4 respectively; $z = 3.082$, $P = .002$.

Belly sizes taken from sightings of dependent female cubs aged 12 months or more, and from independent adolescent females (if more than one female was in a group an average was taken). All year: Ns $= 74$, 75 sightings, $\overline{X}$s $= 6.1$, 5.3 respectively; Mann-Whitney U test, $z = 1.956$, $P = .05$.

Two 7-month-old cubs watch a neonate Thomson's gazelle regain its feet after having chased it and knocked it over. It had been released for them by their mother. (Drawing by Dafila Scott.)

6
BENEFITS OF FAMILY LIFE FOR CUBS

In common with most mammals, carnivores give birth to altricial young that are born with poor motor coordination, are often unable to mount an effective defense against predators, and cannot forage for themselves. It is the difficulty of prey acquisition, however, that is thought to set the order apart from other mammals. Specifically, carnivores are believed to depend on their parents for longer periods of time following weaning than other mammalian orders and to do so because it takes time for young to perfect their prey-catching techniques (Bekoff, Daniels, and Gittleman 1984). Similar arguments have been made for seabirds that have to acquire complex feeding skills (Ashmole and Tovar 1968). Surprisingly, neither of these propositions has been tested empirically, although it is known that carnivores have a longer period between weaning and sexual maturity than other mammalian orders, except primates, once the effects of body weight have been removed (Read and Harvey 1989). Given that the lengths of life history stages, such as gestation, weaning, and maturity, covary positively and significantly in mammals, it may be safe to assume that the period between weaning and independence (not reported by Read and Harvey) is relatively longer for carnivores than for other orders as well.

The second assumption, that offspring leave their parents only once they have mastered hunting techniques, has never been examined critically because the nocturnal or crepuscular habits of most carnivores and their secretive nature hamper close observation (Bekoff 1989). In this chapter, I document the ontogeny of hunting behavior in cheetah cubs in order to determine whether offspring do indeed rely on their mothers for solid food up to the time of separation.

An alternative explanation for extended offspring dependence is that parents may be able to enhance juvenile survival by defending progeny after weaning if predation on offspring is high. I therefore examined both vigilance and antipredator behavior of mothers and offspring in order to determine the extent to which cubs rely on their mothers to detect sources of danger and defend them over the period of dependence. In this way the various benefits that cheetah cubs derive from parental care and the relative importance of these benefits are assessed.

Cub Growth in the Lair

Cubs weighed approximately 350 g at birth, with cubs of lighter mothers weighing less than those of heavier mothers, males weighing more than females, and those in litters of four or five weighing less than those in litters of two or three (Laurenson 1992). Cubs grew at an average of 44.6 g per day, with males and females growing at similar rates, but cubs in larger litters growing faster than those in litters of two or three.

Maternal food intake affected cub growth rates through lactation since cubs were not provided with solid food while in the lair. When mothers ate more than 1.5 to 2.0 kg per day, cub growth was roughly constant, but when maternal intake fell below this, growth rates dropped off sharply, and cubs lost weight when maternal intake fell to 0.7 g per day (Laurenson, in press-a). Cub growth rates declined the greater the distance their mother traveled per day if maternal intake was high, but growth rates were apparently unaffected by travel if her food intake was already low (Laurenson 1992).

Transition to Solid Food after Leaving the Lair

Within days of leaving the lair, cubs were introduced to solid food. On these first occasions, cubs approached and sniffed the carcass gingerly but then backed away. Cubs returned to the carcass when they heard their mothers churr, and after roughly three exposures, lost their fear and sat next to it or played nearby. At 2 months of age, following emergence, each cub spent an average of 6.1% ($N = 6$ litters) of daylight hours eating but 10.3% ($N = 7$ litters) on the nipple. Offspring feeding bouts at a kill were interspersed with long gaps (fig. 6.1) during which time cubs sometimes tried to nurse. For example, I saw a 2-month-old cub leave a neonate Thomson's gazelle carcass and suckle for 14 minutes while her brother and mother ate for over half an hour. Cubs of this age may have experienced

Fig. 6.1 Young cubs show disinterest in the Thomson's gazelle carcass from which their mother is feeding. One is asleep while the other is surveying its surroundings.

difficulties in digesting meat if their alimentary tracts were still immature (Henning 1981).

At 3 months, each cub spent the same proportion of the day eating solids (6.6%, $N = 3$ litters) but only 4.2% ($N = 4$ litters) nursing. Their mother still had to open up gazelle carcasses since cubs of this age could not sever the abdominal wall for themselves. Once the carcass was eviscerated cubs nibbled at stomach contents but clearly found them distasteful; in contrast, older cubs passed over them. By 4 months, each cub nursed for an average of only 1.2% ($N = 5$ litters) of the day, while feeding remained at 6.2% ($N = 5$ litters).

Food Intake of Cubs

The percentage of time that cubs spent eating declined as they grew older (fig. 6.2) [1]. In part this reflected the slow, laborious way that young cubs with small teeth and mouths chewed meat. Nevertheless, offspring maintained approximately the same food intake as they grew older (fig. 6.3) [2], an estimated average of 0.05 kg per daylight hour (SE = 0.01, N = 43 litters). These calculations assumed that a young cub ate one-third as much meat as its mother per unit time, two-thirds as much when middle-aged, and an equal amount when old (see chap. 3), but I suspect this was a generous estimate for very young cubs whose feeding skills were poorly developed. If so, then cub intake may have initially risen with age. The amount cubs ingested was unaffected by litter size, partially because mothers made an increasing but nonsignificant number of kilograms of meat available to offspring in larger litters (Caro 1989b). Given, first, that

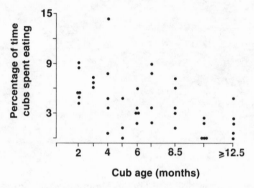

Fig. 6.2 Percentage of 15-minute scans that cubs spent eating, plotted against cub age in months; each point represents an average for all cubs in a litter. Single-day watches were excluded.

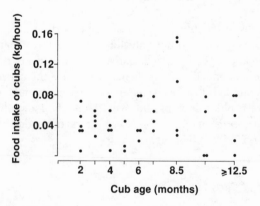

Fig. 6.3 Number of kilograms of meat that cubs ate per hour, plotted against cub age in months; each point represents an average of all cubs in a litter. Single-day watches were excluded.

weight of prey captured by mothers per hour did not change with cub age (chap. 5); second, that intake of mothers, but not cubs, declined as offspring matured (chap. 5); and third, that there was little aggression over meat, it is possible that mothers refrained from eating to maintain offspring consumption, as suggested for mothers feeding in the presence of two or more sons (Caro 1990). The extent to which mothers hold back from eating in different circumstances requires further and more detailed investigation.

In summary, each cub ate approximately 0.6 kg of meat during daylight hours. Over 24 hours, young and middle-aged cubs probably ate little in addition to this because their mothers rarely hunted at night; however, 0.6 kg per day may have been a low figure for old cubs that occasionally fed after dark. Cubs were able to obtain additional nutrition from milk until they were approximately 16 weeks old.

Development of Hunting Behavior in Cubs

ACCOMPANYING THE MOTHER

Offspring accompanied their mother on most hunts (72.3%, $N = 642$ hunts) but with increasing frequency as they grew older (fig. 6.4) [3]. Young cubs sometimes sat and waited as their mother began to stalk prey; in these cases they may have assumed that their mother was stalking a predator, as this was cubs' usual response to danger. In other instances cubs failed to realize that their mother was hunting. For example, I saw 2-month-old cubs walk ahead of their stalking mother but flee from her when she rushed at the prey. In cases that caught my attention because cubs were left for more than just a few minutes, offspring were, on average, left alone for 38 minutes ($N = 43$ hunts, SE $= 5.3$) while their mother was an estimated 230 m away ($N = 36$ hunts, SE $= 30.1$). If the hunt was successful, the mother either churred to her offspring to rejoin

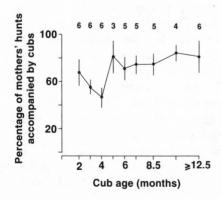

Fig. 6.4 Mean (and SE) percentage of mothers' hunts on which cubs accompanied their mothers, plotted against cub age in months; families in which mothers were seen to hunt once or less are excluded. Numbers of litters are shown above the graph.

her or, if the prey was not too heavy or too distant, carried it back to them. As a case in point, a mother dragged a half-grown Thomson's gazelle 150 m to cubs that failed to arrive. If, on the other hand, the hunt failed, she returned to her cubs, calling them from about 100 m away.

After 4 months cubs generally followed their mother on hunts unless they were asleep. Once a mother and her 6-month-old son left to hunt an adult male Thomson's gazelle, but her sleeping daughter did not follow despite her brother calling (yipping) her from 80 m away. Though she woke briefly and sat up during their absence, she never noticed that they had left; her brother finally returned and awakened her 27 minutes later.

A minimum of 16.4% of mothers' hunts failed as a result of cubs' activities (Caro 1987b), and offspring hanging back reduced the chances of cubs being seen by prey. Nevertheless, this behavior made cubs more vulnerable to predation because their mother was sometimes too far off to see them and her attention was on her quarry. For instance, two adult spotted hyenas approached 8.5-month-old cubs to within 5 m while their mother was resting 200 m away after making a kill; however, the hyenas left of their own volition.

A second cost of this behavior was that young cubs could not always hear their mother call and sometimes missed a meal. One hungry mother ate an entire neonate Thomson's gazelle by herself, 600 m from the cubs that failed to join her. On another occasion, a mother alone consumed a neonate of the same species after failing to attract her cubs from 500 m away, despite churring 21 times and waiting 42 minutes before eating. Cubs sometimes prevented their mother from feeding, too. After killing an adult female Thomson's gazelle, a mother called her cubs from 600 m away but they could not hear her in the strong wind. As she moved 20 m toward them, seven vultures closed in on the carcass, forcing her to run back. After leaving and returning to the kill nine times in 45 minutes, she gave up and rejoined her family, having only picked at the flesh. Similar observations to these have been reported for grizzly bears (Murie 1981).

Cheetah cubs accompanied their mothers as soon as they were mobile and before they were weaned, in common with other cats (e.g., tigers: Schaller 1967; lions: Schaller 1972c). Young bears also leave the den at a comparatively early age before weaning (e.g., giant pandas: Schaller et al. 1985). In social canids, however, pups may be weaned before quitting the den but are provisioned by pack members regurgitating meat (e.g., wolves: Mech 1970; wild dogs: Malcolm and Marten 1982). In contrast to these families, lactation is prolonged in hyenids. Brown hyenas are nursed for up to 9 months in the den but their diets are supplemented with food items carried to them, whereas spotted hyenas remain at the den for 10 to 15 months and have to rely on their mothers' milk for the entire period (Mills 1990; Hofer and East 1993). Factors underlying these family differences are poorly understood, but the energetic costs of travel by mothers and prey dispersal must be important.

HUNTING BEHAVIOR PATTERNS AND PREY PREFERENCES

When cubs first accompanied their mother on hunts they simply trotted after her or else ran or walked toward prey, but they rarely showed any hunting behavior (fig. 6.5). Nevertheless, they chased inappropriate prey from an early age (table 6.1). As cubs grew older, the frequency of all hunting patterns increased [4]. Cubs were nonetheless incompetent at hunting. Sometimes they gazed at far-off prey and yipped, a vocalization used to call family members, suggesting they wanted to attract prey to them! As cubs reached middle age, they turned their hunting activities from inappropriate to appropriate prey except in regard to chasing. At 8.5 months they began to rush at prey before being seen instead of just chasing the quarry once it was in flight. In old cubs, stalking became the commonest hunting activity, and for the first time appropriate prey items were chased more often than inappropriate prey.

Small and medium-sized birds made up the majority of inappropriate prey items hunted by young cubs (table 6.2). Cubs always chased birds on the ground but these took flight at 3 to 4 m away and were never caught.

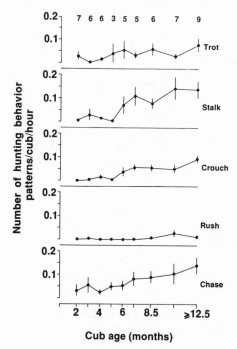

Fig. 6.5 Mean (and SE) number of times cubs, averaged across each litter, trotted, stalked, crouched at, rushed at, or chased appropriate prey items per hour, plotted against cub age in months. Numbers of litters are shown above the graphs.

TABLE 6.1 Mean Frequencies of Hunting Behaviors Performed by Cubs

	Cub age		
	Young	Middle-aged	Old
Number of litters	19	13	22
Trot			
App.	0.016	0.042	0.055
Inapp.	0	0.001	0.001
Stalk			
App.	0.006	0.061	0.106
Inapp.	0.010	0.010	0.016
Crouch			
App.	0.004	0.031	0.054
Inapp.	0.002	0.005	0.007
Rush			
App.	0.001	0.001	0.014
Inapp.	0	0.001	0.001
Chase			
App.	0.005	0.021	0.072
Inapp.	0.032	0.044	0.042

Note: Mean frequencies per hour at which cubs (averaged across the litters) showed five different hunting behavior patterns toward appropriate and inappropriate prey (see table 6.2 for list of inappropriate prey).

TABLE 6.2 Percentage of Instances in which Different Inappropriate Species Were Hunted by One or More Cubs

	Cub age		
	Young	Middle-aged	Old
Number of hunts	58	78	68
Lizards	6.9	14.1	1.5
Small birds	29.3	15.4	17.6
Medium birds	20.7	17.9	8.8
Large birds	8.6	7.7	5.9
Vultures	17.2	14.1	14.7
Carnivores	10.3	26.9	38.2
Large mammals	6.9	3.8	10.3
Other	0	0	2.9

Note: Small birds were usually passerines; medium birds included Egyptian geese, plovers, francolins, spurfowl, white-bellied and black-bellied bustards; large birds included secretary birds, kori bustards, crowned cranes, and storks; vultures included eagles too; all birds were hunted when on the ground. Carnivores included servals, wildcats, bat-eared foxes, dwarf, banded, and Egyptian mongooses, and golden and black-backed jackals. Large mammals included zebras, elands, giraffes; the Alcephalinae were treated as appropriate prey. "Other" was a leopard tortoise and a porcupine.

Middle-aged and old cubs chased small carnivores more often than other types of inappropriate prey. Usually these were jackals attracted to cheetahs' kills. It was unlikely that cubs were trying to keep them off the carcass since jackals rarely stole meat while cheetahs were eating. In other contexts too, jackals proved almost irresistible to cubs. They rose from resting specifically to chase jackals that would otherwise have passed by unaware of their presence. Cubs normally gained on small carnivores but then gave up before making contact. Nonetheless I did see a serval outdistance an old cub that seemed to be running at full speed. On another occasion I saw cubs slap a jackal to the ground. Its hindleg was broken and the four cubs surrounded and pinned it down for 25 minutes. Middle-aged cubs also explored sloping rock faces, where they chased agama lizards into crevices. Enormous prey such as giraffes were the quarry in a tenth of old cubs' inappropriate hunts but were always abandoned before contact.

INITIATING FAMILY HUNTS

Hunts of appropriate prey involving the mother were occasionally initiated by offspring from the age of 6 months onward (fig. 6.6a), but cubs did not assume substantial responsibility for initiating hunts until they were 12.5 months old or older [5]. Although maternal hunting rates remained fairly constant as cubs matured, the rate of appropriate hunts initiated by cubs in which mothers did not participate increased as cubs reached 10.5 months of age [6] (fig. 6.6b). Now approximately one in three family hunts was made without the mother (compare the heights of the two curves in figure 6.6b over this period).

Irrespective of their mother's involvement, cubs rarely captured and killed prey themselves (fig. 6.7) despite their growing responsibility in hunting. Neither did they help the family capture prey in more subtle ways by, for instance, chasing prey so that their mother could subsequently cut it off at corners. Only in the oldest category did the total number of kills made by cubs approach that of their mothers.

REASONS THAT CUBS' HUNTS FAILED

The family hunts in which cubs participated failed primarily as a result of prey noticing the cubs approaching (table 6.3). Often a family hunt was ruined because cubs sat up, walked forward, or moved from a crouched position to an advancing stalk while gazelles had their heads up. Middle-aged cubs were particularly culpable. Sometimes one cub would simply become uninterested and walk off at an oblique angle, alerting the quarry.

Cubs became more adventurous as they grew older. Increasingly they began to chase prey (see above), even when it was too far off to be caught or when it was already gaining on their mother; mothers would follow

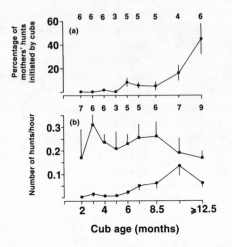

Fig. 6.6 (*a*) Mean (and SE) percentage of hunts of appropriate prey in which mothers participated (i.e., hunted) that were initiated by cubs, plotted against cub age in months; families in which mothers were seen to hunt only once were excluded. (*b*) Mean (and SE) number of hunts per hour in which mothers participated (solid squares), and mean number of hunts per hour in which cubs *but not their mothers* participated (solid circles), plotted against cub age in months. Numbers of litters are shown above the graphs.

cantering on behind the cubs. This behavior accounted for the rise in hunts failing as a result of the family being outrun (see table 6.3). It may also have contributed to hunts being abandoned at short distances from prey (see chap. 5), since mothers might have given up before initiating a chase in other circumstances. Cubs also began to make contact with prey, but even old cubs were wary of slapping it down. I judged almost a quarter of cubs' hunts to be thwarted because the cubs were "not hunting seriously." Such hunts typically consisted of chasing appropriate prey for a short distance (50 to 100 m) but then decelerating even though the cheetah was gaining on it. Admittedly cheetahs may have been "testing" prey by running at the herd, as do wild dogs (Reich 1981) and spotted hyenas (Kruuk 1972), but this seemed improbable given their different hunting style. Without knowledge of how a cheetah perceived its chances of catching prey, I therefore classified these hunts as not being serious.

To conclude these sections, different facets of hunting behavior developed at different rates, as reported in other studies (mammals: e.g., Leyhausen 1965; birds: e.g., Marchetti and Price 1989). Cubs first tried out some behaviors on inappropriate prey, then switched to appropriate items employing the new behavior patterns. Later, they began to initiate family hunts at an increasing rate. Comparisons with other carnivores are

difficult because reports of offspring incompetence in free-living carnivores are usually anecdotal. Only a handful of studies have quantified the
ontogeny of predatory behavior in the wild (see Watt 1993); moreover,
these have been on species only distantly related to the cheetah. For example, young polar bears hunted very little, only 4% of the time as year-
lings and 7% as 2-year-olds, compared with 35–53% of the time for adult
females; and young bears spent little time lying in wait for seals (Stirling
and Latour 1978). Other studies have reported an increasing representation of larger prey items in the stomachs of older individuals (e.g., bobcats:

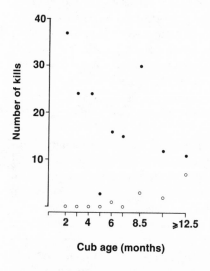

Fig. 6.7 Total number of kills made
by all mothers (solid circles) and by
all cubs (open circles) observed at
different cub ages in months. Since
different numbers of litters were
watched at each age, totals can be
compared only within age groups,
not across them.

TABLE 6.3 Reasons for Failures of Family Hunts of Appropriate Prey that
Resulted from Cubs' Hunting Activities

| | Cub age | | | |
	Young	Middle-aged	Old	Total
Number of hunts	11	29	78	118
Seen by prey	27.3	65.5	35.9	42.4
Started rush too early	9.1	3.4	9.0	7.7
Does not dare	27.3	10.3	5.1	8.5
Outrun	0	0	7.7	5.1
Not serious	18.2	20.7	24.4	22.9
Other	9.1	0	11.5	8.5
Unknown	9.1	0	6.4	5.1

Note: Failures are separated according to different reasons and expressed as a percentage. Hunts in
which the mother participated and those in which she was not involved are combined; maternal hunts in
which cubs only followed their mothers but did not hunt are excluded.

Litvaitis, Stevens, and Mautz 1984), or items that are difficult to catch (e.g., otters: Watt 1993), but it is not always clear whether differences in preference or competence are responsible for these effects. The more numerous laboratory studies (e.g., Rasa 1973; Vincent and Bekoff 1978) cannot, of course, identify changes in prey preferences or responsibility for initiating hunts. Thus it is difficult to make comparative statements about the development of predation in free-living carnivores at present.

CUB PLAY

Among carnivores play is often assumed to serve as practice for hunting behavior (Bekoff 1989), despite little supportive evidence (reviewed in Martin and Caro 1985). For example, Prater (1935) noted that cheetah cubs knock each other over during play with a characteristic paw slap that is later used to knock prey off balance. In cheetahs, play could be divided into four categories: locomotor play, noncontact social play, contact social play, and object play. These peaked at different ages but all declined as cubs grew older. Cubs played for 3.4% of the day, averaged over the period of dependence (Caro, in press).

Locomotor play may have aided cubs in developing the ability to escape predation, because it occurred at high rates in very young cubs and carried costs in terms of being conspicuous to predators. Litters whose members stalked and crouched at family members often during play also stalked and crouched at prey frequently, suggesting that these aspects of noncontact social play may have been causally linked to approaching prey and could also have served as practice for hunting. Litters showing more frequent contact social play and object play also showed higher rates of contacting live prey released for them by their mothers. These two forms of play therefore may have served as practice for contact predatory skills (Caro, in press). Although these findings provide preliminary evidence that play may facilitate aspects of hunting and antipredator behavior in cheetahs, they are not conclusive.

Maternal Encouragement of Offspring's Hunting Skills

CHANGES WITH CUB AGE

Mothers provisioned cubs while their hunting skills developed but additionally provided them with opportunities to perform predatory behavior. Mothers did this in three ways. First, they pursued and knocked down quarry but instead of suffocating the victim allowed it to stand and run off. By the time the prey had risen, the cubs had normally arrived. Second, mothers carried live animals back to their cubs before releasing them, repeatedly calling (churring) to their cubs. Third, and less often, mothers ran slowly during their initial chase of prey and allowed their cubs to overtake them and thus be the first to knock down the prey themselves.

As a released prey fled, cubs cantered after it and tried to slap its hind-quarters. Some of their slaps missed the prey altogether, some slaps made contact but failed to knock it off balance, and some knocked it over. Usually the victim rose again and ran off with the cubs following, but if it stayed down (which was unusual) they pawed at it. During this time, the mother cantered or trotted after her cubs and retrieved the prey for them if it escaped. There was a cost to releasing prey, however: it escaped from the mother and cubs on 3 out of 36 occasions when cubs were given the opportunity to play, thereby delaying the family's next meal.

The proportion of prey that mothers released for cubs and the way in which it was killed changed as cubs grew older (fig. 6.8) [7]. Mothers of 2-month-old cubs usually killed prey by suffocation (Thomson's gazelles) or biting through the skull (hares), and rarely released it. When cubs were 3 to 4 months old mothers sometimes let the prey go but normally intervened and killed it after a 5- to 15-minute period of cubs chasing and knocking it over; cubs very rarely dispatched prey at this age (fig. 6.8b).

When cubs were between 5 and 7 months old, mothers released almost one-third of the prey items that they caught. Cubs now started to suffocate prey themselves, hence the percentage of prey killed by mothers declined. This pattern remained more or less unchanged up to the time cubs reached 8.5 months, with mothers still releasing 30% of their captures.

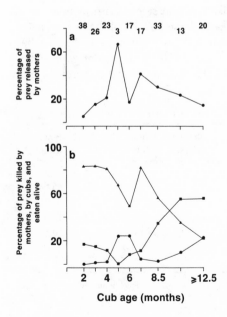

Fig. 6.8 (a) Percentage of prey caught by mothers that they released for their cubs, plotted against cub age in months. (b) Percentage of prey that were killed by mothers (solid triangles), by cubs (solid circles), or that died being eaten alive (solid squares), plotted against cub age in months. Numbers of kills are shown above the graphs.

Now, however, offspring would disembowel prey or tear it apart while a family member, either mother or littermate, held onto the windpipe. When cubs were 10.5 months old or older, about half the kills were eaten alive, with mothers killing prey infrequently. The popular myth that cheetahs are "clean killers," killing their prey before eating it, runs counter to these data; many prey animals must have suffered badly while being eviscerated or at best have been in shock. The proportion of prey released for cubs showed a slight decline during this final period.

Some changes could be discerned in cubs' responses to live prey released by mothers. The proportion of chases in which cubs got close enough to make contact with prey showed a marginal increase with cub age [8]. Although cubs had little opportunity to contact prey under other circumstances, these improvements cannot be ascribed to increased opportunities to interact with prey because cubs also chased each other during social play (Caro, in press) and maturational changes may have taken place.

HUNGER AND PREY TYPE

Two other factors besides cub age influenced whether mothers released prey for their cubs. First, hungrier mothers were slightly more likely to kill prey than to release it for their cubs [9]. Their decision was probably influenced by the latency to start eating and the possibility of the victim escaping. The likelihood that mothers would refrain from killing prey was unrelated to the cubs' belly sizes averaged across the litter [9].

Second, mothers were more likely to release certain prey items than others (table 6.4). In particular, they released 30.9% of the live neonates and fawns that they captured but only 4.0% of adult and subadult gazelles [10]. Fawns were much easier to recapture than were older gazelles because they could not turn as sharply (FitzGibbon 1990a) and probably ran

TABLE 6.4 Proportions of Different Types of Prey Released by Mothers

Species	Number released	Number killed immediately	Percentage released
Hare	5	28	15.2
Neonate and fawn Thomson's gazelle	23	55	29.5
Neonate and fawn Grant's gazelle	2	1	66.7
Half-grown Thomson's gazelle	3	17	15.0
Subadult Thomson's gazelle	0	9	0
Adult Thomson's gazelle	2	39	4.9
Other[a]	1	5	16.7

[a] Other consisted of three neonate wildebeests, an adult female reedbuck, a subadult male Grant's gazelle, and an adult dik-dik, which was released.

Fig. 6.9 Two middle-aged cubs attempt to capture an adult male Thomson's gazelle released for them by their mother. This male was old and had a severe mange infestation.

more slowly. Neonates were unsteady on their feet and in some cases failed to recognize cheetahs as predators. I once watched a neonate Thomson's gazelle playing with two 5-month-old cubs for 30 minutes while the cheetah mother rested. The gazelle playfully headbutted one of the cubs six times, twice skipped, and once tried to nurse, wagging its tail almost constantly, typical of infant-mother interactions; it was eventually eaten alive by the cubs. The two cases in which an adult male Thomson's gazelle was released by a mother were unusual. One very old male had mange on its hindquarters, neck, and head and was too weak to escape (fig. 6.9). Another male ran into a shallow lake where the cubs chased it into deep water. It drowned while the mother watched from the bank. Subsequently the cubs pulled it out and ate it.

Though hares were released by mothers (see table 6.4), they sometimes escaped from cubs by disappearing down a hole. Cubs managed to kill hares on only 6 of the 13 occasions that they chased them, whereas mothers had substantially higher capture rates on hares (table 6.5) [11].

Indeed, I saw a mother take over chasing a hare and catch it after it had outmaneuvered her 10-month-old son using swift turns. Whether their ability to evade cubs made mothers release proportionately fewer hares than neonate gazelles is unknown, but it is worth noting that mothers maimed two of the five hares but none of the neonate gazelles they released [12]. These hares appeared to have suffered a cerebral or spinal injury in that they ran erratically or in a slow circle. Whether mothers were inclined to injure hares in their cubs' presence or whether the lagomorph's small head predisposed it to serious injury in the jaws of a cheetah, I could not tell.

Aspects of maternal encouragement have been seen in other wild felids. Schaller (1967) saw a tigress pull a buffalo down and then leave it for her cubs to kill, toppling it again for them when it stood up. He also saw a lioness carry a live gazelle fawn to her cubs (Schaller 1972c). In domestic cats, changes in the mother's behavior have been studied in some detail. Mothers first eat prey in front of the kittens instead of consuming it away from the den; then they carry live prey to their offspring and allow them to play with it, recapturing it if it escapes; and finally they simply make intention movements toward the prey while the young catch and kill it (Baerends-van Roon and Baerends 1979; Caro 1980b). In these and other carnivore examples, a mother presents her offspring with the opportunity to interact with prey and prevents it from escaping (termed "opportunity teaching" by Caro and Hauser 1992). Further descriptions from primates and raptors, in particular, indicate that mothers in certain species undertake guided instruction of their naive offspring without obtaining an immediate benefit for themselves (see Caro and Hauser 1992 for a review).

Maternal encouragement showed flexibility in cheetahs in that it varied according to prey type and hunger. Mothers might therefore have been responsive to their cubs' predatory competence, releasing more prey to

TABLE 6.5 Outcome of Hunts of Hares by Mothers and by Cubs

	Mothers	Cubs
Hunt successful	28	6
Hare goes down a hole	1	5
Hare outruns cheetah	2	1
Hunt not serious	0	1
Other	2	0
Total	33	13

Note: Five cases of mothers releasing hares, or holding back while their cubs took over the chase, are included as mothers' successes. Hares chased by cubs included those released for them by mothers and those that they flushed themselves.

TABLE 6.6 Summary of Age-Related Events in the Development of Hunting Behavior in Cheetah Cubs

Young cubs	Middle-aged cubs	Old cubs
Nurse		
Accompany mother on hunts	Accompany mother on hunts	Accompany mother on hunts
Chase inappropriate prey	Hunt appropriate prey with mother	Hunt appropriate prey with and without mother
	Initiate hunts	Increasingly initiate hunts
	Opportunities to knock prey over provided by mother	
		Begin to make kills

litters that were poor at hunting rather than gearing their behavior simply to their cubs' age. Unfortunately I could not examine this systematically, but domestic cat mothers are sensitive to their offspring's interactions with prey (Caro 1980b). In cheetahs, no data were available to show that cubs' skills improved as a result of mothers' encouragement, as required by formal definitions of teaching (Caro and Hauser 1992), because families were not observed longitudinally during development.

The major events in the development of hunting behavior are summarized in table 6.6. In spite of increasing participation in their mother's hunts, to the extent that they initiated a number of them, and in spite of maternal encouragement, cubs were inept at hunting and captured only 13 of 185 prey items (7.0%) without the help of their mothers. One can dismiss the alternative possibility that cubs could hunt but lacked the motivation because they initiated hunts and participated in many themselves (see fig. 6.6). One can also dismiss the idea that mothers' superior prey-catching techniques masked those of cubs, since offspring's success rates were still poor in hunts in which mothers did not participate (see table 6.5). In short, maternal provisioning was a critical aspect of postweaning care because cubs relied almost entirely on their mothers for solid food from the time they emerged from the lair until separation from her. Other benefits of parental care are examined in the next two sections.

Changes in the Vigilance of Cubs

In analyses of the ontogeny of vigilance, the proportion of their time individuals allocate to monitoring their surroundings, their ability to detect an event once they are looking up, and even their ability to recognize a source of danger or prey item once it has been detected need to be examined separately, as each may change independently as young mature. Cubs showed a steady increase in the percentage of time they spent monitoring their surroundings during the midday rest period as they grew older (fig. 6.10) [13]. Concomitant with this, older cubs were less relaxed than younger ones, spending a greater proportion of time lying alert [14], a measure of unease in cheetahs, and they spent less time lying flat out [15]. For instance, cubs of 2 and 3 months allocated most of their rest period to nursing or lying flat out asleep, although they might indulge in short bouts of play around midday.

At kills, where vigilance is associated primarily with antipredator behavior (Caro 1987a), cubs looked up from the carcass at increasing rates as they grew older [16]. In contrast, the percentage of time cubs spent off the carcass did not decline significantly with age [16]. The discrepancy between these measures occurred because old cubs spent short bouts of time off the carcass while young cubs spent a relatively large proportion of time away from the carcass but monitored their surroundings at low rates when they returned to feed.

Based on whether a cheetah stared intently at a passing predator and visually monitored its movements, cubs 6 months or younger completely missed seeing approximately a third of the dangerous predators that passed by. In comparison, mothers spotted an average of nine out of ten predators throughout the period of cub dependency (fig. 6.11) [17] (but see Laurenson, in press-b, for a lower estimate). Up to the age of 10 months, cubs rarely caught sight of predators before their mother did (fig. 6.12), achieving this in only about a fifth of instances, despite there usually being two or three cubs in the family but only one mother. When

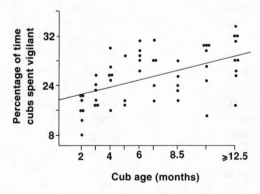

Fig. 6.10 Percentage of 5-minute scans during the midday rest period that cubs had their eyes open and were observing their surroundings, plotted against cub age in months; each point represents an average for all cubs in a litter ($y = 18.830 + 1.267x$).

cubs were very small, they had difficulty seeing over vegetation, and as they grew they made little attempt to scan their surroundings systematically. Therefore only cubs of 10 months or older had much chance of spying a predator before their parent.

Vigilance has been found to rise with age in other species, mostly in birds. Scanning by juvenile yellow-eyed juncos increased from very low levels to adult rates during the fledgling period (Sullivan 1988); similar changes occur in white-winged choughs (Heinsohn 1987) and white-fronted geese (Owen 1972). In mammals, few studies have investigated

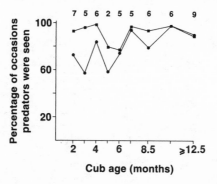

Fig. 6.11 Mean percentage of occasions that mothers (solid squares) or any cub in the litter (solid circles) noticed dangerous predators (lions, spotted hyenas, leopards, other cheetahs of both sexes, striped hyenas, jackals, servals, ratels, and baboons) that I saw pass by the cheetah family, plotted against cub age in months. Numbers of litters are shown above the graph; SEs are omitted for clarity. Note: Laurenson (1992) systematically scanned for predators every 15 minutes and reported much lower rates of predator detection by mothers with newly emerged cubs. Here percentages are probably inflated because passing predators were noted ad lib, but changes in relation to cub age can nevertheless be compared.

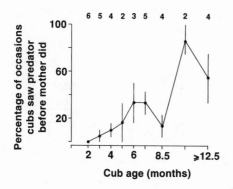

Fig. 6.12 Mean (and SE) percentage of occasions when predators were seen by a family that cubs saw the predator before their mother did, plotted against cub age in months. Numbers of litters are shown above the graph.

the effect of age on vigilance, but at least one, on squirrel monkeys, found that vigilance increased with age in circumstances when youngsters were looking for food (Boinski and Fragaszy 1989).

Compared with their mothers, then, cheetah cubs were generally less vigilant during the day and at carcasses (table 6.7). Only old cubs approached levels of maternal vigilance. As noted above, quantitative measures do not necessarily provide an adequate picture of the differences in how much attention offspring and mothers paid to the environment. For example, mothers might look carefully in several directions when they stood up, and would look ahead when walking. On the other hand, I had the impression that cubs looked at the ground more often when standing

TABLE 6.7 Means (and SEs) of Measures of Vigilance Shown by Mothers and Cubs

	Cub age		
	Young	Middle-aged	Old
Percentage of day spent observing			
	($N = 14$)	($N = 12$)	($N = 15$)
Mother	18.1	17.1	16.1
	(1.5)	(1.9)	(1.2)
Cubs	12.6	13.8	13.0
	(0.8)	(1.1)	(1.1)
Frequency of looking up from carcass per minute			
	($N = 19$)	($N = 12, 11$)	($N = 13, 12$)
Mother	0.47	0.51	0.35
	(0.04)	(0.04)	(0.05)
Cubs	0.30	0.42	0.40
	(0.02)	(0.04)	(0.05)
Percentage of time spent off carcass			
	($N = 19$)	($N = 12, 11$)	($N = 13, 12$)
Mother	31.9	27.0	13.7
	(2.4)	(3.5)	(3.0)
Cubs	23.9	19.0	21.3
	(2.5)	(1.9)	(2.8)
Percentage of time vigilant during midday rest period[a]			
	($N = 19$)	($N = 13$)	($N = 22$)
Mother	52.9	48.0	39.9
	(2.9)	(3.4)	(2.6)
Cubs	21.2	29.4	30.5
	(1.5)	(2.0)	(1.6)

Note: Measures for cubs were averaged across each litter. Sample sizes are given above each measure; if two are given, the second denotes cubs.

[a] Measures are not strictly comparable as infrequent instances of standing and walking were scored as being vigilant for mothers but not for cubs (see text).

and at each other when walking. I attempted to incorporate these qualitative observations into the data by including instances of mothers' walking or standing during the midday rest period as vigilance but excluding these for cubs. Thus the differences between mothers and cubs are not strictly comparable for the last measure in table 6.7, but their magnitude may reflect ability to notice events rather more accurately than the other comparisons therein. In addition, younger cubs failed to see many predators, and were slow to spot those that they did eventually see. Hence the burden of detecting carnivores fell on mothers for most of the period of cub dependency, at least until cubs were 10 months old. Predator detection was thus an important facet of maternal care.

Cub Vulnerability and Antipredator Behavior

On the Serengeti plains, cheetah mothers and their families encountered lions, spotted hyenas, golden jackals, and other cheetahs of both sexes more often than they did other carnivore species, all of which were potential predators. Cubs' vulnerability to these predators went through three distinct stages as they matured (see table 4.2). Cubs were relatively unlikely to be found by predators in the lair, but if they were, were unlikely to escape because their motor coordination was poor. Once they had emerged, they could be seen at a distance, and until roughly 5 months were slow to react and run away from danger. Hence their vulnerability remained high but for different reasons. From 5 months on, they could outsprint most carnivores except other cheetahs.

Before cubs emerged from the lair, their only recourse in response to danger was to hiss and spit at intruders, as noted by Laurenson (pers. comm.) when she entered the lair.

After emergence, young cubs showed a remarkable failure to recognize that they were in danger. Apparently, their only rule of thumb was to scatter when their mother ran. For example, when a mother with two 2-month-old cubs walked and then stalked toward an approaching leopard 50 m away, they followed her for 15 m! The cubs ran off only after their mother fled 5 m when the leopard charged. The leopard watched the cubs and made an intention movement to follow but the cheetah mother charged at that moment and chased her for 5 m. A series of chases and flights between the two cats followed. I suspect that surprise alone saved a cub from being killed. Inability to recognize and then respond to carnivores ahead of time must have been an important cause of the high mortality of young cubs both in and out of the lair.

I saw cubs being killed on two occasions, although other cases have since been witnessed (Laurenson, in press-b). In the first, two of four 2-month-old cubs were dispatched by a lioness. The cubs scattered only when their mother rushed the lioness from 30 m away, but it kept track of their short flight lengths (an estimated 10 to 30 m). In the other instance, the mother only charged at the lioness when it was 25 m off. Though her three 2-month-old cubs were alerted to the predator's presence by the mother's low growling before she charged, the lioness was close enough to follow the cubs' flight paths despite the cheetah mother repeatedly bluff-charging and slapping her on the hindquarters. These anecdotes suggest a selective advantage to mothers, starting their rush at predators from far off, because offspring would scatter further from the predator, reducing their chances of being detected. Cheetah cubs were often unaware of their surroundings not only in regard to danger but also to prey. For instance, a 4-month-old litter spent more than 3 hours resting, unaware that their mother had killed a neonate Thomson's gazelle lying 35 m away!

At 4 months or less, cubs were fearful of a great many species that were relatively harmless, and to which their mothers paid no attention (table 6.8; fig. 6.13). Young vervet monkeys similarly give explicit alarm calls to a wider array of species than do adults; for example, uttering "eagle alarm calls" to a falling leaf (Seyfarth and Cheney 1980). Greater

TABLE 6.8 Instances of Cubs Being Fearful of Relatively Harmless Animals

2 months of age
1. Hisses and runs away from black-bellied bustard 7 m away.
2. Run away from 2 crowned cranes 25 m away.
3. Run off 10 m when giraffe 200 m away.
4. Slink away from Grant's gazelle.
5. Slinks away from hartebeest.
6. Slink away from kori bustard.
7. Back away from an adult male warthog 10 m away.[a]
8. Hisses at secretary bird 8 m away.[b]

3 months of age
1. Slink off when 2 subadult Grant's gazelles spar 35 m away.
2. Run when neonate Grant's gazelle bleats while dying.
3. Run off when vulture hisses at them 20 m away.[a]
4. Slink toward mother when 2 adult warthogs pass by at 30 m.[a]
5. Flee from a warthog 50 m away.[a]
6. Moves around to back of mother when zebra 40 m away.[a]
7. Run to mother when golden jackal howls at them 20 m away.[b]

4 months of age
1. Move away from giraffe 120 m away.
2. Slink off 2 m when 2 giraffes 200 m away.
3. Slinks off to family when bustard 800 m away.
4. Moves to mother when 12 zebras 20 m away.[a]

[a] These species might be harmful to young cubs.
[b] Species known to pose a threat to young cubs.

vulnerability to predators cannot account for the lack of selectivity, since both cheetah cubs and infant vervets made mistakes about species that posed no danger to them (e.g., a crowned crane and a bee-eater respectively). That they mistook harmless objects for dangerous predators is also improbable, since cubs moved away from giraffes that had a larger and different outline from any carnivore. Most probably close proximity of (perhaps unfamiliar) species elicited fear and caused cubs to run off, as put forward for vervets (Seyfarth and Cheney 1986). In support of this idea, many of the frightening stimuli in table 6.8 were nearby, except the giraffe, which may have appeared close due to its size.

I made no systematic attempt to determine how cubs became more selective in their antipredator behavior, but at least four factors may have been involved. First, mothers paid little attention to harmless species and did not flee with their cubs, as they did from dangerous predators. Second, the churring sound that mothers made to beckon offspring that were far away probably provided reassurance, since it was associated with approaching their mother in other contexts. Third, by returning to their mother, cubs had to approach the fear-provoking stimulus, which may

Fig. 6.13 From their daytime resting place in a patch of *Indigofera,* two young cubs intently watch a kori bustard pass by.

have habituated them. Fourth, peering at the animal from behind their mother or over her recumbent body allowed them to experience her tactile stimuli, which must have calmed them in this tense situation. After cubs reached 4 months of age, I never saw them exhibit fearful behavior in response to inappropriate objects other than tourist vehicles.

Once cubs reached 5 months, they seemed more aware that a predator was present, perhaps by noting that their mother was stalking and then looking to see what lay ahead. Now they sat still or ran directly away from the source of danger instead of exploding in all directions. Cubs' anti-predator behavior differed according to the species they encountered (table 6.9). They normally watched or moved away from lions and spotted hyenas at all ages but showed proportionately more offensive behavior toward jackals as they grew older [18]. A passing jackal was a powerful stimulus for cubs to chase after 4 months of age. Whereas young cubs showed defensive behavior to other cheetahs, middle-aged and old cubs gingerly approached and investigated them on approximately one out of four occasions [18]. Older cubs might move toward another cheetah (usually a female) and just observe it, might shadow it for 200 m or so, or occasionally surround it and gaze from 2 m away; this last pattern was most characteristic of older male cubs. Four 6-month-old cubs once

TABLE 6.9 Percentage of Occasions in which Cubs Reacted Defensively or Offensively to Predators They Saw

	Cub age		
	Young	Middle-aged	Old
Lions	(N = 14)	(N = 17)	(N = 17)
Defense	100.0	94.1	100.0
Offense	0	5.9	0
Spotted hyenas	(N = 26)	(N = 57)	(N = 46)
Defense	92.3	91.2	93.4
Offense	7.7	8.8	6.5
Cheetahs	(N = 23)	(N = 22)	(N = 21)
Defense	100.0	77.3	76.2
Offense	0	22.7	23.8
Jackals	(N = 25)	(N = 27)	(N = 24)
Defense	76.0	40.7	33.3
Offense	24.0	59.3	66.7

Note: Situations in which cubs were displaced from a kill or in which their behavior was unknown are excluded. Defense refers to watching, standing their ground, or moving away from predators; offense refers to stalking, approaching, or chasing predators (contact was never seen). Numbers of encounters are given in parentheses.

pinned an adult female cheetah down, charging her when she tried to leave, and even followed her through a shallow lake from which she managed to escape, but this sort of persistent behavior was rare. Over the course of such interactions mothers either stared intently at the other cheetah or cheetah family from a distance, occasionally calling their cubs, or often as not, looked off in another direction. Only rarely did they investigate conspecifics with their cubs.

Benefits of Mothers' Antipredator Behavior

Defense of offspring can involve considerable risks to parents and hence constitutes an important component of parental care (Maestripieri 1992). Defense is expected to vary according to parental, offspring, and predator characteristics so as to maximize the lifetime reproductive success of parents, and has been examined primarily in birds (e.g., Regelmann and Curio 1983). The main finding to emerge from a number of avian studies is that parents' defense of offspring in the nest increases with nestling age, because of the greater parental investment necessary to replace older offspring if they die (Dawkins and Carlisle 1976; Boucher 1977). Nestling vulnerability is high and roughly constant in the nest and so does not mask the effects of offspring's changing reproductive value. Similar findings should be expected for mammals that leave offspring in a den (e.g., carnivores) or hiding place (e.g., hider ungulate species) during the period they are sequestered. After fledging or emergence from the den, parental defense is expected to decline since the offspring's increasing mobility will help them escape and they may be better able to repel attacking predators (see Barash 1975; Grieg-Smith 1980). In addition to testing these predictions, bird studies have also demonstrated that the intensity of parental defense rises with increasing risk to offspring but falls with increasing risk to the parent (Montgomerie and Weatherhead 1988; Redondo 1989). This should apply to mammals as well.

OFFSPRING AGE

Mothers that had cubs in the lair employed stealth and crypticity to avoid detection by predators. They rarely sat up while nursing or resting with their cubs and were more likely to miss passing predators as a result than when they were out in the open (Laurenson 1992; Laurenson, in press-b). On returning to the lair after hunting trips, mothers were more vigilant within 1 km of the lair than farther away, and they often returned to the lair after dark, presumably to avoid detection. Nevertheless, if a predator did discover the lair, mothers attempted to drive it away (Laurenson 1993; Laurenson, in press-b).

Once cubs emerged from the lair, individual mortality rates per unit time increased sharply (Laurenson, in press-b). Mothers now showed heightened vigilance, noticing lions, for example, at greater distances than did females in other reproductive states. Furthermore, they were more likely to be aggressive to spotted hyenas than were lone females or mothers with cubs in the lair (Laurenson, in press-b). In general, mothers with young cubs were more offensive (stalking, chasing, or contacting predators) than mothers of older cubs [19]. They also took offensive or defensive measures against zebras, wildebeests, and warthogs when they were close by (table 6.10); in other circumstances these species elicited little response or were hunted. Since cubs reacted to danger by scattering in all directions and at rather a slow pace, they might have been trampled or gored by these species. It seems unlikely that these maternal responses simply spilled over from heightened reactions to other carnivores because only certain ungulates elicited these reactions. Table 6.10 also shows that species dangerous to cheetahs of all ages (buffaloes, leopards, striped hyenas, baboons) provoked a response whatever the age of the cubs. Baboons steal kills from cheetahs (Frame and Frame 1981) and mothers paid careful attention to them; with young cubs, they moved away at great distances.

In general, then, mothers were most active in defending offspring against predators and large ungulates when cubs were young and vulnerable to predation; however, this behavior declined as offspring grew older. Maternal antipredator behavior was clearly tailored to offspring vulnerability rather than to their reproductive value, since the latter increased as cubs grew older while the former declined as cubs became able to outrun predators. A similar decline in parental defense after offspring have left the security of their birthplace has been reported for stonechats (Greig-Smith 1980).

RISKS OF PREDATION FROM DIFFERENT PREDATORS

The match between maternal antipredator behavior and offspring vulnerability was further brought to light when maternal responses to different predators were examined; however, the danger predators posed to mothers was also evident here (table 6.11). Lions were the most important cause of mortality in young cheetah cubs (table 4.5) and could also kill adult cheetahs (e.g., Guggisberg 1962; Burney and Burney 1979). As lions sought out and chased cheetah families and tried to kill them regardless of maternal behavior, mothers were unable to drive lions off and could only distract them [20]. For example, I saw a mother cheetah stalk toward a lioness sitting 300 m away, but when her 2-month-old son moved, the lioness started a fast, determined stalk in the cub's direction and crouched down 80 m from it. By now the mother cheetah, making deep growling

TABLE 6.10 Mothers' Reactions to Species that Appeared to Pose a Threat to Them or Their Cubs

Mother's behavior	Cub age (months)	Species' behavior	Closest distance from cheetah (m)
Zebra			
Chases off 4 adults for 5 m	2	Follow them	5
Chases off herd for 2 m	2	Flee	13
Chases off 30 zebra for 8 m	2	Flee	10
Defensive stalk through herd	2	Approach	15
Defensive stalk through herd	2	Watch	15
Watches intently	3	Watch	40
Watches adult male intently	3	Watches	25
Crouches defensively at 12 zebras	4	Don't see	20
Slinks away from 16 zebras	4	?	40
Wildebeest			
Stalks 30 with arched back for 5 m	2	?	30
Stalks 35 with arched back for 2 m	2	?	25
Chases 2 for 15 m	7	Flee	20
Warthog			
Watches adult male	2	Doesn't see	10
Chases 2 off somewhat playfully	2	Flee	25
Watches 2 adults intently	3	?	30
Watches single warthog intently	3	?	50
Watches subadult intently	8.5	Approaches	5
Buffalo			
Watches 4 males from 1 m up tree	10.5	?	30
Leopard			
Chases for 50 m	2	Flees, then chases family	2
Striped hyena			
Approaches for 30 m	6	Flee	80
Watches intently	12.5	Doesn't see	500
Baboon			
Leaves and walks 700 m away	4	Walk by	200
Runs 400 m away from adult male	4	Walks by	800
Watches troop of 23 intently	4	Don't see	500
Watches single baboon intently	6	Walks by	60
Slinks away 5 m from single baboon	6	Walks by	25
Watches adult male intently	6	?	?

TABLE 6.10 Continued

Mother's behavior	Cub age (months)	Species' behavior	Closest distance from cheetah (m)
Slinks away from 2	6	Don't see	300
Watches adult male intently	7	Walks by	800
Watches adult male intently	7	Approaches	70
Watches troop of 8 intently	8.5	Don't see	1,000
Flees 80 m from 2 males	12.5	Approach	50
Watches troop of 28 intently	12.5	Approach	?

TABLE 6.11 Mothers' Reactions to Dangerous Common Predators

	Predator species			
	Lion	Spotted hyena	Cheetah	Jackal
Number of encounters	55	157	77	79
Walk or crouch	49.1	53.5	64.9	78.5
Move away	34.5	30.6	24.7	7.6
Hiss or stand up	0	5.1	0	0
Stalk or approach	10.9	6.4	5.2	2.5
Chase	3.6	1.9	5.2	11.4
Slap	1.8	2.5	0	0

Note: Percentage of those encounters in which mothers reacted to the four most common predators, separated according to maternal behavior; situations in which they were displaced from a kill and where mothers' behavior was unknown were excluded. If a mother reacted in several of the ways listed, only the one that brought her into closest proximity to the predator (the most dangerous one) was scored.

noises, was 20 m from the lioness, who chased her for 60 m and then again four more times. The lioness now doubled back to search the 60-cm-high vegetation for the cub, 10 m from where I had last seen it. She made a series of 5-m-long sorties into this vegetation but eventually sat down and looked in the general direction of the cub's last position; the cheetah mother sat 15 m from her. After 40 minutes had elapsed, the lioness left. The cheetah mother moved 120 m from the scene and began calling for her cub. After more walking and repeated churring, she eventually found it 400 m from the place I had last seen it. The mother must have known approximately where the cub had gone, judging from the direction in which she departed, but by advancing so close to the lioness she distracted it (and me) long enough for the cub to run off without us detecting it.

Spotted hyenas were also an important predator on young cubs (see table 4.5), but single hyenas, at least, posed less of a threat to adult cheetahs. They elicited offensive behavior from cheetah mothers with young cubs [21] (fig. 6.14), and would ordinarily flee when mothers ran toward them.

Lone female cheetahs usually avoided mothers with cubs, but male cheetahs would sometimes run at mothers and knock them over, pinning them down as they investigated their reproductive status (chap. 11). Though risks to young cubs were low (males did not approach families with young cubs more often than families with older cubs [22], suggesting, perhaps, that infanticide was uncommon after cubs had quit the lair), mothers were relatively ineffective in protecting either themselves or their cubs against the attentions of males. Consequently they showed little offensive behavior toward cheetahs [23].

Jackals posed little threat to adult cheetahs or their cubs. Mothers with young cubs were somewhat more offensive to jackals than other mothers [24] but only chased them when cubs were 2 or 3 months old (three

Fig. 6.14 An adult female cheetah walks toward a single adult spotted hyena that has moved off in response. Note the cheetah's stiff tense gait.

cases). Later mothers joined their older cubs in playfully pursuing these canids.

Similar differences in cheetah mothers' responses to each of these predators were observed in Laurenson's parallel study (in press-b). She additionally noted that a mother was more likely to attack a predator if it approached her directly, and if vegetation cover was low, both of which increased the probability of cubs being discovered.

It is worth noting that wild dogs and spotted hyenas could potentially run any cheetah down during a prolonged chase. In Asia domestic dogs were used to catch cheetahs, and in parts of southern Africa are still used to tree them. Nevertheless, it must have been far more profitable for wild dogs to pursue ungulate prey than to risk suffering injuries in subduing a cheetah or losing it up a tree.

In short, these observations indicate that mammals as well as birds adjust defense of offspring according to the risks that the predator poses to both their offspring and themselves.

OFFSPRING NUMBER

Predictions concerning the relationship between maternal antipredator behavior and litter size in cheetahs differ according to offspring age because offspring vulnerability changes so radically. Data collated by Laurenson (1992) show that the number of young taken by predators increases with litter size in the lair because the whole litter is killed in most cases. Hence parental investment should increase with litter size (brood loss case of unshared investment: Lazarus and Inglis 1986). Unfortunately there are insufficient cases of mothers defending cubs in the lair to test the prediction empirically.

Between emergence and 4 months of age, however, the relationship between number of cubs lost to predators and litter size is less pronounced, although it is positively correlated. It may be fair to argue, conservatively, that cubs' poor mobility makes it unlikely that only one would be taken, and hence that more would be killed in larger litters. Thus investment should increase with litter size at this stage too. Some evidence supports this; for example, mothers of young cubs were more likely to go on the offensive against spotted hyenas when they had three or four cubs rather than one or two [25], but other evidence is more equivocal (see Caro 1987a).

Predation on cubs older than 4 months was probably independent of litter size since these cubs could outrun predators. In the two reports of predation, one cub was taken from a litter of two and another from a litter of four. Consequently investment should be independent of litter size (fixed loss case: Lazarus and Inglis 1986; but see Forslund 1993) and, with one exception, litter size had little influence on maternal antipredator behavior during this period (Caro 1987a).

In sum, the most cautious interpretation of these results is that evidence does not refute the proposition that parents are willing to incur greater survivorship costs in defending offspring if they can promote the survival of a greater number of progeny. Nevertheless, predictions are complicated by the possibility that individuals respond only to deviations from their expected litter size, not to absolute numbers of offspring, and that larger litters may be more vulnerable to predation (Redondo 1989); these factors were not investigated.

Benefits of Parental Care

Young cubs faced three sorts of difficulty in escaping predation. First, they were slow to discern the presence of a predator until it was very close and hence a threat; second, their reactions to predators were often inappropriate and came too late; and third, they seemed unable to distinguish harmful species from benign. Mothers enhanced the survival of young cubs by detecting predators from a long way off and moving away, or by threatening or attacking predators if they came too close.

In general, cubs of 6 months or older could use their speed to escape lions and spotted hyenas provided they had some warning ahead of time. Yet they were not vigilant enough to spy predators reliably at long distances and only matched adults in this regard once they reached 10.5 months of age. Hence, offspring still profited from maternal vigilance up to this point.

In summary, cubs benefited from the presence of their mother in at least three ways, and not solely through her provisioning. Young cubs gained from their mother's antipredator behavior, vigilance, and nutrition provided through milk and prey that she caught for them. Middle-aged and to some extent old cubs profited from her vigilance and hunting skills, while for offspring in the old cub age group mothers' provisioning was the principal benefit of parental care.

Summary

1. Cubs weighed 350 g at birth and grew at an average of 44.6 g/day in the lair. Mothers introduced cubs to solid food once they emerged from the lair but cubs continued to nurse until they were 4 months old. Cubs ate an estimated 0.6 kg of meat each day over the time they were dependent on their mothers.

2. After leaving the lair, offspring usually accompanied their mothers on hunts but occasionally would wait behind.

3. Young cubs chased inappropriate prey that was ignored by adult cheetahs and did not stalk or crouch at appropriate prey until they were older. Cubs began to initiate family hunts from 6 months of age onward but they rarely killed prey. Cubs approached the killing rate of their mothers only in the oldest age class. Cubs' hunts failed because prey often saw them approaching.

4. Mothers encouraged their cubs to capture prey by releasing live prey for them instead of killing it, principally after cubs reached 5 months of age. Less hungry mothers were more likely to do this, and neonate gazelles were released more than any other prey types.

5. Despite changes in hunting skills, cubs were still incompetent at hunting throughout most of the period they were with their mothers. Maternal provisioning of solid food was therefore critical to juvenile survival.

6. Young cubs were very poor at seeing predators at all and rarely saw them before their mother did. Mothers were more vigilant than their cubs, and maternal vigilance constituted an important component of parental care until cubs were 10 months old.

7. Causes and extent of cub vulnerability went through three phases. In the lair they could not flee from predators if discovered; after emergence when they were easily seen, they were slow at escaping danger; but after 4 months they could outrun predators.

8. Young cubs failed to recognize predators and were slow in responding appropriately to danger after they emerged from the lair. They were also fearful of many harmless objects. Mothers enhanced cub survivorship by detecting predators a long way off and then either moving away or attacking them.

9. Mothers with young cubs were more offensive against predators than mothers with older cubs; in particular, they chased hyenas and jackals away. They could not mount an effective defense against lions or other cheetahs, however. Mothers also attacked ungulate species that were normally disregarded at other times.

10. Mothers took greater risks in defending larger litters when the number of cubs in danger was related to litter size.

11. Cubs benefited from family life in three ways, the importance of which changed as they grew older. Young cubs profited from their mother's antipredator behavior, vigilance, and the milk and solid food she provided; middle-aged cubs from her vigilance and provisioning; while old cubs benefited primarily from the consequences of her hunting proficiency. Hence the long period of offspring dependence in this species is apparently geared to cubs gaining the minimum skills necessary to catch food for themselves.

Statistics

1. Spearman rank order correlation coefficient between the percentage of 15-minute scans that cubs were seen eating, averaged across the litter, and cub age, $N = 41$ litters, $r_s = -.534$, $P < .001$, excluding single-day watches.

2. Spearman rank order correlation coefficient between the number of kg of meat that cubs ate per hour, averaged across the litter, and cub age, $N = 43$ litters, $r_s = .101$, $P > .5$, excluding single-day watches.

3. Spearman rank order correlation coefficient between percentage of hunts in which cubs accompanied their mother and cub age, $N = 46$ litters, $r_s = .396$, $P < .01$.

4. Spearman rank order correlation coefficients between the numbers of times cubs showed different hunting behavior patterns toward appropriate and inappropriate prey items and cub age, $N = 54$ litters for all tests, trot: $r_s = .356$, $P < .02$; stalk: $r_s = .580$, $P < .001$; crouch: $r_s = .658$, $P < .001$; rush: $r_s = .365$, $P < .02$; chase: $r_s = .468$, $P < .002$.

5. Spearman rank order correlation coefficient between the percentage of hunts in which the mother participated that were initiated by cubs and cub age; watches in which only one hunt occurred were excluded, $N = 46$ litters, $r_s = .652$, $P < .001$.

6. Spearman rank order correlation coefficient between the number of hunts in which mothers participated per hour and cub age, $N = 54$ litters, $r_s = -.120$, $P > .2$.

Spearman rank order correlation coefficient between the number of hunts cubs made without their mother participating and cub age, $N = 54$ litters, $r_s = .548$, $P < .001$.

7. Percentage of occasions mothers released live prey for their cubs, young cubs: 9.2% ($N = 87$ prey captured), middle-aged cubs: 32.4% ($N = 37$ prey captured), old cubs: 24.2% ($N = 66$ prey captured), G test, $G_2 = 11.315$, $P = .004$.

Comparing young and middle-aged cubs: $G_1 = 9.517$, $P = .001$. Young and old cubs: $G_1 = 6.402$, $P = .011$. Middle-aged and old cubs: $G_1 = 0.792$, $P > .3$.

8. Spearman rank order correlation coefficient between the percentage of "successful" chases of live prey released by mothers (i.e., chases that finished with cubs contacting the prey) and cub age, $N = 16$ litters, $r_s = .360$, $P = .086$.

9. Mothers' belly sizes when they released prey for cubs ($N = 35$ belly size readings, $\bar{X} = 4.9$, SE $= 0.3$) differed from those when prey was not released ($N = 154$ belly size readings, $\bar{X} = 4.3$, SE $= 0.1$), Mann-Whitney U test, $z = 1.713$, $P = .087$.

Belly size of cubs, averaged across the litter, when prey was released

(N = 35 belly size readings, $\overline{X}$ = 5.6, SE = 0.1) and was not released for them (N = 154 belly size readings, $\overline{X}$ = 5.9, SE = 0.3), z = -0.869, $P > .3$.

10. Percentage of neonate Grant's and Thomson's gazelles released by mothers (30.9%, N = 81 captures by mothers) differed from the percentage of adult and subadult gazelles released (4.0%, N = 50 captures by mothers), G test, G_1 = 16.381, $P < .0001$.

11. Percentage of hares killed by cubs (46.2%, N = 13 chased by cubs) differed from the percentage killed by mothers (84.8%, N = 33 chased by mothers), Fisher test, $P = .01$.

12. Percentage of hares that were maimed (40.0%, N = 5 released by mothers) differed from the percentage of neonate gazelles that were released in a maimed condition (0%, N = 23 released by mothers), Fisher test, $P = .042$.

13. Pearson correlation coefficient between the percentage of time cubs had their eyes open and were monitoring their surroundings, averaged over each litter, and cub age, N = 54 litters, r = .559, $P < .001$.

14. Pearson correlation coefficient between the percentage of 5-minute scans during the midday rest period cubs lay flat out, averaged over each litter, and cub age, $y = 40.677 - 1.261x$, N = 54 litters, $r = -.289$, $P = .034$.

15. Pearson correlation coefficient between the percentage of time cubs lay alert, averaged over each litter, and cub age, $y = 16.919 + 0.760x$, N = 54 litters, $r = .291$, $P = .033$.

16. Spearman rank order correlation coefficient between the frequency with which cubs looked up from the carcass, averaged over each litter, and cub age, N = 44 litters, r_s = .443, $P < .005$.

Spearman rank order correlation coefficient between the percentage of time spent off the carcass while it was available, averaged over each litter, and cub age, N = 44 litters, $r_s = -.185$, $P > .2$.

17. Spearman rank order correlation coefficient between the percentage of occasions predators were seen by any cub and cub age, N = 51 litters, r_s = .355, $P < .02$.

Spearman rank order correlation coefficient between the percentage of occasions predators were seen by the mother and cub age, N = 51 litters, $r_s = -.060$, $P > .05$.

18. Cubs' offensive and defensive responses to different predators, separated by cub age; young vs. middle-aged and old cub categories combined for each of the first three predators due to small sample sizes. Spotted hyenas, Fisher test, $P > .7$; lions, Fisher test, $P > .7$; cheetahs, Fisher test, $P = .009$; jackals, comparing three age groups; G test, G_2 = 10.753, $P = .006$ (see table 6.9).

19. Percentage of occasions that cheetah mothers stalked, chased, or slapped other predators (were offensive), as opposed to watched, stood their ground, or moved away from predators (were defensive), separated by cub age: young (19.1%, $N = 126$ encounters), middle-aged (11.4%, $N = 114$ encounters), and old cubs (6.3%, $N = 128$ encounters), G test, $G_2 = 9.923$, $P = .008$.

20. Percentage of occasions mothers were offensive as opposed to defensive to lions, separated by cub age: young (22.7%, $N = 22$ encounters), middle-aged and old cubs combined (12.1%, $N = 33$ encounters), Fisher test, $P > .3$.

21. Percentage of occasions mothers were offensive as opposed to defensive to spotted hyenas, separated by cub age: young (26.2%, $N = 42$ encounters), middle-aged (8.3%, $N = 60$ encounters), and old cubs (1.8%, $N = 55$ encounters), G test, $G_2 = 14.952$, $P = .005$.

22. Percentage of occasions male cheetahs approached mothers with young cubs (37.5%, $N = 8$ instances) and mothers with middle-aged and old cubs (45.5%, $N = 11$ instances), Fisher test, $P > .3$.

23. Percentage of occasions mothers were offensive as opposed to defensive to cheetahs, separated by cub age: young (5.9%, $N = 34$ encounters), middle-aged and old cubs combined (14.0%, $N = 43$ encounters), Fisher test, $P > .1$.

24. Percentage of occasions mothers were offensive as opposed to defensive to jackals, separated by cub age: young (21.4%, $N = 28$ encounters), middle-aged and old cubs combined (9.8%, $N = 51$ encounters), Fisher test, $P = .098$.

25. Percentage of occasions mothers showed offensive behavior to spotted hyenas when their litters contained 1 or 2 cubs (10.0%, $N = 20$ encounters) and litters of 3 or 4 cubs (40.9%, $N = 22$ encounters), G test, $G_1 = 5.533$, $P = .023$.

A single adolescent female, having flushed and chased a hare, throttles it. (Drawing by Dafila Scott.)

7
HUNTING AND GROUPING IN ADOLESCENCE

Juveniles of many species must learn how to forage. For example, in species in which adults have to employ good judgment and motor coordination in capturing food, or complicated handling skills in processing it, young may be expected to require time to perfect these skills. Among birds, the ability to obtain food often improves with age and experience (Lack 1954, 1966; Ashmole 1963; Marchetti and Price 1989). Juvenile little blue herons at least 9 months of age miss prey more frequently and catch less food per minute than do adults (Recher and Recher 1969), while immature brown pelicans 18 to 24 months of age capture prey in a lower percentage of dives than do adults (Orians 1969a). In regard to handling, oystercatchers take 3 years to become as proficient as adults at breaking open and eating edible mussels (Norton-Griffiths 1968). In some of these species using complex feeding skills, adults continue to supply offspring with food after they have left the nest (e.g., crowned hawk eagles: Brown 1966; great frigate birds: Nelson 1967; eastern kingbirds: Morehouse and Brewer 1968), which may prevent breeding the following season (Ashmole and Tovar 1968).

In mammals, evidence of juveniles possessing poor foraging skills is less well documented. Carnivores' prey-catching techniques may be expected to take time to acquire, but it is usually difficult to monitor the way in which hunting skills or rates of food intake change with age, so indirect methods have been used. For example, stomach contents have shown that young individuals eat different foods from adults, but it is impossible to tell whether this results from differences in food preferences or in hunting skills. Fortunately, the cheetah's diurnal activity pattern and open habitat make it an ideal subject for documenting improvement in hunting skills.

In this mammal, the foundations of predatory behavior are laid during dependency. Trying out hunting skills while being provisioned with food, having prey released in front of them, and perhaps rehearsing predatory skills through play could all potentially facilitate cubs' development of predatory techniques (see Martin and Caro 1985 for a similar argument concerning domestic cats). Nevertheless, cubs were poor hunters at the time of separation from their mothers (see chap. 6), so the most dramatic development in hunting skills must have occurred after independence. This was well known to the sportsmen who took only adult cheetahs from the wild for coursing (Sterndale 1884; Shortridge 1934). In the first half of this chapter, I document changes in hunting techniques and foraging returns as independent cheetahs grow older.

Patterns of grouping in juvenile mammals show a good deal of variation. Among solitary species that give birth to a single offspring (monotoky), juveniles separate from their parents on their own (e.g., orangutans: MacKinnon 1974). In monotokous species that live in groups, juveniles also quit their natal group alone, regardless of whether males or females are the dispersing sex. Examples include yellow baboons, in which single males transfer (Altmann, Hausfater, and Altmann 1988), red colobus, in which single females disperse (Struhsaker 1980), and hamadryas baboons, in which both sexes transfer alone (Kummer 1968). Nevertheless, among ungulates, it is common for juvenile males to form bachelor herds either with members of their own cohort or with older males (Jarman 1974). In polytokous group-living species, it is more common for several juveniles to leave their natal group together, as in lions (Packer et al. 1988), wild dogs (Frame et al. 1979), and dwarf mongooses (Rood 1987b), in which, respectively, groups of juvenile males, females, and both sexes leave their natal group as a unit.

In polytokous solitary species, however, littermates also quit their mother as a group, and mixed-sex juvenile groups are common. For example, two or three grizzly bear cubs from the same litter will continue to associate for 4.5 months or so after losing contact with their mother (Murie 1981). While we know that groups of male siblings may later have enhanced access to females in certain species (Packer et al. 1988), in general the advantages of mixed-sex juvenile groups remain mysterious.

Ordinarily felids are solitary and polytokous, with adolescents of both sexes remaining together once they have separated from their mother (table 7.1). Such groups are temporary in the sense that they last only an order of months, but are stable in that littermates actively seek to remain in one another's company. For example, in cheetahs, if one moves, the

TABLE 7.1 Recorded Instances of Littermates Remaining Together after
Leaving Their Mother in Felids

Species	Comments
North American lynx	"A pair of lynxes (yearlings or 2-yr-olds) separated from their mother were followed about 3 miles. They hunted abreast several yards apart in wooded areas but followed one another in the open" (Saunders 1963).
European lynx	"The young cling together for a certain time after being left by the mother, then the brood gradually disbands" (Stroganov 1969).
	"They [siblings] stay together for some time longer [after being chased away by mother's new suitors] but the group gradually breaks up each going its own solitary way" (Guggisberg 1975).
Bobcat	"The older and larger bobcats seem to be solitary, but the young often travel in groups of two or three. Twice in the winter of 1940–41 groups of three young were located and on another occasion two were found traveling together" (Marston 1942).
Cougar	"Many litters maintain their identity for a period after leaving their mother. There are 9 cases of 3 or more immature cougars in the yearling and long-yearling class travelling together" (Robinette, Gaswiler, and Morris 1961).
	"Breeding pairs and recently independent siblings formed cohesive units, but they were of brief duration" (Seidensticker et al. 1973).
Snow leopard	"The litter does not disband in the winter but continues hunting together" (Novikov 1962).
	"When 2 or 3 large animals associate they represent . . . independent cubs in a litter which has not yet split" (Schaller 1977).
	"Other than breeding pairs, female-offspring groups, or recently independent siblings, physical contact between individuals is the exception" (Jackson and Ahlborn 1989).
Jaguar	"Two siblings will live and hunt together for a few months while searching for their own territory" (Mondolfi and Hoogesteijn 1986).
Tiger	"The litter does not disband for 2–3 years" (Novikov 1962).
	"At 17 months we saw the 4 cubs on their own more frequently. Akbar, the dominant male sibling took charge of his brothers and sister. At 21 months old Akbar left. At 22½ months Hamir left. Babar (a male) and Laximi (a female) remained together for yet another 2 months (to 24½ months)" (Thapar 1986).
	"At 18 months both cubs still used their mother's home range but spent long periods of time away from her. They shared several kills and spent more time with each other than with their mother" (Sunquist and Sunquist 1988).

TABLE 7.1 Continued

Species	Comments
Cheetah	"Groups consist of litters broken away from their mothers. Females leave such groups and become solitary before their first estrus but male sibs may remain together. The 2 males and 1 female stayed together for approximately 1 month after leaving their mother. Two females stayed together 1 month after leaving mother. Brothers or single males may form bonds with others of their own sex" (Schaller 1972c).
	"Subadults often stay together after they have become independent of their mother. The females do so for only a few months until they become pregnant, but brothers may keep one another company for longer" (Bertram 1979).
	"Siblings remain together for several months after leaving mother. One by one the females, when 17–23 months old, leave their littermates" (Frame 1984).

others will follow, and if members become separated, they will spend hours calling and looking for one another until reunited. Since adolescent felids reportedly face difficulties in capturing prey, it is tacitly assumed that they stay with one another to increase hunting success (or perhaps to avoid injury costs during prey capture; see some of the references in table 7.1), but this has never been investigated.

Unlike most other cats, male cheetah littermates form lifelong associations and might therefore be expected to maintain contact with one another as adolescents. In cheetahs, therefore, the question is, why do adolescent females continue to remain with their brothers and sisters after separating from their parent? In the second half of the chapter, the benefits that females gain from associating with siblings are examined by comparing adolescent females living alone with adolescent females living in the company of male or female littermates. Some of the single adolescent females had earlier lived with siblings, whereas others were subjects on whom I had no genealogical information and might therefore have had no littermates or might have separated from them already. On balance, then, single females were probably slightly older than females in groups, assuming equivalent ages of separation from their mothers.

Last, limited data on female home ranges and male dispersal are presented. Sex-biased dispersal is often viewed as a mechanism to avoid inbreeding (Greenwood 1980; Pusey 1980; Clutton-Brock 1989a). In most wild populations of birds and mammals, parent-offspring and full-sib matings are rare, constituting between 0% and 6% of all observed pairings (Ralls, Harvey, and Lyles 1986). In theory, limited dispersal and inbreeding might be a cause of the extreme lack of genetic variation observed in cheetahs; therefore dispersal has a direct bearing on this problem, the causes of which are under debate (O'Brien et al. 1987; Pimm et al. 1989; O'Brien 1989). Also, knowing the potential for inbreeding in wild populations would be helpful to zoo managers developing guidelines for acceptable levels of inbreeding in small pools of captive individuals.

Changes in Prey Preferences with Age

The size of prey that independent females attempted did not rise steadily with age, although it was somewhat greater in young adult females than in other age classes (fig. 7.1) [1]. Annual home ranges of adolescent, young adult, and adult females were roughly similar in extent as they all followed the Thomson's gazelle migration (see below and chap. 8), so that differential availability of prey was unlikely to confound this result. Indeed, Thomson's gazelles made up a similarly large proportion of the hunting quarry of females in each of the age classes (table 7.2), although none was quite as high as the 89% reported by Schaller (1968).

Younger females (i.e., adolescents and young adults) chased after inappropriate species rarely pursued or eaten by adults, just as older cubs had done. These were large and dangerous prey such as adult zebras and warthogs, very small prey, usually birds, or medium-sized predators that

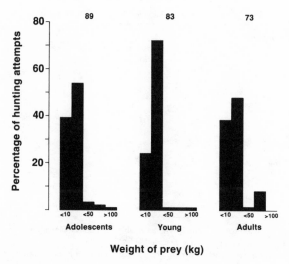

Fig. 7.1 Percentage of hunting attempts made on prey of different body weights (<10, 11–20, 21–50, 51–100, >100 kg) by adolescent, young adult, and adult females. Numbers of hunting attempts are shown above the histograms.

they were unlikely to catch (table 7.3). There are only occasional reports of adult cheetahs eating such items, usually from other parts of Africa (Pienaar 1969).

Why did younger females continue to exhibit this immature behavior? There may have been benefits in rehearsing hunting skills in circum-

TABLE 7.2 Percentage of Hunting Attempts Made by Adolescent, Young Adult, and Adult Females on Different Types of Prey

	Age			
	Adolescent	Young adult	Adult	Total
Number of hunts	101	101	66	268
Hares	5.9	10.9	4.5	7.5
Thomson's gazelles	76.2	73.3	83.3	76.9
Other	5.9	5.9	9.1	6.7
Unknown quarry[a]	11.9	9.9	3.0	9.0

[a] Usually mixed herds of Thomson's and Grant's gazelles.

TABLE 7.3 Number of Inappropriate Species Pursued by Female Cheetahs of Differing Ages

	Age		
	Adolescent[a]	Young adult	Adult
Total number of hours watched	657.4	290.2	293.6
Adult zebra	1	1	
Adult ostrich	1		
Warthog	1	1	
Caracal		1	
Serval	1		
Jackal	8	4	2
Bat-eared fox	2	1	
Vulture or eagle	2	1	1
Bustard	2	1[b]	1
Gamebird	3		
Other bird	2	2	1

Note: These pursuits are not recorded as hunts in table 7.2. Interactions with scavengers during and immediately after carcass consumption were excluded.

Jackals: golden and black-backed; vultures: lappet-faced and white-headed; eagle: steppe eagle; bustard: white-bellied, black-bellied, and Kori; gamebird: spurfowl and sand grouse; other bird included chanting goshawk.

[a] Pursuits by single adolescent females and adolescent sibgroups containing females were combined.
[b] A nestling Kori bustard was caught and consumed.

TABLE 7.4 Characteristics of Hunts of Inappropriate Prey by Adolescent, Young Adult, and Adult Female Cheetahs

	Age		
	Adolescent[a]	Young adult	Adult
Number of inappropriate hunts	23	12	5
Number per hour watched	0.035	0.041	0.021
Average distance chased (m)	56	17	20
Average distance abandoned (m)	18	8	2
Average belly size of huntress	6.6	6.3	5.4

[a] Hunts of adolescent females and sibgroups were combined in the table.

stances additional to those provided by appropriate prey. Furthermore, hunts of inappropriate prey were of little cost because they took place infrequently, chases were short, and there was little risk of injury as chases were abandoned at some distance from the quarry (table 7.4). That cheetahs were unable to discriminate different prey types seems improbable since most inappropriate hunts occurred when females were reasonably satiated (their belly sizes were greater than 5), and they normally abandoned their hunts prior to contact even if prey were small and posed no threat. Nevertheless, there was no question that adolescents still had much to learn about the behavior and even identity of potential prey items. I once watched an adolescent female stalking a sleeping neonate wildebeest. She acted warily, sniffing and finally patting it gently, which awakened it. Only once it fled did she chase and kill it; apparently she had not encountered sleeping prey before.

Changes in Hunting Behavior with Age

HUNTING SUCCESS

Females became increasingly successful at catching hares and neonate gazelles as they matured. Hunting success on larger prey did not increase significantly, however (fig. 7.2) [2]. In spite of this, the combined effect of changing prey preferences and hunting success resulted in a greater proportion of older females' kills being made up of quarry larger than hares or neonate gazelles (fig. 7.3) [3].

There were two main reasons why younger females were poor at catching prey. First, young adults began their hunts at greater distances from prey than did adult females; figure 7.4 suggests that adolescents did the same, although this was not significant [4]. Both classes of younger females seemed overeager to start hunting or, put another way, were poor at judging whether they had a reasonable chance of approaching ungulate herds undetected. As a consequence of starting their hunts more than 100 m away, younger females were detected by prey somewhat more often than were adults [5]. Second, younger females were rather more likely to let their quarry escape [6] because, having started the chase, they held back and did not press their pursuit. It was as if they did not dare chase prey properly and catch up with it. A surprisingly high proportion of almost one in ten of their hunts failed for this reason (table 7.5). As a consequence, younger females abandoned chases at greater distances from the quarry (fig. 7.4) [7]. Both of these predilections limited their opportunities for practicing and refining skills necessary for securing prey at the end of a chase (fig. 7.5).

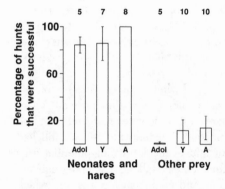

Fig. 7.2 Mean (and SE) percentage of hunts on neonate gazelles and hares (left) and other (larger) prey (right) that were successful for adolescent (Adol), young adult (Y), and adult (A) females. Numbers of individuals are shown above the bars.

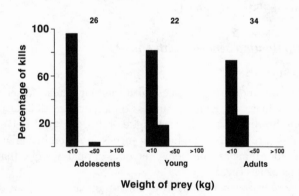

Fig. 7.3 Percentage of kills of prey of different body weights (<10, 11–20, 21–50, 51–100, >100 kg) made by adolescent, young adult, and adult females; numbers of kills are shown above the histograms. The adolescent kill in the 21–50 kg range was made when a neonate eland was stumbled upon while it was lying out away from its mother.

There were other age-related differences in the reasons that hunts failed, but these were of lesser import (table 7.5). For instance, older females sometimes abandoned their hunts because they entered an open area where there was very little cover between themselves and the prey, and they were often outrun by prey. In part, both of these differences reflected adults' greater persistence once they had started to hunt prey.

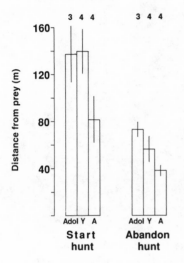

Fig. 7.4 Mean (and SE) distance in meters at which adolescent (Adol), young adult (Y), and adult (A) females started to hunt prey other than neonate gazelles and hares. The distance at which they abandoned failed hunts is also shown. Only those individuals seen to hunt five or more times were included. Numbers of individuals are shown above the bars.

TABLE 7.5 Reasons Hunts by Adolescent, Young Adult, and Adult Females Failed

	Age		
	Adolescent	Young adult	Adult
Number of hunts	74	54	37
Seen by prey	44.6	37.0	24.3
Prey run off not seeing cheetah	14.9	5.6	18.9
Terrain too open	1.4	7.4	8.1
Start rush too early	5.4	13.0	5.4
Outrun or outmaneuvered	1.4	1.9	8.1
Unable to pull prey down	0	0	0
Did not dare	8.1	9.3	0
Not serious	12.2	7.4	18.9
Other	10.8	5.6	8.1
Unknown	1.4	13.0	8.1

Note: Failures are expressed as a percentage of the number of failed hunts.

Fig. 7.5 A single adolescent female unsuccessfully attempts to knock over a Grant's gazelle fawn that she discovered hiding in tall vegetation on the short grass plains.

COMPONENTS OF HUNTING

The percentage of hunts in which different components of hunting behavior were exhibited changed little as females grew older [8]. Furthermore, the rate at which hunting behavior patterns occurred in each hunt changed little (table 7.6) except for bouts of trotting and chasing. Older females trotted toward prey between bouts of stalking in order to reduce the distance to the prey, rather than just trotting toward prey on first seeing it. Adolescent and young females sometimes required more than one chase in order to catch prey (table 7.6) because they failed to knock it over by slapping it, or did not pin it down and bite it once it had fallen over. In both situations the victim usually ran off again, triggering additional chases. In contrast, adult females normally caught prey after one chase. Adults appeared confident in securing their prey, especially if it was a neonate Thomson's gazelle. To take an extreme case in point, one adult female waited 32 minutes while a nearby fawn, still wet after parturition,

TABLE 7.6 Frequency of Hunting Behaviors Performed by Adolescent, Young Adult, and Adult Females

	Age		
	Adolescent	Young adult	Adult
Trotting	1.13	1.39	1.50
	(23)	(23)	(12)
Stalking	1.68	1.91	1.85
	(53)	(53)	(33)
Crouching	1.86	1.92	1.56
	(22)	(24)	(18)
Rushing	1.05	1.00	1.00
	(19)	(19)	(11)
Chasing	1.21	1.22	1.00
	(19)	(23)	(11)

Note: Average number of times behavior patterns were seen in hunts in which they occurred at least once are shown; the number of hunts is given in parentheses. Hunts of neonate gazelles and hares were excluded.

watched her. The cheetah walked 6 m away from it, lay down in an alert posture, and closed her eyes before finally returning to kill and eat it. When any adult female got close to a neonate gazelle she acted as if she understood it could not escape (fig. 7.6). Occasionally independent cheetahs of all ages used local topography such as an erosion terrace or bush to approach prey unseen, even to the point of running at right angles to the quarry in order to remain hidden.

To summarize these results, certain aspects of hunting behavior, such as choosing the right distance at which to begin a hunt, took a long time, up to 3.5 years, to develop. Other aspects showed a more steady and rapid improvement with age, such as the proportion of hunts in which females went undetected and the distances at which they abandoned the quarry. Females may have become better at choosing vulnerable prey, at choosing the right locations or circumstances in which to hunt, or at crouching or halting during their stalk when the prey looked up. In the absence of systematic data, but based on observations of a large number of hunts, I believe the third issue was of major consequence, while the first two were minor. Older females appeared to take greater notice of prey's vigilance and movements and adjusted their hunting behavior patterns accordingly.

While the principal ontogenetic changes in cheetahs' predatory behavior involved approaching prey unseen, the literature on predatory development in other carnivores centers on the ontogeny of contact motor patterns or killing, since nearly all observations have been made in the laboratory (e.g., Rasa 1973; Leyhausen 1979; Pellis and Officer 1987; but

Fig. 7.6 A neonate Thomson's gazelle fawn tries to nurse from an adult female cheetah that looks elsewhere. She subsequently killed and ate it.

see Watt 1993). Parallels between cheetahs and other species can nevertheless be found. For example, cheetahs' reduction in eagerness is similar to increased frequency of "lying still hunts" shown by maturing polar bear cubs waiting for seals to appear at breathing holes in the ice (Stirling and Latour 1978). Increased daring is reminiscent of changes seen in the hunting behavior of sandwich terns: older birds tended to plunge-dive from higher heights than first-winter individuals and apparently had greater fishing success as a result (Dunn 1972). Finally, cheetahs' growing ability to secure prey once they had contacted it mirrors decreases in handling time and speed of employing the killing bite, as reported in many laboratory studies (e.g., Caro 1980a).

Changes in Foraging Success with Age

Since the kills of older females tended to be larger in size than those of adolescents (figs. 7.3, 7.7) and since the rate of hunts did not change with age [9], one would expect older females to experience greater food intake

Fig. 7.7 An adult female scans her surroundings for predators as she finishes off an adult male Thomson's gazelle caught that morning.

per unit time. In my small sample of closely observed females, adults ate more, but not significantly more, kilograms of meat per hour than other age groups [10]. I was suspicious of these data, however, because I often decided to follow single females after failing to locate a target family or group of males. This meant that formal observations might begin as late as midmorning, with the consequence that my female subjects may have made a kill and eaten before I arrived. Belly sizes of these focal females thus provided a better measure of overall foraging success as they represented the sum total of daytime and nighttime intake combined. Average belly size showed a marginally significant increase with female age, with the major differences being found between adults and the other age groups (fig. 7.8) [11]. This finding was replicated across a wider sample of individuals but only in the dry season, when adolescents suffered particularly badly [12]. In the wet season there were no strong differences between age categories, implying that adolescents and young females could find sufficient numbers of neonates and hares to maintain belly sizes equivalent to those of adult females. These results provide strong evi-

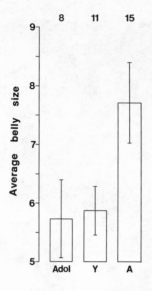

Fig. 7.8 Mean (and SE) average belly size of adolescent (Adol), young adult (Y), and adult (A) females. Numbers of individuals are shown above the bars.

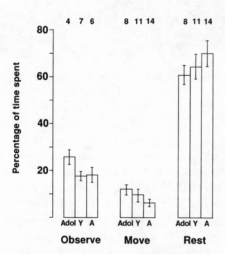

Fig. 7.9 Mean (and SE) percentage of 15-minute scans adolescent (Adol), young adult (Y), and adult (A) females spent observing, moving, and resting. Numbers of individuals are shown above the bars.

dence that the disproportionate number of family dissolutions in the wet season was adaptive (chap. 4), since it allowed adolescents to maintain a food intake that almost matched that of older age groups.

Adolescents' belly sizes were more likely to fall below the critical figure of 4 on the 14-point scale [13], the point at which cheetahs normally began to hunt. Consequently, in comparison to young females, adolescents spent a greater proportion of time sitting up observing their surroundings, an activity associated with looking out for prey (fig. 7.9) [14]. They also

spent twice as much time moving as adults [14]. Laurenson (1992) similarly found that young females traveled farther each day than adult females because they spent a greater proportion of the day searching for
lagomorphs and neonate gazelles concealed in tussocks of grass. More
time spent in these activities resulted in a reduced, though nonsignificant,
proportion of the day spent resting (fig. 7.9) [14].

To summarize, adolescents in particular, but young females as well,
found it difficult to catch enough food. The resulting energetic costs must
have been compounded by their moving more and resting somewhat less
than adults. The effect of poor hunting abilities on adult survival are unknown but may emerge when demographic analyses are complete. In raptors facing analogous challenges in learning how to hunt, mortality is high
in the postfledging period (Newton 1986).

Aspects of reproduction might also be affected by low foraging returns.
Females could conceive successfully at approximately 37.3 months (see
chap. 4), an age at which they chose to hunt smaller prey than adults,
had poorer hunting success, and were nutritionally stressed. Laurenson
(1991b) suspected that one young female abandoned her litter because
she could not catch sufficient food.

It has been argued that the cheetah's specialized prey-catching technique, its high-speed chase, and the dewclaw on its forefoot, which may
aid in hooking quarry (Burton 1950), might make it difficult to learn how
to capture prey (see Eaton 1970d). Comparative data indicate that the
period between independence and maturity, when cheetahs are honing
their hunting skills, is nevertheless shorter in cheetahs than in other members of the Felidae relative to their body weight (fig. 7.10). Indeed, chee-

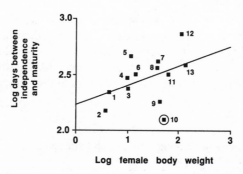

Fig. 7.10 $\log_{10}$ number of days between independence and maturity (H in app. 6)
plotted against $\log_{10}$ female body weight for species of felids, $y = 2.224 + 0.174x$,
$N = 13$, $r^2 = .174$. 1, European wildcat; 2, African wildcat; 3, caracal; 4, ocelot; 5,
clouded leopard; 6, European lynx; 7, leopard; 8, snow leopard; 9, cougar; 10,
cheetah (circled); 11, jaguar; 12, tiger; 13, lion.

tahs are the first species to reproduce after independence once body weight has been taken into account. Presumably, other felids face their own problems. They too use a concealed approach toward prey, must get close before launching an attack (perhaps closer than a cheetah, given their slower speeds), and require a firm grip in order to subdue prey. Quantitative observations on predatory development in other felids would clearly be useful.

The Influence of Grouping on Prey Preferences and Hunting

Adolescent cheetahs living in groups attempted to catch a greater proportion of prey larger than hares or neonate gazelles than adolescent females living alone (table 7.7) [15]. These large prey were usually adult and subadult Thomson's gazelles but occasionally wildebeest neonates. This finding provides intraspecific support for Earle's (1987) conclusion that prey size is strongly correlated with total mass of the predator group size across species. Lone adolescents' reluctance to hunt large prey items was exemplified by the hunting techniques of certain individuals. For example, one used the tactic of sneaking up to a herd of Thomson's gazelles without being seen, but instead of attempting to hunt an adult, she waited for fawns to appear when they stood up to nurse. If she spotted none after half an hour or so, she would move on to another gazelle group, yet despite her patience she failed to notice a number of fawns that did stand up to suckle! Another adolescent, a male this time, searched tussocks for hidden prey, but would only sit and watch nearby Thomson's gazelles and would not hunt them. Laurenson also saw a young female behaving in the same way.

There were no significant differences in overall rates of hunting [16] or in hunting success on either neonates and hares or other sorts of prey [17] when single adolescent females were compared with adolescent groups. Nor were there differences in the proportion of hunts in which the initiator of a sibgroup hunt trotted, stalked, crouched at, rushed, or chased

TABLE 7.7 Number of Hunting Attempts on Different Sizes of Prey by Adolescent Cheetahs

	Hares and neonate gazelles	Larger prey
Single adolescent females	29	71
Adolescent groups containing a female	22	150

prey, compared with single adolescent females; in the distance at which hunts, rushes, or chases began from the prey, or even in the distance at which failed hunts were abandoned. Moreover, the reasons that single adolescent females failed to catch prey were very similar to those of adolescent groups (table 7.8), with one exception. Adolescent groups started their rush too early almost four times as often as did single adolescents [18], most likely because one of the siblings was too eager to get to the quarry.

SIMULTANEOUS HUNTING BY SIBGROUP MEMBERS

In 66.7% of 15 hunts of neonate gazelles or hares, and in 66.9% of 118 hunts of other prey types, sibgroup members hunted at the same time. Yet simultaneous hunting had no effect on hunting success [19].

Sibgroup members also chased both neonate prey and larger prey simultaneously (75.0% of the 12 hunts where chasing occurred and 51.2% of 41 hunts, respectively). Large prey items were more likely to be caught if they were chased by more than one littermate (table 7.9) [20]. The reason was that one group member would take over from its sibling and topple the prey if the initiator of the chase held back from slapping the victim down, as occurred relatively frequently among younger females (see table 7.5). In fact, the first littermate to start hunting killed the prey in only 36.4% of the 11 successful hunts in which more than one adolescent chased the prey. I had insufficient data to test whether one individual was consistently braver than its siblings. Of the four sibgroups I saw making more than one kill (excluding neonates or hares), responsibility for

TABLE 7.8 Reasons that Hunts by Single Adolescent Females and Groups of Adolescents Containing a Female Failed

Number of hunts	Groups 130	Single adolescents 74
Seen by prey	42.3	44.6
Prey run off not seeing cheetah	13.1	14.9
Terrain too open	0.8	1.4
Start rush too early	20.0	5.4
Outrun or outmaneuvered	3.1	1.4
Unable to pull prey down	1.5	0
Did not dare	5.4	8.1
Not serious	8.5	12.2
Other	3.1	10.8
Unknown	2.3	1.4

Note: Failures are expressed as a percentage of the number of failed hunts.

subduing the prey was divided evenly in two of them (1:1, 3:2, 2:0, 2:0:0 kills). Simultaneous chasing was not successful because sibgroup members cut prey off at corners. In contrast to these data on chasing, there was no increase in hunting success if more than one group member contacted the prey because hunts in which contact was made were always successful [21].

The key finding to emerge from my observations of sibgroups hunting was that they enjoyed greater success on subadult and adult Thomson's gazelles if members chased the prey simultaneously. This was because there was a greater chance of an adolescent being brave enough to contact the prey if more than one was on hand at the end of a chase. I could not distinguish whether this was simply an effect of numbers, or whether adolescents became braver in the presence of siblings. Sibgroups' preference for larger prey and their ability to rely on companions resulted in larger prey making up a greater proportion of their kills (fig. 7.11) [22]. This result highlights a number of issues concerning cooperative hunting (see also chap. 12).

First, sibgroup members hunted cooperatively in the sense of hunting simultaneously (Packer and Ruttan 1988), but did not always exhibit the same hunting patterns during hunts and were not coordinated in time or

TABLE 7.9 Outcome of Hunts when Adolescent Group Members Chased Prey Larger than Neonate Gazelles or Hares either Simultaneously or Alone

	Success	Failure
Alone	3	17
Simultaneously	11	10

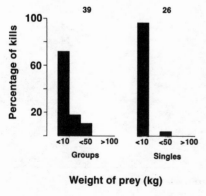

Fig. 7.11 Percentage of kills of prey of different body weights (<10, 11–20, 21–50, 51–100, >100 kg) made by sibling groups containing females and by single adolescent females. Numbers of kills are shown above the histograms. The one single adolescent kill in the 21–50 kg range was a neonate eland that was stumbled upon.

space in the sense of adjusting their positions and speeds so as to remain coordinated. Nor did they perform different but complimentary actions directed toward the same quarry, as reported for chimpanzees hunting red colobus in the Tai Forest, Côte D'Ivoire (Boesch and Boesch 1989). Second, the effect of their simultaneous behavior was extremely specific. It was simultaneous chasing, rather than taking part in the hunt or toppling prey together, that increased hunting success; it was specific to larger prey items where bravery became an issue; and it was specific only to adolescents (see chap. 10), the age group that was reticent in capturing even medium-sized prey items. Nevertheless, evidence that such communal hunting is an adaptation to promote the capture of larger prey cannot be assessed without examining per capita foraging returns experienced by adolescents in groups.

Adolescent Grouping and Foraging Success

Although sibling groups caught larger prey than lone adolescents, they did not experience greater per capita foraging returns because they had to share prey with littermates (fig. 7.12). This was confirmed using a variety of measures. The proportion of time spent eating and the number of kilograms of meat eaten per hour did not differ significantly between female adolescents living alone and those living with siblings [23]. By chance most watches took place in the dry season when poor conditions would be expected to highlight any differences in foraging returns, yet no significant differences were found when only dry season watches were compared. Two females were observed both in a sibling group and, at later dates, subsequently alone: one female fed more while she was with

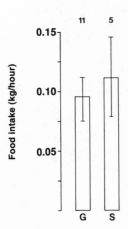

Fig. 7.12 Estimated mean (and SE) kilograms of meat eaten per hour by adolescent females in sibgroups (G) and single adolescent females (S) watched for 12 or more hours. Numbers of individuals are shown above the bars.

TABLE 7.10 Food Intake of Two Adolescent Females with Siblings and Later when Alone

	Hours watched	Kg/hour	Time spent eating (%)
Female 1			
With two brothers	45.6	0.18	4.8
Alone	56.2	0.03	2.8
Female 2			
With one brother	64.8	0.07	2.9
Alone	70.9	0.23	8.0

her brothers, the other fed less (table 7.10). Though anecdotal, this finding highlights the lack of consistent difference in foraging success in the two samples. In addition, average belly size and variation in belly size were similar among my focal adolescent females [24]. Last, sightings showed that adolescent females were equally likely to fall below the hunger threshold of 4 whether they lived alone or with siblings [25].

In sum, preference for larger prey items and their greater representation in the diet of groups did not mean that females in groups ate more than females living on their own. It is therefore difficult to argue that simultaneous chasing of large prey was an adaptation to increase individual foraging success. That simultaneous chasing occurred in only half the hunts of larger prey supports this. Instead, larger prey items simply compensated for having to share food with siblings, with the result that adolescent females suffered no foraging costs by continuing to associate with littermates. Among adolescent cheetahs, therefore, there is no evidence for cooperative hunting in the sense of group members enjoying enhanced per capita foraging returns compared with solitary animals. Furthermore, foraging efficiency cannot explain why female adolescents chose to remain with their brothers and sisters.

The Influence of Grouping on Adolescents' Vigilance

The presence of companions allowed adolescent females to be more relaxed than those living alone, as determined from their time budgets, postures, and vigilance. In groups, adolescent females spent less time observing their surroundings [26], about the same amount as that recorded for old cubs (see table 6.7). During the midday rest period, they spent less time lying alert and sitting up, and more time lying flat out (the most relaxed posture) than lone adolescent females [27] (fig. 7.13). For the two females who were watched with brothers and subsequently without them, the percentage of time they lay flat out showed a sharp decline after they lost their littermates (female 1: before, 17.7%; after, 6.4%; female 2: before, 29.6%, after, 4.0%). Finally, individual females in groups spent less time being vigilant than single adolescent females during the midday rest period (fig. 7.14) [28]. Again, vigilance of sibgroup members mirrored that of old cubs, whereas vigilance of single adolescents was, on average, a third as great again (see table 6.7). Becoming independent therefore represented a smooth transition with respect to vigilance for cubs with littermates but was a time of change for single adolescents.

Females in sibgroups were able to lower their personal vigilance without compromising that of the group because the proportion of time that at least one group member had its eyes open was very similar to that for singletons (fig. 7.14) [28]. High levels of vigilance ensured that cheetahs

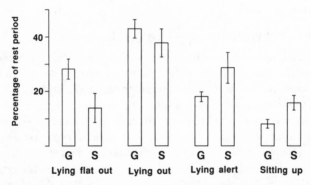

Fig. 7.13 Mean (and SE) percentage of 5-minute scans during the midday rest period that adolescent females in groups (G) (N = 12 individuals) and single adolescent females (S) (N = 8 individuals) spent in different postures.

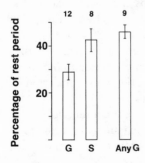

Fig. 7.14 Mean (and SE) percentage of 5-minute scans during the midday rest period that adolescent females in groups (G) (N = 12 individuals), single adolescent females (S) (N = 8 individuals), and any adolescent group member (AnyG) (N = 9 groups) looked at their surroundings.

were rarely surprised by predators, although Laurenson once noted a hyena approaching to within 2 m of a cheetah before being seen.

Reduction in individual vigilance without lowering that of the group occurs in other species (Bertram 1980; Ward 1985) and usually allows individuals to spend more time foraging, as, for instance, in downy woodpeckers (Sullivan 1984). Groups of adolescent cheetahs benefited by being more relaxed during the rest period, however, not because of increased foraging. In some species, individuals benefit from grouping by detecting danger earlier than solitary individuals (Lazarus 1979) and can hence escape predators more effectively, as described for wood pigeons escaping from a goshawk (Kenward 1978). Early detection of predators (and prey) was unlikely to be a benefit of grouping for adolescent cheetahs, however, because the proportion of time at least one group member was vigilant did not exceed the proportion of time a singleton was vigilant. Lowering of personal vigilance to the point where groups do not experience improved predator detection has also been reported in house sparrows (Barnard 1980).

WAS SIBGROUP VIGILANCE COORDINATED?

Despite a group-related reduction in personal watchfulness, adolescents did not share vigilance in any systematic way. For example, one individual was no more likely to scan its surroundings during the midday rest period if its partner had closed its eyes. Indeed, the reverse was true; it was more likely that littermates would look up together or that none would look up than would be expected by chance [29]. Periods of vigilance overlapped because group members simultaneously monitored an animal for several minutes as it passed by, and during the long stretches when the group was undisturbed subjects closed their eyes at the same time. My observations provided no hint that a sibgroup member checked whether a littermate was looking up before closing its own eyes.

Sibgroup members did not look in different directions so as to increase the likelihood of detecting prey or predators when they monitored their surroundings at the same time. In four sibgroups, members looked in the same quadrat simultaneously more often than expected by chance, and in the other five there was no evidence of coordination [30]. Resting locations partially explained these findings. If cheetahs lay on a hillside, they could normally scan only down and out, and if they relaxed in the shade of a rock, they could not see behind them. Also, they were all alerted by the same stimuli as described above.

These findings indicate that adolescents did not use a sentinel system in the sense of coordinating their vigilance or taking turns in guarding and alerting group members to danger, although confounding variables such as location and passing animals were not controlled. Thus far, sentinels have been reported only in cooperatively breeding birds and mammals, for example, in Florida scrub jays (McGowan and Woolfenden 1989) and in meerkats (Moran 1984). Individuals living in other sorts of groups apparently distribute their periods of vigilance at random with respect to one another (e.g., Bertram 1980). In line with this, present evidence indicates that female cheetahs reduced their personal vigilance in sibgroups because they felt more relaxed and not because they relied on kin to monitor surroundings in an organized fashion.

Deterrence of Predators

Why might adolescent cheetahs be more relaxed in groups than when they were on their own? Reduction in the threat posed by other predators is a possibility. Fully grown cheetahs were sometimes killed by lions (Burney and Burney 1979), and I had no doubt spotted hyenas could do the same. Adult male cheetahs also killed adolescents (Kuenkel 1978; H. van Lawick, pers. comm.). The data show that spotted hyenas were more likely to approach single cheetahs (including stealing their kills) but to move away from groups (table 7.11) [31]. In contrast, much larger lions never moved off on seeing cheetahs (table 7.11) [32] and could always displace them. Nevertheless, lions were encountered only about a third as often as hyenas (42 vs. 156 encounters with all cheetah age-sex groups except families, including those in which predators' behavior was not recorded). Passing male cheetahs were also affected by group size. Males were somewhat less likely to approach groups than to approach single conspecifics [33]. Having seen members of male groups launch attacks on

TABLE 7.11 Behavior of Spotted Hyenas and Lions upon Seeing Cheetahs

	Approach	Stay or pass by	Move away
Spotted hyenas			
Single cheetahs	28	9	1
Groups of cheetahs	23	12	12
Lions			
Single cheetahs	10	6	0
Groups of cheetahs	7	1	0

Note: The number of times each predator (either alone or in groups) approached, stayed resting or passed by, or actively moved away from cheetahs was separated according to whether cheetahs were alone or in a group. To increase sample sizes adolescent, young adult, and adult cheetahs of both sexes were combined, but families of cheetahs were excluded because they contained vulnerable cubs (see Laurenson, in press-b). Instances in which hyenas and lions failed to see the cheetahs were excluded. Complementary data on interactions between cheetahs were not available.

cheetahs from different directions, I assumed that a group of adolescents could attack a predator in the same way, although I never witnessed such a fight. If so, a spotted hyena or male cheetah must have been intimidated by an adolescent group, since they were roughly the same size as each of its members.

I had no evidence as to whether adolescent groups were more likely to be seen by predators than single adolescents; they rested for equivalent proportions of the day, so this seemed unlikely [34]. I suspect discovery was primarily related to whether the cheetahs had a kill and vultures were present. It is important to note that the antipredator benefits of grouping did not accrue as a result of the cheetahs' behavior, but as a consequence of predators' differential response to the cheetahs' group size. For when adolescent female cheetahs in groups were compared with those living alone, the former were no bolder toward spotted hyenas or lions than the latter [35].

CONCLUSIONS

In short, my chief finding was that groups of cheetahs were less likely to be harassed by predators than were single cheetahs. By keeping company, adolescents apparently reduced close encounters with dangerous carnivores and consequently lowered their chances of injury or death compared with adolescents living alone. In addition, if a group was actually attacked, each individual would have a reduced probability of being the victim since some would almost certainly escape (see Kuenkel 1978).

Antipredator benefits derived from grouping are normally examined in potential prey species such as passerines or ungulates. In such cases benefits stem from a reduction in the probability of being the victim of predation (Hamilton 1971; Bertram 1978a), from lowering the success rates of predatory attack through enhanced vigilance (Powell 1974), or even from confusing the predator (Pitcher 1986). More rarely prey may deter predators, but examples are restricted to relatively large prey: muskoxen defending themselves against wolves (Mech 1970) or buffalo against lions (Sinclair 1977). Yet large carnivores must now be added to this list, since their sharp teeth and claws represent a threat equivalent to that of a large bovid, deterring other predators in the same way.

Surprisingly, the informal hypothesis that group living conferred foraging benefits on adolescents was not supported: though adolescent group members tackled larger prey, they had to share it among themselves. Finally, turning to speculation, since females in sibgroups were more relaxed and less vigilant than adolescents living alone, it is conceivable that the associated reduction in stress allowed them to grow faster and so reproduce earlier. While I have absolutely no information on this, if true, it would be an additional benefit over and above the antipredator consequences of temporary group living. Zoological institutions could provide valuable data on the relationship between activity, growth, and reproduction.

Reasons for the Dissolution of Sibgroups

Littermates were never seen parting company, but the Frames saw two sisters together leave their sister and brother before becoming solitary themselves (Frame and Frame 1981). This indicated that sibgroups could split up in a piecemeal fashion. Two pieces of evidence suggested that females must have left their brothers rather than vice versa. First, females were the principal instigators of group movements in mixed-sex litters, with males following their sisters' lead (chap. 5). They were hungrier than males and often tried to rouse the group when distant herds of gazelles appeared (chap. 5; fig. 7.15). I suspect that females' greater hunger stemmed from their smaller body size and reduced stomach capacity compared with males, not because they were displaced from kills. In all four mixed-sex sibgroups I observed feeding, females spent a lower proportion of time on the carcass than their brothers, despite incidents of aggression being absent or very low. I noticed also that their belly sizes declined at a faster rate after meals.

Second, I was impressed that females were less concerned about maintaining contact with their brothers than vice versa. In two situations I found members of a sibling group apart and, by luck, could keep track of all participants. In the first, a female and her two brothers moved off, leaving a third, probably ill, brother resting some 1.5 km away. At the end of the day it was the two males that returned to their brother, with their sister lagging some way behind. In the second incident, I saw a male calling for his sister 400 m away for 10 minutes, but she did not call to him.

From an ultimate standpoint, there were no foraging benefits to females taking up a solitary existence, as shown in this chapter, and there were costs, since females on their own were at greater risk from predators. Thus an additional cost of group membership must have arisen to force females to quit their siblings, the most plausible of which is avoidance of mating with brothers (Packer 1979). Yet the limited demographic data presented in chapter 4 showed that females first conceived successfully 5.7 months after leaving their siblings, and that females did not quit mixed-sex sibgroups earlier than they did all-female groups. Both findings speak against incest being an important concern. On the other hand, reports of adult males pinning down mixed-sex sibling groups and investigating the female (Kuenkel 1978; Frame and Frame 1981) suggest that

Fig. 7.15 Vigilance among sibgroup members. A female scans the surroundings while her three brothers doze in the shade of a kopje during the midday rest period.

some females might have been ready to mate while in the company of brothers. Until we have better data on the onset of both estrus and male mating activity in the wild, and on the timing of separation of littermates from a larger sample, it is difficult to dismiss the sib-mating avoidance hypothesis with any certainty.

Whatever the ultimate factors that promote the breakup of adolescent groups, inbreeding avoidance would probably prevent continued association with brothers once young females became reproductively active. The reasons that adult female cheetahs live alone are under debate (see chap. 12).

Female Philopatry

Once sibgroups split up, daughters remained within their natal range (figs. 7.16 and 7.17). Sons showed a similar pattern, at least initially, and I once saw a pair of brothers meet up with their sister 3 months after all were last seen together (although I did not know the exact date of separation). Instead of gingerly approaching and sniffing each other's noses as siblings did after losing each other for a few hours (see Frame and Frame 1981 for an excellent photograph), the brothers chased their sister and one slapped and bit her, reminiscent of males' behavior toward other females (chap. 11).

Once daughters became solitary, their ranges overlapped their mother's by 61.8% ($N = 6$ daughters, SE $= 8.9\%$) (see figs. 7.16, 7.17, and 7.18). Figure 7.19 shows that the ranges of two female full siblings also overlapped by an average of 73.1%. Frame and Frame (unpublished data) suggested that sororal range overlap fell between 30% and 90%. Ranges

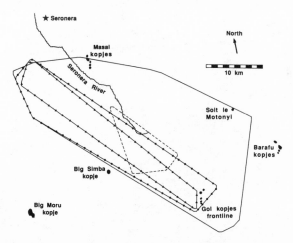

Fig. 7.16 Location of a mother's range (solid line), and her offspring's ranges, first as a sibgroup (dashed line) 53 to 57 days after last being seen with their mother, and subsequently when the pair of sons (solid triangles) and the daughter (solid circles) had separated (136 to 265 days and 135 to 550 days respectively after last being seen with their mother). None were radio-collared. Topography as in fig. 2.11.

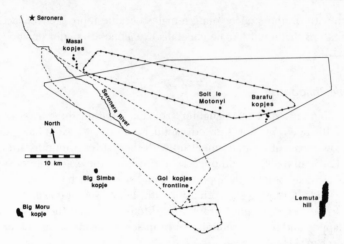

Fig. 7.17 Location of a mother's range (solid line), and her offspring's ranges, first as a sibgroup (dashed line) 23 to 287 days after last being seen with their mother, and subsequently when the trio of sons (solid triangles) and the daughter (solid circles) had separated (332 to 448 days and 372 to 790 days respectively after last being seen with their mother). Only the mother was radio-collared. Topography as in fig. 2.11.

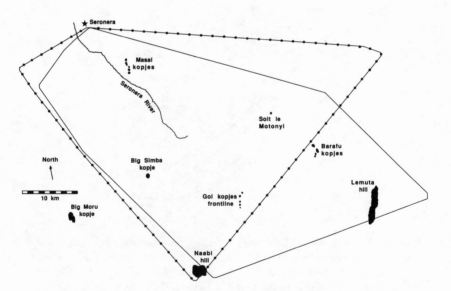

Fig. 7.18 Home ranges of a mother (solid line) from 19 September 1987 to 30 May 1990 and her daughter (solid circles) from 25 June 1987 to 22 July 1990. Both were radio-collared. Topography as in fig. 2.11.

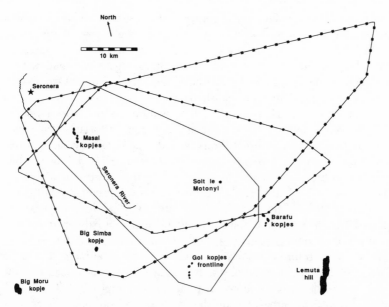

Fig. 7.19 Home ranges of a mother (solid line) from 14 February 1986 to 11 July 1990 and two of her daughters from the same litter, the first from 6 November 1988 to 27 May 1990 (solid circles), and the second from 1 May 1989 to 15 July 1990 (solid squares). All were radio-collared. Topography as in fig. 2.11.

of females belonging to the same matriline did not appear to overlap more than ranges of nonrelatives (compare figs 5.15 and 7.19 for example), although I did not test this systematically. Females probably benefited from philopatry through their familiarity with seasonal distributions of Thomson's gazelles and possibly through knowledge of predator distributions, potential lair sites, and dry season water supplies, each of which might promote cub survival.

Male Dispersal

Some males stayed in their natal range until they were 3 years old, whereas others moved away as described by Frame (1984). Figure 7.17 shows the area covered by three males 332 to 448 days after they were last seen with their mother; their sister, seen over more than three times as long a time period, was far more philopatric. These males moved to the southeastern portion of Gol kopjes and remained there from February to June 1989, scent-marking occasionally, possibly with a view to setting up residence. I did not consider them residents because the trio was very young, it did not remain there or return next wet season, and this area was never used by other males as a territory over the course of the study. Unfortunately, these males were not sighted again, but Frame has presented important records to show that territorial males eventually set up residence some distance from their natal range (18 km and 20 km, Frame 1984; Frame and Frame, unpublished data).

Regarding nonterritorial males, there is little evidence for or against their moving away from the natal range. Two nonterritorial, sexually mature singletons from different litters ranged over areas they had covered with their sibgroups. I did not know the extent of their natal ranges, but extensive overlap between sibgroup and natal ranges in other families (see figs. 7.16 and 7.17) suggested that these males' adult ranges might have overlapped those of their mothers and sisters. Ordinarily, however, I expected that independent males would be unable to determine their chances of becoming resident without consulting the local demography, and would therefore check areas away from their natal range, as would future territory holders. Also, sightings indicated that most males, especially nonresidents, were more shy than females, implying that they had arrived from natal areas outside the study area where encounters with tourists were minimal. Both arguments led me to conclude that virtually all males emigrated from their natal range. If this is correct, then the cheetah's genetic monomorphism cannot be attributed to contemporary inbreeding between close relatives.

WHY DO MALE CHEETAHS DISPERSE?

In common with most mammals, then, male cheetahs dispersed while females were the more philopatric sex (Clutton-Brock 1989a). Why did males leave? Inbreeding avoidance is probably the evolutionary cause of sex-biased dispersal in cheetahs as in other birds and mammals (Cockburn, Scott, and Scotts 1985). Though cheetahs show a marked lack of genetic variability compared with other species, polymorphisms are detectable using two-dimensional polyacrylamide gels (O'Brien et al. 1983), and moderate levels of genetic diversity are apparent in portions of mitochondrial DNA (Menotti-Raymond and O'Brien 1993). The frequency of polymorphic loci was 4% and average heterozygosity was 0.014 in East African individuals (O'Brien et al. 1987). Any genetic variability opens up the possibility that the benefits of outbreeding could outweigh the high mortality suffered by incoming males when trying to gain access to a territory (chap. 8). On a more proximate level, sightings data show that adolescent males avoid territories held by residents (chap. 8), so harassment by males or competition for territories might force males to disperse (Dobson 1982). Even males still in mixed-sex sibgroups were chased and killed by residents (Kuenkel 1978; H. van Lawick, pers. comm.). Harassment specifically from fathers (Moore and Ali 1984) seemed unlikely as males must have encountered them infrequently in the course of their ranging. In conclusion, inbreeding avoidance as well as competition for mates and harassment by males are all candidate causes of male-biased dispersal in this species.

Summary

1. When cubs left their mother, their concealed approach toward prey and their abilities to chase prey at high speed and knock it over were all poorly developed. Dramatic improvements occurred over the next 2 years.

2. Prey preferences showed little change between adolescent, young adult, and adult females. All hunted Thomson's gazelles in approximately three-quarters of their hunts, as summarized in app. 8. Adolescent and young females pursued a variety of inappropriate prey in addition to the usual species.

3. Some evidence indicated that hunting success increased with age. Prey larger than neonate gazelles or hares made up a significantly greater proportion of the kills of older females.

4. Adolescent and young females were seen by prey when approaching more often than were adults, and on many occasions did not dare complete their hunts or secure prey efficiently.

5. Younger females had smaller belly sizes than adult females, especially during the dry season. They were hungrier than adults, and adolescents, in particular, spent a greater proportion of time moving and monitoring their surroundings.

6. The behavior of adolescents living with littermates and female adolescents living alone was compared. Those in groups attempted to capture larger prey, which resulted in these items making up a greater proportion of their kills (see app. 8).

7. Members of sibgroups normally hunted prey together although this had no effect on hunting success. Simultaneous chasing, however, enabled one group member to take over the chase and topple prey if its partner held back.

8. Per capita foraging success of females in adolescent groups was no greater than that of single adolescents, however, because members of sibgroups had to share food. Foraging efficiency cannot explain why female adolescents continued to remain with brothers and sisters.

9. Adolescent females in groups were more relaxed and less vigilant than females living alone, although overall group vigilance matched that

of singletons. Group members did not appear to monitor their surroundings in an organized sentinel system.

10. Cheetahs in groups were less likely to be harassed by spotted hyenas and by male cheetahs than were single cheetahs, lowering the chances of sibgroup members being injured by these predators. Antipredator benefits can explain continued association between cheetah littermates after independence.

11. Females seemed less concerned about losing contact with their littermates than were males and may have eventually left their brothers on account of greater hunger. There are insufficient data to assess the ultimate reasons that sibgroups broke up, although incest avoidance is a candidate.

12. Sibgroups remained mostly within their natal range. After littermates split up, daughters' ranges overlapped with their mothers' by 61.8%, but sons moved out of their natal range, probably to avoid inbreeding.

Statistics

1. Percentage of hunting attempts made on prey that weighed more than 10 kg by adolescent (60.7%, $N = 89$ attempts), young adult (75.9%, $N = 83$ attempts), and adult females (61.6%, $N = 73$ attempts), G test, $G_2 = 5.548$, $P = .068$.

2. Percentage of hunts on hares and neonate gazelles by adolescent ($N = 5$ individuals), young adult ($N = 7$ individuals), and adult females ($N = 8$ individuals) that were successful, $\bar{X}s = 84.3\%$, 85.7%, and 100.0% respectively, Kruskal-Wallis test, $H = 5.925$, df = 2, $P = .052$.

Percentage of hunts on prey other than hares and neonates by adolescent ($N = 5$ individuals), young adult ($N = 10$ individuals), and adult females ($N = 10$ individuals) that were successful, $\bar{X}s = 0.9\%$, 11.6%, and 13.8% respectively, Kruskal-Wallis test, $H = 1.251$, df = 2, $P > .5$.

3. Percentage of kills that were prey other than hares or neonate gazelles made by adolescent (7.7%, $N = 26$ kills), young adult (25.9%, $N = 27$ kills), and adult females (44.8%, $N = 29$ kills), G test, $G_2 = 10.478$, $P = .008$.

4. Estimated distance in meters that hunts started from prey other than neonate gazelles or hares, comparing young adult ($N = 4$ individuals) and adult females ($N = 4$ individuals) seen to hunt five or more times, $\bar{X}s = 139.6$, 81.7 m respectively, t test, $t = 2.15$, $P = .075$.

Comparing adolescent ($N = 3$ individuals) and adult females ($N = 4$ individuals) seen to hunt five or more times, $\bar{X}s = 137.3$, 81.7 m respectively, $t = 1.84$, $P > .1$.

5. Percentage of hunts that failed because prey saw the cheetah: ado-

lescent and young adult females combined (41.4%, N = 128 hunts) and adult females (24.3%, N = 37 hunts), G test, G_1 = 3.743, P = .059.

6. Percentage of hunts that failed because females did not dare catch the prey: adolescent and young adult females combined (8.6%, N = 128 hunts) and adult females (0%, N = 37 hunts), Fisher test, P = .055.

7. Estimated distance in meters that adolescent (N = 3 individuals), young adult (N = 4), and adult females (N = 3) seen to hunt five or more times abandoned their hunts of prey other than neonate gazelles and hares, $\bar{X}$s = 73.6, 56.5, 38.2 m respectively, $F_{2,8}$ = 4.597, P = .047 on logged data.

8. Percentage of hunts in which adolescent (N = 65 hunts), young adult (N = 71 hunts), and adult females (N = 43 hunts) showed different patterns of hunting behavior; hunts of neonate gazelles and hares were excluded. Stalking, 81.5%, 74.6%, 76.7% respectively, G test, G_2 = 0.970, P > .6.

Crouching, 33.8%, 33.8%, 41.9% respectively, G_2 = 0.905, P > .6.
Trotting, 35.4%, 32.9%, 27.9% respectively, G_2 = 0.671, P > .7.
Rushing, 29.2%, 26.8%, 25.6% respectively, G_2 = 0.195, P > .9.
Chasing, 33.9%, 47.9%, 25.6% respectively, G_2 = 0.894, P > .6.

9. Frequency with which adolescent (N = 5 individuals), young adult (N = 8 individuals), and adult females (N = 7 individuals) watched for 12 or more hours hunted per daylight hour, $\bar{X}$s = 0.31, 0.36, 0.24 hunts/hr respectively, Kruskal-Wallis test, H = 1.141, df = 2, P > .4.

10. Comparison of kilograms ingested per daylight hour for adolescent (N = 5 individuals), young adult (N = 8 individuals), and adult females (N = 7 individuals) watched for 12 or more hours, $\bar{X}$s = 0.11, 0.09, 0.15 kg/hr respectively, Kruskal-Wallis test, H = 2.934, df = 2, P > .2.

11. Average belly sizes of adolescent (N = 8 individuals), young adult (N = 11 individuals), and adult females (N = 15 individuals), $\bar{X}$s = 5.7, 5.9, 7.7 respectively, $F_{2,31}$ = 3.066, P = .061, on logged data.

Adolescents vs. young, t test, t = -0.32, P > 0.7; young vs. adults, t = -1.99, P = .058; adolescents vs. adults, t = -1.92, P = .068 on logged data.

12. Belly sizes of females taken from sightings, wet season: adolescent (N = 13 sightings), young adult (N = 30 sightings), and adult females (N = 153 sightings), $\bar{X}$s = 6.3, 7.4, 6.9 respectively, Kruskal-Wallis test, H = 1.658, P > .3.

Dry season: (Ns = 15, 21, 144 sightings respectively), $\bar{X}$s = 4.7, 6.9, 6.1 respectively, H = 9.042, P < .02.

13. Percentage of sightings that adolescent (N = 28 sightings), young adult (N = 51 sightings), and adult females (N = 297 sightings) had belly sizes of 4 or less on the scale of 1 to 14, 39.3%, 13.7%, 25.3% respectively, G test, G_2 = 6.684, P = .038; adolescents vs. young, G = 6.477, P = .010;

young vs. adults, $G = 3.551$, $P = .073$; adolescents vs. adults, $G = 2.404$, $P = .108$.

14. Percentage of 15-minute scans adolescent ($N = 4$ individuals), young adult ($N = 7$ individuals), and adult females ($N = 6$ individuals) watched for two or more days spent observing, $\bar{X}$s $= 25.8\%, 17.6\%, 18.2\%$ respectively, $F_{2,14} = 2.576$, $P > .1$; adolescents vs. young, $t = 2.58$, $P = .030$; young vs. adults, $T = -0.18$, $P > .8$; adolescents vs. adults, $t = 1.67$, $P > .1$.

Percentage of 15-minute scans adolescent ($N = 8$ individuals), young adult ($N = 11$ individuals), and adult females ($N = 14$ individuals) spent moving, $\bar{X}$s $= 12.1\%, 9.5\%, 6.3\%$ respectively, $F_{2,30} = 1.827$, $P > .1$; adolescents vs. young, $t = 0.74$, $P > .4$; young vs. adults, $t = 1.05$, $P > .3$; adolescents vs. adults, $t = 2.29$, $P = .033$.

Percentage of 15-minute scans adolescent, young adult, and adult females spent resting (Ns as for moving), $\bar{X}$s $= 60.8\%, 64.4\%, 70.4\%$ respectively, $F_{2,30} = 0.943$, $P > .4$; adolescents vs. young, $t = -0.55$, $P > .5$; young vs. adults, $t = -0.83$, $P > .4$; adolescents vs. adults, $t = -1.30$, $P > .2$.

15. Percentage of hunting attempts that were made on prey other than hares or neonate gazelles by single adolescents (71.0%, $N = 100$ attempts) and adolescent groups (87.2%, $N = 172$ attempts), G test, $G_1 = 10.550$, $P = .001$ (see table 7.7).

16. Number of hunts per hour made by single adolescents ($N = 5$ individuals) and adolescent groups ($N = 8$ groups) watched for 12 or more hours, $\bar{X}$s $= 0.31, 0.27$, Mann-Whitney U test, $U = 17$, $P > .1$.

17. Hunting success on hares and neonate gazelles for single adolescents ($N = 5$ individuals) and adolescent groups ($N = 4$ groups), $\bar{X}$s $= 84.3\%, 100.0\%$, Mann-Whitney U test, $U = 4$, $P > .1$.

Hunting success on prey other than hares or neonate gazelles for single adolescents ($N = 5$ individuals) and adolescent groups ($N = 9$ groups), $\bar{X}$s $= 0.9\%, 8.7\%$, $U = 13$, $P > .1$.

18. Sibgroup hunts failed because a member started its rush too early more often than did those of single adolescents, G test, $G_1 = 9.143$, $P = .047$ (see table 7.8).

19. Hunting success on all types of prey for sibgroups when members hunted simultaneously (23.6%, $N = 89$ hunts) or hunted alone (15.9%, $N = 44$ hunts), G test, $G_1 = 1.085$, $P > .3$.

20. Hunting success on prey larger than neonate gazelles or hares for sibgroups when members chased prey simultaneously (52.4%, $N = 21$ hunts) or chased prey alone (15.0%, $N = 20$ hunts), G test, $G_1 = 6.671$, $P = .012$ (see table 7.9).

Hunting success on neonates or hares for sibgroups was 100% whether members chased them simultaneously (N = 10 hunts) or chased them alone (N = 5 hunts).

21. Hunting success was 100% whether prey was contacted by more than one sibgroup member (N = 9 hunts) or by one member only (N = 19 hunts).

22. Percentage of kills that were prey other than hares or made by single adolescents (7.7%, N = 26 kills) and adolescent groups (46.2%, N = 39 kills), G test, G_1 = 12.305, P = .001.

23. Percentage of time that single adolescent females (N = 8 individuals) and females in sibgroups (N = 12 individuals) spent eating per daylight hour watched, 5.3%, 2.8%, Mann-Whitney U test, U = 35, P > .1.

Number of kilograms of meat eaten per hour for single adolescent females (N = 5 individuals) and for females in sibgroups (N = 11 individuals) watched for 12 or more hours, $\bar{X}s$ = 0.11, 0.10 kg/hr respectively, Mann-Whitney U test, U = 24, P > .7.

24. Average belly sizes of single adolescent females (N = 8 individuals) and females in sibgroups (N = 12 individuals), $\bar{X}s$ = 5.7, 6.3, Mann-Whitney U test, U = 41, P > .1.

Standard deviations in belly sizes of single adolescent females (N = 4 individuals) and females in sibgroups (N = 9 individuals) seen three or more times, $\bar{X}s$ of SDs = 1.6, 1.7, U = 16, P > .1.

25. Percentage of sightings in which belly sizes were 4 or less for single adolescent females (N = 28 sightings) and females in sibgroups (N = 47 sightings), 39.3%, 40.4%, G test, G_1 = 0.001, P > .9.

26. Percentage of 15-minute scans that single adolescent females (N = 8 individuals) and females in sibgroups (N = 12 individuals) spent observing during the day, $\bar{X}s$ = 19.1%, 10.8%, t test, t = 2.52, P = .022.

27. Percentage of midday rest period that single adolescent females (N = 8 individuals) and adolescent females in sibgroups (N = 12 individuals) spent lying flat out, $\bar{X}s$ = 13.9%, 28.2% respectively, t test, t = −2.30, P = .033.

Lying out, $\bar{X}s$ = 37.8%, 42.9% respectively, t = −1.12, P > .2 on logged data.

Lying alert, $\bar{X}s$ = 28.6%, 18.1% respectively, t = 1.87, P = .077 on logged data.

Sitting up, $\bar{X}s$ = 15.8%, 8.1% respectively, t = 2.66, P = .016.

28. Percentage of midday rest period single adolescent females (N = 8 individuals) and females in sibgroups (N = 12 individuals) spent observing their surroundings, $\bar{X}s$ = 42.4%, 28.9% respectively, t test, t = 2.45, P = .025.

Percentage of midday rest period single adolescent females (N = 8 individuals) and *any* adolescent group member (N = 9 groups) spent observing their surroundings, $\bar{X}$s = 42.4%, 46.0% respectively, $t = -0.682$, $P > .5$.

29. Number of 5-minute scans during the midday rest period when both sibgroup members or neither of them were looking up at the same time, and the number each was looking up by itself were entered into a 2 × 2 table. Most sibgroup members were more likely to be looking up or not to be looking up at the same time than expected by chance. G tests for 4 MF sibgroups: (a) $G_1 = 13.040$, $P = .0003$; (b) $G_1 = 29.284$, $P = .0001$; (c) $G_1 = 48.588$, $P = .0001$; (d) $G_1 = 20.344$, $P = .0001$; and one FF sibgroup (e) $G_1 = 19.683$, $P = .0001$.

G tests and Fisher tests for 2 MMF sibgroups comparing each sibgroup member with each other one separately, (f) $G_1 = 41.270$, $P = .0001$; $G_1 = 42.598$, $P = .0001$; $G_1 = 63.745$, $P = .0001$, (g) Fisher tests $P = .011$, $P = .036$, $P = .019$; and one FFF sibgroup (h) $G_1 = 13.590$, $P = .0001$; $G_1 = 16.999$, $P = .0001$; $G_1 = 5.726$, $P = .01$.

Fisher tests for 1 MMMF sibgroup comparing each member with each other one separately (i) $P = .039$; $P > .4$; $P = .029$; $P = .005$; $P = .026$; $P = .009$.

30. Sibgroup members looked in the same quadrat more often than expected by chance in four sibgroups (expected values: same 0.25, different 0.75). Binomial test $z = 2.177$, $P < .03$; $\chi^2 = 7.348$, df = 1, $P < .01$; binomial test $z = 2.177$, $P < .03$; $\chi^2 = 9.012$, df = 1, $P < .01$; and in five no coordination was found, $\chi^2 = 1.333$, df = 1, $P > .2$; binomial test $z = .447$, $P > .6$; binomial test $z = -1.000$, $P > .3$; $\chi^2 = 0.067$, df = 1, $P > .7$; $\chi^2 = 0.008$, df = 1, $P > .9$.

31. The number of times spotted hyenas approached, stayed resting or passed by, or moved away from independent cheetahs was affected by whether cheetahs were alone or in a group, G test, $G_2 = 7.608$, $P = 0.042$ (see table 7.11).

32. The number of times lions approached, vs. the number of times they stayed resting, passed by, or moved away (combined) from independent cheetahs was unaffected by whether cheetahs were alone or in a group, Fisher test, $P > 0.1$ (see table 7.11).

33. Male cheetahs approached single cheetahs 29 times but groups of cheetahs 16 times, binomial test $z = -1.789$, $P = .073$.

34. Percentage of 15-minute scans that single adolescent females ($N = 8$ individuals) and females in sibgroups ($N = 12$ individuals) spent resting during the day, $\bar{X}$s = 60.8%, 68.1%, $t = -1.41$, $P > .1$.

35. Responses of single adolescent females to spotted hyenas were to approach or watch them on 68% of occasions but to move away on 32% ($N = 25$ occasions), whereas sibgroups did this on 77.6% and 22.5% of 49 occasions respectively, G test, $G_1 = 0.775$, $P > .3$.

Responses of single adolescent females to lions were to approach or watch them on 50.0% of occasions but to move away on 50.0% ($N = 8$ occasions), whereas sibgroups did this on 60.0% and 40.0% of 5 occasions respectively, Fisher test, $P > .4$.

Responses to male cheetahs were too few to test.

A pair of resident males sniff a low kopje before urinating on it themselves. (Drawing by Dafila Scott.)

8
THE MATING SYSTEM

For females, the principal factor limiting reproductive success is access to resources. For males, which can potentially inseminate many mates, reproductive success is instead limited by access to females (Bradbury and Vehrencamp 1977; Emlen and Oring 1977; Wrangham 1980; Clutton-Brock 1988). This difference is especially striking in mammals, in which pregnancy and lactation impose great energetic demands on females but not on males (Gittleman and Thompson 1988). Mammalian mating systems are therefore determined largely by the way in which resources essential to female reproduction influence female dispersion in space and time.

Clutton-Brock (1989b) has outlined a framework of contingencies necessary to explain the diversity of mating systems in mammals. Aside from a small minority of mammals in which paternal care is a prerequisite for offspring survival, forcing males to be monogamous (Kleiman 1977), males do not assist in rearing young. In most species a male either defends resources on which a group of females depend (resource defense polygyny or promiscuity), as, for example, when a male yellow-bellied marmot defends a feeding territory belonging to a group of females (Armitage and Downhower 1974); or defends the ranges of several single females (most carnivores: Macdonald 1983). If, however, female groups are unstable, or females are solitary and their ranges too large to be defended, males defend dispersed or clumped mating territories within a portion of females' home ranges. For example, male pronghorn defend discontinuous territories that are visited by small groups of females (Kitchen 1974), while solitary female white rhinoceroses visit clumped male territories (Owen-Smith 1975). In some species in which females form stable groups, however, males defend small groups of females (harem defense polygyny or promiscuity) (red deer: Clutton-Brock, Guinness, and Albon 1982) or large groups (buffalo: Sinclair 1977). In those species in which females mate during migration, males may defend individual females, small harems, or temporary territories for as long as they can (e.g., wildebeest: Watson 1969), or set up leks which females visit in order to mate (e.g., Uganda kob: Buechner 1961). Finally, if females are solitary or live at a low population density, males may search for estrous females over wide areas, briefly consorting with them and defending them against rivals (e.g., orangutans: MacKinnon 1974).

Female group size and female ranging patterns, overlaid by the degree to which females breed synchronously (Gosling 1986), are the principal factors determining whether males defend feeding or mating territories, defend females themselves, form temporary territories, or roam in search of receptive females (Sandell and Liberg 1992). In the first part of this chapter, females' ranging patterns are documented in order to provide the background to which male cheetahs' defense systems can be related.

Serengeti cheetahs are promiscuous. Males associate with females only at mating, provide no parental care, and attempt to mate with as many females as possible. Females live alone (chap. 3); range over wide areas (Frame 1984); breed throughout the year (chap. 4), although more conceptions occur in wet season months; and almost certainly mate with different males over successive breeding attempts. If they encounter a group of males, they may mate with more than one during a single period of receptivity (Caro and Collins 1987b). Since female cheetahs in the Serengeti are solitary, migratory, and live at low densities (Myers 1975a), it is difficult to predict in advance the type of mating system shown by males, except to guess that males are perhaps likely to employ more than one tactic to secure matings.

Previous studies of some carnivores have found that males use more than one behavioral tactic. In some species, males may either hold an exclusive territory or move and mate over a wide area shared with other males (e.g., martens: Taylor and Abrey 1982; North American lynxes: Bailey et al. 1986; see Lott 1991 for a review). In most studies, however, transient males are mentioned only in passing and resident males holding an exclusive territory are assumed to achieve most of the matings. If, however, female density declines, a threshold will be reached when it pays a male to move around in search of receptive females rather than sequestering a diminished number of females on his territory (Liberg and Sandell 1988; Sandell 1989; Whitehead 1990). In partial support of this conclusion, recent studies have shown that transient males include adults as well as young immigrants and that roaming males can achieve the majority of matings in at least some species (brown hyenas: Mills 1982; stoats: Sandell 1986).

Previous publications on Serengeti cheetahs (Caro and Collins 1986, 1987a,b; Durant et al. 1988) reported that males did indeed show more than one behavioral tactic, with some holding a territory and some roaming over large areas, and that male territories were centered on areas where females temporarily aggregated during the course of their extensive annual movements. Nevertheless, many questions and obvious omissions remained in these earlier publications. First, and most important, female densities inside and outside territories were not known with certainty because data on sightings of females were not controlled for observers' visits to different areas. If, for instance, males' territories were scanned for females more often than other areas, the number of sightings there would be inflated. Second, territories were not occupied continuously. There were long periods when no males were found in areas previously patrolled by residents, and several years into the study males took up residence in areas that were previously unoccupied, implying that the benefits of territoriality might change over time. Third, nonterritorial males moved through territories, calling into question the effectiveness of territorial behavior altogether.

After data on female ranging are presented, the potential reproductive benefits of territoriality for males are therefore reevaluated using a more extensive data set spanning 10 years. The distribution of females now takes account of the number of observers' visits to territories and other parts of the study area, thereby removing an important source of potential bias. As a necessary preamble, however, differences in behavior, physiology, longevity, and patterns of ranging between territorial and nonterritorial males are compared. Finally, the cheetah's peculiar mating system is described and discussed in the light of current theory.

Female Ranging Behavior

The average size of a female home range was 833.0 km² ($N = 19$ home ranges, SE = 85.1; see app. 9). During the wet season, most females in the study area were found on the intermediate or short grass plains. As figure 8.1 shows, they moved into the Ngorongoro Conservation Area east of Barafu kopjes, some as far as Lemuta Hill (see also fig. 7.17), as well as south of Gol kopjes. In the dry season, females moved northwest into the Seronera area and remained there from July to September, but some moved farther west into the woodlands (see female 3 in fig. 8.1). Their ranging followed the Thomson's gazelle movements on and off the plains (see Durant et al. 1988 for a discussion). In general, the majority of wet season sightings were on the plains, whereas dry season sightings were near the plains-woodland border (see female 1 in fig. 8.1). Nonetheless, there were numerous exceptions, depending on the time the gazelles started their migration, whether females were restricted to a lair, and possibly, individual differences between females. As examples of this last point, Laurenson and I found one female only in the vicinity of Gol kopjes (the mother with the most southerly range in fig. 5.15) and another only around Seronera, irrespective of season, but we were unsure whether these ranges represented the complete extent of their movements because of difficulties with radiotelemetry. Females' annual movements therefore showed broad predictability although their individual movements varied according to local conditions.

Females exhibited a variety of movement patterns within their ranges, from walking only a few hundred meters during the day, especially if they had eaten a large meal, to moving locally and hunting for several weeks in an area of roughly 30 km², then traveling 5–10 km to another area in the course of a day or so. I noted a mother and four recently emerged 2-month-old cubs covering 12 km in a 12.5-hour stretch in this way. Fe-

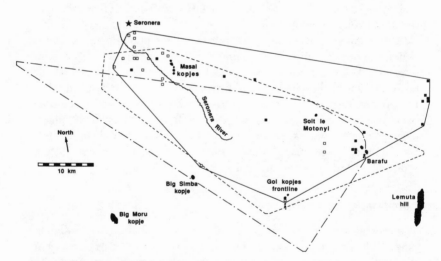

Fig. 8.1 Location and size of the home ranges of three representative females living in the Serengeti over the same time period. Female 1 (solid line), 20 October 1986 to 8 November 1989; grid squares in which the first sighting of the day was made in the wet season (solid squares) and in the dry season (open squares) are shown for this range only. Female 2 (dashed line), 13 October 1986 to 20 April 1989. Female 3 (dashed and dotted line), 3 November 1986 to 27 October 1987. To our knowledge, these females were not relatives. Topography as in fig. 2.11.

males also made longer, sustained treks from one part of their range to another; Laurenson recorded a female traveling 33 km almost due east over 5 days. At the onset of the rains, when the bulk of the gazelle population had left for the plains, small concentrations sometimes remained behind. When these became unprofitable, female cheetahs were forced to move long distances in order to catch up with the larger herds.

Female cheetahs' annual home ranges overlapped extensively (see fig. 8.1), and at certain times of year up to 20 females collected in small, 50-km² areas (see chap. 12 and below). Females did not defend their ranges, although they sometimes marked by urinating and defecating on termite mounds after scanning for prey. I did not get the impression that they sought out termitaria for marking purposes as in Namibia (D. Morsbach as reported to P. Gros, pers. comm.). If during day-to-day movements females noticed each other, they sat and stared from up to 2 km away until one eventually walked off. It was very rare for one to approach another (two cases). I heard only three reports of females sharing carcasses (M. Iwago, K. Laurenson, and J. Root, pers. comms.); one of these was a mother and her independent daughter, both of whom had litters of young cubs.

Except in lions and some domestic cat populations, other female felids also avoid one another (see Leyhausen 1979). In species such as bobcats (Bailey 1974), females actively defend mutually exclusive home ranges (i.e., territories, sensu Burt 1943) whereas in other species, such as servals (Geertsema 1985), female ranges overlap to varying degrees in space but usually not in time (see table 12.2). Variation in territorial defense also occurs within species according to circumstance. Territorial tiger mothers tolerate their daughters staying on within their natal range for several months after they become independent (Sunquist 1981), and in the height of the dry season, lion prides on the Serengeti plains move west into areas normally inhabited and defended by other prides (C. Packer and A. Pusey, pers. comm.).

Resident and Nonresident Males

DEFINITIONS

Territorial (also called resident) males were defined as those males that were repeatedly seen in the same small area of the park over a period of months, and that urine-marked the area. The clearest form of marking occurred when a male positioned himself 1 m or less from a vertical tree trunk or rock surface, lifted his tail to the vertical position, and pointed his penis backward to urinate horizontally or 60° upward, either as a spray or in a single stream of urine. Most often a male would tread with his hindfeet at the same time. Such a male also marked by urinating close to the ground in a semi-squatting position, repeatedly raking the ground with his hindfeet over and around his urine (fig. 8.2). Males urine-marked prominent landmarks throughout their territory, such as solitary trees, rocks and termite mounds far from others, the undersides of trunks and branches of fallen trees, and rocks and bushes on kopjes. Less often, males clawed at trees, or flattened grass by rolling in it as seen in tigers (Smith, McDougal, and Miquelle 1989). They also deposited feces on prominent features, which may have been mixed with anal gland secretions judging from the white mucus that I occasionally noticed. Typically, territorial males would spend up to a minute smelling a landmark intensely and then urinate and defecate on it, either in the morning while moving or in the evening after leaving their daytime resting spot, or both. The same places were visited often, but irregularly, within the course of a month. Middens never built up because feces had normally blown away or had possibly been consumed by vultures. If I had been absent from a territory for several days or weeks, I would start looking for residents near these landmarks.

Nonterritorial males (also called nonresidents or floaters) were defined as individuals that were seen in several different areas of the park, often many kilometers apart. They covered ground at a faster rate than territorial males [1], usually remaining in a small area for just a matter of days. Despite investigating prominences intensely, they urinated and defecated far less frequently than territorial males [2] and failed to seek conspicuous landmarks for this purpose. Instead they squatted in grass or on low termite mounds surrounded by many others [3]. I also had the impression that they raked the ground less vigorously than territorial males. Nonterritorial males consisted of adolescents that had recently achieved independence, young adult and adult males, and old males; territorial males, on the other hand, were never adolescent (Caro and Collins 1987b).

Distinctions between nonterritorial and territorial males were normally clear-cut except for two minor problems. On rare occasions nonresidents scent-marked, making it necessary to observe males several times (not scent-marking) before being completely confident of their status. Second, territorial males sometimes made brief journeys out of their territories, usually for 1 or 2 days but sometimes for up to several weeks. As a digression, I had records of 14 out of 26 residents making 18 excursions in total. On average, these extended 19.5 km (SE = 3.4) from the territorial boundary (excluding one male whose territorial boundary was problematic); one pair of residents traveled 65 km out of their territory. Excursions occurred in both wet (10 instances) and dry seasons (8 instances) and coincided with the territory being devoid of prey and females. Territorial males were found with a female on 2 of the 15 excursions during which they were located on the ground, indicating, perhaps,

Fig. 8.2 A radio-collared resident male urinates on a low rocky outcrop in a semi-squatting position; his left hindleg is raking backward. There were no prominent bushes on this kopje on which to spray-urinate.

that they had left in search of the opposite sex. Males scent-marked in 5 out of 9 excursions on which they were followed for several hours. Although potentially exploring new territories, they failed to settle and quickly returned to their own areas.

These infrequent excursions sometimes made short-term occupancy difficult to interpret. In other words, if I saw a male for whom I had no prior records scent-mark in an area for a month or two but then disappear, I could not always tell whether it was a floating male attempting to establish a territory but failing, or a resident from outside the study area on a brief foray.

I did not investigate cheetah scent marking in great detail, but it had all the characteristics associated with territoriality (Macdonald 1985). Scent marks were deposited in places that increased their chances of being perceived and that roughly corresponded to defended areas, as judged by fights witnessed between male cheetahs. Despite this, some nonresidents still entered territories (see below), in common with many other species (Ralls 1971). This was not a result of intruders being unable to detect scent marks, since even I could smell them at close range. Feces that an adolescent left on the hood of my vehicle adhered to it and gave off a pungent smell 3 days later. After 6 days, they still caught the attention of a young adult male downwind of the Land Rover, although I could no longer detect any odor. Though marking did not deter intruders, it may have intimidated them. I once saw two territorial males investigate a small kopje at the border of their range earlier marked by neighboring residents. Within minutes of sniffing the kopje, they sped back toward the center of their territory.

Richardson (1991) regards scent marks in carnivores as a cheap form of display for residents that conveys the message, "If I catch you in my territory, I will kill you." In species living at low densities where meetings are rare, as in cheetahs or aardwolves, intimidation through scent marking may be the best way of excluding intruders, providing it is backed up intermittently by honest threat. Field and laboratory studies have demonstrated that scent marks can cause anxiety among intruders (Mykytowycz et al. 1976; Macdonald 1979), so there is some basis to this idea. In contrast, in ungulates living at high densities where individuals meet much more frequently, it has been suggested that scent marking may enable the resident to be identified by intruders because they can match his smell to that of the area (Gosling 1982). Thus scent marking in cheetahs probably signaled to nonresidents that the area was occupied and that all cheetahs within it should be avoided (unless they could be unequivocally recognized as female); marks may also have carried additional information about the residents themselves.

BEHAVIORAL DIFFERENCES

Nonterritorial males showed skulking behavior. They often made their extensive movements after dark and were frequently located in tall vegetation. They rarely rested on rocky outcrops where they could be visible to resident cheetahs, who might attack them on sight [4]. If they did rest above the ground, it was at a lower height than residents [4]. For these reasons nonresidents were difficult to locate.

Nonresidents seemed less relaxed than residents, judging from their body postures. Table 8.1 shows that nonresidents spent a lower proportion of the midday rest period lying flat out and a greater proportion lying alert and sitting up than did residents. In short, floaters were ill at ease and tried to remain inconspicuous.

Males may have assumed nonresident status because they had assessed the probability of winning a fight against a resident but decided against trying, at least until demographic conditions or factors such as personal body size changed for the better. That nonresidents weighed less than residents gave some support to this possibility [6]. Alternatively, nonresi-

TABLE 8.1 Mean (and SE) Percentage of 5-Minute Scans that Nonresident and Resident Nonadolescent Male Cheetahs Spent in Different Body Postures during the Midday Rest Period

Body posture	Nonresidents ($N = 9$ individuals)	Residents ($N = 13$ individuals)	t value	P value
Lying flat out	20.0 (3.7)	29.8 (2.1)	−2.32	.031
Lying out	45.9 (5.3)	46.3 (2.3)	−0.09	.932
Lying alert	22.9 (3.1)	15.6 (1.8)	2.15	.044
Sitting up	10.4 (2.3)	5.2 (0.9)	1.99	.060

Source: Caro, FitzGibbon, and Holt 1989.

dents may have attempted but failed to take over a territory in the past or may have been ousted from one. Nonresidents may even have had a reduced probability of winning due to the prior residency advantage found in some territorial species (Davies 1978).

PHYSIOLOGICAL DIFFERENCES

Nonresidents showed elevated cortisol concentrations in a sequence of blood samples taken during a standardized electroejaculation procedure (fig. 8.3), as seen by their significantly higher acute adrenal response up to an hour after the last stimulus [5]. Based on comparative studies of experimentally induced stress, these elevated cortisol levels indicate that nonresidents were physiologically stressed compared with residents, corroborating behavioral observations (see Caro, FitzGibbon, and Holt 1989). Fear of being located and killed by residents may have caused nonresidents' physiological and behavioral stress. The effect of social circumstances on endocrinological parameters has also been documented for free-living baboons (Sapolsky 1987).

MEASURES OF CONDITION

Differences between the two male strategies were also found in hematology studies and measures of condition. Nonresidents had high white blood cell counts compared with residents [7], possibly suggesting a higher level of chronic bacterial or viral infection (fig. 8.4). Nonresidents also had significantly raised eosinophil levels [8], which is a diagnostic feature of a broad range of parasitic infections and allergic respiratory diseases (Schalm, Jain, and Carroll 1985; Duncan and Prasse 1986). Hemoglobin concentrations, red blood cell counts, packed cell volumes, and mean cell volumes did not differ significantly between the two samples, regardless of whether nonresidents that subsequently became territorial were included or not.

Nonresident males were in poor condition compared with resident males (table 8.2). They had thinner vertebral musculature, as measured by palpation of the muscles on either side of the spine [9], the mange on their pinnae was more extensive [10], and 50% had coarse coats as opposed to residents, all of whose coats were in soft and sleek condition [11]. Some of the nonresidents had ulcerated mouths and gingivitis, sebaceous

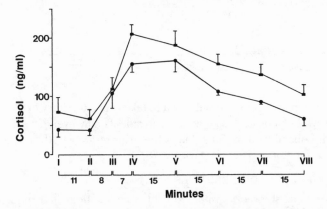

Fig. 8.3 Mean (and SE) serum cortisol concentrations (ng/ml) for four nonresident (squares) and four resident (circles) male cheetahs. Cheetahs were serially bled before (I), during (II, III, IV) and after (V, VI, VII, VIII) electroejaculation. Figures along the x-axis denote the number of minutes between blood samples (see Wildt et al. 1984; Wildt, O'Brien et al. 1987 for details). (From Caro, Fitz-Gibbon, and Holt 1989.)

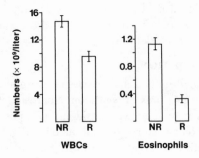

Fig. 8.4 Mean numbers (and SE) of white blood cells (× 10⁹/liter) and eosinophils (× 10⁹/liter) from nonresident (NR) (N = 8 individuals) and resident (R) (N = 5 individuals) male cheetahs (there were no adolescents in either sample).

exudate on the chest and groin, extensive hair loss and mange, a waxy discharge from the ears, or swollen lymph nodes. One individual had severe dermatitis, another had erythematous lesions, and a third had either osteomyelitis or an abscess on its foot.

There is ample evidence from laboratory studies on a broad range of species to show that various stressors such as forced exercise or exposure to cold cause pathogenic responses (Seyle 1971). The hormones secreted during times of physical or psychological stress, adrenaline and glucocorticoids, inhibit the immune system (Munck, Guyre, and Holbrook 1984), and individuals more readily succumb to diseases during periods of chronic immunosuppression. Thus nonresidents' stress may have been an important negative influence on their health.

Nonetheless, it is difficult to determine whether males in poor condition were forced to take on a floating lifestyle because they were unable to mount a serious challenge against residents or, conversely, whether being a nonresident resulted in ill health. Three indirect arguments favor the second hypothesis. First, nonresidents did not appear to be suboptimal individuals. Though lighter than residents, they did not have appreciably smaller linear dimensions [12] nor did they bear physical abnormalities, which respectively might have indicated poor condition during development or congenital ill health. Second, animals in poor condition might be expected to rest extensively in order to recover, yet the opposite was true. Floaters covered much longer distances than did residents (see below) and at a faster rate, which must have exacerbated their poor condition. Third, at least one of the floating males had previously held a territory (see table 8.2), but his residence terminated at about the time his male partner disappeared, so for him at least, poor health was unlikely to have been responsible for his change in status. In short, circumstantial evidence does not support the argument that ill health forced males to float. Rather, it points to males being unable to take over a territory, perhaps for demographic reasons (see chap. 9), and as a consequence experiencing the stress and extensive ranging associated with the floating lifestyle, which in turn resulted in poor condition.

In a number of other mammals males show alternative behavioral tactics (Lott 1991). Some of these are age-dependent, as in elephant seals, in which young males copulate surreptitiously with females while older males hold harems (Le Boeuf 1974). Since no cheetah male became territorial during adolescence, tactics were in part age-related (see Caro and Bateson 1986). This was not surprising since competitive ability in mammals generally improves markedly with age (Poole 1989; Dunbar, Buckland, and Miller 1990). In other mammals the tactic adopted by a given male is contingent upon social and demographic circumstances. Male hamadryas baboons base their decision on whether to take over a

TABLE 8.2 Status and Condition of Nonresident and Resident Male Cheetahs

Number	DPV	Mange	Coat	Condition
Nonresident males that never held a territory				
1.	1.5	4.0	C	Hair loss on chest (exchloriation or mange) with circular erythematous red lesions. Encrustations on all paws, limb joints, ears (also ulcerated). Mange around anus; exudate in groin. Ulcerative gingivitis with papules under tongue, one ulcer on gums, three lower incisors missing; waxy discharge from ears; 37 ticks; lymph nodes swollen.
2.	2.0	0	S	Hair loss at elbow. Inflamed gums on one side, old scar on right thigh, 16 ticks.
3.	2.0	0.5	S	Yellow sebaceous discharge in groin; lesion on left rump; 12 ticks.
4.	2.0	0	S	Calluses on elbows; one tick.
5.	2.0	5.0	S	Osteomyelitis or abcess in swollen left front paw with exudate. Cranial nipples encrusted and enlarged; all legs mangy and encrusted on plantar aspects. Calluses on elbows, shoulder, carpus rump. Two upper incisors missing. Waxy discharge from ears; 43 ticks; lymph nodes swollen.
6.	3.0	0	S	Waxy discharge from ears; 47 ticks including around eyes and penis.
7.	2.0	1.0	S	Puncture wound on chin; 3 ticks.
8.	2.0	1.0	—	10 ticks.
9.	—	—	C?	Mouth and throat ulcerated, otherwise no other data taken.
10.	—	—	—	Hair loss on chest, elbows, shoulder, and base of tail; extensive mange and ticks.
Nonresident males that once held a territory before examination				
11.	1.0	2.0	C	Hair loss on chest, back, right thigh (dermatitis). Upper canines broken with nerves exposed, one remaining incisor broken at gum level; gums inflamed; right side mouth infected; 1 tick; lymph nodes swollen.
Nonresident males that subsequently held a territory after examination				
12.	2.0	3.5	C	Tongue tip missing; two upper and one lower incisor missing. Calluses on elbows; tear in left ear.
13.	2.0	1.0	C	Calluses on elbows; 14 ticks; scar on right flank.
14.	1.0	2.0	C	Calluses on elbows; 4 ticks; 2 wounds on foreleg.
Resident males at time of examination				
15.	3.0	0	S	Right pinna missing. Scar measuring 3.5 × 5 cm on flank but flesh hardened, scar on jaw. Left ear waxy; 8 ticks.
16.	3.0	0	S	38 ticks.
17.	3.0	0	S	Scars on two right paws; upper two incisors missing; slight waxy discharge from ears; 50 ticks.
18.	3.0	0	S	Two upper and one lower incisor missing; 32 ticks.

TABLE 8.2 Continued

Number	DPV	Mange	Coat	Condition
19.	3.0	1.0	S	Four ticks; small scar on knee, one lymph node slightly enlarged.
20.	—	—	—	No data taken.
21.	3.0	0	S	Scar on nose; 13 ticks.
22.	—	0	S	Some scratches on nose and legs.
23.	—	—	—	No data taken. (Vestigial pendulous dewclaws on hindlimbs.)
24.	—	—	—	No data taken.

Note: Adolescents were not included. Unless stated, pelage, eyes, mouth, teeth, ears, and lymph nodes were examined; absence of mention signifies that no abnormality was detected. DPV = Dorsal processes of vertebrae; 3, thick muscle, difficult to palpate; 2, palpable with pressure, 1, vertebrae easily palpable. Mange, average of independent score for each ear. 0, none, through 5, entire pinna covered with sarcoptic infestation. Coat: S, soft; C, coarse. Male 7 was currently a member of a pair; male 11 was formerly a member of a pair, males 13 and 14, 19 and 20, 23 and 24 were each members of a pair; and males 16, 17, and 18 were members of the same trio.

female unit or enter it as a follower on factors such as the proportion of males who are harem-holders and local birth rates (Dunbar 1984). As young adults, cheetahs probably made their reproductive decisions on similar criteria, such as age of current residents or personal body condition, although empirical work is needed in this area. Finally, in common with mammals such as bighorn sheep, in which the same individuals employ different behavioral tactics to secure matings during the rut (Hogg 1984), male cheetahs sometimes switched tactics, for example, shifting from being territorial to floating when they lost a male partner.

DIFFERENCES IN LONGEVITY

It was difficult to determine precisely how long males lived in the wild. Birth dates were usually unknown, although cheetahs could be classified as adolescents, young adults, or adults when first seen (see chap. 3). Unless a male was radio-collared, his disappearance from our records could mean that he had left the study area, either temporarily or permanently, had died and been eaten by scavengers, or simply that we could not find him. Therefore, in order to determine whether males that had disappeared were likely to be sighted again, separate frequency distributions of intersighting intervals were constructed for territorial and nonterritorial males, as intervals differed between them [13]. For each type of male, the mean intersighting interval plus two standard deviations was added to the last date the male was seen, and if this fell before the study terminated (or matchings of that male ceased to be made), the male was presumed to have disappeared permanently from the study area. Judging from the fact that all 16 radio-collared males remained within the study area (except one last located beyond it at time of writing) and that 11 out of 11 died within it irrespective of their status, it was assumed that the great majority of disappearances were the result of deaths within the study area. Males could thus be divided into those that were *known* to have died ($N = 11$ males) and those whose disappearances were so long that they were *presumed* to have died ($N = 26$ males).

Using these methods, estimated minimum ages of the 10 males seen over the longest time period were between 6.0 and 8.4 years ($\bar{X} = 6.9$, SE = 0.2). This corresponded closely to more exact ages of three territorial males whose birth dates were known. Two of these disappeared from their territory when they were 6.2 years old and in a badly wounded state (males A and C: A. Owensen, pers. comm.), while the third vanished from the territory when he was 8.1 years old (male B).

Comparing males of different status, estimated maximum life spans of the three oldest territorial and three oldest nonterritorial males were very similar: 8.1, 7.1, and 6.9; and 8.4, 7.4, and 7.0 years respectively. Territorial males were in better health than nonterritorial males, however, and might therefore be expected to live longer. Table 8.3 shows the average number of days between first and last sighting for males that were resident and nonresident, separated by age category at first sighting. In each category, resident males were resighted over a longer time span than nonterritorial males, significantly so for adults, and for males lumped together irrespective of their age class when first seen [14]. This second result was notable because younger males, who made up a greater proportion of the combined nonresident sample, would be expected to live longer (assuming similar survivorship curves as adults), yet residents were still seen over a longer time frame.

Emigration of nonterritorial males was unlikely to explain these differences, since monthly fixes taken on nine radio-collared floaters showed that they never left the study area (see fig. 8.9). Rather, the results indicate that nonterritorial males lived for shorter spans of time than did residents on the Serengeti plains. Nonterritorial adult males probably had a lower chance of surviving, either as a result of poor health or poor competitive ability. I had definite records of two floaters who died as a result of ill health (not diagnosed) but none of territorials. I had five records of floaters who died in or on the border of an occupied territory, suggesting they had been killed in a fight with a conspecific, but only two of resident males. Nevertheless, the sample size was too small to assess the relative importance of these and other causes of mortality of males of different status. In contrast to these comparisons, there was no evidence that males in groups (those last seen in the company of a male partner) lived longer than single males [15].

TABLE 8.3 Mean ($\pm$ SE) Number of Days between First and Last
Sighting of Males

	Age class when first seen			Irrespective of age class when first seen
	Adolescent	Young adult	Adult	
Residents				
	1,202.0	528.5 $\pm$ 258.5	758.9 $\pm$ 145.7	757.7 $\pm$ 124.2
	($N = 1$)	($N = 2$)	($N = 12$)	($N = 15$)
Nonresidents				
	548.8 $\pm$ 389.7	467.9 $\pm$ 187.4	353.2 $\pm$ 163.1	425.2 $\pm$ 117.3
	($N = 4$)	($N = 7$)	($N = 11$)	($N = 22$)

Note: Residents include males who were or subsequently became resident; nonresidents include males who were nonresidents or subsequently lost their territories and became nonresidents. Only males known to be dead or presumed dead based on the extrapolation method (see text) were included. Groups of males that disappeared together were assigned a single figure, but if one member continued to be sighted, individuals were treated separately. N refers to numbers of groups or individuals. Approximate ages at death can be calculated by adding 504 days to figures for adolescents, 910 days to young adults, and 1,176 days to adults, i.e., their approximate age when they entered that age class.

Very few studies have compared relative longevity associated with different mating tactics. In calculations of the reproductive payoffs of alternative life histories, copulations per unit time are usually reported together with the age at which morphs or subjects using various tactics enter the breeding population (e.g., Shuster and Wade 1991). Termination of breeding is frequently assumed to occur at the same time for all individuals. Since tactics normally incur differential costs (e.g., song sparrows: Arcese and Smith 1985), calculations of relative breeding life span must incorporate measures of longevity to be accurate. For example, male hooknose salmon are reproductively active for 50% longer than jacks, which greatly affects calculations of lifetime fitness for salmon (Gross 1985; van den Berghe and Gross 1986). The same is true of cheetahs, in which resident males were expected to survive, on average, 1.8 times as long as floaters (757.7 vs. 425.2 days: table 8.3).

Location of Territories

Figure 8.5 shows the location and extent of the areas used by all the resident males during the 10-year study period. A number of points emerge from the figure. There were eight foci of territoriality where new residents settled time and again: the base of Oldonya Rongai, Simba kopjes, Naabi Hill, Gol kopjes, the woodlands around Ndutu, and the Zebra–Barafu–Soit le Motonyi kopjes complex; Loliondo kopjes and Hidden Valley were also occupied by males (see fig. 2.11 for locations). Note that

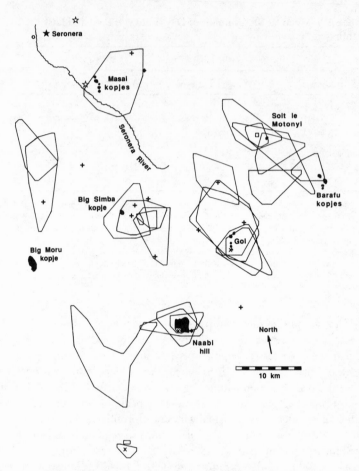

Fig. 8.5 Location and extent of 26 territories on the Serengeti plains, derived by the minimum polygon method for all males that were residents from March 1980 to July 1990. (Hidden Valley territory in the southwest followed drainage lines and consequently was not derived by the minimum polygon method). Territories overlap as a result of sequential, not simultaneous, residence. Occasional long-distance forays made by residents from their core areas were excluded from the polygons. When members of a resident coalition disappeared but other member(s) retained tenure, the combined size of the territory before and after the event is portrayed for the sake of clarity. Also shown are grid squares in which dead cheetahs were found, separated into the following categories to avoid possible bias in number of visits by observers: dead radio-collared males (plus signs, $N = 11$); dead males that were not collared (solid diamonds, $N = 2$), females (open circle, $N = 1$), cheetahs of unknown sex located by chance on the ground (crosses, $N = 3$), and male cheetahs that died after being very ill (open stars, $N = 2$). A pair of males that died close to or within Ndutu territory (P. Moehlman, pers. comm.) is not shown as the exact grid square was not known. Topography as in fig. 2.11.

overlap between territories at these foci signifies sequential, not simultaneous, residence. Even in the northeastern corner of the study area, where three territories at Zebra, Barafu, and Soit le Motonyi were each occupied by a different pair of males at the same time in 1981, there was no spatial overlap between them then. Additionally, at least one group of males occupied a portion of the floor of Ngorongoro Crater (off fig. 8.5 to the southeast). Finally, I had reliable reports of males scent-marking in the woodlands on the north side of Banagi Hill (just northwest of Banagi: P. Swan, pers. comm.) and at the crossing of the first wooded tributary of Olduvai Gorge that is encountered on the road south to Ngorongoro Crater (W. Baker, pers. comm.).

ECOLOGICAL FACTORS ASSOCIATED WITH LOCATION OF TERRITORIES

Thomson's gazelles aggregated on the short grass plains in the wet season, and in the vicinity of Seronera for the first two-thirds of the dry season (fig. 8.6). Within both areas territories were located in places where gazelles were numerous; however, they were not sited specifically in regard to prey concentrations. As reported elsewhere (Caro and Collins 1987a), there were no appreciable differences in abundance of Thomson's gazelles, or presence and absence of Grant's gazelles and wildebeests, inside and outside territories, based on the number of months herds were found there. Furthermore, points outside but immediately adjacent to territorial boundaries did not differ from points inside in the number of months high (>100), medium (11 to 100), or low (0 to 10) numbers of gazelles were found there in either wet or dry seasons, again suggesting that the delineation of boundaries was not simply related to prey concentrations (Caro and Collins 1987a). Although there is inevitable sampling error attached to estimates of local abundance of herbivores, the absence of any association between territory location and gazelle concentrations over a 25-month period suggests that males were not defending feeding territories against other males.

That territories were sequentially occupied in the same areas instead suggested that their siting was contingent more upon constant environmental features, or associated factors, than on the vagaries of prey movements, which differed within and between years according to local rainfall. Common to the territories was vegetation cover, or some associated factor. Oldonya Rongai, Loliondo kopjes, Soit le Motonyi, and Ndutu each included portions of the woodlands as well as plains (similar to the landscape shown in fig. 2.9), while the isolated kopje and drainage systems at Simba, Gol, Zebra, and Barafu, and at Naabi Hill, were all wooded to differing extents (fig. 8.7; see fig. 2.5). The deep drainage of Hidden Valley supported large shrubs, bushes, and thick grassy tussocks. The only possible exception to this pattern was a territory set up for 7 months approximately 5 km north of Gol kopjes, but even this was centered on the Semetu Valley drainage, which contained an occasional tree (see fig. 2.11).

In contrast, males did not set up residence in the large interstices between the territories shown in figure 8.5, such as the "five hills"; or to the east of the park boundary near Southeast kopjes or Merua kopje; or in the "triangle" (see fig. 2.11). These regions were virtually devoid of all trees and bushes although they supported large concentrations of Thomson's gazelles in the wet season (see fig. 8.6). Absence of territories in these areas reinforced the hypothesis that cover was important.

I do not view freestanding water as a key factor in the location of territories because the quantity of rainfall did not differ inside and outside territories (Caro and Collins 1987a). Water could be found everywhere on the plains during the rainy season, while in the second half of the dry

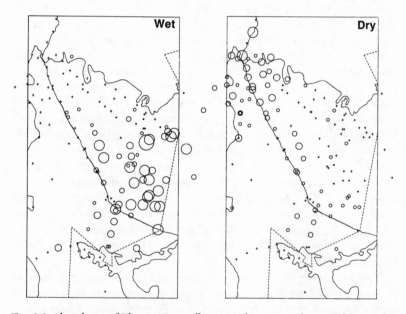

Fig. 8.6 Abundance of Thomson's gazelles at 142 locations, 1 km in radius, on the Serengeti plains during the wet (November to May) and dry (June to October) seasons between February 1982 and July 1985. Each month gazelles were counted and numbers were then divided into seven categories: 1–10, 11–50, 51–100, 101–200, 201–500, 501–1,000, >1,000. Circle sizes represent the median category for monthly counts over all the years that gazelles were counted during that season, increasing in area in proportion to the median number in these categories. Points at which no gazelles were seen are denoted by +. (Note: Gazelles were not counted in the Hidden Valley region.) (From Durant et al. 1988.)

Fig. 8.7 A drainage in Barafu territory, showing low bushes and trees that af-
forded shade. The depression, in which standing water might be found for only
two months of the year, allowed cheetahs to get close to Thomson's gazelles undetected as they fed on the short grass plain in the background. A small kopje with
trees can be seen in the far background.

season it was difficult to find water anywhere on the plains. Only in
months when rain was sparse did water remain in kopjes and drainages on
which territories were sited. While presence of water was probably critical for lactating females (Laurenson 1992, 1993), other cheetahs may have
been able to slake their thirst by lapping blood from the peritoneal cavity
of prey that they captured (Estes 1991).

    In short, my working hypothesis is that sufficient cover together with
adequate concentrations of gazelles affected siting of territories insofar as
these features attracted females (see below). Cheetahs, particularly females, hunted a greater proportion of the available gazelle groups found
in high vegetation (>30 cm) than those found in low vegetation (Fitz-
Gibbon 1990c), so they may have been drawn to areas with vegetation
cover. In addition, cheetahs of both sexes used sparse riparian vegetation
to approach prey undetected, and they sometimes ran along deep drainages to get closer to their quarry. Furthermore, the steeply rolling topog-

raphy surrounding kopje systems allowed them to stalk prey from over, or more usually from below, the brow of a hill. In the absence of these features, cheetahs were easily seen by prey on the short grass plains. Vegetation also provided shade during the heat of the day.

Once I realized the importance of vegetation, I made stringent efforts to locate other territories in areas that contained cover. As a result, I am certain that males did not set up residence at Semetu kopjes and am fairly sure that the areas north of Kiombobo kopjes and around Simuyu kopjes were not occupied by territorial males either. Despite favorable cover, these areas never contained large concentrations of gazelles in either wet or dry seasons (fig. 8.6), again indicating the combined importance of both cover and prey concentrations. No resident males were found in the tourist area around Mukoma Hill or at Masai kopjes throughout the study, although the Frames knew of a male (called Paka) who held a territory in this last area in the mid-1970s (Frame and Frame 1981). I cannot explain this anomaly, as cover was plentiful, similar to that found around Loliondo kopjes, and many Thomson's gazelles collected there in the dry season (fig. 8.6). I am sure tourists were not responsible for this absence, as visitor numbers were higher in the 1970s than in the 1980s (fig. 2.2a). My study area did not include Moru kopjes, Oldonya Olbaye, or the Ngare Nanyuki drainage east of the park boundary, so I cannot comment on these regions.

The total area of the plains occupied by lions was greater than that covered by cheetah male territories because pride ranges were contiguous. The distribution of pride ranges was approximately similar, however, with prides being absent east of the park border (Packer et al. 1988). Despite the presence of large numbers of ungulates for some of the year (Maddock 1979), the flat topography and very short grass of this eastern region made it very difficult for either species to make concealed approaches toward prey.

Size of Territories

The average size of male territories was 37.4 km^2 ($N = 22$ territories, SE = 5.2) (or 48.3 km^2 if non-radio-collared males were excluded; see app. 10). This represented only 4.5% of the average size of a female home range. Moreover, the largest single area occupied by a resident male (74.8 km^2) was still only 19.0% of the smallest female range (394.5 km^2). Among terrestrial carnivores, it is very unusual for male territory size to be smaller than female range size (Sandell 1989), but in the sea otter, an aquatic carnivore, males do have smaller home ranges than females

(Loughlin 1980; Ribic 1982). In some other groups of birds and mammals increasing female home range size is associated with reduced male territory size, since very large female areas are no longer defensible by males. In both reduncine antelopes (Clutton-Brock 1989b) and tetraonid grouse (Bradbury et al. 1986) the area defended by males is much diminished when female ranges are large. The same pattern holds for felids (fig. 8.8). In the majority of cats in which females live alone, either in small mutually exclusive ranges or in areas that show varying degrees of overlap, single males usually defend three or four female ranges against other males (e.g., Bailey 1974). In lions, the only felid whose breeding unit comprises more than one female, several males defend the relatively large pride range, or sometimes more than one pride range, against other groups of males (Pusey and Packer 1987). Cheetahs are exceptional, as males defend much smaller areas that females visit in order to obtain resources. In common with other species, such as Grevy's zebra (Rubenstein 1986) or gazelles (Walther, Mungall, and Grau 1983), in which resources important for females are dispersed widely, cheetah male territories are discontinuous (see fig. 8.5) (see also Gosling 1986).

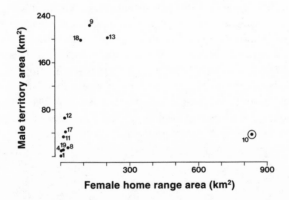

Fig. 8.8 Male territory size plotted against female home range or territory size in km² for some species of felids. 1, European wildcat (1.2, 0.8 km² for male and female areas respectively: from Corbett 1978); 4, ocelot (10.0, 3.0: Ludlow and Sunquist 1987); 8, snow leopard (15.4, 29.3: Jackson and Ahlborn 1989); 9, cougar (223.0, 127.0: Seidensticker et al. 1983); 10, cheetah (circled) 37.4, 833.0: this study); 11, jaguar (33.4, 10.5: Rabinowitz and Nottingham 1986); 12, tiger (66.0, 16.8: Sunquist 1981); 13, lion (203.1, 203.1: Schaller 1972); 17, bobcat (42.1, 19.3: Bailey 1974); 18, North American lynx (198.5, 86.5: Mech 1980); 19, serval (11.6, 9.5: Geertsma 1985); see also table 12.2.

ECOLOGICAL CAUSES OF EXPANDED FEMALE HOME RANGE SIZE

The key feature distinguishing cheetah female home ranges from those of other female cats is their size (see fig. 8.8). Increased home range size can result from a number of factors, one of which is a decrease in prey density that makes food difficult to find. Among felids, home range size has been shown to increase with declining prey density in both bobcats (Litvaitis, Sherburne, and Bissonette 1986) and North American lynxes (Ward and Krebs 1985). Alternatively, range size will increase if prey is located in small patches of high density separated in space. In this second situation, foragers might "trap-line," moving from one high-quality patch to the next (Bradbury 1981). In Serengeti cheetahs, it is the patchiness of prey that accounts for expanded ranges, not low prey density. Serengeti has a high ungulate biomass compared with national parks such as Nairobi or Kruger (Schaller 1972c), and on the plains Thomson's gazelle densities alone reach the order of 85–110/km², or more than 1,000 kg/km² (numbers from Campbell et al. 1990 and Dublin et al. 1990). Because of localized rainfall patterns and differences in soil quality on the short grass plains, green flushes arise separated in space and time, causing Thomson's gazelles to form localized concentrations lasting a few weeks to a maximum of 5 months (figs. 2.12, 2.13). Female cheetahs move over large areas in search of these ephemeral but rewarding prey concentrations, locating them either by trial and error or by knowing potential sites in advance.

Expanded home ranges are associated with great overlap in individual patterns of movement in carnivores and male ungulates (Grant, Chapman, and Richardson 1992). For instance, in Idaho mountain lions, females had almost completely overlapping ranges when ungulates were concentrated at low elevations during winter (Seidensticker et al. 1973). Where patches of prey were variable in density, ranges of female lynxes also showed overlap, with several of them working the same high-density patch (Ward and Krebs 1985). Movements of female cheetahs show a similar pattern.

Location and Size of Nonresident Male Ranges

Figure 8.9 shows the extent of the ranges of 10 nonresident males on whom there were extensive sightings. Ranges showed great overlap in both space and time: for example, seven of the ranges in the figure were occupied simultaneously between April 1986 and May 1987. Most of the wet season sightings of floaters were made in the eastern half of their ranges on the short grass plains; they moved as far east as Barafu kopjes and beyond, into the Ngorongoro Conservation Area, and as far south as Naabi Hill. Their movements took them through many territories occupied at the time (see fig. 8.5). During the dry season nonresidents tended to move northwest into the vicinity of Seronera and Mukoma plain. These seasonal movements mirrored the migration of both female cheetahs and Thomson's gazelles (Durant et al. 1988).

Nonetheless, there were many exceptions to this general pattern, with occasional sightings of males on the eastern park boundary in dry season months and near Seronera in the wet season. Some males also went west

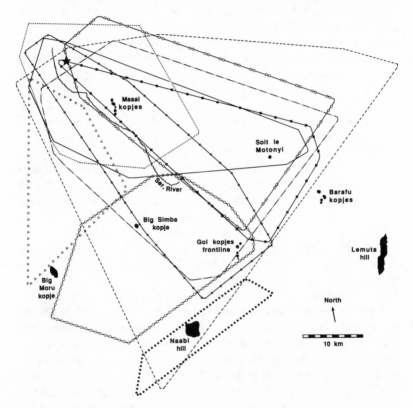

Fig. 8.9 Location and size of home ranges utilized by 10 nonresident males between June 1981 and July 1990, derived by the minimum polygon method. A, dotted line; B, dashed line; C, solid line and open squares; D, dashed line and double dots; E, solid line and solid squares; F, solid line only; G, solid line and solid triangles; H, open triangles; I, dashed line and open circles; J, solid circles. All ranges were derived from 10 or more sightings except those of I and J, which are shown in order to highlight different patterns of ranging. Seronera is shown as a star; topography as in fig. 2.11.

and southwest, but I had insufficient sightings of nonterritorial males around Ndutu, and none at Oldonya Olbaye or Moru kopjes, and thus could not determine the proportion using more southerly sections of the plains-woodland ecotone. Certain floating males may have left the plains traveling directly north or northeast in the dry season, but again I had no records on this.

Not every nonresident male used such extensive ranges: some ventured only a small distance out onto the plains in the wet season and survived on the prey remaining around Seronera and on the plains-woodland border (see ranges A and H in fig. 8.9). (Smaller ranges could not be attributed to our following a male for a short span of time. Floater A's range was a quarter the size of floater B's but was generated from following him for 51 months, whereas B was followed for 46 months.) Yet other nonterritorial males showed a different pattern of ranging, moving between the woodland border around Ndutu to the Simba kopjes and Naabi Hill areas (ranges I and J).

Ranges of nonterritorial males averaged 777.2 km² based on the minimum polygon method ($N = 9$ ranges for which there were more than 10 sightings, SE = 153.0). The largest range covered by a nonterritorial male was 1,892.6 km² over a period of 46 months. Males showed all sorts of movements within their ranges, sometimes staying in a 5-km² area for up to 2 weeks, making steady progress across the plains, or traveling long distances in a matter of days. For example, a male moved from just west of Barafu kopjes to the junction of the Seronera River and the main road in 95 hours, a minimum straight-line distance of 40.3 km. The average area covered by a nonterritorial male was 20.1 times the average size of a territory.

If nonresidents saw a female in the course of their ranging, they approached her, investigated her, and sometimes remained with her in anticipation of estrus. Mate searching over wide areas has been documented across a wide range of mammals including orangutans (MacKinnon 1974), sperm whales (Best 1979), elephants (Barnes 1982), greater kudu (Owen-Smith 1984), polar bears (Ramsay and Stirling 1986), eastern grey kangaroos (Jarman and Southwell 1986), and thirteen-lined ground squirrels (Schwagmeyer 1988). In these species, the strategy is apparently associated with females that range widely in search of unpredictable food sources and live at a low population density, making them impossible for males to defend in any number (Gosling 1986; Clutton-Brock 1989b). In addition, mate searching may be promoted by breeding asynchrony, which exacerbates the reproductive costs of attempting to defend females over time (Gosling 1986). All these conditions pertained to Serengeti cheetahs.

Ranging Behavior of Nonresidents in Relation to Residents

If scent marks in conjunction with the possibility of physical attack were effective in repelling intruders from a region of the plains, one would expect that floating males would more often be found outside than inside territorial boundaries. To test this, I compared the number of sightings of adult and young adult floaters inside territorial boundaries in the months when the territories were occupied by owners (termed "active" territories) with the number of sightings outside territories or within them in months when no resident held tenure. To correct for the number of visits that I and my colleagues made to different areas of the park to search for cheetahs, the total number of times that floating males were seen in a given grid square was divided by the number of times that the square was scanned with binoculars (with the stipulation that it could not be scanned more than once on the same day) to give an index of floating males for each square. This index did not differ significantly between squares that were inside "active" territories and those elsewhere in space or time [16]. In contrast, the index of adolescent males found in squares inside "active" territories was lower than that in other squares [17].

Thus adolescents that were probably not yet sexually active respected territorial boundaries, whereas older, reproductively active nonresidents entered territories. In doing so they ran the risk of being attacked by residents, based on records of territorial males fighting and killing nonresidents of all ages (Kuenkel 1978; Frame and Frame 1981; Caro 1989a). That nonresidents were found on territories at all suggests that they had not been detected by the owners as they passed through, or that the floaters were of an equivalent or larger group size than the residents, making them formidable opponents. Single males were at a disadvantage in fights with male groups (see chap. 9) and were therefore likely to be especially careful to avoid confrontation with residents. Systematic and anecdotal data support this. Floating males living in groups of two or three were more likely to be found inside "active" territories (29.3% of 58 sightings) than were single floaters (16.4% of 280 sightings) [18]. And I once observed the resident trio (A, B, and C) at Gol kopjes and a group of three adult floaters 900 m apart eyeing each other for 50 minutes before the nonresidents moved off without showing signs of fear.

In conclusion, territorial behavior was effective in intimidating adolescent males and single males. Presence of territorial males in the area also may have interfered with floaters' willingness to spend long periods of time guarding receptive females, since this would increase their chances of being located by residents, but I have no data on this.

Benefits Associated with Territoriality

Significantly more females were seen on territories while they were occupied by residents than were seen outside them or on territories that were not currently occupied, once observers' visits had been taken into account [19]. This means that resident males had the possibility of encountering more females per unit time than did nonresidents. I was more likely to see females pass by when I was conducting behavioral observations on territorial males than on nonresident males [20]; if I could see them, males would certainly have been able to spot them too. Indeed, sightings made of males guarding females were more than four times as common on "active" territories than elsewhere, devalued for searching in different areas [21].

These results show that active territories were specifically centered on areas that females visited in large numbers. Females might stay for many weeks in these areas hunting Thomson's gazelles and hares. Mating territories sited in areas regularly visited by females in search of food are found in a variety of antelopes, including Coke's hartebeest (Gosling 1974) and puku (Rosser 1992; see Estes 1974 and Gosling 1986 for reviews), although relative numbers of visiting females have rarely been quantified. Females in these species and in cheetahs might additionally have entered particular territories to mate with certain males, as suggested for puku (Rosser 1992).

DO FEMALES CHOOSE TO MATE WITH CERTAIN MALES?

If females visited territories to choose mates, one might have expected them to visit territories when they were occupied by residents. As table 8.4 shows, this was true for only some territories. At Gol kopjes, Naabi Hill, and Oldonya Rongai, females were encountered more often when males were in residence, once observers' visits had been taken into account. But at Simba kopjes, Loliondo kopjes, and the Zebra kopjes and Soit le Motonyi area, the number of females encountered was unaffected by whether males were in residence. At Ndutu, more females were seen when residents were absent. This territory's size was an underestimate, however, because thick vegetation hindered effective searching for territorial males (and females), and it was only occupied for a short period, so I do not attach importance to this last result. If females had been visiting territories to choose mating partners, they should have left vacant territories as quickly as possible and searched elsewhere once they could not locate the resident; however, this was not the case.

Second, potentially receptive females, that is, lone adult and adolescent

TABLE 8.4 Index of Females Seen on Territories When Males Were or Were Not in Residence

Territory	Owners		z-value on Mann-Whitney U test	P value
	Present	Absent		
Gol	0.0170 (346)	0.0106 (283)	7.513	<.0001
Naabi	0.0201 (71)	0.0035 (64)	5.121	<.0001
Rongai	0.0086 (113)	0.0070 (98)	2.359	.018
Simba	0.0052 (132)	0.0095 (118)	− 0.221	>.8
Loliondo	0.0134 (278)	0.0121 (280)	0.806	>.4
Zebra/Soit le Motonyi	0.0099 (134)	0.0093 (134)	0.377	>.7
Ndutu	0 (20)	0.0116 (20)	− 2.612	.009

Note: Mean numbers of females seen on territorial foci when males were or were not seen in residence were divided by the number of visits to different grid squares during times of owners' presence and absence. Number of searches of grid squares in territories when owners were present or absent are given in parentheses. To be conservative, foci were defined as those grid squares used by two or more sets of occupants in a given area (i.e., the overlap of superimposed territories shown in fig. 8.5). Hidden Valley territory was omitted as it was searched so rarely, and Barafu territory was omitted because records of observers' visits had not been initiated while it was occupied.

females and mothers with old cubs (chap. 4), did not visit active territories more often than other parts of the study area [22]. As females were encountered more often on active territories than elsewhere irrespective of their reproductive condition, it appeared that females returned to these areas containing prey and cover to feed and not specifically to mate. Thus, the location of territories was sensitive to the distribution of females in general, not to that of receptive females in particular. Third, male territories were far apart, which must have made it difficult to choose between males, although it must be said that individual females sometimes moved between territories in a few days.

In conclusion, there was no evidence that females visited male territories in order to choose between different residents. Yet once on a territory, the possibility that a female chose to mate with certain members of the male groups, either residents or floaters, cannot be discounted on the basis of these arguments.

Alternative Tactics among Males

Male cheetahs thus showed two behavioral tactics for acquiring mates on the Serengeti plains: holding a mating territory or roaming in search of females. Though some males started out and remained as floaters all their lives, others showed both tactics. Those males that held territories as adults moved over a wide area as adolescents before they settled. Other males became floaters after vacating a territory. For example, fig. 8.10 shows the range of a male who held Soit le Motonyi territory until his coalition partner disappeared, at which time he stopped scent-marking and covered an area 14.6 times as large. This change is well within the bounds of those found in other carnivores, studies of which have documented a 50-fold range increase for individual males during the breeding season (e.g., stoats: Erlinge and Sandell 1986).

Alternative mating tactics are often associated with females appearing at two or more different locations in the environment; for example, if one section of the population is sedentary while another ranges widely (Thornhill and Alcock 1983). For example, in digger bees, some males defend a series of small territories over positions from which virgin females will emerge, while others hover on the edge of an emergence site searching for passing virgins on the wing in a form of scramble competition (Alcock, Jones, and Buchmann 1977). Similarly, in some populations of topi, some males defend territories on which females feed while others defend portions of mobile female groups (Jewell 1972).

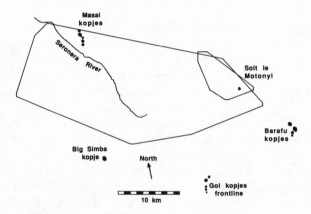

Fig. 8.10 The location and area (33.4 km²) used by a male while he held a territory with his coalition partner, and subsequently when he lost his partner and floated over an area of 486.5 km², as derived by the minimum polygon method. Topography as in fig. 2.11.

The distribution of female cheetahs conformed to this pattern. Although the majority of females collected at relatively high densities where gazelles and cover were plentiful during certain periods of the year, other females were found elsewhere feeding on pockets of gazelles in areas of localized rainfall. The idiosyncratic movements of females within their home ranges made female concentrations somewhat unpredictable, enabling males to encounter females either on mating territories or outside them. In these circumstances, the relative reproductive payoffs of the two male tactics need not be the same (see chap. 9) and may be altered by demographic factors. Declining female density, for example, will devalue the benefits of waiting for females on territories and result in an increased proportion of roving males in the population (Liberg and Sandell 1988; Sandell and Liberg 1992).

Summary

1. Females had annual home ranges that stretched from west of Seronera to beyond the eastern park boundary, covering 833 km² on average. These ranges were undefended and showed great overlap. During the wet season most females were found on the short grass plains, but in the dry season they moved northwest, following the Thomson's gazelles.

2. Territorial, also called resident, males stayed in small areas of the plains which they scent-marked, whereas nonterritorial or nonresident males, also called floaters, moved over much larger areas and did not scent-mark.

3. Nonterritorial, also called floating, males were less relaxed than residents, exhibited signs of physiological stress, and were in poor condition. Circumstantial evidence suggested that a floating lifestyle resulted in ill health rather than vice versa. Residents were estimated to live longer than nonresidents.

4. Throughout the 10-year study, territories were focused on eight different centers where residents settled again and again. Their location was contingent on a combination of adequate cover and a reasonable number of Thomson's gazelles being present.

5. Male territories averaged 37.4 km² in area and, in contrast to those of other felids, were far smaller than the size of a female home range.

6. Ranges utilized by nonresident males averaged 777.2 km² in area and overlapped with many others. Floating males normally moved from the short grass plains in the wet season to the western plains-woodland boundary in the dry season.

7. Adult nonresidents were found inside territories as well as outside, but adolescent males and single floating males had greater respect for territorial boundaries.

8. Female cheetahs were more often sighted inside territories occupied by residents than outside, once observers' searching patterns had been taken into account. Males set up territories in areas where females aggregated for the purposes of feeding. There was no evidence that female choice was responsible for the cheetah's unusual mating system.

9. Although female concentrations were greater on territories, some females were found elsewhere. This enabled males to employ two reproductive tactics to locate females: settling on a territory or roving in search of mates.

Statistics

1. Median number of 500 × 500 m grid squares covered per day by resident (N = 18 individuals or groups) and nonresident (N = 12 individuals or groups) males sighted three or more times, $\bar{X}$s = 0.61, 1.15 respectively, Mann-Whitney U test, U = 51, P < .02. Distances calculated from intersighting intervals of >100 days were discarded to avoid circuitous routing. Median values were used because nonresidents remained in one small area for several days and then moved a long distance.

2. Mean rate of any type of urination for residents (N = 19 individuals) and nonresidents (N = 20 individuals), $\bar{X}$s = 0.84, 0.02/hr, Mann-Whitney U test, U = 2, P < .002.

Mean rate of defecation (Ns as above), $\bar{X}$s = 0.17, 0.03/hr, U = 56.0, P < .002.

3. Average height above ground that residents (N = 10 individuals or groups) and nonresidents (N = 6 individuals or groups) urinated or defecated, $\bar{X}$s = 1.1, 0.2 m, Mann-Whitney U test, U = 2.5, P < .002.

4. Percentage of midday rest period spent above ground level for residents (N = 15 individuals or groups) and nonresidents (N = 15 individuals or groups), $\bar{X}$s = 12.2%, 4.8%, Mann-Whitney U test, U = 65, P < .1.

Maximum height that residents (N = 15 individuals or groups) and nonresidents (N = 14 individuals or groups) were seen to rest above ground during the midday rest period, $\bar{X}$s = 2.2, 0.8 m, Mann-Whitney U test, U = 58.5, P < .005.

5. Comparison of cortisol concentrations between resident and nonresident male cheetahs before electroejaculation, N = 4, 4 individuals respectively, I: $\bar{X}$s = 42.4, 74.6 ng/ml, t = −1.23, P > .2 (see legend of fig. 8.3 for roman numerals denoting timing of blood samples).

During electroejaculation, N = 4, 4 individuals, II: 40.9, 61.3 ng/ml, t = −1.41, P > .2; III: 104.5, 112.2 ng/ml, t = −0.24, P > .8; IV: 154.3, 206.3 ng/ml, t = −2.53, P = .045.

After electroejaculation, N = 4, 4 individuals, V: 160.9, 187.7 ng/ml,

$t = -0.88$, $P > .4$; VI: 106. 8, 154.1 ng/ml, $t = -2.63$, $P = .039$; $N = 4$, 3 individuals, VII: 89.4, 136.6 ng/ml, $t = -3.16$, $P = .025$; VIII: 59.1, 100.8 ng/ml, $t = -2.11$, $P = .089$.

6. Comparison of body weight of nonresidents ($N = 10$ individuals) and residents ($N = 8$ individuals) controlling for belly size at time of immobilization (none were adolescents), $\bar{X}s = 38.3$, 43.8 kg, $F_{1,15} = 6.253$, $P = .024$.

7. Comparison of white blood cell counts of nonresidents ($N = 8$ individuals) and residents ($N = 5$ individuals) (none were adolescents), $\bar{X}s = 14.7, 9.6 \times 10^9$/liter, t test, $t = 1.92$, $P = .08$.

Same comparison including three nonresidents that subsequently became territorial ($N = 11$ individuals), $\bar{X}s = 13.6, 9.6 \times 10^9$/liter, $t = 1.74$, $P = .103$.

8. Comparison of eosinophil levels of nonresidents ($N = 8$ individuals) and residents ($N = 5$ individuals) (none were adolescents), $\bar{X}s = 1.13$, 0.33×10^9/liter, t test, $t = 3.30$, $P = .007$.

Same comparison including three nonresidents that subsequently became territorial ($N = 11$ individuals), $\bar{X}s = 1.17, 0.33 \times 10^9$/liter, $t = 3.26$, $P = .006$.

9. Vertebral musculature of nonresidents ($N = 12$ individuals) was thinner than that of residents ($N = 6$ individuals), median values 2.0, 3.0 on a 3-point scale, Mann-Whitney U test, $U = 3$, $P < .002$ (see table 8.2).

10. Mange on the ears of nonresidents ($N = 12$ individuals) was more extensive than that on residents ($N = 7$ individuals), median values 1.0, 0 on a 6-point scale, Mann-Whitney U test, $U = 17.5$, $P < .05$ (see table 8.2).

11. Comparison of coat quality of nonresidents ($N = 12$ individuals) and residents ($N = 7$ individuals), Fisher test, $P = .034$ (see table 8.2).

12. Linear dimensions of nonresident and resident male cheetahs. Head and body: $N = 14$, 10 individuals respectively, $\bar{X}s = 120.6$, 125.1 cm, $t = -1.58$, $P > .1$.

Tail: $N = 14$, 10 individuals, $\bar{X}s = 67.4, 69.0$ cm, $t = -1.09$, $P > .2$.

Hindfoot: $N = 14$, 10 individuals, $\bar{X}s = 27.6, 28.0$ cm, $t = -0.94$, $P > .3$.

Chest girth: $N = 11$, 10 individuals, $\bar{X}s = 67.9, 70.9$ cm, $t = -1.76$, $P = .094$.

13. Intersighting intervals for territorial males ($N = 298$ intervals in total, $\bar{X} = 356$ days, SD $= 62.5$, range 1–479 days) and nonterritorial males ($N = 154$ intervals in total, $\bar{X} = 59.2$ days, SD $= 94.3$, range 1–451 days) that were not located using radiotelemetry, t test, $t = -2.81$, df $= 224.37$, $P = .005$.

14. Number of days between first and last sighting for territorial and nonterritorial males, as derived from radio-collared animals known to

have died and individuals presumed dead using the extrapolation method. Using all ages when first seen: $N = 15$ individual or groups of territorial males, 22 individual or groups of nonterritorial males, Mann-Whitney U test, $z = 2.249$, $P = .015$.

First seen as adults only: $N = 12, 11$, $U = 28$, $P = .02$.

First seen as young adults only: $N = 2, 7$, $U = 6$, $P > .8$.

First seen as adolescents: too few to test.

15. Number of days between first and last sighting for single males and groups of males whose members disappeared together (a single figure was taken for groups whose members disappeared at the same time). Males of all ages: $N = 23$ single males, 14 groups, $\bar{X}s = 559.3, 561.1$ days respectively, Mann-Whitney U test, $z = -0.908$, $P > .3$.

Adults only: $N = 13, 10$, $\bar{X}s = 499.2, 650.2$, $U = 42$, $P > .1$.

Territorial males only, all ages: $N = 3, 12$, $\bar{X}s = 1,269.0, 629.9$, $U = 6$, $P > .1$.

Territorial males only, adults only, $N = 2, 10$, $\bar{X}s = 1,302.5, 650.2$, $U = 4$, $P > .1$; there were too few groups of floaters to make other comparisons.

16. Number of sightings of young adult and adult floating males inside and outside "active" territories, corrected for visits to different grid squares, $N = 2,743, 8,933$ visits to grid squares respectively. Index $\bar{X}s = 0.0026, 0.0014$ respectively, Mann-Whitney U test, $z = -0.0955$, $P > .9$; in this analysis floaters included a few males whose status was unknown.

17. Number of sightings of adolescent floating males inside and outside "active" territories, corrected for visits to different grid squares, $N = 2,743, 8,933$ visits to grid squares respectively. Index $\bar{X}s = 7.4 \times 10^{-5}$, 0.0004 respectively, Mann-Whitney U test, $z = -1.829$, $P = .067$.

18. Percentage of sightings of single floaters (16.4%, $N = 280$ sightings) and groups of floaters (29.3%, $N = 58$ sightings) found inside territories, G test, $G_1 = 4.794$, $P = .022$.

19. Number of sightings of females (mothers, lone adults, and adolescents combined) inside and outside "active" territories, corrected for the number of observers' visits to different grid squares, $N = 2,743, 8,933$ visits to grid squares respectively. Index $\bar{X}s = 0.0127, 0.0078$ respectively, Mann-Whitney U test, $z = -2.445$, $P = .011$.

20. Rate at which I observed female cheetahs (irrespective of reproductive status) pass by from my position next to territorial males ($N = 15$ individuals or groups) and nonterritorial males ($N = 10$ individuals or groups) watched for 12 or more hours, $\bar{X}s = 0.037, 0.010/\text{hr}$, Mann-Whitney U test, $U = 39$, $P = .05$.

21. Number of sightings of males and unrelated females seen together inside and outside "active" territories, corrected for the number of ob-

servers' visits to different grid squares, $N = 2,743, 8,933$ visits to grid squares respectively. Index $\bar{X}s = 0.0004, 8.6 \times 10^{-5}$ respectively, Mann-Whitney U test, $z = -3.028, P = .0025$.

22. Number of sightings of potentially receptive females (mothers with old cubs, lone adults, and adolescents combined) inside and outside "active" territories, corrected for the number of observers' visits to different grid squares, $N = 2,743, 8,933$ visits to grid squares respectively. Index $\bar{X}s = 0.0095, 0.0062$ respectively, Mann-Whitney U test, $z = 1.143$, $P > .2$.

DKS

A pair of adult males groom each other. This was often a prelude to moving off together as evening approached. (Drawing by Dafila Scott.)

9
TERRITORIALITY AND
MALE GROUP SIZE

In mammals in which groups of males are territorial, males usually defend the entire area occupied by a group of females against other male intruders, as in lions (Schaller 1972c; Packer and Pusey 1982) and chimpanzees (Wrangham 1979; Goodall 1986). It is relatively uncommon for a male mammal to defend only a portion of a female's home range, and in those species where this occurs, almost invariably a single male guards such patches against other single males (e.g., Coke's hartebeest: Gosling 1986). In a tiny proportion of mammals, however, two to four males defend a small fraction of a female's range against other males. The best-known examples are waterbuck and white rhinoceroses, in which one or as many as three satellite males live permanently within an alpha male's territory and may help defend it (Wirtz 1981, 1982; Owen-Smith 1972, 1975). These subordinate males are tolerated by the alpha but apparently do not mate. In waterbuck, secondary males may later inherit the alpha's territory, whereas in white rhinoceroses, they may be in a strong position to challenge neighboring alpha males for territory ownership. In neither species, however, are the reproductive payoffs for alpha and beta males well documented.

Serengeti cheetahs show some similarity to these two ungulates because groups of two or three males defend small territories in which females collect (chap. 8). Earlier work on cheetahs argued that the reproductive benefits of joint territorial defense were probably shared among group members, and that these benefits were sufficiently great that it paid

233

a male to form a permanent association with a sibling, or occasionally with a nonrelative, because larger groups had a competitive advantage in fights over territory ownership (Frame 1984; Caro and Collins 1986, 1987b). Moreover, cheetah male groups also resemble groups of male lions, in which reproductive success is shared fairly equally, at least in small groups of the size seen in cheetahs (Packer et al. 1991). On the other hand, in the white rhinoceros and the waterbuck, species with mating systems superficially similar to the cheetah's, mating is shared very unevenly between males. In addition, two-fifths of individually known male cheetahs remained single and did not form groups with other males (despite the fact that nonrelatives sometimes joined up together, Caro and Collins 1987b). Both of these latter facts suggested that reproductive benefits might be unevenly distributed within male groups. It therefore seemed necessary to examine the assumption of shared benefits more closely, and this is attempted in chapter 11.

Other questions also remained outstanding from this early work. Based on the theory that male reproductive success is limited by access to females in most species, and hence that male behavior and social relations are shaped by female distribution (Trivers 1972; Bradbury and Vehrencamp 1977; Wrangham 1980), cheetah male groupings were assumed to promote greater mating opportunities. Group living nevertheless affects many aspects of behavior other than reproduction. For carnivores, a considerable literature centers on the hunting and foraging benefits that individuals are thought to accrue from living in social groups (Mech 1970; Kruuk 1972) as well as on cooperative hunting (Packer and Ruttan 1988). Therefore it is important to examine the effects of group size on these activities in male cheetahs, since they might influence survival. This issue is tackled in chapter 10.

TABLE 9.1 Composition of Male Coalitions on the Serengeti Plains

	3 littermates	2 littermates & 1 nonrelative	2 littermates	2 nonrelatives	Unknown
Frames' study	0	3	2	1	13
This study[a]	2	6	20	1	4
	(0,2)	(5,1)	(11,9)	(1,0)	(1,3)
Total	2	8[b]	22	2	17

Note: Independent males of all ages were included.
[a] Numbers in parentheses are the numbers of coalitions that were territorial and nonterritorial, respectively.
[b] One coalition was represented in both studies.

Last, earlier publications on male Serengeti cheetahs were based on demographic records from the first 5 years of the 1980s. But during the second half of the decade it became apparent that single males could secure territories for extended periods of time, calling into question the benefits of group membership in attaining residency. In this chapter, changes in the pattern of residency over time are explored, and the relationship between group size and territoriality is reassessed using the expanded 10-year data set. At the end, the reproductive consequences of living in groups are estimated from data presented in this and the previous chapter.

Coalitions of Males

COMPOSITION OF COALITIONS

Of the 110 males individually recognized in the first half of the study before February 1985, 40.9% lived alone, 40.0% lived in groups of two, and 19.1% lived in groups of three (Caro and Collins 1986). Coalitions of males had a stable composition because the same individuals were always encountered together. Whereas *coalition* is a term used to describe a short-term interaction between two or more individuals that act together in an aggressive or competitive context against a third party (Harcourt and de Waal 1992), *alliance* is a better descriptor for associations of male cheetahs. An alliance denotes an enduring relationship in which individuals repeatedly aid one another in competitive situations and maintain their relationship through activities such as sharing food and mutual grooming; these qualities are characteristic of male cheetah groups (see chaps. 10 and 11). Unfortunately, *coalition* is now entrenched in the literature on male felids, and I have continued to use it.

Coalition members were usually brothers, although some were nonrelatives. From the Frames' study it was known that male littermates remained together after separating from their mother and were never sighted separately (except in one instance when two brothers left a sister and brother) and that only one out of six coalitions was composed solely of nonlittermates (table 9.1; Frame and Frame 1981; Frame and Frame, unpublished data). In this study, members of one trio were originally seen separately as a pair and as a singleton, and in another instance, a pair of males was subsequently seen as part of a permanent trio. Nevertheless, there were insufficient genealogical records to determine directly the proportion of coalitions composed of nonlittermates. Neither I nor my coworkers paid special attention to photographing cubs, which would have subsequently enabled us to trace the origins of ad~~ult and young~~ adult coalition members that we later encountered. Also, an unknown proportion of coalitions emigrated in from outside the study area. Instead, we used a variety of indirect methods to determine relatedness between coalition members.

First, and most generally, the distinctive patterns of black and white bands on the tails of the members of 11 coalitions were found to resemble each other, as did the tails of male littermates. This analysis was based on a procedure that compared observed quantitative differences in tail banding to a frequency distribution generated by randomly allocating coalitions, and family members, to each other (Caro and Durant 1991). Second, a sample of 33 coalitions was examined to find out whether members were siblings. Six coalitions were assessed using genealogical records, 22 by qualitative observations of members sharing distinctive spot patterns or similar tail markings, and 4 by knowing that they had recently separated from their mother. In the remaining coalition, members had very different tolerance of observers, possibly suggesting that one male had been raised in a litter habituated to tourists and the other had not (Caro and Collins 1986). This second method indicated that most pairs were composed of littermates but that most trios included a nonrelative that had joined two littermates. When combined with earlier genealogical data, 70.6% of the 34 coalitions were judged to contain littermates only, while 94.1% contained at least some littermates. These proportions changed little if adolescents were removed from the calculations (see below). Separating coalitions in this study according to their status, 35.3% of resident coalitions ($N = 17$ coalitions) contained a nonrelative (see table 9.1). The makeup of coalitions might be expected to vary according to the male composition of litters reaching independence and entering the adult population.

It is appropriate to juxtapose data on Serengeti cheetah coalitions with those on lions. Male coalitions in lions were larger than in cheetahs, typically containing two to six adult males but reaching as many as nine (Packer et al. 1991). This was because females living in the same pride may give birth to male cubs synchronously, which then disperse together, usually when new males take over their natal pride (Hanby and Bygott 1987; Pusey and Packer 1987). Also, whereas 29.4% of cheetah coalitions contained nonrelatives, 42% of breeding coalitions of lions did so (Packer and Pusey 1982). Male lions can gain access to a pride of females only if they have a partner, and extra-pride males are prevented from fathering cubs by coalition residents (Packer et al. 1991). Since virtually all females live in prides, single nomadic males are forced to join with nonrelatives in order to father offspring.

In lions, nonrelatives were found only among coalitions containing two or three members; in trios this usually consisted of a pair of relatives and an unrelated third, as in cheetah trios. Larger coalitions of lions consisted only of relatives. Packer and colleagues argue that within-coalition variance in reproductive success increases with coalition size because mixed paternity of litters is rare and larger coalitions have a lower per capita number of pride females available to them. Whereas nonbreeding relatives can enjoy inclusive fitness benefits from living in a large coalition, nonrelatives cannot, and they are only able to benefit when reproductive success is divided equally (Packer et al. 1991; see also Vehrencamp 1983). Unfortunately, comparable data on reproductive success among cheetah coalition members were not available.

TIMING OF FORMATION OF COALITIONS

Cheetah males remained with male siblings but were also prepared to join nonrelatives after adolescence. Time of joining was determined from examining group size at different ages and from case studies. First, there were significantly fewer trios of adolescent males (the group size containing the greatest proportion of nonrelatives) than trios of young or adult males [1] (table 9.2), implying that nonrelatives joined up toward the end of adolescence or just after it. It was improbable that low numbers of adolescent trios reflected a temporary drop in trios entering the independent population since there were also few dependent litters containing three males over the first 5 years of the study. Indeed, the number of dependent litters containing three males differed significantly from the numbers of trios of young adults and adults but not from the number of trios of adolescents [2].

Second, anecdotal evidence suggested that unrelated males joined up during adolescence. Frame knew of one coalition, A, B, and C (also called males 152, 122, and 153 respectively in Frame 1980; and Tanu, Tisa, and Tatu respectively in Kuenkel 1978) in which B joined up with littermates A and C within months of their having left their mothers, who had occupied overlapping home ranges. Soon after, this coalition set up residence outside their natal ranges at Gol kopjes nearby (Frame 1980). FitzGibbon (pers. comm.) noted that males P, Q, and R had joined up when P was a young male but when siblings Q and R were adolescents; this occurred at

TABLE 9.2 Number of Males Found in Different-Sized Groupings in the First Half of the Study

	Adults	Young adults	Adolescents	Cubs[a]
Trios	16	5	0	2
Pairs	23	9	12	16
Singletons	28	6	11	29

Source: Caro and Collins 1986.

[a] Dependent litters aged 6 months or older containing different numbers of male cubs.

almost exactly the time that all three began to show territorial behavior at Oldonya Rongai. We also discovered that adolescent L joined adolescent siblings J and K; however, they did not occupy a territory in the study area.

Of the six resident coalitions that contained nonrelatives, three formed just before they took up residence on a territory. Unrelated males may have therefore joined up to mount an effective challenge against current territory holders. As males could not become resident until they were young adults, perhaps because they did not attain adult body weight until that time, territorial challenges may explain why coalitions formed during or at the end of adolescence. Unrelated male lions similarly form coalitions just before a pride takeover (Packer and Pusey 1982).

Unfortunately, I never witnessed males joining up, but occasionally I saw single males investigate each other and then part company again. My notes record a young adult male watching an adult male for 5 minutes from 200 m away before running toward him. The adult ran off for 10 m but quickly settled down, hissing and yipping only once, while the young male sniffed around him. Then the two rested 1 m apart for 90 minutes (as coalition members do; chap. 11). On waking, growling commenced and the young male moved off, but as soon as the adult began to leave the youngster ran back, chased after him, and slapped him down before he got away. Interest in other cheetahs was characteristic of younger males (and females), but I could not tell whether this incident was an attempt to form a coalition or not.

Finally, a most interesting case concerned sibling males Cre and Cro, who occupied the south and west portion of the floor of Ngorongoro Crater for at least 6 years. They were reliably reported to have joined up with a third, younger male at the approximate time that three new territorial males took up residence in the northern portion of the Crater floor (R. Kuenkel, pers. comm.). Despite the increase in coalition size, Cre and Cro disappeared a few months later. This last record indicates that nonrelatives may join forces under particular demographic circumstances when superior numbers would be important in fending off a challenge or setting up a territory (as in the cases of A, B, and C and P, Q, and R), rather than joining up at a specific age.

COMPARISONS WITH OTHER SPECIES

In general, it is difficult to draw parallels between coalitions in cheetahs and in nonfelid species. Coalitions have recently been documented in male slender mongooses (Waser et al., in press), but few behavioral data are available. Among primates, for which there is the most information, individuals within groups often support each other against other members of the same group (Harcourt 1989; de Waal 1989). In the short term, for instance, middle-ranking and usually older male savannah baboons form coalitions against a high-ranking, younger male in order to take over an estrous female (Noe and Sluijter 1990). In the longer term, in cercopithecines, both maternal rank and support received from mothers are critical in determining daughters' eventual rank in the troop (Lee and Johnson 1992). Moreover, individuals compete with each other to form alliances with dominant animals (Seyfarth 1977), and this has been advanced as a key element distinguishing primate alliances from those of other species (Harcourt 1992). In cheetahs and lions, however, coalitions serve to increase competitive ability in intergroup conflicts, and dominance relations are not exhibited between coalition members in either species (chap. 11; Packer and Pusey 1982). Furthermore, while felid coalitions may last a lifetime, coalitions among male primates are usually shorter, occurring in brief fights over estrous females, although they may form repeatedly between the same individuals (e.g., Packer 1977; Hunte and Horrocks 1987).

These differences notwithstanding, a principal factor affecting the composition of coalitions in any species is degree of kinship. This is because even when the prize is indivisible, supporters will receive indirect fitness benefits through relatives; a coalition partner's defection will be less of a cost; and familiarity may enhance cooperation through reciprocity (Wrangham 1982; Harcourt 1989). Examples include Bewick's swans intervening on behalf of their offspring in contests (Scott 1980), and female relatives in many primate species defending contested resources against other female groups (Wrangham 1980) or their offspring against infanticidal males (Hrdy 1977). Since the majority of cheetah coalitions were made up of relatives, they parallel those of primates.

Relationship between Coalition Size and Residence

OBTAINING ACCESS TO A TERRITORY

During the first 5 years of the study, 30.8% ($N = 13$ individuals or groups) of young adult and 23.8% ($N = 46$ individuals or groups) of adult males held territories, whereas adolescent males never became residents regardless of coalition size (Caro and Collins 1986, 1987b). Of these older age groups, 8.8% of 35 singletons obtained a territory, whereas 60.0% of 25 coalitions did so [3]. In Frame's earlier study (pers. comm.), coalitions were also more likely to become residents than singletons, but the difference during his time was less marked: only 36.8% of 19 coalitions became resident, whereas as many as 13.0% of his 23 singletons did so [3].

The most plausible explanation for the disproportionate number of coalitions becoming residents was their numerical advantage, which enabled them to take over a territory by force more easily than could a single male. In the few fights that have been witnessed, a group of males had a great advantage over a singleton because the latter could not protect himself from bites and slaps coming from two or three directions. Also, while one coalition member could use his weight to pin an opponent down and attempt to suffocate it with a bite to the neck, his partner could deliver repeated bites to the haunch and genitals (Kuenkel 1978; Frame and Frame 1981; Caro 1989a). Indeed, single males normally acquired a territory only when a vacancy appeared and were less likely to displace residents from a territory than were coalitions (table 9.3) [4]. In other species too, larger coalitions defeat smaller ones: winning groups of acorn woodpeckers were twice the size of losing groups (Hannon et al. 1985), and larger groups of capuchin monkeys won a greater percentage of intergroup encounters than did smaller ones (Robinson 1988).

TABLE 9.3 Methods by which Male Cheetahs Took Up Residence on a Territory

Group size	Displaced residents	Took up a vacant territory	Retained even though companion(s) disappeared	Unknown
Singletons	0	5	2	3
Pairs	4	2	1	7
Trios	3	2	0	2

TABLE 9.4 Circumstances Surrounding the Deaths of Males

Status of dead male	When the dead male was found on a territory, was it occupied by other males?		Not found on a territory
	Yes	No	
Residents	2[a]	3[b]	
Nonresidents	5	1	1
Males of unknown status	1[c]	1	
Sex unknown	1	0	

Note: Number of instances during the whole study when dead males (or their radio collars) were found on territories, separated according to whether the territories were occupied by residents at the time. A male found dead outside a territory was included. A female, two males that died of illness outside territories, and two cheetahs of unknown sex that died on territories but on unknown dates were excluded.

[a] Territories were taken over by new residents.

[b] Three residents on three different territories were found dead on their own territories, which subsequently became vacant.

[c] Represents a pair of males that died next to each other; they were almost certainly nonresidents (P. Moehlman, pers. comm.).

Competition over territories was an important cause of mortality, as shown by the location of males found dead in the study area (see fig. 8.5): males were more likely to die inside or on the immediate borders of territories than outside them [5]. Moreover, more males died on territories at the time they were occupied than when residents were absent (table 9.4). The timing of one of these deaths coincided with a takeover. On 6 January 1987, male S_2 was seen on his territory at Simba kopjes, but on the 26th he was located from the air at Soguna kopjes, 37.5 km from his territory boundary (see fig. 9.2). At the end of March, S_2 was dead on his territory, and we know that P, Q, and R had clearly established residence there by May. Unfortunately, this was a period of changeover in personnel on the project, and both the death of S_2 and the appearance of P, Q, and R at Simba could have occurred any time after 26 January. On the basis of this circumstantial evidence, however, it is tempting to speculate that S_2 encountered P, Q, and R on Simba and moved far away to Soguna to avoid them, or that P, Q, and R arrived in his absence, but when he returned to his area he was killed by them!

LENGTH OF TENURE

Previously, we reported that length of tenure, as estimated by the number of months between first and last sighting on a territory, increased with coalition size during the first half of the study (Caro and Collins 1987b). The median number of months spent in residence was 4 (interquartile range 3.5–9.5 months) for three singletons, 7.5 (2.8–16.0) for twelve pairs, and 22 (18.5–24.5) for three trios, using all the data available at that time. This increase was only significant ($P < .1$) if the pair of males that held Ngorongoro Crater was omitted from analysis.

Without the aid of radiotelemetry, it is difficult to gather accurate information on residence patterns in carnivores. An animal may appear to be absent from a territory because researchers are unable to find it, because it has temporarily left but will return later, because it has permanently left the territory, or because it is dead. Also, if residents are not radio-collared, the situation in the first half of the study, records may be affected by the observer's rate of searching. Unfortunately I did not record my searching systematically until 20 months into the study. Extent of cover can also affect the likelihood of locating resident males. An unrelated but additional problem is that length of tenure for males who were already resident before the study began and for those who were still resident when the study ended will be underestimates. In analyzing the relationship between tenure and male group size over the whole 10-year period, I therefore took a conservative measure that excluded these equivocal data as well as a generous measure that used all of the data (as shown in fig. 9.1). Both measures indicated that there was no effect of

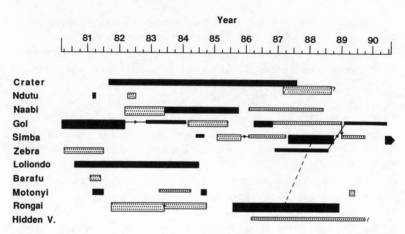

Fig. 9.1 Months in which different territorial males were resident on the Serengeti plains and floor of Ngorongoro Crater. Figures at the top refer to years, starting 1 January; 1 April, 1 July, and 1 October are also shown for each year. Black or dotted bars show that territory ownership changed hands; widths of bars indicate the size of coalition in residence (thinnest, one male; middle-sized, two males; fattest, three males). Horizontal arrows show that the territory was still owned by the same coalition although the number of its members was reduced. Vertical and oblique arrows show that a male switched territories; dashed line indicates that a trio occupied two territories simultaneously. Months in which residents were not seen were still shown provided residents were located on their territories in a subsequent month (residents could be located several times in a month). Ngorongoro Crater was not visited before September 1981, Ndutu before March 1981, Rongai before October 1981, or Hidden Valley before March 1986. Question marks show that we did not know when or if males had terminated their tenure after the last date shown, as the areas were not subsequently visited. The arrow after July 1990 at Simba shows it was still occupied at the time of writing. Identities of resident males, reading from left to right, are as follows. (Note: some different males were assigned the same initials, but none changed coalition partners.) An asterisk (*) in legend denotes that males may have been in residence before the dates shown. *Crater:* Cre* and Cro* (they were later joined by a third male sometime after March 1987, not shown; three new males shared a different part of the crater floor for 5 months in 1987). *Ndutu:* N* and U*; O and Y. *Naabi:* X, Y, and Z; 2 and 3; Mr Universe. *Gol:* A, B, and C had occupied Gol kopjes from October 1977 onward, male B continued after A and C disappeared; Bt and N; A_1 and B_1; Onear; Zebedee. *Simba:* Paris; S_1 and S_2, S_2 continued after S_1 disappeared; P, Q, and R; Onear; Simba Athletic. *Zebra:* M* and N*; Zebedee. *Loliondo:* D* and E*. *Barafu:* M* and H*. *Soit le Motonyi:* W* and E*; Our Man; 144a and 144b; Nelson and Napoleon. *Oldonya Rongai:* B*, S*, and A*, B and A continued after S disappeared; P, Q, and R. *Hidden Valley:* "Ndutu male."

TABLE 9.5 Number of Instances of Termination of Residence by Males under Different Circumstances

Reason	Male group size		
	1	2	3
Ousted from territory by other males	5 or 4[a]	1	1
Territory left vacant because male or his coalition partner died	2	1	2
Territory left vacant because male or his coalition partner disappeared	0	2	0
Territory left vacant but reasons unknown	2 or 3[a]	7	0
No longer held a territory but circumstances completely unknown	1	2	1

Note: Total number of entries here is four fewer than in table 9.3 because three instances of coalition partners retaining the territory after loss of companions are omitted, and one territory was still occupied at time of writing.

[a] It was unknown whether one singleton vacated his territory or was displaced by another single male.

group size on length of tenure [6]. Thus, while members of larger groups may have enjoyed somewhat longer stays on their territories from March 1980 to February 1985, group size had no effect on length of tenure over the whole decade.

This was very surprising, since over the whole study, single resident males were more likely to be displaced by other males (usually by a coalition) than were groups of males (table 9.5). In contrast, resident coalitions were rarely displaced, implying that they vacated their territories voluntarily [7]. Moreover, in the first 5 years of the study, length of tenure was somewhat greater for larger coalitions. One explanation for this discrepancy between singletons' poor ability to fend off challenges and long periods of residence (principally in the second half of the study) is that they were rarely faced with coalitions contending for their territory (see below).

TERRITORY SIZE AND QUALITY

Despite coalitions' superior competitive ability, larger groups did not hold larger territories than smaller groups [8]. Nor did territory size diminish in the three situations in which coalition members continued to retain a territory after the loss of a companion(s) (fig. 9.2). Assuming that a single male occupied the maximum size range he could defend and patrol successfully, it seemed improbable that a coalition would cover a greater area, given that members traveled together. Alternatively, territory size may have been determined by the spatial boundaries of female concentrations, which were unrelated to group size of resident males.

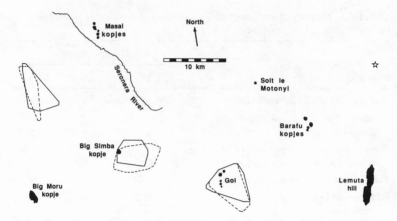

Fig. 9.2 Locations and sizes of territories occupied by males before (continuous line) and after (dashed line) a member of their coalition had disappeared. Right: Gol kopjes was occupied by A, B, and C (44, refers to the number of sightings used to determine the area) and subsequently by B (22). Center: Simba was occupied by S_1 and S_2 (11) and subsequently by S_2 (25). Left: Oldonya Rongai was occupied by B, S, and A (11) and subsequently by B and A (6). The low number of sightings in the last territory probably explains its diminished area. Open star shows the location of the grid square to which S_2 moved just before he was replaced by a trio (see text). Topography as in fig. 2.11.

The number of .females on "active" territories, taking observers' searching into account, showed no relation to residents' group size [9]. This shows that males did not settle on their territories in an "ideal free" manner (Fretwell 1972). If they had, three times as many females would have been encountered on those territories occupied by trios as those occupied by singletons. Lack of association between male group size and female distribution did not appear to result from sampling territories under different demographic conditions (see below) because female indices on territories did not increase with male group size in either the first or the second half of the study [10]. In both periods indices were high on territories owned by single males. Thus although territories were centered on areas of greatest female traffic (chap. 8), males did not settle in a manner in which each successive male set up residence on a site where he would obtain the highest per capita female encounter rates at time of settlement. Of course we know this because coalition members remained together and became residents at the same time; nevertheless the findings raise the specter of resident singletons having higher per capita reproductive success than each member of a resident coalition.

To summarize, coalitions had the competitive edge in fights, were better able to acquire territories, and were less likely to be ousted from territories than singletons. Nevertheless, larger groups of males did not enjoy longer tenure over the whole study, they did not occupy larger territories, and their territories did not hold greater numbers of females while they were in residence compared with those occupied by smaller groups of males. Ability to acquire residence was therefore the principal benefit of coalition membership.

COMPARISONS WITH OTHER SPECIES

At this point it is worth summarizing first the similarities and then the differences between cheetah and lion male coalitions. Larger coalitions of lions are better able to obtain residency within a pride, the most marked difference being between singletons and pairs (Bygott, Bertram, and Hanby 1979; Packer et al. 1988). This closely replicates findings for cheetahs, in which the greatest difference was between singletons and coalitions (Caro and Collins 1986; 1987b). Larger coalitions of lions also enjoyed longer periods of tenure, which was an important component of reproductive success (Packer et al. 1988); this was similar to cheetahs in the first half of the study. The average length of time that lions held tenure was 33 months, well within the range shown by cheetahs, although lions' upper limits were much greater (130 months). In lions, the number of pride females available to males did not increase with coalition size (Packer et al. 1988). This result in some sense mirrored the finding that the number of females encountered on territories was unrelated to cheetah male group size. Nevertheless, larger coalitions of lions gained access to a greater number of females because they occupied more prides during their careers, either sequentially or simultaneously; trios of male cheetahs were sometimes able to hold more than one territory at a time as well (see below).

The main difference between the two species was that larger coalition size in lions conferred greater per capita reproductive success on members, as measured by DNA fingerprinting (Packer et al. 1991), whereas larger coalitions of cheetahs did not encounter a greater number of females on territories. The problem here is that the number of females that we sighted may have been a poor approximation of the number of cubs fathered by males, and that some matings might have occurred off territories.

Broadening the comparison to include other species, two more general points emerge from the demographic data. First, there were only three out of eighteen instances (16.7%) of a resident inheriting a territory after his coalition partner(s) disappeared, one of these cases being that of two males that continued in residence as a team (Oldonya Rongai; see fig. 9.1). This contrasts with waterbuck, in which five out of twelve changes (41.7%)

in territory ownership resulted from a male taking over a territory that he had previously occupied as a satellite (Wirtz 1982). Second, of the seventeen new occupations of territories on which I had records, only two (11.8%) were by males that had previously held a territory elsewhere in the study area, and both of these had been singletons. Satellite waterbuck males acquired neighboring territories in 16.7% of cases, and white rhinoceros beta males took over neighboring territories in three out of eleven cases (27.3%) (Owen-Smith 1975). In contrast to these ungulates, therefore, coalition membership in cheetahs did not enhance the probability of subsequently holding a territory alone or the chances of becoming resident on a nearby territory. Thus the cheetah's apparent similarity to these species, which also have a social organization with more than one male holding a relatively small area compared with a female's range, broke down in regard to the benefits experienced by "supernumerary" males. The picture of the cheetah that emerges is of a species whose mating system has no parallel among mammals, being different from those of ungulates in the way males obtain reproductive benefits and from that of lions in the way females are distributed.

Changes in the Pattern of Residence over Time

If the study had terminated in February 1985, it would have been assumed that single males had very little chance of becoming resident on a territory, but as figure 9.3 shows, single males began to acquire territories at an increasing rate from 1986 onward and retained them for considerable periods (see fig. 9.1). Consequently, an increasing proportion of territories came under the control of singleton males as the study progressed (fig. 9.4), which was the principal reason why the relationship between tenure and group size was lost when all years were considered together. This decline in the relative advantages of coalition membership in relation to residence was reminiscent of Frame's study period, when the probability of a single male becoming resident, although low, was greater than between 1980 and 1985. Moreover, one of his successful singletons held a territory for as long as 47 months.

At least three explanations are possible for the changed pattern of occupancy in the second half of the study: observers' inability to locate resident coalitions, reduced profitability of residency, and a decline in competition over territories.

There were two personnel changes during the second half of the study: C. FitzGibbon took over after I left in February 1985, and K. Laurenson started in October 1987. Our searches for cheetahs together during my visits to the field indicated that they were just as good at finding any type of cheetah association as A. Collins or I. It is conceivable that FitzGibbon and Laurenson were less assiduous at visiting potential territories than

Collins and I had been, given that male demography was not their primary interest, but this seemed unlikely on three counts. First, both of their studies necessitated locating cheetahs every month, and this required regular visits to areas of high cheetah concentrations out on the short grass plains, such as Barafu and Zebra kopjes, during times when one might expect males to set up residence. Second, through monthly correspondence, I monitored residence patterns and continually badgered them to check specific territories for new males, which they did with good humor. And third, one of the principal goals of my six visits to Serengeti over this period was to find new residents, so I spent much time searching vacant

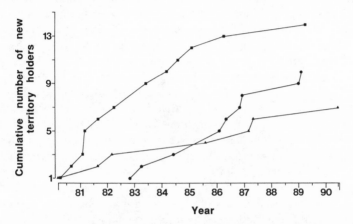

Fig. 9.3 Cumulative number of new territory holders who were single males (solid triangles), pairs (solid squares), and trios (solid circles), plotted against year of the study. 1 January (above the year numeral) and 1 July are shown on the x-axis. Earlier publications used demographic data up until February 1985.

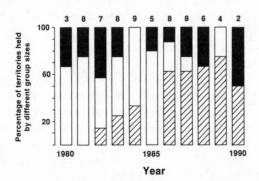

Fig. 9.4 Percentage of territories held by resident singletons (hatched), pairs (open), and trios (solid) during each year of the study. Number of territories held each year is shown above the bars.

territories in both wet and dry seasons. These arguments, together with the fact that there was no decline in the proportion of territories that were occupied over each year of the study [11], implied that we did indeed keep track of all the residents in the study area throughout the decade. Thus changes in personnel cannot readily explain alterations in residence patterns over time.

If territories became less profitable in terms of females in the second half of the study, they may have become unattractive to coalitions, allowing single males to set up residence with relative impunity. Sandell (1986), for example, has argued that it will pay a male carnivore to quit his exclusive range and move around in search of individual females if female densities decline. The number of females seen on territories between November 1981 (when observers' searching was first recorded) and February 1985 (the last month on which earlier publications were based), devalued by observers' visits to them, was greater than from March 1985 to the end of the study in July 1990 [12]. Yet I am loath to attach much weight to this result since the mean index of the number of females seen on territories was lower in the first than in the second half of the study, although the mean ranks on which the Mann-Whitney U test was based were higher. After February 1985 "active" territories were marginally less profitable than other areas [13], although this result was again difficult to interpret for the same reasons.

That certain coalitions took up residence during the second half of the study and incurred the costs of being territorial implied that residence was still a profitable strategy, at least for some individuals. Furthermore, nonresident coalitions did not remain floating within the study area for many months, as would be expected if returns outside territories were particularly high. Instead, floating coalitions passed through the study area, probably in search of vacant territories elsewhere. Putting all these arguments together with the fact that territoriality per se did not decline over the course of the study (only the proportion of resident coalitions), it is difficult to explain the increased representation of singletons on territories in terms of reduced female densities.

RELAXED COMPETITION OVER TERRITORIES

The third hypothesis, reduced competition over territories, was the most probable explanation for why single males were successful in holding territories later on in the study. Sightings of nonterritorial coalitions declined between the 1980–84 and 1985–90 periods from an average of 7.8 to 4.5 per year, resulting in relatively fewer floating coalitions compared with floating singletons in the study area after 1984 [14]. This decline probably stemmed from a reduction in the size of litters entering the adolescent population, as measured from sightings [15]. This may, in turn, have been related to increasing numbers of lions and spotted hyenas in the park (Borner et al. 1987), which are arguably the main cause of mortality of young cheetah cubs (Laurenson, in press-c). More specifically, there was a decline in sightings of litters 8 months and older containing two or more males, which would be likely to enter the adolescent population together [16]. With fewer coalitions as contenders for territories, single males had the opportunity to take up residence and retain tenure for longer periods than in the early 1980s. Similarly, small coalitions of lions held prides in the 1960s when cub survival was poor (G. Schaller, pers. comm.)

Relaxed competition would also explain why single males were able to occupy territories sequentially in later years. A male called Onear moved from Gol to Simba kopjes in January 1989 after P, Q, and R stopped being seen at Simba, and male Zebedee moved from Zebra to Gol kopjes (fig. 9.5; see also fig. 9.1). Zebedee was slightly larger than Onear (39.5 vs. 37.0 kg), and the latter had a large scar that could have affected his fighting ability (fig. 9.6), but it was unknown whether Zebedee ousted Onear from Gol.

Fewer contending coalitions might also explain why P, Q, and R were able to occupy two territories at the same time: first Oldonya Rongai in August 1985 and in addition Simba in May 1987 (fig. 9.5; see also fig. 9.1). P, Q, and R occupied both areas during both seasons and moved between them rapidly, judging from the facts that they were seen at Simba 2 days after being on the Rongai territory and that only 1 out of their 34 sightings was made in the intervening corridor. (Although they scent-marked in the corridor, their use of it was never properly assessed because high grass

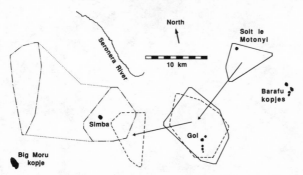

Fig. 9.5 Boundaries of territories occupied sequentially. Zebedee moved from the area north of Zebra kopjes to Gol kopjes (solid lines), Onear moved from Gol kopjes to Simba kopjes (dashed lines). Also shown are the boundaries of the Simba kopjes and Oldonya Rongai territories (dotted and dashed lines) that were occupied simultaneously by P, Q, and R. The corridor between them is represented by dotted lines, although its position is very uncertain (see text). Topography as in fig. 2.11.

and numerous warthog burrows made driving and searching there unpleasant.) The only other possible case of simultaneous occupation was that of A, B, and C. These males held Naabi from October 1977 to November 1978; in December and January they were seen at Gol kopjes, but were back at Naabi in January and March 1979 (G. Frame, pers. comm.). By the time I arrived in March 1980 they were occupying Gol kopjes only. Whether they held residence on both territories sequentially or simultaneously in the period between our studies is unknown.

In short, the working hypothesis is that relaxed competition allowed single males to hold territories, to hold them for many months, and to occupy territories sequentially; and allowed trios to occupy more than one territory at a time. An analogous change in the pattern of territoriality resulting from changing demographic parameters has been reported in pronghorn antelope. Byers and Kitchen (1988) observed a progressive decay in male territorial behavior which they attributed to catastrophic winter mortality that removed 75% of males. This shifted the age distribution toward young males, with the consequence that territorial defense by the few remaining old males was no longer effective against large numbers of raids by young males. In turn, this forced females to leave territories and seek calmer matings elsewhere; defending males then abandoned their territories.

The importance of demography in affecting competitive interactions is also seen in other species. For example, in group-living primates in which contests between group members over resources are common, females

Fig. 9.6 Onear, the resident male at Simba kopjes, had a 5 × 3.5 cm hardened scar on his right haunch from the day he was first seen. The outer part of his right pinna was also missing, possibly as a result of an earlier fight.

form strong bonds, usually with relatives, and support each other in agonistic encounters against third animals (e.g., in macaques). In contrast, in
primates that do not reside in cohesive groups (e.g., patas monkeys:
Chism, Rowell, and Olson 1984) or in which group members fission into
foraging parties (bonobos: White 1988), competition among group members is reduced and coalitions between group members are uncommon
(Wrangham 1980; van Schaik 1989; van Hooff and van Schaik 1992).

Reproductive Consequences of Male Strategies

It was not possible to estimate the reproductive consequences of male
behavior directly because mating was never observed during 10 years of
observation. Moreover, the sequential nature of matings by coalition
members reported from captivity and from the wild (S. Cable, pers.
comm., in Caro and Collins 1987b) would additionally hinder estimates of
per capita mating success. DNA fingerprinting analysis would be the best
method of ascertaining the proportion of cubs fathered by different
males, but in practice it was difficult to locate many of the floaters moving
through such a large area. Moreover, many of the males, both nonresident
and resident, were relatively shy (i.e., tameness 2 or more) and could not
be approached to within the necessary 15 m or so to immobilize them
using a blowpipe or a darting rifle. I considered using a more powerful
rifle that could cut through the relentless wind on the plains that often
blew the dart off course, but was loath to do so since there was a danger
that the dart would splinter a thin bone or injure an important muscle.
Obtaining skin biopsy samples would have been subject to the same problems (Karesh, Smith, and Frazier-Taylor 1987). In the face of these difficulties, I abandoned the idea of large-scale blood sampling and elected to
carry out rough calculations based on demographic information.

The average index of sightings of females inside and outside "active"
territories was 0.0128 and 0.0078 respectively, which took the number of
searches in different areas into account. The average number of sightings
of floaters, devalued by differential searching, was 0.0026 inside and
0.0014 outside "active" territories, or a ratio of 0.65 to 0.35. Occasional
forays by territorial males outside "active" territories were disregarded;
residents were always assumed to be on "active" territories. Thus floaters
had potential access to $(0.0128 \times 0.65) + (0.0078 \times 0.35) = 0.0111$
devalued females, whereas residents had access to $(0.0128 \times 1) = 0.0128$
devalued females per unit time. For both types of males, I assumed males
started to breed as young adults; however, resident males lived 1.78 times
as long as floaters (757.7 : 425.2 days: see table 8.3) so lifetime encounter
rates with devalued females had to be adjusted accordingly (residents:
$0.0128 \times 1.78 = 0.0228$; floaters: $0.0111 \times 1 = 0.0111$). These calcula-

tions assume that floaters inside "active" territories were as likely to encounter and mate with females as were residents. Of 63 sightings of
floaters inside "active" territories, 5 (7.9%) were of floaters in the company of females, whereas females were with territorial males in 8 of 149
sightings (5.4%) [17]. Thus floaters had roughly the same chance of encountering females on territories as did residents, but the numbers were
very small. (Contrary to the data, I suspect that floaters might actually
encounter fewer females on territories than do residents. While trying to
remain discreet, they might fail to see passing females and could ill afford
to encounter every female for fear of being chased off or attacked by pa-
trolling residents.)

To estimate the fitness payoffs of living in groups of different sizes, it
was necessary to determine the percentage of males in each group size
that did or did not become territorial within the study area. Using data
from Caro and Collins (1987b), these were, respectively, 8.8% and 91.2%
for singletons, 70.6% and 29.4% for pairs, and 37.5% and 62.5% for trios.
Multiplying lifetime encounter rates for the two strategies for each male
group size ($\times$ 100) gave payoffs of $0.201 + 1.012 = 1.213$ for singletons,
$(1.610 + 0.326)/2 = 0.968$ for pairs, and $(0.855 + 0.694)/3 = 0.516$ for
trios. These calculations assume that reproductive payoffs were divided
equally among group members and, in the absence of any systematic data
on this issue, indirect behavioral observations presented in chapter 11 indicate that this may be a reasonable assumption.

In short, per capita lifetime reproductive payoffs for males in each
group size were apportioned as 45.0% for single males, 35.9% for males
in pairs, and 19.1% for males in trios. This distribution of payoffs across
group size closely corresponded to the actual distribution of males in different-sized groups: of 110 males, 40.9% lived as singletons, 40.0% in
pairs, and 19.1% in trios (Caro and Collins 1987b). In essence, the calculations show that, for single males, the reduced reproductive returns of
floating were balanced by not having to share matings with coalition
partners.

At face value, similarity in the proportions of males found in each
group size and per capita payoffs associated with them indicates that
males were behaving in an ideal free way (Fretwell 1972); that is, that
males distributed themselves according to group size and territorial status
in such a way that each individual received an equivalent payoff with respect to the potential number of females he could encounter. Nonetheless, at least four points make me question this overall conclusion.

First, the ideal free model assumes that individuals are "ideal" in their
assessments, in this case of their chances of encounters with females, and
that they are "free" to go to the area of their choice, with no individual
being able to prevent another from so doing. While it is plausible that

male behavior was finely tuned to reproductive returns insofar as males probably joined up with others when access to territories was at stake, they were certainly not free to become residents wherever they wanted. Intruders were killed by residents, as determined from both direct observations and locations at death. The evidence suggests that nonterritorial males were unable to make a serious challenge against residents, being disadvantaged by factors such as low body weight, ill health, and stress (see chap. 8). Instead, cheetahs conform to a despotic model in which some individuals monopolize an unfair share of female encounters through territorial behavior.

Second, I suspect that most floating coalitions of males eventually took up residence outside the study area because they passed quickly through it; it was the floating singletons that remained on the plains (chap. 8). Their being in a numerically strong position to challenge residents outside the study area explains why floating coalition members continued to associate despite experiencing low female encounter rates outside "active" territories. If they had stayed within the study area, they should have parted company to avoid competition over estrous females. If these coalitions settled elsewhere in the park, the reproductive returns of pairs and trios as calculated above are underestimates of unknown magnitude.

Third, my calculations are very crude, being based on multiplying a series of mean values together, which can produce an enormous error variance in the final product. Fourth, and least persuasive, there are very few mammalian examples in which different behavioral tactics yield equivalent reproductive payoffs when individuals show an asymmetry in their ability to hold resources (but see Dunbar 1984 for a possible exception). Admittedly our understanding of intraspecific variation in mammalian behavior is still at a descriptive stage (Lott 1991), but alternative tactics in mammals are often age-related, with young males obtaining a low proportion of matings (Caro and Bateson 1986; Kropowski 1993). As examples, young red deer stags attempt to disrupt harems held by older and more competitive males (Clutton-Brock et al. 1979) and young elephant seals attempt to intercept females on their way to and from the beach (LeBoeuf 1974). In other mammals, subordinates simply try to make the best of a bad situation (Davies 1982; Dunbar 1982). As examples, subordinate bighorn rams attempt to copulate by coursing and blocking females' movements while the dominant rams tend ewes (Hogg 1984). In some topi populations, males that set up resource defense territories or occupy the periphery of a lek arena obtain lower reproductive benefits than those on successful leks (Gosling and Petrie 1990). Cheetahs should probably be bracketed with these latter two examples because males that were unable to bid for territories took on a roaming lifestyle.

At present, then, the cheetah data are of insufficient resolution to determine whether the two strategies have equivalent reproductive payoffs or whether single floating males are making the best of a bad situation, but a series of arguments favor the second possibility, the most important of which is that floaters are disadvantaged compared with residents.

Summary

1. Males lived alone or in permanent groups of two or three males. These coalitions were usually composed of littermates, although many of the trios were made up of two brothers and a nonrelative.

2. Nonrelatives apparently joined forces in circumstances in which superior numbers would allow them to take over a territory or fend off a challenge from intruders; this usually occurred in their second or third year of life.

3. Coalitions were more likely to occupy a territory than were singletons because of their numerical advantage in fights. Competition over territories was an important source of male mortality because many males were found dead either inside or on the borders of territories.

4. Length of tenure on territories was unrelated to coalition size over the 10-year study period, contrary to earlier results. Territory area was unrelated to the size of the male group in residence.

5. In contrast to the first half of the study, single males were successful in securing and retaining tenure of territories in the second half. The best explanation is that there were fewer coalitions of males attempting to become resident after 1985.

6. During this period of relaxed competition, some single males occupied territories sequentially, and a trio occupied two territories simultaneously.

7. Rough calculations show that lifetime reproductive payoffs for male cheetahs living in different-sized groups were matched by the proportion of males found in coalitions of different sizes, implying that males distributed themselves in different-sized groupings in an ideal free way.

8. Nonetheless, competition over territories and the fact that nonresident males, usually singletons, were phenotypically disadvantaged compared with residents suggested that they had not chosen the floating strategy voluntarily. More likely, these individuals were forced to follow a strategy with low reproductive returns, indicating that population-wide payoffs of different grouping patterns were not equivalent.

Statistics

1. There were no trios of adolescent males, but 23 pairs and singletons of adolescent males combined, compared with 5 trios of young adult

males, and 15 pairs and singletons of young adult males combined over the first 5 years of the study, Fisher test, $P = .016$.

Adolescent males (Ns as above) compared with 16 trios of adult males and 51 pairs and singletons of adult males combined, Fisher test, $P = .005$.

Young adult and adult males (Ns as above), Fisher test, $P > .2$.

2. Of dependent litters 6 months or older, 2 contained trios of male cubs, and 45 contained pairs or singletons of male cubs combined, compared with no trios of adolescent males, and 23 pairs and singletons of adolescent males combined over the first 5 years of the study, Fisher test, $P > .4$.

Male cubs (Ns as above) compared with trios of young adult males, and pairs and singletons of young adult males combined (Ns as above), Fisher test, $P = .019$.

Number of trios, pairs, and singleton dependent male cubs ($N = 2, 16, 29$ respectively) compared with trios, pairs, and singletons of adult males ($N = 16, 23, 28$ respectively), G test, $G_2 = 10.149, P = .012$.

3. Number of singletons compared with coalitions that acquired a territory from 1980 to 1985, G test, $G_1 = 19.178, P = .0001$ (see text).

In Frame's study from 1973 to 1978, Fisher test, $P = .061$ (see text).

4. Compared with coalitions, single males were more likely to acquire a territory as a result of a vacancy appearing than by displacing residents, Fisher test, $P = .029$ (see table 9.3).

5. Ten males died inside or on the borders of territories (this included the male dying in the corridor between Simba and Oldonya Rongai while P, Q, and R occupied both territories; see fig. 8.5), whereas one died outside them, binomial test, $P = .012$; analysis was restricted to males located by radiotelemetry to avoid the possibility of more assiduous searching for carcasses inside territories.

6. Estimated number of months males were resident on a territory between March 1980 and July 1990, including data from three territories from Frame's earlier study (G. Frame, pers. comm.). The first, conservative measure excluded males that may have been resident before March 1980 ($N = 6$ individuals or groups), those that were definitely ($N = 2$) or possibly ($N = 2$) resident in July 1990, those resident when Frame's study ended ($N = 1$), males that occupied a territory for 3 months or less ($N = 6$), that might be making a visit from outside the study area, and residents of Ngorongoro Crater ($N = 2$) that may have been subject to different demographic pressures (above Ns are not necessarily exclusive of one another). For males that retained tenure after they lost a coalition partner(s), months between the last sighting of their partners and their first sighting subsequent to the loss were not included as months of residence. Kruskal-Wallis test comparing singletons ($N = 9$ individuals, $\bar{X} = 20.9$ months,

median = 17.0, interquartile range 13.0–27.0), pairs (N = 6 pairs, $\bar{X}$ = 16.0, median = 16.0, IQ range 8.5–22.0), and trios (N = 3 trios, $\bar{X}$ = 36.0, median = 40.0, IQ range 15.0–53.0), H = 2.350, df = 2, $P > .3$.

Estimated number of months males were resident on a territory between March 1980 and July 1990, including data from three territories from Frame's earlier study (pers. comm.) using a less conservative measure that included all demographic information (the second coalition to occupy Ngorongoro Crater was, however, excluded as data were of poor quality; see fig. 9.1). Kruskal-Wallis test comparing singletons (N = 11 individuals, $\bar{X}$ = 22.3 months, median = 20.0, interquartile range 12.0–28.0), pairs (N = 16 pairs, $\bar{X}$ = 17.6, median = 12.0, IQ range 4.0–26.0), and trios (N = 5 trios, $\bar{X}$ = 26.0, median = 20.0, IQ range 8.5–46.5), H = 2.280, df = 2, $P > .3$.

7. Single males were more likely to lose territories because they were displaced by incoming males whereas coalitions were more likely to vacate them, Fisher test, P = .047 or $P > .1$, depending on which figures in table 9.5 were used.

8. Territory size occupied by single males (N = 8 individuals, $\bar{X}$ = 40.9 km², SE = 8.2), pairs of males (N = 10 pairs, $\bar{X}$ = 32.8 km², SE = 6.7), and trios (N = 4 trios, $\bar{X}$ = 41.8 km², SE = 18.6) excluding territories derived from less than five sightings, Kruskal-Wallis test, H = 0.522, df = 2, $P > .7$.

9. Number of sightings of females (mothers, lone adults, and adolescent females combined) on "active" territories occupied by singletons, pairs, and trios, corrected for the number of observers' visits to different grid squares, N = 1,163, 952, 628 different grid squares visited respectively. Index $\bar{X}$s = 0.0140, 0.0102, 0.0139 respectively, Kruskal-Wallis test, H = 2.309, df = 2, $P > .3$.

10. Number of sightings of females on "active" territories occupied by singletons, pairs, and trios, corrected for the number of observers' visits to different grid squares from November 1981 to February 1985, N = 203, 661, 287 different grid squares visited respectively, Index $\bar{X}$ ranks = 608.5, 573.5, 558.7 respectively, Kruskal-Wallis test H = 7.179, df = 2, P = .028. Note: Contrary to $\bar{X}$ ranks, index $\bar{X}$s did not increase with male group size (0.0146, 0.0106, 0.0147 respectively) so the significant result should be treated with caution.

From March 1985 to July 1990, N = 960, 291, 341 different grid squares visited respectively, Index $\bar{X}$s = 0.0142, 0.0092, 0.0133 respectively, Kruskal-Wallis test, H = 6.424, df = 2, P = .040.

11. Spearman rank order correlation coefficient between the proportion of territories visited each year that were held at least once by residents during that year and year of the study (1990 was excluded as it was incomplete), N = 10, r_s = −0.098, $P > .5$.

12. Number of sightings of females inside "active" territories before and after February 1985, corrected for visits to different grid squares (three occupied territories that spanned the two halves of the study were represented twice), $N = 776$, 1,096 different grid squares visited respectively. Index $\bar{X}$ *ranks* = 978.7, 906.6, Mann-Whitney U test, $z = -4.772$, $P < .0001$. Note: Contrary to the $\bar{X}$ ranks, index $\bar{X}$s were lower before February 1985 than after (0.0120, 0.0138 respectively) so the significant result should be treated with caution.

13. Number of sightings of females inside and outside "active" territories in the second half of the study (March 1985 to July 1990), corrected for the number of observers' visits to different grid squares, $N = 1,805$, 6,907 different grid squares visited respectively. Index $\bar{X}$ ranks = 4314.6, 4367.5 respectively, Mann-Whitney U test, $z = -1.712$, $P = .087$. Note: Contrary to the $\bar{X}$ ranks, index $\bar{X}$s were higher inside than outside territories (0.0125, 0.0107 respectively) so the result should be treated with caution.

Number of sightings of females inside and outside "active" territories in the first half of the study (November 1981 to February 1985), corrected for the number of observers' visits to different grid squares, $N = 1,093$, 6,911 different grid squares visited respectively, index $\bar{X}$s = 0.0126, 0.0056 respectively, $z = -13.879$, $P < .0001$.

14. Comparison of the number of sightings of nonterritorial coalitions and singletons between 1980 and 1984 ($N = 134$ sightings) and between 1985 and 1990 ($N = 204$ sightings); coalitions accounted for 23.1% of sightings in the first period and 13.2% in the second, G test, $G_1 = 5.465$, $P = .0182$.

15. Comparison of the number of sightings of litters of 8 months or older containing one cub of either sex and more than one cub of either sex between 1980 and 1984 ($N = 235$ sightings) and between 1985 and 1990 ($N = 261$ sightings); litters of more than one cub accounted for 78.7% of sightings in the first period and 62.5% in the second, G test, $G_1 = 15.881$, $P = .0001$.

16. Comparison of the number of sightings of litters of 8 months or older containing one male cub and more than one male cub between 1980 and 1984 ($N = 161$ sightings) and between 1985 and 1990 ($N = 122$ sightings); litters of more than one male cub accounted for 50.3% of sightings in the first period and 31.2% in the second, G test, $G_1 = 10.601$, $P = .0012$.

17. Proportion of sightings of floaters and residents seen with females on territories, Fisher exact test, $P = .181$ (see text).

A trio of males attempt to topple a 2-year-old wildebeest together. Simultaneous involvement of this kind was unusual. (Drawing by Dafila Scott.)

10

FORAGING SUCCESS AND COOPERATIVE HUNTING IN MALE GROUPS

Why do carnivores live in groups? Because some of these species capture prey considerably larger than themselves, it is easy to believe that there might be advantages to hunting in groups, and hence that communal hunting is an important selective pressure driving group living in this order (Kruuk 1975; Wilson 1975). For example, groups of 1 to 3 spotted hyenas set out to hunt wildebeests in Ngorongoro Crater, but their average group size was 10.8 when they hunted heavier zebras (Kruuk 1972). In coyotes, the percentage of mule deer in the winter diet increased with pack size, as determined by scat analysis (Bowen 1981).

Unfortunately, a change in prey preference is far from sufficient evidence that communal hunting is evolutionary cause of sociality. To reject or accept the idea that communal hunting is responsible for group living, data on prey preferences, the behavior and success of individuals hunting in groups, changes in food intake with group size, and some estimate of the relative importance of food for individual fitness all need to be collected (see chap. 1). Not surprisingly, it has proved extremely difficult to obtain all of these measures on any one species, although studies of Harris's hawks (Bednarz 1988) and lions (Packer, Scheel, and Pusey 1990) have approached this. In Serengeti male cheetahs hunted diurnally, and I saw complete sequences of numerous hunts. This provided me with an opportunity to collect extensive data on male cheetahs living alone and in coalitions of two and three individuals.

Prey Preferences and Male Group Size

Larger groups of male cheetahs attempted to capture heavier prey than did smaller groups of males (fig. 10.1), with prey larger than Thomson's gazelles (i.e., >20 kg) making up a significantly greater proportion of their attempts [1]. Larger groups hunted wildebeests more often than did smaller groups [2]. Also, coalitions selected wildebeests out of mixed-species groups of Thomson's gazelles and wildebeests, whereas only one singleton, male B, was observed to do this. It was common to see a trio notice a herd of wildebeests from as far off as 3 km and walk directly toward them through herds of Thomson's gazelles, which scattered in their wake, yet make no attempt to hunt these smaller prey. The relationship between male group size and proportion of attempts on large prey held both in the wet season, when wildebeests were in the study area, and in the dry season, when they were mainly absent but when hartebeests, topi, warthogs, and Grant's gazelles were still patchily distributed over the plains and were resident along the woodland edge [3]. Conversely, larger groups of males hunted significantly fewer Thomson's gazelles than smaller groups in both wet and dry seasons [4]. The result would have been even stronger had I excluded a single male, B, who had formerly

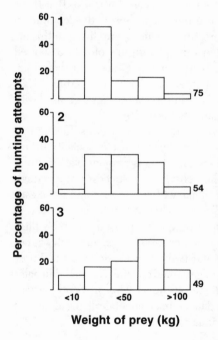

Fig. 10.1 Percentage of hunting attempts made on prey of different body weights by single males (1), by pairs (2), and by trios (3) when the quarry was known. Prey were divided as to whether they weighed <10, 11–20, 21–50, 51–100, or >100 kg. Number of hunts is shown to the right of the histograms. Prey that were stumbled upon (hares, neonate Thomson's and Grant's gazelles) rather than actively chosen by cheetahs are excluded from the figure.

been a member of a trio (A, B, and C) before his companions disappeared. Alone on his territory, he attempted to capture 8 yearling and 1 2-year-old wildebeest (seven successfully) in a total of 11 hunting attempts. As a coalition member, he had frequently captured wildebeests, had initiated 10 out of 16 hunts, and had led the approach in 8 out of 13 for which I had records. His preference for hunting large quarry might therefore have developed while he was with his companions.

Coalitions' preference for large prey items was also apparent in the way they hunted. First, there was a greater likelihood that more than one group member would participate in a hunt of large prey than in a hunt of small prey (table 10.1) [5]. Second, larger groups of males apparently tried harder to catch large prey than small prey because their hunts lasted longer [6] although they were no worse at hunting large prey (see below). Third, during hunts of large prey, but especially during unsuccessful hunts, the time spent in energetically costly all-out sprints increased with male group size, as judged from the behavior of the leading male, suggesting that members were particularly keen to catch their quarry [7]. It was difficult to explain these findings in terms of the extra work required to hunt large quarry because expected success rates were not particularly low (D. Scheel, pers. comm.).

Males could choose wildebeests and juvenile and adult Thomson's gazelles because they could see them standing or feeding, but hares and neonate gazelles were hidden and were usually flushed from vegetation as cheetahs walked through it. The number of attempts on these small, concealed prey did not differ between singletons and coalitions [8]. This was surprising, since encounter rates with concealed prey might be expected to rise with group size, as males often walked parallel to one another, disturbing a greater area than would a singleton. Discrepancies in distances traveled by males or in local hare densities might explain this result, but I think a difference in hunting styles was more probable. Whereas

TABLE 10.1 Participation of Coalition Members in Hunts of Small and Large Prey

Coalition member hunts	Prey weighing	
	<20 kg	>20 kg
Alone	16	15
With a partner	26	69

Note: Number of hunts in which only one or more than one member of a coalition hunted the same herd of prey or quarry at the same time (hunts of neonate gazelles and hares were excluded).

coalitions usually started to walk purposefully in the direction of a herd of prey, singleton males would sometimes walk from tussock to tussock, examining each in turn. Their more active searching for concealed prey might therefore have made up for the greater number that two or three males would flush in their wake.

An association between larger hunting parties and selection of larger prey items has been noted for many other carnivores. For example, the mean group size of spotted hyenas hunting subadult gemsbok in the Kalahari was 3.0 but was 4.8 when hunting adults (Mills 1990); and in Serengeti, it was most common for one wild dog to hunt a Thomson's gazelle but for five to hunt a wildebeest (Fanshawe and FitzGibbon 1993).

Because many predators divide up medium-sized or large prey among all group members once it is captured, there is little incentive for individuals to participate actively in hunting unless the probability of hunting success can be greatly enhanced, the chance of encountering prey increased, or the costs of pursuing or subduing prey ameliorated by their participation (Packer and Ruttan 1988). There is evidence for and against each of these points, depending on the study. First, in many studies of large carnivores, hunting success on a specific prey item does not improve with predator group size, as when Ngorongoro hyenas hunt adult wildebeests or zebras (Kruuk 1972). In others, however, it does improve, as in lions hunting a variety of prey species in Etosha National Park, Namibia (Stander 1992b). Second, although predator group size is unlikely to affect the chance of encountering prey for most predators, especially those in open ecosystems supporting high prey densities, Scheel (1993) noted that large groups of Serengeti lions encountered buffaloes more often than small groups. Third, though pursuit costs might decline if additional group members cut prey off at corners, for example, there are only occasional and anecdotal accounts of this at present. Fourth, the costs of subduing prey might decrease with group size, possibly making it profitable for an individual to aid a valuable group member in tackling prey. Though such costs might initially decline with increasing group size, it is difficult to see how additional individuals in group sizes over five could substantially lower such costs (see Mech 1970) and thereby explain, say, the hunting payoffs for twenty-five hyenas hunting zebras in Ngorongoro Crater (Kruuk 1972).

Given the equivocal evidence on each of these points, it is entirely plausible that in many situations some or even most of the individuals setting out to hunt large quarry are not hunting at all. Rather, the initiator is forced to target a large prey item once surrounded by several conspecifics in order to ameliorate the now large costs of sharing her booty. Work on the decisions that individuals make at the start of the hunt under different social conditions is badly needed.

Hunting Behavior and Male Group Size

Male cheetahs in larger groups hunted no more or less frequently than males in smaller groups, nor did they spend a greater or lesser proportion of the day hunting [9]. Hunting success, measured as the percentage of hunts of all types of prey that resulted in kills, did not increase significantly with male group size [10]. Approximately three-quarters of hunts by singleton males and pairs of males, and about half of those by trios, were unsuccessful, and broadly, their hunts failed for similar reasons (table 10.2). Prey spotted approaching singletons and coalitions to the same extent despite the latter involving more cheetahs, and this was an important reason for failure in all group sizes. Prey running off without seeing the cheetahs and males failing to make a serious hunting attempt were also important reasons for failures. Irrespective of group size, hunts rarely failed because cheetahs were outrun or outmaneuvered, or because they could not bring prey down. My notes show that single males failed to topple large prey on only one out of nine occasions.

When hunts were divided according to size of prey attempted, large male groups were not significantly more likely to catch small prey (weighing <20 kg) than were smaller groups, although there was an increase in hunting success with group size [11]. On larger prey weighing >20 kg, hunting success differed significantly, but this was a consequence of pairs having poor hunting success and did not result from a linear rise in success as group size increased [12]. Although these results are somewhat equivo-

TABLE 10.2 Percentage of Hunts by Young Adult and Adult Males that Failed for Different Reasons

	Male group size		
	1	2	3
Number of failed hunts	39	73	31
Seen by prey	28.2	24.7	22.6
Prey run off without seeing cheetahs	17.9	19.2	25.8
Terrain too open	5.1	5.5	3.2
Start rush too early	7.7	2.7	0
Outrun or outmaneuvered	7.7	5.5	3.2
Unable to pull prey down	2.6	0	3.2
Prey defended by self or others	0	5.5	0
Miscellaneous antipredator behavior	2.6	8.2	0
Prey too big or did not dare	0	4.1	3.2
Not serious	25.6	11.0	29.0
Other	2.6	13.7	9.7

cal, they do not demonstrate any clear effect of male group size on hunting success. In short, larger male groups attempted to capture a higher
proportion of heavy prey but were not especially successful in catching
these large prey items. Nonetheless, their preference for attempting large
prey meant that these items made up a somewhat greater proportion of
their kills, especially the kills of trios (fig. 10.2) [13].

Across species, association between size of hunting party and hunting
success varies enormously depending on both the prey and the predator
under scrutiny. A well-known example is that of spotted hyenas hunting
wildebeest calves in the Crater (Kruuk 1972). When one hyena was involved, the success rate was 15%, but if two or three took part, they were
successful on 74% of occasions because one could subdue the calf while
the other kept the mother at bay. In contrast, when adult wildebeests were
hunted, there was no relationship between success rates (at around 40%)
and the number of hyenas present at the end of the chase.

Packer and Ruttan (1988) compared the expected hunting success of
groups whose members cooperated (cooperators) with that of groups
whose members joined the hunt but did not actively participate (cheaters)
in a number of species. They found that when the hunting success of singletons was low, as in hyenas hunting wildebeest calves, it was worthwhile
for a companion to cooperate since its effect on hunting success overcame

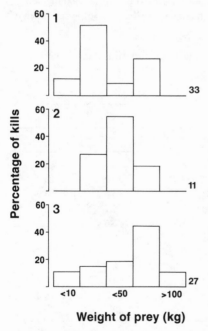

Fig. 10.2 Percentage of kills of prey of
different body weights made by single
males (1), by pairs (2), and by trios (3).
Prey were divided as to whether they
weighed <10, 11–20, 21–50, 51–100,
and >100 kg. Number of kills is shown
to the right of the histograms. Prey that
were stumbled upon (hares, neonate
Thomson's and Grant's gazelles) rather
than actively chosen are excluded from
the figure.

the costs of joining (see also Stander and Albon, 1993). When singleton hunting success was already high, however, as in hyenas hunting adult wildebeests, a partner could do little to improve the outcome and this could not outweigh the costs of active participation. They also compared observed hunting success for cheetahs against expected values for group members that cooperated or cheated using data reported by Eaton (1970b). Those data showed an increase in success rates at group size two, but then a decline at group sizes three and four, and so differ from those reported here. Eaton's data represented only four cheetah groups, however, and included a mother with three cubs, a pair of adult males, and a mother with four adult-sized cubs. Since hunting behavior differs according to the sex, age, and reproductive status of predators in general (Caro

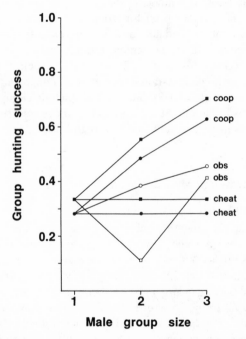

Fig. 10.3 Group hunting success for male cheetahs plotted against male group size on prey weighing 20 kg or less, mostly Thomson's gazelles (circles), and more than 20 kg, mostly wildebeests (squares). Solid points show the expected group size–specific hunting success if groups were composed entirely of cooperators $(H_n = 1 - (1 - H_1)^n)$ or entirely of cheaters $(H_n = H_1$, where H_1 is the probability that a single male will catch prey, and H_n is the probability that a group of n individuals will catch prey; see Packer and Ruttan 1988). Open points show the observed values based on 115 hunts by singletons, 70 hunts by pairs, and 26 hunts by trios on small prey, and on 27, 53, and 46 hunts respectively on large prey.

and FitzGibbon 1992) and cheetahs in particular (this study), it is inappropriate to combine data in this fashion.

Applying Packer and Ruttan's model to the data presented here (fig. 10.3), it can be seen that, for small prey, observed hunting success fell below the values expected if group members were cooperating but above the values expected if members were cheating. On large prey, cheating appeared prevalent. In other words, the model predicted that coalition members would rarely participate actively in other members' hunts but would do so occasionally—exactly what was found when the behavior of group-living males was examined in detail (see below). In general, then, the observed lack of cooperation supports the model, which predicted little cooperation when hunting single prey, when hunting relatively large prey, and when success rates were reasonably high, all characteristics of the cheetah data set. The model's prediction that increased cooperation was likely to occur at small predator group sizes was not supported. Like cheetahs, several other predators hunt single, relatively large prey items that are subsequently divided up among group members, and have singleton hunting success rates between 20% and 40%. Their group members too show little or no cooperation in the sense of enhancing hunting success (Packer and Ruttan 1988). Such species include chimpanzees hunting red colobus in Gombe Stream National Park (Busse 1978) and lions hunting various ungulates in Queen Elizabeth National Park, (van Orsdol 1984).

Foraging Success and Male Group Size

MEAN FORAGING RETURNS

Taking all group sizes together, males on average ate 0.05 times each daylight hour they were watched. When the occasional nighttime meal was taken into account, as determined from an increase in overnight belly size, they ate one meal every 1.25 to 1.50 days (i.e., every 30 to 36 hours). Individual males living in larger groups spent a slightly greater proportion of the day eating from carcasses [14], not because they ate more meals [15] but because their large carcasses lasted longer. Figure 10.4 shows the foraging success of individual males living in different-sized groups. Despite great variation in foraging efficiency within each group size, individuals in larger groups tended to consume more meat per daylight hour than individuals living in smaller groups, with the major difference lying between pairs and trios [16].

A number of confounding factors could account for this finding. First, males in different group sizes might have been sampled during different seasons when food was more or less abundant. Males in each group size were, however, observed for a similar number of hours in wet and dry seasons (totals for singletons were 193.2 hours and 267.6 hours respectively; for pairs 262.7 and 127.6; and for trios 173.8 and 106.4). These ratios were especially well matched for pairs and trios, yet per capita intake was more than twice as high for trios as for pairs. Moreover, during the dry season when wildebeests had left the study area, coalitions of males (usually residents) could still find large prey, such as Grant's gazelles, hartebeests, topi, and warthogs on both plains and woodland border territories, while these prey species were always available to singletons (usually floaters) on the plains-woodland border. In the wet season all group sizes were out on the plains where they could normally encounter wildebeests. For these reasons, differential prey availability was unlikely to confound the association between group size and foraging success.

Nighttime feeding might also have affected the result. If singletons dined disproportionately at night, daytime observations on time spent feeding and meat ingested would underestimate total intake. Fortunately, overall foraging success could be estimated from belly sizes taken when males were first sighted each day because they represented a combination of night and daytime foraging. Across sightings made on consecutive days, belly sizes of single males were no more likely to increase or remain the same (both of which would indicate an overnight meal) than were belly sizes of coalition members [17]. Furthermore, on those nights when belly sizes did increase, singletons did not apparently consume more than coalition members during hours of darkness [18]. In fact, male belly sizes rose sharply with male group size during the wet season when all sightings

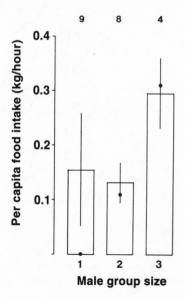

Fig. 10.4 Per capita mean number of kilograms of meat eaten per daylight hour by nonadolescent male cheetahs living alone (denoted as 1), in coalitions of 2, and in coalitions of 3; bars show SEs, dots show medians. Males were observed for a minimum of 12 or more daylight hours; numbers of individuals or coalitions watched are shown above the bars.

were considered, while belly sizes were also greater for coalition members than for singletons in the dry season, though not significantly (table 10.3) [19]. This confirms that per capita food intake increased with male group size, irrespective of season.

VARIANCE IN FORAGING RETURNS

Individuals might be sensitive to long periods without food that could lead to starvation (Clark 1987; Houston et al. 1988). Nevertheless, variation in belly size showed no relation to male group size when standard deviations in individuals' belly sizes were compared [20]. Belly sizes of males in smaller groups were, however, more likely to drop below size 4, the point at which cheetahs started to hunt, suggesting that they were hungrier [21].

In sum, males in larger groups had a higher per capita food intake, principally because a greater proportion of their diet consisted of large prey. As the proportions of large kills and large prey attempted showed significant increases with male group size, but hunting rates and success did not, my working hypothesis is that prey preferences were primarily responsible for the increased representation of large prey in the diet and higher foraging returns. In an attempt to evaluate the relative importance of hunting rates, hunting success, and prey preferences, however, I multiplied group size averages for these variables together but sequentially set each variable as that for a particular group size. Products were affected as much by altering the proportion of large prey attempted as by altering hunting frequencies or success rates on large prey, which suggested that the latter variables were as influential in determining the proportion of large prey captured as were attempts on large prey. The importance of prey preferences in affecting per capita food intake should therefore be treated with caution.

The optimal foraging group size was three for male cheetahs in the Serengeti. While demographic factors and the number of sibling males reaching independence together constrained group size (chap. 9), it was

TABLE 10.3 Mean ($\pm$ SE) Belly Sizes of Males

	Singletons	Pairs	Trios
Wet season	6.1 ± 0.3 (133)	6.7 ± 0.3 (73)	7.0 ± 0.4 (45)
Dry season	6.0 ± 0.2 (142)	6.9 ± 0.4 (56)	6.3 ± 0.6 (21)

Note: Numbers of sightings from which figures were derived are shown in parentheses. For each coalition, an average was taken of its male members. Trios' low belly sizes in the dry compared with the wet season may have been caused by reduced prey density on territories.

not limited by food availability. Members of larger coalitions of four or five (reported from other regions; Graham 1966) could still have satisfied individual needs by capturing adult male or female wildebeests, which were well within their hunting capabilities.

EXPLANATIONS FOR HIGH FORAGING RETURNS IN MALE GROUPS

Assuming that a high plane of nutrition was beneficial for males, what prevented singletons from increasing their intake? First, it is possible that single males were at greater risk of injury when tackling large quarry than were coalition members that could tackle prey together, but that I had observed an insufficient number of dangerous predatory attempts to pick this up. At present, I am not disposed toward this argument because coalition members jointly tackled prey on only 18.8% of occasions (see table 10.6), implying that they did not seek to ameliorate potential injury costs in this way. I did see a single male pursue an adult male wildebeest, the last in a passing line of eleven animals, catch up with it after a short 10-m chase, grasp its haunches, and climb up on its back. At this point the wildebeest kicked with both back legs simultaneously, dislodging the cheetah, who did a backward somersault 1.5 m into the air and landed on all paws at once, apparently unhurt. Clearly, this was a dangerous situation for the cheetah, but without a large number of records it is impossible to say whether risks of injury in capturing large prey were greater for singletons than for coalition members.

A second possibility was that groups containing fewer males chose smaller prey because they were actually less successful at hunting large items starting at a given distance from them (H. Kaplan, pers. comm.). Thus if trios were better hunters than singletons but were also more keen to initiate hunts on a given prey type from a long distance off, then they would be more likely to alert prey, and this factor would mask differences in success rates across group size. Since I did not record changing prey availability on a microlevel (though I tried at the start of the study but found it too difficult), I could not calculate males' willingness to hunt, or the distance from which they approached prey once they had seen it.

There may be some merit to this idea because prey were more likely to run off without seeing the cheetahs as male group size increased (see table 10.2), possibly implying that male group members started their hunts farther away and so gave prey greater opportunity to flee for other reasons. Arguing against it, an equivalent proportion of hunts across group sizes failed because males were seen by prey, suggesting that any group size–related differences in approach distance had little effect on hunting success. In short, without data on success rates standardized for encounter rates with prey, the possibility that singletons were worse hunters at a given distance from the quarry cannot be eliminated. According to this argument, then, males in smaller groups might have chosen smaller prey items, and consequently have suffered reduced foraging returns, in order to compensate for their lower hunting success on large prey items at long distances from herds.

A third and rather different alternative is that a higher plane of nutrition might not have conferred marked benefits on singleton males. Recall that estimates of longevity did not differ between single males and coalition members (chap. 8), implying that any importance of increased food intake was overshadowed by other factors. Admittedly, well-fed males might be able to avoid starvation during times of prey scarcity or a run of unsuccessful hunts, be better prepared to ward off the challenge of infectious disease (see Sinclair 1977), or use their weight to good advantage in fights by pinning their opponent down. Yet singletons were in a position to have increased their hunting rates, given that they spent so much of the day resting and given that females employed this strategy during lactation (Laurenson 1992). The fact that they did not calls into question the benefits of additional foraging returns for these individuals. Thus without definitive evidence on the effects of foraging success on reproduction and survival, the possibility remains that males in coalitions may have simply preferred to hunt large ungulates because smaller prey would have provided insufficient foraging returns per hunt. Coalition members had to share all but the smallest items more or less equally with their partners (table 10.4). Thus males in coalitions may have tried for large wildebeests to satisfy group members' needs, a factor that single males could ignore (the limited needs hypothesis). Since differences in prey preferences did not spring from an inability of single males to capture large prey, or from group-living males having markedly greater hunting success on large prey items, this hypothesis requires attention.

To explore this in more detail, I monitored situations in which male cheetahs left a carcass voluntarily while there was still meat on it in order

TABLE 10.4 Mean (± SE) Percentage Difference among Group Members in Time Spent Eating Different-Sized Prey

	Pairs	Trios
Small (neonate Thomson's gazelles and hares)	53.8 ± 10.5 (13)	38.8 ± 6.4 (8)
Middle-sized (neonate Grant's gazelles, subadult and adult Thomson's gazelles)	—	9.2 ± 2.0 (6)
Large (wildebeests)	6.4 ± 1.5 (5)	5.8 ± 1.4 (15)

Note: Numbers of carcasses are shown in parentheses. For trios, the mean of the three differences was used.

to estimate how much a male could eat during a meal. On average, a male could ingest an estimated maximum of 12.5 kg per meal (SE = 0.8, N = 17 males) with 16.5 kg being the largest meal ever eaten. For a singleton, therefore, there was little point in taking prey larger than a neonate wildebeest with approximately 12 kg of meat on it (table 10.5). Remember, irrespective of group size, cheetahs were unable to defend their carcasses against terrestrial scavengers larger than a jackal; nor could they cache their carcasses. On the other hand, members of a pair or trio would be completely satisfied with nothing smaller than a yearling wildebeest (22.5 or 15.0 kg) to fill their respective stomachs. For a singleton, the weight of flesh of an adult male Thomson's gazelle (10 kg) was close to the maximum he could eat at one sitting (2.5 kg short) but represented a large deficit for members of pairs or trios (7.5 kg and 9.2 kg short of their per capita maxima respectively). Therefore it was unsurprising that coalitions usually chose wildebeests while single males usually picked Thomson's gazelles.

Table 10.5 also shows the age-sex class of prey most often attempted by each group size from the middle and large range of prey items. As male group size rose, the amount of per capita flesh available on its "modal" prey item increased. Specifically, a single male would be best off hunting a 2-month-old wildebeest to fill his stomach capacity, but in most months

TABLE 10.5 Kilograms of Flesh on the Most Common Prey Items in the Serengeti Available to Individual Cheetahs Feeding in Different-Sized Groups

Prey	Estimated weight of prey	Estimated weight of flesh available for each male[a]		
		Male group size		
		1	2	3
Adult female TG	17.7	7.1	3.6	2.4
Adult male TG	20.0	(10.0)	5.0	3.3
Neonate W	20.5	12.1	6.1	4.0
2-month-old W	29.1	17.6	8.8	5.9
4-month-old W	38.2	23.1	(11.6)	7.7
Yearling W	84.0	45.0	22.5	(15.0)
2-year-old W	143.7	55.2	27.6	18.4
Adult female W	182.1	62.8	31.4	20.9
Adult male W	201.1	69.3	34.7	23.1

Note: Parentheses denote the prey item most often attempted by each group size of those shown in the table. Lines denote the size of prey below which individuals in each group size would be fully satisfied and would have to leave meat uneaten because they would be physically unable to consume more. TG, Thomson's gazelle; W, wildebeest. All weights in kg.

[a] From Blumenschine and Caro 1986.

wildebeests of this age were unavailable because of this species' pronounced birth peak (Estes and Estes 1979). If, instead, he caught an adult male Thomson's gazelle, he could experience a potential shortfall of roughly 2.5 kg. A pair of males would be best off hunting a yearling wildebeest, but if a 4-month-old wildebeest was captured instead, members would each suffer only an approximate 1 kg shortfall. A trio could ill afford to attempt anything smaller than a yearling wildebeest to satisfy group needs, but once they caught one there was 2.5 kg to spare for each member of the trio. Therefore, individual males in larger groups would have had a greater opportunity to gorge themselves at these large carcasses.

At present, I cannot distinguish between the limited needs hypothesis, the hunting success standardized for encounter rate idea, and costs of prey capture being greater for smaller groups of males. More extensive data on the risks of injury during prey capture and the effects of food intake on males' reproduction and survival would help evaluate these possibilities.

General Consequences of Uneven Weight Distribution of Prey

The limited needs hypothesis illustrates the effect that distribution of prey sizes can have on predators' individual foraging efficiencies. If prey size (or more precisely, weights of edible flesh per carcass: Caro 1989b) were to increase linearly across abundant (here used as a proxy for relatively easy to catch) prey species, different-sized predator groups might adjust their prey preferences to satisfy only the combined needs of their members and nothing more. Assuming that hunting rates did not change with group size and that multiple kills were unusual, this would result in individuals consuming equivalent amounts irrespective of predator group size. In most ecosystems, including Serengeti, however, there are large gaps in the size distribution of abundant prey, preventing individuals in groups of differing size from equalizing intake without adjusting hunting rates. Depending on the exact weight distribution of abundant prey, some predator group sizes will experience increased per capita foraging returns while others will suffer lower intake rates (fig. 10.5). Thus the relationship between group size and per capita foraging returns is likely to be different for the same predator species living in different ecosystems. It will also be different for each predator species living in the same ecosystem because each species will select a different size range of prey and have a different stomach capacity. The ease with which various prey species can be captured will affect group size–related intake rates as well.

For example, in contrast to male cheetahs, Serengeti lionesses did not experience changes in per capita daily food intake or variance in intake rate with group size in times of prey abundance (Packer, Scheel, and

Pusey 1990). In times of prey scarcity both measures were significantly higher for solitary lionesses than for females in groups of two to four because they had to divide up food. In groups of five to seven lionesses that captured buffaloes, foraging returns rose to levels experienced by single females even after sharing prey. A single lioness (141 kg, Wilson 1968) weighs three times as much as a male cheetah (41 kg, this study) and can subdue heavier prey; her modal prey are adult zebras and wildebeests in Serengeti (Schaller 1972c). Male cheetahs in groups can switch from Thomson's gazelles to plentiful young wildebeests weighing twice as much as they do in order to increase per capita intake, but a lioness with companions either has to share a wildebeest or zebra (which she can sometimes consume entirely herself over several meals), suffer the costs of hunting more often, or attempt larger prey. In Serengeti there is a large gap in prey size between wildebeests and zebras (adult females 163 and

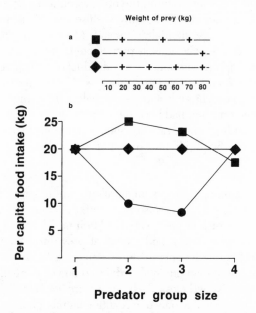

Fig. 10.5 Distribution of prey species (a) and group size–related per capita foraging returns (b) in three hypothetical ecosystems: (a) Presence of available prey of a certain weight is denoted by +. Square, ecosystem where prey of intermediate size is abundant; circle, ecosystem where prey of intermediate size is absent; diamond, ecosystem where prey shows a linear increase in size; (b) Per capita foraging returns plotted against predator group size in each ecosystem. Predators are arbitrarily assumed to weigh 20 kg and to be capable of capturing prey of a maximum size of 1.25 times the combined weight of their group. Hunting rate is invariate across group sizes so that only one prey animal can be caught. Group members then eat the entire carcass, dividing it equally between them.

302 kg respectively) and the next step of prey up: elands, buffaloes, and giraffes (adult females 460, 750, 828 kg respectively: weights from Sachs 1967 and Smithers 1983). In attempting larger prey, a lioness would have to switch from subduing prey up to twice her own weight to tackling prey three to five times her size (Caro 1989b). In general, single felids are loath to do this (Packer 1986), as apparently are two to four lionesses, although five or more will take on a buffalo. In short, gaps in the size distribution of abundant ungulate species help to explain why individual foraging returns rise with group size in (smaller) male cheetahs but decline or remain static in (larger) lionesses living on the Serengeti plains.

Communal Hunting by Coalition Partners

Coalition members spent their time in close proximity to one another (<200 m), and if one left to hunt, the others would almost invariably follow (although not necessarily hunting themselves). Thus hunting group size was the same as residential group size. Moreover, in those hunts in which more than one male actively participated, all the males would usually attempt to capture the same prey individual once a chase had begun, and were never seen to make multiple kills. There appeared to be five possible ways in which adult and young males (those that had been together for some time and had become accustomed to one another's hunting styles) might hunt cooperatively, and an additional two ways in which partners might be helpful in the context of scavenging.

SIMULTANEOUS HUNTING

To start with, coalition partners might all attempt to get as close as possible to prey without being seen so that more than one cheetah would be in place to start a rush at prey. Thus coalition members might all be expected to stalk, trot toward, and crouch at prey during the same hunt. Indeed, in 66.7% of 84 hunts made by pairs and in 72.9% of 59 hunts made by trios, more than one male exhibited one or more of these three hunting patterns. Nonetheless, such hunts were actually slightly less successful than those in which only one coalition member hunted (table 10.6) [22]. This corroborates the failure of hunting success to conform to the cooperation model (see fig. 10.3). It is therefore possible that males were simply trying to be close by when the quarry was brought down while deceiving companions that they were hunting seriously, given the little additional energy cost of these behaviors compared with walking. Alternatively, simultaneous hunting merely reflected individuals' motivation for hunting the quarry independently. In a third of all lions' hunts some individuals refrained from hunting, either remaining immobile or stalking only a very short distance (Scheel and Packer 1991), in a manner very similar to male cheetahs. In both species, therefore, not all individuals present at the onset of a hunt chose to participate in it.

SIMULTANEOUS CHASING

Cheetahs might cooperate in chasing if they could reduce the distance to fleeing prey, either by cutting corners or by alternating the lead position during fast sprints when their companion began to tire. Members of pairs and trios chased prey together in, respectively, 38.7% of 31 hunts and 40.6% of 32 hunts in which chasing occurred, but prey was no more likely to be caught than when it was chased by only one of the males (table 10.6) [23]. Often simultaneous chasing consisted of one male chasing the prey fast while the other(s) ran on behind, tracking him and the prey's flight path fairly closely but apparently not trying very hard, as described for some wild dog hunts (Reich 1981). Very rarely did I see cheetahs cut prey off at corners or switch lead positions during a chase. Prey was usually quite far off when a cheetah started its rush (30 m minimum) and ran directly away, making it difficult for males to cut corners in the initial stages. If the flight path described an arc, it might be more feasible to take shortcuts to the prey or for one male to overtake its tiring companion later on in the hunt. Yet chases were normally so short, less than 10 seconds in duration, that such opportunities were very limited.

Chases were energetically costly, as judged by experiments showing that cheetahs overheat during prolonged running (Taylor and Rowntree 1973), by the time it takes them to recover breath after a chase (Estes 1991), and by the long pauses that sometimes occurred before eating (Caro 1987a). In addition, cheetahs were occasionally lightly injured during chases; two females limped after unsuccessful pursuits. These costs and the limited benefits must have prevented males from joining chases more often, and additionally made it unlikely that males would try to de-

TABLE 10.6 Outcome of All Hunts in which One or More Members of a Coalition Were Involved

	Prey killed	Prey escapes
Coalition member hunts prey		
Alone	15	29
With a partner	19	80
Coalition member chases prey		
Alone	21	17
With a partner	9	16
Coalition member contacts prey		
Alone	24	2
With a partner	6	0

ceive their partners about their willingness to catch prey. More likely each was trying to get close enough to the prey to knock it over, or at least be on hand to start eating straight away.

The benefits of simultaneous chasing in other carnivores have yet to be ascertained. Compared with male cheetahs, Serengeti lionesses simultaneously rushed at prey in a higher proportion of hunts (65%) (though they did not necessarily chase it), but the benefits of such joint action remain unclear since so few kills were witnessed (Scheel and Packer 1991). In wolves, which chase prey over much longer distances, pack members have been seen strung out in line behind a moose when pursuing it through snow. They made shortcuts to one side when the moose veered off, but the effect of this on hunting success was unknown (Mech 1970). Wild dogs, in which several pack members can be involved in chasing one victim, do cut corners, thereby reducing the distance to the quarry (Estes and Goddard 1967; Kruuk and Turner 1967). Estes and Goddard concluded that they would gain little from running in relays since the lead dog has ample speed and endurance for any chase. Indeed, recent quantitative evidence shows that the rate at which dogs gained on their quarry when it started to zigzag did not increase when more dogs were involved in the hunt (Fanshawe and FitzGibbon 1993), questioning the import of running in a relay or cutting corners for this species.

CONTACTING PREY SIMULTANEOUSLY

Male cheetahs might cooperate in using their combined weight to bring prey to the ground after it had been contacted. This occurred in 9.1% of 11 hunts made by pairs and in 23.8% of 21 hunts made by trios in which prey was contacted (fig. 10.6). Nonetheless, prey was so likely to be killed once contacted that hunting success did not improve if prey was toppled by more than one male (table 10.6) [24].

Climbing onto an ungulate or trying to pull it over might be energetically costly and was definitely dangerous. Aside from the male I saw kicked high into the air, I witnessed another being tossed in the same fashion, and on three occasions saw males being butted and knocked over; in one of these cases a male was trampled by a wildebeest mother. Though none of these incidents resulted in males being visibly injured, cheetahs were wary of wildebeests that approached too close and charged them. An instance of a lame wildebeest chasing two male cheetahs away demonstrates just how formidable they could be. Males were particularly concerned by zebras and would crouch defensively: I saw zebras surround and then drive off a pair of males, and K. Laurenson saw a female being chased by a zebra. Finally, P. Swan saw elands charge and toss one of three males in a coalition, and in most parts of Africa cheetahs run from herds of eland (C. Hillman, pers. comm.). I suspect that males rarely helped one

Fig. 10.6 A pair of males (D and E) attempt to pull over a yearling wildebeest simultaneously. Note the lack of coordination. The male on the left of the picture is using his weight to twist the victim's neck and so make it fall to its left, while the male on the right of the picture has bitten the wildebeest's right hindleg and is pulling backward in order to make it topple to the right.

another topple prey because the benefits were insubstantial and the costs were relatively high.

Lurid descriptions of the way several carnivores can bring down and dispatch a victim indicate that communal hunting in this terminal stage could well enhance success rates on large prey, in some species, though no formal comparisons have been made to my knowledge. Among canids and hyenids large ungulate prey is brought to a halt and executed by individuals repeatedly slashing and tearing at the haunches, genitals, abdomen, and neck region until the victim is pulled down or simply falls over from shock and exhaustion, and is then devoured alive (Kleiman and Eisenberg 1973). Though such attacks seem uncoordinated, the presence of additional attackers must reduce the victim's chances of escaping and hasten its demise, thereby lowering risks of injury to each predator.

Felids usually grab prey in the head or neck region, and additional group members can probably help only by throwing prey to the ground where it is less mobile. For example, Schaller (1972c) described how four male lions toppled and slaughtered a bull buffalo using this technique. Cats kill prey by breaking the braincase, by separating the neck vertebrae, or by clamping their jaws around the throat or muzzle (Kleiman and Eisenberg 1973). Additional group members can therefore help little in preventing escape or killing the victim, since it will die anyway, but they could speed the process by disemboweling it during suffocation, as witnessed in groups of cheetahs.

DRIVING RESCUERS AWAY

A fourth way in which cheetah males might cooperate would be to drive off animals that came to rescue the victim. Once a wildebeest calf was contacted, was brought to the ground, or was being throttled by a cheetah, the presumed mother or occasionally another wildebeest sometimes turned on the cheetah and chased it off the victim. In other circumstances ungulates milled around a captured conspecific, approaching to within 30 m. If in these situations one coalition partner ran at the ungulate giving aid and kept it from reaching the victim, the latter always died. If, however, the mother was not prevented from getting near her calf, she could knock the cheetah off her offspring and was always able to rescue it (table 10.7) [25]. Despite these demonstrable benefits, males rarely drove defenders away because ungulates attempted to rescue conspecifics only infrequently.

Keeping a mother at bay is probably the most consistent and important benefit yet demonstrated for communal hunting in carnivores. A single golden jackal was successful in only 14.3% of chases of gazelle fawns because it was constantly attacked by the fawn's mother. Pairs were always successful because the mother chased one jackal while the other subdued the offspring (Lamprecht 1978a). Single spotted hyenas hunting wildebeest calves (discussed earlier) were always driven away from the calf, whereas groups had a 100% success rate because one dealt with the calf while the other took on the mother if she attacked (Kruuk 1972). A similar benefit has now been reported for groups of wild dogs hunting wildebeests (Fanshawe and FitzGibbon 1993). In wolves, Mech (1970) de-

TABLE 10.7 Outcome of All Hunts in which Prey Was Captured by a Coalition Partner and Conspecific Prey Attempted to Rescue It

	Prey subdued and killed	Prey captured but eventually escapes
Conspecific prey attempt to rescue victim	0	3
Conspecific prey attempt to rescue victim but kept away by coalition partner	5	0

scribed a mother moose being driven away by pack members while others concentrated their attacks on her calf, eventually killing it. These observations demonstrate both that maternal defense by relatively large ungulates can be a potent force in promoting offspring survival (see chap. 12) and that several species of carnivores, including cheetahs, can circumvent this antipredator strategy by hunting communally.

HERDING PREY

Last, males might coordinate their behavior by fanning out or by herding prey toward a concealed partner. In presenting a broad front by fanning, cheetahs could increase their chances of encountering any prey that scattered. Pairs and trios often advanced toward herds of wildebeests in this way but I did not record it systematically and have no information on its effects.

On two occasions I saw prey gallop past a concealed coalition member while running from the other male, but it escaped in both instances. Intuitively it seemed that ambushing could work well for predators that stalk their prey. Of 795 lion hunts observed by Stander (1992b) in Etosha National Park, 40.4% involved some lions fanning out and encircling prey while others waited or advanced, slowly adjusting their movements to one another; 30.3% involved similar but less coordinated activities; and 29.3% were solo or uncoordinated hunts. Well-coordinated hunts had higher success rates than other group hunts. Moreover, certain individuals repeatedly occupied center and wing positions and compensated for one another's roles, and were more successful if they occupied their preferred positions (Stander 1992a).

Schaller (1972c) described similar encircling behavior in Serengeti lions, which caused prey to bolt and run close enough to be captured by a lioness that remained hidden in the grass; however, this occurred infrequently. If such hunts constituted cases of cooperation, Scheel and Packer (1991) argued that "refraining" individuals, those that hung back, should participate as often in the final rush as "pursuing" lions that made the detours. In fact "refraining" lions took little part in rushes, implying that in Serengeti they were not coordinating their activities with pride members but were letting others do the work.

Etosha consists of flat, open terrain, and has sparse vegetation and relatively low prey density compared with Serengeti. As a consequence, hunting success of solitary lions is far lower (2.3%) than it is in East Africa (11% to 29%; Schaller 1972c; Elliot et al. 1977; van Orsdol 1981), suggesting that lions would benefit from hunting in groups (Packer and Ruttan 1988). Indeed, Stander (1992a) has argued that coordinated stalking and pursuit is the only means by which large ungulates can be reliably caught in open habitat.

Sophisticated communal hunting has also been described in chimpanzees living in the Tai forest, Côte d'Ivoire (Boesch and Boesch 1989).
Here 91% of hunts involved two or more animals and 63% involved collaboration between participants. Collaboration was defined as hunters
performing different complementary actions all directed at the same prey,
usually red colobus monkeys. Here some individuals took the role of drivers, while others captured prey by pursuit, blocked escape routes, or am-
bushed prey. Chimpanzees in East Africa rarely hunt in this fashion or
with such sophistication (Busse 1978). Comparative studies of both chimpanzees and lions show that differences in ecology rather than cognitive
capacity best explain the extent of collaboration during hunts.

Interspecific Competition

Before concluding any discussion of group size and foraging in carnivores,
the relationship between group size and interspecific competition must
be considered. This is necessary because data on foraging success based
on observed hunts might be confounded if animals in different-sized
groups supplemented their diets to varying extents through scavenging.
The issue has beleaguered estimates of foraging success in groups of lions
(Packer 1986), and although cheetahs scavenge rarely, this behavior has
been reported from both Serengeti (Caro 1982) and Kruger National Park
(Pienaar 1969). Also, cheetah groups of different sizes might themselves
be subject to differential scavenging pressure dependent on their effectiveness at defending carcasses.

SCAVENGING BY MALES

Table 10.8 shows that males scavenged infrequently, that they normally
procured little meat in this fashion, and that they usually scavenged from
female cheetahs with cubs, atypically showing no sexual interest in them.
Scavenging was too infrequent to affect group size–related food intake.
Rates of scavenging by group size could not be calculated accurately as
some incidents occurred during ad lib observations, but there was no obvious change with male group size.

Proximity to dangerous predators and low foraging returns must have
accounted for infrequent scavenging in cheetahs. In order to encounter
carcasses regularly, cheetahs would need to pinpoint their positions by
observing vultures descending to a spot, as do lions (Houston 1974) and
spotted hyenas (Kruuk 1972). Yet if either predator were already present,
it would prevent cheetahs from gaining access to meat. Worse, lions kill
adult cheetahs. In addition, I once saw cheetahs being followed by hyenas
from 20 to 50 m away for several hours, which made them uneasy and

inhibited their hunting. It would therefore be unwise for cheetahs to seek out carcasses and court harassment. If only vultures were present, they might have already consumed much flesh before cheetahs arrived, and large numbers (>50) sometimes made cheetahs nervous. Both G. Schaller and K. Laurenson (pers. comms.) saw cheetahs being driven from a carcass by them. These considerations help explain why males primarily poached from female cheetahs. After watching a female make a kill they could race over and drive her from it well before other scavengers arrived. They also explain why cheetahs (usually females in my experience) took over from any jackals that they saw pursuing gazelle fawns; scavengers would not yet have arrived and jackals would relinquish the chase to them. Simply encountering a carcass fortuitously was extremely unusual (although I saw a family do this once; Caro 1982) as the high density of spotted hyenas and vultures in the study area meant that even carcasses as large as buffaloes disappeared within 48 hours.

SCAVENGING FROM MALES

Of the 110 carcasses that I watched males consume until they left them, 12.7% were stolen by spotted hyenas and none by lions. Earlier studies conducted on the plains reported similar figures (13%, Schaller 1972c;

TABLE 10.8 Known Instances of Scavenging by Male Cheetahs in This Study

Prey species	Weight of flesh on carcass	Estimated weight available to males	Estimated weight eaten by males	Species from which males scavenged
Singletons				
Neonate Thomson's gazelle	1.7	1.7	1.7?	Mother and 1 (3-month) cheetah
Subadult male Thomson's gazelle	5.5	5.5	0.8	Mother and 2 (9-month) cheetahs
Pairs				
Adult hare	0.9	0.9	0.9	Mother and 1 (6-month) cheetah
2-year-old wildebeest	55.2	37.7	13.7	2 spotted hyenas
Zebra (age & sex unknown)	?	?	0	1 striped hyena
Trios				
Large neonate Grant's gazelle	7.5	7.5	7.4	Mother and 3 (4-month) cheetahs

Note: All weights in kg.

"nearly 10%," Frame and Frame 1977b) despite hyena densities being lower at that time (Borner et al. 1987). Cheetahs had already eaten a third of the flesh on these carcasses, however, losing 65.2% (SE = 13.2%) of the meat on the nine carcasses for which I had accurate flesh estimates. Assuming that the number of kills and proportion of flesh stolen are representative, males lost approximately 9.2% of the flesh that they captured to hyenas.

Hyenas located a greater proportion of the kills of single males than the kills of coalitions [26], perhaps because a singleton took roughly twice as long as a pair to consume a given carcass. In Serengeti, numerous factors affect the length of time that carcasses persist (Blumenschine 1987). For instance, they are less likely to be discovered in riparian habitat, but are more likely to be discovered where local hyena densities are high in the proximity of active dens, or at wildebeest aggregations, which attract many hyenas from long distances away (Hofer and East, in press). For example, male B lost five yearling wildebeest carcasses to hyenas at Gol kopjes while the wildebeest migration was there. Given these confounding variables and the small sample of 14 appropriated carcasses, I am skeptical that single males necessarily faced a genuine handicap in regard to hyenas. Indeed, larger carcasses, characteristic of coalitions' diets, were more likely to be found by hyenas than smaller ones since they lasted longer [27]. Also, losses of edible flesh to hyenas were higher from carcasses weighing more than 20 kg (an average of 75.5% lost from six carcasses) than from carcasses weighing less than 20 kg, more often consumed by singletons (an average of 44.7% lost from three carcasses). For all these reasons I am confident that differential loss of carcasses to scavengers could not explain belly size differences seen in male groups of differing size.

Once a cheetah kill had been discovered, male group size had no influence on whether the carcass could be defended against scavengers. Almost without exception, single spotted hyenas and lions could drive cheetahs of both sexes off kills. Indeed, even pairs of males would stop hunting when hyenas were close by, presumably because their kill might be stolen; I once saw a trio terminate their hunt when they heard lions roaring although they could not see them. In contrast, male and female cheetahs continued to eat in the presence of jackals. These observations contradict the hypothesis that cheetahs benefit from group living by defending carcasses more effectively (Eaton 1979; Lamprecht 1981). No data were presented to support this claim, and any such advantages can be only trivial.

In general, willingness to contest a resource must, for both parties, depend on the magnitude of the costs of forgoing eating weighed against the risks of injury in a fight. I took no systematic data on the costs to cheetahs and hyenas, but some anecdotes suggest that both parties took numerical advantage and hunger into account. One of two males chased an adult hyena from a yearling wildebeest while the other cheetah was killing it, but both left when a second, juvenile hyena arrived 75 seconds later. A single male cheetah ate the shoulder of his yearling wildebeest carcass for 4 minutes while an adult hyena ate the flank; he even followed while the hyena attempted to drag the carcass off. Finally, two males displaced an adult and a subadult spotted hyena with very full bellies from a 2-year-old wildebeest carcass; the hyenas left when one of the males showed a defensive threat from 25 m away (see table 10.8). In other species, the same factors apparently apply. One or two lions relinquished carcasses in the face of 20 to 40 spotted hyenas (Packer 1986), and the length of time for which wild dogs fed at carcasses was longer when the ratio of dogs to spotted hyenas was high (Fanshawe and FitzGibbon 1993).

Reasons for Grouping in Males

Results presented in this chapter show that overall foraging success increased with group size for male cheetahs living on the Serengeti plains because groups of males attempted larger prey items that had sufficient meat on them to satisfy all group members. Interspecific competition and communal hunting played virtually no role in improving per capita group intake. In fact, coalition members behaved selfishly, often hunting at the same time but rarely in a coordinated fashion, and their hunting success did not profit as a consequence. Collaboration was restricted to occasional instances of driving conspecific prey away. No other carnivore study has shown that foraging success increases consistently with group size. Stander (1992b) demonstrated that pairs of Etosha lionesses had significantly higher per capita foraging returns than singletons in the dry season, but returns then dropped for group sizes of three and above. In the wet season, there was no clear relationship between foraging success and group size.

Could enhanced foraging returns be the evolutionary cause of grouping in male cheetahs? Male reproductive success in mammals is usually limited by access to females, not by access to food (Trivers 1972). Food intake would likely be an important determinant of fitness only if it enabled males to attain more matings. Although enhanced food intake might, in theory, result in increased survivorship, estimates of longevity were no greater for males in groups than for singletons (chap. 8). Enhanced food intake might also have resulted in greater body weight, which could have affected the outcome of disputes over territory ownership between similar-sized groups, but any such effect would have been dwarfed by group size, which was the key determinant of access to territories, and hence to females, when competition was intense (chap. 9). In short, there is little support for the hypothesis that elevated foraging returns are the selective agent causing male cheetahs to live in groups, although they may be a side benefit of grouping. It is even more difficult to argue that communal hunting drives group living, since it contributes little to foraging success. Grouping in male cheetahs is best explained as a response to intraspecific competition.

Summary

1. Male cheetahs living in groups accompanied one another on hunts; thus hunting and residential group sizes were the same. Weights of prey attempted increased with male group size because coalitions focused primarily on wildebeests while singletons concentrated on Thomson's gazelles.

2. More than one member of a coalition was likely to participate in a hunt if large prey was the quarry. In other carnivores, size of prey attempted also increases with the number of individuals setting out to hunt.

3. There were no consistent differences in the rates at which different-sized groups of males hunted, or in their hunting success on either large or small prey.

4. Comparison of observed hunting success with that expected if coalition members were either hunting cooperatively or were cheating indicated there was little active coordination between coalition members during group hunts.

5. Preference for large prey probably resulted in these items making up a greater proportion of the kills of larger male groups as summarized in app. 11.

6. Individual males in larger groups spent a greater proportion of the day eating and, per capita, ate more per unit time. Variance in food intake did not change with group size. Neither sampling bias nor differential nighttime foraging confounded these results. Single males were thinner in both wet and dry seasons and were more often hungry than those in coalitions.

7. Smaller groups may have experienced lower per capita foraging returns because high risks of injury prevented them from regularly tackling large prey, or because they actually had lower hunting success at a given distance from prey. Measures of hunting were too insensitive to uncover either factor. Alternatively, males in larger groups may have preferred

large prey in order to satisfy group members' needs that smaller groups could afford to ignore. Since coalition members' large carcasses had a great deal of meat on them, they could eat to capacity, but singletons were sometimes left short.

8. Available flesh on prey does not increase linearly across different age and sex classes and species of prey within an ecosystem. Thus the association between per capita foraging returns and predator group size will differ for each predator species that has a different stomach capacity and which targets a different suite of prey. This may explain why individual food intake rose with group size in male cheetahs but declined or remained unchanged with increasing group size in lionesses.

9. Coalition members hunted together at the same time in about two-thirds of their hunts, chased prey simultaneously in about two-fifths of their hunts, and rarely attempted to bring down prey together. In none of these activities did joint participation improve the chances that prey would be captured.

10. When wildebeests defended a calf that had been caught by cheetahs, coalitions could improve their success rates if one member kept the rescuer at bay while the other throttled the victim. Similar advantages to this form of communal hunting have been reported in other carnivores. Cheetahs did not drive prey toward concealed coalition partners.

11. Very occasionally males scavenged kills, usually from female cheetahs, but this was too infrequent to affect the relationship between food intake and group size.

12. Cheetahs lost 12.7% of their carcasses to spotted hyenas but this was equivalent to 9.2% of the meat they might have eaten. Evidence that singletons lost more to hyenas than did coalitions was weak.

13. Although increased coalition size resulted in greater per capita foraging returns, group size probably had far greater impact on reproductive success through its effect on intraspecific competition between males. Grouping in male cheetahs can best be viewed as a response to intraspecific competition, with greater food intake being a secondary consequence of group living.

Statistics

1. Number of hunting attempts made on prey that weighed >20 kg by nonadolescent male singletons, pairs, and trios over the whole year, $N = 141, 112, 68$ hunts respectively, 20.6%, 47.3%, 64.7%, G test, $G_2 = 43.508, P < .001$.

2. Total number of hunting attempts made on wildebeests by nonadolescent male singletons, pairs, and trios when the quarry was known,

N = 132, 114, 69 hunts respectively, 12.9%, 32.5%, 56.5%, G test, G_2 = 42.696, P = .0001.

3. Number of hunting attempts made on prey that weighed >20kg by nonadolescent singletons, pairs, and trios in the wet season: N = 99, 72, 53 hunts respectively, 21.2%, 54.2%, 73.6%, G test, G_2 = 44.676, P < .001.

Dry season: N = 42, 40, 15 hunts respectively, 19.0%, 35.0%, 46.7%, G test, G_2 = 4.914, P < .1.

4. Number of hunting attempts made on Thomson's gazelles by nonadolescent singletons, pairs, and trios over the whole year (neonate gazelles excluded): N = 141, 112, 68 hunts respectively, 61.0%, 29.5%, 17.6%, G test, G_2 = 46.321, P < .001.

Wet season: N = 99, 72, 53 hunts, 56.6%, 22.2%, 13.2%, G test, G_2 = 37.61, P < .001.

Dry season: N = 42, 40, 15 hunts, 71.4%, 42.5%, 33.3%, G test, G_2 = 10.067, P < .01.

5. Coalition members (excluding adolescents) simultaneously hunted prey that weighed >20 kg more often than they simultaneously hunted prey that weighed <20 kg (neonate gazelles and hares excluded), G test, G_1 = 5.950, P < .02 (see table 10.1).

6. Time that nonadolescent singletons, pairs, and trios spent in hunts of large prey that weighed >20 kg, N = 21, 35, 32 hunts respectively, $\overline{X}$s = 6.3, 8.0, 12.3 min, Kruskal-Wallis test, H = 5.544, P < .1.

7. Time that nonadolescent singletons (N = 4 individuals), pairs (N = 11 coalitions), and trios (N = 2 coalitions) spent in unsuccessful rushes and chases (combined) of large prey that weighed >20 kg, using data on the leading group member only, $\overline{X}$s = 4.8, 15.7, 47.5 sec, Kruskal-Wallis test, H = 9.139, P < .02.

8. Number of hunting attempts made on neonate gazelles and hares by nonadolescent singletons and coalitions of all sizes, N = 141, 180 hunts, 16.3%, 16.7%, G test, G_1 = 0.007, P > .9.

9. Frequency with which nonadolescent singletons (N = 11 individuals), pairs (N = 5 coalitions), and trios (N = 5 coalitions) hunted per daylight hour watched, $\overline{X}$s = 0.15, 0.22, 0.15 hunts/hr respectively, $F_{2,24}$ = 0.948, P > .4 on logged data.

Percentage of the day that nonadolescent singletons (N = 10 individuals), pairs (N = 8 coalitions), and trios (N = 4 coalitions) hunted per daylight hour watched, $\overline{X}$s = 1.24, 1.99, 1.45, $F_{2,19}$ = 1.155, P > .3 on logged data.

10. Hunting success of nonadolescent singletons (N = 10 individuals), pairs (N = 10 coalitions), and trios (N = 5 coalitions) on all types of prey, 22.6%, 24.8%, 47.1%, $F_{2,22}$ = 1.659, P > .2.

11. Hunting success of singletons, pairs, and trios on all prey that

weighed <20 kg, N = 115, 70, 26 hunts respectively, 28.1%, 38.3%, 45.5%, G test, G_2 = 3.508, P > .1.

A similar pattern was seen when comparing hunting success on all prey that weighed <20 kg of nonadolescent singletons (N = 6 individuals), pairs (N = 5 coalitions), and trios (N = 3 coalitions) that were seen to hunt >10 times; 27.8%, 53.2%, 44.6%, Kruskal-Wallis test, H = 2.229, df = 2, P > .3.

12. Hunting success of singletons, pairs, and trios on all prey that weighed >20 kg, N = 27, 53, 46 hunts respectively, 33.3%, 11.3%, 41.3%, G test, G_2 = 12.763, P < .01.

Comparing singletons and pairs: G_1 = 5.405, P < .02; singletons and trios: G_1 = 0.461, P > .4; pairs and trios: G_1 = 12.081, P < .001.

A similar pattern was seen when comparing hunting success on all prey that weighed >20 kg of nonadolescent singletons (N = 6 individuals), pairs (N = 5 coalitions), and trios (N = 3 coalitions) that were seen to hunt >10 times, 14.9%, 8.2%, 38.9%, Kruskal-Wallis test, H = 4.796, df = 2, P < .1.

Comparing singletons and pairs: Mann-Whitney U test, U = 13, P > .7; singletons and trios: U = 3, P > .1; pairs and trios: U = 0, P = .036.

13. Percentage of all kills made by nonadolescent singletons, pairs, and trios that weighed >20 kg over the whole year: N = 41, 30, 29 kills respectively, 22.0%, 20.0%, 65.5%, G test, G_2 = 17.664, P < .001.

Wet season: N = 31, 22, 23 kills respectively, 25.8%, 27.3%, 69.0%, G test, G_2 = 12.512, P < .002.

Dry season: N = 10 kills (singletons), N = 14 kills (coalitions combined), 10.0%, 21.4%, Fisher test, P > .3.

14. Percentage of 15-minute scans individual nonadolescent singletons (N = 10 individuals), pairs (N = 8 coalitions), and trios (N = 4 coalitions) watched for 12 or more hours spent eating per day; for each coalition, an average was derived from group members' percentages, $\bar{X}$s = 2.2%, 3.3%, 5.9%, $F_{2,19}$ = 2.719, P = .092 on logged data.

15. Number of meals nonadolescent singletons (N = 11 individuals), pairs (N = 11 coalitions), and trios (N = 5 coalitions) watched for 12 or more hours were seen to eat per daylight hour watched, $\bar{X}$s = 0.04, 0.06, 0.08, $F_{2,24}$ = 1.235, P > .3 on logged data.

16. Kilograms eaten per hour by individual nonadolescent singletons (N = 9 individuals), pairs (N = 8 coalitions), and trios (N = 4 coalitions) watched for 12 or more hours. Means, medians, and interquartile ranges respectively, 0.15, 0, 0–0.23 kg/hr; 0.13, 0.11, 0.07–0.21 kg/hr; 0.30, 0.31, 0.17–0.41 kg/hr; Kruskal-Wallis test, H = 5.237, df = 2, P < .08.

Comparing singletons and pairs: Mann-Whitney U test, U = 22, P > .1; singletons and trios: U = 7, P > .1; pairs and trios: U = 4.5, P < .07.

Kilograms eaten per hour by individual nonadolescent singletons (N =

6 individuals), pairs ($N = 7$ coalitions), and trios ($N = 4$ coalitions) watched for 20 or more hours. Means, medians, and interquartile ranges respectively, 0.22, 0.06, 0–0.51 kg/hr; 0.14, 0.12, 0.11–0.27 kg/hr; 0.30, 0.38, 0.30–1.69 kg/hr; Kruskal-Wallis test, $H = 4.939$, df $= 2$, $P < .1$.

Comparing singletons and pairs: Mann-Whitney U test, $U = 17.5$, $P > .1$; singletons and trios: $U = 5$, $P > .1$; pairs and trios: $U = 1.5$, $P < .02$.

17. Percentage of sightings made on consecutive days in which belly sizes increased or did not change overnight (with no meal, it would decline) for nonadolescent singletons ($N = 37$ consecutive sightings) and coalitions ($N = 41$ consecutive sightings) (coalition members' bellies were averaged at each sighting), 48.6%, 51.2%, G test, $G_1 = 0.026$, $P > .8$.

18. Mean overnight change in belly size for nonadolescent singletons ($N = 5$ individuals) and coalitions ($N = 5$ individuals) that were sighted on consecutive days at least once, for those nights in which belly size increased or did not change, $\bar{X}$ increase in size, 3.0, 3.1, Mann-Whitney U test, $U = 11$, $P > .4$.

19. Belly sizes of nonadolescent males increased with group size (coalition members' bellies were averaged at each sighting), wet season: Kruskal-Wallis test, $H = 7.896$, df $= 2$, $P < .01$ (see table 10.3).

Dry season: $H = 2.540$, df $= 2$, $P > .3$ (see table 10.3).

20. Standard deviations of belly sizes of nonadolescent singletons ($N = 10$ individuals), pairs ($N = 10$ coalitions), and trios ($N = 4$ coalitions) seen five or more times (coalition members' bellies were averaged at each sighting), average standard deviations 2.6 (SD $= 0.3$), 2.7 (SD $= 0.2$), 2.2 (SD $= 0.4$) respectively, Kruskal-Wallis test, $H = 1.300$, $P > .5$.

21. Percentage of sightings (excluding consecutive sightings of the same males) that nonadolescent singletons ($N = 239$ sightings), pairs ($N = 97$ sightings), and trios ($N = 50$ sightings) had belly sizes of <4 (coalition members' bellies were averaged at each sighting), 38.1%, 23.7%, 18.0% respectively, G test, $G_2 = 12.159$, $P = .003$.

22. Hunts were less successful when more than one coalition member hunted prey than when only one member was involved, G test, $G_1 = 3.582$, $P < .1$ (see table 10.6).

23. Hunts were no more successful when more than one coalition member chased prey than when only one member chased it, G test, $G_1 = 2.265$, $P > .1$ (see table 10.6).

24. Hunts were no more successful when more than one coalition member contacted prey than when only one member contacted it, Fisher exact test, $P = .655$ (see table 10.6).

25. In hunts in which conspecifics tried to defend a captured ungulate the victim was killed if the rescuer was driven off by another male cheetah

but the victim escaped if the rescuer was able to get to the calf and displace the cheetah, Fisher exact test, $P = .018$ (see table 10.7).

26. Spotted hyenas located 24.4% of singletons' 41 kills but only 5.8% of coalitions' 69 kills, G test, $G_1 = 7.757$, $P < .01$.

27. Spotted hyenas located 22.2% of 36 kills weighing >20 kg but only 8.1% of 74 kills weighing <20 kg, G test, $G_1 = 4.071$, $P < .05$.

Two adult males (right) watch a female move away from them to the left. Her cub is in the background. (Drawing by Dafila Scott.)

11
THE BEHAVIOR OF MALES
IN COALITIONS

Alliances between individuals are common in group-living primates (Harcourt and de Waal 1992). The most common form of alliance occurs between mothers and their immature offspring, although adult members of both sexes may form alliances against other groups, or against individuals within the group, or both. Male mountain gorillas that remain in their natal group help repel extra-group males (Harcourt and Stewart 1981), while in gray langurs a coalition of males will collectively oust a breeding male from his harem (Hrdy 1977). Within groups, male chimpanzees form alliances to increase their dominance rank (Nishida 1983) and male baboons form short-term coalitions that enable one of them to steal an estrous female from a competitor (Bercovitch 1988; see Smuts 1986 for a review).

In most non-primate mammals, alliances between females and between males are less common and less well understood. Females living in groups rarely defend territories together, although there are exceptions, such as some microtine rodents (Cockburn 1988) and lions (Packer, Scheel, and Pusey 1990). Within groups, female spotted hyenas support offspring in fights, resulting in a matrilineal dominance hierarchy within each clan (Frank 1986). Outside primates, coalitions of males are restricted to carnivores, in which, for instance, groups of male lions defend prides against other coalitions (Bygott, Bertram, and Hanby 1979), and delphinids, in which coalitions of male bottle-nosed dolphins steal females from other males (Connor, Smolker, and Richards 1992). Details of the behavior of individuals within coalitions in these non-primate species and the ways in which coalitionary relationships are maintained are sketchy; consequently, I decided to explore these aspects in cheetahs.

Many studies of male primates have sought to determine the direct reproductive payoffs of forming alliances, measured in terms of access to estrous females, or more indirectly, access to groups of females which in turn provide mating opportunities. Yet there are other potentially important short-term costs and benefits for males living in small groups that are only indirectly related to reproduction. Further on in this chapter, therefore, I examine possible short-term benefits that male cheetahs might gain from cohabiting, exclusive of the direct reproductive and foraging advantages discussed in the two previous chapters. Short-term costs of competing over food and females are also documented. This leads into a discussion of the behavior of males and females in each other's presence. Last, the issue of dominance in the context of male relationships is tackled. If one male obtains predominant access to resources at the expense of his partner in most circumstances, then the latter may best be viewed as a nonreproductive helper rather than a partner with equal privileges.

Behavior between Coalition Members

AFFILIATIVE BEHAVIOR

Coalition partners were extremely tolerant of one another's close proximity. During the midday rest period they spent approximately 10% of the time in contact, and were less than 1 m apart for over 50% of the time (table 11.1). In many circumstances coalition members were only partially in shadow and had the opportunity to seek larger patches of shade behind trees or rocks some meters away, but they still chose to stay next to their companions.

Grooming is considered to be an important affiliative interaction in felids (Macdonald et al. 1987). During the day, partners groomed each other approximately once every 5 hours (table 11.2), usually licking each other on the face, ears, and neck. Bouts varied from a single lick to prolonged sessions lasting 3 minutes. Males tugged pieces of vegetation and ticks out of each other's fur using their incisors, and would swallow ticks and hippoboscid flies found on their partners. In some coalitions, partners initiated an equivalent number of grooming bouts (four out of six pairs, and two out of five trios) while in others the distribution of grooming bouts was other than expected by chance [1]. Once a male had begun to lick another, grooming was reciprocated on more than 50% of occasions (table 11.2). Very occasionally purring was heard during these interactions.

BEHAVIOR TOWARD NONLITTERMATES WITHIN COALITIONS

Although coalitions were characterized by amicable relations, the majority of interactants were relatives. Therefore it was also important to examine the behavior of males in coalitions containing nonlittermates. One of the adolescent trios that I followed had 55 days earlier consisted only of littermates J and K; the third male, L, had joined sometime later. Over a 4-day observation period, there were many instances of aggression

TABLE 11.1 Mean (and SE) Percentage of Time that Coalition Members Spent at Different Distances from One Another during the Midday Rest Period

Distance	Pairs ($N = 11$)	Trios ($N = 6$)	Combined ($N = 17$)
0–1 m	53.2 (9.7)	52.9 (4.1)	53.1 (6.3)
2–5 m	24.9 (6.6)	35.2 (3.1)	28.6 (4.5)
> 5 m	21.9 (7.2)	11.5 (4.7)	18.3 (5.0)
In contact	13.6 (3.4)	9.0 (2.5)	12.0 (2.4)
Total number of hours watched	108.6	100.0	208.6

Note: Coalitions were watched during the midday rest period for between 3 and 27 hours each; figures for trios were calculated from the average of distances between the three males. Ns refer to number of coalitions.

TABLE 11.2 Bouts of Grooming Initiated and Reciprocated by Coalition Members

	Pairs	Trios	Combined
	($N = 7$)	($N = 5$)	($N = 12$)
Grooming bouts per hour[a]	0.12 (0.03)	0.20 (0.02)	0.19 (0.03)
	($N = 6$)	($N = 5$)	($N = 11$)
Percentage reciprocated[b]	56.8 (14.0)	64.6 (6.0)	60.3 (7.8)

Note: Only males watched 20 or more hours were included. Ns refer to number of coalitions. The reduced sample size for reciprocation is because no grooming was observed in one pair.

[a] Mean (and SE) number of grooming bouts that individual males in coalitions initiated per hour.

[b] Mean (and SE) percentage of times that a bout of grooming was reciprocated (i.e., the recipient started to groom the actor before the actor's bout had finished).

by J, and especially by K, toward L. For instance, L was slapped by K on the only occasion L tried to groom him and when L sniffed the same object as K. Bouts of play often led to aggression if L tried to join in; for example, a play run made by L ended with the brothers standing over him while he lay in a defensive threat posture. L was sensitive to this aggression, and when J ran toward him trying to initiate a play bout, he would not flee playfully. Nonetheless, I had the impression that tension waned between K and L over my 4 days' observation. In addition to the behavioral discrimination shown by members of this trio, L spent a lower proportion of the midday rest period in contact with another coalition member than did J and K, and was usually farther away from them than they were from each other, though rarely more than 5 m (table 11.3). L would even rest entirely in the sun to be near J and K while they lay in the shade.

Two other trios were also observed in which two individuals were littermates but the third was not. When behavioral observations began, B, the nonlittermate, had been together with littermates A and C for at least 4 years; whereas P had been with littermates Q and R for at least 12.5 months but no longer than 20 months. This provided a limited opportunity to examine whether relationships between unrelated coalition members changed over time. The differences in daytime proximity shown by J and K to L were no longer evident in the more established trios (table 11.3). For both J, K, and L and P, Q, and R, however, the distribution of grooming was significantly different from that expected [1], with both L and P grooming coalition partners least in their respective trios, although B groomed his companions as expected. Thus discrimination on the basis of kinship continued for longer with regard to grooming than to resting proximity.

Grooming is an important means by which some female primates garner the support of high-ranking individuals, as, for example, in vervets (Seyfarth 1980). Consequently females may compete for the opportunity to groom females of high rank; thus dominant individuals may receive more bouts of grooming than subordinates (Seyfarth 1977). In other species of Old World primates, however, grooming is preferentially targeted at relatives (Gouzoules and Gouzoules 1986). Male cheetahs showed parallels to the second, kin-based model with respect to grooming. Grooming was distributed more or less evenly among members of coalitions composed only of littermates, implying a lack of dominance relations. Moreover, males preferred to groom relatives in coalitions in which nonrelatives were present, at least in the first year or so. Later, males directed a substantial proportion of grooming at nonrelatives as, for example, do female bonnet macaques (Silk 1982).

TABLE 11.3 Percentage of 5-Minute Scans that Members of Three
Coalitions Spent at Different Distances from One Another during the
Midday Rest Period

Distance	JKL			PQR			ABC		
	J–K	K–L	J–L	Q–R	Q–P	R–P	A–C	A–B	C–B
0–1 m	87.2	37.0	34.8	49.8	46.9	64.3	54.0	74.9	36.0
2–5 m	7.4	60.7	59.3	35.3	31.4	21.4	29.3	22.9	46.4
> 5 m	5.4	2.4	6.0	14.8	21.7	10.5	16.7	2.2	17.6
In contact	28.8	4.5	3.8	18.1	5.6	22.8	6.7	27.9	6.8

Source: Adapted from Caro 1993.

Note: Littermates J and K had just joined up with nonlittermate L; littermates Q and R had been
together for over a year with nonlittermate P; and littermates A and C had been together for at least
4 years with nonlittermate B. The coalitions were watched for 11.5, 21.0, and 16.5 hours respectively
during the midday rest period.

MAINTAINING VISUAL CONTACT

In 181 sightings of coalitions that were seen more than once (and hence
could be definitely classified as coalitions) members were found together
on 92.8% of occasions. Under most circumstances coalition partners were
careful not to lose contact with one another. Ordinarily a male that rose
from resting and walked off would be followed by his companion(s). If
not, he might look around and call his partner by yipping, might sit and
wait for him before moving off again, or if that failed, would return to his
partner and perhaps groom him before walking off once more. If a male
began hunting, his partners nearly always followed, either walking or participating in the hunt, but very occasionally a male completed an unsuccessful hunt alone and then returned to his companions, who were
watching. I only saw males lose each other once, when encountering a
female. A of A, B, and C pursued a female into a large kopje; although B
and C searched for the couple, they could not locate them. The three
males were seen together again 2 days later. M. Deeble (reported to
K. Laurenson, pers. comm.) also saw a member of a trio lose his partners
for at least 2 days when they split up while searching for an estrous female.
In a parallel case, a 7-month-old cub that had been parasitic on a pair of
males for over a month lost contact with them when they chased a female
into tall herbs (see chap. 4). Only in the context of chasing after females
were males unwilling to wait for each other.

RELOCATING COALITION PARTNERS

On the few occasions when I found companions apart, they seemed dis-
tressed, searching and calling for each other for most of the day outside

the rest period. For example, I located male B of B, S, and A from 1.5 km away first by hearing him call in the still early morning air and only later by seeing him. He walked between termite mounds, climbing each one, where he sat or stood scanning the surroundings, and for 20 minutes yipped and churred almost continuously; my notes record that the churring was as loud as a small generator. In another instance a member of a different trio walked 1 km, searching in patches of herbs and calling 191 times in the space of 30 minutes, until one of his partners, suddenly appeared and the two simply walked off together. If no female was involved, territorial males, at least, could usually relocate one another well within a day because their movements were by definition restricted. I was always astonished at the way in which cheetahs knew where a companion (or in the case of a mother, her cub) had last been visible. Once, having immobilized a coalition member in high grass to attach a radio collar, I saw his companions return right to the spot where he was last seen walking, although they had been over 200 m away at the time. They then waited 30 m from the car until he recovered an hour later.

Compared with lions, which roar (Hast 1989), male cheetahs were at a disadvantage in locating lost partners. Though lion coalitions split up into subgroups within their territory, which could be more than 100 km² in size (van Orsdol, Hanby, and Bygott 1985), they could quickly regroup if challenged by intruders because their roars could be heard at a distance of 3 to 4 km (Schaller 1972c). Stevenson-Hamilton (1954) reported hearing lions roar from 8 km away. Separated cheetahs could not contact one another in this way, but their territories were smaller, facilitating reunion. Floating coalition members, however, would be hard pressed to find one another again, except by chance.

Short-Term Benefits of Group Living

Having described the behavior of males in coalitions, I now examine the short-term benefits of coalition membership in terms of support in competitive interactions and in sharing vigilance.

FIGHTS BETWEEN MALE GROUPS

Group size probably had a stronger influence than any other factor in determining the outcome of contests between male cheetahs, as reflected by larger coalitions' long lengths of tenure under conditions of strong competition (Caro and Collins 1987b; chap. 9). Thus the most parsimonious explanation for why coalition members stayed in such close proximity was the danger of encountering another group of males. Though it is intuitively obvious that numerical superiority in contests would be advantageous, very few cheetah fights have been seen in the wild and the means by which additional companions enhance the probability of winning a fight is not fully appreciated.

There is descriptive information on four fights between males. (1) Frame and Frame (1981) described how territorial males A, B, and C killed a male that had become separated from his two companions. They chased and caught him, and repeatedly bit his legs, body, and neck, creating puncture wounds and cracking bones. After resting briefly, they bit and tore his flesh again, and one finally suffocated him. (2) Tanzania National Park rangers (pers. comm.) saw territorial males X, Y, and Z kill an intruding male at the entrance to the rangers' sleeping quarters at Naabi Hill. One of the trio lay on the intruder's chest, pinning him to the ground, and throttled him while the other two bit his flank and genitals. (3) Kuenkel (1978) saw males A, B, and C attack a sibling group of two males and a female; A choked one of the two males to death. (4) I witnessed a fight between X, Y, and Z and a single male. First, a male ran past the three coalition members without noticing them. X, Y, and Z then pursued him and one slapped him to the ground, after which they all smelled the ground nearby. Then, while the singleton lay on his back with paws extended, ready to strike, two of the trio sniffed his genitals and one bit his flank. Next, the threesome moved 15 m away, but as soon as the singleton moved off they returned, slapped him down, and, while one male held the intruder down with his weight and bit the upper part of his chest, the other two bit the intruder's thighs repeatedly, dislodging a considerable amount of fur. Though the singleton flailed at them and yelped continuously, he never managed to inflict a single bite on any one of the trio, although he did survive the encounter. The trio left after 8 minutes, and two of them scent-marked immediately. In all these four cases weight as well as presence of companions would have been an advantage in keeping an adversary pinned to the ground so that others could attend to him at will.

Finally, I also saw males B, S, and A resting beneath a tree with a single male perched 4 m above. As I came upon them, I saw B saunter toward the tree, looking up at the male, so I guessed the singleton must have fled from the coalition and scurried 3 m up to the first branch just before I arrived. For the rest of the day, 8 hours and 35 minutes, the singleton had to keep his balance standing on a branch (except for 45 minutes' sitting) and did not descend until 80 minutes after the trio had left.

These records indicate that single males that lived alone or had temporarily lost their companions were at tremendous disadvantage if they encountered a coalition. Coalitions that noticed other cheetahs seemed more confident than singletons, as judged by a greater willingness to go and investigate groups of cheetahs as opposed to simply watching them [2], although this failed to reach significance when conspecifics in general were considered [2]. McLaughlin (1970) recorded an incident of a resident male, whose coalition partner had temporarily disappeared with a female, spotting a pair of floating males 1 km off. He approached to within 50 m of them but then stopped and turned in the opposite direction; on the way back to his initial position, he scent-marked a tree. In contrast, the behavior of coalitions was less timid. As an extreme example, a resident pair chased an adult leopard that I had inadvertently frightened out of a stand of tall *hypoestes* vegetation for 15 m, giving up 15 m from it. It was my impression that the males mistook the leopard for a female cheetah, which were often found in this area near Zebra kopjes; the incident suggested that they were willing to investigate anything resembling a cheetah without hesitation! Since adult leopards can kill adult cheetahs (Bailey 1994) they were unlikely to have been playing with it knowingly.

In response to a group of cheetahs smaller than their own, males were more ready to attack than to sit and watch them pass by, but they preferred to watch groups of equivalent size, although this failed to reach significance [3]. Other than the regular patrols that males made of their territories, however, coalitions did not seek out opportunities to attack other males, as reported for chimpanzees (Goodall 1986). Nevertheless, it is possible that P, Q, and R extended their territory from Oldonya Rongai to Simba kopjes in this way at the beginning of 1987 when S_2 disappeared (chap. 9). In conclusion, being unable to rely on companions, singletons were forced to show restraint in approaching and attacking other cheetahs, especially groups of cheetahs. Since it was difficult to discriminate a group of males from a mother with large cubs at a distance, singletons showed restraint to all groups irrespective of their composition.

In contrast to cheetahs, male lions were often found in groups that were smaller than the total size of their coalition for periods of up to several days. As fights between male lions were as severe as those between male cheetahs (see photograph in Iwago 1986), at least two explanations are possible. Encounters with intruding coalitions may have been less common in lions than in cheetahs, but this seemed unlikely given their greater densities on the plains (app. 2) and equivalent lengths of tenure on the territories (chap. 9). More probably, lions could summon help by roaring, as described earlier. In addition, different subsets of a coalition might have been able to notify and deter nomadic males through simultaneous roaring without necessarily joining up to repel them.

VIGILANCE

Lowered individual vigilance levels might also be an important benefit of group living for male cheetahs. Individual vigilance declines with group size in many species of birds and mammals (Elgar 1989), and almost all empirical work on vigilance (e.g., Lazarus 1979; Underwood 1982) has been based on studies of grazing herbivores or granivores that have to feed for much of the day; time spent vigilant is therefore time lost to feeding. In carnivores, which are less constrained by feeding time budgets, there may be less of a premium on reducing personal vigilance. Furthermore, herbivores often live in herds or flocks that are subject to predation, hence their vigilance is classically thought of as a means of detecting danger rather than of monitoring conspecifics or locating new sources of food (Bertram 1978a). Again in contrast, carnivores may look up to detect passing prey or conspecifics, as well as sources of danger (Caro 1987b). Hence for reasons of opportunity cost and predation risk, the relationship between vigilance and group size may be different for predators than for prey.

The proportion of time individual male cheetahs spent with their eyes open during the midday rest period and the percentage of time they spent observing their surroundings throughout the day did not decline significantly with group size (fig. 11.1) [4]. These results support the idea that male cheetahs were on a relatively relaxed time schedule; indeed, the predominant activity of all male group sizes was resting: singletons rested for 71.3% of the day ($N = 11$ individuals), pairs, 71.3% ($N = 8$ coalitions), and trios, 72.1% ($N = 5$ coalitions). As a result, larger groups enjoyed increased vigilance because the proportion of time that any group member had its eyes open was greater than that for singletons [5]. In addition, the average percentage of time during which any one of the four 90° quadrants of the environment was observed by any male rose linearly with group size from the 25% that a singleton could cover while it had its eyes open (fig. 11.1) [5].

As male cheetahs were rarely subject to predatory attack compared with ungulates in Serengeti, were they looking out for predators? For cheetah mothers, neither vigilance during the midday rest period nor the proportion of time spent observing during the course of the day were statistically associated with antipredator behavior, as measured by the percentage of instances mothers reacted to predators or defended their cubs (Caro 1987a). Rather, these two measures of vigilance were strongly correlated with percentage of time spent hunting, suggesting mothers were being vigilant in order to locate prey. If males were vigilant for the same reasons, coalition members might be expected to look out for passing prey less than singletons, given their lower levels of hunger (as measured by significantly larger belly sizes, chap. 10). Yet coalition members were no less vigilant than singletons, implying that hunger was not the principal causal factor behind males' surveillance (table 11.4).

If males maintained vigilance in order to locate other males early on, and thus gain the benefit of surprise or be able to slink off unnoticed, one might expect that individual coalition members would be less vigilant than singletons given the reduced dangers they faced in encounters with conspecifics, yet this was not the case.

Last, if males were chiefly on the lookout for females, then individual male vigilance should not decline with group size. The first male to see a female would immediately run to her to have the best chance of mating if she was in estrus; I recorded that in only 1 out of 26 cases when a coalition member saw and ran to a female did he wait for his companion. Furthermore, M. Deeble (reported by K. Laurenson, pers. comm.) saw three males sniff a rock on which a female may have urinated, become extremely agitated, and each run off in a different direction searching for

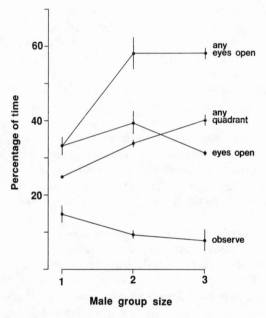

Male group size

Fig. 11.1 Mean percentage (and SE) of time that individual males living in groups of 1, 2, and 3 were vigilant. From the top: Percentage of time that any male had his eyes open during the midday rest period ($N = 10$ individuals, and 7 and 5 coalitions respectively). Average percentage of time any 90° quadrant of the environment was being observed by any male that had his eyes open during the midday rest period ($N = 10$, 7, and 5 respectively). (For each segment, the total number of times it was monitored by any male was divided by the total number of scans during which any male had his eyes open; an average was then taken for the four segments.) Percentage of time each male had his eyes open during the midday rest period ($N = 10$, 7, and 5 respectively). Percentage of time each male observed his surroundings throughout the day ($N = 11$, 8, and 5 respectively).

her. The one that found her mounted immediately. Although another coalition member found the pair a few minutes later, no further matings were observed over the next 3 days. Thus the observed relationship between group size and individual vigilance supports the idea that males were principally on the lookout for females in order to further their own reproductive interests, though predators, prey, and other males could also be monitored at the same time (table 11.4).

Vigilance at kills did not change with male group size either. Males in larger groups did not look up less often or spend a lower percentage of time off the carcass than those in smaller groups [6]. Again, in cheetah mothers, vigilance at kills was statistically associated with antipredator behavior, as determined by the percentage of instances a mother defended her cubs in other circumstances, but it was not associated with measures of hunting (Caro 1987a). As carcasses attracted dangerous predators (chap. 10), this was likely to be true for males as well. Also, males were unlikely to be on the lookout for additional prey with a kill at their feet (although they might still be searching for females).

Given that time spent eating was being compromised and that there was potential for feeding competition at all but the largest carcasses, it was surprising that individual vigilance levels did not drop among coalition members. Two explanations are possible. Either males were still scouting for reproductive opportunities, or they had to see an approaching predator for themselves. In support of the second point, any male that noticed a far-off predator simply watched it intently for a while and then quickly resumed eating. Being so similar to the normal pattern of feeding bouts, this behavior gave partners little clue to the presence of impending danger. Once the predator was within 10 m, however, the cheetah would bolt, prompting his companions to follow suit irrespective of whether they

TABLE 11.4 Hypotheses for the Principal Reasons Why Males Were Vigilant

Hypothesis	Predicted change with increasing group size	Observed change with increasing group size
Looking out for prey	Decline with group size as less hungry	No change
Looking out for males	Decline with group size as singletons more vulnerable	No change
Looking out for females	No change as each male wants to see a female first	No change

had seen it beforehand. Thus males benefited little from one another's surveillance at carcasses. In general, males were relatively bold in the face of hyenas (chap. 10) and spent a smaller proportion of time off carcasses looking around than did mothers with cubs ($\bar{X}$ = 20.7, SE = 2.0, N = 16 individuals or coalitions; $\bar{X}$ = 26.5%, SE = 2.0, N = 38 families that made kills).

To summarize these results, males did not lower their vigilance levels when living in coalitions. In most species, a negative association has been found between vigilance and group size, with only 7 out of 32 bird species and 1 out of 20 mammals showing a positive correlation or no relation, as found in this study (Elgar 1989). All but 1 of those 52 studies were of herbivorous, granivorous, or insectivorous species, however, which may have been under tight time budgets, forcing them to relax personal vigilance in the presence of conspecifics. Even in the one predator study, of bald eagles at salmon piles, competition over food was intense and vigilance (for humans) initially declined with increasing group size (Knight and Knight 1986). Although many of the studies failed to control for confounding variables such as time of day, distance from cover, objects obstructing the view of other group members, competition over food, and edge effects, making them open to alternative interpretation, these factors were not pertinent to cheetahs relaxing during their midday rest period (see chap. 5). The lack of association between individual vigilance and group size in cheetah males therefore appears robust, especially since it was seen during the midday rest period, throughout the day, and at kills. More generally, the cheetah findings suggest that individual predators will not necessarily reduce personal vigilance in groups if feeding time budgets are unconstrained. In addition, in species or age classes that are relatively immune from predation and in which flight and alarm responses are infrequent, individuals are unlikely to benefit from conspecifics' vigilance. In the case of male cheetahs, group members were not notified if their companion saw something threatening in the environment (see Packer and Abrams 1990 for a parallel argument concerning prey). The relative importance of relaxed time budgets and selfishness in relation to vigilance requires further investigation.

Short-Term Costs of Group Living

While males kept company, searched for one another if they became separated, groomed one another, and benefited from mutual support during intergroup competition, there were costs to living together as well. These costs were manifested as competition over carcasses and over females.

AGGRESSION AT KILLS

Males in coalitions bit or slapped each other, or slapped the carcass itself, on 57.8% of the 45 occasions when they were observed eating together, and growling was heard on 51.1% of these occasions. At small kills, one male usually attempted to monopolize the prey by carrying it off every time his companions approached, growling at the same time. In this tense atmosphere, a companion did not approach his partner head on in order to gain a scrap of meat, presumably because of danger of blows to the face. Rather, he waited until his companion moved and then fed on any scraps that had fallen off the carcass. Occasionally a male walked up to and quickly sat down on his partner's haunches (to be far from his partner's teeth, perhaps), causing the latter to stop eating for a moment or else move off quickly without a good grip on the meat. Then the instigator would make a lunge at the morsel.

It was at intermediate-sized kills that rates of aggression were highest, however (table 11.5) [7]. Here all the males fed from the carcass simultaneously, and toward the end, competed for the remaining scraps still attached to the skeleton that could not be carried off. Now cheetahs stopped chewing and fastened onto the carcass with their jaws, sometimes growling softly; or, if competition escalated, made sharp downward jabs with their front paws that might contact the other cheetah, the carcass, or the ground. They often kept their eyes closed under these circumstances. Occasionally a male let go of the meat, nipped his opponent, and then

TABLE 11.5 Mean (and SE) Rates of Aggressive Behavior among Coalition Members at Kills

	Size of kill[a]		
	Small (N = 9)	Intermediate (N = 4)	Large (N = 9)
Aggression	1.46 (0.52)	5.65 (5.16)	0.21 (0.08)
Growling	2.82 (1.64)	1.05 (0.45)	0.29 (0.13)

Note: Rates of aggression (slapping and biting combined) and growling per male per hour by coalition members (pairs and trios of males combined) at small, intermediate, and large kills are shown. Average rates of behavior were calculated for each coalition eating different-sized prey, then a mean of these figures was calculated; thus the same coalition might be represented at different-sized kills. Ns refer to number of coalitions.

[a] Small kills consisted of hares and neonate Thomson's gazelles; intermediate kills of neonate Grant's gazelles, half-grown, subadult, and adult Thomson's gazelles; large kills of wildebeests.

tried to regain a hold with his mouth. At large carcasses rates of aggression and growling were low.

Heightened aggression between group members at small kills is found in other carnivores such as wolves (Zimien 1986) and spotted hyenas (Kruuk 1972). Nevertheless, escalated fighting between group members did not occur in cheetahs or in these species, presumably because the payoffs of winning scraps of meat were minor compared with the risks of injury to self or valuable companions.

COMPETITION OVER FEMALES

Having sighted a female, males usually approached her cautiously, sometimes stalking her, but chased after and slapped her down if she fled. Despite the great majority of lone females being pregnant or else having cubs in a lair (chap. 4), and hence being unreceptive, males approached 68.9% of lone females that they saw ($N = 45$ occasions). To a lesser extent, they investigated mothers with cubs [8], some of which could have been receptive (see table 4.8). One reason that males failed to visit every female is that they already knew the identity and reproductive condition of some of them: while following cheetah families, I noticed that males might visit on one day but then not approach the family on subsequent days. Males may also have mistaken some females for males and stayed away.

Males approached females to determine whether they were in estrus. Males also guarded females in anticipation of estrus or after mating (as reported by M. Deeble). Since I saw no matings, I assumed that none of the females were in estrus when I saw them. This assumption was supported by the fact that males churred (or stuttered) in only four, and females in only two, of twenty-seven lengthy encounters together; stuttering is often a prelude to mating in captivity (D. Lindburg, pers. comm.).

When coalition members encountered a female, they sometimes threatened one another by growling or hissing, but overt aggression between them occurred in only one of seven coalitions, that one containing a nonlittermate. Here brothers A and C were aggressive only to their unrelated companion (table 11.6) [9]. Though this incident is suggestive, the sample size is clearly too small to show that relatedness is an important factor in determining intermale aggression. Data from lions show that male aggression over females depended on whether ownership was undecided rather than on kinship (Packer and Pusey 1982).

I had no information on whether aggression between males was more pronounced when females were in estrus. In the report of the pair of males mating at Naabi Hill, males competed to mount the female by pushing each other off her with their heads (S. Cable, pers. comm.). M. Deeble (pers. comm. to K. Laurenson) noted that the coalition member that arrived at the female first would not let his partner come close. In contrast,

TABLE 11.6 Number of Aggressive Behaviors among Members of a Coalition during Encounters with Females

		Behavior received by		
		A	B	C
Behavior directed by	A		6	0
	B	7		11
	C	0	2	

Note: Total number of slaps and bites (combined) that males A, B, and C directed at one another during their five encounters with females in which aggression was seen (out of a total of eight). Males A and C were littermates, whereas B was not.

McLaughlin (1970) reported one male mounting a female while his partner slept or watched for prey, showing little interest.

In free-living lion coalitions, one male monopolizes an estrous female exclusively, with escalated aggression occurring only when ownership is unclear. Over the course of time each male in a small coalition probably encounters estrous females a similar number of times, thereby reducing the selective pressure to be aggressive over every mating opportunity (Packer and Pusey 1982; Packer et al. 1991). The low levels of intragroup aggression in free-living male cheetahs might therefore reflect approximately equivalent access to females over time (see below).

Behavior of Males and Females in Each Other's Presence

Once males surrounded a female (fig. 11.2), they set about sniffing the vegetation close to where she lay and, less often, attempted to smell her vulva. On average, males sat an estimated 6 m from the female but sometimes less than 1 m away. In general, coalition size had little influence on male behavior in the presence of a female (table 11.7). Singletons and pairs could not surround a female and limit her movements as well as trios could, however, and as a consequence singletons more often approached and sniffed where she had been sitting. Also, males in smaller groups groomed themselves more frequently. Singletons' self-grooming rates were, on average, ten times higher than the rate of intermale grooming when females were absent (see table 11.2; I did not record rates of self-grooming in situations when females were absent). I guessed that frequent grooming in the presence of a female was a displacement activity associated with fear of being close to a strange cheetah.

The female tried to break away from males whenever possible. The males, having sniffed where she had lain or sat, then walked or trotted after her, so these behavior patterns were strongly correlated with her

Fig. 11.2 A pair of males (males 2 and 3, to the right and in the foreground) and a single male (center left) surround a mother (center and partially obscured) and her 12-month-old cub (far left) at Naabi Hill. Note the intent interest shown by the males toward the female, while the cub looks elsewhere.

leaving (see table 11.8). Pursued females were invariably caught and knocked to the ground where, yipping loudly, they lay dorsally or laterally in a defensive threat posture and struck out if the male(s) came too close. In one case, a female that was larger than the single male still showed fear through frequent yipping and churring. A female growled if a male sniffed vegetation too close to her, and might yip and slap him if he came close enough to sniff the female herself. If she was slapped down by a male, she would often slap him back, and reciprocal bouts could last up to 5 seconds; however, I never saw males biting females, as reported by H. van Lawick (pers. comm.). Once slapped, males and females usually moved off a meter or two. Finally, the rate at which males rolled over was correlated with both the rate at which females rolled over and the rate at which females groomed themselves. I have no satisfactory explanation for the function of these activities, but self-grooming may reflect levels of tension among the participants, as suggested earlier.

Females' behavior differed little in the presence of different numbers of males, except that they growled more at large groups, perhaps because they were more fearful of them (table 11.9). Rates of rolling and of self-grooming (of all parts of the body including the genitals) were correlated in females [10], and have been used to identify estrus in captivity (Florio and Spinelli 1967; Foster 1977). Males stayed with a female for as little as

TABLE 11.7 Mean Rates of Behavior per Hour Shown by Individual Males toward Females They Encountered

| | Male group size | | | | |
	1 (N = 4)	2 (N = 6)	3 (N = 2)	H value	P value
Approach	4.5	4.3	0.8	4.673	< .1
Sniff object	8.0	6.2	1.2	5.417	< .1
Sniff female	0	0.3	0.1	1.848	> .3
Slap female	0	1.4	0.1	3.776	> .1
Yip	0.4	0.5	0.1	0.184	> .9
Growl	0	0	0.1	2.341	> .3
Roll over	0.7	0.6	0.9	0.159	> .9
Groom self	2.2	0.5	0.1	5.273	< .1
Move off	1.9	3.0	0.7	4.154	> .1
Average distance (m)	3.2	6.6	11.9	2.099	> .3

Source: Caro 1993
Note: Individual rates were averaged for coalitions. Also shown is the average distance spent from the female. H values on Kruskal-Wallis tests (df = 2) and significance levels are also shown; Ns refer to number of coalitions.

TABLE 11.8 Spearman Rank Order Correlation Coefficients between Rates of Male Behavior and Rates of Female Behavior during Encounters

| | Female behavior | | | | | |
Male behavior	Slap male	Yip	Growl	Roll over	Groom self	Move off
Approach	.085	.070	− .191	.179	− .094	.648****
Sniff object	.310	.207	.351*	.462***	.039	.827****
Sniff female	.927****	.856****	− .090	− .087	− .112	.094
Slap female	.887****	.669****	.295	.250	− .143	.629****
Yip	− .135	− .139	− .173	− .100	− .032	− .005
Growl	− .113	− .114	− .096	− .175	− .143	− .110
Roll over	− .141	− .010	.027	.419**	.425**	− .031
Groom self	− .129	− .035	− .134	.113	.532****	− .019
Move off	− .403**	− .511****	− .181	− .054	− .225	− .386*

Note: N = 26 occasions. Individual rates were averaged for coalition members.
****$P < .01$, ***$P < .02$, **$P < .05$, *$P < .1$.

TABLE 11.9 Mean Rates of Behavior per Hour Shown by Females toward Males in Different Group Sizes

	Male group size				
	1 (N = 7)	2 (N = 10)	3 (N = 9)	H value	P value
Slap male	0.3	2.6	0.3	1.058	> .5
Yip	6.9	20.1	2.3	1.613	> .3
Growl	0	1.2	3.0	8.379	< .02
Roll over	2.0	0.9	0.8	1.700	> .3
Groom self	2.3	0.2	0.3	3.810	> .1
Move off	1.6	2.4	0.8	2.200	> .3

Source: Caro 1993

Note: H values on Kruskal-Wallis tests (df = 2) and significance levels are also shown; Ns refer to number of occasions a different female was seen with males in each group size.

3 minutes or as long as 2 days. The majority of associations dissolved because males left. Uncommonly, and only if a male slept, a female would slink off in a low stalking posture, frequently looking back at him. Cubs normally stayed within 50 m of their mother during the course of her interaction with males, occasionally growling at them.

COMPARISONS WITH CAPTIVE OBSERVATIONS

How do these observations match those of cheetahs in captivity? Estrous behavior is difficult for observers to identify even in captivity (Fitch, Millard, and Tenaza 1985), but it is now recognized that elevated frequencies of behaviors such as rubbing, genital licking, urine spraying, or keeping the tail erect (see Varaday 1964; Herdman 1972a,b; King 1986) can predict estrus in some individuals (Sarri 1991; S. Wells, unpublished data). None of these behaviors occurred at high rates in free-living females accompanied by males, however, although females did roll and groom themselves relatively often in the presence of singletons (see Foster 1977; Brand 1980). It is therefore difficult to make comparisons between this study and the captive situation because most females observed in this study were probably not in estrus, while interactions between males and nonestrous females are rarely reported from captivity. That said, estrous females may be persistently pursued by males for as long as 3 days in captivity, whereas it was atypical for free-ranging males to maintain such extreme interest for extended time periods. Captive males often scent-marked in the presence of a female (Sarri 1991), but this was infrequent in my experience.

In captivity, females have produced litters as a result of a single mating with a single male (Thompson and Landreth 1973; Lindburg et al. 1993)

or by being introduced to several males (Tennant and Craig 1977). Some fighting was common between cohabiting males (including littermates) when they were introduced to an estrous female, but reports differ as to whether one male maintained exclusive access to the female in terms of mating or staying close to her (Eaton 1974). Furthermore, opinion is divided as to whether competition between males increases female libido (Benzon and Smith 1974) or interferes with breeding (Skeldon 1973; Tennant and Craig 1977). Observations on estrous females in the wild are too limited to determine the extent to which coalition members fought or maintained exclusive access to females. In summary, then, the principal differences between ex situ and in situ observations may stem from whether females were in estrus and not from the captive context itself.

How Egalitarian Are Coalitions?

In this final section, I examine whether all the males in a coalition obtain equivalent benefits. In the absence of data on mating success, it was difficult to assess the individual reproductive advantages of coalition membership because any enhanced access to females experienced by territorial coalitions during periods of intense competition might have been enjoyed by the dominant member only. Across many primate species, however, there are reliable positive correlations between male dominance rank, usually measured as access to food, and male mating success among individuals of the same age class, at least when few males are present in the troop (Cowlishaw and Dunbar 1991). If a parallel relationship existed in male cheetahs, one might be able to hazard a guess as to whether mating access was unequal. Accordingly, I tried to determine whether one male within a coalition gained disproportionate access to food or females or was primarily responsible for initiating most social behavior and hunting activity.

Coalitions were evenly split as to whether one member initiated significantly more bouts of grooming or whether grooming was distributed equitably [see 1]. In only six of fifteen coalitions did members differ significantly in the number of group movements they initiated [11]. When coalitions hunted, one member initiated hunts significantly more often than the other in only one of seven coalitions [12]. This same male also led in more hunts than his partner, but in five other coalitions there was no such disparity [13].

An alternative way to describe the data is to show the percentage difference in each male's contribution to initiating these activities (table 11.10). On average, one male initiated each of the four activities nearly twice as often as his partner(s) although no male was entirely responsible for any one of them (i.e., a percentage difference near 100%).

TABLE 11.10 Percentage Differences among Members of Coalitions in Activities Performed

Activity	N	Mean	SE
General activities			
Initiates grooming	12	28.3	4.4
Initiates movements	16	30.3	6.6
Initiates hunts	11	29.3	4.2
Leads hunts	10	28.6	5.2
Feeding			
Time spent eating	10	14.9	5.5
Average belly size	15	4.9	1.7
Percentage of time off carcass	10	31.3	28.4
In female company			
Average distance to female	5	33.5	13.5
Rate of approaching female	4	15.9	5.4
Rate of sniffing in female's presence	5	11.0	0.8

Note: For pairs, the lesser score of the two individuals was subtracted from the greater, divided by their combined total, then multiplied by 100 to give a percentage difference; for trios, an average of the three differences was divided by the three males' total score. Means (and SE) were then calculated across coalitions. Scores range between 0% and 100% with higher scores indicating greater differences between males. For the first four activities, analysis was restricted to those coalitions for which there were six or more records; average belly size, to those for which there was more than one record; and the rest, to males observed at more than one kill or with more than one female. N refers to number of coalitions.

Regarding benefits that might be shared between members, individuals, on average, differed by approximately 25% in the time they spent eating, although their average belly size estimates were almost equivalent during the course of behavioral observations (table 11.10). At kills, one coalition member spent approximately twice as much time off the carcass scanning the surroundings as the other(s), on average. In the presence of a female, the average distance that one male stayed from her was almost twice that of the other male(s), but there was less difference in the rates at which coalition members approached females or at which sniffing occurred.

Although responsibility for group activities and the benefits that males enjoyed were unevenly matched, it seemed improbable that one coalition member could consistently dominate others because size differences between them were small. In a sample of coalitions, heavier males weighed, on average, only an eighth more than their partners (table 11.11), limiting their ability to monopolize females or carcasses. Moreover, in none of the intensively watched coalitions did one individual score consistently higher than his partner(s) across all of eight activities measured (table 11.12).

This was true of both pairs and trios, including trios that contained nonlittermates. In particular, males that spent more time eating were not necessarily those that stayed closer to females they encountered, so that any ability to dominate at kills did not reflect an ability to monopolize potential mates (as judged from behavior toward females that were out of estrus).

In a final analysis, I used a somewhat larger sample of coalitions for which there were additional data on some of the eight measures. Across coalitions, the chief instigator or performer of one behavior was no more likely to be the chief performer of another in any of fifty-five paired comparisons between measures, except for two. Individuals that groomed their partners more than vice versa tended to be those that initiated group movements more often [14]. After a rest period, one male would often start to groom his companion, apparently rousing him, before he initiated a movement. Also, males that initiated hunts would usually be those that led them [15]. Initiators of hunts were not always those that initiated group movements, however, nor were they necessarily those that ate more at kills [16].

In conclusion, the lack of strong differences in responsibility for initiating behavior or in sharing group benefits and the failure to find consistent asymmetries on behavioral measures between coalitionary males both signified that coalitions were relatively egalitarian associations and, by extension, that mating access might be relatively equal. In the absence of paternity exclusion studies, DNA fingerprinting, or repeated observations of coalition members mating with females, the working hypothesis is that coalition members had roughly similar reproductive success. It

TABLE 11.11 Weights and Linear Measurements of Coalition Members

Name	Weight (kg)	Chest girth (cm)	Head & body (cm)	Tail (cm)	Hindfoot (cm)
S_1	40.5	67	116	69	28.0
S_2	46.5	71	122	74	29.5
A	45.5	—	127	71	29.0
B	40.5	—	123	69	27.0
Cre	47.0	77	132	72	28.5
Cro	48.0	75	134	71	27.0
P	51.0	72	136	74	29.0
Q	42.5	70	118	63	28.0
R	45.0	72	122	68	28.5

TABLE 11.12 Identity of Males within Coalitions that Performed Activities More Frequently than Their Partners

Name[a]	Hours watched	Initiate groom	Initiate move	Initiate hunts	Time spent eating	Most vigilant at kills	Belly size	Distance from female	Sniffing female
2, 3	52.1	—	2	2	2	3	23[b]	2[b]	3
W, E	68.9	E	E	W	W	E	WE	—	—
M, H	84.9	M	M	Hm	M	H	H	M	M
D, E	49.4	DE	D	E	E	D	De	—	—
M, N	51.0	Mn	N	N	N	M	M	N	M
B, A	21.0	Ba[b]	B	—	—	—	A	—	—
P, Q, R	62.6	R	Pr	R	R	Qp	PR	—	—
J, K, L	39.8	K	K	Kl	J	K	L	—	—
X, Y, Z	94.1	XY	Y	YZ	Y	Z	Y	Y[b]	XYZ
B, S, A	73.3	S	B	Ba	B	S	A	—	—
A, B, C	50.2	Ca	BC	B	C	B	C	Ba	B

Note: Only coalitions observed for 20 or more hours are included. If individuals performed an activity the same number of times, both are named; if they differed by a score of 1 or a very small percentage, the lower-scoring individual is shown in lowercase. J, K, and L was a coalition of adolescent males.

[a] Individuals that were definitely not littermates of their coalition partners are italicized.

[b] Denotes small sample size.

therefore seems improbable that one of the littermate coalition members was a nonreproductive helper (see Emlen 1991), although males obtained inclusive fitness benefits through aiding kin.

COMPARISONS WITH OTHER MAMMALS

These preliminary findings are similar to those made for coalitions of lions, in which males in small coalitions of two or three show little variance in reproductive success as determined from DNA fingerprinting analysis; although some males in larger coalitions father no cubs (Packer et al. 1991). In contrast to cheetahs and lions, primate coalitions are less egalitarian. In those species in which coalitions repel extra-group males, such as mountain gorillas (Fossey 1983) or gelada baboons (Dunbar 1984), only one male gets predominant access to mates. In those species in which coalitions expel a breeding male from a one-male group, such as gray langurs, only one of the members will achieve breeding status (Hrdy 1977). In other species in which males form coalitions to increase dominance rank, such as chimpanzees, only one male achieves the top position at the expense of his partner (de Waal 1982; but see Goodall 1986). Nevertheless, the subordinate partner may subsequently be in a stronger position to change affiliations and oust the new alpha male (Nishida 1983). Last, in those species in which males cooperate to compete directly for females, such as savannah baboons, recent data show that benefits are not necessarily distributed evenly between coalition partners (Noe 1990), although this varies between populations (Packer 1977; Smuts 1985; Bercovitch 1988). Van Hooff and van Schaik (1992) have argued that coalitions are likely to be more egalitarian when conflict between groups is common than when intragroup conflict is prevalent because when larger groups win against smaller groups, as in cheetahs and lions, coalition members can ill afford to dominate other group members to the point at which they quit the group (Vehrencamp 1983).

Considering their variability, it is unwise to categorize all primate examples together, but they seem to differ from male coalitions in felids in two ways. First, alliances between primates are commonly short-lived, terminating when a rank reversal or a takeover has occurred, although alliances between male gorillas (Stewart and Harcourt 1986) and male chimpanzees (Goodall 1986) can last a very long time. In contrast, male felid coalitions usually last a lifetime, though admittedly we know little about their dynamics as they are forming. Second, in contradistinction to most primate examples, there is no dominance hierarchy among felid coalition members, which probably results in an egalitarian distribution of reproductive and other payoffs when coalitions are small. This may be a factor in why felid coalitions last so long. Following on from this, Harcourt

(1992) has suggested that only primates attempt to cultivate alliances with dominant group members and compete for such allies.

How can the behavior of cheetah males living in coalitions be categorized in terms of cooperation? In fights members gain from one another's support, and their enhanced competitive ability allows them to take over and defend a territory where females collect, at least when competition is intense. While it is costly to give aid in fights, all participants in a coalition benefit in terms of retaining access to an area of high female density (chap. 9). Regarding prey acquisition, the situation is similar. All members may incur minor costs from participating in a hunt but these can result in immediate foraging benefits. Coalition members did not cooperate over vigilance, and in the presence of females, showed little evidence of anything other than selfish behavior.

These descriptions do not conform to models of reciprocal altruism, in which one individual aids another at some cost to itself in anticipation that the recipient will return the favor in the future (again at a cost) and so provide the actor with a net benefit (Trivers 1971; Koenig 1988; see also Cheney and Seyfarth 1987 on cases in which there are strong cost-benefit asymmetries). Rather, costly acts, such as driving defending wildebeests away, result in immediate personal gain. Behavior shown by coalition partners therefore appears to be mutualistic (Wrangham 1982) or synergistic (Maynard Smith 1983) in that all partners benefit as a result. Again, Harcourt (1992) perceives lack of reciprocation as a factor distinguishing nonprimate alliances from those of primates. Simultaneous cooperation is a term that has been applied to situations in which participants act at the same time and all receive benefits (Rothstein and Pierotti 1988), as, for example, in fights against other cheetah males. For other situations in which only one coalition member suffers a cost, say in hunting, but both benefit, by-product mutualism (Brown 1983) or by-product beneficence (Rothstein and Pierotti 1988) may be more appropriate terms. These points apply whether or not coalition partners are littermates, but any cost-benefit calculation of males' behavior needs to incorporate inclusive fitness considerations when partners are related.

Summary

1. Members of coalitions rested in close proximity, groomed one another, and searched for their companions if they became separated.

2. In a recently formed trio littermates rested closer to each other and instigated more grooming of companions than did the nonlittermate, but these differences were no longer evident in a coalition that had been together for some time.

3. In fights, single males were at great disadvantage when attacked by

groups of males and were less likely to approach groups of cheetahs than were coalitions.

4. Individual male vigilance levels did not decline with increasing group size. This contrasted with most other studies conducted on prey species in which individuals are primarily watching for predators. It is argued that males were on the lookout for females rather than predators, prey, or other males, and could ill afford to lower their vigilance and let their partner spot a female and mate with her first.

5. Escalated aggression between coalition members was never seen at prey carcasses, but low-level aggression was observed at small and intermediate-sized kills.

6. Overt aggression between males in the presence of nonestrous females was seen in only one of seven coalitions. In this case brothers were aggressive only to their unrelated companion.

7. Once males had encountered a female, single males were more likely to groom themselves, and appeared nervous. They were less able to control a female's movements than was a male coalition and as a consequence spent more time sniffing vegetation when the female moved off. Females showed similar rates of behavior in the presence of different numbers of males, aside from growling more often at large groups.

8. Within coalitions, no one male predominated in initiating social activity or hunts, and males shared access to food and females almost equally. It is therefore argued that they probably shared mating opportunities fairly equally as well. The lack of dominance and the long duration of felid coalitions contrast with the characteristics of those observed in primates.

Statistics

1. Number of grooming bouts initiated by individual coalition members compared with that expected by chance. Pairs, using binomial tests: Cre and Cro, 5 and 8 respectively, $P > .4$; W and E, 2 and 6, $P > .1$; D and E, 2 and 6, $P > .2$; M and N, 12 and 11, $P = 1.0$; N and Bt, 11 and 29, $z = -2.688$, $P < .01$; M and H, 28 and 13, $z = -2.186$, $P < .03$. Trios, df = 2: P, Q, and R, 6, 8, and 25, $\chi^2 = 16.760$, $P < .001$; J, K, and L, 12, 19, and 0, $\chi^2 = 17.872$, $P < .001$; X, Y, and Z, 22, 22, and 12, $\chi^2 = 3.571$, $P < .1$; B, S, and A, 8, 12, and 9, $\chi^2 = 0.896$, $P > .9$; A, B, and C, 11, 6, and 11, $\chi^2 = 1.786$, $P > .3$. Only coalitions in which 6 or more bouts of grooming were observed are included.

2. Single males investigated groups of cheetahs on 11.8% of 17 occasions when they saw them, whereas pairs and trios (combined) investigated groups on 60.9% of 23 occasions when they noticed them, Fisher exact test, $P = .048$.

Single males investigated other cheetahs on 40% of 40 occasions when they saw them, whereas pairs and trios (combined) investigated other cheetahs on 57.8% of 45 occasions when they noticed them, G test, $G_1 = 2.692$, $P = .102$.

3. Males attacked male groups smaller than their own on 71.4% of 7 occasions (the encounter between B, S, and A and the treed male was considered an attack; see text), whereas they watched groups equal in number on 70.0% of 10 occasions (one of these cases was a friendly interaction); Fisher exact test, $P = .104$.

4. Percentage of midday rest period that individual males (watched for 12 or more hours) had their eyes open and were looking at their surroundings, singletons ($N = 10$ individuals), pairs ($N = 7$ coalitions), and trios ($N = 5$ coalitions), $\bar{X}s = 33.2\%, 39.4\%, 31.3\%$; $F_{2,19} = 2.495$, $P > .1$.

Percentage of 15-minute scans that individual males spent observing, singletons ($N = 11$ individuals), pairs ($N = 8$ coalitions), and trios ($N = 5$ coalitions), $\bar{X}s = 14.8\%, 9.3\%, 7.9\%$; $F_{2,21} = 2.316$, $P > .1$, using logged data.

5. Percentage of midday rest period any individual male (watched for 12 or more hours) had his eyes open and was looking at his surroundings, singletons ($N = 10$ individuals), pairs ($N = 7$ coalitions), and trios ($N = 5$ coalitions), $\bar{X}s = 33.2\%, 58.1\%, 58.1\%$; $F_{2,19} = 25.109$, $P < .0001$.

Percentage of midday rest period that a 90° quadrant of the environment was observed by any male watched for 12 or more hours (Ns as above), $\bar{X}s = 25.0\%, 34.0\%, 40.2\%$; $F_{2,19} = 127.963$, $P < .0001$.

6. Frequency at which singletons ($N = 4$ individuals), pairs ($N = 7$ coalitions), and trios ($N = 5$ coalitions) watched for 12 or more hours looked up per minute at carcasses, $\bar{X}s = 0.37, 0.49, 0.37$ respectively; $F_{2,13} = 0.716$, $P > .5$, on logged data.

Percentage of time males watched for 12 or more hours spent off carcasses looking around (Ns as above), 25.9%, 16.0%, 23.0% respectively, $F_{2,13} = 1.085$, $P > .3$.

7. Comparison of individual rates of male aggression per hour while feeding on small ($N = 9$ coalitions), intermediate ($N = 4$ coalitions), and large prey ($N = 9$ coalitions), Kruskal-Wallis test, $H = 6.870$, df $= 2$, $P < .05$ (see table 11.5).

Growling, $H = 3.658$, df $= 2$, $P > .1$ (see table 11.5).

8. Males investigated lone females more often (68.9% of 45 occasions) than they investigated mothers with cubs (27.5% of 40 occasions), G test, $G_1 = 14.971$, $P = .0001$.

9. Brothers A and C each directed no slaps and bites to the other but 6 and 2 respectively (i.e., 8) to nonrelative B, sign test, $P = .008$.

10. Spearman rank order correlation coefficients between the rates at which females rolled over and the rates at which they groomed them-

selves, $N = 26$ female-male associations, $r_s = 0.517$, $P < .01$ (see table 11.6).

11. Number of movements initiated by individual coalition members compared with that expected by chance. Pairs, using binomial tests: Cre and Cro, 13 and 17 respectively, $z = -0.548$, $P > .5$; W and E, 14 and 18, $z = -0.530$, $P > .5$; D and E, 27 and 23, $z = -0.424$, $P > .6$; M and N, 20 and 40, $z = -2.452$, $P < .02$; Bt and N, 4 and 10, $P > .1$; M and H, 22 and 19, $z = -0.468$, $P > .6$; B and A, 8 and 6, $P > .7$; males 2 and 3, 30 and 15, $z = -2.087$, $P < .04$; B and U, 8 and 1, $P = .04$; A and B, 5 and 2, $P > .4$; N and U, 7 and 0, $P = .016$. Trios, df = 2: P, Q, and R, 9, 6, and 8, $\chi^2 = 0.608$, $P > .7$; J, K, and L, 8, 16, and 6, $\chi^2 = 5.600$, $P < .1$; X, Y, and Z, 10, 16, and 11, $\chi^2 = 1.675$, $P > .3$; B, S, and A, 16, 4, and 13, $\chi^2 = 7.092$, $P < .05$; in other trios there were too few initiations to test.

12. Number of hunts initiated by individual coalition members compared with that expected by chance. Pairs, using binomial tests: W and E, 10 and 3 respectively, $P < .1$; D and E, 8 and 11, $P > .6$; M and N, 2 and 6, $P > .2$; Bt and N, 2 and 4; M and H, 3 and 4; males 2 and 3, 4 and 2, $P = 1.000$. Trios: J, K, and L, 6, 10, and 9, $\chi^2 = 1.039$, df = 2, $P > .5$; in other trios there were too few initiations to test.

13. Number of hunts in which individual coalition members led compared with that expected by chance. Pairs, using binomial tests: W and E, 10 and 3 respectively, $P < .1$; D and E, 6 and 13, $P > .1$; M and N, 4 and 7, $P > .5$; M and H, 4 and 3, males 2 and 3, 3 and 3, $P = 1.0$. Trios: J, K, and L, 6, 10, and 9, $\chi^2 = 1.039$, df = 2, $P > .5$; in other trios there were too few hunts to test.

14. There were 10 coalitions in which one male both groomed his companion and initiated movements more frequently than did his partner(s), 3 in which this did not occur, and 1 coalition in which individuals scored the same on one of the two measures, sign test, $N = 13$, $P = .004$.

15. There were 11 coalitions in which one male both initiated hunts and led in them more frequently than did his partner(s), 1 in which this did not occur, and 2 coalitions in which individuals scored the same on one of the two measures, sign test, $N = 12$, $P = .006$.

16. There were 4 coalitions in which one male initiated both movements and hunts more frequently than did his partner(s), 8 in which this did not occur, and 2 coalitions in which individuals scored the same on one of the two measures, sign test, $N = 12$, $P > .3$.

There were 5 coalitions in which one male both initiated hunts and ate more at kills than his partner, and 6 in which this did not occur, sign test, $N = 11$, $P = 1.00$.

An adult female cheetah walks past a small group of adult wildebeests, which inspect her. Adult wildebeests were never attempted by females in Serengeti. (Drawing by Dafila Scott.)

12
EVOLUTION AND ECOLOGY
OF CHEETAHS

This chapter examines the broad significance of three important themes that emerge from the book, with the following aims: to place cheetahs in evolutionary perspective in relation to other felids, to determine whether the ecological factors that underlie the cheetah's breeding system apply to other species, and to reexamine the issue of cooperative hunting. Each of these areas has theoretical implications that extend beyond cheetahs.

Recently, it has become apparent that variations in life history traits, such as age at maturity or interbirth interval (see Stearns 1976; Boyce 1988), can best be explained as adaptive solutions to differential patterns of mortality, not to differences in basal metabolic rate or brain size as assumed in the past (Harvey, Promislow, and Read 1989; Read and Harvey 1989; Promislow and Harvey 1990; Harvey, Pagel, and Rees 1991). Thus species in which mortality rates are high might be expected to reproduce faster than those in which mortality is low. In the first part of the chapter, I assess whether the rate of mortality in cheetahs (see chap. 4) is substantially higher than that found in other cats, and if so, whether cheetahs have life histories characteristic of rapidly reproducing species.

Second, carnivores are of central importance in the study of animal breeding systems because they exhibit such wide variation in social organization, both between and within families (Bertram 1979; Moehlman 1989). For example, in some group-living species all females breed, while in others some females are reproductively suppressed (Creel and Creel 1990). Yet other species have nonbreeding helpers, offspring from previous years that stay on to help raise subsequent litters (Rood 1978; Moehlman 1979). Despite our detailed knowledge of carnivore breeding systems, however, there have been relatively few systematic attempts to relate this variation to ecological forces, and this is particularly true of felids. Since cheetahs have a social organization unique among felids and mammals in general, they provide additional scope for examining the ecological factors underlying variation in breeding systems.

The third issue is cooperative hunting. Hunting and foraging among social carnivores have attracted much attention because group hunting, especially of large prey, has been viewed as a form of cooperation and could therefore be an advantage of group living (Kruuk 1975; Sunquist and Sunquist 1989). To demonstrate a causal connection between communal hunting and group living it is necessary to measure the consequences of group hunting, namely, per capita foraging returns, but such data are available from only a few studies. Since several segments of cheetah society hunt in groups, cheetahs provide additional opportunities to examine the effects of group hunting more closely and perhaps contribute to a consensus on whether cooperative hunting can be responsible for group living in large carnivores.

Cheetah Life Histories in Relation to Other Felids

MORTALITY

Cheetah cub mortality was the highest reported for non-hunted populations of felids (table 12.1). While strict comparisons between studies are problematic because cubs in different studies were first sighted or radiotagged at different ages, juvenile mortality from emergence to independence is considerably greater in cheetahs than that reported for most other cats. No study other than Laurenson's (in press-b) has measured postnatal mortality prior to emergence from the lair, but when this is included, 94–96% of cheetah cubs died between birth and independence. Mortality stemmed primarily from predation and to a lesser extent from abandonment, but was unrelated to radio-collaring or observation schedules (Laurenson and Caro, in press). In chapter 4 I argued that high juvenile mortality characterized cheetahs' evolutionary history since savannah regions probably supported high predator densities and a migratory prey base in the past, as they do today.

Longevity in cheetahs is relatively short for their body weight in comparison with felid species (fig. 12.1) or genera. Longevity is usually derived from the age of the oldest individual recorded in captive institutions (Gittleman 1984) and therefore underestimates mortality rates in the wild. Indeed, Laurenson (in press-c) estimated the mean life expectancy of females to be 6.9 years, based on those that died while radio-collared, far shorter than the 11.7 years reported from captivity; nonetheless, over-estimates from captivity are assumed to be similar across species. She also estimated the probability of adolescent females dying each year to be 0.153; adult females, 0.227; and old females, 0.55, all far lower than for cubs.

LIFE HISTORY TRAITS

In species in which juvenile mortality is high as a result of extrinsic factors, age at maturity is expected to be brought forward in order to keep the high-risk juvenile stage as short as possible (Horn 1978; Reznick and Endler 1982; Stearns 1992). In support of this idea, age at maturity in cheetahs was somewhat earlier than in other felid species or genera of

TABLE 12.1 Juvenile Mortality among Non-Hunted Felid Populations

Location	Measure	% mortality	Source
Cheetah			
Serengeti	0–2 months	71	Laurenson, in press-b
	2 months to independence	81–86[a]	
	Birth to independence	94–96	
Cougar			
Utah	3–10 months	28	Hemker et al. 1986
	10 months to dispersal	8	
	Contact to dispersal	33[a]	
Leopard			
Chitwan	First year	42	M. and F. Sunquist, pers.
	On to dispersal	16	comm.
	Contact to dispersal	58[a]	
Kruger	Cubs	50[a]	Hornocker and Bailey 1986
	Tagged subadults	32	
Lion			
Ngorongoro	12 months	29–42	Elliott and Cowan 1978;
	18 months	36–73[a]	van Orsdol, Hanby, and Bygott 1985
Serengeti	12 months	48–73	Schaller 1972c; van Orsdol,
	18 months	56–78[a]	Hanby, and Bygott 1985
Queen	12 months	14–60	van Orsdol 1981, 1982
Elizabeth	18 months	14–80[a]	
Tiger			
Chitwan	First year	34	Smith and McDougal 1991
	Second year	17	
	Contact to independence	58[a]	

[a] Indicates approximately comparable periods.

equivalent body weight (fig. 12.2), paralleling that found across families of mammals (Promislow and Harvey 1990). This finding runs counter to the idea that species having to acquire complex feeding skills might delay maturity, as put forward for large seabirds by Ashmole and Tovar (1968).

In species in which extrinsic adult mortality is high, components of fecundity such as gestation length, age at weaning, interbirth interval, and age at independence might be expected to be shortened so that more reproductive iterations can be completed before death (Charnov and

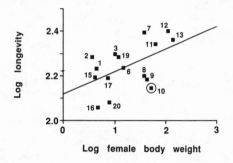

Fig. 12.1 $\log_{10}$ maximum longevity (months) reported from captivity (from Gittleman 1984) plotted against $\log_{10}$ female body weight (kg) for felids (see app. 6); $y = 2.116 + 0.101x$, $r^2 = .275$. 1, European wildcat; 2, African wildcat; 3, caracal; 6, European lynx; 7, leopard; 8, snow leopard; 9, cougar; 10, cheetah (circled); 11, jaguar; 12, tiger; 13, lion; 15, leopard cat; 16, jungle cat; 17, bobcat; 19, serval; 20, fishing cat.

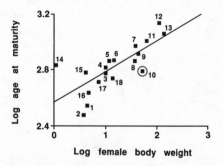

Fig. 12.2. $\log_{10}$ age at sexual maturity (age in days at birth of first offspring) plotted against $\log_{10}$ female body weight (kg) for felids (see app. 6); $y = 2.565 + 0.219x$, $r^2 = .558$. 1, European wildcat; 2, African wildcat; 3, caracal; 4, ocelot; 5, clouded leopard; 6, European lynx; 7, leopard; 8, snow leopard; 9, cougar; 10, cheetah (circled); 11, jaguar; 12, tiger; 13, lion; 14, black-footed cat; 15, leopard cat; 16, jungle cat; 17, bobcat; 18, North American lynx; 19, serval.

Schaffer 1973; Partridge and Harvey 1988). In cheetahs, however, these components were no shorter than expected from their body weight (fig. 12.3); comparisons across genera revealed much the same pattern. One explanation for the lack of predicted associations is that longevity in captivity is a poor measure of the rate of adult mortality in the wild and that the latter is not appreciably higher in cheetahs than in other species. An alternative possibility is that age at independence and interbirth intervals could not be advanced or shortened without old cubs starving since they still relied on food provided by their mothers (see fig. 6.7). That mothers conceived before their previous litter had left (see table 4.8) suggests they were extending the period of parental care as much as possible. Rather than going the route of altering these life history traits, chee-

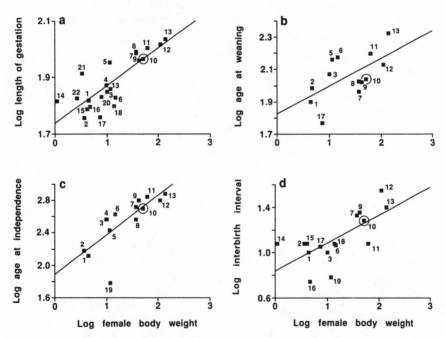

Fig. 12.3 (a) Log$_{10}$ gestation length (days), $y = 1.737 + 0.134x$, $r^2 = .677$; (b) log$_{10}$ age at weaning (days), $y = 1.823 + 0.171x$, $r^2 = .365$; (c) log$_{10}$ age at independence (days), $y = 1.876 + 0.491x$, $r^2 = .584$; (d) log$_{10}$ interbirth interval (months), $y = .834 + 0.246x$, $r^2 = .474$; all plotted against log$_{10}$ female body weight (kg) for felids (see app. 6). 1, European wildcat; 2, African wildcat; 3, caracal; 4, ocelot; 5, clouded leopard; 6, European lynx; 7, leopard; 8, snow leopard; 9, cougar; 10, cheetah (circled); 11, jaguar; 12, tiger; 13, lion; 14, black-footed cat; 15, leopard cat; 16, jungle cat; 17, bobcat; 18, North American lynx; 19, serval; 20, fishing cat; 21, margay; 22, jaguarundi.

tahs have apparently advanced the age at maturity, which consequently reduced the time between independence and age at first breeding (see fig. 7.10). The cheetah's rapid resumption of breeding following the loss of an unweaned litter cannot be systematically compared with other free-living cats as data are not available.

Fecundity can also be increased through production of large litters. Average litter size was higher in cheetahs than in all other felids except the European wildcat (fig. 12.4a). Indeed, litters of eight cheetah cubs have been born in the wild (Graham 1966). Results were even more marked in comparisons across genera. Since there is a trade-off between offspring number and offspring weight (Smith and Fretwell 1974; Stearns 1976), it was unsurprising that neonate weight was somewhat lower in cheetahs than in other species (fig. 12.4b). In response to low birth weight, perhaps, Laurenson (in press-a) found that cheetahs had higher individual and litter growth rates for a given metabolic weight than other solitary felids (fig. 12.5), which could be viewed as an adaptation for passing through the period of high juvenile mortality risk as quickly as possible.

Finally, in circumstances in which juvenile mortality is high and mothers are unable to mitigate its effects, they are expected to put little effort into each reproductive iteration (Schaffer 1974; Hirshfield and Tinkle 1975). Given that cheetahs had very low juvenile survivorship, especially

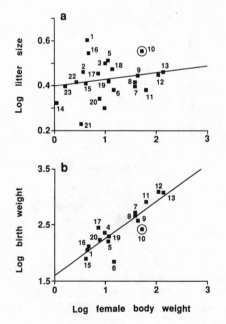

Fig. 12.4 (a) Log$_{10}$ average litter size, $y = 0.397 + 3.063e^{-2}x$, $r^2 = .043$; (b) log$_{10}$ birth weight of individual cubs (g), $y = 1.586 + 0.667x$, $r^2 = .757$, plotted against log$_{10}$ female body weight (kg) for felids (see app. 6). 1, European wildcat; 2, African wildcat; 3, caracal; 4, ocelot; 5, clouded leopard; 6, European lynx; 7, leopard; 8, snow leopard; 9, cougar; 10, cheetah (circled); 11, jaguar; 12, tiger; 13, lion; 14, black-footed cat; 15, leopard cat; 16, jungle cat; 17, bobcat; 18, North American lynx; 19, serval; 20, fishing cat; 21, margay; 22, jaguarundi; 23, rusty-spotted cat.

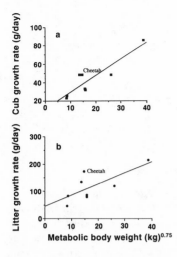

Fig. 12.5 (*a*) Offspring growth rate, $y = 10.9 + 1.81x$; (*b*) litter growth rate, $y = 43.7 + 4.14x$, plotted against female metabolic body weight, across seven large (>10 kg) felid species. (From Laurenson, in press-a.)

before emergence from the lair, that predators accounted for 73.2% of cub losses (Laurenson, in press-b), and that mothers were usually ineffectual in driving them away (chap. 6), it was not surprising that cheetah litter weight relative to maternal weight was lower than in most other felid species or genera once female body weight had been taken into account (fig. 12.6). Relative litter weight amounted to less than 2% of mothers' weight in cheetahs (see also Oftedal and Gittleman 1989). Low litter birth weights might alternatively or additionally be an adaptation to minimize the possible effect of slowing pregnant females when chasing prey (see Shine 1980). Since felids show low neonate weights compared with other carnivore families (Gittleman 1986b), the cheetah must be viewed as committing very relative reproductive effort per iteration.

In short, cheetahs have evolved to reproduce more rapidly than most other felids and can be crudely characterized as living fast and dying young. Large litters constituting little maternal expenditure can be viewed as an adaptation to circumstances in which offspring survival is unpredictable or unlikely. While all cubs usually disappeared in those litters that were attacked by predators or were abandoned by their mothers (Laurenson, in press-b), most survived in litters that were not afflicted by these pressures. Thus a large litter of small cubs would yield high fitness in those few reproductive bouts that were successful, but a light litter would minimize losses in the majority of bouts that were unsuccessful (see Promislow and Harvey 1990).

In passing, the notion that the cheetah possesses a suite of intercorrelated canid traits—namely, a gracile skeleton, nonretractile claws, a cursorial lifestyle, and large litter size—may be misplaced. Whereas its skeletal features are probably an adaptation to the high-speed chase

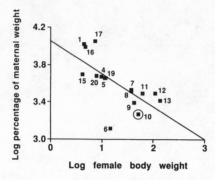

Fig. 12.6 Log_{10} weight of litter (birth weight × litter size) divided by mother's body weight × 100, plotted against log_{10} female body weight (kg) for felids (see app. 6); $y = 4.050 - 0.349x$, $r^2 = .458$. 1, European wildcat; 4, ocelot; 5, clouded leopard; 6, European lynx; 7, leopard; 8, snow leopard; 9, cougar; 10, cheetah (circled); 11, jaguar; 12, tiger; 13, lion; 15, leopard cat; 16, jungle cat; 17, bobcat; 19, serval; 20, fishing cat.

(chap. 2), large litter size appears to be an independent evolutionary response to high mortality.

Comparative analyses of Felidae indicate similarities between the cheetah and the European wildcat and the jungle cat. These species reach sexual maturity relatively early and have large litter sizes for their body weight; moreover, jungle cats have relatively short life spans in captivity. Little is known about the extent or sources of mortality in the wild, or even about the ecology of these species (but see Corbett 1979), but one might predict juvenile mortality to be high. Leopards are also interesting in that they show an opposite suite of characteristics from the cheetah, having a relatively long interbirth interval and small litter size for their body weight, perhaps in response to their longer life span.

Cheetah Social Organization in Relation to Other Felids

SOCIALITY AMONG MALES

In most felids, females and males live alone (Seidensticker and Lumpkin 1991), and males rarely occupy an area greater than three times that of a female (table 12.2; note, for example, that ocelot males are at the upper end of this range). Therefore, if females defended exclusive ranges against other females, one male could monopolize only three or four females, on average. Male cheetahs and male lions may live in groups, however. The principal advantage of group living for male cheetahs on the Serengeti plains was their ability to gain access to small territories and defend them against other males. Nomadic females collected on these territories in

TABLE 12.2 Ecological and Home Range Characteristics of Felids

Felid Density	R or M prey	Female range Size	Female range O/E	Male range Size	Male range O/E	Males alone or in groups
Bobcats						
1. In Minnesota eating snowshoe hares, white-tailed deer, porcupines						
4.5	R	38	E	62	O	Alone
2. In Idaho eating rabbits						
5.4	R	19.3	E	42.1	O	Alone
3. In Oregon eating mountain beavers						
77	R	2	(O)	11	—	(Alone)
4. In San Diego eating?						
152.5	R	1.8	E	3.0	O	(Alone)
Ocelots						
5. In Venezuela eating rodents, crabs, iguanas						
40	R	3.4	(O)	10.4	E	Alone
6. In Peru eating rodents, birds, reptiles						
80	R	2.1	E	7.0	—	Alone
Servals						
7. In Ngorongoro Crater eating *Otomys, Arvicanthis, Mus*						
41.7	R	9.5	O	11.6	O	Alone
North American lynxes						
8. In Alaska eating hares						
1.7	R	66.5	—	783	—	Alone
9. In Alberta eating hares						
6.2	R	28[a]	O	28[a]	O	Alone
10. On Cape Breton Island eating hares						
20	R	25.5	—	19	—	(Alone)
European lynxes						
11. In Swiss Alps eating roe deer, chamois, hares						
1.2	—	115.5	—	362.5	—	Alone
Snow leopards						
12. In Nepal eating bharal						
7.5	M	29.3	O	5.4	O	Alone
Leopards						
13. In Sri Lanka eating sambar						
3.3	R	8	O	9	E	Alone
14. On Serengeti plains-woodland border eating impalas, bushbuck, Thomson's gazelles						
3.3–4.7	R	14.1–50	O	57.5	(E)	Alone
15. In Serengeti woodlands eating impalas, Thomson's gazelles						
10.4	R	15.9	—	17.8[b]	(O)	Alone
16. In Zimbabwe eating dassies, klipspringers						
16.7	R	18[a]	O	18[a]	(E)	Alone
Cougars						
17. In Utah eating mule deer						
0.4	M	685	O	826	—	(Alone)
18. In Florida eating armadillos, white-tailed deer						
0.9	R	193	O	519	(O)	Alone

TABLE 12.2 Continued

Felid Density	R or M prey	Female range		Male range		Males alone or in groups
		Size	O/E	Size	O/E	
Cougars - Continued						
19. In the Diablo range in California eating black-tailed deer, wild pig, tule elk						
1.8	R	66.5	E	157.5	O	(Alone)
20. In Idaho eating elk, mule deer						
1.4–6.1	M	20–268	O	40–453	(E)	Alone
21. In the Sacramento area in California eating deer, rabbits						
6.3	R	21.5	O	30	O	(Alone)
Cheetahs						
22. In Masai Mara G.R. eating Thomson's gazelles, impalas, Grant's gazelles						
2.5^c	R	79.9	O	16.2	E	Groups
23. In Nairobi N.P. eating Thomson's gazelles, impalas, Grant's gazelles						
25	R	79	O	102	—	Groups
24. On Serengeti plains eating Thomson's gazelles, wildebeests, hares						
40	M	833	O	37.4	E	Groups
Jaguars						
25. In Pantanal in Brazil eating cattle						
4	R	31.5	O	56.5	E	Alone
26. In Belize eating armadillos, peccaries, anteaters						
15.4	R	10.5	E	33.4	O	Alone
Tigers						
27. In Sikhote-Alin in Russia eating wapiti, wild pig						
0.2–0.9	M	73–250	E	800–900	O	Alone
28. In Chitwan in Nepal eating chital, sambar, hog deer						
2.6	R	18	E	66	E	Alone
29. In Kahna in India eating chital, sambar, barasingha						
6.4	R	40	(E)	48	E	Alone
30. In Ranthambhore in India eating sambar, chital, wild boar						
10	R	30	O	27.5	O	Alone
Lions						
31. In Kalahari eating gemsbok						
2	M	187	O	187	E	Groups
32. In Kruger N.P. eating wildebeests, impalas, zebras						
13	R	93	O	93	E	Groups
33. In Serengeti woodlands eating wildebeests, zebras, Thomson's gazelles						
12–18	R	65–142	O	65–142	E	Groups
34. On Serengeti plains eating wildebeests, zebras						
10–25	M	149–226	O	149–226	E	Groups
35. In Nairobi N.P. eating hartebeests, zebras, wildebeests						
24	M	26	O	26	E	Groups
36. In Ngorongoro Crater eating wildebeests, zebras, gazelles						
22–38	R	45–88	O	45–88	E	Groups
37. In Queen Elizabeth N.P. eating kob, topi, warthogs						
11–52	R	39–68	O	39–68	E	Groups
38. In Lake Manyara N.P. eating wildebeests, impalas, zebras						
38	R	22	O	22	E	Groups

Note: Data were taken from studies in which densities, food items, and ranging patterns are all reported. Prey are given in order of importance. Felid densities are per 100 km². R refers to resident prey, M, to migratory. Ranges are in km²; O refers to overlapping, E, to exclusive ranges; (O) denotes some overlap but not extensive; (E), not quite exclusive; (Alone), assumed but not stated in source.

ᵃ Mean of male and female ranges.

ᵇ Young animal only.

ᶜ Underestimates as does not report densities of temporary female aggregations.

Sources: 1. Berg 1979. 2. Bailey 1974. 3. Wittmer and DeCalesta 1986. 4. Lembeck 1986. 5. Ludlow and Sunquist 1987. 6. Emmons 1986. 7. Geertsema 1985. 8. Bailey et al. 1986. 9. Brand, Keith, and Fischer 1976; Nellis, Wetmore, and Keith 1972. 10. Parker, Maxwell, and Morton 1983. 11. Haller and Breitenmoser 1986. 12. Jackson and Ahlborn 1989. 13. Eisenberg and Lockhart 1971. 14. Schaller 1972c; Cavallo 1990; Bailey 1994. 15. Bertram 1978b, 1982. 16. Smith 1977. 17. Hemker, Lindzey, and Ackerman 1984. 18. Belden 1986; Maehr, Land, and Roof 1991. 19. Hopkins, Kutilek, and Shreve 1986. 20. Hornocker 1969, 1970; Seidensticker et al. 1973. 21. Sitton and Wallen 1976. 22. Burney 1980. 23. McLaughlin in Burney 1980. 24. Schaller 1972c; this study. 25. Schaller and Crawshaw 1980; Crawshaw and Quigley 1991. 26. Rabinowitz 1986; Rabinowitz and Nottingham 1986. 27. Matjushkin, Zhivotchenko, and Smirnov 1977; Bragin 1986. 28. Sunquist 1981. 29. Schaller 1967; Panwar 1987. 30. Thapar 1986. 31. Eloff 1973b. 32. Smuts 1976, 1978, 1979; Smuts, Hanks, and Whyte 1978. 33. Schaller 1972c; Van Orsdol, Hanby, and Bygott 1985. 34. Schaller 1972c; Van Orsdol, Hanby, and Bygott 1985. 35. Rudnai 1973a,b. 36. Elliot and Cowan 1978; Van Ordsol, Hanby, and Bygott 1985. 37. Van Ordsol, Hanby, and Bygott 1985. 38. Makacha and Schaller 1969.

relatively large numbers, attracted by a combination of abundant cover and reasonably high concentrations of Thomson's gazelles that aggregated there during the course of their migration. Male lions, on the other hand, benefited from group living because they were better able to gain access to female prides, could hold prides for longer, and could occupy several prides during their reproductive careers (Packer et al. 1988). Thus high or localized female densities apparently drive male sociality in these species.

Male sociality in lions and cheetahs cannot be a consequence of large litter size because other felids produce litters of two (or more) cubs (see app. 6), a quarter of which would be a pair of males, on average. As littermates remain together after leaving their mother in several species (see table 7.1), brothers could continue to associate if it was in their reproductive interests.

If localized or high densities of females are responsible for group living in males, females should either be widely dispersed or live at low densities in other felids in which males are solitary. In order to test this, female home range overlap was taken as a measure of localized female distribution (see Leyhausen 1965) and overall density was used as an approximation of female density because the latter measure was unavailable in most studies. (This assumed that adult sex ratios were roughly equivalent across species.) Mean densities for each species were calculated from the studies outlined in table 12.2, and species were dichotomized by whether females had overlapping or exclusive ranges, based on the modal category across studies.

The first prediction, that males were more likely to live in groups where females had overlapping ranges, was not upheld [1], although males did not form alliances in species in which female ranges were primarily exclusive. The second prediction, that males were more likely to live in groups where densities were high, was not supported either [2]. Certainly no males lived together in species in which female densities were low, but males were equally likely to live alone whether densities were low or high.

In those species above the median density and in which female ranges overlapped, however, males usually lived in groups, while in species in which these factors were not congruent, males lived alone (table 12.3) [3]. (Unfortunately, the effect of an interaction between density and female range overlap could not be tested directly owing to small sample size.) The exception was servals living at high density in Ngorongoro Crater. There female range overlap was extensive in both time and space (the latter 79%: Geertsema 1985). These factors should have promoted intense competition between males and the formation of alliances, but they did not, and my hypothesis cannot account for asociality among male servals.

In conclusion, the evidence indicates that high female density and extensive range overlap together are important in favoring formation of alliances between males insofar as they increase the premium on male competition. Nonetheless, there are exceptions, and more work incorporating seasonality of mating opportunities is required to test the importance of these factors for felid social organization.

What are the ecological factors that promote high female densities and clumping? Female density is positively correlated with prey density both

TABLE 12.3 Species of Felids Separated according to Whether Densities Were Higher than the Median and Female Ranges Overlapped

	Densities higher than median and female ranges overlap	Densities lower than median and/or female ranges are exclusive
Males may live in groups	Cheetah Lion	
Males live alone	Serval	Bobcat Cougar European lynx Leopard North American lynx Ocelot Snow leopard Tiger

Note: Data for jaguars were equivocal (see table 12.2).

within populations (e.g., North American lynxes: Brand, Keith, and Fischer 1976; Ward and Krebs 1985) and across populations (e.g., lions: van Orsdol, Hanby, and Bygott 1985); prey density must therefore be important. Female range overlap is primarily affected by the distribution and predictability of food. Females may be clumped in areas where prey is found in stable, rich patches, since these can be defended by a group of females or by single females living in exclusive ranges (see Liberg and Sandell 1988). Females may also become seasonally clumped if they feed on and follow migratory prey that aggregate on limited feeding pastures at certain times of year. Nevertheless, a combination of these ecological factors appears to be important in driving intense competition between males and formation of alliances. For example, in Idaho and Nepal, where cougars and snow leopards respectively concentrate in valleys during winter following migratory ungulates, female densities appear too low (see table 12.2) to favor strong intermale competition (Hornocker 1969, 1970; Seidensticker et al. 1973; Jackson and Ahlborn 1989).

Living at low densities is characteristic of species living at the top of the trophic pyramid. Maintaining exclusive ranges is a strategy to reduce feeding competition, which is especially important for predators that feed opportunistically on resources that have a low rate of renewal. Thus being an exclusively carnivorous family at the top trophic level may predispose felids to asociality.

ASOCIALITY AMONG FEMALES

Two related hypotheses have been advanced to explain why most female cats are asocial but why female lions live in prides. Packer (1986) first proposed that in those species in which females characteristically take large prey and which live in open habitats and at high female population densities, there would be selection favoring group living. This is because large carcasses last for some time and are particularly likely to be seen by other females in open habitats, especially where conspecifics are numerous. Under such circumstances it would pay a female to share her visible carcass with conspecific relatives rather than inevitably relinquishing it to unrelated conspecifics. Packer argued that only in lions were these three conditions met.

In a later paper I considered several ways in which two or more adult female cats with attendant cubs might be able to compensate for having to share food if they were to become social (Caro 1989b). I suggested that it would be difficult for social mothers to carry back large prey items to a common den, as felids have relatively weak neck musculature. If, on the other hand, a group attempted to increase its food intake but mothers avoided increasing their hunting rates by hunting alternately, cubs would have to travel very large distances to be present at each kill. Thus the principal means of providing for additional group members were either to hunt more often or to capture larger prey. Among Serengeti cheetahs the former would be difficult because mothers with young cubs already spent a large proportion of their time hunting and searching for prey to feed themselves and their cubs, and were probably near the upper limit of the time they could allocate to these activities. Regarding the latter, it would be difficult to provide for additional group members by catching prey larger than Thomson's gazelles if females were to become social since females' hunting success declined and time spent hunting increased with prey size attempted. Only if hunting success rose with female group size would this be possible, but this seemed unlikely since hunting success did not rise significantly with group size in males (chap. 10). Thus to realize increased intake by taking large prey, I argued that a hypothetical group of female cheetahs would have to face the prospect of hunting almost continuously in Serengeti.

Two facts now make me question this line of argument. First, Laurenson's new data (1992) demonstrate that female cheetahs show preferences for larger prey (subadult and adult Thomson's gazelles) and increase their hunting success on these items during lactation, indicating that improvements in intake rates are possible by these means. Second, groups of males have higher per capita foraging returns than singleton males (chap. 10), implying that females might be able to achieve this too if they lived in groups. Thus the question of whether a hypothetical group of female cheetahs could provide for themselves and their cubs is still open.

Nevertheless, the formation of female groups would be greatly facilitated in ecosystems where prey weighing the same or up to twice as much as an adult female cat was abundant. This is the size of prey that felids prefer (Packer 1986; Caro 1989b), and its availability would enable them to capture prey more frequently and with greater ease. Empirical evidence shows that in 17 of 21 field sites, prey of equivalent or up to twice the size of the female felid under consideration was absent or was present only in low numbers. Thus for most members of the Felidae, an uneven weight distribution of prey, with small items being numerous, but prey close to a female's body weight being scarce, constrains opportunities for females to provide for additional group members. Only in lions, which live in areas containing numerous prey slightly larger than themselves, are the costs of feeding other group members greatly reduced, allowing lionesses to capitalize on the advantage of group living. Though the ecological factors considered by this hypothesis could account for the absence of sociality in most populations, they could not account for all of them (Caro 1989b).

Packer's and Caro's hypotheses are similar in that both stress the diverse benefits that sociality might bring for female felids and both propose that foraging costs prevent the formation of groups. More important, both recognize the significance of large prey in allowing for sociality, and neither suggests that the ability of a group to catch large prey favors sociality. The hypotheses differ in that Caro's considers availability of large abundant prey as the only factor necessary for felids to be social, whereas Packer's also considers high female density and open habitat to be important. In my view, however, there are problems in linking the three factors together (Caro 1989b). First, lions living at low densities, or in woodland habitats with low visibility, should not be social, but pride size remains relatively constant across lion populations living at different densities and in different habitats (Eloff 1973a; van Orsdol, Hanby, and Bygott 1985). Second, there are other species in which the three factors are congruent. For example, in Ranthambhore National Park, visibility is good, and female tigers there used to live at densities equivalent to savannah lions before a recent wave of poaching (Jackson 1992). They killed large sambar, were attracted to each other's kills by vultures, and competed over carcasses (Thapar 1986), yet they did not live in groups. A similar situation pertains in temperate or subarctic regions where snow and open habitat allow carcasses to last for long periods. Here female lynxes and bobcats sometimes live at high densities and feed on large prey, but are nevertheless asocial. Third, solitary, and presumably unrelated, females in several species have been reported as forming temporary aggregations at carcasses (tigers: Schaller 1967; cougars: Seidensticker et al. 1973), yet female relatives do not band together to defend the kills.

In a subsequent paper dealing only with lions, Packer, Scheel, and Pusey (1990) argued that cooperative defense of cubs against infanticidal males and defense of pride territories against other female groups were the positive benefits that lionesses accrued from forming groups. These factors do not explain why only lions are social, however, as other felids' offspring are subject to infanticide (Packer and Pusey 1984) and other felid populations are found at substantially higher densities than lions (see table 12.2). Females in these populations might similarly benefit from cooperative range defense. The issue therefore reverts to the permissive factors allowing females to forage together, and although size of available prey seems important, the details by which it prevents or allows for sociality remain unresolved.

Although female cheetahs do not associate with one another in Serengeti, there are occasional reports of adult females living together in other regions of Africa. In Graham and Parker's (1965) survey of East African cheetahs, for example, there were two reports of two adult females being seen in the company of males, although I suspect these were adolescent sisters. More convincing data come from Namibia, where McVittie (1979) reported that 23 of 123 sightings of adult females were of two females associating together with or without cubs. McVittie's data came from information provided by farmers, some of which was definitely unreliable due to inaccuracies, and some of the cheetahs had been caught in box traps (D. Morsbach, pers. comm.). It is therefore possible that single animals were repeatedly caught in the same place and were later assumed to belong to a group of females. Nevertheless, interviews carried out in other parts of southern Africa indicate that group sizes there may be larger than in East Africa (P. Gros, pers. comm.), and the problem warrants further investigation.

Cooperative Hunting and the Evolution of Sociality

CHEETAHS

For cooperative hunting to evolve, group members must accrue greater per capita foraging returns by hunting simultaneously than by hunting alone, as a result of their collaborative actions during the hunt. For cooperative hunting to be the principal selective force in the evolution of sociality, it must be shown that rate of food intake is the key factor affecting fitness in the group under consideration. These stringent criteria incorporate all the essential elements of previous formulations of cooperative hunting (chap. 1). In earlier chapters it was shown that three different segments of cheetah society hunted together in groups: mothers and cubs, adolescent groups, and male coalitions. Did any of these groups hunt cooperatively?

Group hunting by mothers and cubs, even old cubs, can be categorically rejected as evidence of cooperative hunting. Despite old cubs accompanying their mothers on hunts (see fig. 6.4), and initiating an increasing proportion of hunts as they grew older (see fig. 6.6), the food intake of mothers with old cubs was lower than that of lone adult females, and cubs' intake increased after they became independent (see table 5.4).

Among adolescents, groups made significantly more attempts on prey larger than neonate gazelles and hares than did adolescents living alone. This preference for large prey, combined with hunting success similar to that of single adolescents, resulted in a greater proportion of groups' kills being of large prey (see fig. 7.11). When groups hunted, one individual would often take over from its sibling and topple the prey if its partner held back; hesitancy in contacting prey was a hallmark of inexperienced adolescents' attempts to secure prey. Despite their capturing larger prey, however, per capita foraging returns were no greater for female adolescent group members than for single adolescent females because group members had to share the adult and subadult Thomson's gazelles that they caught (see fig. 7.12). As their per capita food intake was no higher than that of singleton adolescents, groups could not be said to hunt cooperatively (table 12.4).

In male coalitions, larger groups of males attempted heavier prey more often than smaller groups due to their focusing more extensively on wildebeests (see fig. 10.1). Hunting success did not show a linear increase with group size, and males' simultaneous participation in hunts did not improve their outcome except when one drove a defending wildebeest mother away, but this occurred rarely. Nevertheless, preference for larger prey resulted in heavier prey making up a greater proportion of groups' kills (see fig. 10.2), and this, in turn, meant that group members experienced greater per capita foraging returns (see fig. 10.4). Since prey preferences rather than simultaneous hunting accounted for greater food intake, male cheetahs could not in the normal sense of the phrase be said to hunt cooperatively (table 12.4).

If, however, group size–related prey preferences changed as a result of individuals' becoming braver in the presence of companions, this could in a very general sense be regarded as a form of cooperation. Nonetheless, it is clear that the principal benefits that males accrued from living in groups stemmed from enhanced competitive ability in fights over territories. Thus foraging benefits were unlikely to be the evolutionary cause of group living in male cheetahs.

In passing, it is noteworthy that all segments of cheetah society attempted larger prey under conditions of increasing demand. Adult females showed preferences for larger prey when lactating, mothers when they had large litters of old cubs, adolescents when accompanied by siblings, and males in the company of other males. The type of prey attempted is probably the element of the hunt over which predators have the most control, since hunting success is in part determined by the actions of the prey, and foraging success by competition from conspecifics and heterospecific scavengers.

Teasing apart both hunting and foraging success in male and adolescent cheetahs is instructive because it demonstrates that generalizations about the effects of carnivore group size on components of predation cannot be made even for the same species living in the same habitat! Since foraging returns and hunting success can vary independently, measurement of both, as well as determining the means by which hunting success changes with group size, is necessary before we can confidently decide that animals hunt cooperatively. Even if these criteria are met, cooperative hunting may still not be the evolutionary cause of group living. To illustrate these points, I have reexamined studies of other predators for evidence of cooperative hunting.

Table 12.4 is a summary of the best behavioral studies of hunting in

TABLE 12.4 Effects of Increasing Group Size on Hunting and Foraging in Various Predators

Species	Preference for large prey	Hunting success	How simultaneous hunting affects success	Per capita food intake	Can cooperative hunting account for grouping?
Adolescent cheetah	Increases	No effect	Taking over, making contact	No effect	No
Male cheetah	Increases	No effect	Keeping mother at bay	Increases	No
Serengeti lion	Increases in dry season	Increases B, no others	Not given	No effect	No
Etosha lion	No effect	Increases	Driving, ambushing	Increases?	No
Wild dog	Increases	Increases W, no effect TG	Hold W or chase mother W off, no effect TG	No effect, or not clear	No?
Spotted hyena	Increases	Increases W calves, no effect others	Keeping W mother at bay	Not given	?
Wolf	Increases	Not given	Keeping moose mother at bay	Not given	?
Golden jackal	Not given	Increases	Keeping TG mother at bay	Not given	?
Chimpanzee	Not given	Increases	Driving, blocking, ambushing	Not given	?
Harris's hawk	Not given	Increases	Converging on, flushing, relays	Increases	Yes?

Sources: Cheetahs: Data from this study. Serengeti lions: Packer, Scheel, and Pusey 1990; Scheel and Packer 1991. Etosha lions: Stander 1992a,b; Stander and Albon 1993. Wild dogs: Fuller and Kat 1990; Fanshawe and FitzGibbon 1993. Spotted hyenas: Kruuk 1972; Mills 1985; Mills 1990. Wolves: Mech 1970. Golden jackals: Lamprecht 1978a. Chimpanzees: Boesch and Boesch 1989. Harris's hawks: Bednarz 1988.

Note: B, buffalo; W, wildebeest; TG, Thomson's gazelle.

carnivores. In those studies for which data on foraging returns are available, per capita intake fails to increase with group size in all but one, and in none can cooperative hunting account for group living. In most studies, however, there are insufficient data on group size–related per capita foraging returns to assess whether cooperative hunting occurs. In addition, two striking points emerge from the table. First, preference for larger prey increases with group size in most species, although it is difficult to distinguish whether groups can capture large prey more easily or whether they need to capture larger items to satisfy group demands. Second, keeping prey at bay is clearly an important advantage of hunting in groups for many species. Each study is now examined in more detail.

LIONS

In Serengeti lions, large groups of five or six lionesses were more likely to be near herds containing buffaloes when they started to hunt than were smaller groups, indicating a preference for this species (Scheel 1993). In analyzing the role of group members while hunting, Scheel and Packer (1991) found that individuals were more likely to refrain from pursuing warthogs, indicating a lack of cooperation when this species was hunted, but were more likely to pursue zebras and buffaloes, which were difficult to capture. Indeed, buffaloes were never stalked by solitary lions and could only be killed through the combined efforts of a group. In times of prey abundance, per capita foraging success did not change with group size (Packer, Scheel, and Pusey 1990). During periods of prey scarcity, the foraging success of singletons was higher than per capita success in groups of two to four, but in groups of five to seven foraging success was equivalent to that of single females because these large groups took buffaloes. As per capita foraging success did not increase with group size, Serengeti lions cannot be said to hunt cooperatively.

Lions in the more open habitat of Etosha National Park showed a different pattern of hunting behavior. Here there was no effect on group size on the type of prey attempted, but lions had higher success rates in larger groups when zebras, wildebeests, or all prey were considered (Stander 1991b; Stander and Albon 1993). This was primarily due to group members coordinating their activities, with most prey fleeing from one lioness but being captured by another from an ambush position (Stander 1991a, b). In the dry season lionesses in groups had higher intake than solitary females, although intake did not increase beyond group sizes of two. In the wet season, there was no clear pattern of intake except that groups of one to three had significantly higher intake than groups of four to seven. These observations lend partial support to the proposition that lionesses hunt cooperatively, since groups' foraging returns were higher than solitaries' in the dry season, and coordinated group hunts and group size were primarily responsible for increasing hunting success (Stander and Albon 1993). Nevertheless, foraging returns did not show a consistent increase with group size and actually declined with group size in the wet season.

However these data are interpreted, communal hunting was unlikely to account for group living in Etosha lions for the following reasons. In the dry season, lions in all pride sizes were most often found in groups of two, corresponding to high daily food intake, but were rarely found in groups of six or seven, which had the second highest rate of food intake. During the wet season, when per capita foraging returns were greatest in groups of one to three, large prides foraged in groups of five or six animals (Stander 1991b). Group size therefore appeared related to factors other than foraging returns.

WILD DOGS

Fanshawe and FitzGibbon (1993) observed the hunting behavior of a wild dog pack on the Serengeti plains. When it split up to hunt, larger parties tended to hunt wildebeests while smaller ones hunted gazelles; very small parties of one or two dogs concentrated on fawns. Pack members returned to a den often to regurgitate food to pups, so pack demand was the same irrespective of the number of dogs hunting. Thus larger hunting parties may have chosen wildebeests because they could capture large prey more easily, not because their need was greater. Hunting success did not increase with party size when Thomson's gazelles were pursued, but it did when wildebeests were hunted. One dog held onto the muzzle of an adult wildebeest while the others disemboweled it; with wildebeest calves, some dogs chased the mother off while the others caught her offspring. In addition, a larger number of dogs enabled them to keep scavenging spotted hyenas away from the carcass for longer. Meat yields were calculated by dividing the weight of the prey item by the number of dogs hunting it and multiplying by the probability they would be successful. Yields increased up to party size four when hunting wildebeests but declined from party size one when hunting gazelles. Unfortunately, it is difficult to conclude that per capita foraging returns necessarily increased with size of hunting party because Thomson's gazelles constituted the majority of wild dog kills in Serengeti (see Fuller and Kat 1990 for a review); because all pack members fed from the kill, not just those hunting it; and because pack size varied over the period of Fanshawe and FitzGibbon's study.

In a separate study, in an area bordering the Masai Mara Game Reserve but still in the Serengeti ecosystem, Fuller and Kat (1990) conducted observations on a pack whose members dropped in number during the period of study. Here, the amount of meat ingested by each dog per hunt was reported for different pack sizes. Intake rates per dog per hunt were not significantly higher at larger than at smaller pack size [4], and kill rates were almost exactly the same for both. Unfortunately, hunting party sizes were not reported. Current evidence therefore indicates that wild dogs in the Serengeti ecosystem do not hunt cooperatively since per capita intake does not increase with group size, but a new study that follows packs of different size continuously and records hunting party size and per capita food intake is obviously required.

OTHER SPECIES

Complete data sets reporting all the necessary variables are unavailable for other large carnivores. In Ngorongoro Crater, spotted hyenas preferred to hunt zebras in large groups but smaller-sized wildebeests and Thomson's gazelles in small groups (Kruuk 1972). Hunting success, however, did not increase with group size except when wildebeest calves were hunted. In this situation, the wildebeest mother could attack only one hyena at a time while the other dealt with her calf. In the Kalahari, spotted hyenas were more likely to hunt springbok and gemsbok calves in small groups, but gemsbok adults, wildebeests, and eland in large groups (Mills 1985; 1990). Again, hunting success did not increase with group size. Unfortunately, per capita intake rates were not reported in either study.

In wolves, preferences for large prey also increased with group size, and pack members were able to keep a defending moose mother at bay (Mech 1970); however, per capita food intake was not reported. Rates of food intake were also unknown for golden jackals hunting gazelle fawns alone or in pairs (fig. 12.7). A similar problem is faced in the Tai chimpanzee study despite evidence of sophisticated collaboration between party members when hunting red colobus. Thus it is not yet possible to say that per capita intake rates in hunting groups exceed those of single individuals and hence that these animals hunt cooperatively. In conclusion, there is no current basis on which to say that group hunting might be an evolutionary cause of sociality in these species.

Although the advantages of group living are not completely understood in the examples shown in table 12.4, they are increasingly regarded as being unrelated to hunting. Grouping is seen as a means of enhancing territorial defense (lionesses: Packer, Scheel, and Pusey 1990; male chimpanzees: Wrangham 1979; Nishida and Hiraiwa-Hasegawa 1986) or territory size (wolves: Peterson, Woolington, and Bailey 1984); as a way of defending carcasses more effectively against intra- or interspecific competitors (spotted hyenas: L. Frank, pers. comm.); as a way of obtaining greater access to females (male lions: Bygott, Bertram, and Hanby 1979; male cheetahs: this study); or as an antipredator strategy (adolescent cheetahs: this study). Alternatively, grouping may arise from constraints on

Fig. 12.7 Having chased the defending mother away, a pair of golden jackals begin to disembowel a Thomson's gazelle fawn that they have found lying out in a patch of tall vegetation on the short grass plains.

breeding opportunities brought about by few territories being available, a shortage of sexual partners, or prohibitively high costs of independent reproduction (possibly wolves, jackals, and wild dogs: see Emlen 1984 and references therein).

Large carnivores are therefore subject to the same selection pressures that affect other mammals and birds: the need to maintain a territory, escape predation, and obtain access to mating partners. The chapters in this book bring this message home with even greater force than do comparisons between species, since different age-sex classes of cheetahs live in groups for different reasons. Grouping allows males to enhance their competitive edge when contending for areas of high female density, adolescents to reduce harassment from predators, and families to further the mother's reproductive success while cubs are protected from predators and provided with food. There are multiple reasons for group living in this asocial species.

Perhaps the strongest evidence for group living arising as a result of cooperative hunting comes from Harris's hawks (Bednarz 1988). Preliminary evidence shows that hunting success increases with group size as a result of simultaneous hunting, and that as a consequence, per capita food intake is greater in larger groups. The search for an association between sociality and cooperative hunting may therefore be more profitable outside the group-living carnivores!

Summary

1. Cheetahs' life history traits, breeding system, and group hunting behavior are examined from a comparative perspective.

2. Cheetahs have the highest juvenile mortality yet recorded for non-hunted populations of cats in the wild. To compensate, cheetahs reach maturity relatively early, and have relatively larger litter sizes than other felids. Mothers produce offspring of low birth weight and have relatively light litters in order not to waste expenditure on young that have a low chance of survival.

3. In cheetahs and in lions, high densities and localized female distributions set up conditions for intense male competition and formation of alliances between males. In other felid species, this combination of factors is rarely encountered, and reduced competition over females favors asociality in males.

4. Two related hypotheses suggest that presence of large prey permits female felids to be social, although both stress that foraging benefits are not the key to group living. In most species, females may be unable to secure sufficient food to feed additional group members because their habitats lack abundant prey the same size or up to twice the body weight of a female. Alternatively, benefits of group living may be manifested only in those rare situations in which female density is high and in which carcasses are large and can be seen from some distance, since it will pay females to live in groups and share their carcasses with kin. Neither hypothesis is wholly satisfactory.

5. According to strict definitions of cooperative hunting, adolescent cheetahs did not hunt cooperatively since per capita foraging success in groups was no greater than that of singletons. Males in coalitions did not hunt cooperatively either since their higher per capita food intake compared with single males did not result from behavior while hunting quarry simultaneously but from a preference for larger prey. Therefore even within the same species it is risky to make generalizations about the effects of group size on either hunting or foraging success in carnivores.

6. In most large carnivores preferences for large prey increased with group size, and keeping prey at bay was a common feature of group hunting. Unfortunately, few studies report per capita foraging returns, but in the majority of those that do, per capita foraging success did not increase with group size. In populations in which it did, grouping patterns did not reflect optimal foraging group sizes. Though limited, current evidence therefore suggests that cooperative hunting is not responsible for group living in any carnivore.

Statistics

1. Among cheetahs, lions, cougars, leopards, North American lynxes, servals, and snow leopards, in which female ranges were primarily overlapping, males lived in groups in the first two (28.6%), but among bobcats, ocelots, and tigers, in which female ranges were primarily exclusive, none lived in groups, Fisher test, $P = .467$. Comparisons across populations revealed a similar pattern, with males forming alliances in 45.8% of the 24 populations in which female ranges overlapped, and no males forming alliances in the 10 populations in which female ranges were exclusive.

2. Among cheetahs, lions, bobcats, jaguars, ocelots, and servals, in which densities were higher than the median ($9.5/100$ km^2), males lived in groups in the first two (33.3%), but among cougars, European lynxes, leopards, North American lynxes, snow leopards, and tigers, in which densities were lower than the median, none lived in groups, Fisher test, $P = .228$. Comparisons across populations revealed a similar pattern, with males forming alliances in 47.4% of the 19 populations in which densities were higher than the median (8.8/km^2), and 10.5% forming alliances in the 19 populations in which densities were lower than the median.

3. In 66.7% of the three felid species in which densities were higher than the median and females had overlapping ranges, males lived in groups, but none lived in groups in the eight species in which this did not apply, Fisher test, $P = .055$ (see table 12.3). Comparisons across populations revealed a similar pattern, with males forming alliances in 64.3% of the 13 populations in which densities were higher than the median and female ranges overlapped, and 10.0% forming alliances in the 20 populations in which this did not apply.

4. Number of kilograms ingested per wild dog per hunt when the pack size was 28–29 animals compared with when it was 19–21 animals for days when both the morning and evening hunts were observed, $Ns = 10$, 4 days respectively, $\bar{X}s = 3.2$, 2.7 kg (summing morning and evening returns), Mann-Whitney U test, $U = 11.5$, $P > .1$.

Including days when any hunt was observed in either the morning or the evening, or both, $Ns = 17, 9$ days, $\bar{X}s = 2.1, 1.7$ kg (summing morning and evening returns if both were observed), $U = 64$, $P > .1$ (reanalyzed from Fuller and Kat 1990).

A 2-month-old cub born in captivity on a weighing scale. (Drawing by Dafila Scott.)

13
CONSERVATION OF CHEETAHS IN THE WILD AND IN CAPTIVITY

The cheetah's gracile, canid-like morphological features and the extremely fast sprint it uses to capture prey have fostered a popular mythology that the species is overly specialized and hence doomed to extinction (Quammen 1985). There is some merit to the idea that specialists are more prone to extinction than generalists if ecological conditions change because they are often adapted to a specific habitat or to eating a restricted diet. This is unlikely to apply to cheetahs because they occupied habitats ranging from woodlands to semidesert across Africa, the Middle East, and Asia until recently, and they still take prey items varying in size from mole rats to buffalo calves (app. 3).

Nevertheless, there are other reasons for believing that cheetahs have only a moderate chance of persisting through the next century. The cheetah's absolute numbers in Africa are low despite its wide distribution (Myers 1975a), and it has virtually disappeared from Asia. In areas where they are found, cheetahs survive at low densities compared with other large carnivores (chap. 2; app. 2). The species exhibits an extreme lack of genetic variability which may, in theory, increase its susceptibility to disease and compromise its ability to adapt to future environmental conditions (O'Brien et al. 1983, 1985; but see Caughley 1994; Caro and Laurenson 1994). Furthermore, efforts to breed this species in captivity have generally met with little success (Marker and O'Brien 1989; Marker-Kraus and Grisham 1993). In this chapter I attempt to unravel the importance of the different problems that cheetahs face in the wild and in and in captivity, and suggest possible conservation solutions that arise from the findings of this and other studies.

Status in the Wild

The cheetah was one of the first mammals whose total numbers were estimated in the wild. Myers (1975a) gathered extensive data on the distribution and abundance of cheetahs in Africa based on 648 interviews and correspondence with 304 people who had direct experience of cheetahs. In addition, he conducted 1,400 interviews and conversations, and received almost 300 letters from people with field experience in Africa. His survey of 28 countries showed that cheetahs numbered between 7,300 and 22,950 in sub-Saharan African during the early 1970s (table 13.1). North of this, small populations were present in areas such as the Hoggar and Air mountains on the Niger-Libya border. A relict population of perhaps 200 individuals existed and probably still survives in the Kosh Yeilagh area of Iran and possibly northwestern Afghanistan (Jackson 1990). A total of between 7,000 and 25,000 cheetahs were thought to be living in the wild in the early 1970s.

Myers suggested that the African population might decline to 7,400 by 1980, but there are no data to support or refute this prediction. Estimates in the 1990s are currently unknown but are presently the subject of a detailed study (Gros 1990). Since the 1970s changes have occurred in some of the six countries where Myers recorded cheetahs as being especially numerous. These include erection of wildlife fences in Botswana and the persecution of cheetahs on farmlands in Namibia and Zimbabwe. In Kenya, agriculture has spread quickly with a consequent reduction in habitat available to cheetahs. Only in Tanzania and Zambia have environmental conditions remained relatively similar to those in the 1970s. I would guess that subpopulations of perhaps 250 or more interbreeding

TABLE 13.1 Cheetah Numbers in the Early 1970s in Sub-Saharan Africa

Region	Estimated numbers
East Africa (Kenya, Tanzania, Uganda)	1,600–4,650
Miombo woodland zone (Angola, Malawi, Mozambique, Zambia)	800–3,300
Southern Africa (Botswana, Namibia, South Africa, Zimbabwe)	2,850–7,300
West Africa (Burkina Faso, Cameroon, Chad, Mauritania, Niger)	800–2,600
Northeastern Africa (Ethiopia, Sudan, Somalia)	1,150–4,500
Equatorial rainforest region (Zaire)	100–500
Total	7,300–22,950

Source: Adapted from Myers 1975a.

cheetahs may now be found only in Botswana, Kenya, Namibia, Tanzania, Zambia, Zimbabwe, and in the Kruger National Park, South Africa.

Threats to Cheetah Populations Outside Protected Areas

HABITAT DESTRUCTION

Many problems are cited as afflicting cheetahs in the wild, but the principal ones contributing to their range reduction are habitat destruction and loss of the ungulate herds on which they depend (Myers 1975a). Collecting information on habitat encroachment and loss of prey on a continent-wide scale is difficult, and there are currently no quantitative data sets to support these claims. Another medium-sized carnivore, the wild dog, formerly had a geographic distribution similar to that of the cheetah, but has suffered a substantial range reduction over the last 10 years (Fanshawe, Frame, and Ginsberg 1991). It is possible that the current distribution of cheetahs parallels the present distribution of wild dogs if habitat loss and persecution are primarily responsible for the cheetah's demise. I suspect that the relative importance of habitat loss and reduction in ungulate biomass differs by region. In Kenya and Zimbabwe, spreading agriculture has squeezed habitat available for cheetahs, while in Tanzania and Zambia, increasing use of firearms must have been important in lowering ungulate densities. In the Sahel, a series of droughts during the 1980s combined with increased numbers of livestock and new agricultural practices have condensed wildlife habitat between agricultural areas and the true desert (Le Houérou and Gillet 1986), but greater use of vehicles by hunting parties has also reduced ungulate populations there over the last 20 years (Newby 1990).

DIRECT EXPLOITATION

Cheetahs are listed in Appendix I of CITES. In Namibia, however, 6,782 were shot as vermin, for trophies, or were exported live between 1980 and 1991 according to CITES reports (Marker-Kraus and Grisham 1993). Since this figure does not include illegal offtake, it suggests that Joubert and Mostert's (1975) estimate of 6,000 cheetahs alive in Namibia in the 1970s may have been an underestimate and further, that Morsbach's (1984/86) figure of 2,500 alive a decade later may have been too large. In Zimbabwe, farmers can take out a permit to shoot "nuisance" cheetahs, and limited trophy hunting occurs. In both countries human exploitation is almost certainly the key factor depressing the cheetah population size. Sustained persecution is lower elsewhere. CITES reported an international trade averaging 87 live animals and 101 skins and trophies annually between 1985 and 1989. In 1991 an export quota system was established for trophies and live animals, allowing export of 150 cheetahs from Namibia, 50 from Zimbabawe, and 5 from Botswana. An unknown number of live animals end up in the Middle East for coursing purposes. In most countries where cheetahs are still found, a handful are kept as pets, but this cannot represent a serious threat to the continental population.

Threats to Cheetah Populations Inside Protected Areas

RELATIONS WITH LARGE PREDATORS

Within protected areas the principal threats to cheetahs come from other predators and from humans, although disease may also be important. Interspecific competition between predators can occur when one predator depletes the resources of another, or displaces it from prey it has captured. Predators may also kill each other (termed intraguild predation, Polis, Myers, and Holt 1989). Rough calculations suggest that Serengeti cheetahs are unlikely to be limited by a reduction in available food as a consequence of predation by other carnivores. Cheetahs removed an estimated 3,970 adult Thomson's gazelles from the plains each year (app. 12) or 5,134 from the ecosystem (app. 2). This latter figure amounted to between 3.9% and 5.9% of the adult annual recruitment using the population size in 1986 and 5.1% to 7.7% in 1989. As other large carnivores took between 35.6% and 74.1% (app. 2), the shortfall suggests that cheetahs could not be held in check by shortage of Thomson's gazelles. Laurenson (in press-c) has independently argued that food availability has little effect on cheetah numbers in Serengeti because of the high prey biomass in the 15–60 kg range, low rates of cub abandonment as a result of prey scarcity, and reproductive and growth rates comparable to those of cheetahs in captivity. Nevertheless, interspecific competition over available prey cannot be discounted in other areas.

Based on observations of lions and spotted hyenas stealing kills made by cheetahs, competition over carcasses is often cited as having an adverse influence on cheetahs in the wild (Myers 1977). The calculations in chapter 10, however, suggest that hyenas take only 9% of the flesh that male cheetahs procure on the Serengeti plains, an area where hyena densities are high. In other, more closed habitats with lower visibility, kleptoparasitism is likely to be of even lesser import. Thus other predators' effect on cheetahs' food intake may be less severe than previously assumed, and trivial compared with factors that limit reproduction directly.

Several lines of evidence indicate that sympatric carnivores have a major impact on cheetah population growth rates as a result of direct predation. Using a model to estimate cub recruitment, Laurenson (in press-c) found juvenile and adult mortality to be the most important factors affecting lifetime reproductive success, while fecundity had relatively little

influence. Since rates of cub mortality were far higher than those estimated for adolescents or adults, and predation was the most important
source of cub mortality, accounting for 73.2% (see table 4.3), she concluded that predation could be the critical factor in determining cheetah
abundance in Serengeti. She further argued that an observed reduction
in the average size of old, but not young, litters between the period from
1969 to 1976 (Frame 1975/76) and the period from 1987 to 1990 may
have been attributable to the increase in lion and spotted hyena numbers
on the plains (fig. 13.1) (Hanby and Bygott 1979). These predators characteristically take a portion of the litter after it emerges from the lair (see
table 4.4).

Circumstantial evidence indicates that large carnivores are important
predators of cheetah cubs in other regions. In areas where large predators
are absent, as in small reserves in South Africa, cheetah litter sizes are
large. For example, the average size of 10-month-old litters was 4.0 (N =
9 litters) on farmlands in Namibia (McVittie 1979), approximately double
that in Serengeti. In such areas population growth rates are extremely
rapid, and resulting densities are high (Anderson 1984). Conversely, extremely high densities of lions and spotted hyenas may be the cause of
cheetahs' virtual absence from Ngorongoro Crater. More systematically,
Laurenson (in press-c) found that cheetah biomass was negatively correlated with the biomass of lions across nine protected areas once the effects
of prey biomass in the 15–60 kg range had been removed (fig. 13.2). She
has therefore marshaled preliminary evidence to indicate that predation
on cubs is responsible for the cheetah's low density over most of its range
(0.3 to 5/100 km^2: Myers 1975a). Although this requires substantiation, it
has potentially solved the mystery posed by Schaller (1972c) of "some

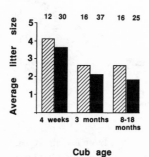

Fig. 13.1 The average size of cheetah litters on the Serengeti plains at different
cub ages during the early and mid-1970s (hatched bars: Frame 1975/76) and late
1980s (solid bars). The only significant difference is found in the oldest age class
of cubs. Sample sizes are shown above the bars. (From Laurenson, in press-c).

unknown factor or factors keep the population depressed and seemingly stable at a low level."

Tackling the problem of predator-induced juvenile mortality is difficult because reducing numbers of large predators in national parks would defeat conservation goals, and would be viewed adversely by the public. Translocating lions and spotted hyenas is impractical because of cost, and there are few areas in which to place them. Constructing artificial lairs that prevent access by larger predators but are attractive to cheetahs is probably impossible. Capturing already mated free-living females, allowing them to raise cubs in secure enclosures adjacent to or within a protected area, and then releasing them, would be intrusive and expensive, and there is no guarantee that it would work! Breeding cheetah litters in captivity to an age at which they can escape predation and then releasing them into the wild is impractical at present, since females are reluctant to mate under captive conditions (see below).

If the limit on cheetah numbers is set by lion and hyena predation on cubs, then any project for artificially increasing cheetah numbers would be effective only so long as the program was operating. A reinforced cheetah population would decline to former levels in a density-dependent fashion as soon as the project ceased. Only where cheetah densities are artificially low as a result of hunting, for example, might a release program allow permanent increase in the population. Given these difficulties, it is worth considering ways to protect cheetahs outside national parks. For example, we might expect cheetah densities to be high in hunting blocks

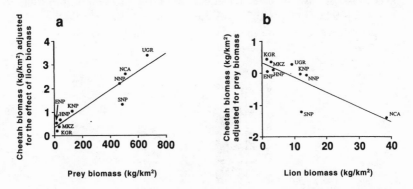

Fig. 13.2 (a) The relationship between cheetah biomass and prey biomass across nine protected areas, taking lion biomass into account. (b) The relationship between cheetah biomass and lion biomass, taking prey biomass into account. ENP, Etosha National Park; HNP, Hwange National Park; KGR, Kalahari Gemsbok National Park; KNP, Kruger National Park; MKZ, Mkomazi Game Reserve; NCA, Ngorongoro Conservation Area; NNP, Nairobi National Park; SNP, Serengeti National Park; UGR, Umfolozi Game Reserve. (From Laurenson, in press-c.)

or in areas used by pastoralists where lion and hyena numbers are low. Conservation efforts and funds might therefore be targeted at encouraging people to be more tolerant of cheetahs in rangeland habitats.

TOURISM

In East Africa, opinion is divided as to the effects of tourists on wildlife in national parks (e.g., Caro 1986a and letters in *Swara Magasine* volumes 9[6], 10[1, 4, 5], 11[1]). Cheetahs, in particular, are thought to suffer badly as a result of tourism. Their diurnal activity pattern and relative timidity make them particularly susceptible to visitors disrupting their hunts and driving them from kills. For example, Henry (1975) stated that "concentrations of more than six vehicles sharply diminish hunting activity" and suggested that cheetahs are more crepuscular in Amboseli National Park as a result of tourist pressure. Effects of tourism vary by area (Burney 1981): in Amboseli large aggregations of tourist vehicles often cluster around cheetahs, but in the Masai Mara Game Reserve, where visibility is lower, harassment is somewhat less common despite high visitor numbers. The same is true in Serengeti, where tourist numbers are lower.

Burney (1980) conducted a detailed study of relations between cheetahs and humans in the Masai Mara Game Reserve, which hosts a large number of tourists per annum (40,000 in 1978 during his study). He noted that vehicles stayed with cheetahs for 17.6 minutes on average ($N = 415$ visits) and approached to 17 m ($N = 337$ visits) on average. When cheetahs were on kills, these figures changed to an average of 21.8 minutes and 22 m (52 and 49 measurements respectively). By observing tourists from far away, approaching cheetahs, Burney found that cheetahs fell into two categories: those that tolerated vehicles and those that fled from them at long distances. (In Serengeti, I found that cheetahs exhibited a more normal distribution in wariness, possibly due to my larger sample size.) Cheetahs were strongly affected by the behavior of tour drivers and their clients in the Mara. When vehicles were driven directly toward them, cheetahs were more likely to move off, but were significantly more likely simply to shift position or not respond if the vehicle made a circling or oblique approach without pointing directly at them (see also chap. 3). Cheetahs were significantly more likely to leave if tourists vocalized, as opposed to making mechanical sounds with camera shutters or banging on the side of the car. If tourists got out of the car, cheetahs would either run off or shift position, but were little affected if tourists remained screened by the vehicle. Using these data, recommendations were made as to how to locate wildlife more efficiently, and how to approach and observe it with minimum disturbance (Burney 1982a).

More important, chases more often ended in a kill when vehicles were within 100 m of cheetahs than when they were absent, though not signifi-cantly so. Despite clear (and often memorable) cases of tourists fright-ening prey away or distracting cheetahs, Burney found that vehicles sometimes drew the attention of prey, gave tame cheetahs cover from which to stalk, or woke cheetahs up, causing them to notice prey that had approached to within chasing range.

Burney concluded that cheetahs were little affected by the presence of tourists in the reserve during the late 1970s, and that tourism in general had only a very minor impact on cheetahs' survival in the wild. (His con-clusion must hold even if occasional incidents of vehicles killing cubs are included.) The number of visitors has increased sharply in the Masai Mara since the 1970s, and it would therefore be instructive to repeat Burney's study under this new pressure. Furthermore, it is not clear whether Bur-ney's results can be generalized to more open habitats.

Conservation Implications of Reduced Genetic Variability

It is not, however, the threats to population viability in the wild that have captured the attention of conservation biologists in recent years. Rather, these have been overshadowed by a series of surprising discoveries made in the course of a genetic survey of the species. In a study of fifty-five cheetahs originating in Transvaal and in Namibia, O'Brien et al. (1983) found a complete absence of genetic variation at each of 47 allozyme loci. Two-dimensional gel electrophoresis of 155 proteins from six animals re-vealed a percentage polymorphism of 3.2% and an average heterozygosity of 0.013, both far lower than in other Felidae sampled (Newman et al. 1985) and lower than in other mammalian populations, which average 14.7% polymorphisms and 0.036 heterozygosity. A parallel study of chee-tah seminal quality found spermatozoa that were ten times less concen-trated than in domestic cats subjected to the same electroejaculatory regime. Seventy-one percent of sperm were morphologically abnormal, compared with 29.1% in cats, and crucially, they showed only 54.0% as opposed to 77.0% motility (Wildt et al. 1983). These findings corrobo-rated the genetic results since spermatozoal morphology and develop-ment are under strict genetic influence (Wildt, Bush, et al. 1987). A genetic and reproductive analysis of free-living East African cheetahs, mostly from Serengeti, confirmed these results, detecting only two allo-zyme polymorphisms in an electrophoretic survey of the products of 49 genetic loci (O'Brien et al. 1987; Wildt, O'Brien, et al. 1987).

Additional evidence of depauperate variation in the cheetah's genome came from fourteen reciprocal skin grafts performed between pairs of unrelated cheetahs (O'Brien et al. 1985). Eleven of fourteen grafts were accepted and three showed slow rejection. In marked contrast, skin from domestic cats was rejected quickly by cheetahs within the second week following the operation. These results suggested that the major histocompatibility complex (MHC) was unusually invariate in cheetahs. The MHC is normally a highly polymorphic group of tightly linked loci in vertebrates that encodes cell surface antigens responsible for cell-mediated rejection of allogenic skin grafts.

POSSIBLE CAUSES OF REDUCED GENETIC VARIABILITY

From a genetic standpoint, cheetahs resemble populations suffering from known founder effects, as in island introductions, or those that have suffered genetic depletion through severe persecution by humans (O'Brien et al. 1983). Mammalian examples of the latter include northern elephant seals and black-footed ferrets (Bonnell and Selander 1974; O'Brien et al. 1989). Cheetahs are very unusual among vertebrates in having apparently suffered this fate without documented human influence or being confined to an island (O'Brien and Evermann 1988). O'Brien and colleagues therefore conjectured that a major population bottleneck or, more probably, a series of less severe bottlenecks (Nei, Maruyama, and Chakraborty 1975) might have occurred at the end of the Pleistocene some 10,000 years ago. They argued that such events would be necessary to elicit the extremes of inbreeding required to produce the observed homozygosity.

Analyses of mitochondrial DNA and hypervariable minisatellite loci have subsequently confirmed the approximate timing of the bottleneck (Menotti-Raymond and O'Brien 1993). These show that while the cheetah is depauperate in genetic variation for nuclear coding loci, moderate levels of genetic diversity have accumulated in portions of DNA not subject to strong selection. Back calculations based on relative divergence of mtDNA in felids and mutation rates of variable number of tandem repeat loci in other species place the last bottleneck at the end of the Pleistocene between 6,000 and 20,000 years ago.

Within the last 100 years, chance founder effects or a second bottleneck, resulting perhaps from persecution by farmers or the skin trade, may have led to slightly lower genetic variability in the southern than in the East African population (O'Brien et al. 1987).

Unfortunately it is difficult to envisage a population being reduced to a few interbreeding individuals without it going extinct for demographic or environmental reasons. For example, R. Lacy (pers. comm.) has calculated that in the absence of mutation, a population size of 10 cheetahs lasting 45 to 90 generations, or 100 cheetahs lasting 459 to 918 generations, or the equivalent, would be required to cause the 10- to 100-fold reduction in genetic variability compared with other mammals. Even if the high juvenile mortality rate observed in modern populations had kept the intrinsic rate of population growth low over a protracted time period, such scenarios seem improbable.

Nevertheless, alternatives to the population bottleneck hypothesis also seem unlikely, at least for cheetahs (see Pimm et al. 1989). Such arguments center on the maintenance of a low effective population size (N_e) in a reasonably large population. This might have occurred if the number of males contributing to the next generation had been low, as, for example, in a highly polygynous species, or if certain females had been consistently more successful at reproducing than others. Evidence from this study lends little support to either possibility, however. Serengeti females encountered and presumably mated with nonresident males both outside and inside territories, as well as with residents (chap. 9), suggesting that the population of potential fathers was large. Even if females had mated only with territorial males, these comprised 25.4% of the male population. Particular females were unlikely to be consistently more successful in contributing to the next generation than others given the unpredictable nature of early juvenile mortality (chap. 4).

Effective population size can also be low compared with the total population size if there is a wide variation in litter size (Franklin 1980). During this study, litters of cubs aged 8 months or older showed little size variation ($\bar{X} = 1.98$, SE = 0.04, $N = 496$ sightings), with 29.8% of sightings being of one cub, 48.6% of two, 15.5% of three, and 6.0% of four; old litters of five or more cubs were never seen. As the vast majority of litters reaching independence contained two or fewer cubs, variation in litter size as judged from Serengeti data is unlikely to have contributed to a low N_e.

Effective population size can also be reduced in situations in which numbers are usually high but periodically drop as a result of an environmental fluctuation or catastrophe, since N_e is equivalent to the harmonic mean across generations. Assessing the extent of nonanthropogenic fluctuations in population size or local extinctions in the past is difficult because cheetah populations have been monitored for such a short time. That said, the Serengeti population has suffered no disease epidemics recently, as have the wild dog and black-backed jackal populations (Gascoyne et al. 1993), nor has it been subjected to parasite infestations, as were lions in Ngorongoro Crater (Fosbrooke 1963). Indeed, the cheetah population has probably remained at approximately the same size since Frame's study or declined only slightly (Frame 1975/76). Therefore limited contemporary evidence does not support the idea that severe fluctuations in effective population size characterized cheetah populations in the past. Although homozygous populations may be relatively susceptible to disease, one cannot conclude that disease was the original cause of reduced genetic variability.

Last, population heterozygosity will be lowered if individuals mate more or less at random and travel long distances to find mates. Selander and Kaufman (1973) have suggested that highly mobile animals are likely to exploit diverse habitats and hence have generalist phenotypes with genomes that are poorly adapted to local conditions, and will, as a consequence, show little variation. Some support for this idea comes from mustelids that have very large territories and disperse widely; these animals exhibit little genetic variability (Simonsen 1982; R. Lacy and M. Foster, pers. comm.). The cheetah's wide ecological and geographic distribution (chap. 2) and broad prey base (app. 3) suggest a wide tolerance for varying ecological conditions despite its morphological specializations. Moreover, cheetahs have the ability to trek long distances (chap. 8): a radio-collared individual released in Etosha National Park returned 450 km home (H. Berry, pers. comm. to P. Gros), and female home ranges in Serengeti are huge compared with those of other felids (table 12.2; see fig. 8.8). In addition, the cheetah's mating system is promiscuous rather than polygynous, as is typical of the family. All these factors predispose the species toward panmixia and might therefore have contributed to lack of genetic variation in the past. Arguing against this, both male and female offspring dispersed rather short distances in Serengeti (chap. 7).

Other explanations for lack of genetic variability, such as assortive mating or evolving to an adaptive optimum, cannot be assessed at present. In short, the causes of cheetahs' reduction of genetic variability in the Pleistocene remain an open question (Pimm et al. 1989). A series of historical population bottlenecks is certainly one candidate explanation, but the possibility that a large population of cheetahs was somewhat panmictic with subpopulations being in periodic contact as a result of catholic food habits and extensive ranging also requires consideration.

MORTALITY AND REDUCED GENETIC VARIABILITY

It has been argued that reduced genetic variability in cheetahs has two consequences that are detrimental to their survival: elevated juvenile mortality and inability to combat infectious disease. Juvenile mortality, usually in utero, increases when individuals start to inbreed as a result of lethal recessive alleles being exposed (Ralls, Brugger, and Ballou 1979; Falconer 1981; Allendorf and Leary 1986; Quattro and Vrijenhoek 1989). At first sight, then, homozygous species such as cheetahs might be expected to show high intrinsic juvenile mortality, as argued by O'Brien and colleagues in their 1985 paper. They reported that juvenile mortality of captive cheetahs (combining stillbirths, premature births, and mortality prior to 6 months of age) was higher than that of most other exotic species in captivity. Yet an independent comparative analysis of neonatal mortality in captivity showed that rates were no higher for cheetahs than for other carnivore or felid species (Loudon 1985). O'Brien et al. pointed out that there was no significant difference in juvenile mortality between inbred (related) and non-inbred (unrelated) pairings in cheetahs, cleverly arguing that this might be expected in a homozygous species in which loci contributing to congenital defects would be no more exposed as a result of matings between relatives than between nonrelatives. On the other hand, no significant differences were found in similar comparisons in 15 of 26 other species shown in their figure 1. Contrary data reporting 26.3% juvenile mortality in 194 non-inbred cheetah cubs but 44.2% in 43 inbred progeny was provided by Hedrick (1987), although the source of his data was unclear. This significantly higher figure is indicative of inbreeding depression, suggesting that cheetahs are still segregating for recessive alleles affecting fitness despite their apparent homozygosity.

Finally, it is worth noting that juvenile mortality derived from combining three juvenile stages is a poor measure of mortality arising from genetic defects, as so many other factors can be involved. For example, it is well known that poor mothering is an important source of offspring mortality in captive cheetahs (Degenaar 1977). At present, then, there is no convincing evidence for elevated juvenile mortality in captive cheetahs as a result of their depauperate genetic variability.

In the wild, Laurenson (in press-b) reported two cubs disappearing from otherwise healthy litters as a result of either congenital problems or accident. This represented just 4.1% of the cubs that died from known causes (see table 4.3). Although cheetah juvenile mortality is higher in nature than that of other non-hunted felid populations (see table 12.1), it stems chiefly from predation and other unpredictable events. Judging from the rapidity with which a subsequent litter is produced after premature loss of the previous one (see table 4.6), stillborn litters and postnatal defects are not obviously prevalent in the wild.

To summarize, indirect evidence indicates that juvenile mortality resulting from lack of genetic variability is no higher in cheetahs than in other species. This is hardly surprising given that cheetah nuclear loci have been depauperate in variability for many generations (Menotti-Raymond and O'Brien 1993) and presumably purged themselves of most deleterious recessives some time ago. Thus juvenile mortality should be no greater for cheetahs than for outbred species (Templeton and Read 1983, 1984).

DISEASE AND REDUCED GENETIC VARIABILITY

The second issue concerns the ability of species with greatly reduced genetic variability to mount an effective defense against infectious disease. In such species, a disease vector that overcomes the defense system of one individual will successfully challenge those of many (O'Brien and Evermann 1988). Examining a case study of disease sweeping through a successful breeding colony of cheetahs at Wildlife Safari, Oregon, O'Brien et al. (1985) noted that 60% of the cheetahs there died from coronavirus-associated diseases, including feline infectious peritonitis (FIP), which is fatal in its effusive form (see also Heeney et al. 1990). In contrast, lions at Wildlife Safari developed comparatively low antibody titers and none developed symptoms of FIP; in domestic cats, average morbidity seldom exceeds 10% in response to this virus. Since cytotoxic T cells require a combination of viral and MHC antigens to clear virus-infected cells, any viral mutation that interferes with the normal expression of MHC molecules in infected cells will invade the host successfully. Hence there will be strong selection for polymorphism at the MHC locus to counter viral adaptations. O'Brien et al. (1985) concluded that reduced variability at the MHC in cheetahs could have dampened their heterogeneous response to possible adaptations in the FIP virus that have evolved to interfere with MHC function. Nevertheless, some captive and free-living individuals showed low titers, and not all the Wildlife Safari cheetahs perished (see Heeney et al. 1990 for discussion). In addition, high seroprevalence to other viral agents shows that some individuals can surmount the challenge of diseases (Brown et al. 1993; Evermann et al. 1993; Caro and Laurenson 1994).

In theory, though, cheetahs must be at greater risk from disease than other, more heterozygous felids, all else being equal. Fortunately, however, several aspects of cheetahs' behavior and ecology place them at low risk of disease. They live at low density, are somewhat asocial, usually feed on fresh kills, and live in dry climates. Indeed, these factors may have allowed them to thrive despite their compromised immune system (T. Young, pers. comm.). Note that many of these factors do not pertain to captive institutions.

What are the practical implications of disease susceptibility? In captivity cheetahs need to be kept separate from other cats that are apparently less susceptible to felid diseases and parasites. Extra strict precautions regarding hygiene are therefore entirely appropriate and could be stipulated by national zoological authorities as a requirement for keeping large numbers of cheetahs at one institution. In the wild, where populations increasingly reside in protected areas, cheetahs should be prevented from coming into contact with domestic cats for the same reason. Use of cats to control rodents in grain stores and villages in Africa is extensive; thus it will be difficult to dissuade farmers living on park borders and management personnel within parks from keeping cats as pets.

In regard to proposed translocations or population reinforcements, the possibility of infecting the wild population must be taken very seriously indeed, and stringent screening procedures need to be employed before any release.

Finally, reduced genetic variability hampers the ability of species to react to environmental perturbations on an evolutionary time scale (Frankel and Soulé 1981; Beardmore 1983). This is the plight of species that lose genetic variability as a result of dropping to very low population sizes (Schonewald-Cox et al. 1983). Natural environments are being rapidly altered by humans through fragmentation, extirpation of selected species, and introduction of exotics. In the long term, therefore, cheetahs may face greater problems adapting to new circumstances than more outbred species. Therefore the best solution is to preserve the integrity of natural ecosystems as much as possible.

Problems in Captive Breeding

DEMOGRAPHY OF THE CAPTIVE POPULATION

Though cheetahs have been kept captive since the Assyrian dynasty (chap. 2), none were apparently bred until 1956, aside from one litter raised in Akbar's great collection (Guggisberg 1975; Sunquist 1992). Sporadic breeding continued during the 1960s (van de Werken 1968) and became well established in Whipsnade Zoological Park, U.K., during that decade (Manton 1970); litters born there now exceed 100. Cheetahs have also been bred with great success at the de Wildt Breeding Centre in South Africa (Brand 1980), which by 1988 had produced a fifth of all captive births worldwide (Marker-Kraus 1990). Several institutions in North America, notably the San Diego Wild Animal Park, California; Wildlife Safari, Oregon; Fossil Rim Wildlife Center, Texas; and Columbus Zoo, Ohio, have had considerable breeding successes too (Lindburg et al. 1985; Marker and O'Brien 1989). Indeed, in North America alone 113 litters were produced at 57 institutions between 1956 and 1986.

Despite these optimistic figures, the captive cheetah population cannot sustain itself as yet, and reproduction is still relatively poor in comparison with other large cats such as Indian lions (Smith 1985) or Siberian tigers (Seal and Foose 1983). Of 385 animals imported into North America between 1956 and 1986, only 36 were captive-born, and only 14.9% of imported individuals reproduced successfully (Marker and O'Brien 1989). Among the 193 animals alive in 1986, only 12 males and 17 females had bred successfully at least once, giving an effective population size of 28.1, or 14.5% of the captive population. Infant mortality is common in captivity, with 33.9% of 1,046 cubs born between 1978 and 1988 failing to reach 6 months of age (Marker-Kraus 1990). Based on the number of mentions made by 44 international zoos in response to a partially open-ended questionnaire, neonatal mortality stemmed principally from poor husbandry (10 mentions) and maternal neglect (10), with cannibalism (5), congenital defects (5), disease (4), and stillbirths (3) playing a lesser role.

In comparison, adult mortality plays a relatively small part in influencing the captive population size. Between 1978 and 1988, 38% of animals lived beyond 5 years of age, a considerable improvement on previous years, while 17% lived to be over 10 years old, and 3% reached 15 years, with wild-caught animals living longer than captive-born (Marker-Kraus 1990). In a number of institutions the main cause of adult mortality is FIP, although renal and hepatic diseases are also important (Marker and O'Brien 1989).

GENETIC SOLUTIONS FOR IMPROVED BREEDING

Reproductive difficulties in captivity must be surmounted if captive cheetahs are to act as a buffer against possible loss of the species in the wild (Soulé et al. 1986). Believing that lack of genetic heterozygosity might be responsible for the cheetah's poor reproductive performance in captivity, Marker and O'Brien (1989) put forward three ways in which the effects of depauperate genetic variability could be ameliorated. First, they counseled that related animals should be prevented from breeding. This is a relatively simple procedure given that pedigree records are kept on this species (Marker-Kraus 1990). Nevertheless, 35.3% of the 201 cubs born between 1987 and 1991 were from matings between related parents (Marker-Kraus and Grisham 1993).

Second, they suggested that individuals originating in East Africa might be bred with those from southern Africa so as to take advantage of the slight differences in allelic frequencies indicated in earlier studies and subsequently confirmed by analysis of DNA variation at the MHC locus (Yuhki and O'Brien 1990). Indeed, Marker-Kraus (1990) argued that some of the success at the Apeldoorn program in Holland and at Whipsnade may have been due to crossing East African founders with individuals from southern Africa, although husbandry practice is clearly a critical confounding factor here. As the genetic difference between cheetah subspecies is ten times less than that between human racial groups, however, it seems sensible to maximize genetic variability in this way while it is still available.

Cheetahs' abilities to combat disease and capture prey are unlikely to be compromised as a result of this policy. The possibility that the species possesses coadapted gene complexes involved in fighting epizootics specific to different geographic regions seems remote, given the absence of geographic or temperature barriers to diseases or their vectors over most of the cheetah's range. Also, cheetahs everywhere hunt ungulates of roughly similar morphology and body weight (app. 3), so the techniques needed to capture them must be fairly similar. Given that experience is so important in the acquisition of hunting skills in both cheetahs (chap. 7) and domestic cats (Caro 1980a), any genetic differences between populations are likely to have only a minor influence on the development of prey-catching skills. Nevertheless, moral objections to introducing new genetic material into an area need consideration if translocations or population reinforcements are eventually carried out.

Third, Marker and O'Brien argued that cheetahs should be imported, either from captive institutions abroad or from the wild, so as to maintain an effective breeding population size of 50 individuals in North America. This would keep the rate of inbreeding below 1% per generation and thereby minimize inbreeding depression (Seal 1985). As of 1991, the effective population size was 48.5 individuals (Marker-Kraus and Grisham 1993); thus importation from the wild, at least at present, appears unnecessary.

While there is unquestionable merit to the first and second ideas, genetics probably plays little role in the cheetah's current inability to sustain itself in captivity (Caro and Laurenson 1994). First, lack of genetic variability is less likely to be of consequence in those species that have been depauperate for some time and may have shed their deleterious recessives already. Second, failure to mate or conceive is the most critical factor slowing captive population growth (Marker-Kraus 1990), although its relative import compared with neonatal mortality has yet to be calculated. Thus genetic monomorphism has little bearing on why most adults fail to breed in captivity and on why only 30% of 43 zoological facilities in North America bred cheetahs between 1987 and 1991 (Marker-Kraus and Grisham 1993). Third, neonatal abnormalities are only one of several causes of postnatal mortality (see above). The great range of offspring mortality across institutions, ranging from 0% to 100%, implies that husbandry is the key factor in offspring survival, not congenital defects, which would likely be constant across institutions.

PHYSIOLOGICAL EXPLANATIONS FOR POOR
REPRODUCTIVE PERFORMANCE

Poor seminal quality is a prime candidate for explaining why so few cheetahs give birth in captivity. Although more than 90% of captive males produced spermic ejaculates, the proportion of pleiomorphic sperm was high (Wildt et al. 1993) and was not an artifact of the electroejaculation procedure (Durrant, Schuerman, and Millard 1985). Unfortunately, the significance of spermatozoal morphology in fertility is controversial (Salisbury and Baker 1966). For example, fertility in domestic bulls and dogs may be affected when primary spermatozoal defects exceed 20% (Chenoworth and Ball 1980; Larson 1980), and they reach 38.6% in captive cheetahs (Wildt et al. 1983). Against this, fertile men exhibit struc-tural defects in 20–35% of spermatozoa, while 29–92.5% of gorillas' spermatozoa are pleiomorphic (Afzelius 1981).

Most interestingly, Wildt et al. (1993) found no difference in ejaculate characteristics or hormonal profiles between proven and unproven breed-ers. This finding can be interpreted in two opposing ways. On the one hand, it suggests that males failing to breed in captivity do so for reasons that are unrelated to the qualities of their sperm, such as dysfunctional libido or husbandry practice. Clearly, retrospective analysis of male be-havior at the time of introduction would help determine whether this was the case. This highlights the importance of maintaining systematic behav-ioral records during breeding attempts (Caro 1993). In the absence of such records, it is worth noting that free-living Serengeti males also exhib-ited low numbers of sperm per ejaculate and a percentage of sperm ab-normalities similar to that of captive animals in North America and South Africa. Their serum testosterone and cortisol levels also mirrored those of captive counterparts (Wildt, O'Brien, et al. 1987) (the latter being a mea-sure of adrenal activity). Yet pregnancies apparently arise without diffi-culty in the wild, judging from the rapidity with which females conceived following the premature loss of a litter (see table 4.6) or normal departure of their offspring (see table 4.8). Furthermore, Lindburg et al. (1993) report that ten of eleven males at the San Diego Wild Animal Park pro-duced pregnancies. Of nineteen pregnancies produced, seventeen oc-curred in a female's first estrus following lactation or introduction into the study, and four of these resulted from a single sperm sample. Findings from the North American survey, from San Diego, and from the wild therefore all agree that males with impaired seminal characteristics are quite capable of siring offspring.

On the other hand, lack of seminal differences between proven and unproven breeders could imply that breeding males were on the thresh-old of infertility. In support of this, Donoghue et al. (1992) found that only 17.3% of all cheetah oocytes inseminated in vitro managed to cleave, approximately half the proportion found in domestic cats or tigers, and that failure to fertilize was best explained by poor sperm motility. Most probably sperm in teratospermic ejaculates lack strong motility. More-over, pleiomorphic sperm are incapable of penetrating the inner zona pel-licuda (Wildt et al. 1993) and hence reaching the oocyte cytoplasm. Since sperm motility combined with sperm morphology regulates fertilization, and both may be impaired in cheetahs, there is a strong case for believing that even proven males are on the threshold of sterility (Wildt et al. 1993).

In contrast to males, captive females appear reproductively sound. Wildt et al. (1993) found that 83.3% of females exhibited no abnormalities of the reproductive tract. Although 51.5% had parovarian cysts, these were similarly common in proven and unproven breeders and were not taken to be indicative of anatomical problems. Two-thirds of the 68 females sampled had ovaries with follicles >2 mm in diameter, which contain oocytes most capable of fertilization in vitro. Also, Donoghue et al. (1992) reported that some oocytes of all 12 females in their study underwent in vitro fertilization. Finally, there were no differences in pituitary sensitivity or ability to produce LH and FSH in females that had or had not bred (Wildt et al. 1993).

These findings were reinforced by those in Serengeti. There, all radio-collared females except one young animal gave birth while they were collared or else had done so previously (see table 4.1), and they rapidly replaced lost litters. In short, the problems that cheetahs face in reproducing in captivity are unlikely to be physiologically or anatomically mediated in females and, at best, can only be partially explained by physiological difficulties in males.

BEHAVIORAL ASPECTS OF POOR BREEDING

It is striking that only a handful of institutions have been really successful in breeding cheetahs in captivity. Between 1980 and 1988, only 9 produced more than ten litters (de Wildt and Varaday, South Africa; Columbus, Winston, and San Diego, U.S.A.; Wassenaar, Holland; Whipsnade, U.K.; Shirahama, Japan; and Moscow, USSR) although 140 held cheetahs between 1978 and 1988 and reproduction occurred in 41 of these (Marker-Kraus 1990). Reproductively sound individuals are likely to be distributed evenly across institutions, thus management decisions and personnel must have had a strong hand in the differential success of programs. Certainly, difficulty in detecting estrous behavior has contributed to poor breeding performance. As a consequence, several institutions have adopted the practice of running males past female enclosures in order to ascertain when females might accept a male.

Unfortunately there are few common threads to the breeding programs that have been successful. Factors mentioned in promoting successful breeding include keeping animals in large enclosures (Seager and Demorest 1978; Fitch, Millard, and Tenaza 1985), keeping them in natural surroundings (Cupps 1985), providing an elevated area from which to survey the terrain, keeping males and females out of sight of each other (N. Hulett, pers. comm.), and even keeping potential prey species in sight (Seager and Demorest 1978). Estrous behavior may be facilitated by moving females, either between zoos or within the zoo itself (Cupps 1985). Furthermore, competition among males may increase a female's receptivity (Benzon and Smith 1975; Cupps 1985; Fitch, Millard, and Tenaza 1985), and females are thought to be selective as to whom they mate with (Brand 1980).

It is difficult to assess the relative importance of these factors, and successful institutions give different priority to different methods. Certainly, free-living cheetahs of both sexes seek out prominences from which to scan, and territorial males spend more of the day on elevated places than do floaters (chap. 8). Transporting females from one area to another may in some way mimic females moving into new areas where they might meet males. Elsewhere I have argued that females are more likely to encounter, and by extension mate with, coalition members, since the majority of female sightings were on active territories, usually held by coalitions of males (Caro 1993). Nevertheless, I have no data on whether competition among free-living males might facilitate estrus nor any data on female choice of males within a coalition. A study of captive cheetahs is currently trying to decipher the efficacy of such captive protocols, focusing particularly on encounters between females and different numbers of males, and on mate choice (N. Wielebnowski, unpublished data).

For some females, minimal disturbance is necessary for successful mothering (Marker-Kraus et al. 1990), but there is a continual tension between staying away and regular veterinary monitoring of cubs' health and weight soon after birth. Provision of several nest boxes may allow mothers to move cubs as they do in the wild (Laurenson 1993). Attention has also focused on nutritional aspects of captive husbandry (Dierenfeld 1993), such as whether zoo diets are deficient in copper (Chance and Wilkinson, unpublished data) and whether estrogens in food containing soybean extract are detrimental to cheetahs' health (Setchell et al. 1987).

Reintroductions

Reintroductions have been attempted in South Africa with unexpected results (see also Adamson 1969). Where cheetahs have been reintroduced into protected areas within their former range, their numbers have risen rapidly in the absence of lions or spotted hyenas. For example, in Pilansberg National Park in Bophuthatswana, South Africa, 6 introduced cheetahs increased to 17 within a year, greatly affecting resident ungulate populations: one cheetah took all the waterbuck calves in the park within a 2-week period (Anderson 1984). This population expansion occurred despite the presence of leopards and brown hyenas. A similar effect was noted in the Suikerbosrand Nature Reserve, where 5 introduced males and 3 females rose to 24 animals in 2 years, resulting in a drop in blesbok and springbok numbers (Pettifer, De Wet, and Muller 1980). Managers were then forced to remove cheetahs from the area.

Where cheetahs are already present and populations are reinforced by introducing additional animals, there is a danger of residents killing them. Pettifer (1981) reported that in Timbavati Nature Reserve, one member of a trio of introduced males, aged 2.5 years, was badly injured by resident males and became incapable of moving any great distance. His partners stayed with him, nevertheless, despite being prevented from hunting for a week and apparently enduring 11 days without food.

A common concern about cheetah reintroductions is that captive-born animals will fail to capture prey and starve, since free-living cheetahs require a protracted period to refine their predatory skills. Pettifer's (1981) study of three reintroduced males (see above) was the only source of information I could find on this point, however. After the predatory skills of the captive-bred trio were tested on a Barbary sheep, they were radio-collared and released. Straight away they captured giraffe calves, impalas, waterbuck, and kudu, each consuming an average of between 2.2 and 4.1 kg per day. As a result of inexperience, perhaps, the males hunted large prey, and one was injured while attempting a buffalo. Although no further attempts were made on buffaloes, this incident showed that lack of selectivity might initially prove a problem in some releases. Based on my Serengeti observations, these males appeared exceptional, and I believe younger or single animals might have more difficulty in feeding. Note, however, that captive rearing may not be an undue impediment to acquiring predatory skills, since newly independent free-living adolescents are incompetent at hunting (chap. 7); more work is clearly needed in this area.

Pettifer's (1981) study makes three further points that are worthy of mention. Though the reintroduced males kept a good distance from lions, they spent long periods at carcasses: an average of over 32 hours at each one. Lack of experience of competition from other predators or scavengers may have accounted for this. Second, they had little fear of people and twice entered camps and raided chickens. This would certainly bring them into conflict with humans in other situations. Last, one of the males died of a snakebite, but whether inexperience played a part in this is of course unknown.

At present, it is fair to say that future cheetah reintroductions hold promise since this species possesses many of the traits advanced by Stanley Price (1989) as facilitating successful reintroductions: tolerance of a wide range of environments and habitats, allowing them to adapt to new situations; being large and thus having a broad range of available foods; being exploratory and hence able to move into new areas; and being amenable to behavioral manipulation. For example, after releasing and periodically feeding a cheetah, Adamson (1969) reduced its reliance on her and successfully returned it to the wild.

In conclusion, the rapid expansion of cheetah populations reintroduced into areas lacking large predators stands in stark contrast to their poor breeding performance in captivity, as does the amount of money and effort spent in the two contexts. If the goal of captive breeding programs is to reintroduce cheetahs into the wild, as is often claimed, it is extraordinary that so few attempts have been made in this direction.

Improving the Cheetah's Chances of Survival

Despite the genuine advances made by zoos in breeding exotic animals (Foose 1983) and despite their successes (Dresser 1988; Seal 1988), the long-term future of most species ultimately lies in the viability of free-living populations in the context of natural ecosystems (Western and Pearl 1989). Currently there is a pressing need to discover the extent to which the distribution of cheetahs has changed throughout Africa and Asia since Myers conducted his study, to estimate the size of subpopulations in different habitats, and to assess the threats that they face in different areas. We also need to know the effective population sizes of subpopulations. Once promising areas for protection can be pinpointed, we need to attract the attention of national and local authorities and help them to set up protected areas. Where the prey base is migratory, these areas need to be large. For example, in Serengeti, females moved well outside park boundaries into the Ngorongoro Conservation Area following the Thomson's gazelles (chap. 8); fortunately, both species are still secure there. In contrast, in Tarangire National Park, Tanzania, which provides a dry season refuge for large concentrations of ungulates, migration routes to wet season pastures are being blocked by farms and ranches (Borner 1985). As migratory species constitute the bulk of the ungulate prey biomass, their loss will result in a diminution of predator numbers, including cheetahs. In addition to the gazetting of new protected areas, increased funding and staffing is needed in most existing reserves to stop poaching (Leader-Williams and Albon 1988), especially of cheetahs' ungulate prey.

Cheetahs may also be able to live outside protected areas, on farms, or in regions inhabited by pastoralists, provided slaughter of wildlife can be prevented. Remember, this species is not dangerous to humans. Such projects will involve integration of economic, sociological, and biological concerns to a far greater extent than hitherto attempted. Great success has been achieved in changing people's attitudes toward carnivores where the safety of livestock (e.g., "red wolves" reintroduced into North Carolina: Parker 1988) or even of people themselves is at stake (e.g., tigers in the Sundarbans: Jackson 1991). In all of these efforts to conserve cheetahs inside and outside protected areas, conservation organizations must be convinced to provide money.

This leads to a final point. In the course of my work on cheetahs, many people have told me of their desire to study the behavior and ecology of the species in some protected area or other in order to gain information necessary to conserve the species effectively. To my mind, such good intentions are misguided. We already know a great deal about the ecology and behavior of free-living cheetahs, much more than about most endangered species, and while detailed studies of individuals in their natural habitat raise new questions about evolution and ecology, they fail to address the conservation of the species head on. Thus for those interested in the long-term future of cheetahs, my advice is to get involved in reintroduction programs or ecological monitoring or enter the world of conservation politics, especially at a local level, rather than fiddling while Rome burns.

Summary

1. Myers estimated that between 7,300 and 23,000 cheetahs survived across a wide geographic area of Africa in the early 1970s, but their range and numbers have almost certainly diminished since then.

2. The principal threats to free-living cheetahs in the wild come from habitat destruction and loss of prey as well as direct persecution. Cheetahs are shot as vermin in Namibia and Zimbabwe. While interspecific competition over carcasses has little effect on cheetah numbers, predation on cubs keeps populations at low density. A detailed study by Burney showed that tourism had little effect on reproduction and survival in the wild.

3. Based on electrophoretic studies, reproductive surveys, and experiments using reciprocal skin grafts, cheetahs show extreme lack of genetic variability compared with other mammals.

4. DNA analyses date the genetic monomorphism to 6,000–20,000 years ago, but its cause remains unknown. Explanations include a population bottleneck occurring in the Pleistocene, or great interchange between subpopulations equivalent to panmictic breeding. Explanations that rely on past populations being large but having a reduced effective population size seem less likely.

5. It has been argued that the consequences of reduced genetic variability are increased juvenile mortality and susceptibility to disease. Evidence of elevated cub mortality in captivity is scant and would not be expected in species purged of deleterious recessives. Inability to combat infectious disease has theoretical and empirical support and needs to be taken more seriously by captive breeders and park managers. Cheetahs may also be poorly equipped to adapt to environmental change on an evolutionary time scale.

6. Though cheetahs now breed in captivity, the number of animals that have produced offspring is low and infant mortality is high. Consequently there are few institutions with strong breeding records.

7. Lack of genetic variability is unlikely to be responsible for poor

reproduction in captivity since it has a questionable impact on juvenile mortality and little influence on cheetahs' willingness to mate. Nevertheless, prevention of close inbreeding and crossing individuals from East Africa with those from southern Africa both require attention.

8. Despite a high degree of spermatozoal defects in male cheetahs, many males are capable of siring offspring in captivity. Females, too, appear reproductively sound. Thus environmental and social impediments specific to captivity may prevent successful breeding. Size of enclosure, ability to scan the environment, moving females, male-male competition, and female choice of mating partners have all been advanced as factors promoting mating, but their relative importance is unknown.

9. Reintroductions are extremely successful in areas without lions or spotted hyenas and result in rapid population growth. Cheetahs possess a number of traits associated with the successful reintroductions of other species.

10. The cheetah's survival principally depends on maintaining viable populations in both protected areas and in multiple-use areas in the wild, with captive breeding programs being only a stopgap measure. We need the commitment of national authorities, local people, and conservation organizations to secure its long-term future.

An adult female drags her Thomson's gazelle kill into the shade. (Drawing by Dafila Scott.)

Appendix 1

Common and Scientific Names of Species Mentioned in the Text

MAMMALS

Order Marsupialia
    Macropus giganteus   Eastern grey kangaroo

Order Primata
    Callithrix jacchus   Common marmoset
    Cebus olivaceus   Wedge-capped capuchin
    Saimiri sciureus   Squirrel monkey
    Cercopithecus aethiops   Vervet monkey
    Erythrocebus patas   Patas monkey
    Macaca mulatta   Rhesus macaque
    Macaca radiata   Bonnet macaque
    Papio cynocephalus   Savannah, yellow, or chacma baboon
    Papio anubis   Olive baboon
    Papio hamadryas   Hamadryas baboon
    Theropithecus gelada   Gelada baboon
    Presbytis entellus   Gray langur
    Colobus badius   Red colobus
    Pongo pygmaeus   Orangutan
    Pan paniscus   Bonobo
    Pan troglodytes   Chimpanzee
    Gorilla gorilla   Mountain gorilla

Order Lagomorpha
    Lepus americanus   Snowshoe hare
    Lepus californicus   Jackrabbit

Order Lagomorpha *Continued*

Lepus capensis	Cape hare
Lepus crawshayi	Savannah hare

Order Rodentia

Spermophilus beldingi	Belding's ground squirrel
Spermophilus tridecemlineatus	Thirteen-lined ground squirrel
Marmota flaviventris	Yellow-bellied marmot
Mus musculus	Domestic mouse
Rattus norvegicus	Domestic rat
Cryptomys sp.	Mole rat
Neotoma floridiana	Wood rat
Erethizon dorsatum	North American porcupine
Hystrix africaeaustralis	Cape porcupine

Order Cetacea

Physeter macrocephalus	Sperm whale
Tursiops truncatus	Bottle-nosed dolphin
Delphinus bairdi	Porpoise
Orcinus orca	Killer whale

Order Carnivora

Canis lupus	Wolf
Canis latrans	Coyote
Canis lupus-latrans hybrid	Red wolf
Canis adustus	Side-striped jackal
Canis aureus	Golden jackal
Canis mesomelas	Black-backed jackal
Lycaon pictus	Wild dog
Otocyon megalotis	Bat-eared fox
Ursus arctos	Grizzly bear
Ursus maritimus	Polar bear
Ailuropoda melanoleuca	Giant panda
Mustela erminea	Stoat or ermine
Mustela nigripes	Black-footed ferret
Martes americana	Marten
Lutra lutra	European otter
Enhydra lutris	Sea otter
Mellivora capensis	Ratel or honey badger
Meles meles	European badger
Helogale parvula	Dwarf mongoose
Herpestes ichneumon	Egyptian mongoose
Herpestes sanguineus	Slender mongoose
Mungos mungo	Banded mongoose
Cynictis penicillata	Meerkat
Proteles cristatus	Aardwolf
Crocuta crocuta	Spotted hyena
Hyena hyena	Striped hyena
Hyena brunnea	Brown hyena
Felis chaus	Jungle cat
Felis libyca	African wildcat
Felis silvestris	European wildcat

Order Carnivora *Continued*

Felis manul	Pallas's cat
Felis margarita	Sand cat
Felis marmorata	Marbled cat
Felis planiceps	Flat-headed cat
Felis nigripes	Black-footed cat
Felis aurata	African golden cat
Felis temmincki	Asiatic golden cat
Felis bengalensis	Leopard cat
Felis rubignosa	Rusty-spotted cat
Felis viverrinus	Fishing cat
Felis colocolo	Pampas cat
Felis tigrinus	Tiger cat
Felis catus	Domestic cat
Felis yagouarundi	Jaguarundi
Felis serval	Serval
Felis weidi	Margay
Felis pardalis	Ocelot
Felis geoffroyi	Geoffroy's cat
Felis concolor	Cougar
Lynx caracal	Caracal
Lynx canadensis	North American lynx
Lynx lynx	European lynx
Lynx rufus	Bobcat
Neofelis nebulosa	Clouded leopard
Panthera pardus	Leopard
Panthera onca	Jaguar
Panthera uncia	Snow leopard
Panthera tigris	Tiger
Panthera leo	Lion
Acinonyx jubatus	Cheetah

Order Pinnipedia

Arctocephalus australis	South American fur seal
Arctocephalus galapagoensis	Galápagos fur seal
Otaria byronia	Southern sea lion
Mirounga angustirostris	Northern elephant seal

Order Proboscidia

Loxodonta africana	African elephant

Order Perissodactyla

Equus burchelli	Burchell's zebra
Equus grevyi	Grevy's zebra
Ceratotherium simum	White rhinoceros

Order Artiodactyla

Phacochoerus aethiopicus	Warthog
Giraffa camelopardalis	Giraffe
Cervus elaphus	Red deer
Cervus unicolor	Sambar
Odocoileus virginianus	White-tailed deer

Order Artiodactyla *Continued*

Alces alces	Moose
Antilocarpa americana	Pronghorn
Tragelaphus scriptus	Bushbuck
Tragelaphus imberbis	Lesser kudu
Tragelaphus strepsiceros	Greater kudu
Taurotragus oryx	Eland
Syncerus caffer	African buffalo
Bubalus bubalis	Indian buffalo
Kobus defassa	Waterbuck
Kobus vardoni	Puku
Adenota kob	Kob
Redunca redunca	Reedbuck
Oryx beisa	Oryx
Oryx gazella	Gemsbok
Hippotragus equinus	Roan antelope
Hippotragus niger	Sable antelope
Alcelaphus buselaphus	Hartebeest
Alcelaphus lichensteini	Lichenstein's hartebeest
Damaliscus korrigum	Topi
Damaliscus lunatus	Tsessebe or sassaby
Damaliscus damaliscus	Blesbok
Connochaetes taurinus	Wildebeest
Raphicerus campestris	Steinbok
Ourebia ourebi	Oribi
Madoqua kirki	Dik-dik
Aepyceros melampus	Impala
Antilope cervicapra	Blackbuck
Litocranius walleri	Gerenuk
Gazella granti	Grant's gazelle
Gazella thomsoni	Thomson's gazelle
Gazella cuvieri	Cuvier's gazelle or edmi
Gazella gazella	Chinkara or Indian gazelle
Antidorcas marsupialis	Springbok
Cephalophus sp.	Duiker
Ovibos moschatus	Muskox
Ovis aries	Domestic sheep
Ammotragus lervia	Barbary sheep
Ovis canadensis	Bighorn sheep

BIRDS

Order Struthioniformes

Struthio camelus	Ostrich

Order Pelicaniformes

Fregata minor	Great frigate bird
Pelecanus occidentalis	Brown pelican

Order Anseriformes

  Cygnus columbianus   Bewick's or tundra swan
  Anser albifrons   White-fronted goose
  Alopochen aegyptiaca   Egyptian goose

Order Ciconiiformes

  Egretta caerulea   Little blue heron

Order Falconiiformes

  Torgos tracheliotus   Lappet-faced vulture
  Trigonoceps occipitalis   White-headed vulture
  Melierax sp.   Chanting goshawk
  Parabuteo unicinctus   Harris's hawk
  Aquila rapax   Steppe or tawny eagle
  Stephanoaetus coronatus   Crowned hawk eagle
  Haliaeetus leucocephalus   Bald eagle
  Sagittarius serpentarius   Secretary bird

Order Galliformes

  Gallus gallus   Domestic chicken
  Numida meleagris   Guinea fowl
  Francolinus sp.   Francolin, spurfowl

Order Gruiformes

  Balearica regulorum   Crowned crane
  Ardeotis kori   Kori bustard
  Eupodotis senegalensis   White-bellied bustard
  Eupodotis melanogaster   Black-bellied bustard

Order Charadriiformes

  Haematopus ostralegus   Oystercatcher
  Larus argentatus   Herring gull
  Larus californicus   California gull
  Sterna sandvicensis   Sandwich tern

Order Pteroclidiformes

  Pterocles sp.   Sand grouse

Order Columbiformes

  Columba palumbus   Pigeon

Order Coraciiformes

  Merops bullockoides   White-fronted bee-eater

Order Piciformes

  Picoides pubescens   Downy woodpecker

Order Passeriformes

  Tyrannus tyrannus   Eastern kingbird
  Aphelocoma coerulescens   Florida scrub jay
  Corcorax melanorhamphos   White-winged chough
  Saxicola torquata   Stonechat
  Passer montanus   House sparrow
  Junco phaenotus   Yellow-eyed junco
  Melospiza melodia   Song sparrow

FISHES

Order Clupeiformes
   Stolephorus purpureus   Anchovy

Order Polynemiformes
   Oncorhynchus kisutch   Coho salmon

Order Perciformes
   Caranx ignobilis   Jack

REPTILES

Order Chelonia
   Geochelone pardalis   Leopard tortoise

Order Squamata
   Agama agama   Agama lizard

INSECTS

Order Hymenoptera
   Centris pallida   Digger bee

Appendix 2

Predator Populations and Numbers of Adult Thomson's Gazelles They Kill in the Serengeti Ecosystem

| | Predator numbers | | Adult gazelles killed/predator/yr | | | | |
| | | | per individual | | per species | | |
	Plains	Wood-lands	Plains	Wood-lands	Plains	Wood-lands	Total
Lion	200	2,600	2.2	3.3	440	8,580	9,020
Cheetah	110	100	35.4	12.4	3,894	1,240	5,134
Leopard	0	800–1,000	0	4.9–5.9	0	3,920–5,900	3,920–5,900
Wild dog	60		6.7		402		402
Hyena	5,200	3,500–4,000	5.6	1.3	29,120	4,550–5,200	33,670–34,320
Grand Total							52,146–54,776

Methods of Estimation

Population estimates for most of the large predators are available from in-depth studies. Regarding prey killed by predators, Schaller (1972c) is still the most useful source of information since little further data have been published. Schaller employed a variety of assumptions and methods of calculation for estimating the number of gazelles killed by different predator species (as summarized below), with the exception of spotted hyenas, for which he cited Kruuk's (1972) data on consumption rates. Predator population structures and social group sizes were assumed to have remained similar to Schaller's estimates for the purposes of analysis.

The lion study population comprises 200 individuals (Packer, Scheel, and Pusey 1990) while another 2,600 are estimated to live in the woodlands and Masai Mara (Hilborn, in press). The "average" lion (summing across age classes and their relative requirements: Schaller 1972c) was estimated to consume 2,468 kg of prey biomass each year. Of this, 2.5% was Thomson's gazelles of average weight 12 kg, giving a rate of 5.14 gazelles/lion/year. The relative proportion of adult gazelles (those greater than 12 months old) in the kill was 65%, and thus each lion killed or scavenged 3.3 adult Thomson's gazelles/year in the woodlands.

Scheel (per. comm.) reports that during his study, lions on the plains made 23 hunts of adult Thomson's gazelles, each of which lasted 0.33 hours on average. From Schaller's data, a lion made 3.8 hunts for every Thomson's gazelle killed, and thus spent 1.25 hours hunting Thomson's gazelles per adult killed. Prides spent 0.08 hours hunting this class of prey per day, which translates into 0.06 adults killed/day, or 22.02/year. Since there are 10 lions per plains pride on average (Packer, Scheel, and Pusey 1990), this is 2.2 gazelles killed/lion/year on the plains.

Cheetah numbers averaged 112.3 (SE = 5.8) adults on the plains between 1981 and 1990. The cheetah population in the woodlands is unknown, although rough calculations can be attempted. I made 24 journeys by road from Seronera to Bologonja (almost entirely through the woodlands), a distance of approximately 120 km, and encountered cheetahs on three occasions (0.001 cheetahs/km). In comparison, I encountered five cheetahs on 84 recorded road journeys from Seronera to the Naabi entrance gate, a distance of approximately 50 km almost entirely across the plains (0.001 cheetahs/km). Despite the similarity, I do not believe that overall densities were the same, because the cheetahs that I found in the woodlands were tame and were encountered either just north of Seronera near the Orangi River, or close to the international border near the Masai Mara Game Reserve. These locations suggest that habituated cheetahs were on temporary excursions from nearby plains habitats frequented by tourists and did not live in the woodlands. In addition, during a subsequent study in which I worked exclusively in the woodlands during a particularly dry period (October to December 1991), I encountered no cheetahs at all. These considerations lead me to suspect that few cheetahs live solely in the woodlands, perhaps 100 at a guess, totaling an absolute maximum of 250 adults throughout the ecosystem.

Rates of adult Thomson's gazelles killed on the plains are taken from dividing the number of gazelles killed by the number of cheetahs in Appendix 12. Thomson's gazelles occupy only some 35% of the northern and central woodlands on an annual basis (calculated from Maddock

1979). Furthermore, there is a diversity of medium-sized prey available for cheetahs throughout all the woodlands (notably impalas). Thus predation rates on gazelles for the 100 woodland cheetahs have been reduced by 35%.

Leopards are found only in the woodlands (but see Frame 1986) and populations are thought to have remained stable since Schaller's time. An adult leopard was thought to consume 1,000–1,200 kg of prey biomass per year, 10% of which was Thomson's gazelles at 12 kg average weight, giving a killing rate of 8.33 to 10.00 gazelles/year (Schaller 1972c). Twenty percent of the leopard population were cubs (<1 year old), which consumed 0.5 of an adult ration, so the effective "consuming adult" population was 90% of the total population size. Adult gazelles made up 65% of the total kill. Thus at a consumption rate of 1,000 kg/year, an "average" leopard would kill $8.33 \times 0.9 \times 0.65 = 4.88$ adults, while at 1,200 kg, the kill would be 5.85 adults/year.

In the past, the wild dog population was recorded chiefly on the plains, but starting in 1987 wild dogs were monitored throughout the whole ecosystem. Following a crash in the 1970s, the population had maintained itself at 30–50 adults, although this has since declined to 29 (Burrows 1990). To include the demands of nonadult animals, a figure of 60 throughout the ecosystem for the late 1980s seems conservative and therefore reasonable.

Schaller (1972c) collected consumption rates for dogs primarily on the plains, but packs living in woodland habitats seek out open grassland areas (Fuller and Kat 1990), so the rates probably apply to dogs throughout the ecosystem. Each dog appeared to kill 36.5 prey/year; although a rate of 55/year is also mentioned. In Schaller's study, one-third, or 12.17, were Thomson's gazelles, although higher proportions have been reported from Serengeti (see Fuller and Kat 1990). The relative proportion of adult gazelles in the kill was 55%, giving a consumption rate of 6.7 adults/dog/year, which can be considered a low estimate.

The number of spotted hyenas utilizing the plains and woodlands was taken from Hofer and East (in press), but 1,500 (from Hilborn, in press) was added to the woodlands figure to include Mara hyenas. Estimates of prey consumption rates were based on dry season fecal samples taken from the plains and woodlands of the western corridor by Kruuk (1972). The two sets of samples give widely differing predation rates, a possible reflection of differential gazelle abundance or vulnerability in the two habitats. However, since many of the roughly 2,100 hyenas in his study area included both plains and woodlands in their annual ranges, Kruuk felt that the different figures could represent maximum and minimum consumption rates over the whole area. Kruuk suggested that the total hyena population of the Serengeti could number 3,000, with some 900 individuals inhabiting the northern, central, and peripheral woodlands. Dividing total kill figures in the woodlands by 3,000 gives a killing or scavenging rate of 1.3 adult gazelles/hyena/year. Dividing kill figures on the plains by 2,100 hyenas that used that area gives 5.6 adult gazelles killed or scavenged there each year. Kruuk's analysis did not distinguish between Grant's and the (much more numerous) Thomson's gazelles. Using his figures will give a slight overestimate of predation rate on the latter species alone.

The table shows that the five major predators in the ecosystem consumed a total of between 52,146 and 54,776 adult gazelles/year, spotted hyenas having the most profound influence. Considering the 1986 Thomson's gazelle wet season population estimate of 572,920 (SE = 64,715) (Dublin et al. 1990), this amounted to 39.5–62.9% of adult annual recruitment (see app. 7). Taking the more recent corrected wet season estimate of 440,845 (SE = 42,285) (Campbell et al. 1990), predators accounted for between 51.4% and 81.8% of recruitment into the 1989 population.

Assuming a stable Thomson's gazelle population, between 18.2% and 60.5% are unaccounted for, suggesting that estimates of predation rates may be too low. Alternatively, many gazelles may die from causes other than predation, such as starvation in the late dry season or disease, and these may be scavenged by other species such as vultures, or else are not located. Finally, there is an unlikely possibility that the Thomson's gazelle population was increasing, although if anything, counts in the 1980s indicate a stable or declining population.

Appendix 3

Percentage Representation of Prey Species in the Diets of Cheetahs in Different Areas of Africa

	East Africa	Nairobi N.P.		Masai Mara G.R.
Source	Graham 1966	McLaughlin 1970	Eaton 1974	Burney 1980
Sample size	173	183	53	96
Method	Survey	Observations supplemented with kills	Observations supplemented with kills	Observations supplemented with kills
Thomson's gazelle	22.0	21.9	9.4	41.7
Grant's gazelle	21.4	24.6	17.0	1.0
Impala	15.6	27.4	35.8	32.3
Oribi	4.0			
Hare	4.0	1.6		3.1
Wildebeest	3.5		1.9	12.5
Coke's hartebeest	2.9	12.0	9.4	
Lichenstein's hartebeest				
Burchell's zebra	2.2	0.6	1.9	1.0
Grevy's zebra	0.6			
Springbok				
Steinbok	2.2	2.2		
Ostrich	2.2		1.9	
Oryx	1.7			
Topi	1.7			5.2
Waterbuck	1.7	1.6	9.4	1.0
Warthog	1.7	2.2	7.5	2.1
Guinea fowl	1.7			
Lesser kudu	1.1			
Greater kudu				
Bushbuck	1.1	1.7		
Kori bustard	1.1			
Roan antelope	0.6			
Duiker	0.6			
Jackal	0.6			
Mole rat	0.6			
Reedbuck		3.8	5.7	
Puku				
Gemsbok				
Buffalo				
Giraffe				
Eland				
Sable antelope				
Tsessebe				
Dik-dik	1.7	0.6		
Gerenuk	2.9			
Caracal				
Mongoose				
Bat-eared fox				

	Serengeti			
Source	Kruuk and Turner 1967	Schaller 1968	Frame 1986	This study
Sample size	33	136	443	424
Method	Observations supplemented with kills	Observations supplemented with kills	Hunts	Mostly observations
Thomson's gazelle	56.0	89.0	59.4	65.8
Grant's gazelle		2.2	9.3	4.0
Impala			0.9	0.2
Oribi		2.2		
Hare	4.0	2.2	6.3	18.4
Wildebeest	26.0	0.7	9.7	9.0
Coke's hartebeest			1.1	0.2
Lichenstein's hartebeest				
Burchell's zebra	4.0		4.3	0.2
Grevy's zebra				
Springbok				
Steinbok			0.2	
Ostrich				
Oryx				
Topi		1.5	1.4	0.2
Waterbuck			0.2	
Warthog			1.1	0.5
Guinea fowl			2.5[a]	
Lesser kudu				
Greater kudu				
Bushbuck				
Kori bustard				0.2
Roan antelope				
Duiker				
Jackal			0.2	
Mole rat			0.2[b]	0.2[b]
Reedbuck		1.5	1.8	0.5
Puku				
Gemsbok				
Buffalo				
Giraffe				
Eland			0.2	0.2
Sable antelope				
Tsessebe				
Dik-dik		0.7	0.5	0.2
Gerenuk				
Caracal			0.2	
Mongoose			0.5	
Bat-eared fox				

	Kalahari	Kafue N.P.	Transvaal	Kruger N.P.
Source	Mills 1984	Mitchell, Shenton, and Uys 1965	Hirst 1969	Pienaar 1969
Sample Size	229	33	47	2,532
Method	Kills	Observations supplemented with kills	Observations supplemented with kills	Mostly kills
Thomson's gazelle				
Grant's gazelle				
Impala		6.1	85.1	68.0
Oribi		3.0		
Hare				
Wildebeest	3.5	6.2	6.4	5.0
Coke's hartebeest	1.7			
Lichenstein's hartebeest		9.1		
Burchell's zebra		3.0		1.8
Grevy's zebra				
Springbok	86.9			
Steinbok	0.9			
Ostrich	3.5			
Oryx				
Topi				
Waterbuck				6.7
Warthog		6.1		0.6
Guinea fowl				
Lesser kudu				
Greater kudu		3.0	8.5	6.8
Bushbuck		3.0		1.1
Kori bustard				
Roan antelope				0.1
Duiker		3.0		2.6
Jackal				
Mole rat				
Reedbuck		12.1		5.3
Puku		45.4		
Gemsbok	2.6			
Buffalo				0.1
Giraffe				0.2
Eland				0.1
Sable antelope				0.3
Tsessebe				0.7
Dik-dik		0.6		
Gerenuk				
Caracal				
Mongoose				
Bat-eared fox	0.9			

[a] Other bird species.
[b] Other rodent species.

Appendix 4

Weights and Measurements of Adult Cheetahs

	Serengeti (this study)[a]	East Africa (diverse, McLaughlin 1970)	Namibia (Labuschagne 1979)	Southern Africa (diverse, McLaughlin 1970)
Weight (kg)				
Males				
Mean	41.4	61.0	53.9	55.0
SD	5.4	3.2	—	6.5
N	(23)	(4)	(7)	(4)
Range	28.5–51.0	58–65	39–59	50–62
Females				
Mean	35.9	52.0	43.0	48.5
SD	5.3	15.6	—	13.4
N	(19)	(2)	(6)	(2)
Range	21.0–43.0	41–63	36–48	39–58
Total length (cm)				
Males				
Mean	190.6	209.4	206.0	201.3
SD	9.2	10.4	—	11.3
N	(24)	(5)	(7)	(14)
Range	172–209.5	198–224	191–221	179–222
Females				
Mean	189.8	207.4	190.0	186.0
SD	9.7	22.6	—	—
N	(16)	(5)	(7)	(1)
Range	174–208	191–236	184–196	—
Head and body (cm)				
Males				
Mean	122.5	127.0		
SD	7.0	4.2		
N	(24)	(2)		
Range	113–136	124–130		
Females				
Mean	124.5			
SD	7.5			
N	(16)			
Range	113–140			
Tail (cm)				
Males				
Mean	68.1	66.0	71.5	72.8
SD	3.4	—	—	7.1
N	(24)	(1)	(7)	(6)
Range	63–74	—	65–76	60–79

[a] Some of the Serengeti females are from Laurenson's study (1992).

	Serengeti (this study)[a]	East Africa (diverse, McLaughlin 1970)	Namibia (Labuschagne 1979)	Southern Africa (diverse, McLaughlin 1970)
Tail (cm)				
Females				
Mean	65.5	73.0	66.7	
SD	4.5	—	—	
N	(19)	(1)	(6)	
Range	59.5–73	—	63–69	
Chest girth (cm)				
Males				
Mean	69.2			
SD	4.1			
N	(21)			
Range	62–77			
Females				
Mean	66.2	52.0	43.0	48.5
SD	3.5	15.6	—	13.4
N	(12)	(2)	(6)	(2)
Range	61–72	41–63	36–48	39–58
Shoulder (cm)				
Males				
Mean		76.8	88.1	79.9
SD		2.8	—	4.9
N		(6)	(7)	(8)
Range		74–81	83–94	74–86
Females				
Mean		75.3	84.7	70.0
SD		8.5	—	—
N		(3)	(6)	(1)
Range		67–84	79–84	—
Hindfoot (cm)				
Males				
Mean	27.7			
SD	1.1			
N	(24)			
Range	25–29			
Females				
Mean	27.3			
SD	0.7			
N	(18)			
Range	26–28.5			
Testes (cm)				
Males				
Mean	3.6 ×	2.2		
SD	0.3	0.2		
N	(16)	(18)		
Range	3.2–4.0	1.9–2.6		

Appendix 5

Description of Subspecies of *Acinonyx jubatus*

Subspecies	Region	Characteristics
Acinonyx jubatus jubatus (Schreber 1776)	South Africa	Small body size; small, well-separated spots
A. j. velox (Heller 1913)	East Africa, west of Kikuyu escarpment	Generally longer hair than *jubatus,* especially on nape and belly; large spots close together covering a similar total area to the background
A. j. raineyii (Heller 1913)	East Africa, east of Kikuyu escarpment	Very similar to *velox* but paler and shorter hair; still has long nape and belly hair; fewer spots on back
A. j. soemmeringii (Fitzinger 1855)	Sudan	Small spots < 1.3 cm diameter widely separated; hindfeet spotted; pale
A. j. hecki (Hilzheimer 1913)	North-West Africa	Small body size, dainty, pale
A. j. venaticus (Griffith 1821)	India and North Africa	Smaller than East African cheetahs, with shorter legs; no long hair on nape and belly; spots small and widely spaced as in *jubatus*
A. j. raddei (Hilzheimer 1913)	Turkestan	Thick, long hair; spots very large; long-haired bushy tail

Source: McLaughlin 1970.

Note: Both *A. j. velox* and *A. j. raineyii* were named previously *A. j. ngorongorensis* by Hilzheimer (1913). Harper (1945) applies this latter name to all cheetahs from Tanzania to Ethiopia and Somalia, with northern forms being paler than those from southern Kenya and Tanzania.

Appendix 6

Life History Variables of Felid Species

Species	A Female body weight (kg)	B Birth weight (g)	C Litter size	D $\dfrac{B \times C}{A}$
1. European wildcat	4.3	114.3	4.00	10.53
2. African wildcat	3.7	—	2.90	—
3. Caracal	10.0	—	3.17	—
4. Ocelot	9.8	231.0	2.00	4.72
5. Clouded leopard	11.4	160.0	3.25	4.56
6. European lynx	14.5	70.0	2.40	1.31
7. Leopard	38.2	527.1	2.50	3.45
8. Snow leopard	37.5	474.6	2.60	3.29
9. Cougar	43.0	383.7	2.78	2.48
10. Cheetah	51.7	266.4	3.60	1.86
11. Jaguar	62.6	823.1	2.40	3.16
12. Tiger	111.5	1,253.3	2.80	3.15
13. Lion	137.4	1,231.0	2.90	2.60
14. Black-footed cat	1.1	—	2.10	—
15. Leopard cat	4.1	80.0	2.56	5.00
16. Jungle cat	4.7	130.9	3.50	9.85
17. Bobcat	7.2	285.6	2.84	11.27
18. North American lynx	13.7	—	2.98	—
19. Serval	11.6	200.0	2.62	4.52
20. Fishing cat	7.8	170.0	2.20	4.79
21. Margay	3.4	—	1.70	—
22. Jaguarundi	2.7	—	2.60	—
23. Rusty-spotted cat	1.6	—	2.50	—
24. Geoffroy's cat	—	65.0	2.30	—
25. Sand cat	—	39.0	3.25	—
26. Pallas's cat	—	—	4.25	—
27. African golden cat	—	—	—	—
28. Asiatic golden cat	—	250.0	1.70	—
29. Tiger cat	—	—	1.50	—
30. Pampas cat	—	—	2.00	—
31. Marbled cat	—	—	—	—

Source: Data collated by Marcella Kelly (see p. 72). Data for each species were gleaned from the following references:

1. Asdell 1964; Corbett and Southern 1977; Ewer 1973; Guggisberg 1975; Hemmer 1976b; Kingdon 1977; Macdonald 1984; Matthews 1941; Meyer-Holzapfel 1968; Miller and Everett 1986; Morris 1965; Novikov 1962; Volf 1965.

2. Asdell 1964; Ewer 1973; Guggisberg 1975; Hemmer 1976b; Kingdon 1977; Roberts 1977; Rosevear 1974; Rowe-Rowe 1978; Smithers 1983; Wilson 1968.

3. Asdell 1964; Ewer 1973a; Guggisberg 1975; Hemmer 1976b; Kingdon 1977; Kralik 1967; Macdonald 1984; Roberts 1977; Rosevear 1974; Rowe-Rowe 1978; Smithers 1983; Stoddart 1979.

E	F	G	H	I	J	K
Weaning (days)	Indepen- dence (days)	Maturity (days)	G − F (days)	Gestation (days)	Interbirth interval (months)	Longevity (months)
79	131.3	352.1	220.9	65.8	10.0	171
—	150.0	300.0	150.0	57.0	12.0	192
118	365.0	600.0	235.0	70.8	10.0	198
—	365.0	660.0	295.0	74.6	—	—
145	270.0	730.0	460.0	89.7	—	—
150	425.8	743.3	317.5	67.4	11.6	172
92	527.4	942.9	415.5	96.8	21.3	247
107	365.0	730.0	365.0	98.2	—	159
105	638.8	821.3	182.5	91.5	22.5	153
109	498.8	622.8	124.1	92.7	19.1	140
157	707.2	1,026.5	319.3	100.8	12.0	220
135	632.0	1,368.8	736.8	104.3	35.3	252
211	759.1	1,147.1	388.0	108.5	25.0	230
—	—	684.4	—	65.5	12.0	—
—	—	603.3	—	61.3	12.0	156
96	—	435.0	—	62.6	5.5	114
59	—	517.1	—	57.3	11.3	155
—	547.5	—	62.8	12.0	—	—
—	60.0	—	—	72.6	6.0	192
—	—	—	—	67.9	—	120
—	—	—	—	82.3	—	—
—	—	—	—	67.1	—	—
—	—	—	—	—	—	—
63	—	—	—	71.0	12.0	—
—	—	—	—	61.0	6.0	93
—	—	—	—	—	—	—
—	—	—	—	—	—	204
—	—	—	—	95.0	—	210
—	—	—	—	74.8	—	—
—	—	—	—	—	—	—
—	—	—	—	—	—	198

4. Asdell 1964; Ewer 1973a; Fagen and Wiley 1978; Guggisberg 1975; Hemmer 1976b; Hershcovitz 1969; Husson 1978; Ludlow and Sunquist 1987; Macdonald 1984; Miller and Everett 1986; Rappole 1988; Schaller 1983.

5. Ewer 1973a; Guggisberg 1975; Lekagul and McNeely 1977; Macdonald 1984; Medway 1978; Miller and Everett 1986.

6. Asdell 1964; Beltran, Delibes, and Aldama 1987; Ewer 1973a; Guggisberg 1975; Haglund 1966; Haller and Breitenmoser 1986; Novikov 1962; Stroganov 1969.

7. Asdell 1964; Bertram 1978b, 1979, 1982; Eisenburg and Lockhart 1972; Ewer 1973a; Guggisberg 1975; Hamilton 1976; Ingles 1965; Kingdon 1977; LeKagul and McNeely 1977; Macdonald 1984; Med-

way 1978; Miller and Everett 1986; Novikov 1962; Phillips 1935; Roberts 1977; Robinette 1963; Rosevear 1974; Schaller 1972c; Stroganov 1969; Sunquist and Sunquist 1988.

8. Ewer 1973a; Guggisberg 1975; Hemmer 1976b; Jackson and Ahlborn 1989; Macdonald 1984; Marma and Yunchis 1968; Miller and Everett 1986; Novikov 1962; Roberts 1977; Schaller 1977; Stroganov 1969.

9. Asdell 1964; Cabrera and Yepes 1960; Ewer 1973a; Grinnell, Dixon, and Linsdale 1937; Guggisberg 1975; Hemmer 1976b; Hershkovitz 1969; Hornocker 1970; Husson 1978; Macdonald 1984; Miller and Everett 1986; Morris 1965; Robinette, Gashwiler, and Morris 1961; Sadlier 1966; Young and Goldman 1946.

10. Asdell 1964; Bertram 1978b, 1979; this study; Crandall 1964; Eaton 1974; Ewer 1973a; Guggisberg 1975; Kingdon 1977; Macdonald 1983; Miller and Everett 1986; Novikov 1962; Pienaar 1969; Rosevear 1974; Schaller 1972c; Smithers 1983.

11. Asdell 1964; Crandall 1964; Ewer 1973a; Guggisberg 1975; Hemmer 1976b; Hershkovitz 1969; Macdonald 1984; Miller and Everett 1986; Morris 1965; Rabinowitz 1986; Rabinowitz and Nottingham 1986; Sadlier 1966; Schaller 1983; Schaller and Crawshaw 1980; Schaller and Vasconcelos 1978.

12. Crandall 1964; Ewer 1973a; Guggisberg 1975; Lekagul and McNeely 1977; Macdonald 1984; Medway 1978; Miller and Everett 1986; Morris 1965; Novikov 1962; Sankhala 1967; Schaller 1967; Singh 1973, 1984; Stroganov 1969; Sunquist 1981; Sunquist and Sunquist 1988; Thapar 1986; Tilson and Seal 1987.

13. Asdell 1964; Bertram 1975a, 1978b, 1979; Crandall 1964; Eloff 1973a,b; Ewer 1973a; Guggisberg 1975; Hanby and Bygott 1987; Kingdon 1977; Macdonald 1984; Miller and Everett 1986; Morris 1965; Packer 1983; Packer and Pusey 1987; Packer et al. 1988; Rosevear 1974; Rudnai 1973a; Schaller 1972c; Smithers 1983; Smuts, Hanks, and Whyte 1978.

14. Asdell 1964; Ewer 1973a; Guggisberg 1975; Macdonald 1984; Miller and Everett 1986; Smithers 1983.

15. Asdell 1964; Ewer 1973a; Guggisberg 1975; Hemmer 1976b; Lekagul and McNeely 1977; Macdonald 1984; Medway 1978; Miller and Everett 1986; Roberts 1977; Stroganov 1969.

16. Acharjyo and Mohapatra 1977; Asdell 1964; Guggisberg 1975; Hemmer 1976b; LeKagul and McNeely 1977; Macdonald 1984; Novikov 1962; Phillips 1935; Roberts 1977; Schauenberg 1979.

17. Asdell 1964; Bailey 1974; Crowe 1975; Ewer 1973a; Gashwiler, Robinette, and Morris 1961; Guggisberg 1975; Hemmer 1976b; Koehler 1987; Litvaitis, Stevens, and Mautz 1984; Macdonald 1984; Miller and Everett 1986; Morris 1965; Parker and Smith 1983; Petraborg and Gunvalson 1962; Provost, Nelson, and Marshall 1973; Rollings 1945; Young 1958.

18. Asdell 1964; Brand and Keith 1979; Carbyn and Patriquin 1983; Ewer 1973a; Hemmer 1976b; Koehler, Hornocker, and Hash 1979; Miller and Everett 1986; Nellis and Keith 1968; Saunders 1964.

19. Asdell 1964; Ewer 1973a; Guggisberg 1975; Hemmer 1976b; Kingdon 1977; Macdonald 1984; Morris 1965; Rosevear 1974; Smithers 1983; Wackernagel 1968.

20. Fagen and Wiley 1978; Guggisberg 1975; Hemmer 1976b; Lekagul and McNeely 1977; Macdonald 1984; Phillips 1935; Roberts 1977; Ulmer 1968.

21. Asdell 1964; Macdonald 1984; Miller and Everett 1986.

22. Asdell 1964; Guggisberg 1975; Husson 1978; Macdonald 1984; Miller and Everett 1986.

23. Asdell 1964; Macdonald 1984; Phillips 1935.

24. Anderson 1977; Asdell 1964; Fagen and Wiley 1978; Guggisberg 1975; Macdonald 1984; Scheffel and Hemmer 1976; Ximenez 1975.

25. Asdell 1964; Guggisberg 1975; Hemmer 1976b; Macdonald 1984; Morris 1965; Roberts 1977; Rosevear 1974.

26. Guggisberg 1975; Macdonald 1984; Roberts 1977.

27. Guggisberg 1975; Kingdon 1977; Macdonald 1984; Rosevear 1974.

28. Ewer 1973a; Guggisberg 1975; Lekagul and McNeely 1977; Macdonald 1984; Medway 1978; Morris 1965.

29. Ewer 1973a; Guggisberg 1975; Husson 1978; Macdonald 1984; Miller and Everett 1986.

30. Guggisberg 1975; Macdonald 1984.

31. Lekagul and McNeely 1977; Macdonald 1984; Medway 1978.

Appendix 7

Adult Recruitment of Thomson's Gazelles between 1985 and 1989

	Adult & subadult males	Adult & subadult females	Ado-lescent males	Ado-lescent females	Fawns & half-growns	Total number counted	% annual adult recruit-ment
1985	8,534 (27.6)	17,829 (57.7)	1,505 (4.9)	1,337 (4.3)	1,681 (5.4)	30,886	
1986	8,437 (27.7)	17,751 (58.3)	1,540 (5.1)	1,406 (4.6)	1,314 (4.3)	30,448	
1987	9,533 (29.7)	18,096 (56.3)	1,090 (3.4)	1,791 (5.6)	1,624 (5.1)	32,134	
1988	6,163 (21.5)	17,401 (60.6)	1,230 (4.3)	1,594 (5.6)	2,305 (8.0)	28,693	
1989	7,708 (26.5)	17,446 (59.9)	906 (3.1)	1,526 (5.2)	1,534 (5.3)	29,120	
Corrected for age class occupance							
1985	8,518 (23.5)	16,492 (45.4)	2,258 (6.2)	4,011 (11.0)	5,043 (13.9)	36,322	25.4
1986	8,052 (23.0)	16,423 (47.0)	2,310 (6.6)	4,218 (12.1)	3,942 (11.3)	34,945	26.7
1987	9,261 (24.7)	16,305 (43.5)	1,635 (4.4)	5,373 (14.3)	4,872 (13.0)	37,446	27.4
1988	4,318 (12.8)	15,807 (47.0)	1,845 (5.5)	4,782 (14.2)	6,915 (20.5)	33,667	32.9
1989	6,349 (19.4)	15,920 (48.5)	1,359 (4.1)	4,578 (14.0)	4,602 (14.0)	32,808	26.7
Average annual recruitment over 5 years							27.8%

Note: Percentages of the total number counted are shown in parentheses.

Methods of Estimation

Figures in the top half of the table were calculated as follows: The numbers of Thomson's gazelles in each of eight age-sex classes (see chap. 3) counted each month were totaled for each year. Counts were not made in January 1986 or March 1987; instead, the proportion that January and March contributed to annual totals in other years was calculated, an average was taken, and this was multiplied by the totals for 1986 and 1987 respectively, and then added to the 11-month totals for those two years. Next, totals of adults and subadults were added together. The total number of fawns was divided by 62 and multiplied by 100 to correct for the average percentage of time this age class remained hidden (FitzGibbon 1988); this figure was then added to the half-growns.

Figures in the bottom half of the table were calculated as follows: The total number of individuals in the fawn and half-grown, adolescent female, and adolescent male classes during the year were divided by the number of months individuals remained in those classes, 4, 4, and 8 months respectively, giving a monthly relative occupance by age class (Bradley 1977), and each was subsequently multiplied by 12. For adults and subadults, the total number counted was devalued by the number of adolescent females and males likely to have entered the adult age class during that year. A female entering the adolescent age class in the first third of the year would have spent up to 8 months as an adult, whereas a female entering in the last third would have spent as few as 0 months as an adult. Therefore it was assumed that adolescent females could be counted as adults in an average of 4 months of the year. As males spent 8 months as adolescents, they could be adults for 0–4 months, or an average of 2 months. The monthly relative age class figure as calculated above was then multiplied by 4 and 2 respectively for females and males and subtracted from the total number of adults and subadults counted for that sex.

The relative totals for adolescent females and males were summed and divided by the corrected adult totals of females and males to give an estimate of the percentage annual recruitment into the adult population each year.

The annual recruitment between 1985 and 1989 varied between 25.4% and 32.9%, while the percentage of the population that were adults during this time ranged between 59.8% and 70.0% as calculated by summing the corrected age class occupance for adult males and females. There is some controversy over the number of Thomson's gazelles in the Serengeti ecosystem during the 1980s which hinges on censusing methods and on whether the population was surveyed under less than ideal conditions (Borner et al. 1987; Dublin et al. 1990). Here I have taken the two most recent estimates, 572,920 (SE = 64,715) from the wet season count of 1986 (Dublin et al. 1990) and a corrected figure of 440,845 (SE = 42,285) counted in May 1989 (Campbell et al. 1990), since these span the years over which recruitment was calculated. With the 1986 figure, adult gazelles would number between 342,606 and 401,044; with an annual recruitment of between 25.4% and 32.9%, 87,022 to 131,943 gazelles would be entering the adult population per year. Taking the 1989 figure, there would be 263,625 to 308,592 adults, thus 66,961 to 101,527 gazelles would be entering the adult population per year. In sum, approximately 67,000 to 132,000 gazelles entered the adult population each year in the second half of the 1980s.

Appendix 8

Hunting Attempts and Kills by Female Cheetahs

Species	Mothers		Adult females		Young females	
	Attempts	Kills	Attempts	Kills	Attempts	Kills
Hare	33	27	3	3	11	11
Thomson's gazelle	484 (80)	140 (73)	53 (11)	24 (11)	74 (10)	14 (9)
Steinbok	1				1	
Grant's gazelle	26 (2)	3 (2)	7 (2)	2 (2)	1	
Topi	1				1	
Hartebeest	1					
Warthog			1			
Wildebeest	10 (4)	1 (1)			1 (1)	
Reedbuck	6	1				
Zebra	1 (1)					
Impala			1		1 (1)	1 (1)
Dik-dik	1					
Eland						
Rat						
Kori bustard					1	1
Unknown	79	1	2		10	
Total	643	173	67	29	101	27

Species	Single adolescent females		Mixed-sex and all-female sibgroups	
	Attempts	Kills	Attempts	Kills
Hare	6	5	6	6
Thomson's gazelle	75 (22)	19 (18)	129 (13)	26 (12)
Steinbok			1	
Grant's gazelle	4 (1)	1 (1)	6(1)	1(1)
Topi	1		1 (1)	
Hartebeest			1	
Warthog	1		1	
Wildebeest			8 (4)	4 (4)
Reedbuck	1		3	
Zebra				
Impala				
Dik-dik				
Eland	1 (1)	1 (1)		
Rat			1	1
Kori bustard				
Unknown	12		16[a]	1[a]
Total	101	26	173	39

Note: Total numbers of hunting attempts and kills witnessed during systematic and ad lib observations made on different types and age-sex classes of prey by independent female cheetahs are shown. Totals include neonates but their number is additionally shown in parentheses; neonates are combined with fawns for Thomson's and Grant's gazelles. While estimates of prey preferences and hunting success can be derived from the table, they will not be strictly accurate since hunts in which the outcome was unknown and ad lib observations of cheetahs being found on a kill are included in the table (the latter is especially pertinent to the adult female data). Such data were excluded from analyses presented in the text, accounting for minor differences between this table and the text.

[a] Includes a hare or neonate Thomson's gazelle.

Appendix 9

Estimation of Female Home Range Size

Frame (1984) had shown that female cheetahs moved over enormous areas of the Serengeti plains each year, so a priori, one would expect it to be difficult to gain an accurate estimate of females' ranging patterns from just a few sightings. Home range areas derived by the minimum polygon method from less than 20 sightings were significantly smaller than ranges derived from a larger sample (fig. A.1; $N = 8$, 23 ranges, Mann-Whitney U test, $z = -2.799$, $P = .005$). Of those females seen at least 20 times, ranges of those that were not radio-collared were smaller than those of radio-collared females since collared individuals could be located in areas

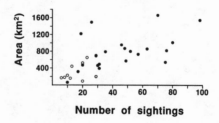

Fig. A.1 Female cheetahs' home range areas (derived by the minimum polygon method) from 1986 onward, plotted against the number of sightings used to generate the ranges. Solid circles denote individuals who were radio-collared (although not all of their sightings were made with the help of radiotelemetry); open circles, individuals without collars.

not normally searched on the ground ($N = 4$, 19 ranges, Mann-Whitney U test, $U = 10$, $P < .05$). Taking only collared females located 20 or more times, the average area they covered was 833.0 km^2 ($N = 19$, SE $= 85.1$, range $394.5-1,269.5$ km^2) over the course of 2 to 4 years. This figure is remarkably similar to Frame's estimate of 800 km^2, which was based on ground sightings only and shows how diligent he was in finding females on the plains.

Appendix 10

Estimation of Male Territory Size

Before average male territory size could be determined with accuracy, it was necessary to decide whether territories derived from just a few sightings or without the aid of radiotelemetry should be included.

Figure A.2 shows the area of each territory, derived by the minimum polygon method, plotted against the number of sightings used to determine its size. Areas generated from fewer than five sightings were under-

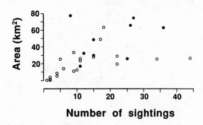

Fig. A.2 Male cheetahs' territory areas, plotted against the number of sightings used to determine their size. Solid circles denote territories in which residents were found using radiotelemetry on at least one occasion; open circles, territories in which residents were never found in this way. In the single case in which one coalition occupied two territories simultaneously, each area is included. For three territories where members of a resident male group were reduced in number, the area of territory both before and after the event is included. One territory was drawn by means other than the minimum polygon method (see fig. 8.5).

estimates, but once these were omitted, neither territories derived from visual sightings only nor those derived with the aid of radiotelemetry showed a significant increase in area with more sightings (residents located only visually: $N = 14$, $r_s = .348$, $P > .1$; residents some of whose sightings were made using radiotelemetry: $N = 9$, $r_s = .218$, $P > .5$). Territory sizes estimated without the help of radiotelemetry could have been underestimates because four of nine territories that were derived in part from radiotelemetry fixes were at the upper end of the size range. In three of these four, however, many of the sightings were acquired visually (17 of 36; 17 of 29; 5 of 8), while the fourth territory (Hidden Valley) was exceptional in that I rarely visited the area. (For this resident, all 26 fixes were made from the air except two when he was seen spray-marking. From these observations and the male's restricted movements over 3.5 years, I concluded he was a resident, but some of his fixes could have been minor forays out of the territory, which would have inflated its size.) The other five territories of collared residents were similar in area to those derived solely by visual means. I therefore retained all territories derived from more than five sightings in calculating the average size of a territory, which came to 37.4 km² ($N = 22$, SE $= 5.2$). If the sample was restricted to collared males only, the average size was 48.3 km² ($N = 9$, SE $= 7.6$).

Appendix 11

Hunting Attempts and Kills by Male Cheetahs

Species	Singletons		Pairs		Trios	
	Attempts	Kills	Attempts	Kills	Attempts	Kills
Hare[a]	9	8	11	10	6	6
Thomson's gazelle[a]	86 (15)	29 (11)	43 (11)	14 (11)	10 (2)	8 (2)
Steinbok[a]			1		1	
Grant's gazelle	13	1	11 (3)	5 (3)	7 (2)	3 (2)
Topi	1		2		2 (1)	1
Hartebeest	1 (1)	1 (1)	3		1	
Warthog	2 (1)	1			3	1
Wildebeest[b]	17 (2)	10 (1)	37 (11)	6 (4)	39 (5)	17 (4)
Reedbuck[b]	2	1	1			
Zebra[b]	1 (1)	1 (1)	5 (1)			
Unknown quarry	1		1			
Totals	133	52	115	35	69	36

Note: Total numbers of hunting attempts and kills witnessed during systematic and ad lib observations made on different types and age-sex classes of prey by nonadolescent independent male cheetahs are shown. Totals include neonates but their number is additionally shown in parentheses; neonates are combined with fawns for Thomson's and Grant's gazelles. For the purposes of analysis prey were separated according to whether they weighed 20 kg or less. While age-sex classes of some species, such as Thomson's gazelles, all fell below 20 kg (marked [a]) and others, such as wildebeests, all fell above 20 kg (marked [b]), different age-sex classes of the remainder were represented in either one or the other category (unmarked). While estimates of prey preferences and hunting success can be derived from the table, they will not be strictly accurate since hunts in which the outcome was unknown and ad lib observations of cheetahs being found on a kill are included in the table. Such data were excluded from analyses presented in the text, accounting for minor differences between this table and the text.

Appendix 12

Number of Adult Thomson's Gazelles Killed by Cheetahs on the Serengeti Plains per Annum

Age-sex class of cheetahs[a]	Approx # independent cheetahs in each class/year	Number of kills seen	Percentage of kills that were adult TGs	Kills/ year	Estimated # adult TG killed/ year
Lone AF	26	(54)	13.8	212	761
Lone YAF	14	(43)	9.3	219	285
Single Adolescents	8	(26)	0	339	0
Adolescent sibgroup	9	(38)	18.4	330	546
Single male	14	(55)	25.7	305	1,097
Pair of males	13	(35)	8.6	228	127
Trio of males	9	(41)	10.1	321	97
AF with cubs in lair	3	(37)	16.6	350	174
YAF with cubs in lair	1	(24)	8.5	269	23
Mother with Y cubs	6	(110)	21.8	292	382
Mother with M-A cubs	3	(31)	41.9	162	204
Mother with O cubs	6	(55)	20.0	228	274
Total	112				3,970

Note: TG denotes Thomson's gazelles; "adult" here includes adult and subadult TG.

[a] A, adult; Y, young; Adol, adolescent; F, female; Y, M-A, and O refer to young, middle-aged, and old cubs respectively.

Methods of Estimation

The mean number of individually recognized independent cheetahs living on the Serengeti plains each year between 1981 and 1990 was 67 females and 45 males. The proportion of adolescent males was taken as 0.209 while those of nonadolescent singletons, pairs and trios were 0.309, 0.291 and 0·191 respectively (from Caro and Collins 1986). For females, the probability of being an adolescent, a young adult, or an adult was derived from the number of months they spent in each category, 8, 20, and 52.8 respectively, with females being assumed to live 6.9 years (Laurenson, in press-c). For females, the ratio of single adolescents to adolescent sib-groups was assumed to be that for males in this age class (11:12: Caro and Collins 1986).

Young adult females and adult females were estimated to be without cubs for 160.4 and 111.7 days respectively for each bout of reproduction (see table 4.6). Both age classes were assumed to have cubs in the den for 49 days and to have cubs accompanying them for 460 days (chap. 4). The probability of maintaining cubs in the den was estimated to be 0.278, and of raising them to independence as 0.097, based on observed rates of litter loss (see table 4.2), and these were multiplied by the number of days spent in the relevant phase of reproduction. A ratio of these two figures was then calculated, and each ratio was multiplied by the probability of being a young adult or adult female as derived above.

To determine the number of females with emerged cubs of different ages, young adult and adult females with emerged cubs (as just calculated) were summed together. Mothers with emerged cubs were assumed to have young, middle-aged, and old offspring for 90, 90, and 280 days respectively, and these were multiplied by the probability of litter survival, 0.55 to reach the start of middle-aged cubhood, and 0.35 to reach independence (see table 4.2). A ratio of these three figures was then calculated, and each ratio was multiplied by the number of females with emerged cubs to give the number of mothers with cubs of different ages.

The number and identity of kills was gleaned from periods of observation and ad lib sampling. "Adult" Thomson's gazelles here include adults and subadults. Kills/year were estimated by adding up the number of adult Thomson's gazelle kills made in total, dividing by the total number of days the age-sex class of cheetah was followed, and then multiplying by 365 (data on adult and young adult females alone and with cubs in the lair were provided by K. Laurenson). Number of adult gazelles killed/year was derived from multiplying the number of kills by the proportion that were adult Thomson's gazelles; pairs of males were reduced by half, trios by a third.

Note that lone adult females and single males had the strongest impacts on the number of adult gazelles taken. If, instead, this calculation had assumed that the population was composed entirely of the easiest age-sex class of predator to monitor (lone adult females in most felid studies), this would have amounted to only 3,277 adult Thomson's gazelles removed. This was 17.5% less than the figure that takes all age-sex classes into account, which highlights the importance of making the individual predator the unit of analysis in studies of predator-prey dynamics.

Bibliography and Comprehensive List of Publications on Cheetahs

This bibliography contains all references cited in the text as well as a comprehensive list of publications on cheetahs compiled by Marcella Kelly and Barbara Wittman. Cheetah references are marked with an asterisk and were included if they contained the word *cheetah* in the title or otherwise referred extensively to cheetahs.

Abbey, H., and Howard, E. 1973. Statistical procedure in developmental studies on species with multiple offspring. *Dev. Psychobiol.* 6:329–35.

*Abbot, S., and Fuller, T. 1971. A fresh look at the cheetah's private life. *Smithsonian* 2(3): 34–42.

Acharjyo, L. N., and Mohapatra, S. 1977. Some observations on the breeding habits and growth of the jungle cat *(Felis chaus)* in captivity. *J. Bombay Nat. Hist. Soc.* 74:158–59.

*Adams, D. B. 1979. The cheetah: Native American. *Science* 205:1155–58.

*Adamson, J. 1966. Pippa returns to freedom in the bush. *Das Tier* 6(12): 4–7.

*Adamson, J. 1969. *The Spotted Sphinx.* London: Collins.

Afzelius, B. A. 1981. Abnormal human spermatozoa including comparative data from apes. *Am. J. Primatol.* 1:175–82.

Alcock, J. 1989. *Animal Behavior: An Evolutionary Approach.* 4th ed. Sunderland, Mass.: Sinauer Associates.

Alcock, J.; Jones, C. E.; and Buchmann, S. L. 1977. Male mating strategies in the bee *Centris pallida* Fox (Hymenoptera; Anthophoridae). *Am. Nat.* 111: 145–55.

Alexander, R. D. 1974. The evolution of social behavior. *Annu. Rev. Syst. Ecol.* 5: 325–83.

*Ali, S. A. 1927. The Moghul emperors of India as naturalists and sportsmen. *J. Bombay Nat. Hist. Soc.* 31:833–61.

*Allen, G. O. 1919. Caracal *(Felis caracal)* and hunting leopard *(Cynailurus jubatus)* in Mazipur, U.P. *J. Bombay Nat. Hist. Soc.* 26:1041.

Allendorf, F. W., and Leary, R. F. 1986. Heterozygosity and fitness in natural populations of animals. In *Conservation Biology: The Science of Scarcity and Diversity,* ed. M. E. Soulé, 57–76. Sunderland, Mass.: Sinauer Associates.

Altmann, J. 1974. Observational study of behaviour: Sampling methods. *Behaviour* 49:227–65.

Altmann, J. 1980. *Baboon Mothers and Infants.* Cambridge, Mass.: Harvard University Press.

Altmann, J.; Hausfater, G.; and Altmann, S. A. 1988. Determinants of reproductive success in savannah baboons, *Papio cynocephalus.* In *Reproductive Success,* ed. T. H. Clutton-Brock, 403–18. Chicago: University of Chicago Press.

Amlaner, C. J., and Macdonald, D. W., eds. 1980. *A Handbook on Biotelemetry and Radio-tracking.* Oxford: Pergamon Press.

*Ammann, K., and Ammann, K. 1984. *Cheetah.* Nairobi: Camerapix Publishers International.

Anderson, D. 1977. Gestation period of Geoffroy's cat bred at Memphis Zoo. *Int. Zoo. Yrbk.* 17:164–66.

*Anderson, J. L. 1982. Can cheetah be conserved in small reserves? *Tshomarelo News* 5:12–13.

*Anderson, J. L. 1984. A strategy for cheetah conservation in Africa. In *The Extinction Alternative,* ed. P. J. Mundy, 127–35. Johannesburg: Endangered Wildlife Trust.

*Anderson, W. I.; Cummings, J. F.; Steinberg, H.; de Lahunta, A.; and King, J. M. 1989. Subclinical lumbar polyradiculopathy in aged domestic, laboratory, and exotic mammalian species—a light and selected electron microscopic study. *Cornell Vet.* 79:339–44.

Andersson, M.; Wiklund, C. G.; and Rundgren, H. 1980. Parental defense of offspring: A model and an example. *Anim. Behav.* 28:536–42.

*Anna, M. 1973. Study of the leopard and the cheetah in Africa south of the Sahara: Their actual situation in the Republique of Chad (in French). Directorate of National Parks and Game Reserves in Chad. Unpublished typescript 4.

Arcese, P., and Smith, J. N. M. 1985. Phenotypic correlates and ecological consequences of dominance in song sparrows. *J. Anim. Ecol.* 54:817–30.

Armitage, K. B., and Downhower, J. F. 1974. Demography of yellow-bellied marmot populations. *Ecology* 55:1233–45.

Arnold, G. W., and Dudzinski, M. L. 1967. Studies of the diet of the grazing animal. II. The effect of physiological status in ewes and pasture availability on herbage intake. *Aust. J. Agric. Res.* 18:349–59.

Arnold, W. 1990. The evolution of marmot sociality: II. Costs and benefits of joint hibernation. *Behav. Ecol. Sociobiol.* 27:239–46.

*Asa, C. S. 1993. Relative contributions of urine and anal-sac secretions in scent marks of large felids. *Amer. Zool.* 33:167–72.

*Asa, C. S.; Junge, R. E.; Bircher, J. S.; Noble, G. A.; Sarri, K. J.; and Plotka, E. D. 1992. Assessing reproductive cycles and pregnancy in cheetahs *(Acinonyx jubatus)* by vaginal cytology. *Zoo Biol.* 11:139–51.

Asdell, S. A. 1964. *Patterns of Mammalian Reproduction.* Ithaca, N.Y.: Cornell Unviersity Press.

Ashmole, N. P. 1963. The regulation of numbers of tropical oceanic birds. *Ibis* 103b:458–73.

Ashmole, N. P., and Tovar, S. H. 1968. Prolonged parental care in royal terns and other birds. *Auk* 85:90–100.

*Ashwood, T. L., and Gittleman, J. L. in press. Behavioral and ecological factors influencing population density in cheetah *(Acinonyx jubatus)*: A critical review. In *Current Mammalogy,* vol. 3, ed. H. G. Genoways. New York: Plenum.

*Averbeck, G. A.; Bjork, K. E.; Packer, C.; and Herbst, L. 1990. Prevalence of hematozoans in lions *(Panthera leo)* and cheetah *(Acinonyx jubatus)* in Serengeti National Park and Ngorongoro Crater, Tanzania. *J. Wildl. Dis.* 26:392–94.

*Baenninger, R. R.; Estes, D.; and Baldwin, S. 1977. Anti-predator behavior of baboons and impala toward a cheetah. *E. Afr. Wildl. J.* 15:327–30.

Baerends-van Roon, J. M., and Baerends, G. P. 1979. *The Morphogenesis of the Behaviour of the Domestic Cat, with Special Emphasis on the Development of Prey Catching.* Amsterdam: North-Holland.

Bailey, T. N. 1974. Social organization in a bobcat population. *J. Wildl. Mgmt.* 38:435–46.

Bailey, T. N. 1994. *The African Leopard: A Study of the Ecology and Behavior of a Solitary Felid.* New York: Columbia University Press.

Bailey, T. N.; Bangs, E. E.; Portner, M. F.; Malloy, J. C.; and McAvinchey, R. J. 1986. An apparent overexploited lynx population on the Kenai peninsula, Alaska. *J. Wildl. Mgmt.* 50:279–90.

*Ban on trade in certain spotted cats. 1970. *IUCN Bull.* 2:137.

Barash, D. P. 1975. Evolutionary aspects of parental behavior: Distraction behavior of the Alpine Accentor. *Wils. Bull.* 87:367–73.

Barnard, C. J. 1980. Flock and feeding time budgets in the house sparrow *(Passer domesticus* L.). *Anim. Behav.* 28:295–309.

Barnes, R. F. W. 1982. Mate searching behaviour of elephant bulls in a semi-arid environment. *Anim. Behav.* 30:1217–23.

*Bartmann, D. W. 1981. The cheetah problem in Namibia/South West Africa. *Zool. Gart.* 51(1):52–64.

*Baudy, R. E. 1971. Notes on breeding felids at the Rare Feline Breeding Center. *Int. Zoo Yrbk.* 11:121–23.

Bauman, D. E., and Currie, W. B. 1980. Partitioning of nutrients during pregnancy and lactation: A review of mechanisms involving homeostasis and homeorhesis. *J. Dairy Sci.* 63:1514–29.

*Baxby, D.; Ashton, D. G.; Jones, D. M.; Thomsett, L. R.; and Denham, E. M. 1982. An outbreak of cowpox in captive cheetah: Virological and epidemiological studies. *J. Hyg.* 89:365–72.

Beardmore, J. A. 1983. Extinction, survival, and genetic variation. In *Genetics and Conservation: A Reference for Managing Wild Animal and Plant Populations,* ed. C. M. Schonewald-Cox, S. M. Chambers, F. MacBryde, and W. L. Thomas, 125–51. Menlo Park, Calif.: Benjamin Cummings.

Bednarz, J. C. 1988. Cooperative hunting in Harris' hawks *(Parabuteo unicinctus)*. *Science* 239:1525–27.

*Beehler, B. A. 1982. Oral therapy for nasal cryptococcosis in a cheetah. *J. Am. Vet. Med. Assoc.* 181:1400–1401.

Bekoff, M. 1989. Behavioral development of terrestrial carnivores. In *Carnivore Behavior, Ecology and Evolution,* ed. J. L. Gittleman, 89–124. New York: Cornell University Press.

Bekoff, M.; Daniels, T. J.; and Gittleman, J. L. 1984. Life history patterns and the comparative social ecology of carnivores. *Annu. Rev. Syst. Ecol.* 15:191–232.

Belden, R. C. 1986. Florida panther recovery plan implementation—a 1983 progress report. In *Cats of the World: Biology, Conservation and Management,* ed. S. D. Miller and D. D. Everett, 159–72. Washington, D.C.: National Wildlife Federation.

Beltran, J. F.; Delibes, M.; and Aldama, J. 1987. Ecology of the Iberian lynx in Donana, Spain. Cong. Int. Union Game Biol. Krakow, August.

*Benzon, T. A., and Smith, R. F. 1974. Male dominance hierarchies and their possible effects on breeding cheetahs. *Int. Zoo Yrbk.* 14:147–49.

*Benzon, T. A., and Smith, R. F. 1975. A case of programmed cheetah breeding. *Int. Zoo Yrbk.* 15:154–57.

*Benzon, T. A., and Smith, R. F. 1977. A technique for propagating cheetahs. In *The World's Cats,* vol. 3(3), ed. R. L. Eaton, 81–97. Carnivore Research Institute, University of Washington, Seattle.

Bercovitch, F. B. 1988. Coalitions, cooperation and reproductive tactics among adult male baboons. *Anim. Behav.* 36:1198–1209.

Berg, W. E. 1979. Ecology of bobcats in northern Minnesota. *Natl. Wildl. Fed. Sci. Tech. Series* 6:55–61.

Berger, J. 1979. Weaning conflict in desert and mountain bighorn sheep *(Ovis canadensis):* An ecological interpretation. *Z. Tierpsychol.* 50:188–200.

Berman, C. M. 1980. Mother-infant relationships among free-ranging rhesus monkeys on Cayo Santiago: A comparison with captive pairs. *Anim. Behav.* 28: 860–73.

*Bernstein, J. J. 1979. Cryptococcus osteomyelitis in a cheetah. *Feline Practice* 9(5): 23.

Bertram, B. C. R. 1975a. The social system of lions. *Sci. Am.* 232:54–65.

Bertram, B. C. R. 1975b. Weights and measures of lions. *E. Afr. Wildl. J.* 13: 141–43.

Bertram, B. C. R. 1976. Studying predators. Handbook 3. African Wildlife Leadership Foundation, Nairobi.

Bertram, B. C. R. 1978a. Living in groups: Predators and prey. In *Behavioural Ecology: An Evolutionary Approach,* ed. J. R. Krebs and N. B. Davies, 64–96. Oxford: Blackwell Scientific Publications.

*Bertram, B. C. R. 1978b. *Pride of Lions.* London: Dent.

Bertram, B. C. R. 1979. Serengeti predators and their social systems. In *Serengeti: Dynamics of an Ecosystem,* ed. A. R. E. Sinclair and M. Norton-Griffiths, 241–48. Chicago: University of Chicago Press.

Bertram, B. C. R. 1980. Vigilance and group size in ostriches. *Anim. Behav.* 28: 278–86.

Bertram, B. C. R. 1982. Leopard ecology as studied by radio tracking. *Symp. Zool. Soc. Lond.* 49:341–52.

*Bertschinger, H. J.; Meltzer, D. G. A.; van Dijk, A.; Coubrough, R. I.; Soley, J. T.; and Collett, F. A. 1984. Cheetah lifeline. *Nuclear Active* 30:2–7.

Best, P. B. 1979. Social organization in sperm whales, *Physter macrocephalus.* In *Behavior of Marine Animals: Current Perspectives in Research,* vol. 3, *Cetaceans,* ed. W. E. Winn and B. L. Olla, 227–89. New York: Plenum Press.

*Bezuidenhout, A. J. 1983. The anatomy of the genital tract of the male cheetah. *Abstr. 22nd World Vet. Cong.*

*Bigalke, R. C. 1964. The speed of the cheetah (*Acinonyx jubatus*). *Afr. Wildl.* 18: 257–58.

*Bigalke, R. C. 1972. Speed of a cheetah. *Afr. Wildl.* 26:1.

*Birkel, R. 1980. Some aspects of husbandry and design in a successful cheetah breeding facility. *Reg. Proc. AAZPA* (Orlando, Fla.) 1980:190–92.

Blumenschine, R. J. 1987. Characteristics of an early hominid scavenging niche. *Curr. Anthropol.* 28:383–407.

Blumenschine, R. J., and Caro, T. M. 1986. Unit flesh weights of some East African bovids. *Afr. J. Ecol.* 24:273–86.

*Blumer, E. S. 1990. Real world applications of reproductive technologies in the management of endangered species. *Annu. Conf. Proc. AAZPA* 1990: 514–19.

*Blyde, D. 1991. Osteochondrosis dissecans in a litter of cheetah cubs at Western Plains Zoo. *Thylaeinus* 16(1): 8–11.

Boesch, C. 1990. First hunters of the forest. *New Sci.* 19 May, 38–41.

Boesch, C., and Boesch, H. 1989. Hunting behavior of wild chimpanzees in the Tai National Park. *Am. J. Physiol. Anthropol.* 78:547–73.

Boinski, S., and Fragaszy, D. M. 1989. The ontogeny of foraging in squirrel monkeys, *Saimiri oerstedi. Anim. Behav.* 37:415–28.

*Bond, J. C., and Lindburg, J. C. 1990. Carcass feeding for captive cheetahs (*Acinonyx jubatus*): The effects of naturalistic feeding program on oral health and psychological well being. *Appl. Anim. Behav. Sci.* 26:373–82.

Bonnell, M. L., and Selander, R. K. 1974. Elephant seals: Genetic variation and near extinction. *Science* 184:908–9.

*Boomker, J., and Henton, M. M. 1980. Pseudotuberculosis in a cheetah. *S. Afr. J. Wildl. Res.* 10:63–66.

Borgerhoff Mulder, M.; Sieff, D.; and Merus, M. 1989. Disturbed ancestors: Datoga history in the Ngorongoro Crater. *Swara* 12:32–35.

Borner, M. 1985. The increasing isolation of Tarangire National Park. *Oryx* 19: 91–96.

Borner, M.; FitzGibbon, C. D.; Borner, M.; Caro, T. M.; Lindsay, W. K.; Collins, D. A.; and Holt, M. E. 1987. The decline in the Serengeti Thomson's gazelle population. *Oecologia* 73:32–40.

*Bottriell, L. G. 1987. *King Cheetah.* Leiden: E. J. Brill.

Boucher, D. H. 1977. On wasting parental investment. *Am. Nat.* 111:786–88.

*Bourgain-Dubourg, A. 1985. *Tender Killers.* New York: Vendome.

*Bourlière, F. 1963. Specific feeding habits of African carnivores. *Afr. Wildl.* 17(1): 21–27.

Bourlière, F. 1964. *The natural history of mammals.* Translated from the French by H. M. Parshley with revisions in English by the author. New York: Knopf.

Bowen, W. D. 1981. Variation in coyote social organization: The influence of prey size. *Can. J. Zool.* 59:639–52.

Bower, J. R. F. 1973. Seronera: Excavations at a stone bowl site in the Serengeti National Park, Tanzania. *Azania* 8:71–101.

Boyce, M. S. 1988. Evolution of life histories of mammals: Theory and patterns from mammals. In *Evolution of Life Histories: Theory and Practice,* ed. M. S. Boyce, 3–30. New Haven: Yale University Press.

Bradbury, J. W. 1981. The evolution of leks. In *Natural Selection and Social Behavior,* ed. R. D. Alexander and D. W. Tinkle, 138–69. New York: Chiron Press.

Bradbury, J. W.; Gibson, R. M.; and Tsai, I. M. 1986. Hotspots and the evolution of leks. *Anim. Behav.* 34:1694–1709.

Bradbury, J. W., and Vehrencamp, S. L. 1977. Social organization and foraging in emballonurid bats. III: Mating systems. *Behav. Ecol. Sociobiol.* 2:1–17.

Bradley, R. M. 1977. Aspects of the ecology of the Thomson's gazelle in the Serengeti National Park, Tanzania. Ph.D. diss., Texas A&M University.

Bragin, A. P. 1986. *Population Characteristics and Social-Spacing Patterns of the Tiger on the Eastern Slopes of the Sikhote-Alin Mountain Range, USSR.* Pacific Inst. Geogr. Record no. 13.

Brand, C. J., and Keith, L. B. 1979. Lynx demography during a snowshoe hare decline in Alberta. *J. Wildl. Mgmt.* 43:827–49.

Brand, C. J.; Keith, L. B.; and Fischer, C. A. 1976. Lynx responses to changing snowshoe hare densities in central Alberta. *J. Wildl. Mgmt.* 40:416–28.

*Brand, D. J. 1975. Cheetah breeding. National Zoological Gardens, Pretoria. Unpubl. typescript. 15 pp.

*Brand, D. J. 1980. Captive propagation at the National Zoological Gardens of South Africa. *Int. Zoo Yrbk.* 20:107–12.

*Brand, D. J. 1983a. A "king cheetah" born. *National Zoological Gardens of South Africa* 1(16):1–3.

*Brand, D. J. 1983b. A "king cheetah" born at the cheetah breeding and research centre of the National Zoological Gardens of South Africa, Pretoria. *Zool. Gart.* 53:366–68.

*Bridges, W. 1955. The cheetah—the mildest cat. *Anim. Kingdom* 58:130–34.

*Briggs, M. B., and Ott, R. L. 1986a. Feline leukemia virus infection in a captive cheetah and the clinical and antibody response of six captive cheetahs to vaccination with a subunit feline leukemia virus vaccine. *J. Am. Vet. Med. Assoc.* 189:1197–99.

*Briggs, M. B., and Ott, R. L. 1986b. Possible feline leukemia virus infection in a captive cheetah and the response of captive cheetahs to feline leukemia vaccination. *Proc. Am. Assoc. Zoo Vet.* 1986:137–39.

*Brock, S. M. 1969. The cat that kills with a silent spring. *Reader's Digest,* June, 60–63.

Bronson, F. H. 1989. *Mammalian Reproductive Biology.* Chicago: University of Chicago Press.

*Broom, R. 1949. Notes on the milk dentition of the lion, leopard and cheetah. *Ann. Transvaal Mus.* 21(2): 183–85.

*Brown, E. W.; Olmstead, R. A.; Martenson, J. S.; and O'Brien, S. J. 1993. Exposure to FIV and FIPV in wild and captive cheetahs. *Zoo Biol.* 12:135–42.

Brown, J. C., and Yalden, D. W. 1973. The description of mammals. 2. Limbs and locomotion of terrestrial mammals. *Mammal Rev.* 3:107–34.

Brown, J. L. 1964. The evolution of diversity in avian territorial systems. *Wils. Bull.* 76:160–69.

Brown, J. L. 1983. Cooperation—a biologist's dilemma. *Adv. Stud. Behav.* 13: 1–37.

Brown, J. L. 1987. *Helping and Communal Breeding in Birds.* Princeton, N.J.: Princeton University Press.

Brown, L. H. 1966. Observations on some Kenya eagles. *Ibis* 108:531–72.

*Bruce, P. 1971. Game digest of the cheetah, *Acinonyx jubatus* (Schreber). Department of Zoology, University of Pretoria. 24 pp. Unpublished typescript.

*Brydon, P. 1987. Rare birth at Western Plains Zoo. *Aust. Zool.* 24:81–83.

Buechner, H. K. 1961. Territorial behavior in Uganda kob. *Science* 133:698–99.

*Burney, D. A. 1980. The effects of human activities on cheetah *(Acinonyx jubatus)* in the Mara region of Kenya. M.Sc. thesis, University of Nairobi.

*Burney, D. A. 1981. Man and the Mara cheetahs. *Wildl. News* (African Wildlife Leadership Foundation, Nairobi) 16(1): 8–11.

*Burney, D. A. 1982a. How to see more game. *Swara* 5(2): 24–26.

*Burney, D. A. 1982b. Life on the cheetah circuit. *Nat. Hist.* 91(5): 50–59.

*Burney, D. A., and Burney, L. 1979a. Cheetah and man. *Swara* 2(2): 24–29.

*Burney, D. A., and Burney, L. 1979b. Cheetah and man: Part 2. *Swara* 2(3): 28–32.

*Burnham, L. 1988. Off and running: The cheetah masterplan may be insurance against extinction. *Sci. Am.* 258:26.

Burrows, R. 1990. Wild dogs. *Conservation Monitoring News* 2:6–7.

Burt, W. H. 1943. Territoriality and home range concepts as applied to mammals. *J. Mammal.* 24:346–52.

*Burton, R. G. 1920. The hunting leopard *(Cynailurus jubatus). J. Bombay Nat. Hist. Soc.* 27:397–98.

*Burton, R. W. 1950. The "dewclaws" of the hunting leopard (cheetah) (*A. jubatus,* Schreber). *J. Bombay Nat. Hist. Soc.* 49:541–43.

*Burton, R. W. 1959. The voice of the cheetah or hunting leopard. *J. Bombay Nat. Hist. Soc.* 56:317–18.

Busse, C. D. 1978. Do chimpanzees hunt cooperatively? *Am. Nat.* 112:767–70.

*Button, C.; Meltzer, D. G.; and Mulders, M. S. 1981a. The electrocardiogram of the cheetah. *J. S. Afr. Vet. Assoc.* 52:233–35.

*Button, C.; Meltzer, D. G.; and Mulders, M. S. 1981b. Saffan induced poikilothermia in cheetah. *J. S. Afr. Vet. Assoc.* 52:237–38.

Byers, J. A., and Kitchen, D. W. 1988. Mating system shift in a pronghorn population. *Behav. Ecol. Sociobiol.* 22:355–60.

Bygott, J. D.; Bertram, B. C. R.; and Hanby, J. P. 1979. Male lions in large coalitions gain reproductive advantages. *Nature* 282:839–41.

Cabrera, A., and Yepes, J. 1960. *Mammiferos Sudamericanos.* Buenos Aires: Historia Natural Eidar, Compañía Argentina de Editores.

*Cade, R. 1965. Cheetah just tolerate humans. *Africana* 2(4): 33–35.

*Caldwell, H., and Howard, J. 1991. First cheetah cub produced by artificial insemination. *AAZPA Communique* (Wheeling, W.V.), Oct.

*Caligiuri, R.; Carrier, M.; Jacobson, E. R.; and Buergelt, C. D. 1988. Corneal squamous cell carcinoma in a cheetah *(Acinonyx jubatus). J. Zoo Anim. Med.* 19:219–22.

Campbell, K. L. I. 1989. Serengeti Ecological Monitoring Programme Report, September.

Campbell, K. L. I.; Kajuni, A. R.; Huish, S. A., and Mng'ong'o, G. B. 1990. *Serengeti Ecological Monitoring Programme.* Serengeti Wildlife Research Centre biennial report 1988–1989.

*Campbell, L. 1983. Moorland cheetah. *E. Afr. Nat. Hist. Soc. Bull.,* May–June, 34–35.

*Cannon, J. 1974. Case report: Toxoplasmosis in cheetah. *Ann. Proc. Am. Assoc. Zoo Vet.* 1974:225–27.

Caraco, T. 1979. Time budgetting and group size: A test of a theory. *Ecology* 60: 618–27.

Caraco, T., and Wolf, L. L. 1975. Ecological determinants of group sizes of foraging lions. *Am. Nat.* 109:343–52.

Carbyn, L. N., and Patriquin, D. 1983. Observations on home range sizes, movements and social organization of lynx, *Lynx canadensis,* in Riding Mountain National Park, Manitoba. *Can. Field Nat.* 97:262–67.

*Cardy, R. H., and R. E. Bostrom. 1978. Multiple splenic myelolipomas in a cheetah. *Vet. Pathol.* 15:556–58.

Caro, T. M. 1980a. The effects of experience on the predatory patterns of cats. *Behav. Neural Biol.* 23:1–28.

Caro, T. M. 1980b. Predatory behaviour in domestic cat mothers. *Behaviour* 74: 128–47.

*Caro, T. M. 1982. A record of cheetah scavenging in the Serengeti. *Afr. J. Ecol.* 20:213–14.

Caro, T. 1986a. Tourism: Too much of a good thing? *Swara* 9(4): 14–17.

*Caro, T. M. 1986b. The functions of stotting in Thomson's gazelles: Some tests of the predictions. *Anim. Behav.* 34:663–84.

*Caro, T. M. 1987a. Cheetah mothers' vigilance: Looking out for prey or for predators? *Behav. Ecol. Sociobiol.* 20:351–61.

*Caro, T. M. 1987b. Indirect costs of play: Cheetah cubs reduce maternal hunting success. *Anim. Behav.* 35:295–97.

*Caro, T. 1989a. The brotherhood of cheetahs. *Nat. Hist.* 6:50–59.

*Caro, T. M. 1989b. Determinants of asociality in felids. In *Comparative Socioecology: The Behavioral Ecology of Humans and Other Mammals,* ed. V. Standen and R. A. Foley, 41–74. Special publication of the British Ecological Society, no. 8. Oxford: Blackwell Scientific Publications.

*Caro, T. M. 1990. Cheetah mothers bias parental investment in favor of cooper-
ating sons. *Ethol. Ecol. Evol.* 2:381–95.
*Caro, T. M. 1991. Cheetahs. In *Great Cats: Majestic Creatures of the Wild,* ed.
J. Seidensticker and S. Lumpkin, 138–47. Sydney: Weldon Owen.
*Caro, T. M. 1993. Behavioral solutions to breeding cheetahs in captivity: Insights
from the wild. *Zoo Biol.* 12:19–30.
*Caro, T. M. In press. Short-term costs and correlates of play in cheetahs. *Anim.
Behav.*
Caro, T. M., and Bateson, P. 1986. Organisation and ontogeny of alternative tac-
tics. *Anim. Behav.* 34:1483–99.
*Caro, T. M., and Collins, D. A. 1986. Male cheetahs of the Serengeti. *Natl. Geogr.
Res.* 2(1): 75–86.
*Caro, T. M., and Collins, D. A. 1987a. Ecological characteristics of territories of
male cheetahs *(Acinonyx jubatus). J. Zool.* 211:89–105.
*Caro, T. M., and Collins, D. A. 1987b. Male cheetah social organization and ter-
ritoriality. *Ethology* 74:52–64.
*Caro, T. M., and Durant, S. M. 1991. Use of quantitative analyses of pelage char-
acteristics to reveal family resemblances in genetically monomorphic cheetahs.
J. Hered. 82:8–14.
*Caro, T. M., and FitzGibbon, C. D. 1992. Large carnivores and their prey: The
quick and the dead. In *Natural Enemies: The Population Biology of Predators,
Parasites and Diseases,* ed. M. J. Crawley, 117–42. Oxford: Blackwell Scientific
Publications.
*Caro, T. M.; FitzGibbon, C. D.; and Holt, M. E. 1989. Physiological costs of be-
havioural strategies for male cheetahs. *Anim. Behav.* 38:309–17.
Caro, T. M., and Hauser, M. D. 1992. Is there teaching in nonhuman animals?
Q. Rev. Biol. 67:151–74.
*Caro, T. M.; Holt, M. E.; FitzGibbon, C. D.; Bush, M.; Hawkey, C. M.; and Kock,
R. A. 1987. Health of adult free-living cheetahs. *J. Zool.* 212:572–84.
*Caro, T., and Laurenson, K. 1989. The Serengeti cheetah project. *Swara* 12(2):
28–31.
*Caro, T. M., and Laurenson, M. K. 1994. Ecological and genetic factors in conser-
vation: a cautionary tale. *Science* 263:485–86.
*Carvalho, C. 1968. Comparative growth rates of handreared big cats. *Int. Zoo
Yrbk.* 8:56–59.
*Caughley, G. 1994. Directions in conservation biology. *J. Anim. Ecol.* 63:215–244.
Cavallo, J. A. 1990. A study of leopard behavior and ecology in the Seronera Valley,
Serengeti National Park, Tanzania. SWRI, TANAPA, COSTECH, MWEKA,
Tanzania. Typescript.
*Chance, C.; Eller, C.; and Wilkinson, A. 1977. A study of communication in chee-
tah. Natal, South Africa. Typescript.
Charnov, E. L., and Schaffer, W. M. 1973. Life history consequences of natural
selection: Cole's result revisited. *Am. Nat.* 107:791–93.
*The cheetah and our national parks. 1974. *Custos* 3(5): 10–12.
*The cheetah appeal. 1974. *Wildl. Survival* (Endangered Wildlife Trust, Johannes-
burg) 1(1): 1–4.

*Cheetah baffles scientists. 1974. *Afr. Wildl.* 28:34–37.

*Cheetah born near Rome. 1966. *Animals* 9:80.

*Cheetah for the Kruger Park. 1973. *Custos* 2(4): 34–37.

*Cheetah in trouble in East Africa. 1972. *Oryx* 11:403.

*The cheetah or hunting-leopard (*Acinonyx jubatus* Erxleben). 1935. *J. Bombay Nat. Hist. Soc.* 37:147–49.

*Cheetah Research Council. 1989. *Research Manual.* Oklahoma City, Ok: AAZPA.

*Cheetah stages a comeback. 1971. *Outdoorman* 1(8): 7.

*Cheetahs bred by private owner in Holland. 1976. *Int. Zoo News* 23(2): 28–29.

*Cheetahs: End of the line? 1985. *Science* 85(6): 6.

*Cheetahs: Wild cats in danger. 1989. *Natl. Geogr. World,* Jan., 3–7.

Cheney, D. L., and Seyfarth, R. M. 1987. The influence of inter-group competition on the survival and reproduction of female vervet monkeys. *Behav. Ecol. Sociobiol.* 21:375–86.

Cheney, D. L., and Wrangham, R. W. 1987. Predation. In *Primate Societies,* ed. B. B. Smuts, D. L. Cheney, R. M. Seyfarth, R. W. Wrangham, and T. T. Struhsaker, 227–39. Chicago: University of Chicago Press.

Chenoworth, P. J., and Ball, L. 1980. Breeding soundness evaluation in bulls. In *Current Therapy in Theriogenology,* ed. D. Morrow, 330–39. Philadelphia: W. B. Saunders.

*Chinery, M. 1979. Killers of the wild: Streamlined cheetah. *Wildlife* (Lond.) 21(8): 6–7.

Chism, J.; Rowell, T. E.; and Olson, D. K. 1984. Life history patterns of female patas monkeys. In *Female Primates: Studies by Women Primatologists,* ed. M. F. Small, 175–90. New York: Alan R. Liss.

*CITES. 1992. Quotas for trade in specimens of cheetah. Eighth meeting of the Convention of International Trade in Endangered Species of Wild Flora and Fauna. Document 8.22 (Rev.): 1–5.

Clark, C. W. 1987. The lazy, adaptable lions: A Markovian model of group foraging. *Anim. Behav.* 35:361–68.

Clark, C. W., and Mangel, M. 1986. The evolutionary advantages of group foraging. *Theor. Popul. Biol.* 30:45–75.

*Clayton, H. 1962. Two cheetahs kill impala. *Afr. Wildl.* 16(3): 203–4.

Clutton-Brock, T. H. 1984. Reproductive effort and terminal investment in iteroparous mammals. *Am. Nat.* 123:212–29.

Clutton-Brock, T. H. 1988. *Reproductive Success: Studies of Individual Variation in Contrasting Breeding Systems.* Chicago: University of Chicago Press.

Clutton-Brock, T. H. 1989a. Female transfer, male tenure and inbreeding avoidance in social mammals. *Nature* 337:70–71.

Clutton-Brock, T. H. 1989b. Mammalian mating systems. *Proc. R. Soc. Lond.* B. 236:339–72.

Clutton-Brock, T. H. 1991. *The Evolution of Parental Care.* Princeton, N.J.: Princeton University Press.

Clutton-Brock, T. H.; Albon, S. D.; Gibson, R. M.; and Guinness, F. E. 1979. The logical stag: Adaptive aspects of fighting in red deer (*Cervus elaphus* L.). *Anim. Behav.* 27:211–25.

Clutton-Brock, T. H.; Albon, S. D.; and Guinness, F. E. 1982. Competition between female relatives in a matrilocal mammal. *Nature* 300:178–80.

Clutton-Brock, T. H.; Albon, S. D.; and Guinness, F. E. 1986. Great expectations: Dominance, breeding success and offspring sex ratios in red deer. *Anim. Behav.* 34:460–71.

Clutton-Brock, T. H.; Guinness, F. E.; and Albon, S. D. 1982. *Red Deer: The Behavior and Ecology of Two Sexes.* Chicago: University of Chicago Press.

Clutton-Brock, T. H., and Harvey, P. H. 1977. Primate ecology and social organisation. *J. Zool.* 183:1–39.

Clutton-Brock, T. H.; Iason, G. R.; Albon, S. D.; and Guinness, F. E. 1982. Effects of lactation on feeding behaviour and habitat use in wild red deer hinds. *J. Zool.* 198:227–36.

Clutton-Brock, T. H., and Parker, G. A. 1992. Potential reproductive rates and the operation of sexual selection. *Q. Rev. Biol.* 67:437–56.

Cockburn, A. 1988. *Social Behaviour in Fluctuating Populations.* London: Croom Helm.

Cockburn, A.; Scott, M. P.; and Scotts, D. J. 1985. Inbreeding avoidance and male-biased natal dispersal in *Antechinus* spp. (Marsupialia: Dasyuridae). *Anim. Behav.* 33:908–15.

*Cohen, M. 1978. A preliminary survey of the cheetah *Acinonyx jubatus* on the Suikerbosrand Nature Reserve. 1–61. Pretoria: Transvaal Provincial Authority.

*Cohn, J. P. 1986. Surprising cheetah genetics. *BioScience* 36:358–62.

*Collier, G. E., and O'Brien, S. J. 1985. A molecular phylogeny of the Felidae: Immunological distance. *Evolution* 39:473–87.

*Comrie-Greig, J. 1985. Cape cobra cheats cheetahs. *Afr. Wildl.* 39(2): 67.

*Conklin, G. F. 1931. *Cheetahs, the Swift Hunters.* New York: Holiday House.

Connor, R. C.; Smolker, R. A.; and Richards, A. F. 1992. Dolphin alliances and coalitions. In *Coalitions and Alliances in Humans and Other Animals,* ed. A. H. Harcourt and F. B. M. de Waal, 415–43. Oxford: Oxford University Press.

*Cooke, C. K. 1974. The cheetah hunt paintings. *Arnoldia* 6(33): 1–4.

*Cooper, A. L. 1926. A curious skin. *Field* 147:690.

*Cooper, A. L. 1927. Notes on *Acinonyx rex* (Cooper's cheetah). *S. Afr. J. Sci.* 24: 343–45.

Cooper, S. M. 1990. The hunting behaviour of spotted hyaenas *(Crocuta crocuta)* in a region containing both sedentary and migratory populations of herbivores. *Afr. J. Ecol.* 28:131–41.

*Copycat, cheetahs genetically weak. 1983. *Int. Wildl.* 13:24.

Corbett, G. B., and Southern, H. N., eds. 1977. *The Handbook of British Mammals.* Philadelphia: Blackwell Scientific Publications.

Corbett, L. 1978. Behaviour of wild cats at Glen Tanar. Annual Report to the Institute of Terrestrial Ecology, Banchory, U.K.

Corbett, L. K. 1979. Feeding ecology and social organization of wildcats *(Felis sylvestris)* and domestic cats *(Felis catus)* in Scotland. Ph.D. diss., Aberdeen University.

*Corkill, N. L. 1929. On the occurrence of the cheetah *(Acinonyx jubatus)* in Iraq. *J. Bombay Nat. Hist. Soc.* 33:700–702.

*Coubrough, R.; Bertschinger, H. J.; and Soley, J. T. 1978. Scanning electron microscopic studies on cheetah spermatozoa. *Proc. Electron Micro. Soc. S. Afr.* 8:57–58.

*Coubrough, R., and Soley, J. T. 1976. Some aspects of normal and abnormal spermatozoa in cheetah. *Proc. Electron Micro. Soc. S. Afr.* 6:5–6.

*Coubrough, R., and Soley, J. T. 1981. The fine structure of interstitial cells of leydig in cheetah. *Proc. Electron Micro. Soc. S. Afr.* 11:57–58.

Cowlishaw, G., and Dunbar, R. I. M. 1991. Dominance rank and mating success in male primates. *Anim. Behav.* 41:1045–56.

Crandall, L. S. 1964. *The Management of Wild Animals in Captivity.* Chicago: University of Chicago Press.

*Crawshaw, G. J.; Brown, J. L.; and Goodrowe, K. L. 1991. Investigation of infertility in a male cheetah *(Acinonyx jubatus).* *J. Zoo Wildl. Med.* 22:119–24.

Crawshaw, P. G., and Quigley, H. B. 1991. Jaguar spacing, activity and habitat use in a seasonally flooded environment in Brazil. *J. Zool.* 223:357–70.

Creel, S. R., and Creel, N. M. 1990. Energetics, reproductive suppression and obligate communal breeding in carnivores. *Behav. Ecol. Sociobiol.* 28:263–70.

Crook, J. H., and Gartlan, J. S. 1966. Evolution of primate societies. *Nature* 210: 1200–1203.

Crowe, D. M. 1975. Aspects of aging, growth, and reproduction of bobcats from Wyoming. *J. Mammal.* 56:177–98.

*Cupps, W. 1985. The cheetah program at the Columbus Zoo: What's worked and what hasn't. *Proc. AAZPA* 1985:552–57.

*Curtis, L., ed. 1972. Seminar on problems of breeding cheetahs. *Proc. AAZPA,* Portland, Oreg. Oklahoma City Zoo, Ok. Typescript.

*Cutting, C. S. 1938. The fastest hunt in the world. *Nat. Hist.* 3:179–84.

*Czekala, N. M.; Callison, L.; Williams, M.; Durrant, B.; Millard, S.; and Lindburg, D. 1991. Fecal steroid hormone analysis as an indicator of reproductive function in the cheetah *(Acinonyx jubatus).* *Proc. Soc. Stud. Reprod., Biol. Reprod. Suppl.* 44:37.

Dacie, J. V., and Lewis, S. M. 1984. *Practical Haematology.* 6th ed. Edinburgh: Churchill Livingstone.

*Darehshuri, B. F. 1978. Threatened cats of Asia: Asiatic cheetah. *Wildlife* (Lond.) 20:396–97.

*Das, A. K. 1985. The imperial cheetahs in Akbar's shikarkhana. *India Magazine,* Aug. 28–39.

*D'Aulaire, E., and D'Aulaire, D. 1971. Nature's golden racer: The cheetah. *Int. Wildl.* 1(1): 12–16.

*Davey, P. 1980. Cheetah attacking leopard: A black serval. *E. Afr. Nat. Hist. Soc. Bull.,* Nov./Dec., 97.

*Davidson, B. C.; Cantrill, R. C.; and Morsbach, D. 1986. The fatty acid composition of the liver and brain of southern African cheetahs. *Prog. Lipid Res.* 25: 97–100.

*Davidson, B. C.; Cantrill, R. C.; and Varaday, D. 1986. The reversal of essential fatty acid deficiency symptoms in the cheetah. *S. Afr. J. Zool.* 21:161–64.

Davies, N. B. 1976. Parental care and the transition to independent feeding in the young spotted flycatcher *(Muscicapa striata).* *Behaviour* 59:280–93.

Davies, N. B. 1978. Territorial defense in the speckled wood butterfly *(Pararge aegeria)*: The resident always wins. *Anim. Behav.* 26:138–47.

Davies, N. B. 1982. Behaviour and competition for scarce resources. In *Current Problems in Sociobiology,* ed. Kings' College Sociobiology Group, 363–80. Cambridge: Cambridge University Press.

Dawkins, R. 1982. *The Extended Phenotype.* Oxford: Freeman.

Dawkins, R., and Carlisle, T. R. 1976. Parental investment, mate desertion and a fallacy. *Nature* 262:131–33.

*Dedekind, H. W. 1979. Cheetah resettled in state forest land. *Afr. Wildl.* 33(2): 49.

*Degenaar, J. P. 1977. Aspects of reproduction in captive cheetah *(Acinonyx jubatus).* M.Sc. thesis, University of Pretoria.

*DeGraaf, G. 1974. The familiar pattern deviation of the cheetah *(Acinonyx jubatus). Custos* 3(2): 2.

*Denis, A. 1964. *Cats of the World.* London: Constable.

de Waal, F. B. M. 1982. *Chimpanzee Politics.* New York: Harper & Row.

de Waal, F. B. M. 1989. Dominance "style" and primate social organization. In *Comparative Socioecology: The Behavioural Ecology of Humans and Other Mammals,* ed. V. Standen and R. A. Foley, 243–63. Oxford: Blackwell Scientific Publications.

de Waal, F. B. M., and Harcourt, A. H. 1992. Coalitions and alliances: A history of ethological research. In *Coalitions and Alliances in Humans and Other Animals,* ed. A. H. Harcourt and F. B. M. de Waal, 1–19. Oxford: Oxford University Press.

de Wit, H. A. 1977. Soil map of the Serengeti Plain. Appendix to *Soils and Grassland Types of the Serengeti Plain (Tanzania).* Thesis, Mededelingen Landbouwhogeschool, Wageningen, 1978.

*Dierenfeld, E. S. 1993. Nutrition of captive cheetahs: Food composition and blood parameters. *Zoo Biol.* 12:143–50.

*Dimijian, C. 1989. Curiosity killed the hat. (Photographs of young cheetahs encountering a hat.) *Nat. Hist.* 11:62–65.

*Dinnes, M. R., and Hendrickson, R. 1970. Liver disease in cheetahs: A preliminary report. *Proc. AAZV* 1970:110–17.

*Divyabhanusinh. 1984. The origin, range and status of the Asiatic (or Indian) cheetah or hunting leopard *(Acinonyx jubatus Veneticus).* Paper presented at the IUCN Cat Specialist Group meeting at Kanha National Park, Madha Pradesh, India, April 1984. Typescript.

*Divyabhanusinh. 1987. Record of two unique observations of the Indian cheetah in Tuzuk-i-Jahangiri. *J. Bombay Nat. Hist. Soc.* 84:269–74.

Dobson, F. S. 1982. Competition for mates and predominant juvenile male dispersal in mammals. *Anim. Behav.* 30:1183–92.

*Dominis, J. 1967. The cheetah. *Africana* 3(3): 19–26.

*Dominis, J., and Edey, M. 1968. *The Cats of Africa.* New York: Time-Life Books.

*Donoghue, A. M.; Howard, J. G.; Byers, A. P.; Goodrowe, K. L.; Bush, M.; Blumer, E.; Lukas, J.; Storer, J.; Snodgrass, K.; and Wildt, D. E. 1992. Correlation of sperm viability with gamete interaction and fertilization in vitro in the cheetah *(Acinonyx jubatus). Biol. Reprod.* 46:1047–56.

*Downes, S. J. T., and Hulett, N. P. 1979. Copper deficiency in cheetah *(Acinonyx jubatus):* A case report. Collisheen Estates, Natal. Unpublished typescript.

*Dragesco-Joffe, A. 1993. *La vie sauvage au Sahara.* Lausanne, Switzerland: Debechaux et Niestle.

Dresser, B. L. 1988. Cryobiology, embryo transfer, and artificial insemination in ex situ conservation programs. In *Biodiversity,* ed. E. O. Wilson, 296–308. Washington, D.C.: National Academy Press.

*Dresser, B. L.; Gosselin, S. J.; Setchell, K. D. R.; Kramer, L.; Johnston, O. J.; Tarr, M. J.; and Ballisteri, W. F. 1985. Possible causes of infertility in captive cheetah. *Proc. AAZPA* 1985:558–59.

*Drummond, D. 1989. Operation cheetah. *Swara* 12(3): 33–35.

Dublin, H. T.; Sinclair, A. R. E.; Boutin, S.; Anderson, E.; Jago, M.; and Arcese, P. 1990. Does competition regulate ungulate populations? Further evidence from Serengeti, Tanzania. *Oecologia* 82:283–88.

*Dubs, B. 1972. Zur operativen Behandlung einer Humerus-Pseudarthrose bei einem Gepard *(Acinonyx jubatus).* Surgical management of humeral pseudoarthrosis in a cheetah. *Dtsch. Tierarztl. Wochenschr.* 79(4): 82–83.

Dunbar, R. I. M. 1982. Intraspecific variations in mating strategy. In *Perspectives in Ethology,* vol. 5, *Ontogeny,* ed. P. P. G. Bateson and P. H. Klopfer, 385–431. New York: Plenum Press.

Dunbar, R. I. M. 1984. *Reproductive Decisions: An Economic Analysis of Gelada Baboon Social Strategies.* Princeton, N.J.: Princeton University Press.

Dunbar, R. I. M.; Buckland, D.; and Miller, D. 1990. Mating strategies of male feral goats: A problem in optimal foraging. *Anim. Behav.* 40:653–67.

Dunbar, R. I. M., and Dunbar, P. 1988. Maternal time budgets of gelada baboons. *Anim. Behav.* 36:970–80.

Duncan, J. R., and Prasse, K. W. 1986. *Veterinary Laboratory Medicine: Clinical Pathology.* 2d ed. Ames, Iowa: Iowa State University Press.

Dunn, E. K. 1972. Effect of age on the fishing ability of sandwich terns *Sterna sandvicensis. Ibis* 114:360–66.

*Durant, S. M.; Caro, T. M.; Collins, D. A.; Alawi, R. M.; and FitzGibbon, C. D. 1988. Migration patterns of Thomson's gazelles and cheetahs on the Serengeti Plains. *Afr. J. Ecol.* 26:257–68.

*Durrant, B. S.; Schuerman, T.; and Millard, S. E. 1985. Non-invasive semen collection in the cheetah *(Acinonyx jubatus). Proc. AAZPA* 1985:257–68.

*Duveen, A. 1961. Hyena chases cheetah. *Afr. Wildl.* 15:80.

*Eardley-Wilmots, S. 1897. The young of the hunting leopard. *Bombay Nat. Hist. Soc.* 11:544–49.

Earle, M. 1987. A flexible body mass in social carnivores. *Am. Nat.* 129:755–60.

*Eaton, K. A.; Radin, M. J.; Kramer, L.; Wack, R.; Sherding, R.; Krakowka, S.; and Morgan, D. R. 1991. Gastric spiral bacilli in captive cheetahs. *Scand. J. Gastroenterol.* (Suppl.) 26:36–42.

*Eaton, K. A.; Radin, M. J.; Kramer, L.; Wack, R.; Sherding, R.; Krakowka, S.; Fox, J. G.; and Morgan, D. R. 1992. Epizootic gastritis in cheetahs associated with gastric spiral bacilli. *Vet. Path.* 30:55–63.

*Eaton, R. L. 1968. Behavioral ecology of hunting in cheetahs. 30th Annual Midwest Fish and Wildlife Conf., Columbus, Ohio.

*Eaton, R. L. 1969a. The cheetah: Beautiful and efficient predator. *Africana* 3(10): 19–23.

*Eaton, R. L. 1969b. The cheetah's survival endangered by man. *Defender Wildl. News* 44(1): 57–60.

*Eaton, R. L. 1969c. Cooperative hunting by cheetah and jackals and a theory of domestication of the dog. *Mammalia* 33:87–92.

*Eaton, R. L. 1969d. Hunting relationships of cheetah with non-prey species. *Mammalia* 33:543.

*Eaton, R. L. 1969e. Notes on breathing rates in wild cheetahs. *Mammalia* 33: 543–44.

*Eaton, R. L. 1969f. The social life of the cheetah. *Animals* 12(4): 172–75.

*Eaton, R. L. 1970a. Group interactions, spacing and territoriality in cheetahs. *Z. Tierpsychol.* 27:461–91.

*Eaton, R. L. 1970b. Hunting behaviour of the cheetah. *J. Wildl. Mgmt.* 34:56–67.

*Eaton, R. L. 1970c. Notes on the reproductive biology of the cheetah. *Int. Zoo Yrbk.* 10:86–96.

*Eaton, R. L. 1970d. The predatory sequence, with emphasis on killing behavior and its ontogeny in the cheetah (*Acinonyx jubatus* Schreber). *Z. Tierpsychol.* 27:492–504.

*Eaton, R. L. 1971a. Cheetah. *Natl. Parks Conserv. Mag.* 45(6): 18–22.

*Eaton, R. L. 1971b. The cheetah: The fastest of the world's land animals is racing toward extinction. *Afr. Wildl.* 25(4): 123–28.

*Eaton, R. L. 1972. An experimental study of predatory and feeding behaviour of the cheetah (*Acinonyx jubatus*). *Z. Tierpsychol.* 31:270–80.

*Eaton, R. L. 1973. Cheetah speed explained. *Afr. Wildl.* 27(1): 43.

*Eaton, R. L. 1974. *The Cheetah: Biology, Ecology and Behaviour of an Endangered Species.* New York: Van Nostrand Reinhold.

*Eaton, R. L. 1976a. The evolution of sociability in the Felidae. In *The World's Cats*, vol. 3(2), ed. R. L. Eaton, 95–142. Carnivore Research Institute, University of Washington, Seattle. Also in *Carnivore* 2:82–88.

*Eaton, R. L. 1976b. A possible case of mimicry in larger mammals. *Evolution* 30: 853–56.

*Eaton, R. L. 1977. Mimicry in African carnivores. In *Proc. 1975 Predator Symposium*, ed. R. L. Phillips and C. Jonkel, 183–90. University of Montana, Missoula.

*Eaton, R. L. 1978. The birth and development of cheetahs in a wild animal park. *Zool. Gart.* 48(2–3): 81–93.

*Eaton, R. L. 1979. Interference competition among carnivores: A model for the evolution of social behaviour. *Carnivore* 2:9–16.

*Eaton, R. L. 1981. *The Cheetah, Nature's Fastest Racer.* New York: Dodd Mead.

*Eaton, R. L., and Craig, S. I. 1973. Captive management and mating behaviour of the cheetah. In *The World's Cats*, vol. 1, ed. R. L. Eaton, 217–54. Winston, Oreg.: World Wildlife Safari.

*Eaton, R. L.; Shorey, D. W.; and Yost, R. 1978. The birth and development of cheetahs in a wild animal park. *Zool. Gart.* 48(2/3): 81–93.

*Eaton, R. L., and York, W. 1970. Breeding cheetahs on a large scale. Lion Country Safari, California, U.S.A. Unpublished typescript.

*Eaton, R. L.; York, W.; and Dredge, W. 1970. The Lion Country Safari and its role in conservation, education and research. *Int. Zoo Yrbk.* 10:171–72.

*Editors. 1935. The wild animals of the Indian Empire and the problem of their preservation. Part III. *J. Bombay Nat. Hist. Soc.* 37(Suppl.): 112–88.

*Egorov, I. 1989. Keeping and breeding cheetahs *(Acinonyx jubatus)* at the Moscow Zoo. Achievements of zoos in breeding rare and endangered species of animals. *Moskva.*

Eisenberg, J. F., and Lockhart, M. 1972. An ecological reconnaissance of Wilpattu National Park, Ceylon. *Smith. Contrib. Zool.* 101:1–118.

Elgar, M. A. 1989. Predator vigilance and group size in mammals and birds: A critical review of the empirical evidence. *Biol. Rev.* 64:13–33.

Elgar, M. A., and Catterall, C. P. 1981. Flocking and predator surveillance in house sparrows: Test of an hypothesis. *Anim. Behav.* 29:868–72.

Elliot, J. P., and Cowan, I. M. 1978. Territoriality, density and prey of the lion in Ngorongoro Crater, Tanzania. *Can. J. Zool.* 56:1726–43.

Elliot, J. P.; Cowan, I. McT.; and Holling, C. S. 1977. Prey capture by the African lion. *Can. J. Zool.* 55:1811–28.

Eloff, F. C. 1973a. Ecology and behavior of the Kalahari lion. In *The World's Cats,* vol. 1, ed. R. L. Eaton, 90–126. Winston, Oreg.: World Wildlife Safari.

Eloff, F. C. 1973b. Lion predation in Kalahari Gemsbok National Park. *J. S. Afr. Wildl. Mgmt. Assoc.* 3(2): 59–63.

Emlen, S. T. 1984. Cooperative breeding in birds and mammals. In *Behavioural Ecology: An Evolutionary Approach,* 2d ed., ed. J. R. Krebs and N. B. Davies, 305–39. Oxford: Blackwell Scientific Publications.

Emlen, S. T. 1991. Evolution of cooperative breeding in birds and mammals. In *Behavioural Ecology: An Evolutionary Approach,* 3d ed., ed. J. R. Krebs and N. B. Davies, 301–37. Oxford: Blackwell Scientific Publications.

Emlen, S. T., and Oring, L. W. 1977. Ecology, sexual selection, and the evolution of mating systems. *Science* 197:215–23.

Emmons, L. H. 1986. Comparative feeding ecology of felids in a neotropical rain forest. *Behav. Ecol. Sociobiol.* 20:271–83.

*Encke, W. 1960. Birth and rearing of cheetahs at Krefield Zoo. *Int. Zoo Yrbk.* 2: 85–86.

*Encouraging figures on the Serengeti cheetah population. 1977. *Africana* 6(5): iv.

*Eriksen, A. 1990. Breeding crocodiles and cheetahs in South Africa. *Int. Zoo News* 37(3): 13–15.

Erlinge, S., and Sandell, M. 1986. Seasonal changes in the social organization of male stoats, *Mustela erminea:* An effect of shifts between two decisive resources. *Oikos* 47:57–62.

*Ervin, A. M.; Junge, R. E.; Miller, R. E.; and Thornburg, L. P. 1988. Hemangiosarcoma in a cheetah *(Acinonyx jubatus). J. Zoo Anim. Med.* 19(3): 143–45.

Estes, R. D. 1974. Social organization of the African bovidae. In *The Behavior of Ungulates and Its Relation to Their Management,* ed. V. Geist and F. Walther, 166–205. Morges, Switzerland: IUCN.

*Estes, R. D. 1991. *The Behavior Guide to African Mammals.* Berkeley: University of California Press.

Estes, R. D., and Estes, R. K. 1979. The birth and survival of wildebeest calves. *Z. Tierpsychol.* 50:45–95.

Estes, R. D., and Goddard, J. 1967. Prey selection and hunting behavior of the African wild dog. *J. Wildl. Mgmt.* 31:52–70.

*Evermann, J. F. 1989. Comparative features of a coronavirus isolated from a cheetah with feline peritonitis. *Virus Res.* 13:15–28.

*Evermann, J. F.; Burns, G.; Roelke, M. E.; McKeirnan, A. J.; Greenlee, A.; Ward, A. C.; and Pfeifer, M. L. 1983. Diagnostic features of an epizootic of feline infectious peritonitis in captive cheetah. *Proc. 26th Amer. Assoc. Vet. Lab. Diag.* 1983:365–82.

*Evermann, J. F.; Henney, J.; Roelke, M.; and O'Brien, S. J. 1988. Biological and pathological consequences of feline infectious peritonitis virus in captive cheetahs. *Arch. Virol.* 102(3–4): 155–72.

*Evermann, J. F.; Laurenson, M. K.; McKeirnan, A. J.; and Caro, T. M. 1993. Infectious disease surveillance in captive and free-living cheetahs: An integral part of the species survival plan. *Zoo Biol.* 12:125–33.

*Evermann, J. F., and McKeirnan, A. J. 1991. Infectious disease surveillance in the cheetah with primary emphasis upon feline coronavirus and feline herpesvirus infections. *Proc. AAZV,* Sept., 191–97.

*Evermann, J. F.; Roelke, M. E.; and Briggs, M. B. 1986. Clinical and diagnostic features of feline coronavirus infections of cheetah. *Feline Practice* 16(3): 21–30.

Ewer, R. F. 1973a. *The Carnivores.* London: Weidenfeld and Nicolson.

*Ewer, R. F. 1973b. The evolution of mating systems in the Felidae, a discussion. In *The World's Cats,* vol. 2, ed. R. L. Eaton, 110–25. Seattle, Wash.: Woodland Park Zoo.

Fagen, R. M., and Wiley, K. S. 1978. Felid paedomorphosis, with special reference to *leopardus. Carnivore* 1:72–81.

Falconer, D. S. 1981. *Introduction to Quantitative Genetics.* 2d ed. London: Longman.

Falconer, D. S. 1981. *Quantitative Genetics.* New York: Ronald.

Fanshawe, J. H., and FitzGibbon, C. D. 1993. Factors influencing the hunting success of an African wild dog pack. *Anim. Behav.* 45:479–90.

Fanshawe, J. H.; Frame, L. H.; and Ginsberg, J. R. 1991. The wild dog—Africa's vanishing carnivore. *Oryx* 25:137–146.

*Fenton, L. L. 1920. The hunting leopard *(Cynailurus jubatus)* in Kathiawar. *J. Bombay Nat. Hist. Soc.* 27:398–99.

*Firouz, E. 1976. Environmental and nature conservation in Iran. *Environ. Conserv.* 3(1): 33–42.

*Fitch, H. M., and Fagan, D. A. 1982. Focal palatine erosion associated with dental malocclusion in captive cheetahs. *Zoo Biol.* 1:295–310.

*Fitch, H. M.; Millard, S.; and Tenaza, R. 1985. Cheetahs. *Zoonooz* 58(5): 4–10.

FitzGibbon, C. D. 1988. Antipredator behaviour in Thomson's gazelles. Ph.D. diss., University of Cambridge.

*FitzGibbon, C. D. 1989. A cost to individuals with reduced vigilance in groups of Thomson's gazelles hunted by cheetahs. *Anim. Behav.* 37:508–10.

*FitzGibbon, C. D. 1990a. Anti-predator strategies of immature Thomson's gazelles: Hiding and the prone response. *Anim. Behav.* 40:846–55.

*FitzGibbon, C. D. 1990b. Mixed-species grouping in Thomson's and Grant's gazelles: The antipredator benefits. *Anim. Behav.* 39:1116–26.

*FitzGibbon, C. D. 1990c. Why do cheetahs prefer male gazelles? *Anim. Behav.* 40:837–45.

*FitzGibbon, C. D. In press. The costs and benefits of predator inspection behavior in Thomson's gazelles. *Behav. Ecol. Sociobiol.*

*FitzGibbon, C. D., and Fanshawe, J. H. 1988. Stotting in Thomson's gazelles: An honest signal of condition. *Behav. Ecol. Sociobiol.* 23:69–74.

*FitzGibbon, C. D., and Fanshawe, J. H. 1989. The condition and age of Thomson's gazelles killed by cheetahs and wild dogs. *J. Zool.* 218:99–107.

Fitzsimons, F. W. 1919. *The Natural History of South Africa. Vol. 1.* London: Longmans, Green and Co.

*Flint, V. 1988. The Asiatic cheetah lives on. *Cat News* 8:11.

*Florio, P. L., and Spinelli, L. 1967. Successful breeding of a cheetah *(Acinonyx jubatus)* in a private zoo. *Int. Zoo Yrbk.* 7:150–52.

*Florio, P. L., and Spinelli, L. 1968. Second successful breeding of cheetahs in a private zoo. *Int. Zoo. Yrbk.* 8:76–78.

Foley, R. 1987. *Another Unique Species: Patterns of Human Evolutionary Ecology.* Harlow: Longmans.

Foose, T. J. 1983. The relevance of captive populations to the conservation of biotic diversity. In *Genetics and Conservation: A Reference for Managing Wild Animal and Plant Populations,* ed. C. M. Schonewald-Cox et al. 374–401. Menlo Park, Calif.: Benjamin Cummings.

Forslund, P. 1993. Vigilance in relation to brood size and predator abundance in the barnacle goose *Branta leucopsis. Anim. Behav.* 45:965–73.

Fosbrooke, H. A. 1963. The *stomoxys* plague in Ngorongoro. *E. Afr. Wildl. J.* 1:124–26.

Fossey, D. 1983. *Gorillas in the Mist.* Boston: Houghton Mifflin.

Foster, J. B., and Kearney, D. 1967. Nairobi National Park game census. *E. Afr. Wildl. J.* 5:112–20.

*Foster, J. B., and McLaughlin, R. 1968. Nairobi National Park game census, 1967. *E. Afr. Wildl. J.* 5:152–54.

*Foster, J. W. 1977. The induction of estrus in the cheetah. In *The World's Cats,* vol. 3, ed. R. L. Eaton, 101–11. Carnivore Research Institute, University of Washington, Seattle.

*Fourie, F. 1972a. Excitement over a tame cheetah. *Custos* 1(3): 15–17.

*Fourie, F. 1972b. Taga, the cheetah. *Custos* 1(10): 2–6.

Fox, M. W. 1975. Evolution of social behavior in canids. In *The Wild Canids,* ed. M. W. Fox, 429–60. New York: Van Nostrand Reinhold.

*Frame, G. W. 1975/76. Cheetah ecology and behaviour. *Serengeti Research Institute Annual Report,* 74–87. P. O. Seronera, via Arusha, Tanzania.

*Frame, G. W. 1980. Cheetah social organization in the Serengeti ecosystem of Tanzania. Paper presented at the Animal Behavior Society, 9–13 June 1980, Colorado State University, Fort Collins, Colorado.

*Frame, G. W. 1983. How cheetah cubs learn to hunt. *Swara* 6(5): 8–9.

*Frame, G. W. 1984. Cheetah. In *The Encyclopedia of Mammals*, vol. 1, ed. D. W. Macdonald, 40–43. London: Allen and Unwin.

*Frame, G. W. 1986. Carnivore competition and resource use in the Serengeti ecosystem in Tanzania. Ph.D. diss., Utah State University.

*Frame, G. W. 1992. First record of king cheetah outside southern Africa. *Cat News* 16:3.

*Frame, G. W., and Frame, L. H. 1975. Cheetah research: Progress report. *Africana* 5(12): ii–iii.

*Frame, G. W., and Frame, L. H. 1976a. Interim cheetah report for the Serengeti Research Institute. Annual Report. Unpublished typescript.

*Frame, G. W., and Frame, L. H. 1976b. The vulnerable cheetah. *Expedition* 6(6): 40–46.

*Frame, G. W., and Frame, L. H. 1977a. Our three years with cheetahs. *Int. Wildl.* 7(1/2): 4–11.

*Frame, G. W., and Frame, L. H. 1977b. Serengeti cheetah. *Wildl. News* 12(3): 2–6.

*Frame, G. W., and Frame, L. H. 1980a. Cheetahs: In a race for survival. *Natl. Geogr.* 157(5): 712–28.

*Frame, G. W., and Frame, L. H. 1980b. "Solitaire": A rare and intimate view of the courtship of a cheetah. *Anim. Kingdom* 6:45–50.

*Frame, G. W., and Frame, L. H. 1981. *Swift and Enduring: Cheetah and Wild Dogs of the Serengeti.* New York: E. P. Dutton.

*Frame, G., and Frame, L. 1993. Serengeti cheetahs. *Swara* 16(5):14–17.

Frame, L. H.; Malcolm, J. R.; Frame, G. W.; and van Lawick, H. 1979. Social organization of African wild dogs *(Lycaon pictus)* on the Serengeti Plains, Tanzania, 1967–1978. *Z. Tierpsychol.* 50:225–49.

Frank, L. G. 1986. Social organization of the spotted hyaena *Crocuta crocuta.* II. Dominance and reproduction. *Anim. Behav.* 34:1510–27.

Frankel, O. H., and Soulé, M. E. 1981. *Conservation and Evolution.* Cambridge: Cambridge University Press.

Franklin, I. R. 1980. Evolutionary change in small populations. In *Conservation Biology: An Evolutionary-Ecological Approach*, ed. M. E. Soulé and B. A. Wilcox, 135–49. Sunderland, Mass.: Sinauer Associates.

Fretwell, S. D. 1972. *Populations in a Seasonal Environment.* Princeton, N.J.: Princeton University Press.

*Fuga, G.; Nuti, M.; Macchioni, G.; and Gadale, O. 1978. A case of relapsing cutaneous larva migrans transmitted by a cheetah *(Acinonyx jubatus).* *Parasitology* 20:139–42.

Fuller, T. K., and Kat, P. W. 1990. Movements, activity, and prey relationships of African wild dogs *(Lycaon pictus)* near Aitong, southwestern Kenya. *Afr. J. Ecol.* 28:330–50.

*Gaerdes, J. 1974. Jagluiperds in Suidwes-Afrika. Bylae tot Nuusbrief XIV/9–10. Des. 73/Jan. 74. S.W.A. Wetenskaplike Vereniging.

*Gaerdes, J. 1975a. Geparden in Sudwestafrika. *Newsl. S. W. Africa Scient. Soc.* 14(9–10) (Suppl.): 1–11.

*Gaerdes, J. 1975b. Geparden in Sudwestafrika. *Newsl. S. W. Africa Scient. Soc.* 14(11): 13–24.

*Gaerdes, J. 1975c. Geparden in Sudwestafrika. *Newsl. S. W. Africa Scient. Soc.* 14(12) (Suppl.): 25–31.

*Gandras, R., and Encke, W. 1966. Case history of a breeding group of cheetahs at the Krefield Zoo. *Int. Zoo Yrbk.* 6:275–76.

Gascoyne, S. C.; Laurenson, M. K.; Lelo, S.; and Borner, M. 1993. Rabies in African wild dogs *(Lycaon pictus)* in the Serengeti region. *J. Wildl. Dis.* 29: 396–402.

Gashwiler, J. S., and Robinette, W. L. 1957. Accidental fatalities of the Utah cougar. *J. Mammal.* 38:123–26.

Gashwiler, J. S.; Robinette, W. L.; and Morris, O. W. 1961. Breeding habits of the bobcat in Utah. *J. Mammal.* 42:76–84.

Geertsema, A. A. 1985. Aspects of the ecology of the serval in the Ngorongoro Crater, Tanzania. *Neth. J. Zool.* 35:527–610.

*Genereaux, L. 1988. Cheetah cub rearing protocol. In *Cheetah: Husbandry and Reproductive Survey and Guidelines,* ed. J. Grisham. AAZPA, Species Survival Plan Program, Oklahoma.

*Genmin sponsors cheetah project. 1989. *Zoon.* 32:6–7.

*Gerhart, J. 1979. Possible interaction of lions, cheetahs, vultures, and tourist vehicles in Amboseli. *E. Afr. Nat. Hist. Soc. Bull.,* Jul./Aug., 92.

*Gilbert, F. 1975. A private cheetah breeding program. *Reg. Proc. AAZPA* 1975: 308–13.

*Gillespie, D., and Fowler, M. 1984. Lymphocytic-plasmacytic colitis in two cheetahs *(Acinonyx jubatus). J. Am. Vet. Assoc.* 185:1388–89.

*Gillespie, D.; Schmeitzel, L.; and Fowler, M. 1984. Possible food hypersensitivity in two cheetahs *(Acinonyx jubatus). Proc. AAZV* 1984:136.

*Gittens, C. 1985. Even cheetahs can be farmed. *Farmer's Weekly* (Zimbabwe) 11: 14–17.

Gittleman, J. L. 1984. The behavioural ecology of carnivores. Ph.D. diss., University of Sussex.

Gittleman, J. L. 1986a. Carnivore brain size, behavioral ecology, and phylogeny. *J. Mammal.* 67:23–36.

Gittleman, J. L. 1986b. Carnivore life history patterns: Allometric, phylogenetic, and ecological associations. *Am. Nat.* 127:744–71.

Gittleman, J. L. 1989. Carnivore group living: Comparative trends. In *Carnivore Behavior, Ecology, and Evolution,* ed. J. L. Gittleman, 183–207. Ithaca, N.Y.: Comstock.

Gittleman, J. L., and Thompson, S. D. 1988. Energy allocation in mammalian reproduction. *Am. Zool.* 28:863–75.

*Glass, G. E., and Martin, L. D. 1978. A multivariate comparison of some extant and fossil Felidae. *Carnivore* 1:80–87.

Godfray, H. C. J. 1991. Signalling of need by offspring to their parents. *Nature* 352:328–30.

Gomendio, M. 1991. Parent/offspring conflict and maternal investment in rhesus macaques. *Anim. Behav.* 42:993–1005.

*Gonyea, W. J. 1976. Adaptive differences in the body proportions of large felids. *Acta Anatomica* 96:81–96.

*Gonyea, W. J., and Ashworth, R. 1975. The form and function of retractile claws in the Felidae and other representative carnivorans. *J. Morphol.* 145:229–38.

Goodall, J. 1986. *The Chimpanzees of Gombe.* Cambridge, Mass.: Belknap Press of Harvard University Press.

*Goodrowe, K. L.; Graham, J.; and Mehren, K. G. 1991. Stimulation of ovarian activity and oocyte recovery in the caracal *(Felis caracal)* and cheetah *(Acinonyx jubatus). J. Zoo Wildl. Med.* 22:42–48.

*Goosen, H. 1986. Striking coat for a king. *S. Afr. Panorama* 31(5): 48–50.

*Gore, M., and Frame, G. 1982. Cheetah learning and losing. *Swara* 5(5): 8–9.

Gosling, L. M. 1974. The social behaviour of Coke's hartebeest *(Alcelaphus buselaphus cokei).* In *The Behaviour of Ungulates and Its Relation to Management,* ed. V. Geist and F. Walther, 481–511. Morges, Switzerland: IUCN.

Gosling, L. M. 1982. A reassessment of the function of scent marking in territories. *Z. Tierpsychol.* 60:89–118.

Gosling, L. M. 1986. The evolution of mating strategies in male antelope. In *Ecological Aspects of Social Evolution,* ed. D. I. Rubenstein and R. W. Wrangham, 244–81. Princeton, N.J.: Princeton University Press.

Gosling, L. M., and Petrie, M. 1990. Lekking in topi: A consequence of satellite behaviour by small males at hotspots. *Anim. Behav.* 40:272–87.

*Gosselin, S. J.; Loudy, D. L.; Tarr, M. J.; Balistreri, W. F.; Setchell, K. D. R.; Johnston, J. O.; Kramer, L. W.; and Dresser, B. L. 1988. Veno-occlusive disease of the liver of captive cheetah. *Vet. Pathol.* 25:48–57.

*Gosselin, S. J.; Setchell, K. D. R.; Harrington, G. W.; Welsh, M.-B. B.; Pylypiw, H.; Kozeniauskas, R.; Dollard, D.; Tarr, M. J.; and Dresser, B. L. 1989. Nutritional considerations in the pathogenesis of hepatic veno-occlusive disease in captive cheetahs. *Zoo Biol.* 8(4): 339–47.

*Gosselin, S. J.; Tarr, M. J.; Balistreri, W. F.; Kramer, L. W.; Setchell, K. D. R.; Johnston, J. O.; and Dresser, B. L. 1986. Dietary considerations in the pathogenesis of hepatic vascular lesions in captive cheetah. *Proc. AAZV* 1986:20.

*Gosselin, S. J.; Tarr, M. J.; Loudy, D. E.; Kramer, L. W.; Setchell, K. D. R.; Johnston, J. O.; and Balistreri, W. F. 1986. Hepatic vascular liver lesions in captive cheetah—dietary pathogenesis. *Hepatology* 6:1175.

Gouzoules, S., and Gouzoules, H. 1987. Kinship. In *Primate Societies,* ed. B. B. Smuts, D. L. Cheney, R. M. Seyfarth, R. W. Wrangham, and T. T. Struhsaker, 299–305. Chicago: University of Chicago Press.

*Graham, A. 1966. East African Wildlife Society Cheetah Survey: Extracts from the report by Wildlife Services. *E. Afr. Wildl. J.* 4:50–55.

*Graham, A. D., and Parker, I. S. C. 1965. East African Wildlife Society Cheetah Survey. Report by Wildlife Services. East African Wildlife Society, Nairobi. Typescript.

Grant, J. W. A.; Chapman, C. A.; and Richardson, K. S. 1992. Defended versus undefended home range size of carnivores, ungulates and primates. *Behav. Ecol. Sociobiol.* 31:149–61.

Graves, J. A., and Whiten, A. 1980. Adoption of strange chicks by herring gulls, *Larus argentatus* L. *Z. Tierpsychol.* 54:267–78.

Gray, J. 1968. *Animal Locomotion.* New York: W. W. Norton.

Greenwood, P. J. 1980. Mating systems, philopatry and dispersal in birds and mammals. *Anim. Behav.* 28:1140–62.

Greig-Smith, P. W. 1980. Parental investment in nest defense by stonechats *(Saxicola torquata). Anim. Behav.* 28:604–19.

Grinnell, J.; Dixon, J. S.; and Linsdale, J. M. 1937. *Fur-Bearing Mammals of California.* Berkeley: University of California Press.

*Grisham, J. 1987. Cheetah *(Acinonyx jubatus)* reproductive evaluations at the St. Louis Zoo. *Reg. Conf. Proc.* AAZPA 1987:440–42.

*Grisham, J. 1988. AAZPA species survival plan program. Husbandry and reproduction of the cheetah: Proposed guidelines in cheetah master plan produced by Special Survival Plan (SSP). April 1988.

*Grisham, J. 1992. *AAZPA Cheetah Husbandry Manual.* Vol. II. Oklahoma City: Oklahoma City Zoological Park.

*Grisham, J., and Lindburg, D. 1989. Cheetah master plan. AAZPA Species survival plan program, 3–10. Oklahoma City: Oklahoma City Zoological Park Publ.

*Grittinger, T. F. 1975. Scent marking behavior of captive cheetahs. *Int. Zoo News* 22(8): 19–20.

*Grittinger, T. F. 1977. Effects of conspecific scent marking among captive male cheetahs. In *The World's Cats,* vol. 3(3), ed. R. L. Eaton, 98–100. Carnivore Research Institute, University of Washington, Seattle.

*Grittinger, T. F., and Ives, J. R. 1979. Scent marking sequences in captive cheetahs. *Carnivore* 2:46–49.

*Grittinger, T. F., and Peneski, T. J. 1984. Seasonal variation in scent marking among captive cheetahs. *Carnivore* 5:40–56.

*Gros, P. 1990. Global cheetah project Phase I: Cheetah status in southern Africa. Typescript.

Gross, M. R. 1985. Disruptive selection for alternative life histories in salmon. *Nature* 313:47–48.

*Grzimek, B. 1964. Speed of cheetah. *Afr. Wildl.* 18:343.

Guggisberg, C. A. W. 1962. *Simba, the Life of the Lion.* London: Bailey Bros. & Swinfen.

*Guggisberg, C. A. W. 1975. *Wild Cats of the World.* New York: Taplinger.

*Gunther, D. R. 1882. Exhibition of flat skin of a leopard*Proc. Zool. Soc. Lond.,* 312.

*Haagner, C. 1975. Cheetah meets more than its match. *Custos* 3(7): 37–42.

*Haghdoost, I. S., and Gharagozlou, M. J. 1983. Feline panleukopenia in two cheetah. (In Persian.) *J. Vet. Faculty* (University of Teheran) 38(2/4): 53–59.

Haglund, B. 1966. Winter habits of the lynx and wolverine as revealed by tracking in the snow. *Viltrevy* 4:245–310.

Hall, V. E., and Pierce, G. H. 1934. Litter size, birth weight and growth rate in the cat. *Anat. Rec.* 60:111–24.

Haller, V. H., and Breitenmoser, U. 1986. Spatial organization of the reintroduced population of the lynx *(Lynx lynx)* in the Swiss Alps. *Z. Saug.* 51:289–311.

Hamilton, P. H. 1976. The movements of the leopards in Tsavo National Park, Kenya, as determined by radio tracking. M.Sc. thesis, University of Nairobi.

*Hamilton, P. H. 1981. The leopard *(Panthera pardus)* and the cheetah *(Acinonyx jubatus)* in Kenya. *Report to U.S. Wildlife Service,* African Wildlife Leadership Foundation and Government of Kenya.

*Hamilton, P. H. 1982. Status of the cheetah in sub-Saharan Africa, with particular reference to Kenya. *Int. Cat Symp.,* Texas A&M, Wildl. Conserv. Mgmt. Dept., Research section, Nairobi. Typescript.

*Hamilton, P. H. 1986a. The leopard, *Panthera pardus,* and the cheetah, *Acinonyx jubatus,* in Kenya: Ecology, status, conservation and management. *U.S. Fish and Wildlife Service,* Washington, D.C.

*Hamilton, P. H. 1986b. Status of the cheetah in Kenya with reference to sub-Saharan Africa. In *Cats of the World: Biology, Conservation and Management,* ed. S. D. Miller and D. D. Everett, 65–76. Washington, D.C.: National Wildlife Federation.

Hamilton, W. D. 1971. Geometry of the selfish herd. *J. Theor. Biol.* 31:295–311.

Hanby, J. P., and Bygott, J. D. 1979. Population changes in lions and other predators. In *Serengeti: Dynamics of an Ecosystem,* ed. A. R. E. Sinclair and M. Norton-Griffiths, 249–62. Chicago: University of Chicago Press.

Hanby, J. P., and Bygott, J. D. 1987. Emigration of subadult lions. *Anim. Behav.* 35:161–69.

Hannon, S. J.; Mumme, R. L.; Koenig, W. D.; and Pitelka, F. A. 1985. Replacement of breeders and within-group conflict in the cooperatively breeding acorn woodpecker. *Behav. Ecol. Sociobiol.* 17:303–12.

*Hanstrom, P. 1949. Cheetahs provide an unusual experience. *Afr. Wildl.* 3(3): 203–9.

Hanwell, A., and Peaker, M. 1977. Physiological effects of lactation on the mother. *Symp. Zool. Soc. Lond.* 41:297–312.

Harcourt, A. H. 1989. Social influences on competitive ability: Alliances and their consequences. In *Comparative Socioecology: The Behavioural Ecology of Humans and Other Mammals,* ed. V. Standen and R. A. Foley, 223–42. Oxford: Blackwell Scientific Publications.

Harcourt, A. H. 1992. Coalitions and alliances: Are primates more complex than non-primates? In *Coalitions and Alliances in Humans and Other Animals,* ed. A. H. Harcourt and F. B. M. de Waal, 445–71. Oxford: Oxford University Press.

Harcourt, A. H., and de Waal, F. B. M., eds. 1992. *Coalitions and Alliances in Humans and Other Animals.* Oxford: Oxford University Press.

Harcourt, A. H., and Stewart, K. J. 1981. Gorilla male relationships: Can differences in immaturity lead to contrasting reproductive tactics in adulthood? *Anim. Behav.* 29:206–10.

*Hardy, N. G. 1959. The cheetah—fastest animal on earth. *Wildlife* (Nairobi) 1(3): 27–30.

Harper, F. 1945. *Extinct and vanishing mammals of the Old World.* Special publication no. 12. New York: American Committee for International Wildlife Protection.

*Harrison, D. L. 1968. The large mammals in Arabia: Oryx, genet, leopard, cheetah, tahr, goat, sheep, deer. *Oryx J. Faun. Preserv. Soc.* 9(5): 357–63.

*Harrison, G. 1989. Who is the fastest? (speediest animal). *Sports Afield* 202: 326.

*Hart, F. R. 1992. Has cheetah management come full circle? *AAZPA Western Regional Conference,* Tucson, Ariz., Mar./April. Unpublished typescript.

Harvey, P. H., and Pagel, M. D. 1991. *The Comparative Method in Evolutionary Biology.* Oxford: Oxford University Press.

Harvey, P. H.; Pagel, M. D.; and Rees, J. A. 1991. Mammalian metabolism and life histories. *Am. Nat.* 137:556–66.

Harvey, P. H.; Promislow, D. E. L.; and Read, A. F. 1989. Causes and correlates of life history differences among mammals. In *Comparative Socioecology: The Behavioural Ecology of Humans and Other Mammals,* ed. V. Standen and R. A. Foley, 305–18. Oxford: Blackwell Scientific Publications.

Harvey, P. H., and Zammuto, R. M. 1985. Patterns of mortality and age at first reproduction in natural populations of mammals. *Nature* 315:319–20.

*Hast, M. H. 1989. The larynx of roaring and non-roaring cats. *J. Anat.* 163:117–21.

Hauser, M. D. 1988. Variation in maternal responsiveness in free ranging vervet monkeys: A response to infant mortality risk? *Am. Nat.* 131:573–87.

Hausfater, G., and Hrdy, S. B. 1984. *Infanticide: Comparative and Evolutionary Perspectives.* New York: Aldine.

Hawkey, C.; Frankel, T.; Ashton, D.; Nevill, G.; Hart, M.; and Alderson, C. 1980. Preliminary report of a study of changes in red blood cells of zoo animals during sedation. In *The Comparative Pathology of Zoo Animals,* ed. R. J. Montali and G. Migadi, 625–32. Washington, D.C.: Smithsonian Institution Press.

*Hawkey, C. M., and Hart, M. G. 1986. Haematological reference values for adult pumas, tigers, leopards, jaguars and cheetahs. *Res. Vet. Sci.* 41:268–69.

*Hedrick, P. W. 1987. Genetic bottlenecks. *Science* 237:963.

*Heeney, J. L.; Evermann, J. F.; McKeirnan, A. J.; Marker-Kraus, L.; Roelke, M. E.; Bush, M.; Wildt, D. E.; Meltzer, D. G.; Colly, L.; Lukas, J.; Manton, V. J.; Caro, T.; and O'Brien, S. J. 1990. Prevalence and implications of feline coronavirus infections of captive and free-ranging cheetahs *(Acinonyx jubatus). J. Virol.* 64:1964–72.

Heinsohn, R. G. 1987. Age-dependent vigilance in winter aggregations of cooperatively breeding white-winged choughs *(Corcovax melanorhampos). Behav. Ecol. Sociobiol.* 20:303–6.

Hemker, T. P.; Lindzey, F. G.; and Ackerman, B. B. 1984. Population characteristics and movement patterns of cougars in southern Utah. *J. Wildl. Mgmt.* 48(4):1275–84.

Hemker, T. P.; Lindzey, F. G.; Ackerman, B. B.; and Button, J. J. 1986. Predictive energetics model for cougars. In *Cats of the World: Biology, Conservation, and Management,* ed. S. D. Miller and D. D. Everett, 333–52. Washington, D.C.: National Wildlife Federation.

*Hemmer, H. 1976a. Fossil history of living Felidae. In *The World's Cats,* vol. 3(2), ed. R. L. Eaton, 1–14. Carnivore Research Institute, University of Washington, Seattle. Also in *Carnivore,* 1979, 2:58–62.

*Hemmer, H. 1976b. Gestation period and post-natal development in felids. In *The World's Cats,* vol. 3, ed. R. L. Eaton, 143–65. Carnivore Research Institute, University of Washington, Seattle.

Hemmer, H. 1978. The evolutionary systematics of living Felidae: Present status and current problems. *Carnivore* 1:71–79.

*Hemmer, H. 1988. Asiatic cheetah. *Cat News* 9:13.

*Hennig, R. 1969. Geparden-Vorkommen in Tunesien. *Z. Saugetierk.* 34:318–19.

*Hennig, R. 1979. The cheetah *(Acinonyx jubatus)* in South West Africa/Namibia and the possibilities for the regulation and conservation of the population. *Z. Jagdwiss.* 25(3): 129–39.

Henning, S. J. 1981. Postnatal development: Coordination of feeding, digestion and metabolism. *Am. Physiol.* 241:199–214.

Henry, W. 1975. A preliminary report on visitor use in Amboseli National Park. Working paper no. 263. Institute for Development Studies, University of Nairobi.

*Herdman, R. 1972a. A brief discussion on reproductive and maternal behavior in the cheetah *(Acinonyx jubatus). Proc. AAZPA* 1972:110–23.

*Herdman, R. 1972b. Captive cheetah reproduction. *Zoonooz* 45(10): 4–12.

*Herdman, R. 1973. Cheetah breeding program. In *The World's Cats,* vol. 1, ed. R. L. Eaton, 255–63. Winston, Oreg.: World Wildlife Safari.

Herrington, S. J. 1986. Phylogenetic relationships of the wild cats of the world. Ph.D. diss., University of Kansas.

Hershkovitz, P. 1969. The evolution of mammals on southern continents. VI. The recent mammals of the neotropical region: A zoogeographic and ecological review. *Q. Rev. Biol.* 44:1–70.

*Heublein, E. 1968. The cheetah . . . a fast cat. *Zoonooz* 41(3): 10–13.

Hilborn, R. In press. A workshop simulation model to evaluate alternative management policies for the Serengeti ecosystem. In *Serengeti II: Research, Conservation and Management of an Ecosystem,* ed. A. R. E. Sinclair and P. Arcese. Chicago: University of Chicago Press.

*Hildebrand, M. 1959. Motions of the running cheetah and horse. *J. Mammal.* 40: 481–95.

*Hildebrand, M. 1960. How animals run. *Sci. Am.* 202:148–57.

*Hildebrand, M. 1961. Further studies on locomotion of the cheetah. *J. Mammal.* 42:84–91.

*Hildebrand, M. 1984. Rotations of the leg segments of three fast-running cursors and an elephant *(Elephas maximus). J. Mammal.* 65:718–20.

*Hildebrand, M., and Hurley, J. P. 1985. Energy of the oscillating legs of a fast moving cheetah, pronghorn, jackrabbit and elephant. *J. Morphol.* 184:23–31.

*Hill, A. 1972. The isolation of *Myocoplasma argini* from captive wild cats. *Vet. Rec.* 91(9): 224–25.

*Hills, D. M., and Smithers, R. H. N. 1980. The "king cheetah": A historical review. *Arnoldia* 9:1–23.

Hilzheimer, M. 1913. Uber neue Geparden nebst Bemerkungen uber die Nomenklatur dieser Tiere. *Sitz.-ber. Gesell. naturf. Freunde Berlin* 5:283–92.

Hirshfield, M. F., and Tinkle, D. W. 1975. Natural selection and the evolution of reproductive effort. *Proc. Natl. Acad. Sci. USA* 72:2227–31.

Hirst, S. 1969. Populations in a Transvaal lowveld nature reserve. *Zool. Afr.* 4: 199–230.

*Hiscocks, K., and Bowland, A. E. 1989. Passage rates of prey components through cheetahs. *Lammergeyer* 40:18–20.

*Hitchins, P. 1975. Last stronghold of the cheetah. *Endangered Wildlife* 1(2): 2–3.

Hofer, H., and East, M. 1993. How predators cope with migratory prey: The commuting system of spotted hyaenas in the Serengeti. III. Attendance and maternal care. *Anim. Behav.* 46:575–89.

Hofer, H., and East, M. In press. Population dynamics, population size, and the commuting system of spotted hyaenas in the Serengeti. In *Serengeti II: Research, Conservation and Management of an Ecosystem,* ed. A. R. E. Sinclair and P. Arcese. Chicago: University of Chicago Press.

Hogg, J. T. 1984. Mating in bighorn sheep: Multiple creative male strategies. *Science* 225:526–29.

*Holeckova, D. 1992. Postnatal development of three cheetahs reared by a dog at Dvur Kalore Zoo. In *International cheetah studbook* 1991, ed. L. Marker-Kraus, NOAHS Center, National Zoological Park, Washington, D.C.

*Holeckova, D.; Sisa, Z.; and Ptacek, M. 1990. Breeding of the cheetah, *Acinonyx jubatus* (Schreber, 1775) at Czechoslovak zoological gardens. *Gazella* 17:49–92.

Holley, A. J. F. 1981. Naturally arising adoption in the herring gull. *Anim. Behav.* 29:302–3.

*Hollister, N. 1911. The nomenclature of the cheetahs. *Proc. Biol. Soc. Wash.* 24:225–26.

*Holmes, M. 1981. Cheetah hunting in the Kalahari. *Afr. Wildl.* 35(6): 22–25.

*Holmes, M. 1983. The "king cheetah." *Koolewong* 12(2): 4–5.

*Holmes, R. G., and Ngethe, S. 1973. Restraint of captive and wild lion *(Panthera leo),* leopard *(Panthera pardus),* and cheetah *(Acinonyx jubatus). Vet. Rec.* 92:290–92.

*Holzinger, E. A., and Silberman, M. S. 1974. Salmonellosis in zoo born cheetah cubs. *Proc. AAZV* 1974:204–6.

*Hoogstraal, H. K.; Wassif, K.; Helmy, I.; and Kaiser, M. N. 1966/67. The cheetah, *Acinonyx jubatus* Schreber, in Egypt. *Bull. Zool. Soc. Egypt* 21:63–68.

Hopkins, R. A.; Kutilek, M. J.; and Shreve, G. L. 1986. Density and home range characteristics of mountain lions in the Diablo Range of California. In *Cats of the World: Biology, Conservation, and Management,* ed. S. D. Miller and D. D. Everett, 223–35. Washington, D.C.: National Wildlife Federation.

*Hopwell, A. T. 1945. Adaptations in the bones of the forelimb of lion, leopard and cheetah. *Zool. J. Linn. Soc.* 40:259–78.

*Hopwell, A. T. 1946. Notes on the interior of the skull of lion, leopard and cheetah. *Zool. J. Linn. Soc.* 41:369–78.

*Hora, J. 1979. Chov geparda *(Acinonyx jubatus)* v zejeti. *Sbornik Severoceske zoologicke zahrady v Liberci* 1:27–44.

*Horii, Y.; Usiu, M.; and Yanagida, T. 1981. Ancylostoma Braziliense de faria, 1910 recovered from imported cheetahs (in Japanese). *Jpn. J. Parasitol.* 30(4):355–61.

Horn, H. S. 1978. Optimal tactics of reproduction and life-history. In *Behavioural Ecology: An Evolutionary Approach,* ed. J. R. Krebs and N. B. Davies, 411–29. Oxford: Blackwell Scientific Publications.

Hornocker, M. 1969. Winter territoriality in mountain lions. *J. Wildl. Mgmt.* 33:457–64.

Hornocker, M. 1970. An analysis of mountain lion predation upon mule deer and elk in the Idaho Primitive Area. *Wildl. Monogr.* 21:1–39.

Hornocker, M., and Bailey, T. 1986. Natural regulation in three species of felids. In *Cats of the World: Biology, Conservation, and Management*, ed. S. D. Miller and D. D. Everett, 211–20. Washington, D.C.: National Wildlife Federation.

*Horzinek, M., and Osterhaus, A. 1978. Feline infectious peritonitus: A worldwide survey. *Am. J. Vet. Res.* 40:1387–92.

Houston, A. C.; Clark, C. W.; McNamara, J.; and Mangel, M. 1988. Dynamic models in behavioral and evolutionary ecology. *Nature* 332:29–34.

Houston, D. C. 1974. Food searching behaviour in griffon vultures. *E. Afr. Wildl. J.* 12:63–77.

Houston, D. C. 1979. The adaptations of scavengers. In *Serengeti: Dynamics of an Ecosystem*, ed. A. R. E. Sinclair and M. Norton-Griffiths, 263–86. Chicago: University of Chicago Press.

*Howard, J. G.; Barone, M. A.; Bush, M.; and Wildt, D. E. 1991. A heterologous salt-stored zonae pelliculae assay for assessing sperm capacitation and the impact of teratospermia in the cheetah *(Acinonyx jubatus)*. *J. Androl.* 12 *(Suppl.* 1): 101.

*Howard, J. G.; Bush, M.; Wildt, D. E.; Brand, D. J.; Ebedes, H.; van Dyk, A.; and Meltzer, D. 1981. Preliminary reproductive physiology studies on cheetahs in South Africa. *Proc. AAZV* 1981:72–74.

*Howard, J. G., and Caldwell, H. 1991. First cheetah cub produced by artificial insemination. *AAZPA Communique* 10:13.

*Howard, J. G.; Donoghue, A. M.; Goodrowe, K. L.; Blumer, E.; Snodgrass, K.; Starnes, D.; Tucker, M.; Bush, M.; and Wildt, D. E. 1992. Successful induction of ovarian activity and laparoscopic intrauterine artificial insemination in the cheetah *(Acinonyx jubatus)*. *J. Zoo Wildl. Med.* 23:288–300.

*Howard, J. G.; Munson, L.; McAloose, D.; Kriete, M.; Bush, M.; and Wildt, D. E. 1993. Comparative evaluation of seminal, vaginal and rectal bacterial flora in the cheetah and domestic cat. *Zoo Biol.* 12:81–96.

Hrdy, S. B. 1976. Care and exploitation of nonhuman primate infants by conspecifics other than the mother. *Adv. Study Behav.* 6:101–58.

Hrdy, S. B. 1977. *The Langurs of Abu.* Cambridge, Mass.: Harvard University Press.

*Huber, W., and Kung, K. 1967. Beobachten au Geparden des Amboseli—Reservates (Kenya). 1. Vorbemeskungen zur Systematik, Verbreitung und Biologie. *Jb. naurh. Mus. Bern.* 1963–1965:147–54.

*Hunt, D. 1968. The capture of cheetah. *Zoonooz* 42:14–17.

Hunte, W., and Horrocks, J. A. 1987. Kin and non-kin interventions in the aggressive disputes of vervet monkeys. *Behav. Ecol. Sociobiol.* 20:257–63.

*Huntley, B. J. 1973. Leopard and cheetah survey: Notes on the Angolan situation. Unpublished typescript.

*Hussain, M. M.; Singh, J.; and Kumar, R. 1988. A note on the repeated xylazine anaesthesia in cheetah *(Acinonyx jubatus)*. *Indian J. Vet. Surg.* 9(2): 160–62.

Husson, A. M. 1978. *The Mammals of Suriname.* Leiden: E. J. Brill.

*Hyslop, N. 1955. Feline enteritis in the lynx, the cheetah and other wild Felidae. *Brit. Vet. J.* 3(9): 573–77.

Ilany, G. 1990. The spotted ambassadors of a vanishing world. *Israelal,* May/June, 18–24.

*Ignatev, R. P. 1983. The first record of a cheetah birth in captivity in the USSR. *Priroda Mosk.* 5:88–89.

Ingles, J. M. 1965. Zambian mammals collected for the British Museum in 1962. *The Puku* 3:75–86.

IUCN. 1972. *Red Data Book.* Morges, Switzerland: IUCN.

IUCN. 1976. *Red Data Book.* Morges, Switzerland: IUCN.

Iwago, M. 1986. The Serengeti: A portfolio. *Natl. Geogr.* 169(5): 560–83.

*Jackson, P. 1984. India's interest in re-introducing cheetahs. *Cat News* 1:13.

*Jackson, P. 1988a. Asiatic cheetah. *Cat News* 9:13.

*Jackson, P. 1988b. Cheetah in Zimbabwe. *Cat News* 8:9–10.

*Jackson, P. 1988c. Cheetah removed from South African Red Data Book. *Cat News* 9:13.

*Jackson, P. 1989. Farmers for cheetah hunting in Zimbabwe. *Cat News* 10:13.

*Jackson, P. 1990. Cheetah surviving in Iran. *Cat News* 13:13.

Jackson, P. 1991. Man versus man-eaters. In *Great Cats: Majestic Creatures of the Wild,* ed. J. Seidensticker and S. Lumpkin, 212–13. Emmaus, Pa.: Rodale Press.

Jackson, P. 1992. Poaching of bones threatens world's last tigers. *Cat News* 17: 2–3.

Jackson, R., and Ahlborn, G. 1989. Snow leopards *(Panthera uncia)* in Nepal— home range and movements. *Natl. Geogr. Res.* 5:161–75.

*Jacobi, E. F. 1982. The cheetah of Pretoria. *Artis. AMST* 28(3): 92–93.

*Jager, H. G.; Booker, H. H.; and Hubschle, O. J. B. 1990. Anthrax in cheetahs *(Acinonyx jubatus)* in Namibia. *J. Wildl. Dis.* 26:423–24.

*James, A. 1962. The puzzle of king cheetahs. *The Field* 24:1018–19.

Janson, C. H. 1992. Evolutionary ecology of primate social structure. In *Evolutionary Ecology and Human Behavior,* ed. E. A. Smith and B. Winterhalder, 93–130. New York: Aldine.

Jarman, P. J. 1974. The social organisation of antelope in relation to their ecology. *Behaviour* 48:215–67.

Jarman, P. J., and Southwell, C. J. 1986. Grouping, associations, and reproductive strategies in eastern grey kangaroos. In *Ecological Aspects of Social Evolution: Birds and Mammals,* ed. D. I. Rubenstein and R. W. Wrangham, 399–428. Princeton: Princeton University Press.

*Jeng, C. R.; Lui, S. K.; Lai, R. Y.; and Chiu, Y. C. 1988. Case report of ollulanus tricuspis infection in cheetahs *(Acinonyx jubatus). J. Chin. Soc. Vet. Sci.* 14: 253–57.

Jewell, P. A. 1972. Social organisation and movements of topi *(Damiliscus korrigum)* during the rut at Inshasha, Queen Elizabeth Park, Uganda. *Zool. Afr.* 7: 233–55.

*Jones, M. L. 1972. The cheetah in captivity: A brief analysis. *Proc. AAZPA* 1972: 126–29.

*Jones, O. G. 1953. Tuberculosis in a cheetah: The use of antibiotics and modern chemotherapeutic agents. *Vet. Rec.* 65(29): 453.

*Joubert, E., and Mostert, P. K. N. 1975. Distribution patterns and status of some mammals in South West Africa. *Madoqua* 9:5–44.

*Junge, R. E., and Miller, R. E. 1988. Persistent regurgitation in a cheetah *(Acinonyx jubatus). J. Zoo Anim. Med.* 18:151–52.

*Junge, R. E.; Miller, R. E.; Boever, W. J.; Scherba, G.; and Sundberg, J. 1991. Persistent cutaneous ulcers associated with feline herpesvirus type 1 infection in a cheetah. *J. Am. Vet. Med. Assoc.* 198:1057–58.

*Karami, M. 1992. Cheetah distribution in Khorasan Province, Iran. *Cat News* 16:4.

Karesh, W. B.; Smith, F.; and Frazier-Taylor, H. 1987. A remote method for obtaining skin biopsy samples. *Conserv. Biol.* 3:261–62.

*Kat, P. W. 1993. Genetics of the cheetah. *Swara* 16(5):13.

*Kaufman, P. H. 1974. Obstructive jaundice in a cheetah. *Proc. AAZV* 1974: 79–84.

*Keh, B., and Hawthorne, R. M. 1977. The induction and eradication of an exotic ectoparasite fly, *Hippobosca longipennis* (Diptera: Hippoboscidae), in California. *J. Zoo Anim. Med.* 8:19–24.

Kenward, R. E. 1978. Hawks and doves: Factors affecting success and selection in goshawk attacks on wood-pigeons. *J. Anim. Ecol.* 47:449–60.

*Khalaf, N.-A. B. 1987. The cheetah *(Acinonyx jubatus)* in Saabrucken Zoo, Germany. *Gazelle* 11:1–11.

*Kieser, J. A., and Groenveveld, H. T. 1991. Fluctuating odontometric asymmetry, morphological variability, and genetic monomorphism in the cheetah *Acinonyx jubatus. Evolution* 45:1175–83.

*King, N. E. 1986. Behavior of a group of cheetahs *(Acinonyx jubatus)* in captivity. Ph.D. diss., University of California, Davis.

Kingdon, J. 1977. *East African Mammals.* Vol. 3A, *Carnivores.* New York: Academic Press.

*Kirch, M. 1984. Gebt unseren Geparden eine chance. *Das Tier,* Apr., 5–7.

*Kirkpatrick, K. M. 1952. A record of the cheetah (*A. jubatus* Erxleben) in Chitoor district, Madras state. *J. Bombay Nat. Hist. Soc.* 50(4): 931–32.

Kitchen, D. W. 1974. Social behaviour and ecology of the pronghorn. *Wildl. Monogr.* 38:1–96.

*Kitchener, A. 1991. *The Natural History of the Wild Cats.* London: Christopher Helm, A. & C. Black.

Kleiman, D. G. 1977. Monogamy in mammals. *Q. Rev. Biol.* 52:39–69.

Kleiman, D. G., and Eisenberg, J. F. 1973. Comparisons of canid and felid social systems from an evolutionary perspective. *Anim. Behav.* 21:637–59.

Knight, S. K., and Knight, R. L. 1986. Vigilance patterns of bald eagles *(Haliaetus leucocephalus)* feeding in groups. *Auk* 103:263–72.

Knowlton, N. 1982. Parental care and sex role reversal. In *Current Problems in Sociobiology,* ed. King's College Sociobiology Group, Cambridge, 203–22. Cambridge: Cambridge University Press.

Koehler, G. 1987. The bobcat. *Audubon Wildlife Report,* 399–409.

Koehler, G. M.; Hornocker, M. G.; and Hash, H. S. 1979. Lynx movements and habitat use in Montana. *Can. Field Nat.* 93:441–42.

Koenig, W. D. 1988. Reciprocal altruism in birds: A critical review. *Ethol. Sociobiol.* 9:73–84.

Konig, B., and Markl, H. 1987. Maternal care in house mice. I. The weaning strategy means for parental manipulation of offspring quality. *Behav. Ecol. Sociobiol.* 20:1–9.

*Korneeva, V. I. 1984. Outbreak of infectious rhinotracheitis in cheetah of Moscow Zoo. *Proc. Int. Symp. Dis. Zoo Anim.* 26:331–34.

Kralik, S. 1967. Breeding the caracal lynx at Brno Zoo. *Int. Zoo Yrbk.* 7:132.

*Kraus, D., and Marker-Kraus, L. 1991. The status of the cheetah *(Acinonyx jubatus).* Data sheet prepared for the IUCN/SSC Cat Specialist Group.

*Kraus, D., and Marker-Kraus, L. 1992. Current status of the cheetah. Cheetah Conservation Fund, NOAHS Center, National Zoological Park, Washington, D.C.

Krebs, J. R., and Davies, N. B. 1978. *Behavioural Ecology: An Evolutionary Approach.* Oxford: Blackwell Scientific Publications.

*Krishnan, M. 1965. The cheetah, cheetal. *J. Wildl. Preserv. Soc. India* 8(1).

*Krishne Gowda, C. D. 1975. Plans for breeding large mammals in India. In *Breeding Endangered Species in Captivity,* ed. R. D. Martin, 309–13. New York: Academic Press.

Kropowski, J. L. 1993. Alternative reproductive tactics in male eastern gray squirrels: "Making the best of a bad job." *Behav. Ecol.* 4:165–71.

Kruuk, H. 1972. *The Spotted Hyena: A Study of Predation and Social Behavior.* Chicago: University of Chicago Press.

Kruuk, H. 1975. Functional aspects of social hunting by carnivores. In *Function and Evolution in Behaviour,* ed. G. Baerends, C. Beer, and A. Manning, 119–41. Oxford: Clarendon Press.

Kruuk, H., and Macdonald, D. 1985. Group territories of carnivores: Empires and enclaves. In *Behavioural Ecology,* ed. R. M. Sibly and R. H. Smith, 521–26. Oxford: Blackwell Scientific Publications.

*Kruuk, H., and Turner, M. 1967. Comparative notes on predation by lion, leopard, cheetah and wild dog in the Serengeti area, East Africa. *Mammalia* 31:1–27.

*Kuenkel, R. 1978. Cheetahs—swift cats of the Serengeti. *Geo* 1:94–110.

Kuhme, W. 1965. Freilandstudien zur Soziologie des Hyanenhundes *(Lycaon pictus lupinus* Thomas 1902). *Z. Tierpsychol.* 22:495–541.

Kummer, H. 1968. *Social Organization of Hamadryas Baboons.* Chicago: University of Chicago Press.

Kurtén, B. 1968. *Pleistocene Mammals of Europe.* London: Weidenfeld and Nicholson.

*Kushnavev, V. P., and Samygin, F. I. 1984. Microsporosis and candidiasis in tigers and cheetahs. *Proc. Int. Symp. Dis. Zoo Anim.* 26:405–8.

*Kymhapeb, B. N., and Cam, H. H. H. 1984. Microsporosis and candidiasis in tigers and cheetah. *IPPEN.*

*Labuschange, W. 1970. A bio-ecological and behavioral study of the cheetah, *Acinonyx jubatus. Progress Report from the Mammal Research Institute,* Apr., June, and Sept., University of Pretoria. Typescript.

*Labuschagne, W. 1974. Ecology and ethology of the cheetah in Kruger and Kalahari Gemsbok National Parks, South Africa. Ph.D. diss., University of Pretoria.

*Labuschagne, W. 1979. 'N Bio-ekologiese en gedragstudie van die jagluiperd *Acinonyx jubatus jubatus* (Schreber 1775). M.Sc. thesis, University of Pretoria.

*Labuschagne, W. 1981. *Aspects of Cheetah Ecology in the Kalahari Gemsbok National Park.* 36th Annual Conference Int. Assoc. Zoo Directors, Washington, D.C.

Lack, D. L. 1954. *The Natural Regulation of Animal Numbers.* Oxford: Clarendon Press.

Lack, D. L. 1966. *Population Studies of Birds.* Oxford: Clarendon Press.

Lack, D. L. 1968. *Ecological Adaptations for Breeding in Birds.* London: Methuen.

*Laemmerzahl, A. F., and Velez, R. A. 1986. The status of cheetahs in the Nairobi National Park—a response to declining herbivore densities. Department of Biology, George Mason University, Va. Unpublished typescript.

Lamprecht, J. 1978a. On diet, foraging behaviour and interspecific food competition of jackals in the Serengeti National Park, East Africa. *Z. Saugetierkunde* 43:210–33.

*Lamprecht, J. 1978b. The relationship between food competition and foraging group size in some larger carnivores: A hypothesis. *Z. Tierpsychol.* 46:337–43.

*Lamprecht, J. 1981. The function of social hunting in larger terrestrial carnivores. *Mammal Rev.* 11(4): 169–80.

Lamprey, H. F. 1964. Estimation of the large mammal densities, biomass and energy exchange in the Tarangire Game Reserve and the Masai steppe in Tanganyika. *E. Afr. Wildl. J.* 2:1–46.

Larson, R. E. 1980. Infertility in the male dog. In *Current Therapy in Theriogenology,* ed. D. Morrow, 646–54. Philadelphia: W. B. Saunders.

*Lasley, W., and Wing, A. 1985. Stimulating ovarian function in exotic carnivores with pulses of GnRH. *San Diego Occasional Papers,* 14–15.

*Last stronghold of cheetah. 1975. *Endangered Wildl.* (Endangered Wildlife Trust, Johannesburg) 1(2).

*Laurenson, M. K. 1991a. Cheetah cub mortality. In *Great Cats: Majestic Creatures of the Wild,* ed. J. Seidensticker and S. Lumpkin, 144. Sydney: Weldon Owen.

*Laurenson, M. K. 1991b. Cheetahs never win. *BBC Wildlife* 9:98–105.

*Laurenson, M. K. 1992. Reproductive strategies in wild female cheetahs. Ph.D. diss., University of Cambridge.

*Laurenson, M. K. 1993. Early maternal behavior of wild cheetahs: Implications for captive husbandry. *Zoo Biol.* 12:31–43.

*Laurenson, M. K. In press-a. Cub growth and maternal care in cheetahs. *Behav. Ecol.*

*Laurenson, M. K. In press-b. High juvenile mortality in cheetahs and its consequences for maternal care. *J. Zool.*

*Laurenson, M. K. In press-c. Implications of high offspring mortality for cheetah population dynamics. In *Serengeti II: Research, Conservation and Management of an Ecosystem,* ed. A. R. E. Sinclair and P. Arcese. Chicago: University of Chicago Press.

*Laurenson, M. K., and Caro, T. M. In press. Monitoring the effects of non-trivial handling in free-living cheetahs. *Anim. Behav.*

*Laurenson, M. K.; Caro, T. M.; and Borner, M. 1992. Female cheetah reproduction. *Natl. Geogr. Res. Expl.* 8:64–75.

Lazarus, J. 1979. The early warning function of flocking in birds: An experimental study with captive quelea. *Anim. Behav.* 27:855–65.

Lazarus, J., and Inglis, I. R. 1978. The breeding behaviour of the pink-footed goose: Parental care and vigilant behaviour during the fledgling period. *Behaviour* 65:62–88.

Lazarus, J., and Inglis, I. R. 1986. Shared and unshared parental investment, parent-offspring conflict and brood size. *Anim. Behav.* 34:1791–1804.

Leader-Williams, N., and Albon, S. D. 1988. Allocation of resources for conservation. *Nature* 336:533–35.

Leakey, L. S. B. 1967. An early Miocene member of the Hominidae. *Nature* 213:155.

Le Boeuf, B. J. 1974. Male-male competition and reproductive success in elephant seals. *Am. Zool.* 14:163–76.

*Leclerc-Cassan, M. 1976. Management (as pets) and principal diseases of wild carnivores (fennec, coati, kinkajou, genet, ocelot, margay, cheetah). *Receuil Med. Vet.* 152:769–79.

*Ledger, J. 1987. Farmers and cheetah. *Endangered Wildlife Trust: A special report,* June 5:15–16.

*Lee, A. R. 1992a. Management guidelines for species kept in captivity. Regent's Park Zoo, London. 50 pp. Unpublished typescript.

*Lee, A. R. 1992b. Management guidelines for the welfare of zoo animals: Cheetah *(Acinonyx jubatus).* Federation of Zoological Gardens of Great Britain and Ireland, London, Sept. 34 pp.

Lee, P. C., and Johnson, J. A. 1992. Sex differences in alliances, and the acquisition and maintenance of dominance status among immature primates. In *Coalitions and Alliances in Humans and Other Animals,* ed. A. H. Harcourt and F. B. M. de Waal, 391–414. Oxford: Oxford University Press.

Le Houérou, H. N., and Gillet, H. 1986. Conservation versus desertization in African arid lands. In *Conservation Biology: The Study of Scarcity and Diversity,* ed. M. E. Soulé, 444–61. Sunderland, Mass.: Sinauer Associates.

Lekagul, B., and McNeely, J. 1977. *Mammals of Thailand.* Bangkok: Karusapa Press.

Lembeck, M. 1986. Long term behavioral and population dynamics of an unharvested bobcat population in San Diego. In *Cats of the World: Biology, Conservation and Management,* ed. S. D. Miller and D. D. Everett, 305–10. Washington, D.C.: National Wildlife Federation.

*Lever, C. 1980. The vanishing cheetah. *Loris* 15(3): 186.

*Lewin, R. 1987. Bottlenecked cheetahs. *Science* 235:1327 and 237:963.

Leyhausen, P. 1965. The communal organization of solitary mammals. *Symp. Zool. Soc. Lond.* 14:249–63.

*Leyhausen, P. 1979. *Cat Behaviour: The Predatory and Social Behaviour of Domestic and Wild Cats* (translated by B. A. Tonkin). New York: Garland.

Liberg, O., and Sandell, M. 1988. Spatial organisation and reproductive tactics in the domestic cat and other felids. In *The Domestic Cat: The Biology of Its Behaviour,* ed. D. C. Turner and P. Bateson, 83–98. Cambridge: Cambridge University Press.

*Lindburg, D. G. 1986. On food and the feeding of exotic animals. *Zoonooz* 59(8): 16–17.

*Lindburg, D. G. 1989. When cheetahs are kings. *Zoonooz* 62(3): 5–10.

*Lindburg, D. G. 1991. On getting cheetahs to reproduce. *Cheetah News: Cheetah SSP Newsletter.* Zoological Society of San Diego Center for Reproduction of Endangered Species: 4–5.

*Lindburg, D.; Durrant, B. S.; Millard, S. E.; and Oosterhuis, J. E. 1993. Fertility assessment of cheetah males with poor quality semen. *Zoo Biol.* 12:97–103.

*Lindburg, D.; Millard, S.; and Lasley, B. 1985. Induced estrus in the cheetah. *Proc. AAZPA* 1985:560–63.

Litvaitis, J. A.; Sherburne, J. A.; and Bissonnette, J. A. 1986. Bobcat habitat use and home range size in relation to prey density. *J. Wildl. Mgmt.* 50:110–17.

Litvaitis, J. A.; Stevens, C. L.; and Mautz, W. W. 1984. Age, sex, and weights of bobcats in relation to winter diet. *J. Wildl. Mgmt.* 48:632–35.

*Lotshaw, R. 1980. The Cincinnati Zoo's successful cheetah propagation program. *Reg. Proc. AAZPA,* Great Lakes Reg. 1980:104–7.

Lott, D. F. 1991. *Intraspecific Variation in the Social Systems of Wild Vertebrates.* Cambridge: Cambridge University Press.

Loudon, A. S. I. 1985. Lactation and neonatal survival of mammals. *Symp. Zool. Soc. Lond.* 54:183–207.

Loughlin, T. R. 1980. Home range and territoriality of sea otters near Monterey, California. *J. Wildl. Mgmt.* 44:576–82.

Loveridge, G. G. 1986. Bodyweight changes and energy intake of cats during gestation and lactation. *Anim. Technol.* 37:7–15.

Loveridge, G. G. 1987. Some factors affecting kitten growth. *Anim. Technol.* 38: 9–18.

*Lowry, A. 1975. Cheetah research project: Etosha National Park. A report presented at the annual meeting of the Professional Officers of the Division of Nature Conservation and Tourism, South West Africa. University of Pretoria. Unpublished typescript.

*Lowry, A. 1976a. Aspects of the cheetah situation in Southern Africa. *Proc. Int. Symp. on Endangered Wildlife in Southern Africa,* ed. J. D. Skinner, 32–35. Johannesburg: Endangered Wildlife Trust.

*Lowry, A. 1976b. Countdown? *Afr. Wildl.* 30(6): 12–14.

*Lowry, A. 1976c. Some thoughts on the possible management of the Etosha National Park cheetah study. A report presented at the Annual Professional Officers Meeting of the Division of Nature Conservation and Tourism, South West Africa. Hardcap Recreational Resort. Unpublished typescript.

Ludlow, M., and Sunquist, M. 1987. Ecology and behavior of ocelots in Venezuela. *Natl. Geogr. Res.* 3:447–61.

*Lumpkin, S. 1992. Cheetahs. *Zoogoer,* July/Aug.

*MacBride, E. W. 1932. The cheetah in Zambia. *Proc. Zool. Soc. Lond.* 814–16.

McClure, P. A. 1981. Sex-biased reduction in food-restricted wood rats *Neotoma floridiana. Science* 211:1058–60.

Macdonald, D. W. 1979. Some observations and field experiments on the urine marking behaviour of the red fox, *Vulpes vulpes* L. *Z. Tierpsychol.* 51:1–22.

Macdonald, D. W. 1983. The ecology of carnivore social behaviour. *Nature* 301: 379–84.

Macdonald, D. W., ed. 1984. *Encylopedia of Mammals*. Vol. 1. London: Allen and Unwin.

Macdonald, D. W. 1985. The carnivores: Order Carnivora. In *Social Odours in Mammals*, ed. R. E. Brown and D. W. Macdonald, 628–722. Oxford: Clarendon Press.

Macdonald, D. W.; Apps, P. J.; Carr, G. M.; and Kerby, G. 1987. Social dynamics, nursing coalitions and infanticide among farm cats. *Adv. Ethol.* 28:1–66.

McGowan, K. J., and Woolfenden, G. E. 1989. A sentinel system in the Florida scrub jay. *Anim. Behav.* 37:1000–1006.

*McKeown, S. 1990. Status of the cheetah within the British Isles. Report to the Joint Management of Species Group Meeting, Nov. 1990. Unpublished typescript.

*McKeown, S. 1991. The cheetah. In *Management Guidelines for Exotic Cats*, ed. J. Partridge, 82–91. Bristol: Association of British Wild Animal Keepers.

*McKeown, S. In press. JMSG regional cheetah studbook. Fota Wildlife Park, Carrigtwohill, Co. Cork.

*McKie, R. 1991. Race against time. *Green Magazine*, Feb., 24–30.

MacKinnon, J. R. 1974. The ecology and behaviour of wild orangutans (*Pongo pygmaeus*). *Anim. Behav.* 22:3–74.

MacKinnon, J., and MacKinnon, K. 1986. *Review of the Protected Areas System in the Afrotropical Realm*. Morges, Switzerland: UNEP & IUCN.

*McLaughlin, R. T. 1970. Aspects of the biology of the cheetah (*Acinonyx jubatus*, Schreber) in Nairobi National Park. M.Sc. thesis, University of Nairobi.

McNab, B. K. 1986. The influence of food habits on the energetics of eutherian mammals. *Ecol. Monogr.* 56:1–19.

MacNair, M. R., and Parker, G. A. 1978. Models of parent-offspring conflict. II. Promiscuity. *Anim. Behav.* 26:111–22.

McNaughton, S. J. 1983. Serengeti grassland ecology: The role of composite factors and contingency in community organization. *Ecol. Monogr.* 53:291–320.

McNaughton, S. J. 1985. Ecology of a grazing ecosystem: The Serengeti. *Ecol. Monogr.* 55:259–94.

McNaughton, S. J. 1988. Mineral nutrition and spatial concentrations of African ungulates. *Nature* 334:343–45.

McNaughton, S. J. 1990. Mineral nutrition and seasonal movements of migratory ungulates. *Nature* 345:613–15.

*McVittie, R. 1979. Changes in the social behaviour of South West African cheetah. *Madoqua* 11(3): 171–84.

Machlis, L.; Dodd, P. W. D.; and Fentress, J. C. 1985. The pooling fallacy: Problems arising when individuals contribute more than one observation to the data set. *Z. Tierpsychol.* 68:201–14.

Maddock, L. 1979. The "migration" and grazing succession. In *Serengeti: Dynamics of an Ecosystem*, ed. A. R. E. Sinclair and M. Norton-Griffiths, 104–29. Chicago: University of Chicago Press.

Maehr, D. S.; Land, E. D.; and Roof, J. C. 1991. Florida panthers: Social ecology of Florida panthers. *Natl. Geogr. Res. Expl.* 7:414–31.

Maestripieri, D. 1992. Functional aspects of maternal aggression in mammals. *Can. J. Zool.* 70:1069–77.

Major, P. F. 1978. Predator-prey interactions in two schooling fishes, *Caranx ignobilis* and *Stolephorus purpureus*. *Anim. Behav.* 26:760–77.

Makacha, S., and Schaller, G. B. 1969. Observations on lions in the Lake Manyara National Park. Tanzania. *E. Afr. Wildl. J.* 7:99–103.

Malcolm, J. R., and Marten, K. 1982. Natural selection and the communal rearing of pups in African wild dogs (*Lycaon pictus*). *Behav. Ecol. Sociobiol.* 10:1–13.

*Manton, V. J. A. 1970. Breeding cheetah at Whipsnade Park. *Int. Zoo Yrbk.* 10:85–86.

*Manton, V. J. A. 1971. A further report on breeding cheetahs at Whipsnade Zoo. *Int. Zoo Yrbk.* 11:125–26.

*Manton, V. J. A. 1972. Captive breeding of cheetahs. In *Proc. Conf. on Breeding Endangered Species as an Aid to Their Survival,* Jersey, May. Unpublished typescript.

*Manton, V. J. A. 1974. Birth of a cheetah to a captive bred mother. *Int. Zoo Yrbk.* 14:126–29.

*Manton, V. J. A. 1975a. Captive breeding of cheetahs. In *Breeding Endangered Species in Captivity,* ed. R. D. Martin, 337–44. New York: Academic Press.

*Manton, V. J. A. 1975b. Cheetah breeding at Whipsnade Park: A report on the first 17 births. *Int. Zoo Yrbk.* 15:157–60.

*Manton, V. J. A. 1979. Breeding of cheetah in close captivity. Paper given to cheetah symposium held in Eastern Transvaal, R.S.A.

*Manton, V. J. A. 1980. A half-century of home bred cheetahs. In *Management of Wild Cats in Captivity,* ed. J. Barzdo, 43–48. *Proc. 4th Symp. Assoc. Brit. Wild Animal Keepers.*

Marchetti, K., and Price, T. 1989. Differences in the foraging of juvenile and adult birds: The importance of developmental constraints. *Biol. Rev.* 64:51–70.

*Marker, L. 1983–1987. *North American Regional Cheetah Studbooks* 1983, 1984, 1985, 1986. Winston, Oreg.: Wildlife Safari Publications.

*Marker, L. 1985a. Factors in cheetah conservation. *Reg. Proc. AAZPA,* 139–44.

*Marker, L. 1985b. North American regional studbook questionnaire survey. Winston, Oreg.: Wildlife Safari Publications.

*Marker, L. 1985c. Summary of the cheetah studbook questionnaire. Winston, Oreg.: Wildlife Safari Publications.

*Marker, L., and Grisham, J. 1993. Captive breeding of cheetahs in North American zoos: 1987–1991. *Zoo Biol.* 12:5–18.

*Marker, L., and O'Brien, S. J. 1989. Captive breeding of the cheetah (*Acinonyx jubatus*) in North American zoos 1871–1986. *Zoo Biol.* 8:3–16.

*Marker-Kraus, L. 1988–1992. *International Cheetah Studbooks.* Washington, D.C.: NOAHS Center, National Zoological Park, Smithsonian Institution.

*Marker-Kraus, L.; Farrington, M.; Kraus, D.; Henkel, U.; and Bounds, D. 1990. International cheetah studbook questionnaire summary. Washington, D.C.: NOAHS Center, National Zoological Park, Smithsonian Institution.

*Marker-Kraus, L., and Kraus, D. 1990. Status of the cheetah in Zimbabwe and Namibia. *Cat News* 12:15–16.

*Marker-Kraus, L., and Kraus, D. 1991. *1991 Annual Report*. Windhoek, Namibia: Cheetah Conservation Fund.

*Marker-Kraus, L., and Kraus, D. 1993. The history of cheetahs in Namibia. *Swara* 16(5):8–12.

Marma, B. B., and Yunchis, V. V. 1968. Observations on the breeding, management and physiology of snow leopards at Kaunas Zoo from 1962 to 1967. *Int. Zoo Yrbk.* 8:66–74.

Marston, M. A. 1942. Winter relations of bobcats to white-tailed deer in Maine. *J. Wildl. Mgmt.* 6:328–37.

Martin, L. D. 1989. Fossil history of the terrestrial carnivora. In *Carnivore Behavior, Ecology, and Evolution*, ed. J. L. Gittleman, 536–68. Ithaca, N.Y.: Cornell University Press.

*Martin, L. D., and Gilbert, B. M. 1978. An American lion *(Panthera atrox)* from natural trap cave north central Wyoming. *Contrib. Geol. Univ. Wyo.* 16(2): 95–102.

*Martin, L. D.; Gilbert, B. M.; and Adams, D. B. 1977. A cheetah like cat in the North American Pleistocene. *Science* 195:981–82.

Martin, P., and Bateson, P. 1986. *Measuring behaviour*. Cambridge: Cambridge University Press.

Martin, P., and Caro, T. M. 1985. On the functions of play and its role in behavioural development. *Adv. Stud. Behav.* 15:59–103.

*Martin, S. N. 1978. Captivity's effect on 5 species of cats. B.A. thesis, Reed College, Portland, Oreg.

Martinez, D. R., and Klinghammer, E. 1970. The behaviour of the whale *Orcinus orca:* A review of the literature. *Z. Tierpsychol.* 27:828–39.

Matjushkin, E. N.; Zhivotchenko, V. I.; and Smirnov, E. N. 1977. The Amur tiger in the USSR. Morges, Switzerland: IUCN.

Matthews, L. H. 1941. Reproduction in the Scottish wild cat. *Proc. Zool. Soc. Lond.* 11:59–77.

Maynard Smith, J. 1964. Group selection and kin selection. *Nature* 201: 1145–47.

Maynard Smith, J. 1976. Group selection. *Q. Rev. Biol.* 51:277–283.

Maynard Smith, J. 1983. Game theory and the evolution of cooperation. In *Evolution from Molecules to Man*, ed. D. S. Bendall, 445–56. Cambridge: Cambridge University Press.

Mech, L. D. 1970. *The Wolf: The Ecology and Behavior of an Endangered Species*. Minneapolis: University of Minnesota Press.

Mech, L. D. 1980. Age, sex, reproduction and spatial organization of lynxes colonizing N.E. Minnesota. *J. Mammal.* 61:261–67.

Medway, L. 1978. *Wild Mammals of Malaya*. Oxford: Oxford University Press.

*Meeker, S. 1976. Cheetah: Earthbound flier. *Natl. Parks Conserv. Mag.* 50(12): 17–20.

*Meeker, W. E. 1973. Breeding cheetahs in a zoo environment. In *The World's Cats*, vol. 2, ed. R. L. Eaton, 172–85. Seattle, Wash.: Woodland Park Zoo.

*Meester, J. 1962. King cheetah in Northern Transvaal. *Afr. Wildl.* 16(1): 81–82.

*Meinertzhagen, R. 1955. The speed and altitude of bird flight (with notes on other animals). *Ibis* 97:114–15.

*Meltzer, D. G. A. 1974. Investigation into the fertility of cheetah males belonging to the Pretoria Zoological Gardens DeWildt Estates. Sept.–Dec. Pretoria. Unpublished typescript.

*Meltzer, D. G. A. 1977. Cheetah breeding. *Redwing* 1977:20–21.

*Meltzer, D. G. A. 1979. Cheetah research. *Zoon.* (Pretoria) (1): 1–3, 16.

*Meltzer, D. G. A. 1987. Reproduction in the male cheetah *(Acinonyx jubatus)* (Schreber 1776). M.Sc. thesis, University of Pretoria, South Africa.

*Meltzer, D. G. A.; Coubrough, R. I.; and Van Dyk, A. 1975. Cheetah breeding: A report on the Pretoria National Zoological Gardens De Wildt Project, Pretoria. Unpublished typescript.

Mendl, M. 1988. The effects of litter size variation on mother-offspring relationships and behavioural and physical development in several mammalian species (principally rodents). *J. Zool.* 215:15–34.

Mendl, M., and Paul, E. S. 1989. Observation of nursing and suckling behaviour as an indicator of milk transfer and parental investment. *Anim. Behav.* 37: 513–15.

*Menendez, I.; Rodriguez Diego, J.; and de la Cruz, J. 1984. Miasis generalizada fatal por larvas de *Cochliomyia* spp. (Diptera: Calliphoridae) en *Acinonyx jubatus* (Carnivora: Felidae). *Revista Salud. Anim.* 6(1): 65–71.

*Menotti-Raymond, M., and O'Brien, S. J. 1993. Dating the genetic bottleneck of the African cheetah. *Proc. Natl. Acad. Sci. U.S.A.* 90:3172–76.

*Meredith, A. L., and Beasey, A. 1991. Ivermectin treatment of ascarids in the cheetah *(Acinonyx jubatus). Vet. Rec.* 129:241–42.

Meyer-Holzapfel, M. 1968. Breeding the European wild cat at Berne Zoo. *Int. Zoo Yrbk.* 8:31–38.

*Millard, S. E.; Durrant, B. S.; and Yamada, J. K. 1988. Vaginal cytology as a management tool in the propagation of captive cheetahs. *Proc. AAZPA* (Wheeling, W.V.): 610.

Miller, S. D., and Everett, D. D., eds. 1986. *Cats of the World: Biology, Conservation, and Management.* Washington, D.C.: National Wildlife Federation.

*Miller-Edge, M. A., and Worley, M. B. 1991. In vitro mitogen responses and lymphocyte subpopulations in cheetahs. *Vet. Immunol. Immunopathol.* 28: 337–49.

*Miller-Edge, M. A., and Worley, M. B. 1992. In vitro responses of cheetah mononuclear cells to feline herpesvirus-1 and *Cryptococcus neoformans. Vet. Immunol. Immunopathol.* 30:261–74.

*Mills, M. G. L. 1973. An unusual case of predation by a leopard in the Kalahari Gemsbok National Park. *Custos* 2(8): 39–41.

Mills, M. G. L. 1978. The comparative socio-ecology of the Hyaenidae. *Carnivore* 1:1–7.

Mills, M. G. L. 1982. The mating system of the brown hyaena, *Hyaena brunnea,* in the southern Kalahari. *Behav. Ecol. Sociobiol.* 10:131–36.

*Mills, M. G. L. 1984a. Kalahari predators and their prey. *Custos* 13(3): 5–9.

*Mills, M. G. L. 1984b. Prey selection and feeding habits of large carnivores in the southern Kalahari. *Koedoe* suppl. 27:281–94.

Mills, M. G. L. 1985. Related spotted hyaenas forage together but do not cooperate in rearing young. *Nature* 316:61–62.

*Mills, M. G. L. 1989. Cheetah and wild dog research in the Kruger National Park in 1988—a progress report. *Quagga* 27:5-6.

Mills, M. G. L. 1990. *Kalahari Hyaenas: Comparative Behavioural Ecology of Two Species.* London: Unwin Hyman.

*Mills, M. G. L. 1991. Thick bush and stronger predators complicate cheetah's hunt. *Custos* 19(12): 16-18.

*Mills, M. G. L., and Biggs, H.C. 1993. Prey apportionment and related ecological relationships between large carnivores in Kruger National Park. *Symp. Zool. Soc. Lond.* 65:253-68.

Mitchell, B. L.; Shenton, J. B.; and Uys, J. C. M. 1965. Predation on large mammals in the Kafue National Park, Zambia. *Zool. Afr.* 1(1): 297-318.

Mock, D. W., and Forbes, L. S. 1992. Parent-offspring conflict: A case of arrested development. *Trends Ecol. Evol.* 7:409-13.

*Modi, W. S.; Wayne, R. K.; and O'Brien, S. J. 1987. Analysis of fluctuating asymmetry in cheetahs. *Evolution* 41:227-28.

Moehlman, P. D. 1979. Jackal helpers and pup survival. *Nature* 277:382-83.

Moehlman, P. D. 1989. Intraspecific variation in canid social systems. In *Carnivore Behavior, Ecology, and Evolution,* ed. J. L. Gittleman, 143-63. Ithaca, N.Y.: Cornell University Press.

*Moll, E. 1976. The cheetah kill and the cheetah killers. *Afr. Wildl.* 30(3): 12-13.

Mondolfi, E., and Hoogesteijn, R. 1986. Notes on the biology and status of the jaguar in Venezuela. In *Cats of the World: Biology, Conservation, and Management,* ed. S. D. Miller and D. D. Everett, 85-123. Washington, D.C.: National Wildlife Federation.

*Monks, E. 1977. The future for Africa's spotted cats. *Africana* 6(4): vi-vii.

Montgomerie, R. D., and Weatherhead, P. J. 1988. Risks and rewards of nest defense by parent birds. *Q. Rev. Biol.* 63:167-87.

Moore, J., and Ali, R. 1984. Are dispersal and inbreeding avoidance related? *Anim. Behav.* 32:94-112.

Moran, G. 1984. Vigilance behaviour and alarm calls in a captive group of meerkats *Suricata suricatta. Z. Tierpsychol.* 65:228-40.

Morehouse, E. L., and Brewer, R. 1968. Feeding of nestling and fledgling eastern kingbirds. *Auk* 85:44-54.

Morris, D. 1965. *The Mammals: A Guide to the Living Species.* London: Hodder and Stotton.

*Morris, R. C. 1936a. Distribution of the hunting leopard *Acinonyx jubatus* Erxl. in India. *J. Bombay Nat. Hist. Soc.* 38:386-87.

*Morris, R. C. 1936b. Further notes on the distribution of the cheetah (*Acinonyx jubatus* Erxl.) in South India. *J. Bombay Nat. Hist. Soc.* 38:610.

*Morrison-Scott, T. 1951. Exhibition of photographs of Arabian cheetah. *Proc. Zool. Soc. Lond.* 121:201.

*Morsbach, D. 1984/86. The behavioural ecology and movement of cheetahs on farmland in Southwest Africa/Namibia. Annual progress reports to Directorate of Nature Conservation and Recreation Resorts, Government of Namibia, Windhoek (summary in English). Typescripts.

*Morsbach, D. 1987. Cheetah in Namibia. *Cat News* 6:25-26.

*Moucha, P.; Vahala, J.; and Ptacek, M. 1991. One case of giardiasis in young cheetahs *(Acinonyx jubatus). Verhandl. Intern. Symp. Erkrank. Zootiere-Eskilstuna* 23:233–35.

*Movchan, V. N., and Opakhova, V. R. 1981. Acoustic signals of cats (Felidae) living in the zoo (in Russian). *Zool. Zh.* 60:601–8.

*Mowlavi, M. 1985. Cheetah in Iran. *Cat News* 2:7.

*Mulder ten Kate, N. 1975. Nursery from the first nest of cheetahs. Wildernislaan 8, Apeldoorn, Netherlands. Unpublished typescript.

Munck, A.; Guyre, P.; and Holbrook, N. 1984. Physiological functions of glucocorticoids in stress and their relation to pharmacological actions. *Endocrinol. Rev.* 5:25–44.

*Munson, L. 1993. Diseases of captive cheetahs *(Acinonyx jubatus):* Results of cheetah research council pathology survey 1989–1992. *Zoo Biol.* 12:105–24.

*Munson, L., and M. B. Worley. N.d. Histological characteristics and prevalence of liver lesions in captive snow leopards and cheetahs. Unpublished typescript.

*Munson, L., and Worley, M. B. 1987. Comparative hepatic histopathology in snow leopards and cheetahs. *Proc. AAZV* 492.

*Munson, L., and Worley, M. B. 1991. Veno-occlusive disease in snow leopards *(Panthera uncia)* from zoological parks. *Vet. Pathol.* 28:37–45.

Murie, A. 1981. *The Grizzlies of Mount McKinley.* Scientific Monograph Series, no. 14. U.S. National Parks Service.

*Murray, M. 1967. The pathology of some diseases found in wild animals in East Africa. *E. Afr. Wildl. J.* 5:37–45.

*Murray, M. 1968. Incidence and pathology of spirocerca-lupi in Kenya. *J. Comp. Pathol.* 78:401–5.

*Murray, M.; Campbell, H.; and Jarrett, W. H. F. 1974. *Spirocerca lupi* in a cheetah. *E. Afr. Wildl. J.* 2:164.

*Myers, N. 1970. Is the cheetah a loser? In *The Web of Life,* ed. R. Herrick, 160–63. New York: Garret Press.

*Myers, N. 1972. Salvaging the spotted cat. *The Ecologist* 2(3): 8–10.

*Myers, N. 1973a. Leopard and cheetah in Ethiopia. *Oryx* 12:197–205.

*Myers, N. 1973b. The spotted cats and the fur trade. In *The World's Cats,* vol. 1, ed. R. L. Eaton, 276–326. Winston, Oreg.: World Wildlife Safari.

*Myers, N. 1974a. An evaluation of the status of the cheetah. *AWLF News* 9: 11–14.

*Myers, N. 1974b. Institutional inputs for cheetah conservation in Africa. *Trans. N. Am. Wildl. Nat. Resour. Conf.* 39 (Denver, Colo., Mar. 31–Apr. 3): 323–31.

*Myers, N. 1974c. Plight of the African spotted cats. *New Sci.* 64(918): 93–98.

*Myers, N. 1974d. Project 693. Cheetah, leopard, and other depleted species in Africa—survey. *World Wildl. Yrbk.* 1973–1974:157–61.

*Myers, N. 1975a. The cheetah *Acinonyx jubatus* in Africa. *IUCN Monogr.* 4: 9–90.

*Myers, N. 1975b. *The Status of the Cheetah in Africa South of the Sahara.* Morges, Switzerland: IUCN.

*Myers, N. 1976a. The cheetah in Africa under threat. *Environ. Aff.* 5(4): 617–47.

*Myers, N. 1976b. Status of the leopard and cheetah in Africa. In *The World's Cats,* vol. 3(1), ed. R. L. Eaton, 48–59. Carnivore Research Institute, University of Washington, Seattle.

*Myers, N. 1977. The cheetah's relationship to the spotted hyaena: Some implications for a threatened species. In *Proc. 1975 Predator Symp.*, ed. R. L. Phillips and C. Jonkel, 191–200. Missoula: University of Montana.

*Myers, N. 1978. Status of the leopard and cheetah in Africa. In *The World's Cats,* vol. 3(3), ed. R. L. Eaton, 53–69. Carnivore Research Institute, University of Washington, Seattle.

*Myers, N. 1982. Conservation strategies for Africa's cats. *International Cat Symposium,* Texas A&M University.

*Myers, N. 1984. Cats in crisis! *Int. Wildl.* 14(6): 42–50.

*Myers, N. 1986a. Behutete Katzen-kindheit. *Das Tier* 8:6–9.

*Myers, N. 1986b. Conservation of Africa's cats: Problems and opportunities. In *Cats of the World: Biology, Conservation and Management,* ed. S. D. Miller and D. D. Everett, 437–66. Washington, D.C.: National Wildlife Federation.

Mykytowycz, R.; Hesterman, E. R.; Gambale, S.; and Dudzinski, M. L. 1976. A comparison of effectiveness of the odours of rabbits, *Oryctolagus cuniculus,* in enhancing territorial confidence. *J. Chem. Ecol.* 2:13–24.

*Naoroji, R. 1979. Some observations on a cheetah family in the Mara. *E. Afr. Nat. Hist. Soc.,* Jan./Feb.: 20–21.

*Nash, W. G., and O'Brien, S. J. 1982. Conserved regions of homologous G-banded chromosomes between the orders in mammalian evolution: Carnivores and primates. *Proc. Natl. Acad. Sci. USA* 79(21): 6631–35.

Neff, N. A. 1983. *The Big Cats: The Paintings of Guy Coheleach.* New York: Abrams.

Nei, M.; Maruyama, T.; and Chakraborty, R. 1975. The bottleneck effect and genetic variability in populations. *Evolution* 29:1–10.

Neill, S. R. St. J., and Cullen, J. M. 1974. Experiments on whether schooling by their prey affects the hunting behaviour of cephalopods and fish predators. *J. Zool.* 172:549–69.

Nellis, C. H., and Keith, L. B. 1968. Hunting activities and success of lynxes in Alberta. *J. Wildl. Mgmt.* 32:718–22.

Nellis, C. H.; Wetmore, S. P.; and Keith, L. B. 1972. Lynx-prey interactions in central Alberta. *J. Wildl. Mgmt.* 36:320–29.

Nelson, J. B. 1967. Etho-ecological adaptations in the great frigate bird. *Nature* 214:318.

*Newman, A.; Bush, M.; Wildt, D. E.; van Dam, D.; Frankenhuis, M. Th.; Simmons, L.; Phillips, L.; and O'Brien, S. J. 1985. Biochemical genetic variation in eight endangered or threatened felid species. *J. Mammal.* 66:256–57.

Newton, I. 1986. *The Sparrowhawk.* Calton, U.K.: Poyser.

Newby, J. E. 1990. The slaughter of Sahelian wildlife by Arab royalty. *Oryx* 24: 6–8.

*Niekerk-Corder, A. 1967. The prince of cats. *Fld. Tide* 9(11): 16–17.

Nishida, T. 1983. Alpha status and agonistic alliance in wild chimpanzees (*Pan troglodytes schweinfurthii*). *Primates* 24:318–26.

Nishida, T., and Hiraiwa-Hasegawa, M. 1986. Chimpanzees and bonobos: Cooperative relationships among males. In *Primate Societies,* ed. B. B. Smuts, D. L. Cheney, R. M. Seyfarth, R. W. Wrangham, and T. T. Struhsaker, 165–77. Chicago: University of Chicago Press.

Noe, R. 1990. A veto game played by baboons: A challenge to the use of Prisoner's Dilemma as a paradigm for reciprocity and cooperation. *Anim. Behav.* 39: 78–90.

Noe, R., and Sluijter, A. A. 1990. Reproductive tactics of male savanna baboons. *Behaviour* 113:117–70.

*Norris, C. G. 1976. Lion and cheetah. Nairobi National Parks. Unpublished typescript.

*Norris, T. 1973. The society's notes: Cheetah identification. *Africana* 5(1): 38.

*Norris, T. 1975. Is this a beginning—of the end . . . ? *Africana* 5(10): i–ii.

Norton-Griffiths, M. 1968. The feeding ecology of the oystercatcher *(Haemotopus ostralegus)*. Ph.D. thesis, University of Oxford.

Novikov, G. A. 1962. *Carnivorous mammals of the fauna of the U.S.S.R.* Israel Program for Scientific Translations, Jerusalem.

Nudds, T. D. 1978. Convergence of group size strategies by mammalian social carnivores. *Am. Nat.* 112:957–60.

O'Brien, S. J. 1989. Reply from O'Brien. *Trends Ecol. Evol.* 4:178.

*O'Brien, S. J. 1991. The genetic peril of the cheetah. In *Great Cats: Majestic Creatures of the Wild,* ed. J. Seidensticker and S. Lumpkin, 146. Sydney: Weldon Owen.

O'Brien, S. J., and Evermann, J. F. 1988. Interactive influence of infectious disease and genetic diversity in natural populations. *Trends Ecol. Evol.* 3:254–59.

O'Brien, S. J.; Martenson, J. S.; Gichelberger, M. A.; Thorne, E. T.; and Wright, F. 1989. Genetic variation and molecular systematics of the black-footed ferret. In *Conservation Biology and the Black-footed Ferret,* ed. E. T. Thorne, M. A. Bogan, and S. H. Anderson, 21–33. New Haven: Yale University Press.

*O'Brien, S. J.; Roelke, M.; Marker, L.; Hart, F.; Goldman, D. G.; Merrill, C. R.; Howard, J. G.; Meltzer, D.; van Dyk, A.; Ebedes, H.; Brand, D. J.; Simonson, J. M.; Simmons, L. G.; Bush, M.; and Wildt, D. E. 1983. The South African cheetah: A multidisciplinary approach reveals a provocative genetic status and natural history. *Proc. AAZV* 1983:16.

*O'Brien, S. J.; Roelke, M. E.; Marker, L.; Newman, A.; Winkler, C. A.; Meltzer, D.; Colly, L.; Bush, M.; Evermann, J. F.; and Wildt, D. E. 1985. Genetic basis for species vulnerability in the cheetah. *Science* 227:1428–34.

*O'Brien, S. J.; Wildt, D. E.; and Bush, M. 1986. The cheetah in genetic peril. *Sci. Am.* 254(5): 84–92.

*O'Brien, S. J.; Wildt, D. E.; Bush, M.; Caro, T. M.; FitzGibbon, C.; Aggundey, I.; and Leakey, R. E. 1987. East African cheetahs: Evidence for two population bottlenecks. *Proc. Natl. Acad. Sci. USA* 84:508–11.

*O'Brien, S. J.; Wildt, D. E.; Goldman, D.; Merrill, C. R.; and Bush, M. 1983. The cheetah is depauperate in genetic variation. *Science* 221:459–62.

*O'Brien, S. J.; Wildt, D. E.; Simonson, J. M.; Brand, D. J.; Ebedes, H.; van Dyk, A.; Meltzer, D.; Simmons, L. G.; and Bush, M. 1981. On the extent of genetic variation of the African cheetah *(Acinonyx jubatus)*. *Proc. AAZV* 1981:74–77.

Oftedal, O. T. 1985. Pregnancy and lactation. In *The Bioenergetics of Wild Herbivores,* ed. R. J. Hudson and R. G. White, 215–38. Boca Rotan, Fla.: CRC Press.

Oftedal, O. T., and Gittleman, J. L. 1989. Patterns of energy output during reproduction. In *Carnivore Behavior, Ecology, and Evolution,* ed. J. L. Gittleman, 355–78. Ithaca, N.Y.: Comstock.

Orians, G. H. 1969a. Age and hunting success in the brown pelican *(Pelecanus occidentalis). Anim. Behav.* 17:316–19.

Orians, G. H. 1969b. On the evolution of mating systems in birds and mammals. *Am. Nat.* 103:589–603.

Owen, M. 1972. Some factors affecting food intake and selection in white-fronted geese. *J. Anim. Ecol.* 41:79–92.

*Owens, R. 1835. On the anatomy of the cheetah, *Felis jubata* Schreb. *Trans. Zool. Soc. Lond.* 1:129–37.

Owen-Smith, N. 1972. Territoriality: The example of the white rhinoceros. *Zoologica Africana* 7:273–80.

Owen-Smith, N. 1975. The social ethology of the white rhinoceros, *Ceratotherium simum* Burchell 1817. *Z. Tierpsychol.* 38:337–84.

Owen-Smith, N. 1984. Spatial and temporal components of the mating system of kudu bulls and red deer stags. *Anim. Behav.* 32:321–32.

Packer, C. 1977. Reciprocal altruism in olive baboons. *Nature* 265:441–43.

Packer, C. 1979. Inter-troop transfer and inbreeding avoidance in *Papio anubis. Anim. Behav.* 27:1–36.

Packer, C. 1983. Once and future kings. *Nat. Hist.* 8:53–63.

Packer, C. 1986. The ecology of sociality in felids. In *Ecological Aspects of Social Evolution: Birds and Mammals,* ed. D. I. Rubenstein and R. W. Wrangham, 429–51. Princeton, N.J.: Princeton University Press.

Packer, C., and Abrams, P. 1990. Should co-operative groups be more vigilant than selfish groups? *J. Theor. Biol.* 142:341–57.

Packer, C.; Gilbert, D. A.; Pusey, A. E.; and O'Brien, S. J. 1991. A molecular genetic analysis of kinship and cooperation in African lions. *Nature* 351:562–65.

Packer, C.; Herbst, L.; Pusey, A. E.; Bygott, J. D.; Hanby, J. P.; Cairns, S. J.; and Borgerhoff Mulder, M. 1988. Reproductive success in lions. In *Reproductive Success,* ed. T. H. Clutton-Brock, 363–83. Chicago: University of Chicago Press.

Packer, C.; Lewis, S.; and Pusey, A. E. 1992. A comparative analysis of non-offspring nursing. *Anim. Behav.* 43:265–81.

Packer, C., and Pusey, A. E. 1982. Cooperation and competition within coalitions of male lions: Kin selection or game theory? *Nature* 296:740–42.

Packer, C., and Pusey, A. E. 1983. Adaptations of female lions to infanticide by incoming males. *Am. Nat.* 121:716–28.

Packer, C., and Pusey, A. E. 1984. Infanticide in carnivores. In *Infanticide: Comparative and Evolutionary Perspectives,* ed. G. Hausfater and S. B. Hrdy, 31–42. New York: Aldine.

Packer, C., and Pusey, A. E. 1987. Intrasexual cooperation and the sex ratio in African lions. *Am. Nat.* 130:636–42.

Packer, C., and Ruttan, L. 1988. The evolution of cooperative hunting. *Am. Nat.* 132:159–98.

Packer, C.; Scheel, D.; and Pusey, A. E. 1990. Why lions form groups: Food is not enough. *Am. Nat.* 136:1–19.

*Pantucci, G. 1985. Il gepardo: Formula uno della savana. *Natura Oggi* 3(5): 96–103.

Panwar, H. S. 1987. Project Tiger: The reserves, the tigers and their future. In *Tigers of the World: The Biology, Biopolitics, Management, and Conservation of an Endangered Species,* ed. R. L. Tilson and U. S. Seal, 110–17. Park Ridge, N.J.: Noyes Publications.

*Paradiso, J. L. 1972. Status report on cats (Felidae) of the world, 1971. *Special Rep. U.S. Fish Wildl. Serv.* Wildlife no. 157: i–iv, 1–62.

*Parham, P. 1991. The pros and cons of polymorphism: A brighter future for cheetahs. *Res. Immunol.* 142:447–48.

*Parihar, N. S.; Charan, K.; and Chakraborty, I. B. 1976. Lipomatosis in a hunting cheetah *(Acinonyx jubatus). Indian J. Vet. Path.* 1:4–5.

Parker, G. R.; Maxwell, J. W.; and Morton, L. D. 1983. The ecology of the lynx on Cape Breton Island. *Can. J. Zool.* 61:771–87.

Parker, G. R., and Smith, G. E. J. 1983. Sex and age specific reproduction and physical parameters of the bobcat on Cape Breton Island, Nova Scotia. *Can. J. Zool.* 61:1771–82.

Parker, W. T. 1988. The red wolf. *Audubon Wildlife Report 1988/89,* ed. W. J. Chandler. San Diego: Academic Press.

Partridge, L., and Harvey, P. H. 1988. The ecological context of life history evolution. *Science* 241:1449–55.

*Patzer, M. 1985. Cat of absolutes. *Signature* 18(5): 20–21.

*Peet, R. L., and Curran, J. M. 1992. Spongiform encephalopathy in an imported cheetah *(Acinonyx jubatus). Aust. Vet. J.* 69(7): 171.

Pellis, S. M., and Officer, R. C. E. 1987. An analysis of some predatory behaviour patterns in four species of carnivorous marsupials (Dasyuridae), with comparative notes on the eutherian cat *Felis catus. Ethology* 75:177–96.

*Pennisi, E. 1993. Cheetah countdown. *Science News* 144(13):200–201.

Pennycuick, L. 1975. Movements of migratory wildebeest populations in the Serengeti area between 1960 and 1973. *E. Afr. Wildl. J.* 13:65–87.

*Pernikoff, D. S.; Boever, W. J.; Gado, M.; and Gilula, L. A. 1986. Vertebral body fracture in a captive cheetah. *J. Am. Vet. Med. Assoc.* 189:1199–1200.

*Pernikoff, D. S.; Sundberg, J. P.; Miller, D. R. E.; Boever, W. J.; and Scherba, G. 1986. Eosinophilic ulcers in association with herpetic dermatitis in sibling cheetahs. *Ann. Proc. Amer. Assoc. Zoo Vet.* 1986:145.

*Peters, G. 1981. The purring of cats (Felidae). *Saugetierkd Mitt.* 29(4): 30–37.

Peterson, R. O.; Woolington, J. D.; and Bailey, T. N. 1984. Wolves of the Kenai peninsula, Alaska. *Wildl. Monogr.* 88:1–52.

Petraborg, W. H., and Gunvalson, V. E. 1962. Observations on bobcat mortality and bobcat predation on deer. *J. Mammal.* 43:430–31.

*Pettifer, H. L. 1981a. Aspects of the ecology of cheetah *(Acinonyx jubatus)* on the Suikerbosrand Nature Reserve. In *Proc. Worldwide Furbearer Conf.* 1: 1121–42.

*Pettifer, H. L. 1981b. The experimental release of captive-bred cheetah *(Acinonyx jubatus)* into the natural envrionment. In *Worldwide Furbearer Conf. Proc.,* ed. J. A. Chapman and D. Pursley, 1001–24. Falls Church, Va.: R. R. Donnelly.

*Pettifer, H. L.; de Wet, J. I.; and Muller, P. J. 1980. The ecology of the cheetah
    (Acinonyx jubatus) on the Suikerbosrand Nature Reserve. Transvaal Division
    of Nature Conservation, Pretoria. Typescript.
*Pettifer, H. L.; DeWet, J. I.; and Muller, P. J. 1981. The experimental relocation
    of cheetahs (Acinonyx jubatus) from the Suikerbosrand Nature Reserve to the
    Eastern Transvaal Lowveld. Transvaal Division of Nature Conservation, Pre-
    toria. Unpublished typescript.
*Pettifer, H. L.; Muller, P. J.; De Kock, J. P. S.; and Zimbatis, N. 1982. The experi-
    mental relocation of cheetahs from the Suikerbosrand Nature Reserve to the
    Eastern Transvaal Lowveld (second progress report). Transvaal Division of Na-
    ture Conservation, Pretoria. Unpublished typescript.
*Pfeifer, M. L.; Evermann, J. F.; Roelke, M. E.; Gallina, A. M.; Ott, R. L.; and
    McKeirnan, A. J. 1983. Feline infectious peritonitis in a captive cheetah. J. Am.
    Vet. Med. Assoc. 183: 1317–19.
Phillips, W. W. A. 1935. The Mammals of Ceylon. London: Daulau and Co.
*Pienaar, U. de V. 1969. Predator-prey relationships amongst the larger mammals
    of the Kruger National Park. Koedoe 12: 108–76.
Pierotti, R. 1991. Infanticide versus adoption: An intergenerational conflict. Am.
    Nat. 138: 1140–58.
Pimm, S. L. 1991. The Balance of Nature? Ecological Issues in the Conservation
    of Species and Communities. Chicago: University of Chicago Press.
Pimm, S. L.; Gittleman, J. L.; McCracken, G. F.; and Gilpin, M. 1989. Plausible
    alternatives to bottlenecks to explain reduced genetic diversity. Trends Ecol.
    Evol. 4: 176–78.
Pitcher, T. J. 1986. Functions of shoaling behaviour in teleosts. In Behaviour of
    Teleost Fishes, ed. T. J. Pitcher, 294–337. Beckenham: Croom Helm.
*Pocock, R. I. 1916a. On the hyoidian apparatus of the lion (F. leo) and related
    species of Felidae. Annu. Mag. Nat. Hist. 8(18): 222–29.
*Pocock, R. I. 1916b. On some cranial and external characteristics of the hunting
    leopard or cheetah (Acinonyx jubatus). Annu. Mag. Nat. Hist. 8(18): 419–29.
Pocock, R. I. 1917. The classification of existing Felidae. Annu. Mag. Nat. Hist.
    Ser. 9, 1: 375–84.
*Pocock, R. I. 1927a. Description of a new species of cheetah (Acinonyx). Proc.
    Zool. Soc. Lond. 1: 245–52.
*Pocock, R. I. 1927b. The new cheetah from Rhodesia. J. Soc. for the Preservation
    of the Empire 7: 17–19.
*Pocock, R. I. 1932. Exhibition of a young cheetah skin. Proc. Zool. Soc. Lond. 2:
    814–16.
*Pocock, R. I. 1951. Catalogue of the Genus Felis. Trustees of the British Museum,
    London.
Polis, G. A.; Myers, C.; and Holt, R. D. 1989. The evolution and ecology of intra-
    guild predation: Competitors that eat each other. Annu. Rev. Ecol. Syst. 20:
    297–330.
Pond, C. M. 1977. The significance of lactation in the evolution of mammals. Evo-
    lution 31: 177–99.
Poole, J. H. 1989. Mate guarding, reproductive success and female choice in Af-
    rican elephants. Anim. Behav. 37: 842–49.

*Porter, S. L., and Simmons, R. L. 1977. The surgical repair of a fractured fibular tarsal bone in a cheetah. *J. Zoo Anim. Med.* 8(3): 20–21.

*Pospisil, J.; Kase, F.; and Vahala, J. 1987. Basic hematological values in carnivores II, the Felidae. *Comp. Biochem. Physiol.* A 87:387–92.

*Pournelle, G. H. 1964. The cheetah . . . associate of aristocracy. *Zoonooz* 37(5): 3–7.

Powell, G. V. N. 1974. Experimental analysis of the social value of flocking by starlings *(Sturnus vulgaris)* in relation to predation and foraging. *Anim. Behav.* 22:501–5.

*Prater, S. H. 1935. The wild animals of the Indian empire. III. Carnivora or beasts of prey. *J. Bombay Nat. Hist. Soc.* 37:112–66.

*Presnell, K. R.; Dingwall, J. S.; and Robins, G. M. 1973. Tension band wiring of fractured tuber calcanei in a cheetah. *J. Am. Vet. Med. Assoc.* 163:549–50.

*Preumont, R. 1973. The cheetah *(Acinonyx jubatus)*. *Rev. Verviet. Hist. Nat.* 30(4–6): 42–44.

Promislow, D. E. L., and Harvey, P. H. 1990. Living fast and dying young: A comparative analysis of life-history variation among mammals. *J. Zool.* 220: 417–37.

Provost, E. E.; Nelson, C. A.; and Marshall, A. D. 1973. Population dynamics and behavior in the bobcat. In *The World's Cats,* vol. 1, ed. R. L. Eaton, 42–67. Winston, Oreg.: World Wildlife Safari.

Pugusek, B. H. 1990. Parental effort in the California gull: Test of parent-offspring conflict theory. *Behav. Ecol. Sociobiol.* 27:211–15.

Pulliam, H. R. 1973. On the advantages of flocking. *J. Theor. Biol.* 38:419–22.

Pulliam, H. R., and Caraco, T. 1984. Living in groups: Is there an optimal group size? In *Behavioural Ecology: An Evolutionary Approach,* 2d ed., ed. J. R. Krebs and N. B. Davies, 122–47. Oxford: Blackwell Scientific Publications.

Pulliam, H. R.; Pyke, G. H.; and Caraco, T. 1982. The scanning behavior of juncos: A game-theoretic approach. *J. Theor. Biol.* 95:89–103.

Pusey, A. E. 1980. Inbreeding avoidance in chimpanzees. *Anim. Behav.* 28: 543–52.

Pusey, A. E., and Packer, C. 1987. The evolution of sex-biased dispersal in lions. *Behaviour* 101:275–310.

*Quammen, D. 1985. The beautiful and the damned: Genetics and aesthetics in the life of a dashing animal. *Outside* 7:21–24.

Quattro, J. M., and Vrijenhoek, R. C. 1989. Fitness differences among remnant populations of endangered Sonoran topminnow. *Science* 245:976–78.

Rabinowitz, A. 1986. *Jaguar.* New York: Arbor House.

Rabinowitz, A. R., and Nottingham, B. G. 1986. Ecology and behaviour of jaguar in Belize. *J. Zool.* 210:149–59.

*Radinski, L. B. 1975. Evolution of the felid brain. *Brain Behav. Evol.* 11:214–54.

Ralls, K. 1971. Mammalian scent marking. *Science* 171:443–49.

Ralls, K.; Brugger, K.; and Ballou, J. 1979. Inbreeding and juvenile mortality in small populations of ungulates. *Science* 206:1101–3.

Ralls, K.; Harvey, P. H.; and Lyles, A. M. 1986. Inbreeding in natural populations of birds and mammals. In *Conservation Biology: The Science of Scarcity and Diversity,* ed. M. E. Soulé, 35–56. Sunderland, Mass.: Sinauer Associates.

Ralls, K.; Lundrigan, B.; and Kranz, K. 1987. Mother-young relationships in captive ungulates: Behavioral changes over time. *Ethology* 75:1–14.

Ramsay, M. A., and Stirling, I. 1986. On the mating system of polar bears. *Can. J. Zool.* 64:2142–51.

Rappole, J. H. 1988. Ocelots' last stand. *Defenders,* Jan./Feb., 30–35.

Rasa, O. A. E. 1973. Prey capture, feeding techniques, and their ontogeny in the African dwarf mongoose, *Helogale undulata rufula. Z. Tierpsychol.* 32: 449–88.

Rasa, O. A. E. 1986. Coordinated vigilance in dwarf mongoose family groups: The "watchman song" hypothesis and the costs of guarding. *Z. Tierpsychol.* 71: 340–44.

*Rawlins, C. G. C. 1972. Cheetahs *(Acinonyx jubatus)* in captivity. *Int. Zoo Yrbk.* 12:119–20.

Read, A. F., and Harvey, P. H. 1989. Life history differences among eutherian radiations. *J. Zool.* 219:329–53.

Recher, H. F., and Recher, J. A. 1969. Comparative foraging efficiency of adult and immature little blue herons *(Florida caerulea). Anim. Behav.* 17:320–22.

*Record cheetah litter born at Lion Country Safari. 1974. *Defenders Wildl. News* 49(1): 34.

Redondo, T. 1989. Avian nest defence: Theoretical models and evidence. *Behaviour* 111:161–95.

Regelmann, K., and Curio, E. 1983. Determinants of brood defense in the great tit *Parus major* L. *Behav. Ecol. Sociobiol.* 13:131–45.

Reich, A. 1981. The Behavior and Ecology of the African Wild Dog *(Lycaon pictus)* in the Kruger National Park. Ph.D. diss., Yale University.

*Reichard, T. A.; Robinson, P. T.; Ensley, P. K.; Meier, J. E.; and Van Winkel, T. 1981. Pancreatitis in a cheetah *(Acinonyx jubatus). Proc. AAZV* 1981: 78–80.

*Resnik, M. 1988. Performing cheetah. *Custos* 17(8): 28–29.

Reznick, D. 1985. Costs of reproduction: An evaluation of the empirical evidence. *Oikos* 44:257–67.

Reznick, D., and Endler, J. A. 1982. The impact of predation on life history evolution in Trinidadian guppies *(Poecilia reticulata). Evolution* 36:160–77.

*Revision of cheetah status in Zimbabwe. 1989. *Cat News* 11:16–17.

Ribic, C. A. 1982. Autumn movement and home range of sea otters in California. *J. Wildl. Mgmt.* 46:795–801.

Richardson, P. R. K. 1991. Territorial significance of scent marking during the non-mating season in the aardwolf *Proteles cristatus* (Carnivora: Protelidae). *Ethology* 87:9–27.

Riedman, M. L. 1982. The evolution of alloparental care and adoption in mammals and birds. *Q. Rev. Biol.* 57:405–32.

Riedman, M. L. 1990. *The Pinnipeds: Seals, Sea Lions, and Walruses.* Berkeley: University of California Press.

Riedman, M. L., and LeBoeuf, B. J. 1982. Mother-pup separation and adoption in northern elephant seals. *Behav. Ecol. Sociobiol.* 11:203–15.

*Rilling, J. 1977. Lion killing cheetah. *E. Afr. Nat. Hist. Soc. Bull.* (7–8): 82.

*Rilling, J. 1978. An unusual cheetah kill. *E. Afr. Nat. Hist. Soc. Bull.* (1–2): 12.

*Roberts, T. J. 1977. *The Mammals of Pakistan*. Ernest Benn, London.

Robinette, W. L. 1963. Weights of some of the larger mammals of Northern Rhodesia. *The Puku* 1:207–15.

Robinette, W. L.; Gashwiler, J. S.; and Morris, O. W. 1961. Notes on cougar productivity and life history. *J. Mammal.* 42:204–17.

Robinson, J. G. 1988. Group size in wedge-capped capuchin monkeys *Cebus olivaceus* and the reproductive success of males and females. *Behav. Ecol. Sociobiol.* 23:187–97.

Rodman, P. S. 1981. Inclusive fitness and group size with a reconsideration of group size in lions and wolves. *Am. Nat.* 118:275–83.

*Rodon, G. S. 1898. Notes on a jackal cub. *J. Bombay Nat. Hist. Soc.* 12:220.

*Rodrigues, J. 1984. Even hot air balloons paid homage to the "King." *Custos* 1:38–43.

Rollings, C. T. 1945. Habits, food and parasites of the bobcat in Minnesota. *J. Wildl. Mgmt.* 9:131–45.

Rood, J. P. 1974. Banded mongoose males guard their young. *Nature* 248:176.

Rood, J. P. 1975. Population dynamics and food habits of the banded mongoose. *E. Afr. Wildl. J.* 13:89–111.

Rood, J. P. 1978. Dwarf mongoose helpers at the den. *Z. Tierpsychol.* 48:277–87.

Rood, J. P. 1986. Ecology and evolution in the mongooses. In *Ecological Aspects of Social Evolution*, ed. D. I. Rubenstein and R. W. Wrangham, 131–52. Princeton, N.J.: Princeton University Press.

*Rood, J. P. 1987a. Cheated cheetah. *Nat. Hist.* 96(12):42–43.

*Rood, J. P. 1987b. Dispersal and intergroup transfer in the dwarf mongoose. In *Mammalian Dispersal Patterns*, ed. B. D. Chepko-Sade and Z. T. Halpin, 85–103. Chicago: University of Chicago Press.

Roosevelt, T. 1910. *African Game Trails; an Account of the Wanderings of a Hunter-naturalist*. New York: Syndicate.

*Rose, M. 1972. The cheetah in Natal. *Afr. Wildl.* 32(3):35.

Rosevear, D. R. 1974. *The Carnivores of West Africa*. Trustees of the British Museum, London.

*Ross, J. 1978. International zoo news. Cincinnati. *Int. Zoo News* 25(7):36–37.

Rosser, A. M. 1992. Resource distribution, density, and determinants of mate access in puku. *Behav. Ecol.* 3:13–24.

Rothstein, S. I., and Pierotti, R. 1988. Distinctions among reciprocal altruism, kin selection, and cooperation and a model for the initial evolution of beneficent behavior. *Ethol. Sociobiol.* 9:189–209.

*Roubin, M.; Grouchy, J. de; and Klein, M. 1974. The Felidae chromosomal evolution. *Annales Genet.* 16(4):233–45.

Rowe-Rowe, D. T. 1978. The small carnivores of Natal. *The Lammergeyer* 25:1–48.

Rubenstein, D. I. 1986. Ecology and sociality in horses and zebras. In *Ecological Aspects of Social Evolution*, ed. D. I. Rubenstein and R. W. Wrangham, 282–302. Princeton, N.J.: Princeton University Press.

*Rucci, S. 1975. Cheetahs along the Kilimanjaro Trail. *Zoonooz* 48(5):12–14.

Rudnai, J. 1973a. Reproductive biology of lions in Nairobi National Park. *E. Afr. Wildl. J.* 11:241–53.

Rudnai, J. 1973b. *The Social Life of the Lion.* Lancaster, England: MTP.

*Sabine, M., and Hyne, R. H. J. 1970. Isolation of a feline picornavirus from cheetahs with conjunctivitis and glossitis. *Vet. Rec.* 87:794–96.

Sacher, G. A. 1959. Relationship of lifespan to brain weight and body weight in mammals. In *The Lifespan of Animals,* ed. G. E. W. Wolstenholme and M. O'Connor, 115–33. Ciba Foundation Colloquia on Aging 5, Churchill, London.

Sacher, G. A., and Staffeldt, E. F. 1974. Relationship of gestation time to brain weight for placental mammals: Implications for the theory of vertebrate growth. *Am. Nat.* 108:593–615.

Sachs, R. 1967. Live weights and body measurements of Serengeti game animals. *E. Afr. Wildl. J.* 5:24–36.

*Sadlier, M. F. S. 1966. Notes on reproduction in the larger Felidae. *Int. Zoo Yrbk.* 6:184–87.

Sadlier, M. F. S. 1980. Milk yield of black-tailed deer. *J. Wildl. Mgmt.* 44:472–78.

Salisbury, G. W., and Baker, F. N. 1966. Nuclear morphology of spermatozoa from inbred and linecross Hereford bulls. *J. Anim. Sci.* 25:476–79.

Sandell, M. 1986. Movement patterns of male stoats *Mustela erminea* during the mating season: Differences in relation to social status. *Oikos* 47:63–70.

Sandell, M. 1989. The mating tactics and spacing patterns of solitary carnivores. In *Carnivore Behavior, Ecology and Evolution,* ed. J. L. Gittleman, 164–82. Ithaca, N.Y.: Cornell Univ. Press.

Sandell, M., and Liberg, O. 1992. Roamers and stayers: A model on male mating tactics and mating systems. *Am. Nat.* 139:177–89.

Sankhala, K. S. 1967. Breeding behavior of the tiger in Rajasthan. *Int. Zoo Yrbk.* 7:133–47.

Sapolsky, R. M. 1987. Stress, social status, and reproductive physiology in free-living baboons. In *Psychobiology of Reproductive Behavior,* ed. D. Crews, 291–322. Englewood Cliffs, N.J.: Prentice-Hall.

Sargent, R. C., and Gross, M. R. 1986. William's principle: An explanation of parental care in teleost fishes. In *Behaviour of Teleost Fishes,* ed. T. J. Pitcher, 275–93. London: Croom Helm.

Sarri, K. J. 1991. Estrous behavior of the female cheetah *(Acinonyx jubatus)* and the male cheetah's response to an estrous female. Senior honors thesis, Washington University, St. Louis.

Saunders, J. K., Jr. 1963. Food habits of the lynx in Newfoundland. *J. Wildl. Mgmt.* 27:384–90.

Saunders, J. K., Jr. 1964. Physical characteristics of the Newfoundland lynx. *J. Mammal.* 45:36–47.

Schaffer, W. M. 1974. Selection for optimal life histories: The effects of age structure. *Ecology* 55:291–303.

Schaller, G. B. 1967. *The Deer and the Tiger: A Study of Wildlife in India.* Chicago: University of Chicago Press.

*Schaller, G. B. 1968. Hunting behaviour of the cheetah in the Serengeti National Park, Tanzania. *E. Afr. Wildl. J.* 6:95–100.

*Schaller, G. B. 1969. The hunt of the cheetah. *Anim. Kingdom* 72(2): 2–8.

*Schaller, G. B. 1970. This gentle and elegant cat. *Nat. Hist.* 79(6): 31–39.

*Schaller, G. B. 1972a. The endless race of life. *Nat. Hist.* 81(4): 38–43.

*Schaller, G. B. 1972b. Predators of the Serengeti. *Nat. Hist.* 81:61–68, parts 2, 3, 4.

*Schaller, G. B. 1972c. *The Serengeti Lion: A Study of Predator-prey Relations.* Chicago: University of Chicago Press.

*Schaller, G. B. 1973. *The Serengeti: The Kingdom of Predators.* London: Collins.

*Schaller, G. B. 1974. *Golden Shadows, Flying Hooves.* London: Collins.

Schaller, G. B. 1977. *Mountain Monarchs: Wild Sheep and Goats of the Himalaya.* Chicago: University of Chicago Press.

Schaller, G. B. 1983. Mammals and their biomass on a Brazilian ranch. *Arq. Zool.* 31:1–36.

Schaller, G. B., and Crawshaw, P. G. 1980. Movement patterns of jaguar. *Biotropica* 12(3): 161–68.

Schaller, G. B.; Jinchu, H.; Wenshi, P.; and Jing, Z. 1985. *The Giant Pandas of Wolong.* Chicago: University of Chicago Press.

Schaller, G. B., and Vasconcelos, J. M. C. 1978. Jaguar predation on capybara. *Z. Saugetierkunde* 43:296–301.

Schalm, O.; Jain, N. C.; and Carroll, E. J. 1985. *Veterinary Hematology.* 4th ed. Philadelphia: Lea and Febiger.

Schauenberg, P. 1979. Reproduction of the jungle cat. *Mammalia* 43:215–23.

Scheel, D. 1993. Profitability, encounter rates and prey choice of African lions. *Behav. Ecol.* 4:90–97.

Scheel, D., and Packer, C. 1991. Group hunting behaviour of lions: A search for cooperation. *Anim. Behav.* 41:697–709.

Scheffel, W., and Hemmer, H. 1976. Breeding Geoffroy's cat in captivity. *Int. Zoo Yrbk.* 15:152–54.

*Scherba, G.; Hajjar, A. M.; Pernikoff, D. S.; Sundberg, J. P.; Basgall, E. J.; Leon-Monzon, M.; Nerurkar, L.; and Reichmann, M. E. 1988. Comparison of a cheetah herpesvirus isolate to feline herpesvirus type I. *Arch. Virol.* 100(1–2): 89–97.

*Schlabing, C. 1989. Beobachtungen und Versuche zum Beutfangverhalten und zur Nahrungsaufnahme des Geparden *(Acinonyx jubatus)* im Frankfurter Zoo. *Zool. Gart.* 59(5–6): 351–401.

*Schlitz durch Streifen. 1987. *Geo* 3:170–82.

*Scholtz, A. T. 1979. Jagluipard in Transvaal: Verspreidingstatus en hervestiging. Transvaal Provincial Authority, Pretoria. P. 8.

Schonewald-Cox, C. M.; Chambers, S. M.; MacBryde, F.; and Thomas, W. L. 1983. *Genetics and Conservation: A Reference for Managing Wild Animal and Plant Populations.* Menlo Park, Calif.: Benjamin Cummings.

*Schuerman, T. 1985. Successful semen collection from a hand-reared cheetah *(Acinonyx jubatus). Anim. Keepers' Forum* 12(12): 436–39.

*Schuling, K. 1990. Verleighende Untersuchungen zum Verhalten des Geparden *(Acinonyx jubatus)* in menschlicher Obhut unter besonderer Berucksichtigung unterschielicher Haltungsbedingungen. Thesis, Westfalische Wilhelms-Universität, Munster.

*Schumann, M. E. 1991. Breeding strategy and field observations of captive cheetahs. *Int. Zoo News* 38(8): 9–19.

Schwagmeyer, P. L. 1988. Scramble-competition polygyny in an asocial mammal: Male mobility and mating success. *Am. Nat* 131:885–92.

*Sclater, P. L. 1877. Report on the additions to the Society's menagerie, in May 1877. *Proc. Zool. Soc. Lond.:* 532.

*Sclater, P. L. 1884. Exhibition of skin of *Felis lanea. Proc. Zool. Soc. Lond.:* 476.

Scott, D. K. 1980. Functional aspects of prolonged parental care in Bewick's swans. *Anim. Behav.* 28:938–52.

Seager, S. W. J., and Demorest, C. N. 1978. Reproduction of captive wild carnivores. In *Zoo and Wild Animal Medicine,* ed. M. E. Fowler, 667–706. Philadelphia: W. B. Saunders and Co.

Seal, U. S. 1985. The realities of preserving species in captivity. In *Animal Extinctions: What Everyone Should Know,* ed. R. J. Hoage, 71–95. Washington, D.C.: Smithsonian Institution Press.

Seal, U. S. 1988. Intensive technology in the care of ex situ populations of vanishing species. In *Biodiversity,* ed. E. O. Wilson, 289–95. Washington, D.C.: National Academy Press.

Seal, U. S., and Foose, T. 1983. Development of a masterplan for captive propagation of Siberian tigers in North American zoos. *Zoo Biol.* 2:241–44.

Seidensticker, J.; Hornocker, M. G.; Wiles, V. W.; and Messick, J. P. 1973. Mountain lion social organization in the Idaho Primitive Area. *Wildl. Monogr.* 35:1–60.

Seidensticker, J., and Lumpkin, S., eds. 1991. *Great Cats: Majestic Creatures of the Wild.* Emmaus, Pa.: Rodale Press.

Selander, R. K., and Kaufman, D. W. 1973. Genic variability and strategies of adaptation in animals. *Proc. Natl. Acad. Sci. USA* 70:1875–77.

*Setchell, K. D. R.; Gosselin, S. J.; Welsh, M. B.; Johnston, J. O.; Balistreri, W. F.; Kramer, L. W.; Dresser, B. L.; and Tarr, M. J. 1987. Dietary estrogens—a probable cause of infertility and liver disease in captive cheetahs. *Gastroenterology* 93:225–33.

Seyfarth, R. M. 1977. A model of social grooming among adult female monkeys. *J. Theor. Biol.* 65:671–98.

Seyfarth, R. M. 1980. The distribution of grooming and related behaviours among adult female vervet monkeys. *Anim. Behav.* 28:798–813.

Seyfarth, R. M., and Cheney, D. L. 1980. The ontogeny of vervet monkey alarm-calling behavior: A preliminary report. *Z. Tierpsychol.* 54:37–56.

Seyfarth, R. M., and Cheney, D. L. 1986. Vocal development in vervet monkeys. *Anim. Behav.* 34:1640–58.

Seyfarth, R. M., and Cheney, D. L. 1988. Empirical tests of reciprocity theory: Problems in assessment. *Ethol. Sociobiol.* 9:181–87.

Seyle, H. 1971. *Hormones and Resistance.* New York: Springer-Verlag.

Sherman, P. W. 1977. Nepotism and the evolution of alarm calls. *Science* 197:1246–53.

Shine, R. 1980. "Costs" of reproduction in reptiles. *Oecologia* 46:92–100.

*Shorter, C. 1979. Cheetah skins. *Swara* 2:30.

Shortridge, G. C. 1934. *The Mammals of South West Africa.* Vol. 1. London: Heinemann.

Shuster, S. M., and Wade, M. J. 1991. Equal mating success among male reproductive strategies in a marine isopod. *Nature* 350:608–10.

Sibly, R. M. 1983. Optimal group size is unstable. *Anim. Behav.* 31:947–48.

Siegel, S. 1956. *Nonparametric Statistics for the Behavioral Sciences.* New York:
McGraw-Hill.

*Siemens, L. 1985. Cheetah in Nakuru National Park. *E. Afr. Nat. Hist. Soc. Bull.*
(May, June, July): 35.

*Silberman, M. S.; Blue, J.; and Mahaffey, E. 1977. Antifreeze (ethylene glycol)
poisoning in a captive cheetah *(Acinonyx jubatus)* population. *Proc. AAZV*
1977:121–22.

Silk, J. B. 1982. Altruism among female *Macaca radiata:* Explanations and analysis
of patterns of grooming and coalition formation. *Behaviour* 79:162–88.

*Simmons, L. 1971. Picorna virus in an epidemic of rhinotracheitis in cheetah.
J. Zoo. Anim. Med. 2(4): 24–25.

Simon, N. 1966. Red Data Book. Vol. 1. Mammalia. International Union for Conservation of Nature and Natural Resources, Survival Service Commission,
Lausanne.

Simonsen, V. 1982. Electrophoretic variation in large mammals. II. The red fox,
Vulpes vulpes, the stoat, *Mustela erminea,* the weasel, *Mustela nivalis,* the pole
cat, *Mustela putorius,* the pine marten, *Martes martes,* the beech marten,
Martes foina, and the badger, *Meles meles. Heridatas* 96:299–305.

Sinclair, A. R. E. 1977. *The African Buffalo: A Study of Resource Limitation of
Populations.* Chicago: University of Chicago Press.

Sinclair, A. R. E. 1979. The Serengeti environment. In *Serengeti: Dynamics of an
Ecosystem,* ed. A. R. E. Sinclair and M. Norton-Griffiths, 31–45. Chicago: University of Chicago Press.

Sinclair, A. R. E.; Dublin, H. T.; and Borner, M. 1985. Population regulation of
Serengeti wildebeest: A test of the food hypothesis. *Oecologia* 65:266–68.

Sinclair, A. R. E., and Fryxell, J. M. 1985. The Sahel of Africa: Ecology of a disas-
ter. *Can. J. Zool.* 63:987–94.

Sinclair, A. R. E., and Norton-Griffiths, M. 1982. Does competition of facilitation
regulate ungulate populations in the Serengeti? A test of hypotheses. *Oecologia*
53:364–69.

Singh, A. 1973. Status and social behavior of the north Indian tiger. In *The World's
Cats,* vol. 1, ed. R. L. Eaton, 176–78. Winston, Oreg.: World Wildlife Safari.

Singh, A. 1984. *Tiger Tiger.* London: J. Cape.

*Singh, J.; Hussain, M. M.; and Kumar, R. 1988. A note on repeated xylazine an-
aesthesia in cheetah *(Acinonyx jubatus). Indian J. Vet. Surg.* 9(2): 160–62.

Sitton, L. W., and Wallen, S. 1976. California mountain lion study. California Dept.
Fish and Game, Sacramento.

*Skeldon, P. C. 1972. The following is a history of the Toledo Zoo cheetahs. *Proc.
AAZPA* 1972:124–29.

*Skeldon, P. C. 1973. Breeding cheetahs *(Acinonyx jubatus)* at Toledo Zoo. *Int.
Zoo Yrbk.* 13:151–52.

*Smeller, J., and Bush, M. 1976. A physiological study of immobilized cheetahs
(Acinonyx jubatus). J. Zoo Anim. Med. 7(3): 5–7.

Smith, C. C., and Fretwell, S. D. 1974. The optimal balance between size and number of offspring. *Am. Nat.* 108:499–506.

Smith, G. L. III. 1985. International studbook of the Indian lion, *Panthera leo persica* (Meyer, 1826). Knoxville, Tenn.: Knoxville Zoological Park.

Smith, J. L. D., and McDougal, C. 1991. The contribution of variance in lifetime reproduction to effective population size in tigers. *Conserv. Biol.* 5:484–90.

Smith, J. L. D.; McDougal, C.; and Miquelle, D. 1989. Scent marking in free-ranging tigers, *Panthera tigris*. *Anim. Behav.* 37:1–10.

Smith, R. M. 1977. Movement patterns and feeding behavior of the leopard in the Rhodes Matapos National Park, Rhodesia. *Arnoldia* 8(13): 58–69.

*Smithers, R. H. N. 1968. Cat of the pharaohs. *Anim. Kingdom* 61:16–23.

*Smithers, R. H. N. 1975. Family Felidae. In *The Mammals of Africa: An Identification Manual,* part 8.1, ed. J. Meester and H. W. Setzer, 1–10. Washington, D.C.: Smithsonian Institution Press.

*Smithers, R. H. N. 1983. *The Mammals of the Southern African Subregion.* Pretoria: University of Pretoria Press.

*Smithers, R. H. N. 1986. South African Red Data Book—Terrestrial Mammals. South African National Scientific Programmes Report #125.

Smuts, B. B. 1985. *Sex and Friendship in Baboons.* New York: Aldine.

Smuts, B. B. 1986. Sexual competition and mate choice. In *Primate Societies,* ed. B. B. Smuts, D. L. Cheney, R. M. Seyfarth, R. W. Wrangham, and T. T. Struhsaker, 385–99. Chicago: University of Chicago Press.

Smuts, G. L. 1976. Population characteristics and recent history of lions in two parts of Kruger National Park. *Koedoe* 19:153–64.

Smuts, G. L. 1978. Effects of population reduction on the travels and reproduction of lions in Kruger National Park. *Carnivore* 2:61–72.

Smuts, G. L. 1979. Diet of lions and spotted hyena assessed from the stomach contents. *S. Afr. J. Wildl. Res.* 9:19–25.

Smuts, G. L.; Hanks, J.; and Whyte, I. J. 1978. Reproduction and social organization of lions from the Kruger National Park. *Carnivore* 1:17–28.

*Sohrabi Haghdoost, I., and Gharagozlou, M. J. 1983. Feline Panleukemia in two cheetahs *(Acinonyx jubatus). J. Vet. Fac. Univ. Tehran* 38(2–4): 53–59.

Sokal, R. R., and Rohlf, F. J. 1981. *Biometry: The Principles and Practice of Statistics in Biological Research.* 2d ed. San Francisco: W. H. Freeman and Co.

*Soley, J. T. 1982. An intercytoplasmic crystal-like inclusion in a leydig cell of the cheetah. *Proc. Electron Micro. Soc. S. Afr.* 12:93–94.

*Soley, J. T., and Coubrough, R. I. 1981. A "pouch-like" defect in the basal plate region of cheetah spermatozoa. *Proc. Electron Micro. Soc. S. Afr.* 11:121–22.

*Sorenson, C., and Norgaard, C. F. 1991. Behavioral criteria and endocrine correlates of estrus in cheetahs: An ongoing study. *Reg. Conf. Proc. AAZPA* 258–64.

Soulé, M. E.; Gilpin, M.; Conway, W.; and Foose, T. 1986. The millennium ark: How long a voyage, how many staterooms, how many passengers? *Zoo Biol.* 5: 101–14.

*Spencer, J. A. 1991. Lack of antibodies to coronavirus in a captive cheetah *(Acinonyx jubatus)* population. *J. S. Afr. Vet. Assoc.* 62:124–25.

*Spencer, J. A., and Burroughs, R. 1991. Antibody response of captive cheetahs to modified-live feline virus vaccine. *J. Wildl. Dis.* 27:578–83.

*Spencer, J. A., and Burroughs, R. 1992. Decline in maternal immunity and anti-
body response to vaccine in captive cheetah *(Acinonyx jubatus)* cubs. *J. Wildl.
Dis.* 28:102–4.

Stacey, P. B., and Koenig, W. D., eds. 1990. *Cooperative Breeding in Birds: Long-
term Studies of Ecology and Behavior.* Cambridge: Cambridge University
Press.

*Stander, P. 1990. Notes on the foraging habits of cheetah. *S. Afr. J. Wildl. Res.* 20:
130–32.

Stander, P. E. 1992a. Cooperative hunting in lions: The role of the individual.
Behav. Ecol. Sociobiol. 29:445–54.

Stander, P. E. 1992b. Foraging dynamics of lions in a semi-arid environment. *Can.
J. Zool.* 70:8–21.

Stander, P. E., and Albon, S. D. 1993. Hunting success of lions in a semi-arid
environment. *Symp. Zool. Soc. Lond.* 65:127–43.

*Standish, R. I. 1971. Fur trade to ban commerce in skins of seven endangered
animals. *Biol. Conserv.* 3:133.

*Standley, S. 1979. Breeding of South-West African cheetahs at Port Lympne.
HELP Newsletter 2:22–25.

Stanley Price, M. R. 1989. *Animal Re-introductions: The Arabian Oryx in Oman.*
Cambridge: Cambridge University Press.

Stearns, S. C. 1976. Life-history tactics: A review of the ideas. *Q. Rev. Biol.* 51:
3–47.

Stearns, S. C. 1992. *The Evolution of Life Histories.* Oxford: Oxford University
Press.

Sterndale, R. A. 1884. *Natural History of the Mammalia of India and Ceylon.*
Canada: Thacker, Spink and Co.

Stevenson-Hamilton, J. 1954. *Wild Life in South Africa.* London: Cassell.

Stewart, K. J., and Harcourt, A. H. 1986. Gorillas: Variation in female relationships. In *Primate Societies,* ed. B. B. Smuts, D. L. Cheney, R. M. Seyfarth,
R. W. Wrangham, and T. T. Struhsaker, 155–64. Chicago: University of Chicago Press.

Stirling, I., and Latour, P. B. 1978. Comparative hunting abilities of polar bear cubs
of different ages. *Can. J. Zool.* 56:1768–92.

*Stock, H. 1975. Feldbeobachten an Geparden und Seiern. *News. S.W. Afr. Sci.
Soc.* 16(4): 5–6.

Stoddart, D. M., ed. 1979. Notes from the Mammal Society—No. 39. *J. Zool.*
(Lond.) 189:523–57.

*Stolk, R. 1992. Cheetah conservation station. *Zoogoer* July/Aug. 1992: 18–23.

*Stranack, F. 1962. Fat distribution in the kidney tubules of the Felidae. *Proc. Zool.
Soc. Lond.* 139:475–82.

Stroganov, S. V. 1969. *Carnivorous Mammals of Siberia.* Israel Program for Scientific Translation, Jerusalem.

Struhsaker, T. T. 1980. *The Red Colobus Monkey.* Chicago: University of Chicago
Press.

*Stuart, C. 1992. The "hunting leopard." *Zoogoer* July/Aug. 1992: 21.

*Stuart, C. T., and Wilson, V. J. 1989. The cats of Southern Africa. IUCN/SSC Cat
Specialty Group. African Carnivore Survey. Chipangali Wildlife Trust.

Sullivan, K. A. 1984. The advantages of social foraging in downy woodpeckers. *Anim. Behav.* 32:16–22.

Sullivan, K. A. 1988. Ontogeny of time budgets in yellow-eyed juncos: Adaptation to ecological constraints. *Ecology* 69:118–24.

*Sunquist, F. 1992. Cheetahs—closer than kissing cousins. *Wildl. Conserv.* 95(3): 38–43.

Sunquist, F., and Sunquist, M. 1988. *Tiger Moon*. Chicago: University of Chicago Press.

Sunquist, M. E. 1981. The social organization of tigers *(Panthera tigris)* in Royal Chitwan National Park, Nepal. *Smithson. Contrib. Zool.* 336:1–98.

Sunquist, M. E., and Sunquist, F. C. 1989. Ecological constraints on predation by large felids. In *Carnivore Behavior, Ecology, and Evolution,* ed. J. L. Gittleman, 283–301. Ithaca, N.Y.: Cornell University Press.

*Swart, W. H. 1978. Annual report on cheetah research project at Motswari. Unpublished typescript.

*Taylor, C. R.; Shkolnik, A.; Dmi'el, R.; Baharav, D.; and Borut, A. 1974. Running in cheetahs, gazelles and goats: Energy cost and limb configuration. *Am. J. Physiol.* 227:848–50.

Taylor, M. E., and Abrey, N. 1982. Marten, *Martes americana,* movements and habitat use in Algonquin Provincial Park, Ontario. *Can. Field Nat.* 96: 439–47.

*Taylor, R. C., and Rowntree, V. J. 1973. Temperature regulation and heat balance in running cheetahs: A strategy for sprinters? *Am. J. Physiol.* 224:848–54.

Templeton, A. R., and Read, B. 1983. The elimination of inbreeding depression in a captive herd of Speke's gazelle. In *Genetics and Conservation: A Reference for Managing Wild Animal and Plant Populations,* ed. C. M. Schonewald-Cox, S. M. Chambers, F. MacBryde, and W. L. Thomas, 241–61. Menlo Park, Calif.: Benjamin Cummings.

Templeton, A. R., and Read, B. 1984. Factors eliminating inbreeding depression in a captive herd of Speke's gazelle. *Zoo Biol.* 3:177–99.

*Tennant, M. B., and Craig, S. 1977. Breeding cheetahs at the Lion Country Safari Parks: A summary. *Int. Zoo Yrbk.* 17:167–69.

Terborgh, J. 1983. *Five New World Primates: A Study in Comparative Ecology.* Princeton, N.J.: Princeton University Press.

*Teunissen, G. H. 1978. Esophageal hiatal hernia. Case report of a dog and a cheetah. *Tijdschr. Diergeneeskd* 103: 742–49.

Thapar, V. 1986. *Tiger.* New York: Facts on File.

*Thomas, W. D. 1965. Observations on a pair of cheetahs at Oklahoma City Zoo. *Int. Zoo Yrbk.* 5:114–16.

*Thompson, P. R.; Sabine, M.; and Hyne, R. H. J. 1971. Herpes virus isolated from cheetahs. *Aust. Vet. J.* 47:458.

*Thompson, R. A., and Landreth, H. F. 1973. Reproduction in captive cheetah. In *The World's Cats,* vol. 2, ed. R. L. Eaton, 162–75. Winston, Oreg.: World Wildlife Safari.

*Thompson, R. A., and Vestal, B. 1974. Survey of conditions associated with breeding cheetah in captivity. *Oklahoma Zoo J.* 2(3).

*Thompson, S. E. 1990. Bringing up baby. *Zoo Life* 1(2): 57–63.

Thornhill, R., and Alcock, J. A. 1983. *The Evolution of Insect Mating Systems.* Cambridge, Mass.: Harvard University Press.

Tilson, R. L., and Seal, U. S., eds. 1987. *Tigers of the World.* Park Ridge, N.J.: Noyes Publications.

*Tong, J. R. 1974. Breeding cheetah at the Berkse Bergen Safari Park. *Int. Zoo Yrbk.* 14:129–30.

Treisman, M. 1975a. Predation and the evolution of gregariousness. I. Models for concealment and evasion. *Anim. Behav.* 23:779–800.

Treisman, M. 1975b. Predation and the evolution of gregariousness. II. An economic model for predator-prey interaction. *Anim. Behav.* 23:801–25.

*Trimen, R. 1887. Extract from a letter referring to *Felis lanea* of Sclater. *Proc. Zool. Soc. Lond.*

Trivers, R. L. 1971. The evolution of reciprocal altruism. *Q. Rev. Biol.* 46:35–57.

Trivers, R. L. 1972. Parental investment and sexual selection. In *Sexual Selection and the Descent of Man, 1871–1971,* ed. B. Campbell, 136–79. Chicago: Aldine.

Trivers, R. L. 1974. Parent-offspring conflict. *Am. Zool.* 14:249–64.

Trivers, R. L. 1985. *Social Evolution.* Menlo Park, Calif.: Benjamin Cummings.

Turner, M. 1987. *My Serengeti Years: The Memoirs of an African Game Warden.* Ed. B. Jackman. London: Elm Tree Books, Hamish Hamilton.

*Ulmer, F. 1957. Cheetahs are born. *American's First Zoo* 9(3): 7.

Ulmer, F. A. 1968. Breeding fishing cats at Philadelphia Zoo. *Int. Zoo Yrbk.* 8: 49–55.

Underwood, R. 1982. Vigilance behaviour in grazing African antelopes. *Behaviour* 79:81–107.

*U.S. to ban trade in eight cat species. 1972. *IUCN Bull.* 3(3): 10.

*Vallat, C. 1971. Birth of three cheetahs at Montpellier Zoo. *Mammalia* 34: 323–25.

*van Aarde, R. J., and van Dyk, A. 1986. Inheritance of the king coat pattern in cheetahs *Acinonyx. J. Zool.* 209:573–78.

van den Berghe, E. P., and Gross, M. R. 1986. Length of breeding life of coho salmon *(Oncorhynchus kisutch). Can. J. Zool.* 64:1482–86.

*Van der Ingh, T. S.; Zwart, P.; and Heldstab, A. 1981. Veno-occlusive disease (VOD) of the liver in cheetahs and snow leopards. *Schweiz. Archiv. Tierheilk.* 123(6): 323–27.

*van de Werken, H. 1967. Preliminary report on cheetahs in zoos and in Africa. *Amsterdam Roy. Zool. Soc.* 1–9.

*van de Werken, H. 1968. Cheetahs in captivity: Preliminary report on cheetahs in zoos and in Africa. *Zool. Gart.* 35:156–61.

*van de Werken, H. 1975. Cheetahs in captivity. *Natura Artis Magistra Roy. Zool. Soc. Amsterdam.* Unpublished typescript.

*Vaneysinga, C. R. 1970. A note on breeding cheetahs under winter conditions. *Int. Zoo Yrbk.* 10:144–46.

van Hooff, J. A. R. A. M., and van Schaik, C. P. 1992. Cooperation in competition: The ecology of primate bonds. In *Coalitions and Alliances in Humans and Other Animals,* ed. A. H. Harcourt and F. B. M. de Waal, 357–89. Oxford: Oxford University Press.

*Van Ingen and Van Ingen. 1948. Interesting shikar trophies: Hunting cheetah *Acinonyx jubatus* (Schreber). *J. Bombay Nat. Hist. Soc.* 47:718–20.

van Orsdol, K. G. 1981. Lion predation in Rwenzori National Park, Uganda. Ph.D. diss., University of Cambridge.

van Orsdol, K. G. 1982. Ranges and food habits of lions in Rwenzori National Park, Uganda. *Symp. Zool. Soc. Lond.* 49:325–40.

van Orsdol, K. G. 1984. Foraging behaviour and hunting success of lions in Queen Elizabeth National Park, Uganda. *Afr. J. Ecol.* 22:79–99.

van Orsdol, K. G.; Hanby, J. P.; and Bygott, J. D. 1985. Ecological correlates of lion social organization *(Panthera leo). J. Zool.* 206:97–112.

*Van Rensburg, I. B. J., and Silkstone, M. A. 1984. Concomitant feline infectious peritonitis and toxoplasmosis in a cheetah. *J. S. Afr. Vet. Assoc.* 55:205–7.

van Schaik, C. P. 1989. The ecology of social relationships amongst female primates. In *Comparative Socioecology: The Behavioural Ecology of Humans and Other Mammals,* ed. V. Standen and R. A. Foley, 195–218. Oxford: Blackwell Scientific Publications.

van Schaik, C. P., and van Noordwijk, M. A. 1985. Evolutionary effect of the absence of felids on the social organization of the macaques on the island of Simeule (*Macaca fascicularis fusca,* Miller 1903). *Folia Primatol.* 44:138–47.

van Schaik, C. P.; Warsano, B.; and Sutrino, E. 1983. Party size and early detection of predators in Sumatran forest primates. *Primates* 24:211–21.

*van Valkenburgh, B.; Grady, F.; and Kurtén, B. 1990. The plio-pleistocene cheetah-like cat *Miracinonyx inexpectatus* of North America. *J. Vert. Paleontol.* 10:434–54.

*van Valkenburgh, B., and Ruff, C. B. 1987. Canine tooth strength and killing behaviour in large carnivores. *J. Zool.* 212:379–97.

*Varaday, D. 1964. *Gara-Yaka: The Story of a Cheetah.* New York: E. P. Dutton.

*Varaday, D. 1966. *Gara Yaka's Domain.* London: Collins.

Vehrencamp, S. L. 1983. A model for the evolution of despotic versus egalitarian societies. *Anim. Behav.* 31:667–82.

*Veselovsky, Z. 1975. Notes on the breeding of cheetah *(Acinonyx jubatus)* at Prague Zoo. *Zool. Gart.* 45(1): 28–44.

Vincent, L. E., and Bekoff, M. 1978. Quantitative analyses of the ontogeny of predatory behaviour in coyotes, *Canis latrans. Anim. Behav.* 26:225–31.

Volf, J. 1965. Breeding the European wild cat at Prague Zoo. *Int. Zoo Yrbk.* 8:38–42.

*Volf, J. 1974. Breeding of cheetah *(Acinonyx jubatus)* at the Prague Zoological Garden. *Lynx Nova Serie Mammalogicke Z. Pravy* 15:45–49.

*Von Henning, R. 1979. Ueber die Geparden in Suedwestafrica/Namibia und Moeglishkeiten ihrer bestandesschonenden Regulierung. *Z. Jagwiss* 25:129–39.

*VonWilhelm, J. H. 1932. Gestation of cheetah. *J. S.W. Afr. Sci. Soc.* 6–71.

*Wack, R. F. 1991a. The response of cheetahs to routine vaccination. M.Sc. thesis, Ohio State University.

*Wack, R. F. 1991b. The vaccination of cheetahs *(Acinonyx jubatus). Ann. Proc. AAZV* 1991:294–97.

*Wack, R. F.; Kramer, L. W.; Cupps, W.; and Currie, P. 1991. Growth rate of 21 captive-born, mother-raised cheetah cubs. *Zoo Biol.* 10:273–76.

*Wack, R. F.; Kramer, L. W.; Cupps, W. L.; and Katz, S. 1990. Antibody titer response of cheetah *(Acinonyx jubatus)* cubs to vaccination. *Ann. Proc. AAZV* 1990:147–49.

Wackernagel, H. 1968. A note on breeding the serval cat at Basle Zoo. *Int. Zoo Yrbk.* 8:46–47.

*Wadsworth, P. F., and Jones, D. M. 1980. Myelipoma in the liver of a cheetah *(Acinonyx jubatus). J. Zoo Anim. Med.* 11(3): 75–76.

*Walker, C. 1978. Cheetah dilemma. *Afr. Wildl.* 32(3): 22.

*Walker, S. 1986. Cheetahs, now and then. *Zoo's Print* 1:18–21.

Walther, F. R. 1969. Flight behavior and avoidance of predators in Thomson's gazelle *(Gazella thomsoni* Gunther 1884). *Behavior* 34:184–221.

Walther, F. R. 1973. On age class recognition and individual identification of Thomson's gazelle in the field. *J. S. Afr. Wildl. Mgmt. Assoc.* 2:9–15.

Walther, F. R.; Mungall, E. C.; and Grau, G. A. 1983. *Gazelles and Their Relatives.* Park Ridge, N.J.: Noyes Publications.

Ward, P. I. 1985. Why birds in flocks do not coordinate their vigilance periods. *J. Theor. Biol.* 114:383–85.

Ward, P., and Zahavi, A. 1973. The importance of certain assemblages of birds as "information-centres" for food finding. *Ibis* 115:517–34.

Ward, R. P. M., and Krebs, C. J. 1985. Behavioral responses of lynx to declining snowshoe hare abundance. *Can. J. Zool.* 63:2817–24.

Waser, P. M.; Keane, B.; Creel, S. R.; Elliott, L. M. and Minchella, D. J. In press. Male associations in a solitary mongoose: are they coalitions? *Anim. Behav.*

Watson, R. M. 1969. Reproduction of wildebeest, *Connochaetes taurinus albojubatus* Thomas, in the Serengeti region and its significance to conservation. *J. Reprod. Fert.* 6 (suppl.): 287–310.

Watt, J. 1993. Ontogeny of hunting behaviour of others *(Lutra lutra* L.) in a marine environment. *Symp. Zoo. Soc. Lond.* 65:87–104.

*Wayne, R. W.; Modi, W. S.; and O'Brien, S. J. 1986. Morphological variability and asymmetry in the cheetah *(Acinonyx jubatus):* A genetically uniform species. *Evolution* 40:78–85.

*Weber, W. J.; Raphael, B. L.; and Boothe, H. W., Jr. 1984. Struvite uroliths in a cheetah *(Acinonyx jubatus). J. Am. Vet. Med. Assoc.* 185:1389–90.

*Weigel, I. 1975. Big felids and cheetah. In *Grzimek's Animal Life Encyclopedia,* vol. 12, ed. B. Grzimek, 335–44. London: Van Nostrand Rheinhold.

*Wemmer, C., and Scow, K. 1978. Communication in Felidae with emphasis on scent marking and contact patterns. In *How Animals Communicate,* ed. T. A. Sebok, 749–66. Bloomington: Indiana University Press.

*West, B.; Wilson, P.; and Hatch, C. 1977. Aelurostrongylus abstrusus infection in a cheetah. *J. Helminthol.* 51:210–11.

Western, D. 1979. Size, life history and ecology in mammals. *Afr. J. Ecol.* 17:185–204.

Western, D., and Pearl, M. C. 1979. *Conservation for the Twenty-First Century.* New York: Oxford University Press.

Western, D., and Ssemakula, J. 1982. Life history patterns in birds and mammals and their evolutionary interpretation. *Oecologia* 54:281–90.

White, F. J. 1988. Party composition and dynamics in *Pan paniscus*. *Int. J. Primatol.* 9:179–93.

Whitehead, H. 1990. Rules for roving males. *J. Theor. Biol.* 145:355–68.

*Whyte, J. 1986. Cheetah under fire. *Zimbabwe Wildl.* 43:17–21.

*Wildt, D. E. 1984. Giving endangered species a second chance. *Zoogoer*, July/Aug.

*Wildt, D. E.; Brown, J. L.; Bush, M.; Barone, M. A.; Cooper, K. A.; Grisham, J.; and Howard, J. G. 1993. Reproductive status of cheetahs *(Acinonyx jubatus)* in North American zoos: The benefits of physiological surveys for strategic planning. *Zoo. Biol.* 12:45–80.

*Wildt, D. E.; Bush, M.; Goodrowe, K. L.; Packer, C.; Pusey, A. E.; Brown, J. L.; Joslin, P.; and O'Brien, S. J. 1987. Reproductive and genetic consequences of founding isolated lion populations. *Nature* 329:328–31.

*Wildt, D. E.; Bush, M.; Howard, J. G.; O'Brien, S. J.; Meltzer, D.; van Dyk, A.; Ebedes, H.; and Brand, D. J. 1983. Unique seminal quality in the South African cheetah and a comparative evaluation in the domestic cat. *Biol. Reprod.* 29:1019–25.

*Wildt, D. E.; Bush, M.; Platz, C. C.; and Seager, S. W. J. 1981. Ovarian activity in the cheetah *(Acinonyx jubatus)*. *Biol. Reprod.* 24:217–22.

*Wildt, D. E.; Chakraborty, P. K.; Meltzer, D.; and Bush, M. 1984. Pituitary and gonadal responses to LH releasing hormone administration in the male and female cheetah. *J. Endocrinology* 101:51–56.

*Wildt, D. E.; Meltzer, D.; Chakraborty, P. K.; and Bush, M. 1984. Adrenal-testicular-pituitary relationships in the cheetah subjected to anesthesia/electroejaculation. *Biol. Reprod.* 30:665–72.

*Wildt, D. E.; Monfort, S. L.; Donohue, A. M.; Johnston, L. A.; and Howard, J. 1992. Embryogenesis in conservation biology—or, how to make an endangered species embryo. *Theriogenology* 37:161–84.

*Wildt, D. E.; O'Brien, S. J.; Howard, J. G.; Caro, T. M.; Roelke, M. E.; Brown, J. L.; and Bush, M. 1987. Similarity in ejaculate-endocrine characteristics in captive versus free-ranging cheetahs of two subspecies. *Biol. Reprod.* 36:351–60.

*Wildt, D. E.; Phillips, L. G.; Simmons, L. G.; Chakraborty, P. K.; Brown, J. L.; Howard, J. G.; Teare, A.; and Bush, M. 1988. A comparative analysis of ejaculate and hormonal characteristics of the captive male cheetah, tiger, leopard, and puma. *Biol. Reprod.* 38:245–55.

*Wildt, D. E.; Platz, C. C.; Seager, S. W. J.; and Bush, M. 1981. Induction of ovarian activity in the cheetah *(Acinonyx jubatus)*. *Biol. Reprod.* 24:217–22.

Wilkinson, G. S. 1992. Information transfer at evening bat colonies. *Anim. Behav.* 44:501–18.

Williams, G. C. 1966. *Adaptation and Natural Selection.* Princeton, N.J.: Princeton University Press.

*Willig, M. R., and Owen, R. D. 1987. Fluctuating asymmetry in the cheetah: Methodological and interpretive concerns. *Evolution* 41:225–28.

Wilson, E. O. 1975. *Sociobiology: The New Synthesis.* Cambridge, Mass.: Harvard University Press.

Wilson, V. J. 1968. Weights of some mammals from eastern Zambia. *Arnoldia* 32(3): 1–20.

*Wilson, V. J. 1986. Cheetah in Zimbabwe. *Cat News* 4:9.

*Wilson, V. J. 1987. Distribution and status of cheetah in Zimbabwe. Report of the Chipangali Wildlife Trust, Zimbabwe.

*Winter, H.; Saan, C.; and Goltenboth, R. 1980. Mast cell leukemia and carcinoma of the duodenum in a cheetah *(Acinonyx jubatus)*. *Kleinter-Prax* 25(8): 499–504.

Wirtz, P. 1981. Territorial defence and territory take-over by satellite males in the waterbuck *Kobus ellipsiprymnus* (Bovidae). *Behav. Ecol. Sociobiol.* 8:161–62.

Wirtz, P. 1982. Territory holders, satellite males, and bachelor males in a high density population of waterbuck *(Kobus ellipsiprymnus)* and their associations with conspecifics. *Z. Tierpsychol.* 58:277–300.

Wittmer, G. W., and DeCalesta, D. S. 1986. Resource use by unexploited sympatric bobcats and coyotes in Oregon. *Can. J. Zool.* 64:2333–38.

*Wolfrom, G. W. 1987. The genetics of cheetahs. *Creat. Res. Soc. Q.* 23(4): 179–80.

*Wolock, C. A. 1986. Aggressive behavior during feeding and non-feeding in captive cheetahs *(Acinonyx jubatus)*. Department of Zoology, Ohio State University, Columbus, Ohio. Unpublished typescript.

Wozencraft, W. C. 1989. Classification of the recent carnivora. In *Carnivore Behavior, Ecology, and Evolution*, ed. J. L. Gittleman, 569–93. Ithaca, N.Y.: Cornell University Press.

Wrangham, R. W. 1979. On the evolution of ape social systems. *Soc. Sci. Inform.* 18:335–68.

Wrangham, R. W. 1980. An ecological model of female-bonded primate groups. *Behaviour* 75:262–300.

Wrangham, R. W. 1982. Mutualism, kinship and social evolution. In *Current Problems in Sociobiology*, ed. King's College Sociobiology Group, 269–89. Cambridge: Cambridge University Press.

Wrogemann, N. 1975. *Cheetah under the Sun.* New York: McGraw-Hill.

Ximenez, A. 1975. *Felis geoffroyi.* Mammalian Species Acct. no. 54, 1–4. American Society of Mammalogists.

*Ygorov, E. V., and Novikova, E. V. 1992. Elaboration of methods of breeding cheetahs in captive conditions. In *International Cheetah Studbook 1991*, ed. L. Marker-Kraus. NOAHS Center, National Zoological Park, Washington, D.C.

*York, W. 1974. Captive breeding of cheetah—a successful management program. *Drum Beat*, 6–20.

*Young, E. 1967. The hand-rearing of the young of the cat tribes. *Afr. Wildl.* 21: 21–27.

*Young, E. 1972. Cheetahs. *Custos* 2(1): 10–12.

*Young, E. 1977. Transvaal farmers involved in important rescue operations. *Fauna Flora* (Pretoria) 29:1–3.

*Young, E. 1980. The cheetah success story. *Fauna Flora* (Pretoria) 38:10–11.

*Young, E., and Naude, T. 1973. Caution in the treatment of cheetahs with mala-thion. *J. S. Afr. Vet. Assoc.* 44:187.

*Young, E.; Zumpt, F.; and Whyte, I. J. 1972. *Notoedres cati* (Hering, 1838) infes-tation of the cheetah: Preliminary report. *J. S. Afr. Vet. Assoc.* 43:205.

Young, S. P. 1958. *The Bobcat of North America.* Harrisburg, Pa.: Stackpole.

Young, S. P., and Goldman, E. A. 1946. *The Puma, Mysterious American Cat.* New York: Dover.

Yuhki, N., and O'Brien, S. J. 1990. DNA variation of the mammalian major histo-compatibility complex reflects genomic diversity and population history. *Proc. Natl. Acad. Sci. USA* 87:836–40.

Zimien, E. 1976. On the regulation of pack size in wolves. *Z. Tierpsychol.* 40:300–341.

*Zinkl, J. G., et al. 1981. Cytauxzoon-like organisms in erythrocytes of two cheetahs. *J. Am. Vet. Med. Assoc.* 179:1261–62.

*Zoological Society of San Diego (CRES). 1989–1992. *Cheetah News.* Biannual cheetah SSP newsletter. Vols. 1–4.

*Zooresearch Consultants. 1986. Genetische Variate en de Gevoeligheid Voor Vi-rusziekten Bij de Cheetah. Utrecht. Unpublished typescript.

*Zwart, P.; von der Hage, M. H.; Schotman, A. J. H.; Dorrestein, G. M.; and Rens, J. 1986. Copper deficiency in cheetah *(Acinonyx jubatus). Erkrankungen Zoo-tiere* 27:253–57.

Author Index

Subject Index